**PHILIP'S**

C000025331

# STREE

# North Essex

## Braintree, Chelmsford, Colchester, Ipswich

www.philips-maps.co.uk

First published in 1999 by

Philip's, a division of
Octopus Publishing Group Ltd
www.octopusbooks.co.uk
2-4 Heron Quays, London E14 4JP
An Hachette Livre UK Company

Third edition 2007
First impression 2007
NESCA

ISBN-10   0-540-09192-8 (pocket)
ISBN-13   978-0-540-09192-8 (pocket)

© Philip's 2007

 **Ordnance Survey®**

## Contents

**II**   **List of mobile speed cameras**

**III**   **Key to map symbols**

**IV**   **Key to map pages**

**VI**   **Route Planning**

**VIII**   **Administrative and Postcode boundaries**

**1**   **Street maps** at 2⅔ inches to 1 mile

**222**   **Index** of towns, villages, streets, hospitals, industrial estates, railway stations, schools, shopping centres, universities and places of interest

## Digital Data

The exceptionally high-quality mapping found in this atlas is available as digital data in TIFF format, which is easily convertible to other bitmapped (raster) image formats.

The index is also available in digital form as a standard database table. It contains all the details found in the printed index together with the National Grid reference for the map square in which each entry is named.

For further information and to discuss your requirements, please contact james.mann@philips-maps.co.uk

# Mobile speed cameras

The vast majority of speed cameras used on Britain's roads are operated by safety camera partnerships. These comprise local authorities, the police, Her Majesty's Court Service (HMCS) and the Highways Agency.

This table lists the sites where each safety camera partnership may enforce speed limits through the use of mobile cameras or detectors. These are usually set up on the roadside or a bridge spanning the road and operated by a police or civilian enforcement officer. The speed limit at each site (if available) is shown in red type, followed by the approximate location in black type.

**A12**
Braintree, Overbridge nr Kelvedon Interchange

**A13**
30 Castle Point, High St (Hadleigh twds London)
30 Leigh on Sea, London Rd
Southend, Bournes Green Chase
Southend, North Shoebury
Southend, Southchurch Boulevard

**A1016**
30 Chelmsford, Waterhouse Lane

**A1017**
30 Sible Hedingham, Swan St
30 Witham / Braintree, Rickstone Rd

**A1023**
30 Brentwood, Chelmsford Rd
30 Brentwood, London Rd
30 Brentwood, Shenfield Rd

**A1025**
40 Harlow, Second Avenue
40 Harlow, Third Avenue

**A1060**
Little Hallingbury, Lower Rd

**A1090**
30 Purfleet, London Rd
30 Purfleet, Tank Hill Rd

**A1124**
30 Colchester, Lexden Rd

**A113**
30 Epping, High Rd

**A1158**
30 Westcliff on Sea, Southbourne Grove

**A1168**
30 Loughton, Rectory Lane

**A1169**
40 Harlow, Southern Way

**A120**
Little Bentley, Pellens Corner
Wix, Harwich Rd nr Colchester Rd

**A1205**
40 Harlow, Second Avenue

**A121**
30 Epping, High Rd
30 Loughton, Goldings Hill (j/w Monkchester Close)
Loughton, High Rd

Waltham Abbey, Farm Hill Rd
Waltham Abbey, Sewardstine Rd

**A126**
30 Grays, London Rd
30 Tilbury, Montreal Rd

**A128**
Chipping Ongar, High St
30 Ingrave/Herongate, Brentwood Rd
40 Kelvedon Hatch, Ongar Rd

**A129**
30 Basildon, Crays Hill
Billericay, Southend Rd
Rayleigh, London Rd
30 Wickford, London Rd
30 Wickford, Southend Rd

**A130**
30 Canvey Island, Long Rd
South Benfleet, Canvey Way

**A133**
30 Elmstead Market, Clacton Rd
Little Bentley, Colchester Rd

**A134**
40 Great Horkesley, Nayland Rd

**A137**
30 Lawford, Wignall St

**B170**
Chigwell, Chigwell Rise
Loughton, Roding Lane

**B172**
Theydon Bois, Coppice Row

**B173**
Chigwell, Lambourne Rd

**B184**
40 Great Easton, Snow Hill

**B186**
30 South Ockendon, South Rd

**B1002**
30 Ingatestone, High St

**B1007**
30 Billericay, Laindon Rd
30 Billericay, Stock Rd
30 Chelmsford, Stock Rd

**B1008**
30 Chelmsford, Broomfield Rd

**B1013**
30 Hawkwell, High Rd
30 Hawkwell, Main Rd
30 Hockley/Hawkwell, Southend Rd
Rayleigh, High Rd

**B1014**
30 South Benfleet, Benfleet Rd

**B1018**
30 Latchingdon, The St
30 Maldon, The Causeway

**B1019**
30 Hatfield Peveral, Maldon Rd
30 Witham, Powers Hall End

**B1021**
Burnham on Crouch, Church Rd

**B1022**
30 Colchester, Maldon Rd
30 Heckfordbridge, Maldon Rd
30 Maldon, Colchester Rd
30 Tiptree Heath, Maldon Rd

**B1027**
30 Clacton-on-Sea, Valley Rd/Old Rd
30 St Osyth, Pump Hill
40 Wivenhoe, Brightlingsea Rd

**B1028**
30 Wivenhoe, Colchester Rd
30 Wivenhoe, The Avenue

**B1033**
30 Kirby Cross, Frinton Rd

**B1335**
40 South Ockendon, Stifford Rd

**B1352**
Harwich, Main Rd

**B1383**
30 Newport, London Rd
Stansted Mountfitchet, Cambridge Rd

**B1389**
30 Witham, Colchester Rd
30 Witham, Hatfield Rd

**B1393**
30 Epping, Palmers Hill

**B1441**
30 Clacton-on-Sea, London Rd
Tendring, Clacton Rd

**B1442**
30 Clacton-on-Sea, Thorpe Rd

**B1464**
30 Bowers Gifford, London Rd

**UNCLASSIFIED**
40 Alresford, St Osyth Rd
30 Aveley, Purfleet Rd
Aveley, Romford Rd
30 Barstable, Sandon Rd
30 Basildon, Ashlyns
Basildon, Clay Hill Rd
40 Basildon, Cranes Farm Rd (j/w Honywood Rd)
30 Basildon, Felmores
Basildon, London Rd, Wickford
30 Basildon, Vange Hill Drive
30 Basildon, Whitmore Way
30 Basildon, Wickford Avenue
30 Billericay, Mountnessing Rd
30 Bowers Gifford, London Rd
30 Braintree, Coldnailhurst Avenue
30 Brentwood, Eagle Way (nr j/w Clive Rd twds Warley Rd)

30 Brentwood, Eagle Way
30 Buckhurst Hill, Buckhurst Way/Albert Rd
30 Canvey Island, Dovervelt Rd
30 Canvey Island, Link Rd
30 Canvey Island, Thorney Bay Rd
Chadwell St Mary, Brentwood Rd
30 Chadwell St Mary, Linford Rd
30 Chadwell St Mary, Riverview
30 Chelmsford, Baddow Rd
30 Chelmsford, Chignall Rd
30 Chelmsford, Copperfield Rd
Chelmsford, Galleywood Rd
30 Chelmsford, Longstomps Avenue
30 Clacton-on-Sea, St Johns Rd
30 Clacton, Kings Parade
30 Clacton, Marine Parade East
30 Colchester, Abbots Rd
30 Colchester, Avon Way
30 Colchester, Bromley Rd
Colchester, Ipswich Rd
30 Colchester, Old Heath Rd
30 Colchester, Shrub End Rd
30 Corringham, Southend Rd
30 Corringham, Springhouse Rd
Danbury, Maldon Rd
30 Daws Heath, Daws Heath Rd
30 Eastwood, Green Lane j/w Kendal Way
30 Eastwood, Western Approaches j/w Rockall
30 Grays, Blackshots Lane
30 Grays, Lodge Lane
Grays, London Rd (nr Angel Rd)
Grays, London Rd (nr Bransons Way)
30 Hainault, Fencepiece Rd
40 Harlow, Abercrombie Way, twds Southern Way
40 Harlow, Howard Way
30 Hawkwell, Rectory Rd
30 Hockley, High Rd
30 Hullbridge, Coventry Hill
30 Laindon, Durham Rd
30 Laindon, High Rd
30 Laindon, Nightingales
30 Laindon, Wash Rd
Langdon Hills, High Rd
30 Leigh on Sea, Belton Way East
30 Leigh on Sea, Belton Way West
30 Leigh on Sea, Blenheim Chase
30 Leigh on Sea, Grand Parade/Cliff Parade
30 Leigh on Sea, Hadleigh Rd
30 Leigh on Sea, Highlands Boulevard
30 Leigh on Sea, Manchester Drive
30 Leigh on Sea, Mountdale Gardens
30 Leigh on Sea, Western Rd
30 Loughton, Alderton Hill
30 Loughton, Loughton Way
Loughton, Valley Hill
30 Maldon, Fambridge Rd
30 Maldon, Holloway Rd
30 Maldon, Mundon Rd
30 Pitsea, Rectory Rd

30 Prittlewell, Kenilworth Gardens
30 Prittlewell, Prittlewell Chase
30 Rayleigh, Bull Lane
30 Rayleigh, Downhall Rd
30 Rayleigh, Trinity Rd, nr Church Rd
30 Rochford, Ashingdon Rd
30 Rochford, Rectory Rd
Rush Green, St Osyth Rd
30 Shoeburyness, Ness Rd
30 South Woodham Ferrers, Hullbridge Rd
30 South Woodham Ferrers, Inchbonnie Rd
30 Southend on Sea, Lifstan Way
Southend, Bournemouth Park Rd
30 Southend, Hamstel Rd
Southend on Sea, Bournemouth Park Rd
30 Southend, Western Esplanade/Westcliff on Sea
30 Springfield, New Bowers Way
30 Stanford le Hope, London Rd
30 Tendring, Burrs Rd, Clacton
30 Tendring, Frinton Rd, Frinton
Tendring, Harwich Rd, Wix Arch Cottages to Cansey Lane
30 Tendring, Osyth Rd, Rush Green
Theydon Bois, Piercing Hill
30 Thorpe Bay, Barnstaple Rd
30 Thorpe Bay, Thorpe Hall Avenue
Waltham Abbey, Paternoster Hill
Weeley Heath, Clacton Rd
Weeley Heath, Clacton Rd
30 West Thurrock, London Rd
30 Westcliff on Sea, Chalkwell Avenue
30 Westcliff on Sea, Kings Rd
30 Wickford, London Rd
30 Wickford, Radwinter Avenue
30 Witham, Powers Hall End
30 Witham, Rickstones Rd

# Key to map symbols

**III**

| | |
|---|---|
| Motorway with junction number | Ambulance station |
| Primary route – dual/single carriageway | Coastguard station |
| A road – dual/single carriageway | Fire station |
| B road – dual/single carriageway | Police station |
| Minor road – dual/single carriageway | Accident and Emergency entrance to hospital |
| Other minor road – dual/single carriageway | |
| Road under construction | **H** Hospital |
| Tunnel, covered road | + Place of worship |
| Speed cameras - single, multiple | **i** Information Centre (open all year) |
| Rural track, private road or narrow road in urban area | Shopping Centre |
| Gate or obstruction to traffic (restrictions may not apply at all times or to all vehicles) | **P** Parking |
| Path, bridleway, byway open to all traffic, road used as a public path | **P&R** Park and Ride |
| | **PO** Post Office |
| Pedestrianised area | Camping site |
| **DY7** Postcode boundaries | Caravan site |
| County and unitary authority boundaries | Golf course |
| Railway, tunnel, railway under construction | Picnic site |
| Tramway, tramway under construction | Important buildings, schools, colleges, universities and hospitals |
| Miniature railway | |
| **Walsall** Railway station | Built up area |
| Private railway station | Woods |
| **South Shields** Metro station | **River Medway** Water name |
| Tram stop, tram stop under construction | River, weir, stream |
| Bus, coach station | Canal, lock, tunnel |
| | Water |
| | Tidal water |
| **Prim Sch** | |
| | **Church** Non-Roman antiquity |
| | **ROMAN FORT** Roman antiquity |

| | | | | | |
|---|---|---|---|---|---|
| Acad | Academy | Inst | Institute | Recn Gd | Recreation Ground |
| Allot Gdns | Allotments | Ct | Law Court | | |
| Cemy | Cemetery | L Ctr | Leisure Centre | Resr | Reservoir |
| C Ctr | Civic Centre | LC | Level Crossing | Ret Pk | Retail Park |
| CH | Club House | Liby | Library | Sch | School |
| Coll | College | Mkt | Market | Sh Ctr | Shopping Centre |
| Crem | Crematorium | Meml | Memorial | TH | Town Hall/House |
| Ent | Enterprise | Mon | Monument | Trad Est | Trading Estate |
| Ex H | Exhibition Hall | Mus | Museum | Univ | University |
| Ind Est | Industrial Estate | Obsy | Observatory | W Twr | Water Tower |
| IRB Sta | Inshore Rescue Boat Station | Pal | Royal Palace | Wks | Works |
| | | PH | Public House | YH | Youth Hostel |

**87**

**58**

Adjoining page indicators

■ The small numbers around the edges of the maps identify the 1 kilometre National Grid lines

■ The dark grey border on the inside edge of some pages indicates that the mapping does not continue onto the adjacent page

**The scale of the maps on the pages numbered in blue is 4.2 cm to 1 km • 2⅔ inches to 1 mile • 1: 23810**

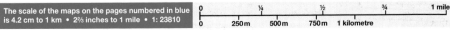

| 0 | ¼ | ½ | ¾ | 1 mile |
|---|---|---|---|---|
| 0 | 250 m | 500 m | 750 m | 1 kilometre |

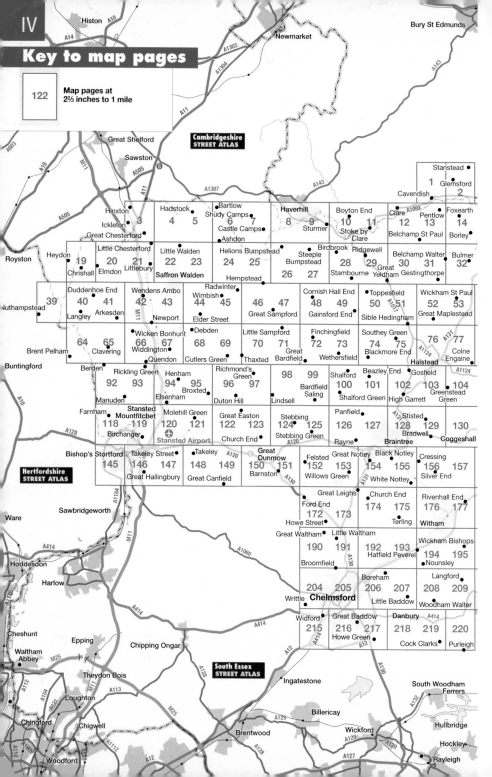

**Suffolk STREET ATLAS**

Framlingham

A14

A140

A1120

Stowmarket

Needham Market

A14

Wickham Market

A12

A1152

Woodbridge

A1141

Whitton

A1214

Ipswich

A1214 Rushmere St Andrew

Sproughton **16** **17** **18**

Long Melford

**15**

Sudbury

Stoke Rose Hill

A1071 Hadleigh Washbrook Belstead A14

A12

A1150

**33** **34** Great Cornard

Middleton

A134

A1071

Capel St Mary

**35** **36** **37** **38**

Wherstead

Freston Woolverstone

**54** **55**
Lamarsh

**56** **57**
Stoke-by-Nayland
Thorington Street

**58** **59**
East Bergholt
Stratford St Mary

Tattingstone
Bentley

Holbrook
**62** **63**

Chelmondiston
Trimley St Mary

**221**

Walton
Felixstowe

Alphamstone Bures

**60** **61**
Brantham

Harkstead

Nayland

Boxted

Pebmarsh

**80** **81**
Little Horkesley

**82** **83**
Langham

Dedham

**84** **85**

Cattawade

**86** **87**
Mistli

**88** **89**
Wrabness

Shotley Gate

**90** **91**
Parkeston Harwich

Mount Bures

**78** **79**
Wormingford

Great Horkesley

Manningtree

Ramsey

Earls
Colne
**105**

Wakes Colne
**106** **107**

West Bergholt

A12

Ardleigh

**110** **111**

Little Bromley

**112** **113**

**114** A120 Wix
**115**

Little Oakley

**116** **117**
Great Oakley

Fordham Heath

Mile End
**108** **109**

Parson's Heath

Great Bromley

Tendring Green

Aldham

Eight Ash Green

Greenstead

Elmstead
Market

Tendring

Beaumont

**131** **132** **133**

Colchester

**136** A133 **137** **138** **139** **140** **141**

**142** **143** **144**
Thorpe-
le-Soken

Kirby-
le-Soken

Marks
Tey

**134** **135**

Wivenhoe Frating Green Weeley

A120

Feering

Easthorpe

Blackheath

Alresford

A133

**158** **159**

**160** **161**
Layer-de-la-Haye

**162** **163**
Malting
Green Abberton

High Park Corner

**164** **165**

Great Bentley

**166** **167**
Thorrington
St Osyth Heath

Weeley Heath

**168** **169**
Little Clacton

Walton-on-the-Naze

**170** **171**
Frinton-on-Sea

Messing
Kelvedon

Birch Green

Great Holland

Tiptree
**178** **179**

**180** **181**
Tolleshunt
Knights

Peldon

**182** **183**
Little
Wigborough

Brightlingsea

**184** **185**

**186** **187**
St Osyth

Great Clacton

**188** **189**
Clacton-
on-Sea

Holland-on-Sea

Great Braxted

Great
Wigborough

East Mersea

**196** **197**
Great Totham

Tolleshunt D'Arcy

West Mersea
**200** **201**

Seawick

**202** **203**
Jaywick

Tolleshunt Major

**198** **199**
Tollesbury

Goldhanger

Heybridge

**210** **211**
Maldon

**212** **213** **214**
Bradwell Waterside

Southminster

Burnham-on-Crouch

Rochford

**Scale**
0 — 5 — 10 — 15 km
0 — 5 — 10 miles

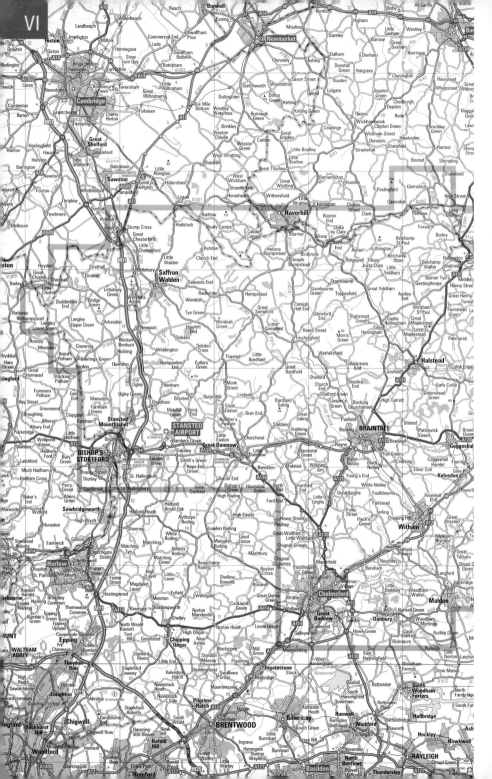

## Route planning

Scale

0       5       10 km

0   1   2   3   4   5   6 miles

# Major administrative and Postcode boundaries

- County and unitary authority boundaries
- District boundaries
- Postcode boundaries
- Area covered by this atlas

## Scale

| 0 | 5 | 10 | 15 km |

| 0 | 5 | 10 miles |

**Suffolk**

**Cambridgeshire**

**Hertfordshire**

**Essex**

**Kent**

**Medway**

**London**

Felixstowe

IP11

IP1 Ipswich IP4 IP5
IP2 IP3 IP10
IP8 IP9
IP7

Harwich

Walton-on-the-Naze
CO14
Great Oakley
CO12
Frinton-on-Sea
CO13
Clacton-on-Sea
CO15
CO16
Manningtree
CO11
St Osyth
Ardleigh
CO7
Wivenhoe
Brightlingsea
East Bergholt
CO1
Colchester
CO4
CO2
CO3
Layer-de-la-Haye
CO5
West Mersea

**Tendring**

**Colchester**

Bures
CO8
CO6
Earls Colne
Coggeshall
Tiptree
Witham
CM8
Tollesbury
CM9
Maldon
Danbury
CM3
Tillingham
CM0
Burnham-on-Crouch
Southminster
SS3
Great Wakering
**Southend-on-Sea**

**Maldon**

Glemsford
CO10
Sudbury
Belchamp St Paul
Castle Hedingham
CO9
Halstead
CM7
Hatfield Peverel
Cold Norton
East Hanningfield
Stock
CM4

**Braintree**

Haverhill
CB9
Steeple Bumpstead
Great Bardfield
Stebbing
Great Dunmow
CM6
Tye Green
Great Leighs
Broomfield
CM1
Chelmsford
CM2
Billericay
CM11
Wickford
SS11
SS12
SS14 SS13
Basildon
SS16
SS15
Canvey Island
SS8
Stanford-le-Hope
SS17

**Chelmsford**

**Basildon**

Clare
CB1
CO10
Great Sampford
CM10
Thaxted
Elsenham
Hatfield Heath
CM22
CM17
CM5
Chipping Ongar
CM15
Brentwood
CM14
CM13
Ingrave
Upminster
RM14
RM16
RM18
Tilbury
DA11 DA12
DA9 DA10
DA1

**Brentwood**

Saffron Walden
CB11
Newport
Clavering
SG9
Stansted Mountfitchet
CM23
CM24
Bishop's Stortford
CM21
Sawbridgeworth
SG12
CM19
Harlow
CM20
Abridge
RM4
RM3
Romford
RM1
RM2
RM5 RM12
RM7
RM6
RM11
RM10
RM13
RM15
RM17
RM19
RM20
DA17
DA18
DA8

**Uttlesford**

**Harlow**

**Epping Forest**

Great Chesterford
CM10
SG8

Waltham Abbey
EN9
EN11
EN8
EN10
EN3
Loughton
IG10
IG7
IG9
IG8
E4
Chingford
E17
E11
IG6
IG5
IG4
IG3 RM8
RM9
Barking
IG11
E6
E12
E7
E13
IG2
IG1
Ilford
IG3

CB10

**West Mersea** CO5

TL TM
TM TR
TL 600 TM
TQ TR
TQ TR
TL TQ
TQ EN3

200

50
40
30
20
10
200
TR
90
80

30
20
10
600
90
80
70
60
50
40
TQ

50
40
30
20
10
200
90
80
70
60
50
40

Suffolk STREET ATLAS

A   B   C   D   E   F

8

7

49

6

IP29

Moor's Farm

Sparrow's Wood

Lower Barn

Wales End Farm

Wales End

Wales Farm

Easty Wood

New Street Farm

PLUM LA

NEW ST

Robb's Farm

CO10

5

48

Ducks Hall

4

Colt's Hall

3

47

Blacklands Hall

CAVENDISH LA

Stour Valley Path

2

Kiln Farm

A1092

MELFORD RD   LOWER RD

WATER LA

THE COLUMBINES

HYDE PARK CNR

PEACOCKS CL

MANOR RD

NETHER RD

CHURCH RD

GENEVYLL CL

THE MALTINGS

PO

BRIDGE COTTS

PENTLOW DR

CLUNNIE ORCH

B1064

PENTLOW LA

Vineyard

Cavendish CE Prim Sch

PH

Cemy

HIGH ST

THE TERRACE

Sue Ryder Foundation Mus

Pentlow Mill

Pentlow Bridge

Pentlow Hall

River Stour

Alder Carr

Scott's Farm

Cavendish

Pentlow

DALHAMS

POOLS ST

QUEEN

STOUR ST

A1092

Pentlow Hall Farm

B1064

1

46

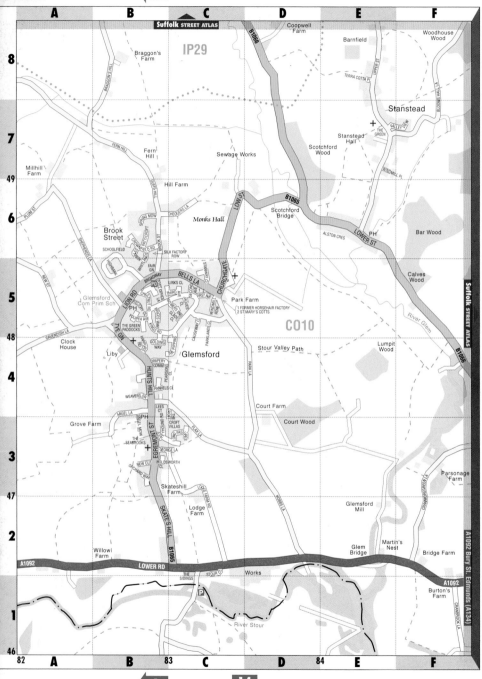

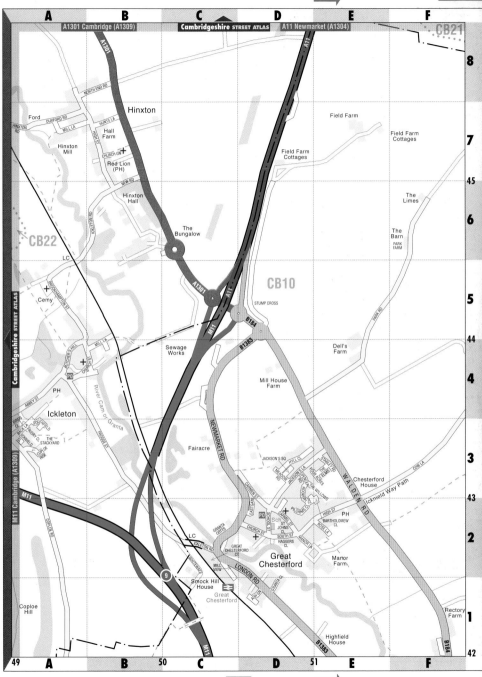

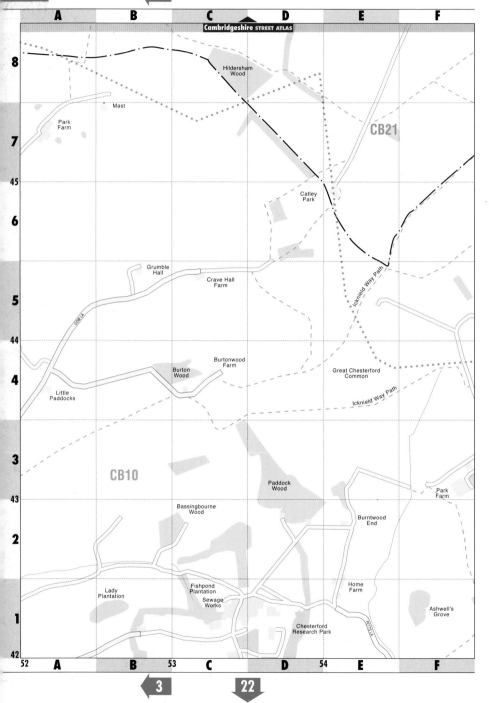

A   B   C   D   E   F

8

Hildersham
Wood

7

Mast

Park
Farm

CB21

45

Catley
Park

6

Grumble
Hall

Crave Hall
Farm

5

Icknield Way Path

COW LA

44

Burtonwood
Farm

4

Burton
Wood

Great Chesterford
Common

Little
Paddocks

Icknield Way Path

3

CB10

Paddock
Wood

Park
Farm

43

Bassingbourne
Wood

Burntwood
End

2

Home
Farm

Lady
Plantation

Fishpond
Plantation

Ashwell's
Grove

Sewage
Works

1

Chesterford
Research Park

PETIS LA

42

52   A   B   53   C   D   54   E   F

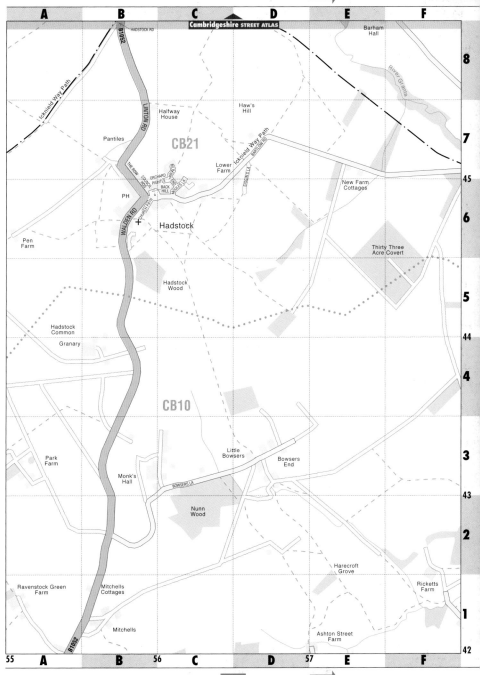

**Cambridgeshire STREET ATLAS**

A  B  C  D  E  F

B1052

HADSTOCK RD

Barham
Hall

8

River Granta

Icknield Way Path

LINTON RD

Halfway
House

Haw's
Hill

7

Pantiles

CB21

Icknield Way Path

45

THE ROW

COUNCIL HOUSE

ORCHARD PIGHTLE

Lower
Farm

SIDGIN'S LA

BARTLOW RD

New Farm
Cottages

BACK
HILL

BELL LA

DULLEA LA

PH

Hadstock

6

WALDEN RD

CHURCH PATH

Pen
Farm

Thirty Three
Acre Covert

Hadstock
Wood

5

Hadstock
Common

Granary

44

CB10

4

Park
Farm

Little
Bowsers

Bowsers
End

3

Monk's
Hall

BOWSERS LA

43

Nunn
Wood

2

Harecroft
Grove

Ricketts
Farm

Ravenstock Green
Farm

Mitchells
Cottages

1

B1052

Mitchells

Ashton Street
Farm

55  A  56  B  C  57  D  E  F  42

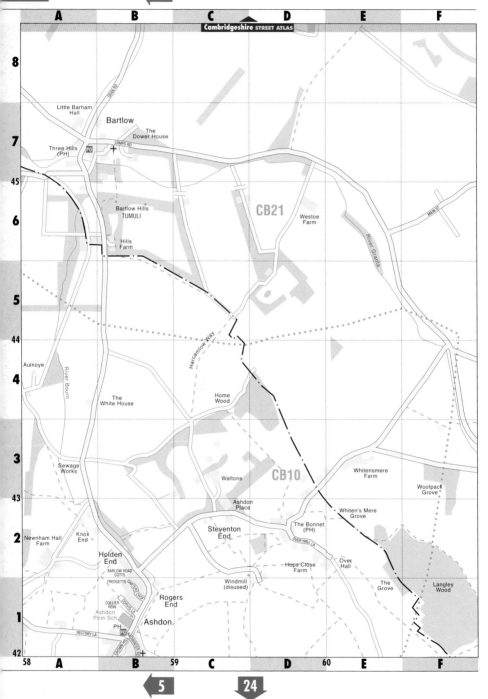

**Cambridgeshire** STREET ATLAS

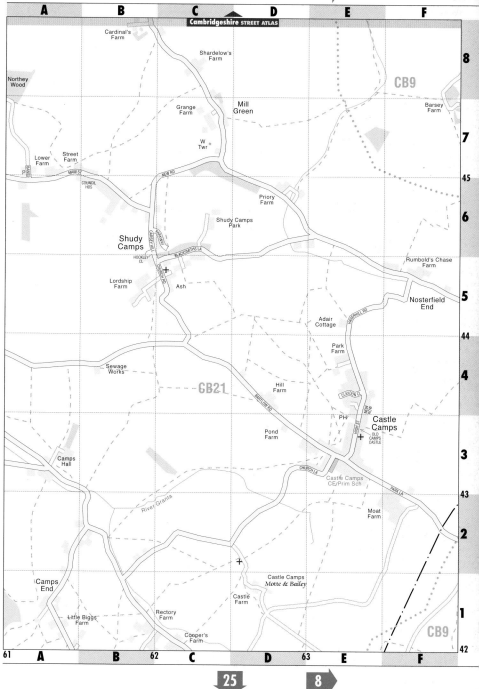

**Cambridgeshire STREET ATLAS**

A B C D E F

8
7
45
6
5
44
4
3
43
2
1
42

Cardinal's Farm

Shardelow's Farm

Northey Wood

CB9

Mill Green

Grange Farm

Barsey Farm

W Twr

Lower Farm
Street Farm

MAIN ST
COUNCIL HOS
NEW RD
CARSEY HILL

Priory Farm

Shudy Camps Park

Shudy Camps

HOCKLEY CL
BLACKSMITHS LA
CHURCH RD

Rumbold's Chase Farm

Lordship Farm

Ash

Nosterfield End

Adair Cottage

VANDHILL RD

Park Farm

Sewage Works

CB21

Hill Farm

CLAYDON CL
HIGH ST
NEW ROW

BARTLOW RD

Camps Hall

Pond Farm

PH

Castle Camps

OLD CAMPS CASTLE

River Granta

CHURCH LA

Castle Camps CE/Prim Sch

PARK LA

Moat Farm

Camps End

Castle Camps Motte & Bailey

Castle Farm

Little Biggs Farm

Rectory Farm

Cooper's Farm

CB9

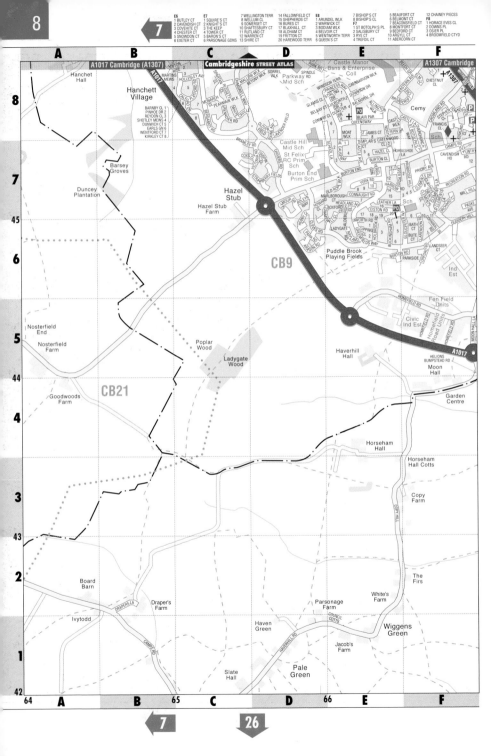

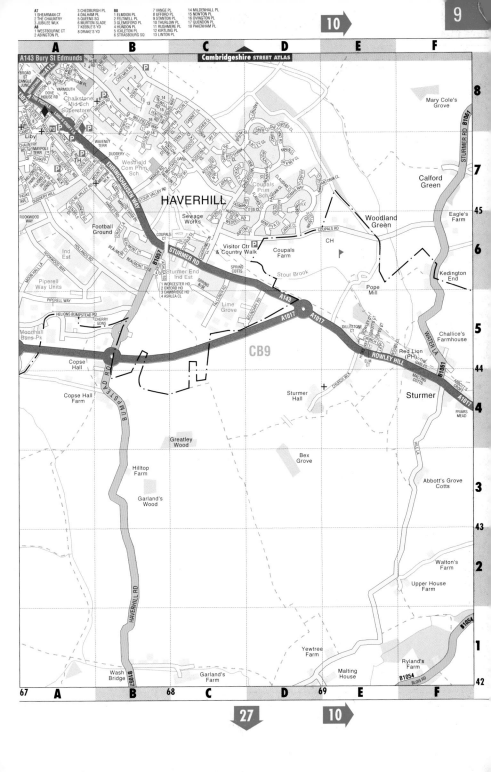

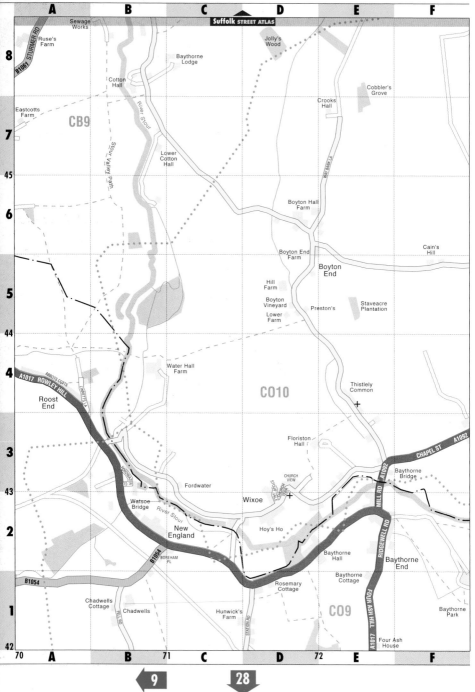

Suffolk STREET ATLAS

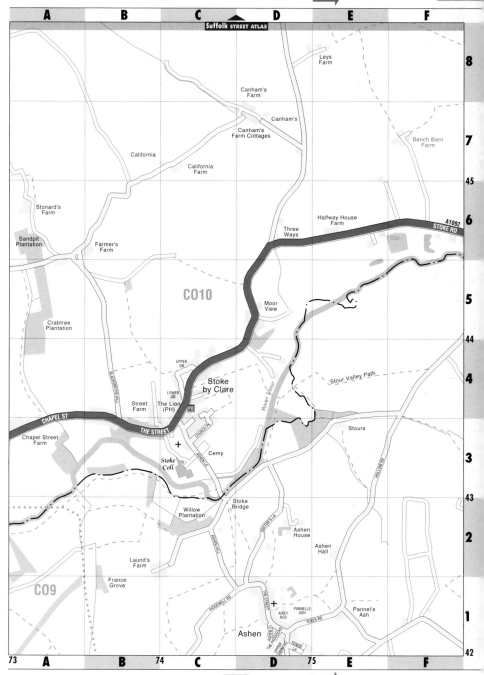

Leys Farm

Canham's Farm

Canham's

Canham's Farm Cottages

Bench Barn Farm

California

California Farm

Stonard's Farm

45

Halfway House Farm

A1092 STOKE RD

Sandpit Plantation

Farmer's Farm

Three Ways

6

CO10

Crabtree Plantation

Moor View

5

44

Stour Valley Path

UPPER GN

Stoke by Clare

4

River Stour

LOWER GN

Street Farm

The Lion (PH)

PO

BLACKSMITHS HILL

Chapel St

Stours

WIXLOW RD

The Street

Chapel Street Farm

CHURCH PK

+

Cemy

3

43

Stoke Coll

ASHEN LA

Stoke Bridge

2

Willow Plantation

Ashen House

VICTORS LA

Ashen Hall

CO9

Laund's Farm

ASHEN HILL

France Grove

RIDGEWELL RD

THE STREET

Pannell's Ash

Ashen

AIREY HOS

+

PANNELLS ASH

FOXES RD

1

42

THE PADDOCKS

ASHEN CL

UPPER GN

FOXES LA

73          74          75

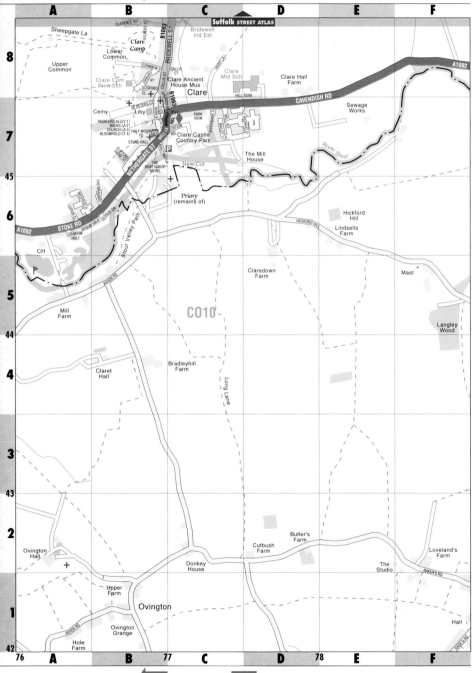

A B C D E F

8

7

45

6

5

44

4

3

43

2

1

42

76 A B 77 C D 78 E F

Sheepgate La

Upper Common

Clare Camp

Lower Common

CLARENCE RD

Clare Cpm Prim Sch

COMMON ST

GILBERT RD

B1063

BRIDEWELL ST

Bridewell Ind Est

HARP LA

Clare Mid Sch

Clare Hall Farm

A1092

GOSFORD ST

St PETERS CT

Libry

Clare Ancient House Mus

B1063

Clare

HILL TERR

CAVENDISH RD

Sewage Works

Cemy

Pashlers Alley 1
Bucks La 2
Church La 3
Bloomfield Ct 4

Half Moon
STONE HALL
YD

CALLIS CT

TH

PARK VIEW

BAILEY LA

HILL ST

River Stout

CLIFTONS CAR DK

NETHERGATE ST

WELL MARKET

Clare Castle Country Park

P

THE BOAT HOUSE MEWS

New Cut

The Mill House

THE GRANARY

STOUR VALE

FREETREE

LYON CL

STOUR RD

Priory (remains of)

Stour Valley Path

A1092 STOKE RD

OANEUM HOLT

Hickford Hill

HICKFORD HILL

Lindsells Farm

ASHEN RD

CH

Claredown Farm

Mast

Mill Farm

CO10

Langley Wood

Claret Hall

Bradleyhill Farm

Long Lane

Ovington Hall

Cutbush Farm

Butler's Farm

Loveland's Farm

The Studio

BAKER'S RD

Upper Farm

Donkey House

Ovington

ASHEN RD

Ovington Grange

Hole Farm

Hall

SAGE RD

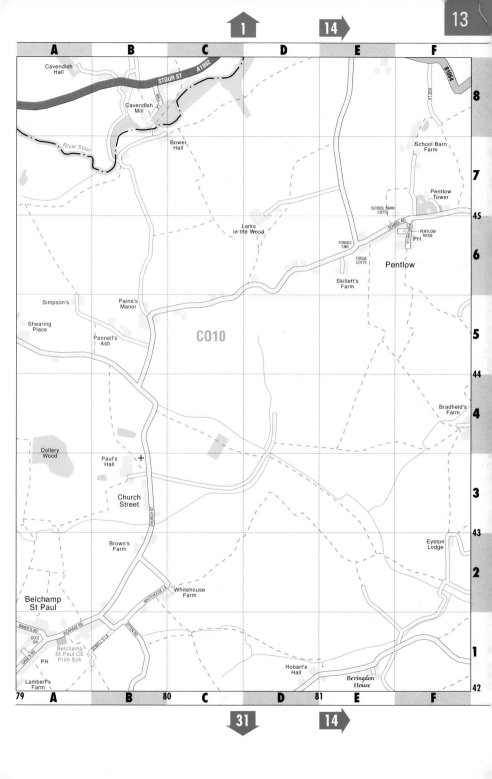

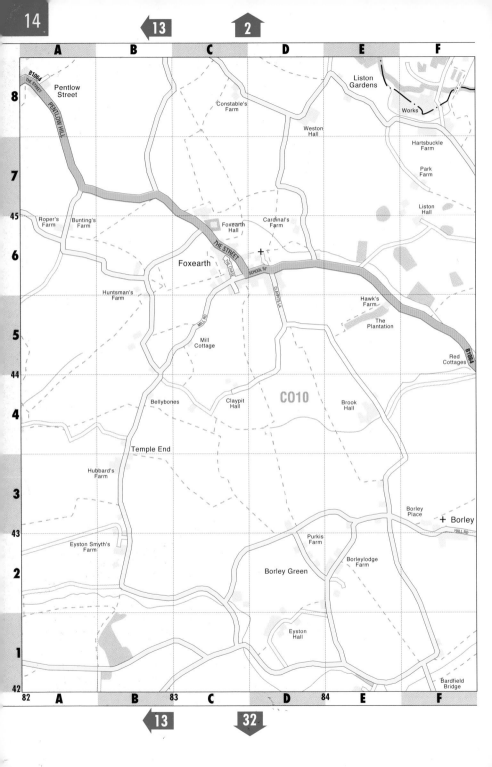

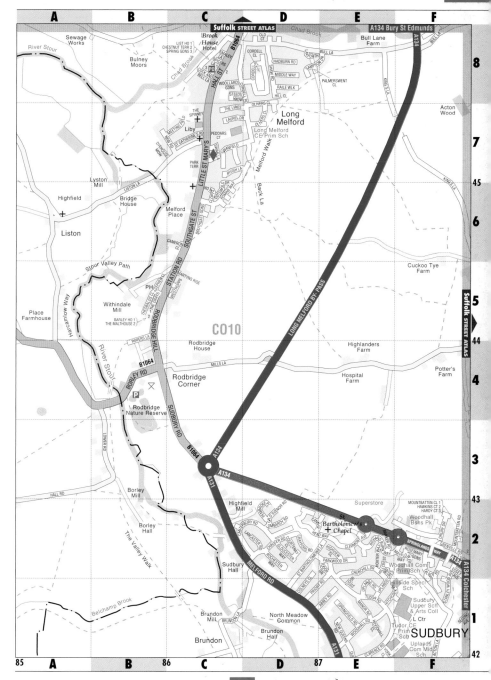

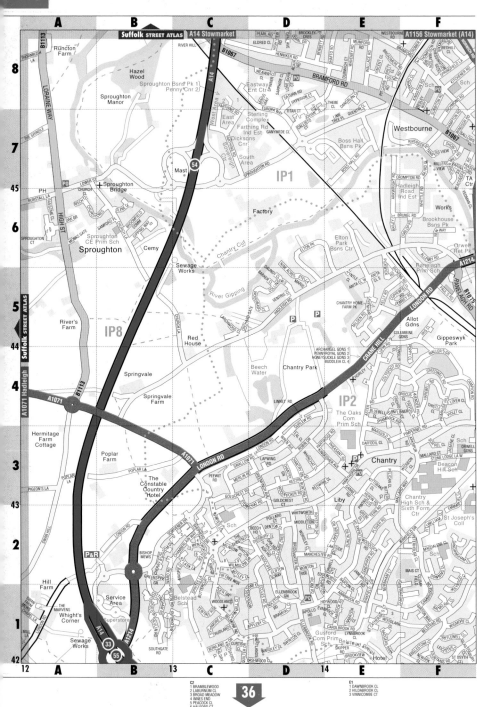

C2
1 BRAMBLEWOOD
2 LABURNUM CL
3 BROAD MEADOW
4 INNES END
5 PEACOCK CL
6 HALFORD CT
7 MERRION CL
8 MATLOCK CL
9 MOTTRAM CL

E1
1 DAWNBROOK CL
2 HILDABROOK CL
3 VINNICOMBE CT

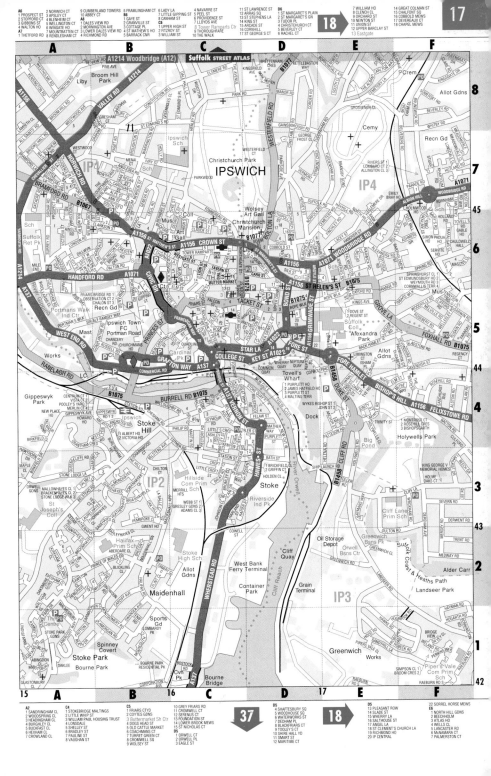

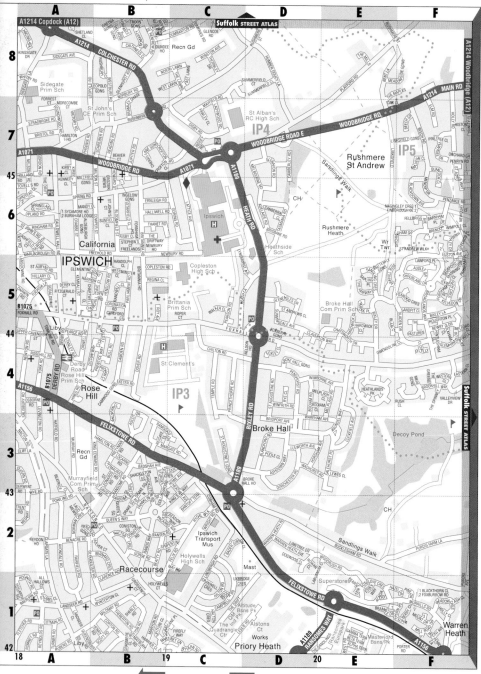

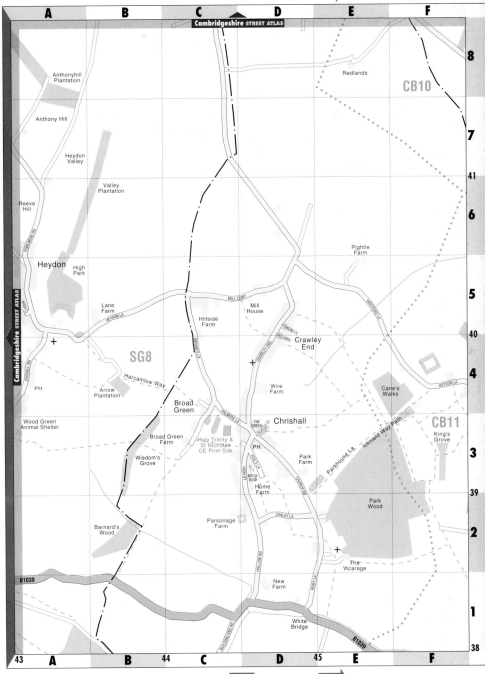

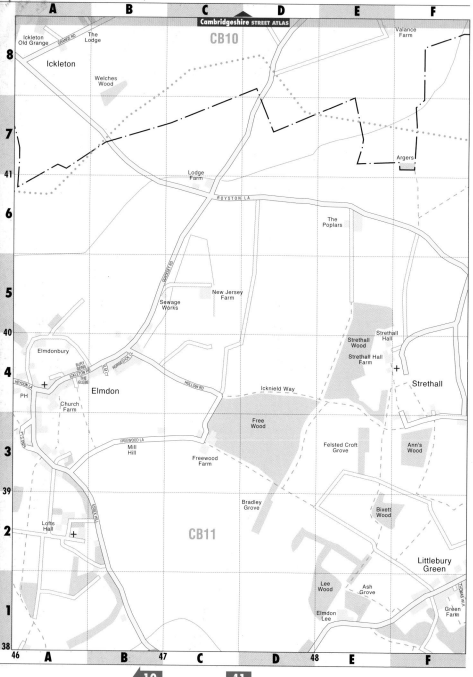

**Cambridgeshire** STREET ATLAS

CB10

Ickleton
Old Grange

GRANGE RD

The
Lodge

Valance
Farm

Ickleton

Welches
Wood

Lodge
Farm

41

ROYSTON LA

Argers

The
Poplars

QUICKSET RD

New Jersey
Farm

Sewage
Works

Strethall
Hall

40

Strethall
Wood

Elmdonbury

BURY DENS

HORNBEACK LA

LEVE LA

THE GLEBE

ICKLETON RD

Strethall Hall
Farm

HEYDON LA

HOLLOW RD

Icknield Way

Strethall

PH

Elmdon

Church
Farm

Free
Wood

Felsted Croft
Grove

Ann's
Wood

FREEWOOD LA

Mill
Hill

Freewood
Farm

39

Bradley
Grove

Bixett
Wood

ESSEX HILL

Lofts
Hall

CB11

Littlebury
Green

THOMAS WLK

Lee
Wood

Ash
Grove

Elmdon
Lee

Green
Farm

38

46

47

48

A  B  C  D  E  F

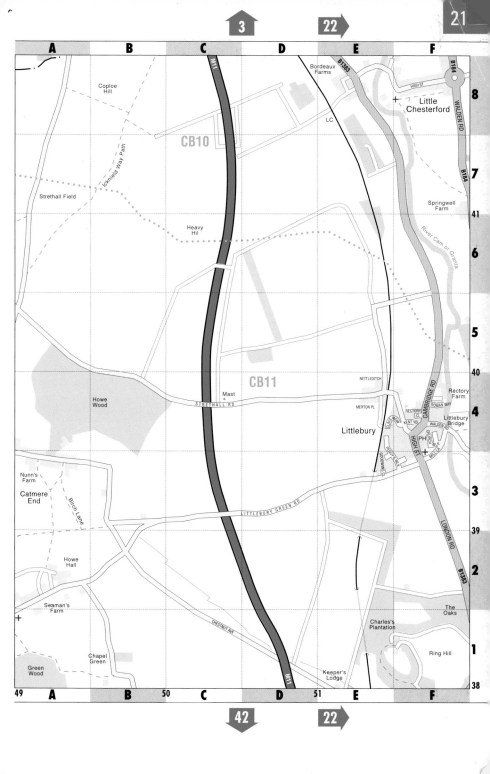

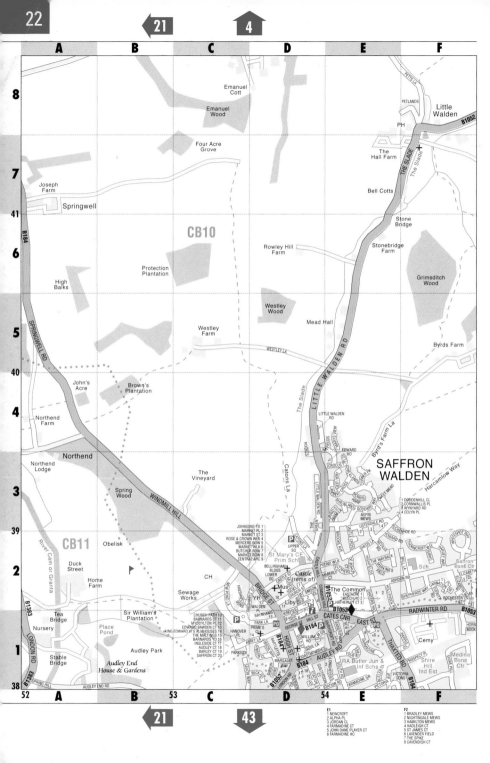

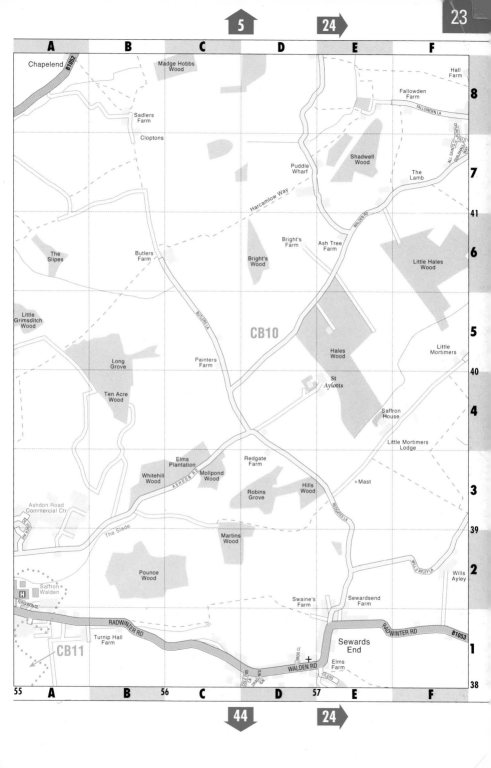

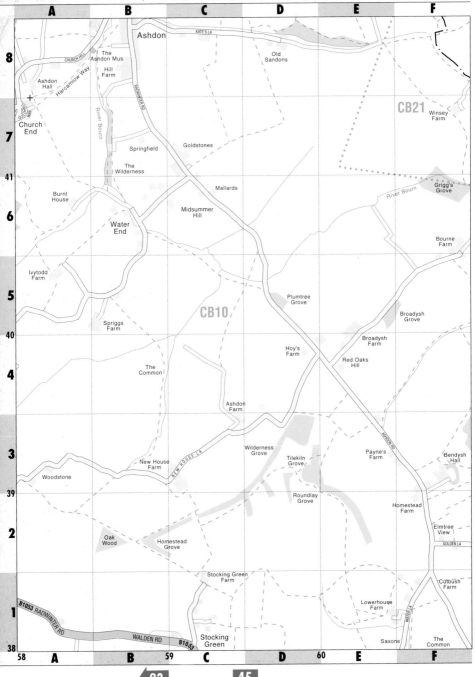

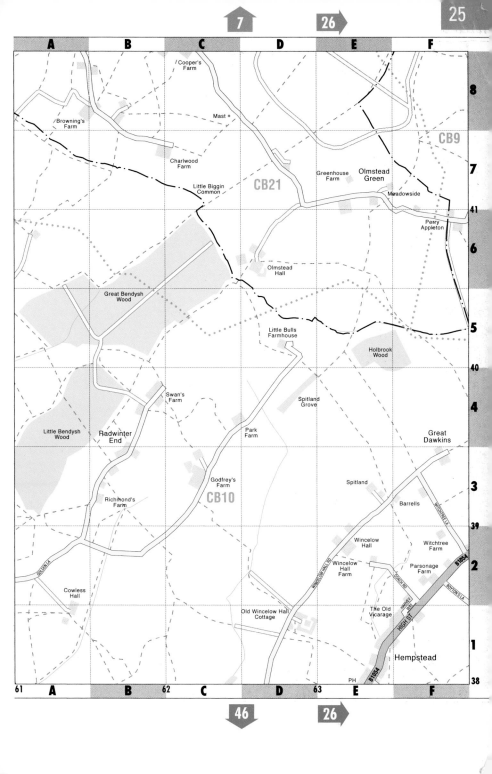

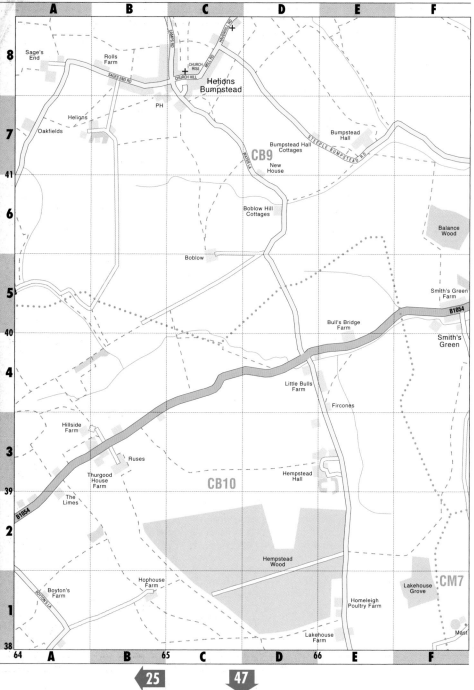

**A**   **B**   **C**   **D**   **E**   **F**

**8**
Sage's End
Rolls Farm
SAGES END RD
CHURCH RISE
CHURCH HILL
CAMPS RD
HAVERHILL RD
MILL RD
Helions Bumpstead
PH

Helions
**7**
Oakfields
Bumpstead Hall
Bumpstead Hall Cottages
STEEPLE BUMPSTEAD RD
B1054
**CB9**
New House

**41**

**6**
Boblow Hill Cottages
Balance Wood

Boblow

**5**
Smith's Green Farm
B1054
**40**
Bull's Bridge Farm
Smith's Green
**4**
Little Bulls Farm
Fircones

Hillside Farm
**3**
Ruses
Thurgood House Farm
Hempstead Hall
**CB10**
**39**
The Limes
B1054
**2**
Hempstead Wood

Boyton's Farm
Hophouse Farm
Lakehouse Grove
**CM7**
**1**
BOYTON'S LA
Homeleigh Poultry Farm
Mast
**38**
Lakehouse Farm

**64**   **A**   **B**   **65**   **C**   **D**   **66**   **E**   **F**

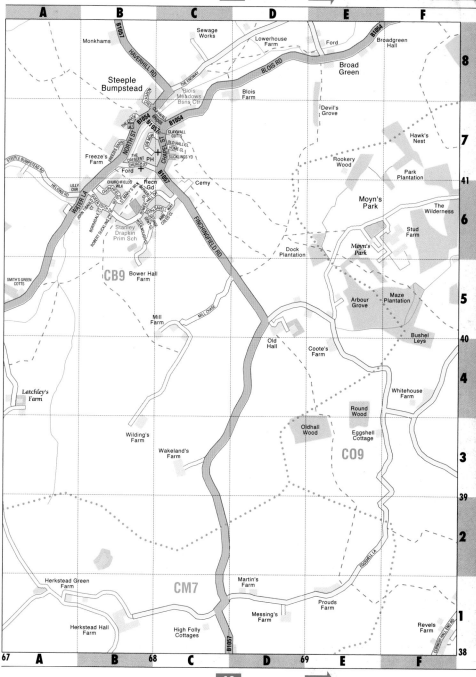

Monkhams

HAVERHILL RD

Steeple
Bumpstead

Sewage
Works

THE LANEWAY

Lowerhouse
Farm

Ford

BLOIS RD

B1054

Broadgreen
Hall

Broad
Green

Blois
Meadows
Bsns Ctr

Blois
Farm

Devil's
Grove

Hawk's
Nest

B1054

B1057

NORTH ST

CLAWWALL

B1057

CHAPEL ST

CLAWWALL
COTTS

OLD HALL CL
HOME CL
SUCKLINGS YD

Rookery
Wood

Park
Plantation

41

Freeze's
Farm

THE CRESCENT
CHURCH ST

PH

Ford

Cemy

Moyn's
Park

The
Wilderness

Stud
Farm

STEEPLE BUMPSTEAD RD

HELIONS RD

LILLY
CNR

WATER LA

Recn
Gd

Stanley
Drapkin
Prim Sch

Moyn's
Park

6

SMITH'S GREEN
COTTS

CB9

Bower Hall
Farm

FINCHINGFIELD RD

Dock
Plantation

Arbour
Grove

Maze
Plantation

Bushel
Leys

5

40

Mill
Farm

MILL CHASE

Old
Hall

Coote's
Farm

Latchley's
Farm

Wilding's
Farm

Wakeland's
Farm

Oldhall
Wood

Round
Wood

Eggshell
Cottage

Whitehouse
Farm

4

CO9

3

39

EGGSHELL LA

2

Herkstead Green
Farm

CM7

Martin's
Farm

Prouds
Farm

Revels
Farm

1

Herkstead Hall
Farm

High Folly
Cottages

B1057

Messing's
Farm

CORNISH HALL END RD

38

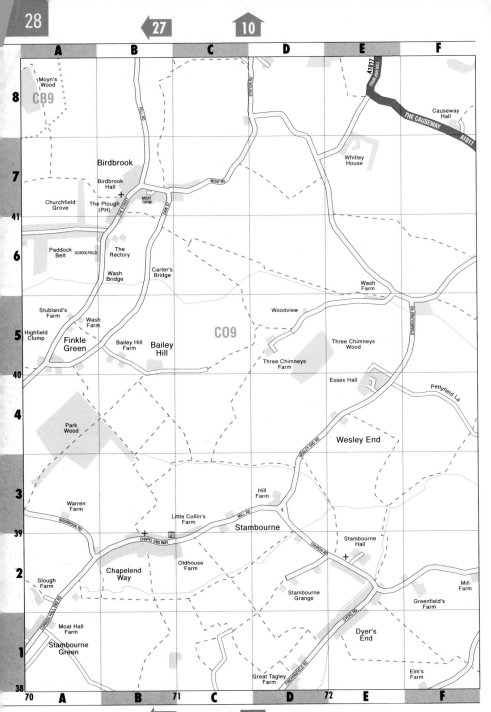

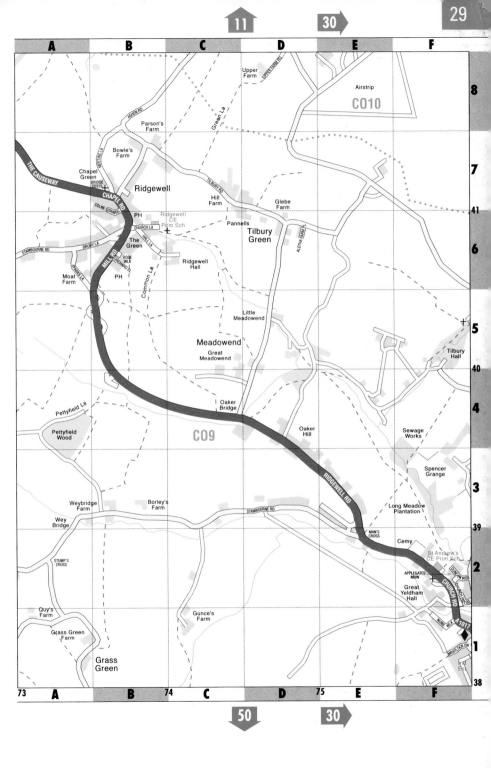

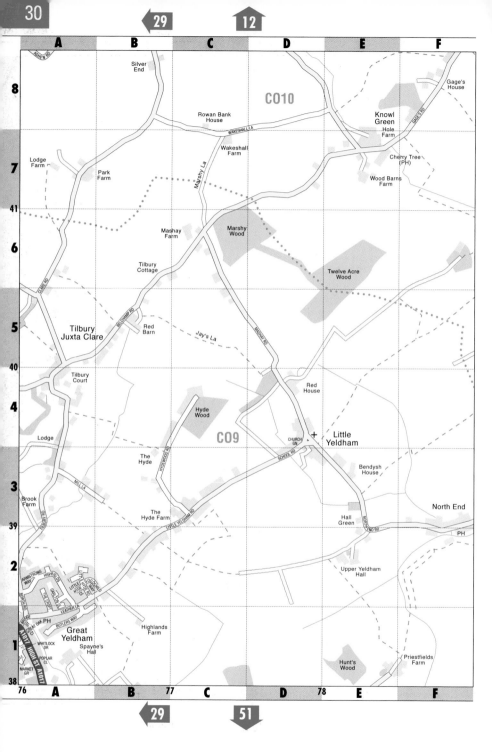

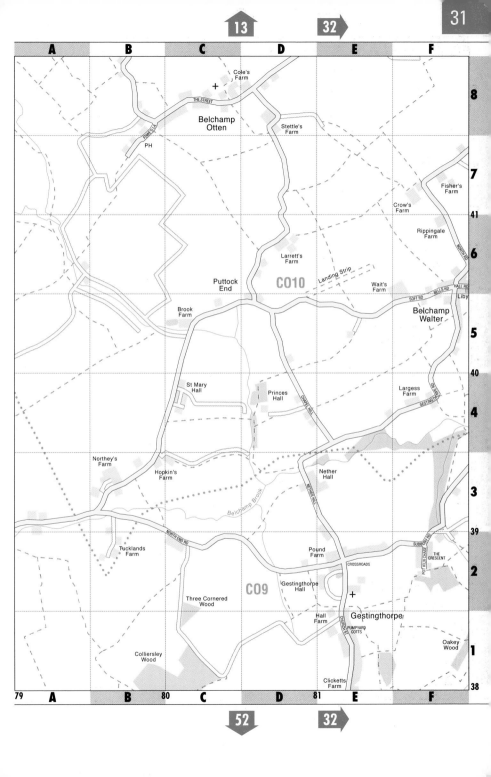

Cole's Farm

THE STREET

Belchamp Otten

Stettle's Farm

PH

Puttock End

CO10

Larrett's Farm

Landing Strip

Crow's Farm

Fisher's Farm

Rippingale Farm

NORTH RD

Wait's Farm

HALL RD

BELLS RD

SOFT RD

Liby

Belchamp Walter

Brook Farm

St Mary Hall

Princes Hall

CHAPEL HILL

Largess Farm

GESTINGTHORPE RD

Northey's Farm

Hopkin's Farm

Belchamp Brook

Nether Hall

NETHER HILL

Tucklands Farm

NORTH END RD

Pound Farm

SUDBURY RD

POT KILN CHASE

THE CRESCENT

CROSSROADS

CO9

Gestingthorpe Hall

Three Cornered Wood

Hall Farm

Gestingthorpe

CHURCH ST

PUMPYARD COTTS

Oakey Wood

Colliersley Wood

Clicketts Farm

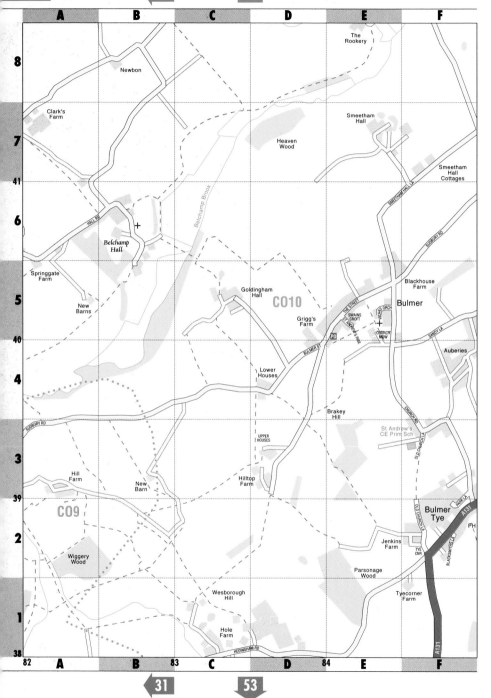

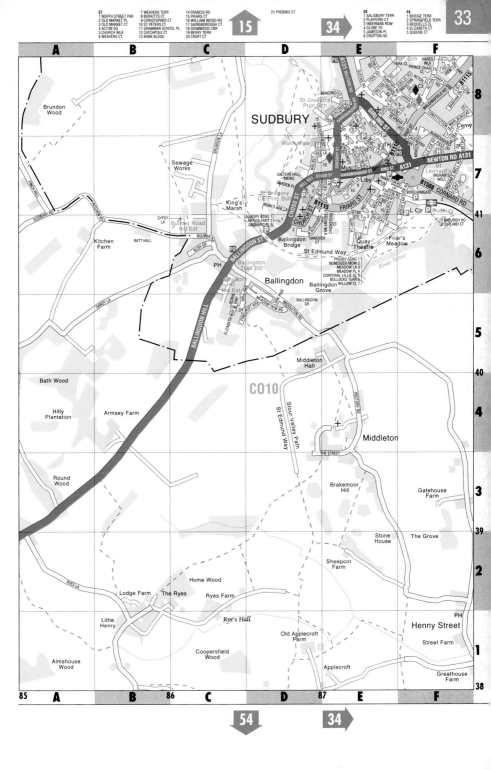

**E7**
1 NORTH STREET PAR
2 OLD MARKET PL
3 OLD MARKET CT
4 ACTON SQ
5 CHURCH WLK
6 WEAVERS CT

7 WEAVERS TERR
8 BURKITTS CT
9 CHRISTOPHER CT
10 ST PETERS CT
11 GRAMMAR SCHOOL PL
12 CATCHPOLE CT
13 BANK BLDGS

14 FRANCIS RD
15 FRIARS CT
16 WILLIAM WOOD HO
17 GAINSBOROUGH CT
18 GRIMWOOD CNR
19 BERRY TERR
20 CROFT CT

21 PHOENIX CT

15

34

**E8**
1 SALISBURY TERR
2 PLAYFORD CT
3 INKERMAN ROW
4 GLOBE YD
5 JAMESON PL
6 CROFTON HO

**F8**
1 BRIDGE TERR
2 SPRINGFIELD TERR
3 REDDELLS CL
4 ELIZABETH CL
5 QUEENS CT

33

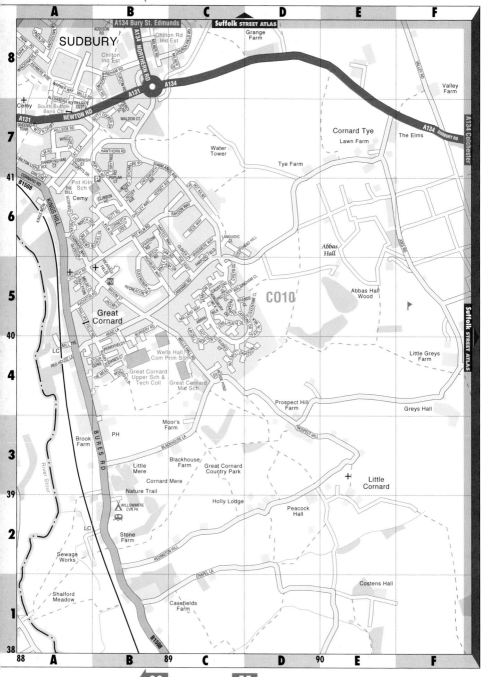

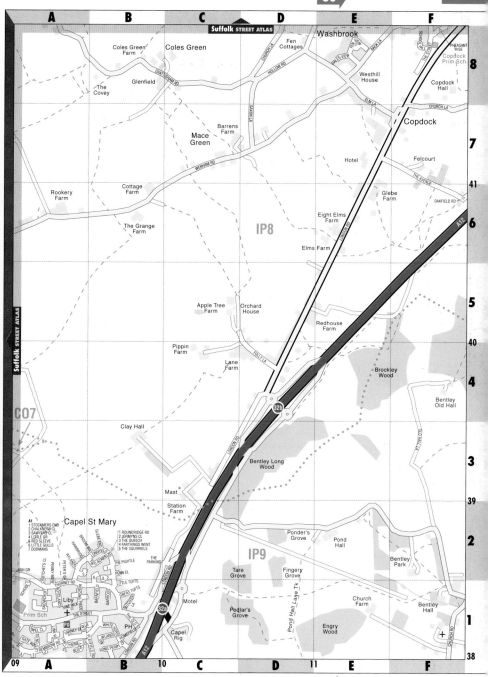

**Suffolk** STREET ATLAS

Washbrook

Coles Green
Farm

Coles Green

Fen
Cottages

PHEASANT
RISE

Copdock
Prim Sch

8

Glenfield

The
Covey

Westhill
House

Copdock
Hall

Copdock

CHURCH LA

ELM LA

Barrens
Farm

Mace
Green

7

Hotel

Felcourt

WENHAM RD

THE AVENUE

Cottage
Farm

41

Rookery
Farm

Glebe
Farm

OAKFIELD RD

The Grange
Farm

Eight Elms
Farm

IP8

6

Elms Farm

A12

Apple Tree
Farm

Orchard
House

5

Redhouse
Farm

Pippin
Farm

40

FOLLY LA

Lane
Farm

Brockley
Wood

4

Clay Hall

32b

Bentley
Old Hall

C07

3

Bentley Long
Wood

Mast

39

Station
Farm

Capel St Mary

Ponder's
Grove

Pond
Hall

2

Bentley
Park

IP9

Tare
Grove

Fingery
Grove

Pond Hall Lane Trk

32a

Motel

Church
Farm

Bentley
Hall

Capel
Rig

Pedlar's
Grove

Engry
Wood

1

A12

A B C D E F

8

33

55 A14

Copdock
Mill

MILL LA

Belstead Brook

GROVE HILL 1
SPECKLED WOOD CL 2
MONARCH WAY 3
GROVE WLK 4
GREEN OAK GLADE 5.

IPSWICH

IP2

Ashground
Plantation

Alder
Carr

CHURCH LA

Belstead
Rise

7

IP8

Belstead
Hall

Belstead

HOLLY LA

GROVE HILL

CHAPEL LA

HOLLY BLUE
CL

SWALLOWTAIL CL 6
SKIPPER RD 7
TORTOISESHELL CL 8
FRITILLARY CL 9
GATEKEEPER CL 10
BOATMAN CL 11
MAYFLY CL 12
LACEWING CL 13
SPRINGTAIL RD 14.

Spring
Wood

15 BLACK ARCHES
16 COPPER GR

LAKEFIELD RD

41

Alder
Carr

Mill Poultry
Farm

Thorington
Hall

A14

6

A12

JACK'S HORNS LA

Blacksmith's
Corner

Street
Farm

BUTT'S LA

THE STREET

Charity
Farm

Spinney
Wood

Wherstead
Wood

Pannington
Hall

Hill
Covert

5

Pannington Hall
Cottage

40

Old Hall
Wood

Clubs
Heath

Bluegate
Farm

4

A137

VALLEY LA

3

Newcome
Wood

Bentley
Manor

Hubbard's Hall
Farm

Tattingstone Trout
Farm

Park
House

39

2

Road
Farm

Holbrook
Park

IP9

A137

1

WHITE HORSE
COTT

PH

WHITE HORSE HILL

SCHOOL RD

Tattingstone
White Horse

CORNHILL RD

Shrub
Wood

38

LEMONS HILL

12 A 13 C 14 E F
B D

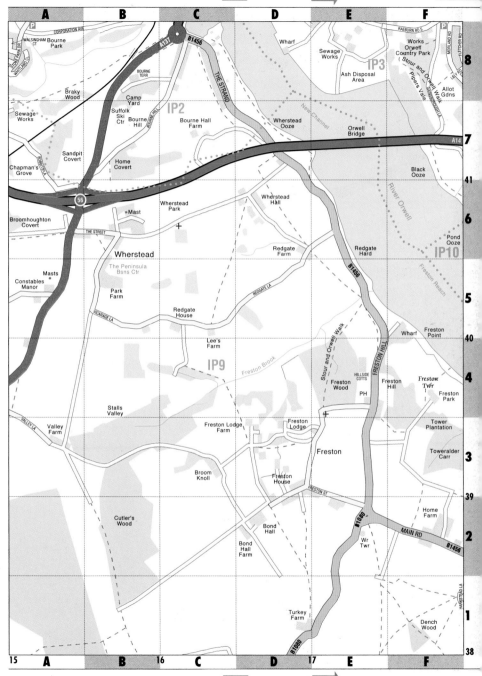

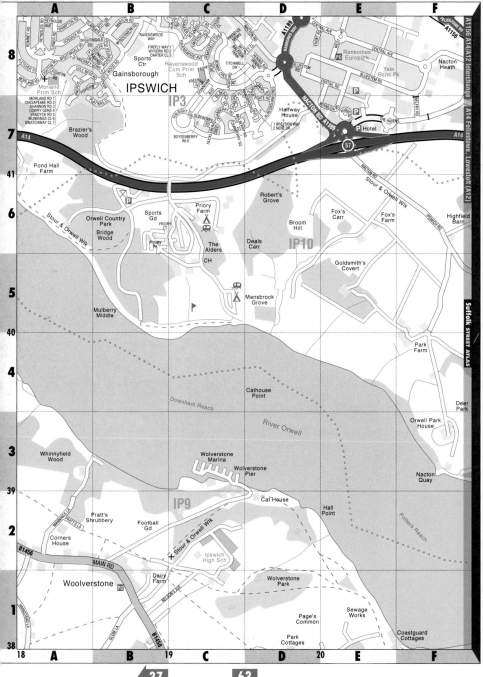

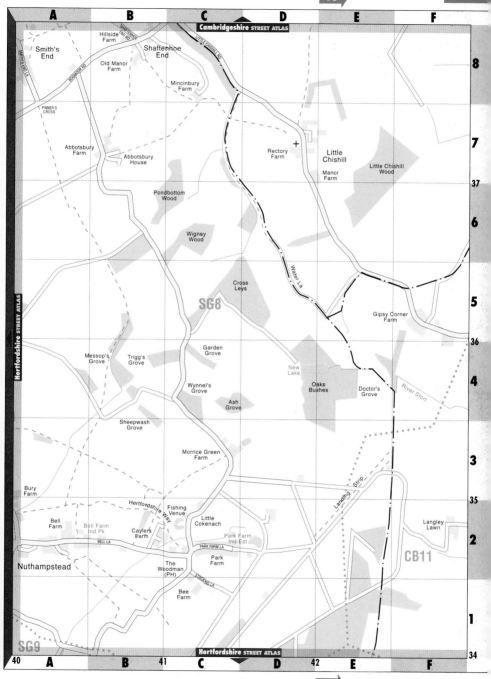

**Cambridgeshire** STREET ATLAS

Hertfordshire STREET ATLAS

**Hertfordshire** STREET ATLAS

8

7

37

6

5

36

4

3

35

2

1

34

A B C D E F

Smith's End

Hillside Farm

Shaftenhoe End

Old Manor Farm

PINNER'S CROSS

Mincinbury Farm

Abbotsbury Farm

Abbotsbury House

Rectory Farm

Little Chishill

Little Chishill Wood

Manor Farm

Pondbottom Wood

Wigney Wood

Walter La

Cross Leys

SG8

Gipsy Corner Farm

Garden Grove

Messop's Grove

Trigg's Grove

Wynnel's Grove

New Lake

Oaks Bushes

Doctor's Grove

River Stort

Ash Grove

Sheepwash Grove

Morrice Green Farm

Landing Strip

Bury Farm

Hertfordshire Way

Fishing Venue

Little Cokenach

Langley Lawn

CB11

Bell Farm

Bell Farm Ind Pk

Caylers Farm

BELL LA

Park Farm Ind Est

PARK FARM LA

Nuthampstead

The Woodman (PH)

Park Farm

STOCKING LA

Bee Farm

SG9

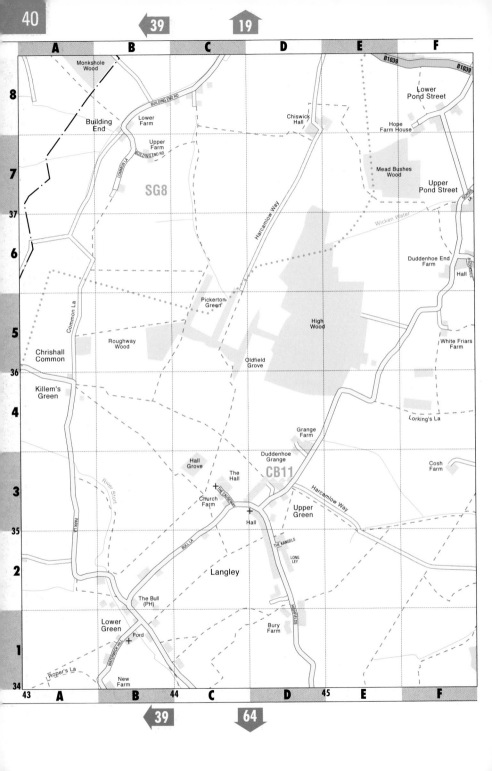

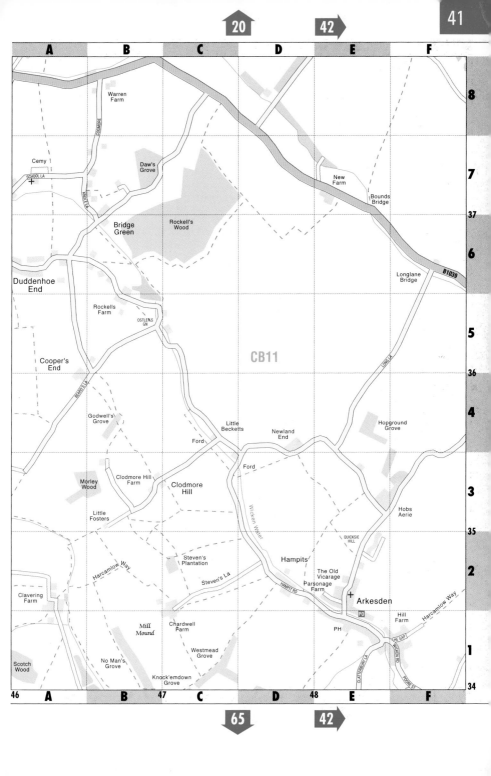

41
21

A B C D E F

8

Bush Pasture Grove

Cups Grove

The Triangle

Strawberry Close Belt

CHESTNUT AVE

Cornwallis Hill

The Willows

7

Mast

Red Leg Plantation

Neville Hill

LONDON RD

B1383

37

6

The Old Vicarage

Wenden Place Farm

MILL LA

THE BEECHES

Railway Cotts

STATION RD

WALDEN RD

PH

B1038

MUTLOW HILL

SILVER ROW

B1038

ROYSTON RD

PH

CHURCH ST

Mutlow Farm

Mutlow Hall

5

CB11

Wenden Hall

Bearwalden Bsns Pk

Audley End

Clanverend Farm

Clanverend Bridge

SHELL LA

DUCK ST

Wendens Ambo

36

Norton End

Rookery Farm

ROOKERY LA

LC

4

Duddenhoe La

Bulse Farm

Mill Farm

Mill Hill

LONDON RD

3

B1383

35

Harcamlow Way

Whiteditch Farm

Tudhope Farm

WHITEDITCH LA

2

Long Plantation

Newport Free Gram Sch

BURY WATER LA

Nursery

Burywater Cotts

TENTERFIELDS

1

Severals Farm

BURY WATER LA

GACES ACRE

SCHOOL LA

M11

34

49 A B 50 C D 51 E F

B1038

WICKEN RD

41
66

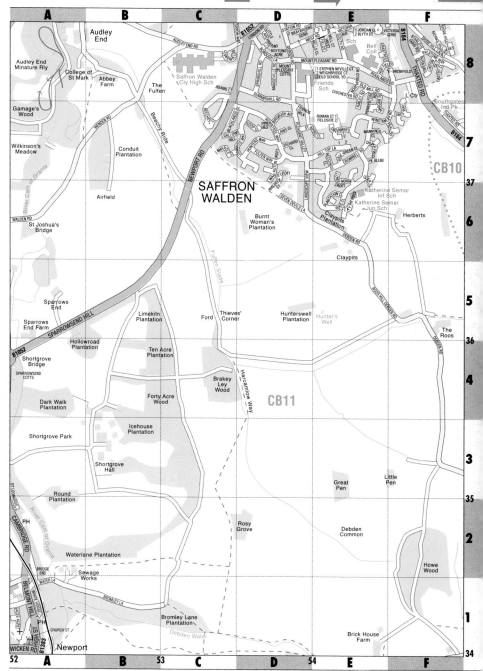

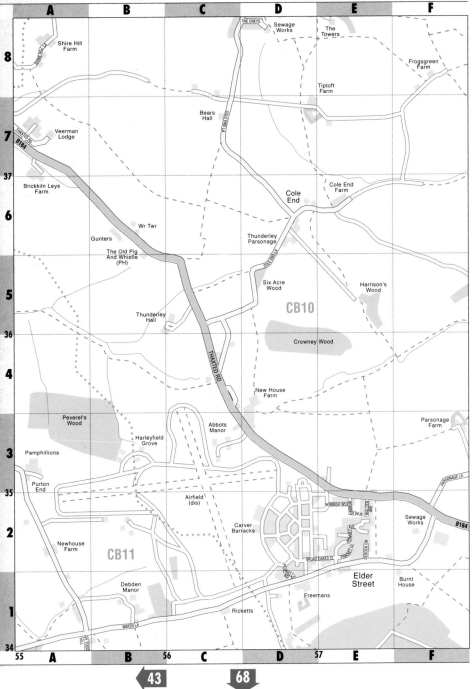

**A**     **B**     **C**     **D**     **E**     **F**

THE DREYS

Sewage Works

The Towers

8

Shire Hill Farm

Frogsgreen Farm

Tiptoft Farm

Bears Hall

7

Veerman Lodge

B184

THAXTED RD

37

Brickkiln Leys Farm

Cole End Farm

Cole End

6

Wr Twr

Thunderley Parsonage

Gunters

The Old Pig And Whistle (PH)

Six Acre Wood

Harrison's Wood

5

Thunderley Hall

**CB10**

THAXTED RD

COLE END LA

36

Crowney Wood

4

New House Farm

Peverel's Wood

Abbots Manor

Parsonage Farm

Harleyfield Grove

3

Pamphillions

PARSONAGE LA

Purton End

35

Airfield (dis)

WIMBISH WLK

Sewage Works

B184

2

Carver Barracks

Newhouse Farm

**CB11**

BROAD OAKES CL

Elder Street

Burnt House

Debden Manor

Freemans

1

Ricketts

WATER LA

34

55    **A**    **B**    56    **C**    **D**    57    **E**    **F**

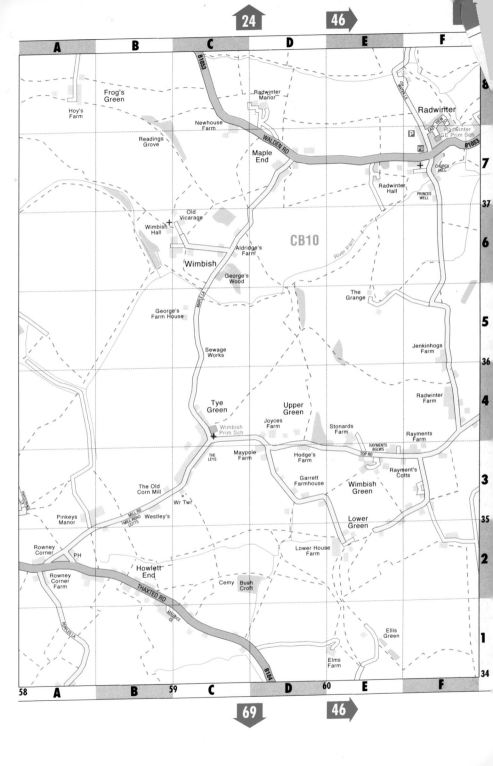

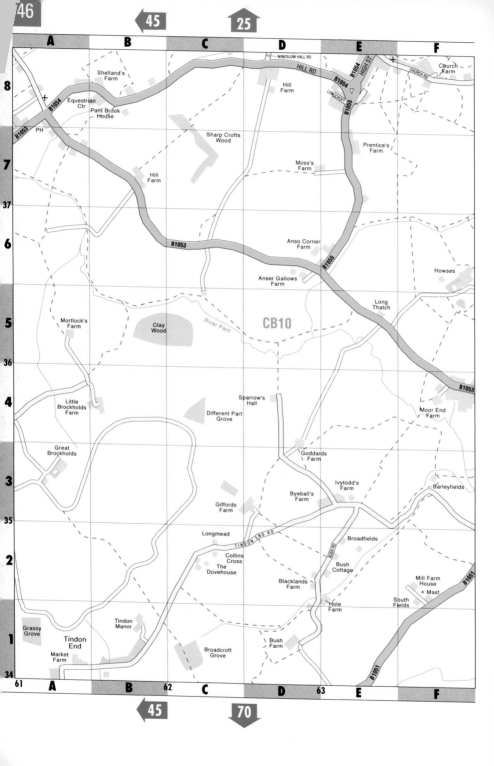

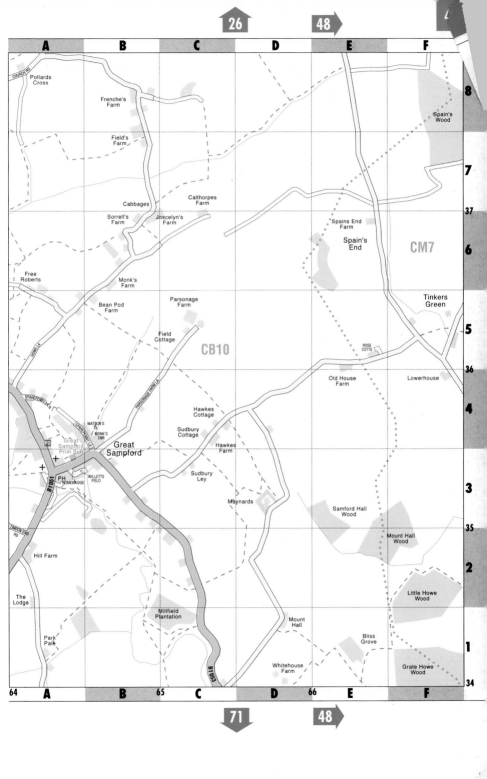

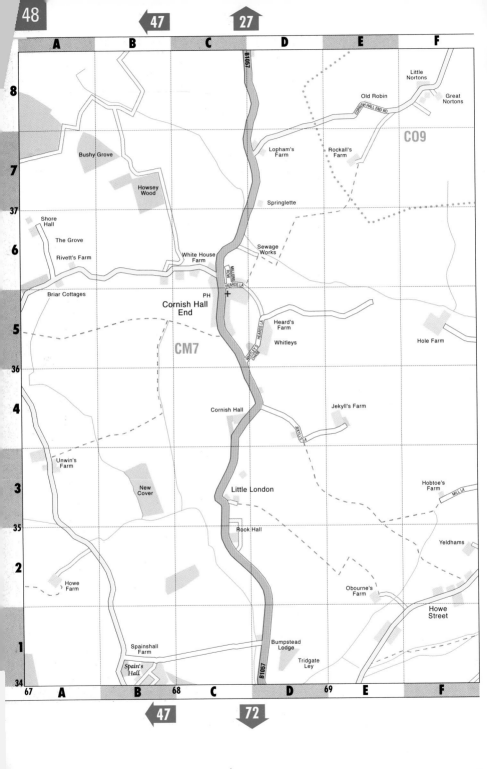

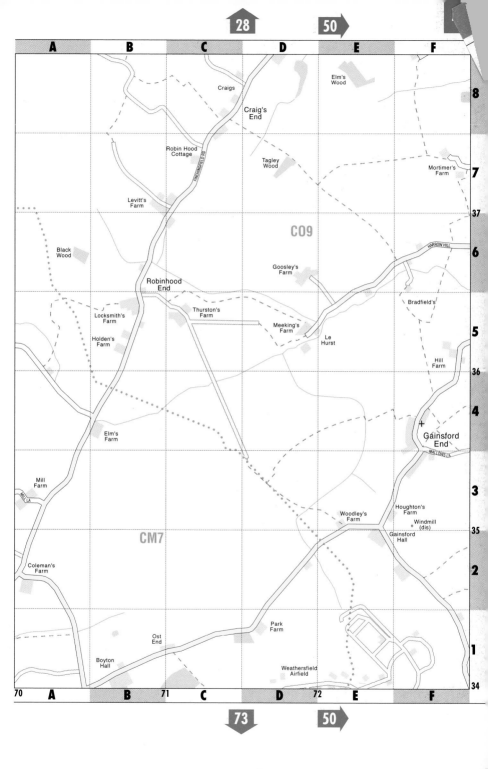

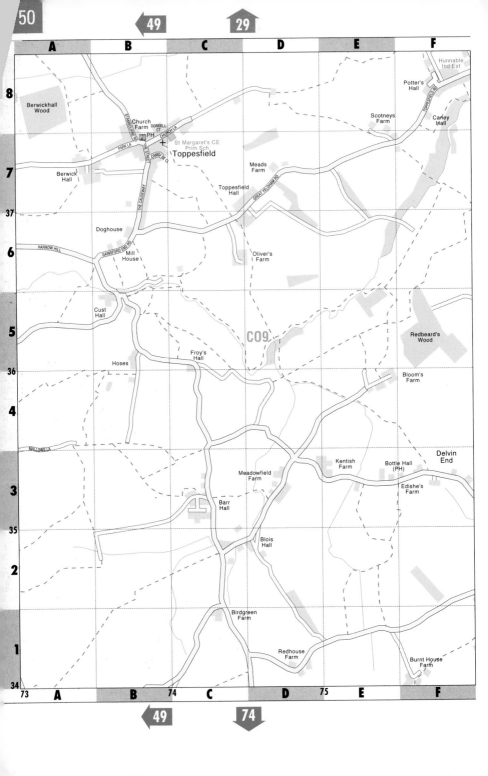

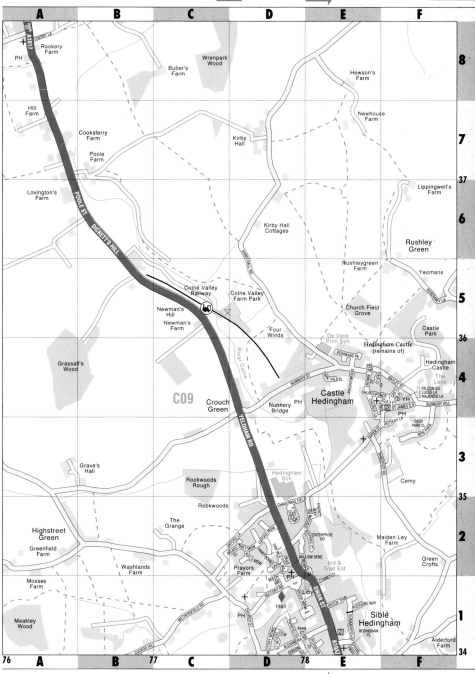

51
31

| | A | B | C | D | E | F |
|---|---|---|---|---|---|---|

**8**

Ridley's Wood

Delvyn's Lane

Delvyn's Farm

CHURCH ST

Audley End

Edeys Farm

PH

Rectory Farm

**7**

**37**

Parkgate Farm

DELVYN'S LA

Crouch House

Great Lodge Farm

**6**

Branwhite's Grove

The Moat

Lawrence's Farm

C09

**5**

Pannells Ash Farm

Rosemary Farm

ROSEMARY LA

Odewells

**36**

SUDBURY RD

Pantile Cottage

Little Chelmshoe House

**4**

ST JAMES'S ST

Kendallscroft Grove

Byham Hall

Little Lodge Farm

New Barn

**3**

Chelmshoe House Farm

Monks Lodge Farm

Monks Lodge

**35**

MONKS LODGE RD

Hosden's Farm

**2**

St Giles CE Prim Sch

ST GILES CL

Link Hills

Hopwell's Farm

Great Maplestead

STONE COTTS

Lucking Street

Luckinghouse Farm

**1**

CHURCH ST

Little Lodge Farm

**34**

Purls Cottage

Barrett's Hall

| 79 | A | B | 80 | C | D | 81 | E | F |
|---|---|---|---|---|---|---|---|---|

51
76

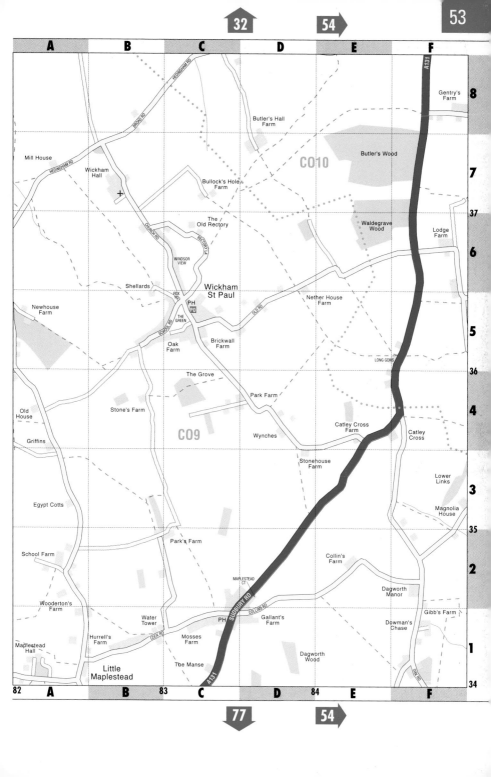

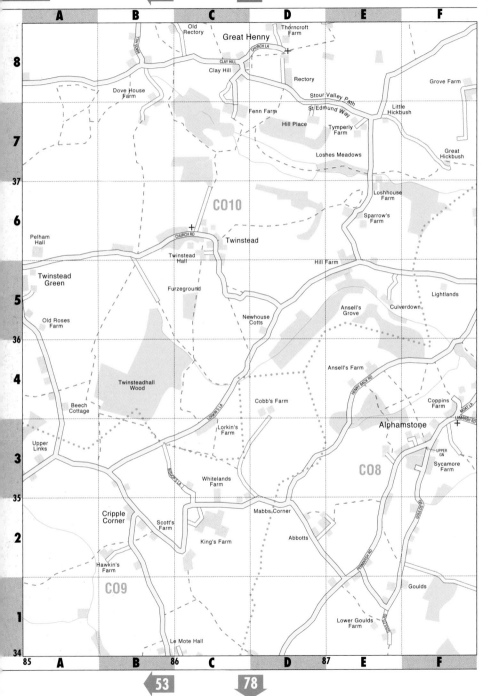

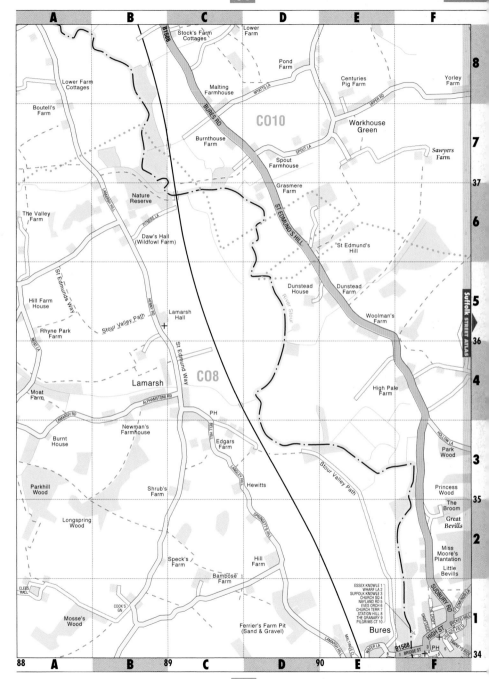

A B C D E F

8

Lower Farm Cottages

Stock's Farm Cottages

Lower Farm

Pond Farm

Centuries Pig Farm

Yorley Farm

Boutell's Farm

Malting Farmhouse

WYATTS LA

CO10

Upper Rd

Warkhouse Green

7

BURES RD

Burnthouse Farm

SPOUT LA

Spout Farmhouse

Sawyers Farm

37

Nature Reserve

Grasmere Farm

St Edmund's Way

Daw's Hall (Wildfowl Farm)

PITMIRE LA

ST EDMUND'S HILL

'St Edmund's Hill

6

The Valley Farm

Hill Farm House

Lamarsh Hall

Dunstead House

Dunstead Farm

Woolman's Farm

5

River Stour

Rhyne Park Farm

Stour Valley Path

HENNY RD

St Edmund Way

36

Moat Farm

Lamarsh

CO8

High Pale Farm

4

ALPHAMSTONE RD

PH

LAMARSH RD

Newman's Farmhouse

Edgars Farm

HOLLOW LA

Park Wood

3

Burnt House

BELL LA

Hewitts

Stour Valley Path

Princess Wood

35

Parkhill Wood

Shrub's Farm

LAMBEY HILL

The Broom

Great Bevills

2

Longspring Wood

SPRINGETTS HILL

Hill Farm

Miss Moore's Plantation

Little Bevills

Speck's Farm

Bambose Farm

ESSEX KNOWLE 1
WHARF LA 2
SUFFOLK KNOWLE 3
CHURCH SQ 4
NAYLAND RD 5
EVES ORCH 6
CHURCH TERR 7
STATION HILL 8
THE GRANARY 9
PILGRIMS CT 10

SUDBURY RD

1

CLEES TRAIL

COOK'S GN

Mosse's Wood

Ferrier's Farm Pit (Sand & Gravel)

LAMARSH HILL

MALTINGS CL

Bures

WATER LA

THE CROFT

DROPT STONE

HIGH ST

DUCKED HILL

PH

B1508

BRIDGE ST

34

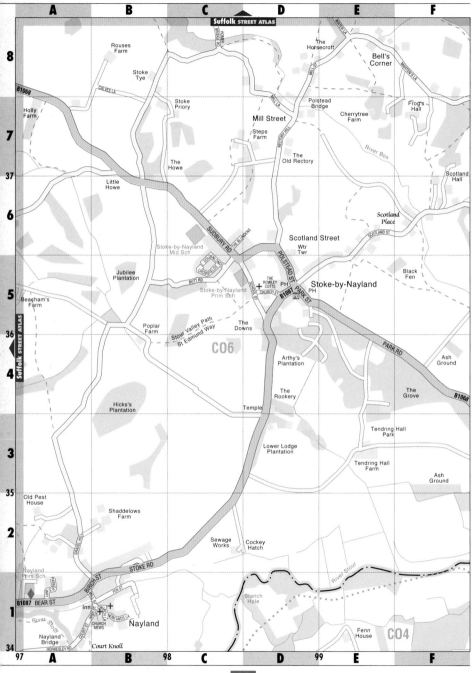

**A** **B** **C** **D** **E** **F**

8

Rouses Farm

Stoke Tye

Stoke Priory

The Horsecroft

Bell's Corner

Frog's Hall

B1068

CALVES LA

Holly Farm

Mill Street

Polstead Bridge

Cherrytree Farm

7

Steps Farm

The Howe

The Old Rectory

River Box

Scotland Hall

37

Little Howe

6

SUDBURY RD

THE BLUNCINS

Scotland Place

SCOTLAND ST

Scotland Street

Wtr Twr

Black Fen

Stoke-by-Nayland Mid Sch

GOLDEN LNDS

CROSSFIELDS

POLSTEAD ST

Jubilee Plantation

BUTT RD

Stoke-by-Nayland Prim Sch

THE ROWLEY COTTS

SCHOOL ST

CHURCH ST

PH

PH

PO

PARK ST

Stoke-by-Nayland

5

Beacham's Farm

Poplar Farm

Stour Valley Path
St Edmund Way

The Downs

B1087

PARK RD

Ash Ground

36

C06

4

Hicks's Plantation

Temple

Arthy's Plantation

The Rookery

The Grove

B1068

Tendring Hall Park

3

Lower Lodge Plantation

Tendring Hall Farm

Ash Ground

35

Old Pest House

Shaddelows Farm

2

Nayland Prim Sch

GRAVEL HILL

STOKE RD

Sewage Works

Cockey Hatch

River Stour

1

B1087 BEAR ST

BIRCH ST

FEN ST

Inn

CHURCH MEWS

Nayland

Stanch Hole

Fenn House

C04

34

Nayland Bridge

HORKESLEY RD

Court Knoll

River Stour

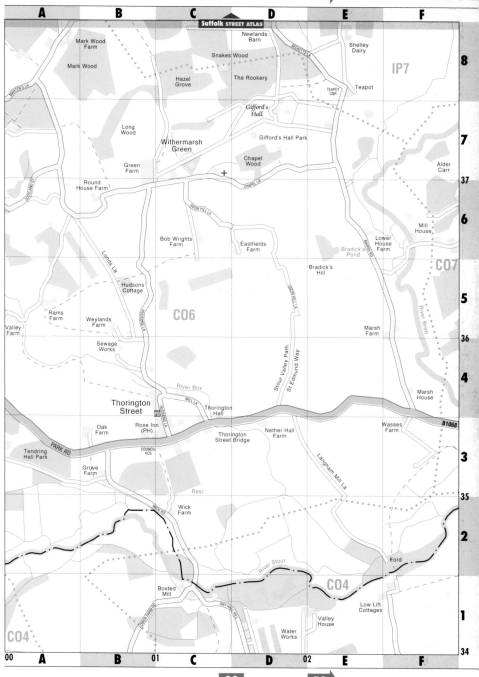

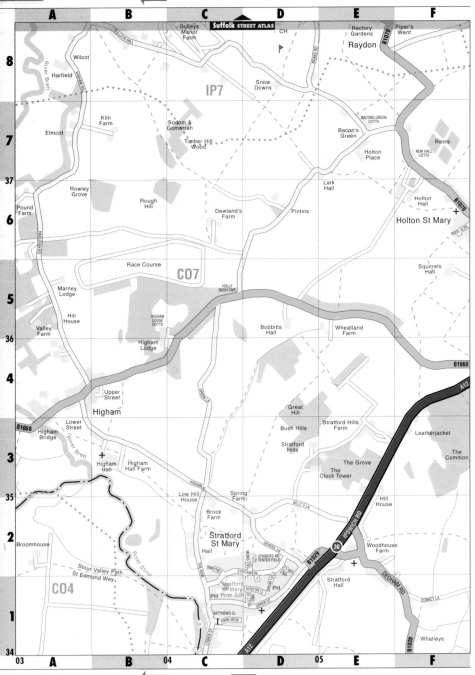

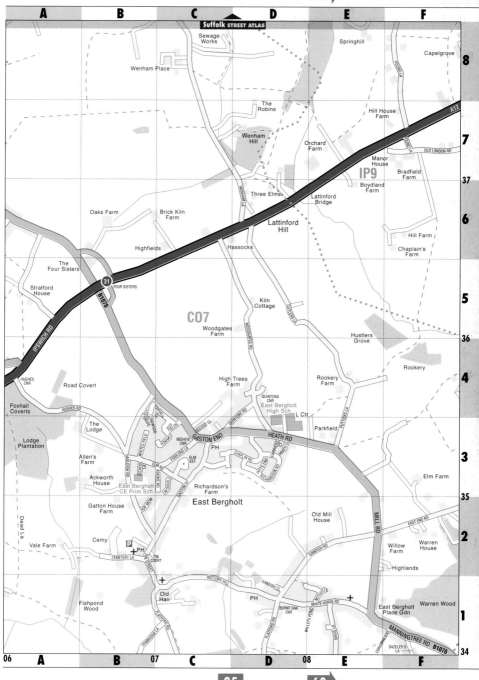

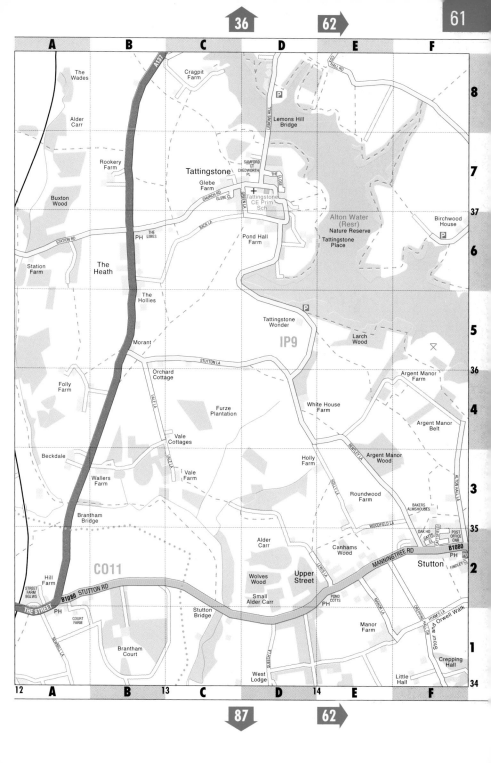

61
37

61
88

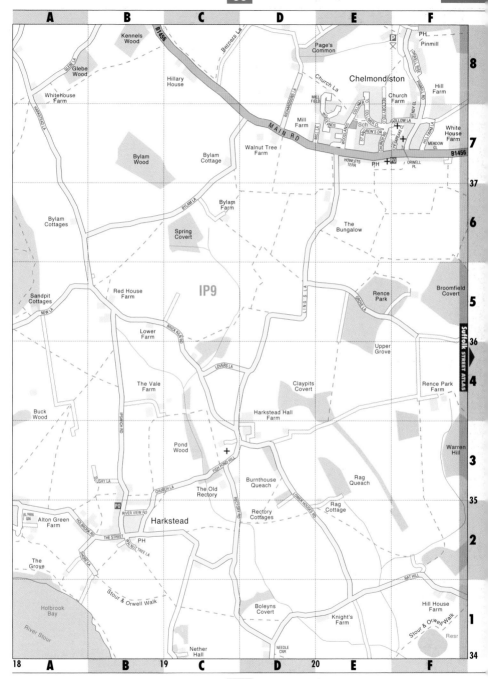

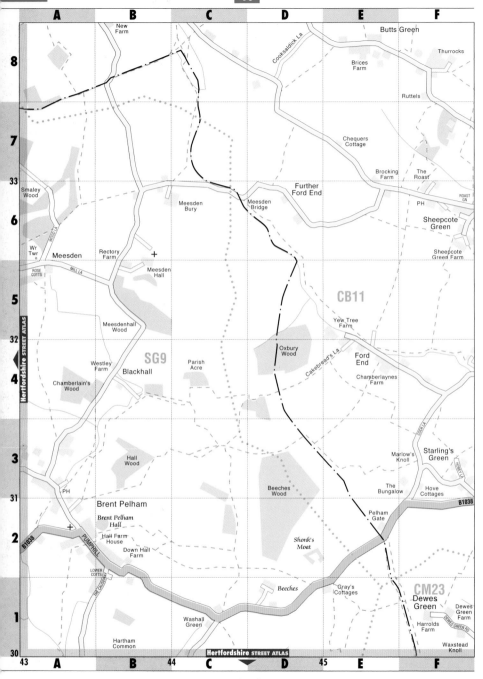

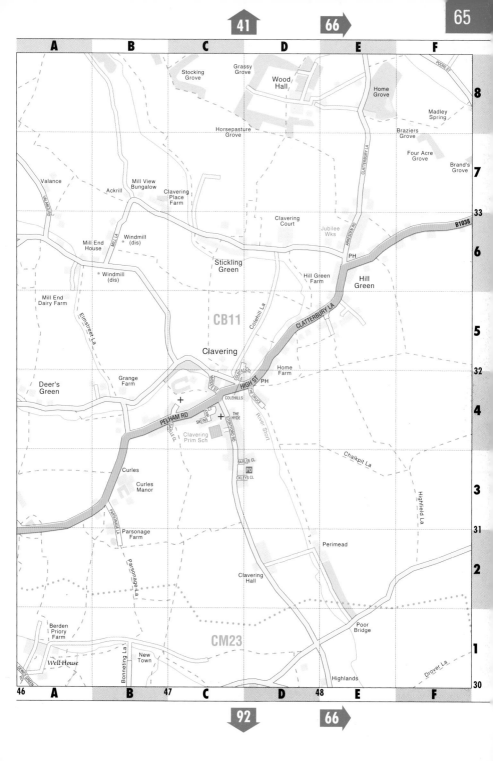

65
42

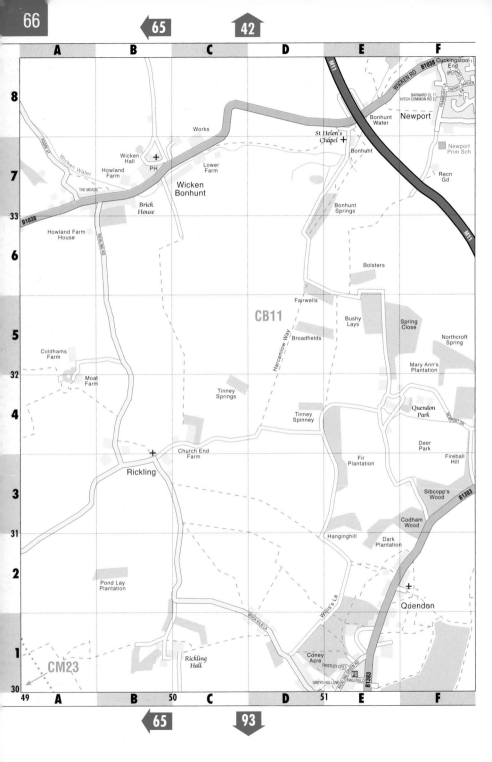

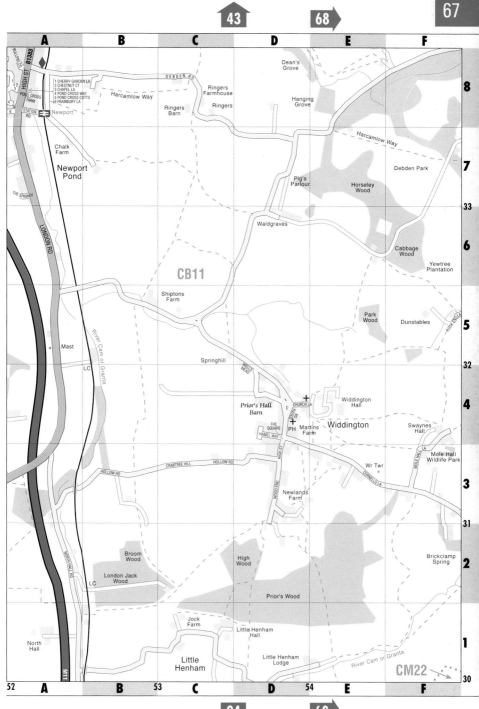

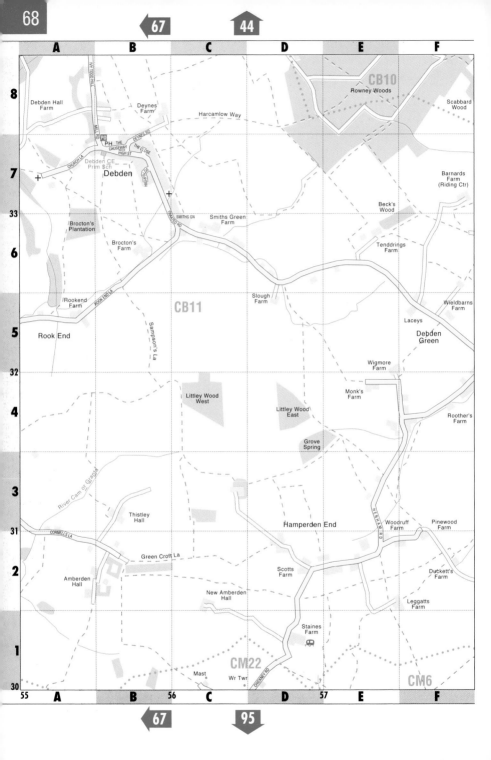

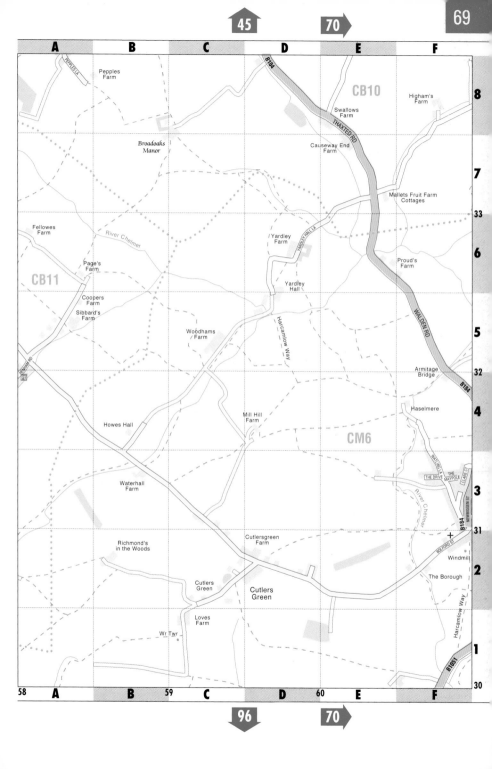

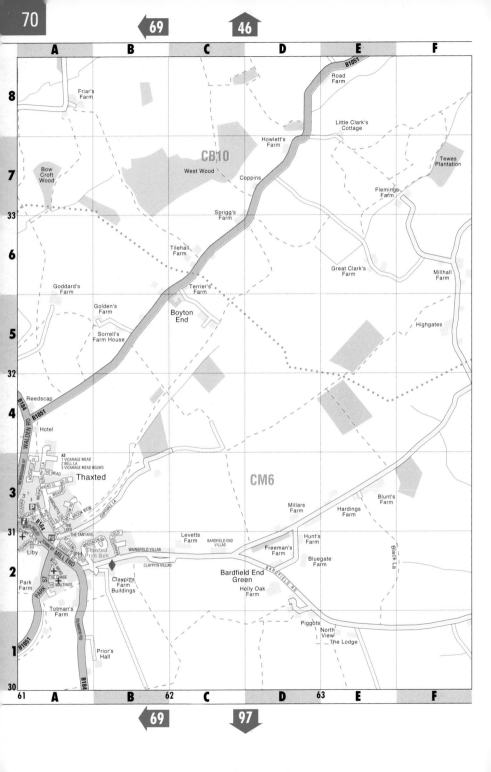

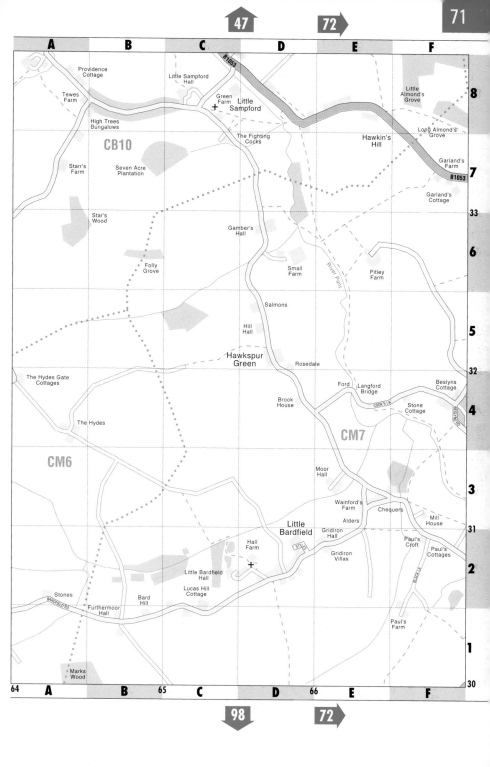

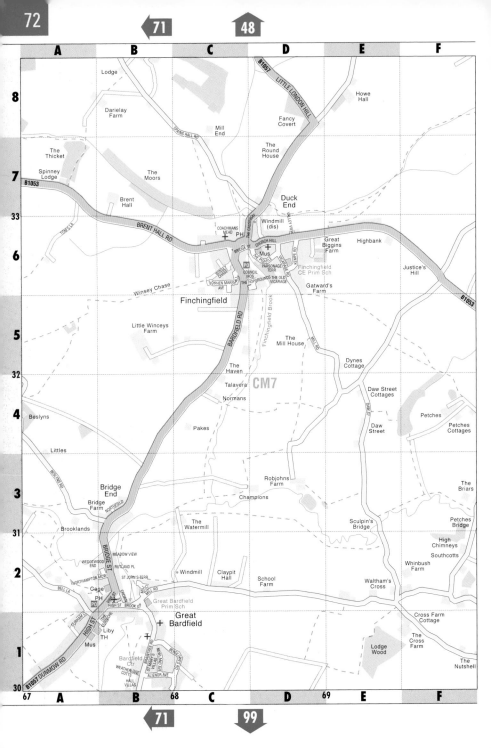

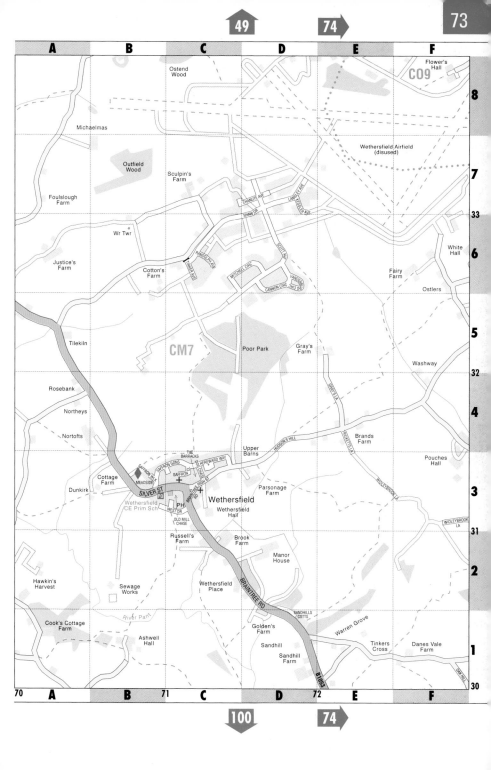

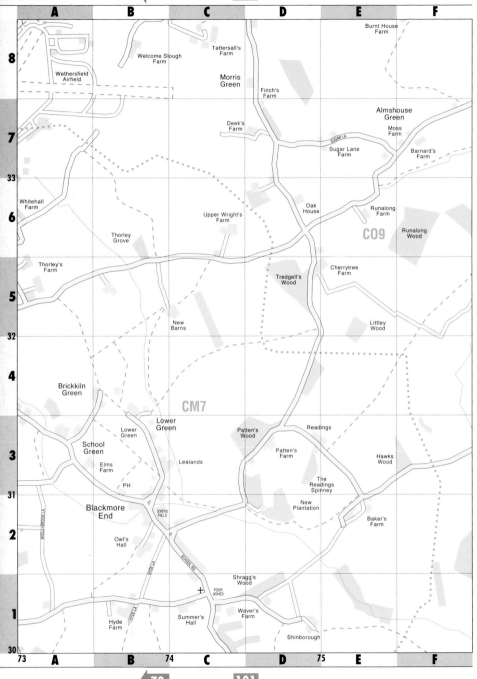

8

Burnt House Farm

Welcome Slough Farm

Tattersall's Farm

Morris Green

Finch's Farm

Wethersfield Airfield

7

Deek's Farm

Almshouse Green

Moss Farm

SUGAR LA

Sugar Lane Farm

Barnard's Farm

33

Whitehall Farm

Upper Wright's Farm

Oak House

Runalong Farm

6

CO9

Thorley Grove

Runalong Wood

Thorley's Farm

Tredgell's Wood

Cherrytree Farm

5

New Barns

Littley Wood

32

Brickkiln Green

4

CM7

Lower Green

Lower Green

Patten's Wood

Readings

School Green

Lealands

Patten's Farm

Hawks Wood

3

Elms Farm

The Readings Spinney

PH

New Plantation

31

Blackmore End

SYERS FIELD

Baker's Farm

2

WIDLEYBROOK LA

Owl's Hall

LYDYELA

SCHOOL RD

Shragg's Wood

FOUR ASHES

Waver's Farm

1

Hyde Farm

Summer's Hall

Shinborough

30

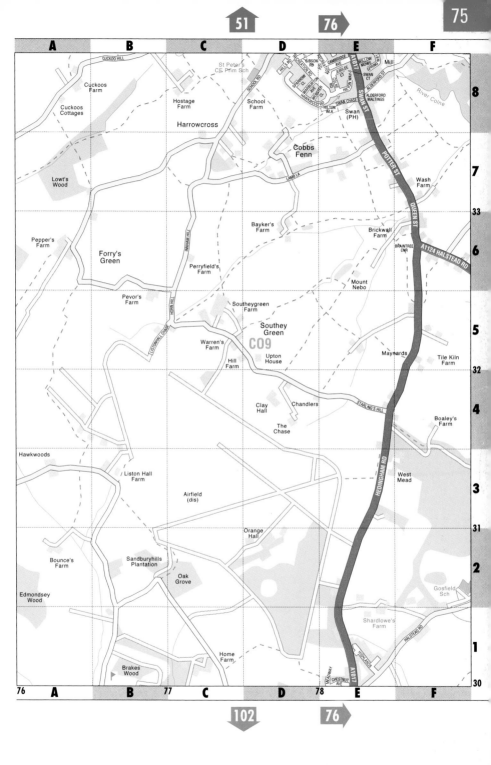

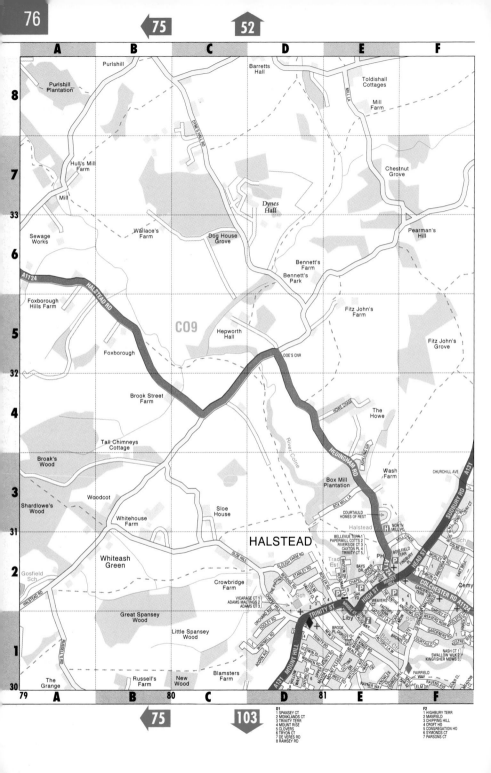

A    B    C    D    E    F

8

7

33

6

5

32

4

3

31

2

1

30

Purlshill

Purlshill
Plantation

Barretts
Hall

Toldishall
Cottages

Mill
Farm

DUKE'S MILL RD

Hull's Mill
Farm

Mill

Dynes
Hall

Chestnut
Grove

Sewage
Works

Wallace's
Farm

Dog House
Grove

Pearman's
Hill

A1124

HALSTEAD RD

Foxborough
Hills Farm

Bennett's
Farm

Bennett's
Park

Fitz John's
Farm

CO9

Hepworth
Hall

DOE'S CNR

Fitz John's
Grove

Foxborough

Brook Street
Farm

HOWE CHASE

River Colne

The
Howe

HEDINGHAM RD

ASHFORD DR

Tall Chimneys
Cottage

Broak's
Wood

Wash
Farm

CHURCHILL AVE

A131

Shardlowe's
Wood

Woodcot

Box Mill
Plantation

BOX MILL LA

COURTAULD
HOMES OF REST

NORTH
MILL PL

SUDBURY RD

Whitehouse
Farm

Sloe
House

Halstead

H

Gosfield
Sch

Whiteash
Green

SLOE HILL

BELLEVUE TERR 1
PAPERMILL COTTS 2
RIVERSIDE CT 3
CAXTON PL 4
TRINITY CT 5.

PH

P

HEAD ST

COLNE RD

Sch

HALSTEAD RD

RUSSELL RD

Crowbridge
Farm

SLOUGH FARM RD

STANLEY RD

Trad
Est

BAYS
DR

CHAPEL

OAK
YD

P

WEAVERS

FACTORY

HIGH ST

P

COLCHESTER RD A131

Cemy

Great Spansey
Wood

VICARAGE CT 1
ADAMS MALTINGS 2
ADAMS CT 3.

ORCHARD RD

Sch

Liby

Sch

Little Spansey
Wood

New
Wood

Blamsters
Farm

A131 MOUNT HILL

TRINITY ST

BROOK
PL

NASH CT 1
SWALLOW WLK 2
KINGFISHER MDWS 3

The
Grange

Russell's
Farm

FAIRFIELD
WAY

RAVENS AVE

ELM DR

HALSTEAD

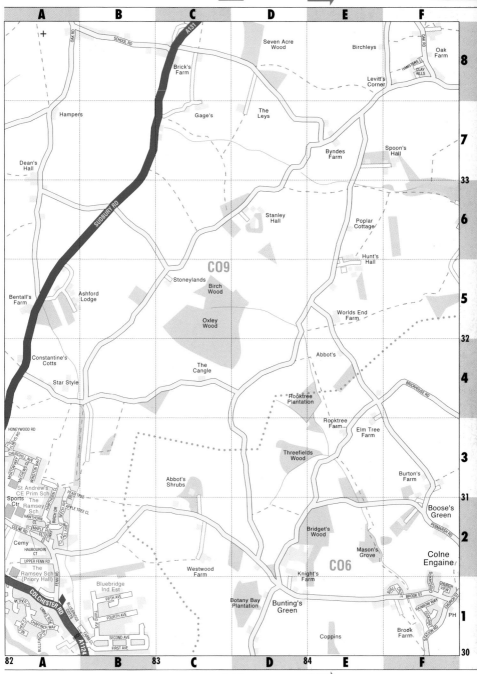

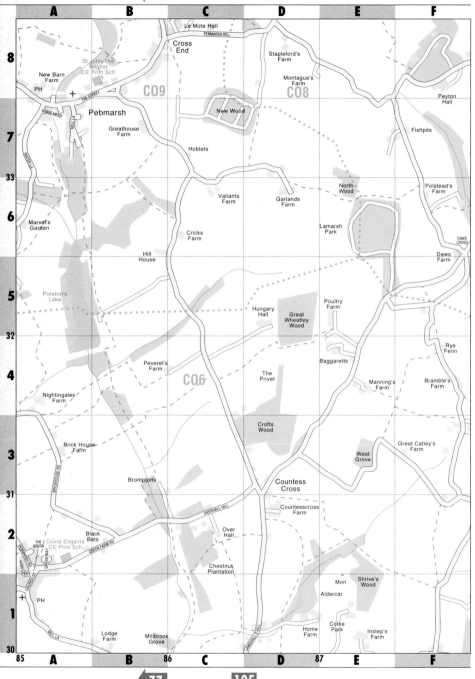

CO9

CO8

CO6

Le Mote Hall
PEBMARSH RD
Cross
End
St John The
Baptist
CE Prim Sch
New Barn
Farm
PH
KINGS MEAD
THE STREET
MILL LA
WIGBELA
Pebmarsh
Greathouse
Farm
Hoblets
Marvel's
Garden
Valiants
Farm
Cricks
Farm
Hill
House
Preston's
Lake
Peverel's
Farm
Nightingales
Farm
Brick House
Farm
Bromptons
BROOKHOUSE RD
Black
Bats
THE
GREEN
Colne Engaine
CE Prim Sch
GREEN WAY
GREEN FARM RD
PEBMARSH RD
HIGH ST
CHURCH ST
PH
MILL LA
Lodge
Farm
Millbrook
Grove
OVERHALL HILL
Over
Hall
Chestnut
Plantation
Stapleford's
Farm
Montague's
Farm
New Wood
Garlands
Farm
North
Wood
Lamarsh
Park
Hungary
Hall
Great
Wheatley
Wood
Poultry
Farm
Baggaretts
The
Privet
Crofts
Wood
Countess
Cross
Countesscross
Farm
West
Grove
Great Catley's
Farm
LANDHALL HILL
Mon
Aldercar
Shrive's
Wood
Home
Farm
Colne
Park
Instep's
Farm
Peyton
Hall
Fishpits
Polstead's
Farm
DAWS
CROSS
Daws
Farm
Rye
Fenn
Manning's
Farm
Bramble's
Farm

8
7
33
6
5
32
4
3
31
2
1
30

A B C D E F

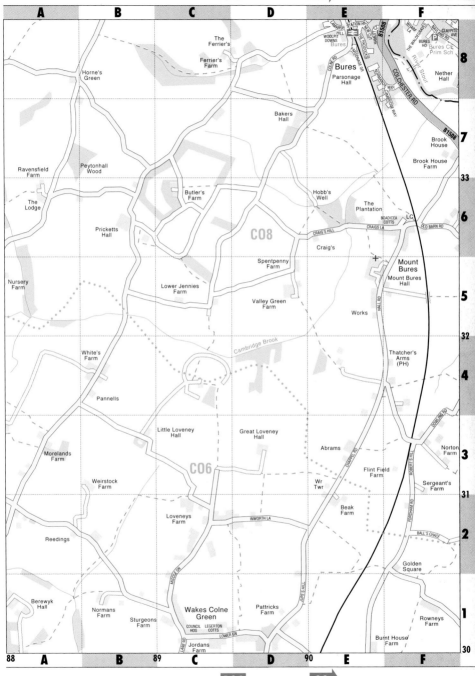

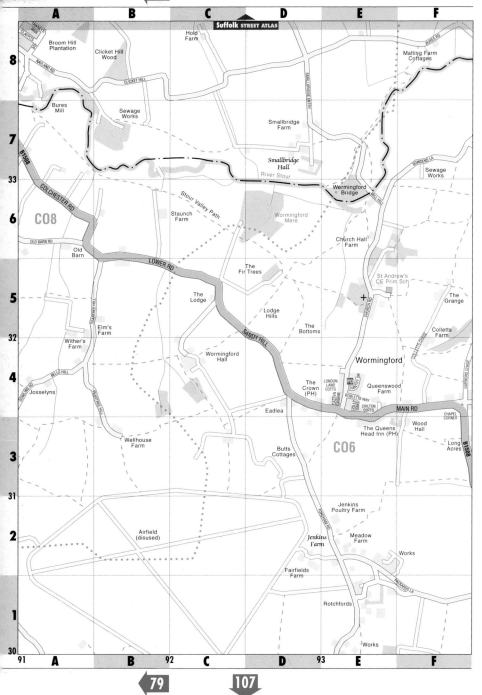

8

Broom Hill Plantation

Hold Farm

Clicket Hill Wood

Malting Farm Cottages

TANNER'S RIDE

CLAYITTS RD

NAYLAND RD

CLICKET HILL

SMALLBRIDGE ENTRY

BURES RD

Bures Mill

Sewage Works

7

Smallbridge Farm

Sewage Works

B1508

COLCHESTER RD

33

Smallbridge Hall

River Stour

Wormingford Bridge

BOWDENS LA

6

CO8

OLD BARN RD

Stour Valley Path

Staunch Farm

Wormingford Mere

Church Hall Farm

MILL HILL

Old Barn

LOWER RD

The Fir Trees

St Andrew's CE Prim Sch

5

The Lodge

Lodge Hills

The Bottoms

The Grange

PEARTREE HILL

CHURCH RD

COLLETTS CHASE

32

Elm's Farm

Wither's Farm

SANDY HILL

Wormingford Hall

Colletts Farm

EDWARDS RD

4

BELLS HILL

Josselyns

ACORN END RD

PEARTREE HILL

The Crown (PH)

LONDON LAND COTTS

Wormingford

Queenswood Farm

ROBLETTS WAY

HOLLY LANE

CHILTON COTTS

MAIN RD

EASTON GREENE

CHAPEL CORNER

Wood Hall

B1508

Eadlea

The Queens Head Inn (PH)

Long Acres

3

Wellhouse Farm

Butts Cottages

CO6

31

TONSTALL RD

Jenkins Poultry Farm

2

Airfield (disused)

Jenkins Farm

Meadow Farm

Works

Fairfields Farm

PACKARDS LA

Rotchfords

1

Works

30

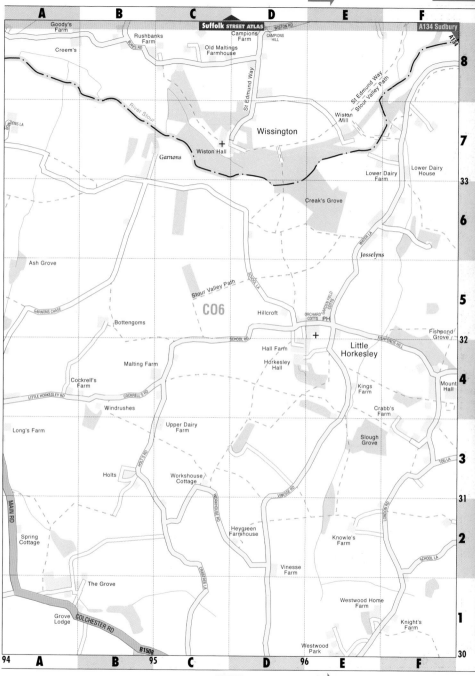

A134 Sudbury

Goody's Farm
Creem's
Rushbanks Farm
BURES RD
Campions Farm
Old Maltings Farmhouse
WISTON RD
CAMPIONS HILL
St Edmund Way
St Edmund Way
Stour Valley Path
River Stour
BURDENS LA
Wissington
Wiston Mill
Garnons
Wiston Hall
Lower Dairy Farm
Lower Dairy House

33

Creak's Grove

6

Ash Grove
Josselyns
WATER LA
GARNONS CHASE

Stour Valley Path
SCHOOL LA
Bottengoms
CO6
Hillcroft
ORCHARD COTTS
GARDEN FIELD COTTS
PH
Fishpond Grove
32
SCHOOL RD
Hall Farm
Little Horkesley
FISHPONDS HILL

Malting Farm
Horkesley Hall
Kings Farm
Mount Hall
4

Cockrell's Farm
COCKRELL'S RD
LITTLE HORKESLEY RD
Windrushes
Crabb's Farm

Long's Farm
Upper Dairy Farm
Slough Grove
TOG LA
3

HOLTS RD
Holts
Workhouse Cottage
WORKHOUSE RD
VINESSE RD
31

Spring Cottage
Heygreen Farmhouse
Knowle's Farm
LONDON RD
2
SCHOOL LA

MAIN RD
The Grove
GRANGE LA
Vinesse Farm
Westwood Home Farm

Grove Lodge
COLCHESTER RD
Knight's Farm
1

B1508
Westwood Park
30

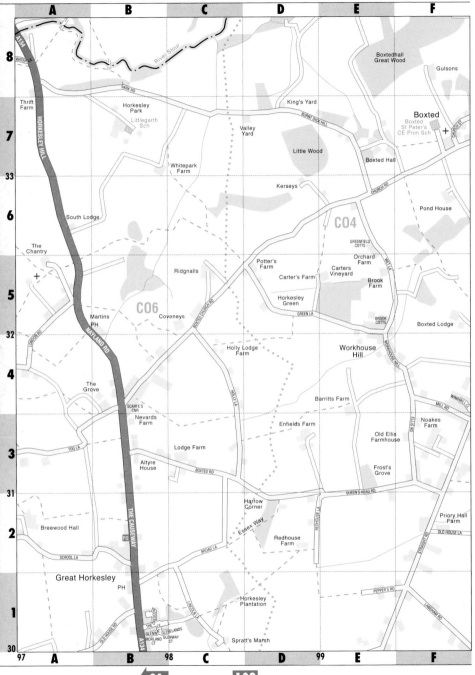

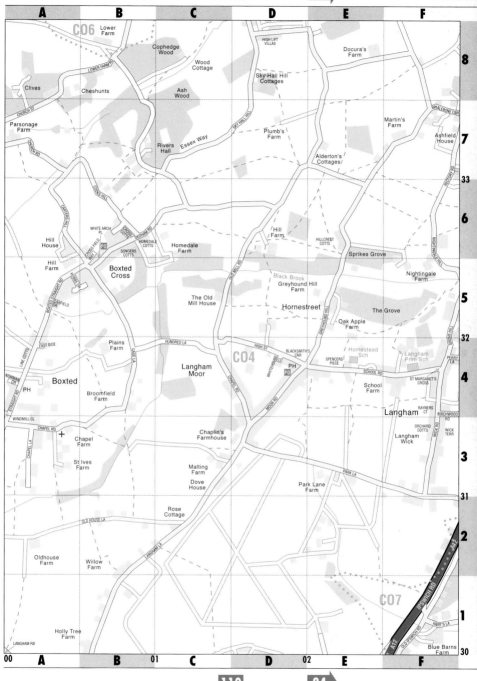

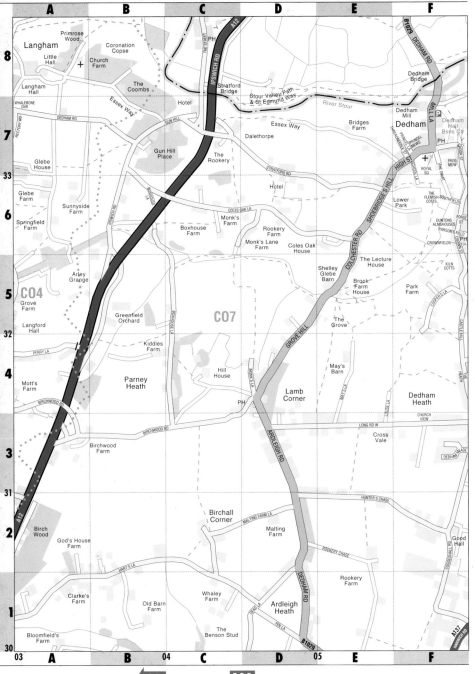

83
58

A B C D E F

8

Langham

Primrose Wood

Coronation Copse

Little Hall

Church Farm

Langham Hall

The Coombs

Essex Way

Hotel

Stratford Bridge

Dedham Bridge

B1029 DEDHAM RD

7

WHALEBONE CNR

RECTORY LA

DEDHAM RD

Gun Hill

Stour Valley Path & St Edmund Way

River Stour

Dedham Mill

Essex Way

Dalethorpe

Bridges Farm

Dedham Mill Bsns Ctr

Dedham

MILL LA

P

33

Glebe House

Gun Hill Place

The Rookery

Stratford Rd

STRATFORD RD

Hotel

HIGH ST

PRINCEL NEWS

PRINCES ST

THORRINGTONS ST

PH

ROYAL SQ

THE DRIFT

FROG MDW

THE FLEMISH SOUTHFIELDS COTTS

FORGE ST

6

Glebe Farm

Sunnyside Farm

IPSWICH RD

MONGLISS LA

Boxhouse Farm

COLES OAK LA

Monk's Farm

Rookery Farm

Coles Oak House

Monk's Lane Farm

SHOEBRIDGES HILL

COLCHESTER RD

The Lecture House

DUNTONS ALMSHOUSES

PARSON'S FIELD

CROWNFIELDS

KILN COTTS

COWER ST

PH

Springfield Farm

5

CO4

Grove Farm

Arley Grange

Greenfield Orchard

BOXHOUSE LA

CO7

Shelley Glebe Barn

Brook Farm House

Park Farm

COOPER'S LA

Langford Hall

32

PERRY LA

Kiddles Farm

The Grove

May's Barn

CASTLE HILL

THE THEE

4

Mott's Farm

BIRCHWOOD RD

Parney Heath

Hill House

MONK'S LA

Lamb Corner

MAY'S LA

LOUSE ST

Dedham Heath

CHURCH VIEW

3

Birchwood Farm

BIRCHWOOD RD

PH

ARDLEIGH RD

LONG RD W

Cross Vale

THE PARADE

DEDHAM

A12

31

Birch Wood

2

God's House Farm

HART'S LA

MALTING FARM LA

Birchall Corner

Malting Farm

DEAD LA

ROOKERY CHASE

HUNTER'S CHASE

DEDHAM RD

Rookery Farm

COLCHESTER RD

Good Hall

1

Clarke's Farm

Old Barn Farm

Whaley Farm

FEN LA

Ardleigh Heath

A137

HARWICH RD

Bloomfield's Farm

The Benson Stud

B1029

30

03 A B 04 C D 05 E F

83
111

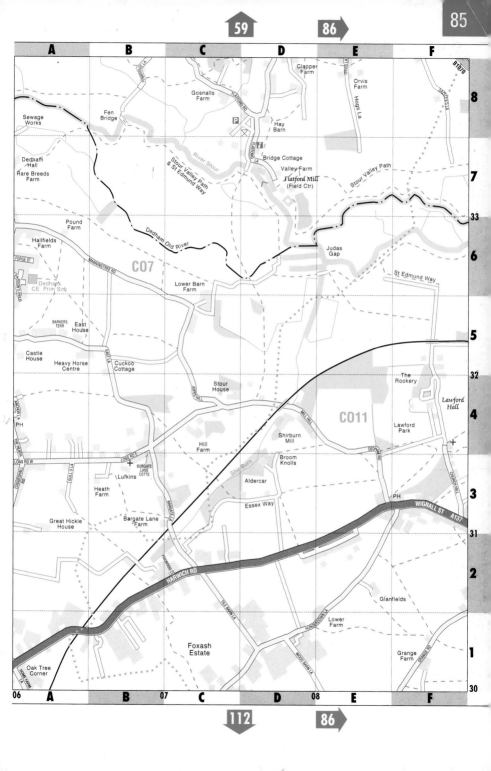

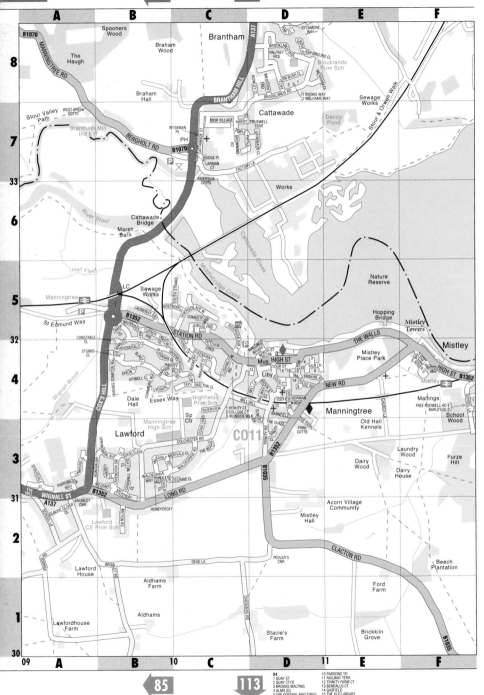

D4
1 QUAY ST
2 QUAY CTYD
3 BROOKS MALTING
4 ALMA SQ
5 THE CENTRAL MALTINGS
6 ST MICHAELS CT
7 YORK ST
8 FALKLANDS DR
9 REGENT ST
10 PARSONS YD
11 RAILWAY TERR
12 TRINITY FARM CT
13 BENDALLS CT
14 GASFIELD
15 THE OLD LIBRARY
16 COMPASS CT

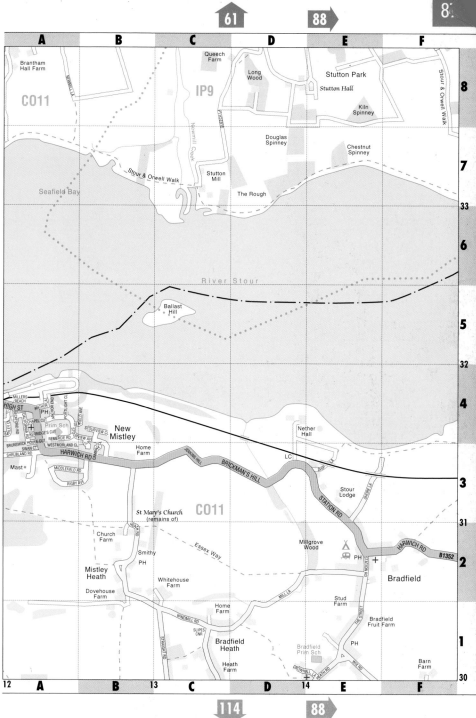

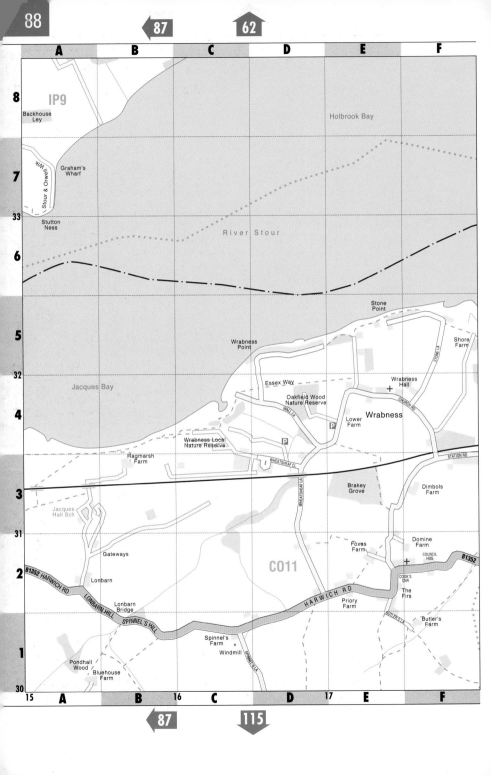

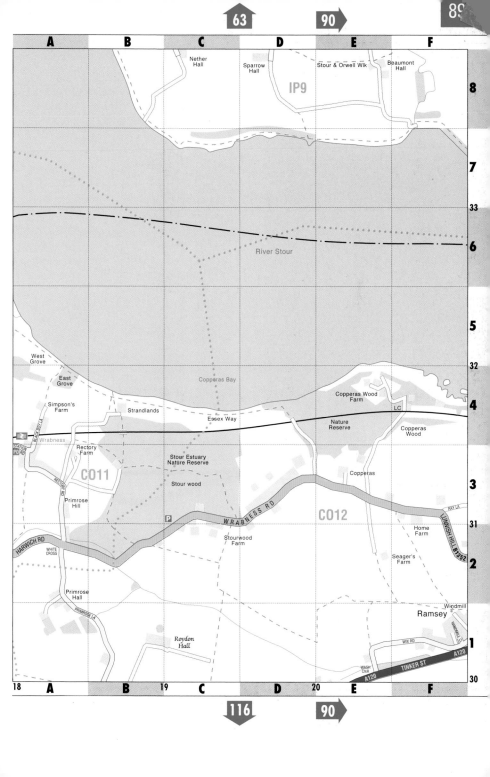

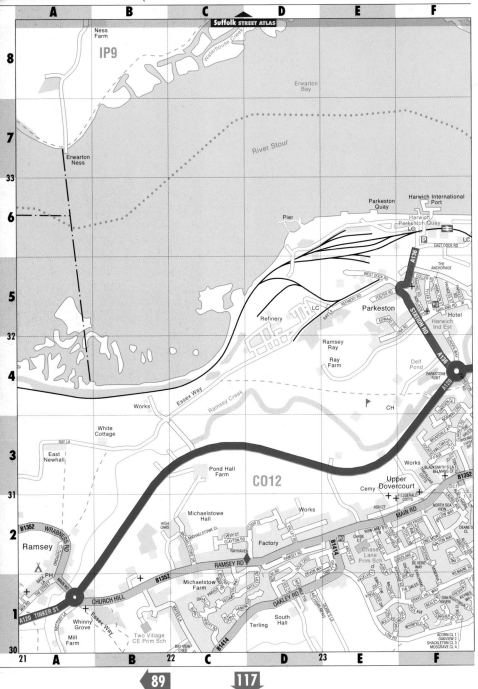

Suffolk STREET ATLAS

A   B   C   D   E   F

Ness
Farm

IP9

Waterhouse Creek

Erwarton
Bay

River Stour

Erwarton
Ness

Parkeston
Quay

Harwich International
Port

Harwich
Parkeston Quay

Pier

EAST DOCK RD

THE
ANCHORAGE

WEST DOCK RD

COLLER RD

Refinery

LC

RAY LA

REFINERY RD

FOSTER RD

Parkeston

STATION RD

A136

Hotel
Harwich
Ind Est

Ramsey
Ray

Ray
Farm

Delf
Pond

PARKSTONE
ROBT

A120

Essex Way

Ramsey Creek

CH

Works

White
Cottage

RAY LA

East
Newhall

Pond Hall
Farm

CO12

Upper
Dovercourt

Cemy

FITZGERALD
COTTS

Works

BLACKSMITH'S LA
BELMANS CT

NORTH SEA
VIEW

Michaelstowe
Hall

HIGH
OAKS

Works

ASH CT

MAIN RD

CHASE
CT

Chase
Lane
Prim Sch

B1352
WRABNESS RD

Ramsey

CLAYTON CT

RAYHAVEN

Factory

RAMSEY RD

B1414

B1352

Michaelstow
Farm

CHURCH HILL

OAKLEY RD

South
Hall

Terling

B1414

A120 TINKER ST

Whinny
Grove

Mill
Farm

Essex Way

Two Village
CE Prim Sch

BAY VIEW
CRES

ACORN CL 1
OAKVIEW 2
SHACKLETON CL 3
MUSGRAVE 4

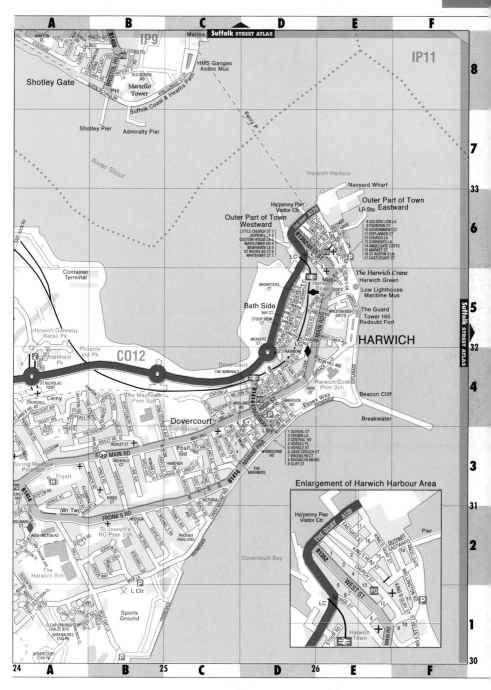

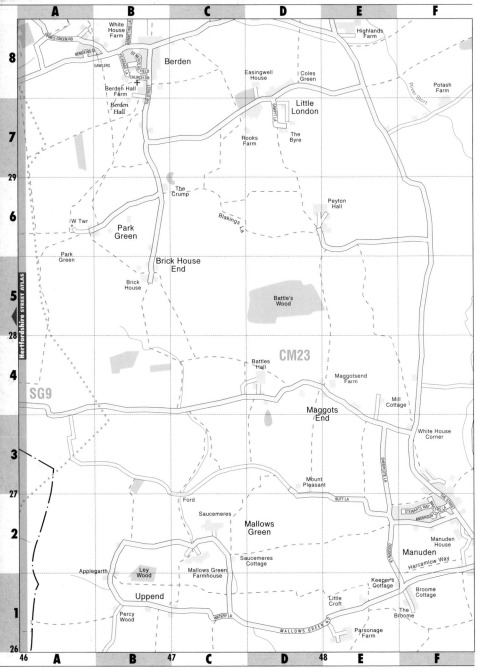

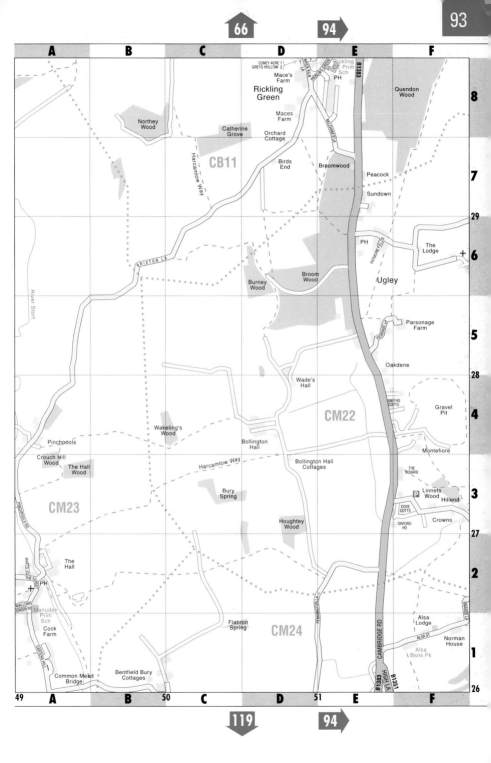

A   B   C   D   E   F

CONEY ACRE 1
GREYS HOLLOW 2
Mace's
Farm
Rickling
Green
Rickling
CE Prim
Sch
PH
BRICK KILN LA
RICKLING GREEN
B1383
Quendon
Wood
**8**

Northey
Wood
Catherine
Grove
Maces
Farm
Orchard
Cottage
CB11
Birds
End
Broomwood
Harcamlow Way
Peacock
**7**

Sundown
**29**

BRIXTON LA
Burney
Wood
Broom
Wood
PH
PATMORE FIELDS
The
Lodge
Ugley
+
**6**

River Stort

Parsonage
Farm
ORFORD LA
**5**

Oakdene
**28**

Wade's
Hall
CM22
SMITHS
COTTS
Gravel
Pit
**4**

Wakeling's
Wood
Bollington
Hall
Bollington Hall
Cottages
Montefiore

Pinchpools
Crouch Hill
Wood
The
Hall
Wood
Harcamlow Way
Bury
Spring
THE
SQUARE
Linnets
Wood
Hillend
DOVE
COTTS
Crowns
ORFORD
HO
P
**3**

CM23
Houghtey
Wood
**27**

The
Hall
PH
PINCHPOOLS RD
WATTS LA
THE STREET
Flatiron
Spring
CM24
PENNINGTON LA
**2**

MALLOWS
GREEN RD
Manuden
Prim
Sch
+
Cock
Farm
Alsa
Lodge
ALSA ST
Norman
House
**1**

CARTERS HILL
Common Mead
Bridge
Bentfield Bury
Cottages
Alsa
Bsns Pk
CAMBRIDGE RD
B1383
HIGH LA
B1351
SAXONS LA
**26**

49   A   B   50   C   D   51   E   F

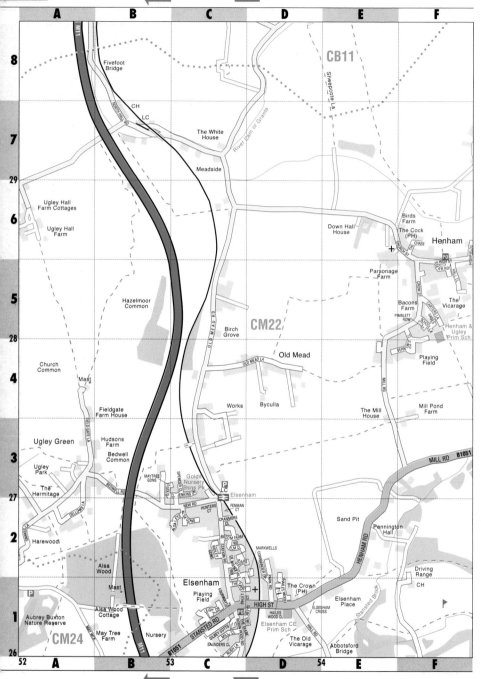

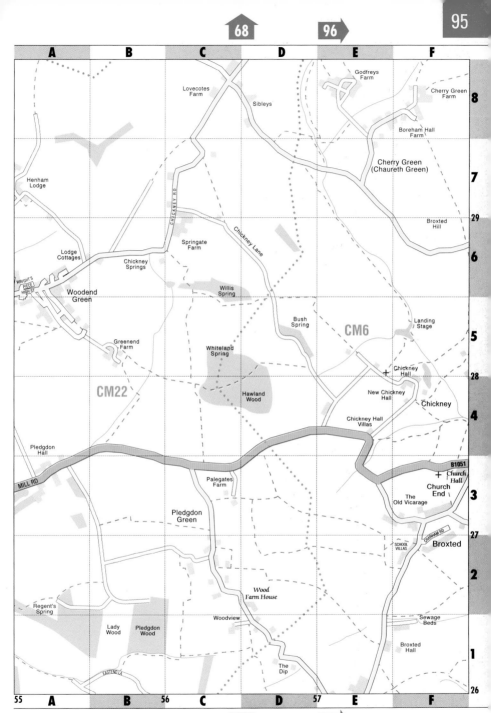

A  B  C  D  E  F

8

Godfreys Farm

Cherry Green Farm

Lovecotes Farm

Sibleys

Boreham Hall Farm

Cherry Green (Chaureth Green)

7

Henham Lodge

29

Broxted Hill

CHICKNEY RD

Chickney Lane

6

Lodge Cottages

Springate Farm

Chickney Springs

Willis Spring

WRIGHT'S PIECE

HIGH ST

Woodend Green

Bush Spring

CM6

Landing Stage

5

Greenend Farm

Whiteland Spring

28

Chickney Hall

CM22

Hawland Wood

New Chickney Hall

Chickney

Chickney Hall Villas

4

Pledgdon Hall

B1051

Church Hall

MILL RD

Palegates Farm

Church End

The Old Vicarage

3

Pledgdon Green

27

GRANHAM RD

SCHOOL VILLAS

Broxted

2

Regent's Spring

Wood Farm House

Woodview

Sewage Beds

Lady Wood

Pledgdon Wood

Broxted Hall

1

The Dip

EASTEND LA

26

55  A  56  B  C  57  D  E  F

**A** **B** **C** **D** **E** **F**

8

Brown's Wood

Home Wood

Stan Brook

Hill Farm

Dairygreen Farm

Warrens Wood

Brickmead

Buckingham's Farm

Stanbrook

7

Horham Hall

Armigers Farm

Hammer Hill Farm

29

Hart's Grove

Sharpes Farm

Armigers

FOLLY MILL LA

6

Sucksted Green

The Stepps

Follymill

River Chelmer

Harcamlow Way

Delfits La

5

Chaureth Hall Farm

CM6

Broadfans Farm

28

Walters Cottage

Brick House Farm

Wolsey's Farm

4

Broadwater Bridge

Tingates

Hill Pasture

Tilty Hill Farm

B1051

Lower Barn

3

Coldharbour Farm

Eseley Wood

Duton Hill

Coldharbour Villas

27

Dutonhill Bridge

Duton Hill Farm

Home Wood

PH

2

Malting Bridge

Mill

Tilty

The Maltings

The Grange

1

Moor End Farm

26

58 **A** **B** 59 **C** **D** 60 **E** **F**

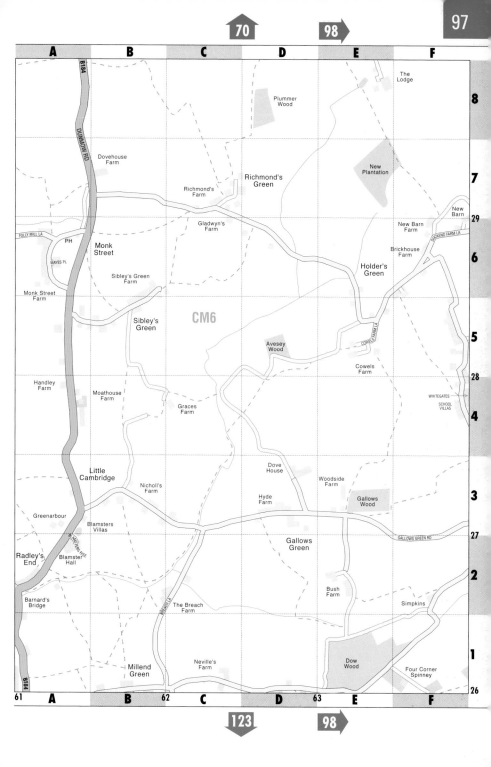

8

7

29

6

5

28

4

3

27

2

1

26

A B C D E F

**CM7**

B1057
DUNMOW RD
B1057

Markswood
Farm

Charity
Farm

The Grove

Oxen
End

Duck End
Farm

Bustard Green Lane

Bustard
Green

Fann's
Farm

Coft
Hall

Frenches
Farm

Daisyley Brook

Porridge
Hall

Brazenhead
Farm

DAISYLEY RD

Templars

**CM6**

Page's
Farm

Tolladay's
Farm

Pratt's
Farm

LUBBERHEDGES LA

Lindsell

Church
End

GALLOWS GREEN RD

LINDSELL LA

Goland's
Bridge

Poplar
Farm

Carter's
Farm

Hill
Farm

Stebbing Brook

Holt's
Farm

Lashley
Hall

Duck End

B1057

Drakeswell

64 A B 65 C D 66 E F

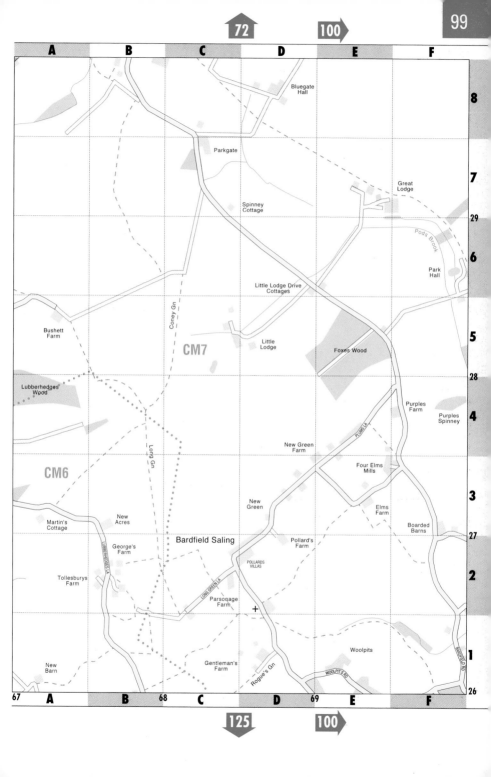

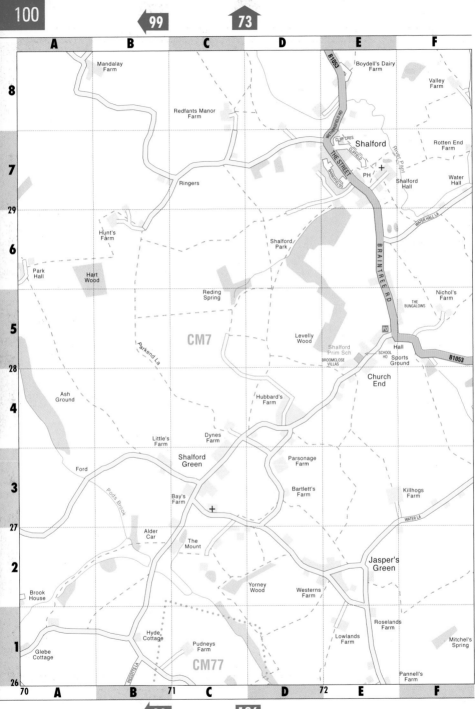

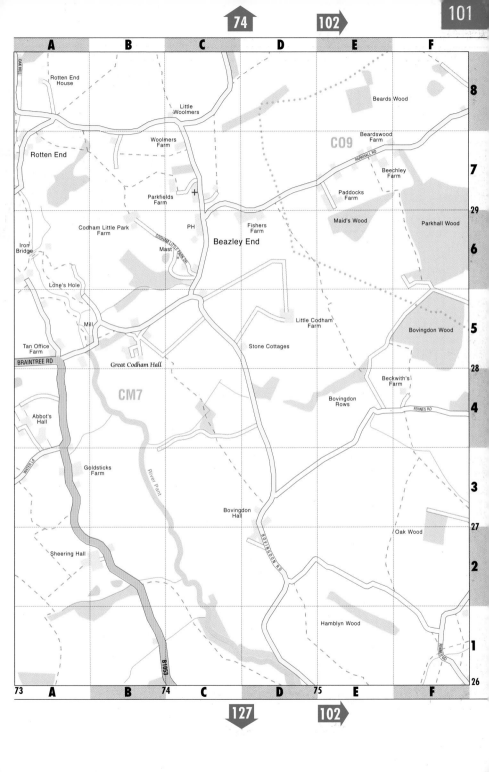

8

7

29

6

5

28

4

3

27

2

1

26

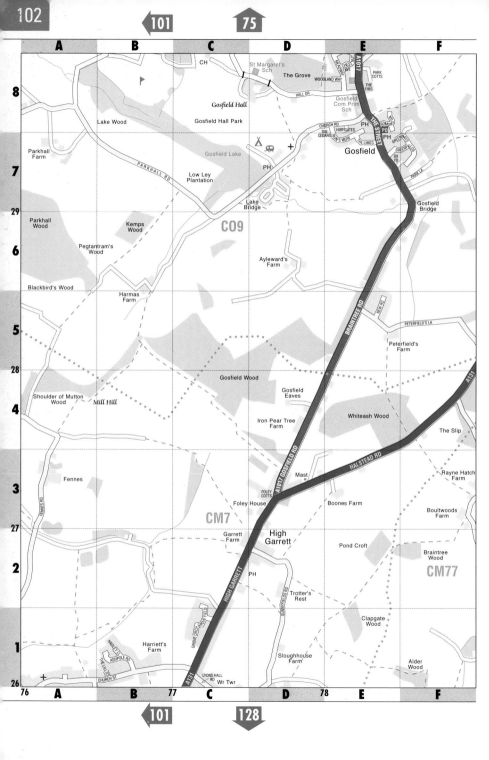

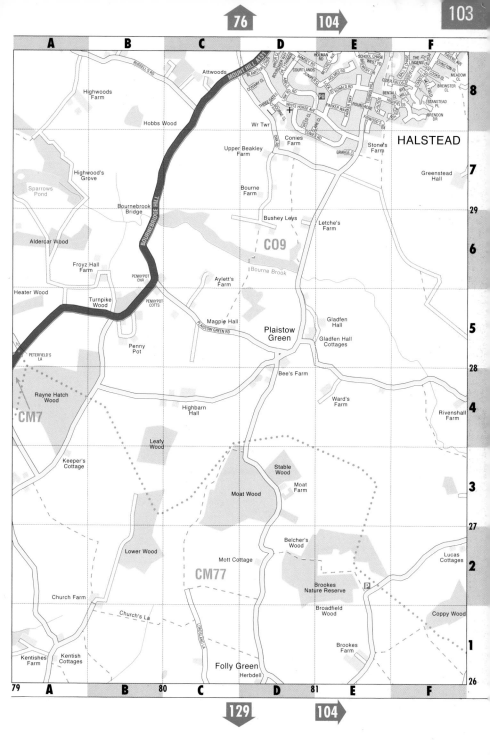

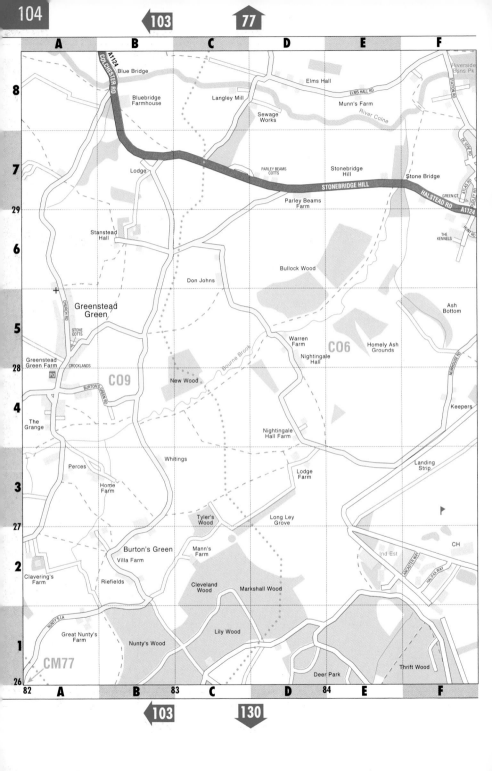

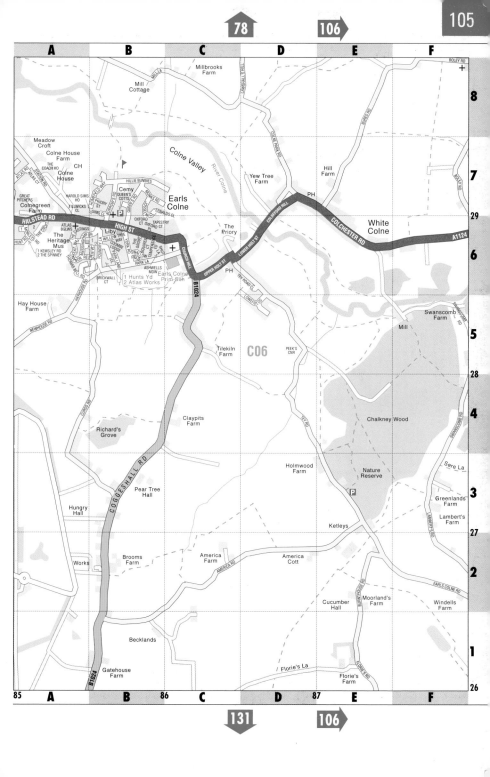

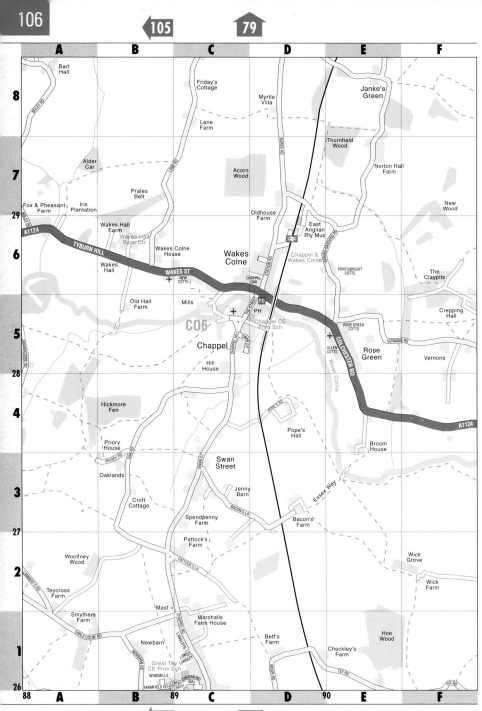

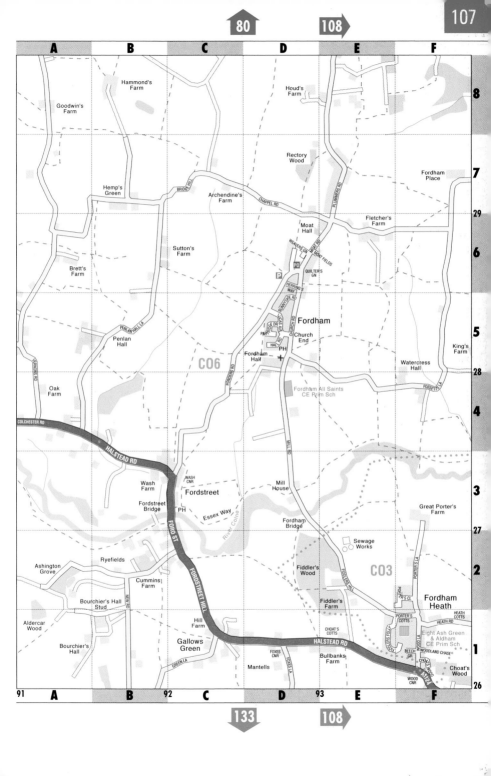

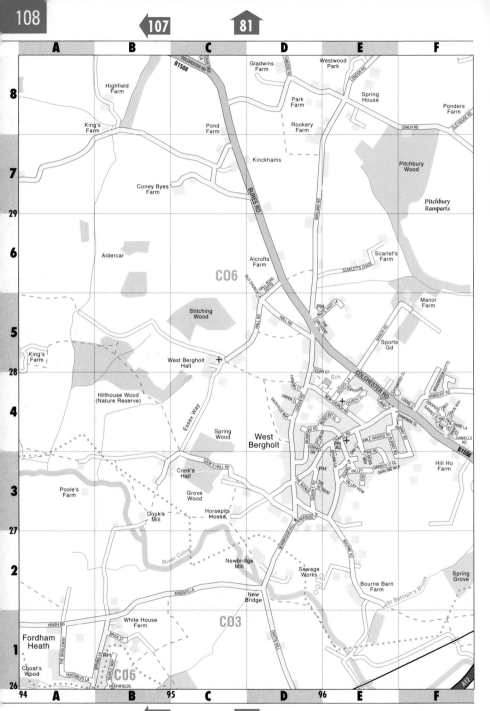

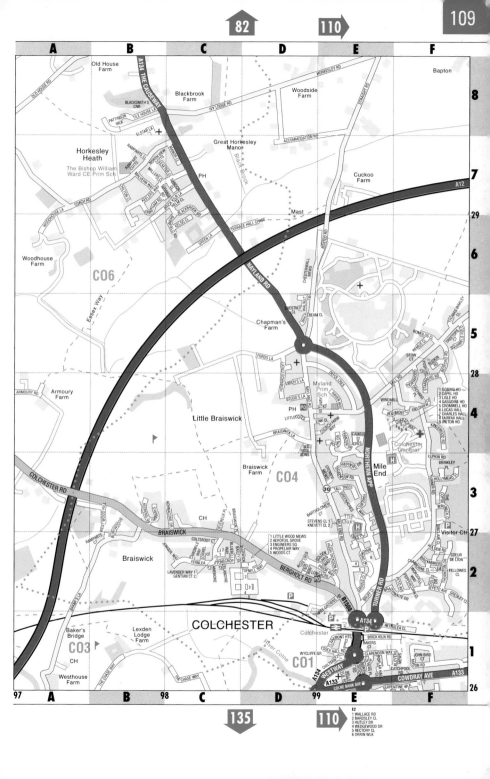

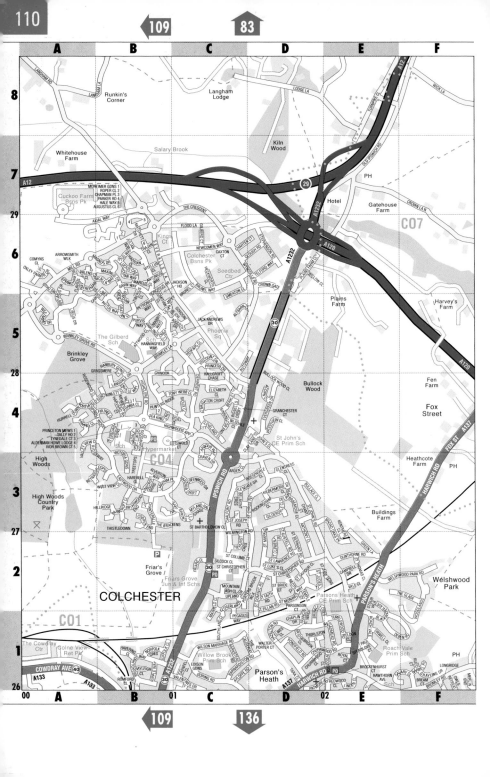

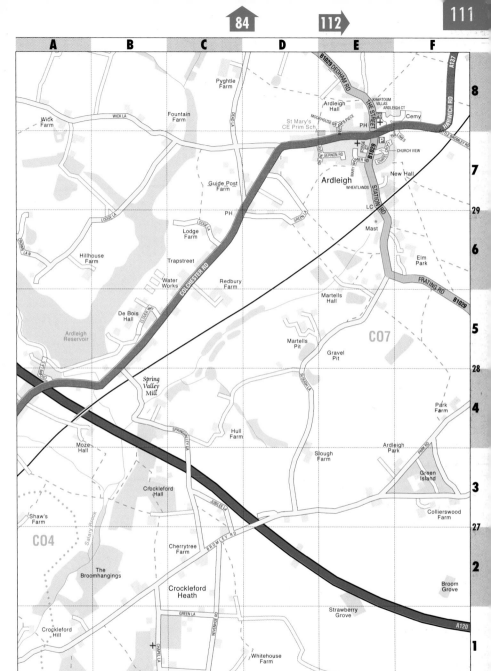

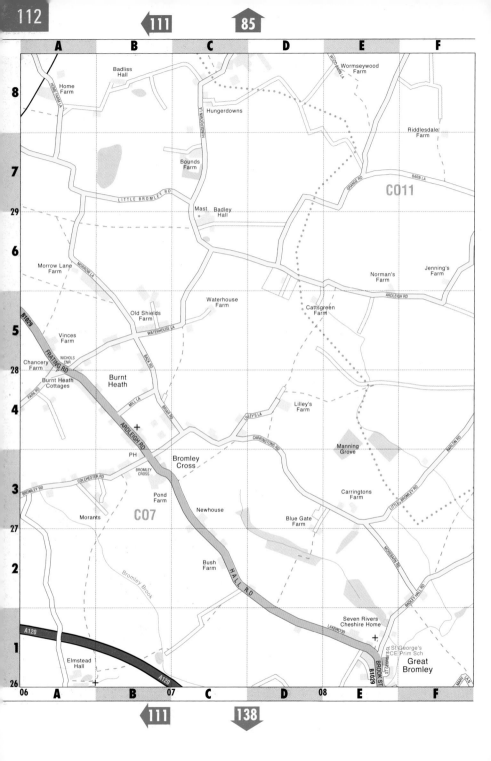

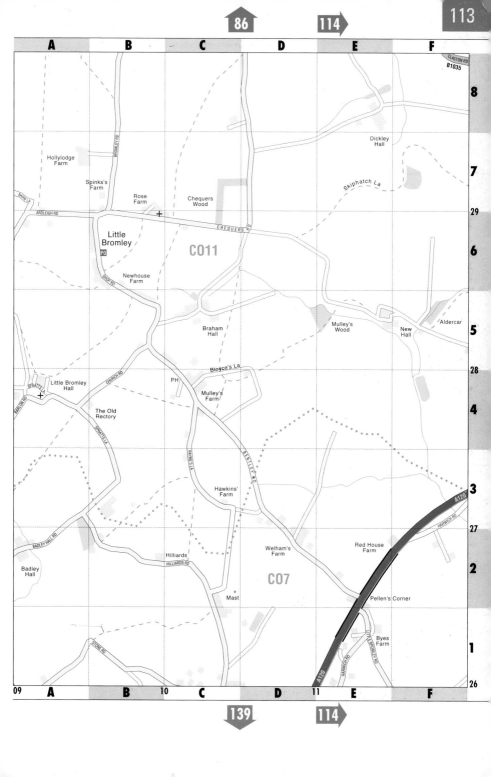

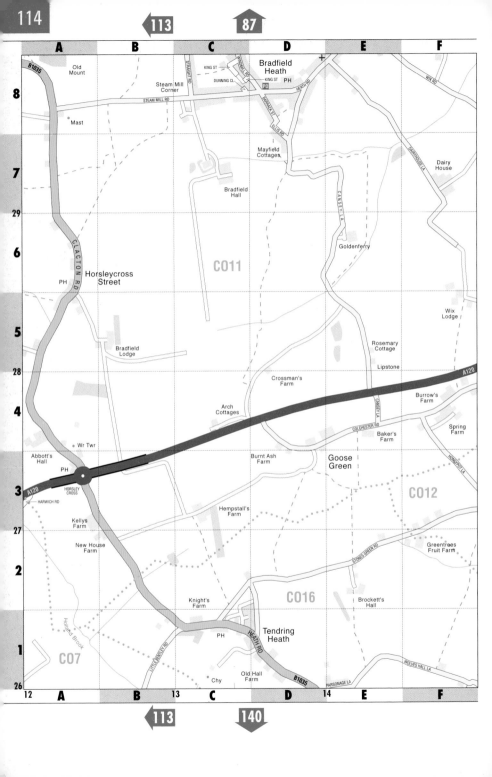

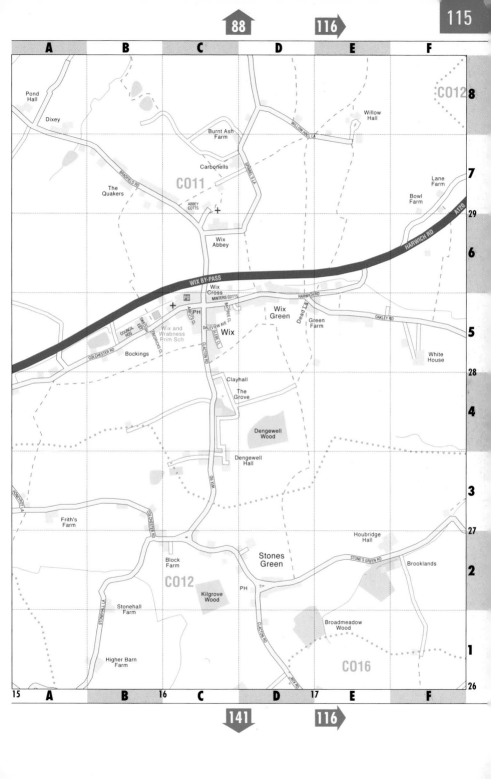

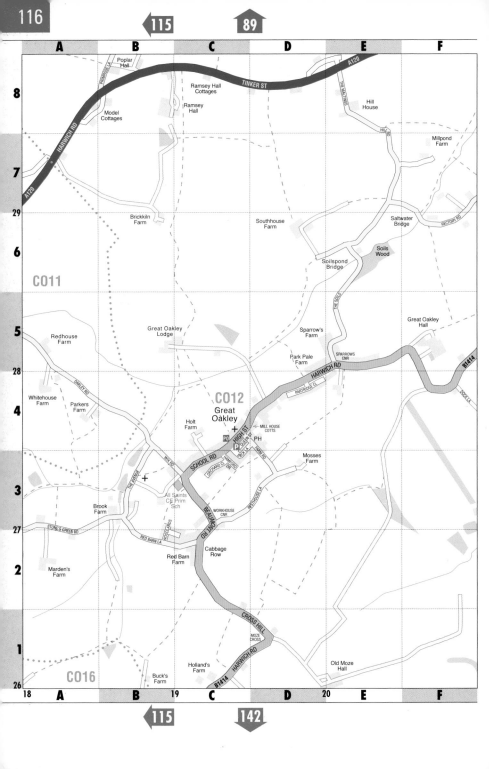

115
89

A B C D E F

8

7

29

6

CO11

5

28

4

CO12
Great
Oakley

3

27

2

1

26

18 A B 19 C D 20 E F

115
142

A120
HARWICH RD
Poplar
Hall
PRIMROSE LA
Model
Cottages
Ramsey Hall
Cottages
Ramsey
Hall
TINKER ST
A120
THE MALTINGS
Hill
House
HILL RD
Millpond
Farm
RECTORY RD

Brickkiln
Farm
Southhouse
Farm
Saltwater
Bridge

Soilspond
Bridge
Soils
Wood
THE SOILS

Redhouse
Farm
Great Oakley
Lodge
Sparrow's
Farm
Great Oakley
Hall

OAKLEY RD
Whitehouse
Farm
Parkers
Farm
Park Pale
Farm
HARWICH RD
SPARROWS
CNR
B1414
DOCK LA

THE AVENUE
WIX RD
Holt
Farm
PARTRIDGE CL
PO
HIGH ST
QUEEN'S
P
PICK LA
FARM RD
PH
MILL HOUSE
COTTS
Mosses
Farm

SCHOOL RD
BEAUMONT RD
LONGWARD CL
HAMFORD CL
RESTHOUSE LA

Brook
Farm
All Saints
CE Prim
Sch
WOOD LA/WS
WORKHOUSE
CNR

STONE'S-GREEN RD
RED BARN LA
Cabbage
Row

Marden's
Farm
Red Barn
Farm

CROSS HILL
MOZE
CROSS
Old Moze
Hall

CO16
Buck's
Farm
Holland's
Farm
HARWICH RD
B1414

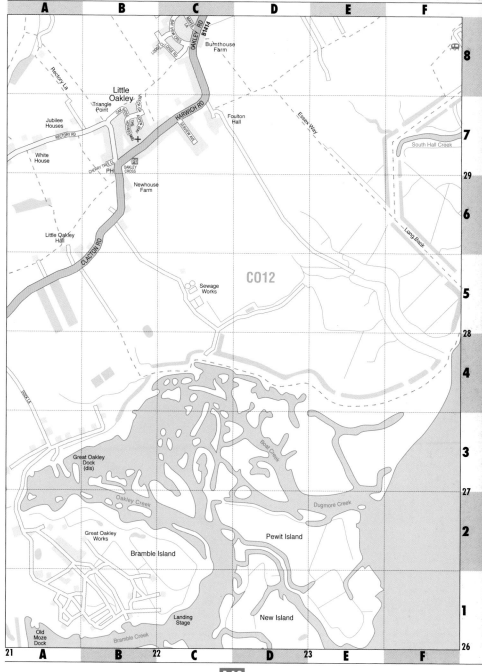

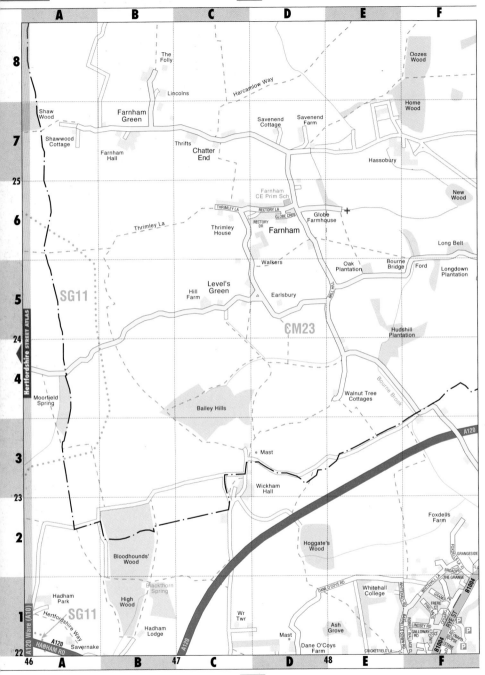

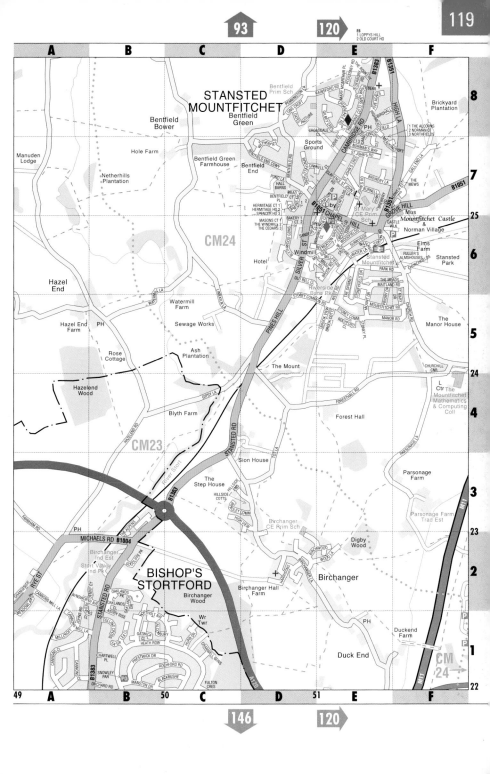

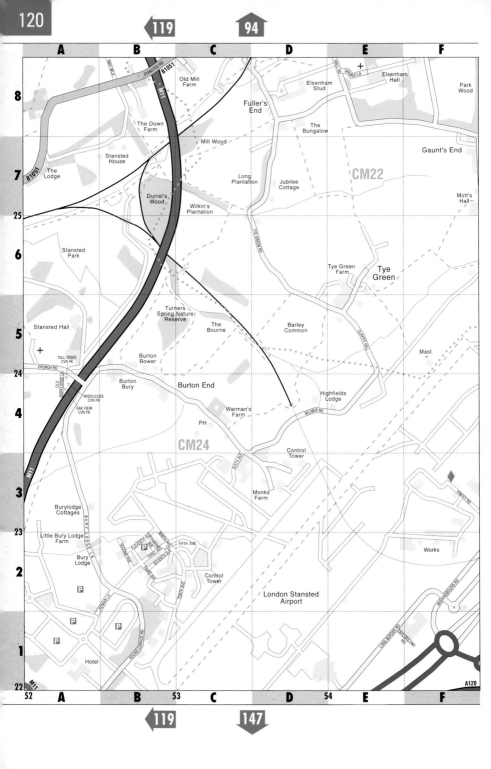

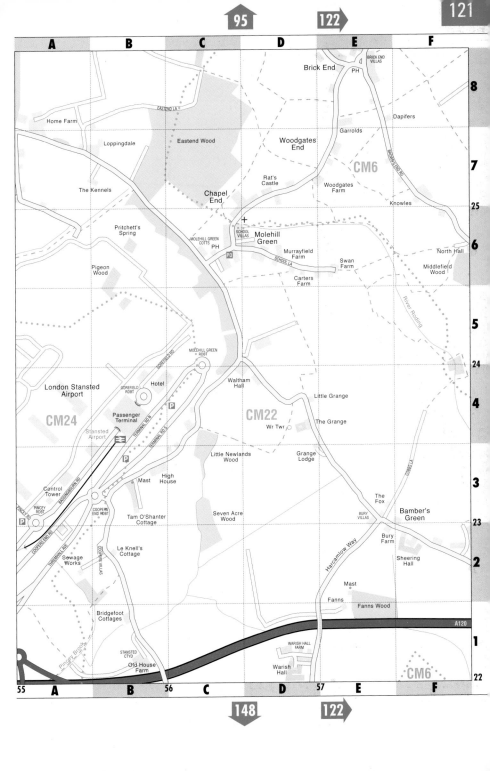

A B C D E F

8

Brick End

BRICK END
VILLAS

PH

Dapifers

Home Farm

EASTEND LA

Garrolds

Loppingdale

Eastend Wood

Woodgates
End

CM6

7

Rat's
Castle

Woodgates
Farm

The Kennels

Chapel
End

Knowles

25

Pritchett's
Spring

MOLEHILL GREEN
COTTS

SCHOOL
VILLAS

Molehill
Green

North Hall

6

PH

PO

Murrayfield
Farm

Middlefield
Wood

Pigeon
Wood

SCHOOL LA

Swan
Farm

Carters
Farm

River Roding

5

MOLEHILL GREEN
RDBT

24

London Stansted
Airport

GOREFIELD
RDBT

Hotel

Waltham
Hall

Little Grange

The Grange

4

CM24

Passenger
Terminal

CM22

Wr Twr

TERMINAL RD S

Stansted
Airport

P

TERMINAL RD N

Little Newlands
Wood

Grange
Lodge

BASSINGBOURN RD

P

Mast

High
House

DORSET RD

3

Control
Tower

PINCEY RD

COOPERS
END RDBT

Tam O'Shanter
Cottage

Seven Acre
Wood

The
Fox

Bamber's
Green

BURY
VILLAS

23

P

Le Knell's
Cottage

COOPERS
VILLAS

Bury
Farm

Sheering
Hall

2

THREMHALL AVE

Sewage
Works

COOPERS END RD

Harcamlow Way

Mast

Fanns

Fanns Wood

Bridgefoot
Cottages

A120

1

Pincey Brook

STANSTED
CTYD

Old House
Farm

WARISH HALL
FARM

Warish
Hall

CM6

22

55 A B 56 C D 57 E F

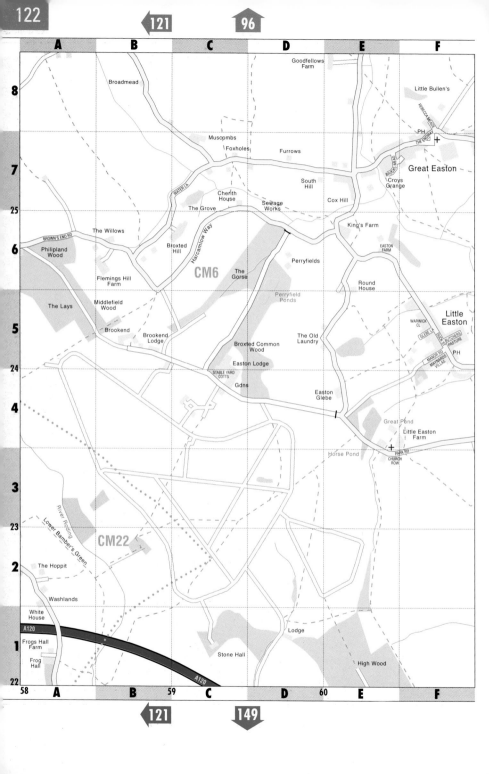

**A** **B** **C** **D** **E** **F**

Goodfellows Farm

8

Broadmead

Little Bullen's

REBECCA MEAD

PH

Muscpmbs

THE STREET

Foxholes

Furrows

Great Easton

7

WATER LA.

South Hill

BROOKS MEAD

Croys Grange

25

Cherith House

Sewage Works

Cox Hill

The Grove

King's Farm

The Willows

EASTON FARM

BROWN'S END RD

Broxted Hill

Perryfields

6

Philipland Wood

Harcamlow Way

CM6

The Gorse

Round House

Flemings Hill Farm

Perryfield Ponds

Little Easton

Middlefield Wood

WARWICK CL.

The Lays

GLEBE LA.

BUTCHERS PASTURE

5

Brookend

The Old Laundry

MANOR RD

PH

Brookend Lodge

Broxted Common Wood

MAYNARDS VILLAS

24

Easton Lodge

STABLE YARD COTTS

Gdns

Easton Glebe

4

Great Pond

Little Easton Farm

PARK RD

CHURCH ROW

Horse Pond

3

River Roding

23

Lower Bamber's Green

CM22

2

The Hoppit

Washlands

White House

A120

Lodge

1

Frogs Hall Farm

Stone Hall

High Wood

Frog Hall

22

A120

58 **A** **B** 59 **C** **D** 60 **E** **F**

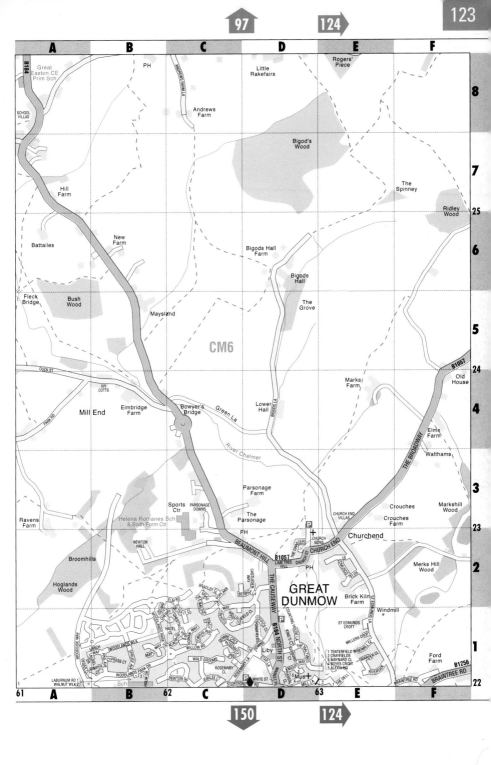

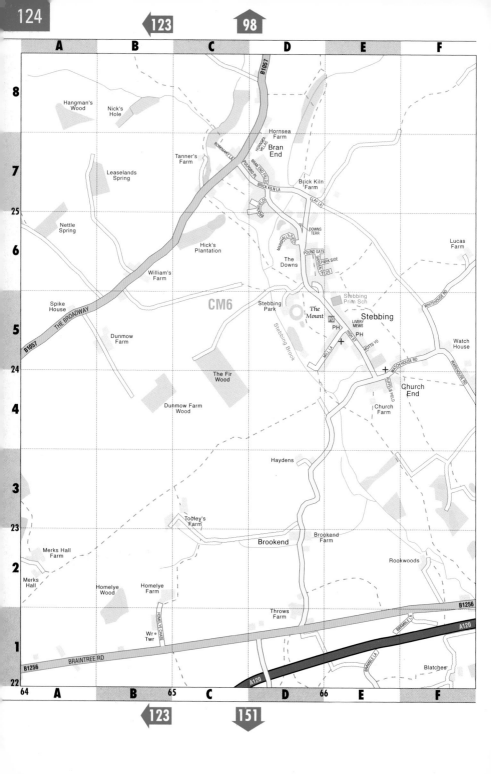

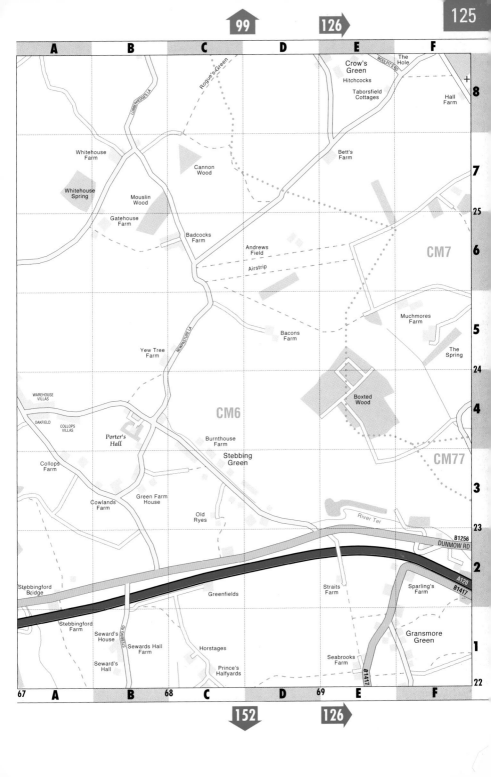

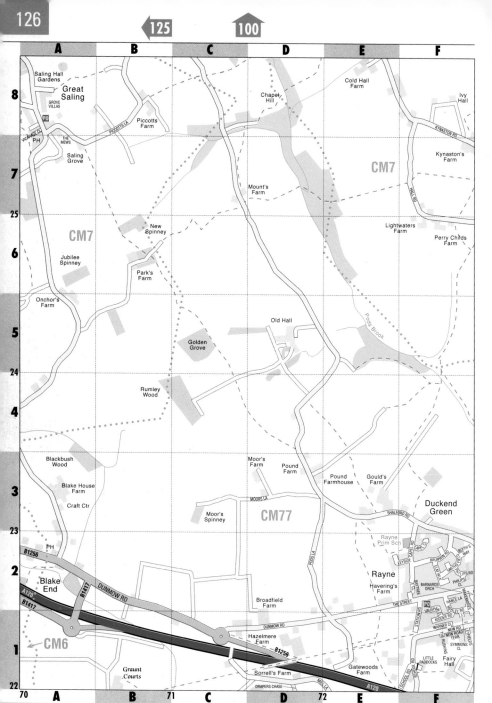

A B C D E F

8

7

25

6

5

24

4

3

23

2

1

22

70 A B 71 C D 72 E F

Saling Hall
Gardens
Great
Saling
GROVE
VILLAS
PO
VICARAGE CL
PH
THE
MEWS
Saling
Grove

PICCOTTS LA
Piccotts
Farm

Chapel
Hill

Cold Hall
Farm

Ivy
Hall

KYNASTON RD

Kynaston's
Farm

CM7

HALL RD

Mount's
Farm

CM7

New
Spinney

Lightwaters
Farm

Perry Childs
Farm

Jubilee
Spinney

Park's
Farm

Onchor's
Farm

Old Hall

Pods Brook

Golden
Grove

Rumley
Wood

Blackbush
Wood

Moor's
Farm

Pound
Farm

Pound
Farmhouse

Gould's
Farm

Duckend
Green

Blake House
Farm

Craft Ctr

Moor's
Spinney

MOORS LA

CM77

SHALFORD RD

Rayne
Prim Sch

CAPEL RD

BLYTH'S
WAY

B1256

PH

Blake
End

B1417

DUNMOW RD

PODS LA

LEYSIDE

BRUNWIN RD

SMITHSON CL

PHILIPS RD

Rayne

BARNARDS
ORCH

PHILLIPS
CL

A120

B1417

CM6

Graunt
Courts

Broadfield
Farm

DUNMOW RD

Hazelmere
Farm

B1256

Sorrell's Farm

DRAPERS CHASE

Gatewoods
Farm

A120

Havering's
Farm

BAYTREE

THE STREET

STATION RD

HANCE LA

NEW ROAD
TERR

PO

VALJOHN

COZEY RD

KIDDER RD

WARNER CL

NEW RD

RUSKINS

MACKMANS

SYMMONS
CL

MILL LA

SCHOOL RD

LITTLE
PADDOCKS

Fairy
Hall

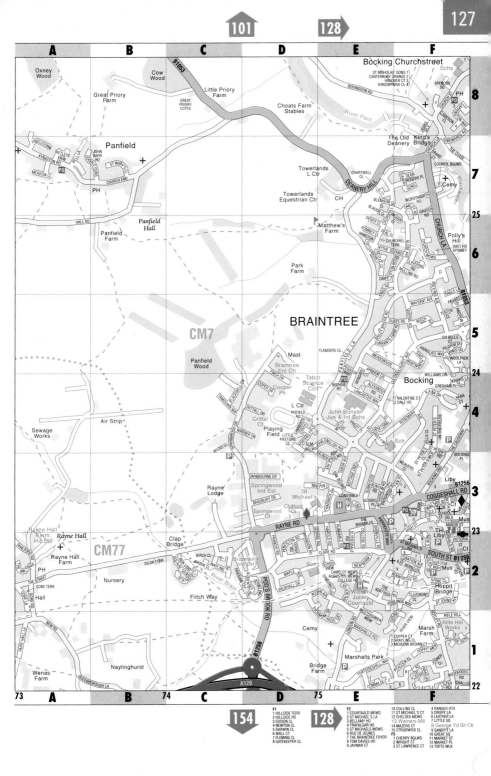

A  B  C  D  E  F

Bocking Churchstreet
Schs

Oxney
Wood

Cow
Wood

B1053

Great Priory
Farm

Little Priory
Farm

GREAT
PRIORY
COTTS

ST NICHOLAS GDNS 1
CANTERBURY GRANGE 2
HANOVER CT 3
KINGSBRIDGE CL 4

SPENCER
SQ

8

PH
PO

BOVINGDON RD

Choats Farm
Stables

River Pant

The Old
Deanery

King's
Bridge

Panfield

JOHN
BARR

ST MARY

PH

KELVEDON RD
KYMSTON RD
MEADOW CL

CHURCH END

CHARTWELL

DEANERY HILL

CHURCH LA

Cemy

7

25

Hall Rd

Panfield
Hall

Panfield
Farm

Matthew's
Farm

Towerlands
L Ctr

Towerlands
Equestrian Ctr

CH

BLENHEIM

BLADON DR

DOVER CL

DEAL CL

ROMNEY CL

WINSTON

CHURCHILL
TERR

HYTHE

Polly's
Hill

OAST HO
SPINNEY

6

Park
Farm

CAMEL

CM7

BRAINTREE

Bocking

B1053

SIX BELLS

WOOLPACK
LA

FRIARS LA

5

24

Mast

Braintree
Ent Ctr

FLANDERS CL

Tabor
Science
Coll

Panfield
Wood

Cooper
Pk

L Ctr

Crittal
BEEHIVE

JOHN BUNYAN
AV

ALEXANDER

LANCASTER WAY

John Bunyan
Jun & Inf Schs

GRESHAM PL

1 VALENTINE CT
2 DALE HO

Sch

ROSMARIN

BOCKING
PL

4

Air Strip

Playing
Field

LITTLE
PASTURE

ASH

ELM

ST PETER'S CL

HILLS CL

PETER ST

WEAVERS

THE FIELDS

Liby

B1256

Sewage
Works

Rayne
Lodge

Springwood
Ind Est

BRADBURY DR

St
Michael's

Chilford

CONSTABLE

GODRIC

RAYNE RD

COGGESHALL RD

PO

MANOR ST

CH

Mus
Liby
VICTORIA
ST

3

23

CM77

Rayne Hall

Rayne Hall
Farm

PH
GORE TERR

Hall

Nursery

Clap
Bridge

GILDA TERR

Broomhills
Ind Est

BIRCH CL

River Brain

BROOK LA

SCHOOL
VIEW

CAMELOT MEWS 1
AUGUSTUS MEWS 2
COLLEGE HO 3

William
Julien
Courtauld

THE
BRAMBLES

COLLEGE

ST MICHAEL'S

CORONATION AV

BOCKINGHAM AV

SOUTH ST

Mus

B1256

Hoppit
Bridge

P

2

Wenas
Farm

Naylinghurst

FARTH HALL LA

NEW RD

Flitch Way

PODS BROOK RD

Cemy

Bridge
Farm

Marshalls Park

B1256

Marsh
Farm

Rifle Hill
Works

1 COPPER CT
2 GRAYLING CL
3 MEADOW BROWN CT

RIFLE HILL

1

22

A120

73  A  B  74  C  D  75  E  F  22

F1
1 HILLSIDE TERR
2 HILLSIDE HO
3 EDISON CL
4 NEWTON CL
5 DARWIN CL
6 WALL CT
7 FLEMING CL
8 GATEKEEPER CL

F2
1 COURTAULD MEWS
2 ST MICHAEL'S LA
3 BELLAMY HO
4 TRAFALGAR HO
5 ST MICHAELS MEWS
6 RUE DE JEUNES
7 THE BRAINTREE FOYER
8 TOM DAVIES HO
9 JAYMAR CT

10 COLLINS CL
11 ST MICHAEL'S CT
12 CHELSEA MEWS
13 Warners Mill
14 MAZERS CT
15 STRUDWICK CL
F3
1 CHERRY BGLWS
2 WRIGHT CT
3 ST LAWRENCE CT

4 RANGER HTS
5 DRURY LA
6 LEATHER LA
7 LITTLE SQ
8 George Yd Sh Ctr
9 SANDPIT LA
10 GREAT SQ
11 MARKET ST
12 MARKET PL
13 TOFTS WLK

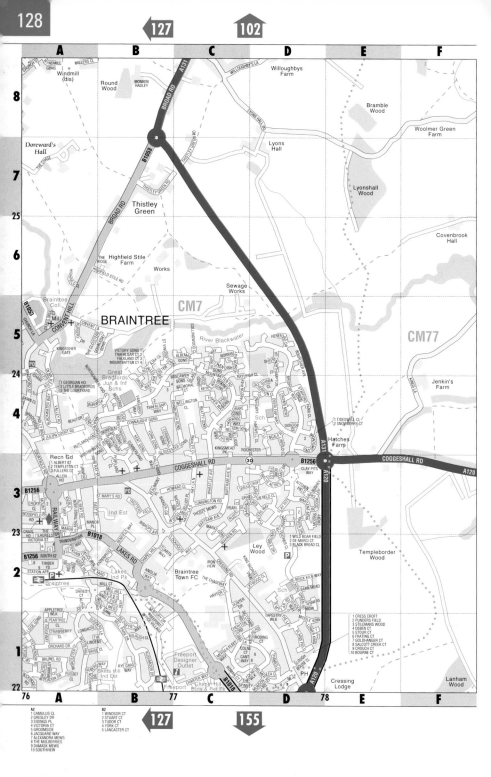

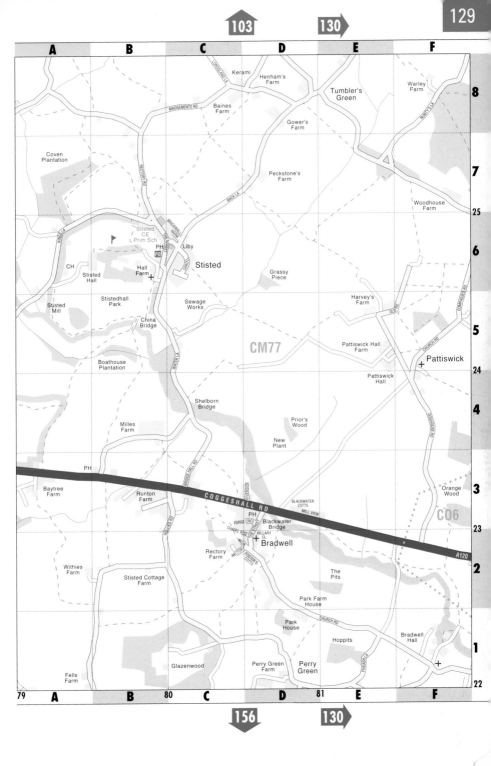

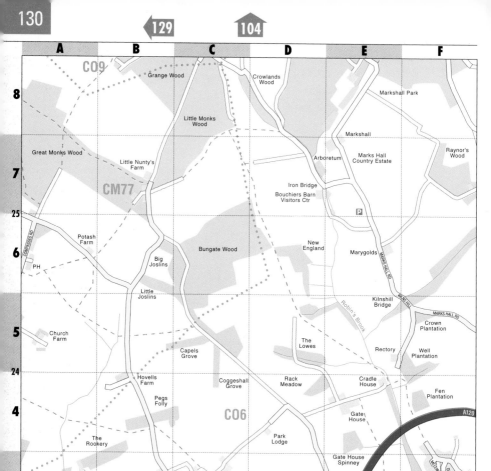

CO9

Grange Wood

Crowlands Wood

Markshall Park

Little Monks Wood

Markshall

Great Monks Wood

Little Nunty's Farm

Arboretum

Marks Hall Country Estate

Raynor's Wood

CM77

Iron Bridge

Bouchiers Barn Visitors Ctr

Potash Farm

Bungate Wood

New England

Marygolds

PH

Big Joslins

Kilnshill Bridge

Crown Plantation

MARKS HALL RD

Little Joslins

Robin's Brook

Church Farm

Capels Grove

The Lowes

Rectory

Well Plantation

Hovells Farm

Coggeshall Grove

Rack Meadow

Cradle House

Fen Plantation

Pegs Folly

CO6

Gate House

The Rookery

Park Lodge

Gate House Spinney

A120

Tilkey

Captain's Wood

Pond Piece

Holfield Grange

Bankfield

Avenue Spinney

Robin's Bridge

Libr

Whiteshill Farm

Stockstreet Farm

A120

COGGESHALL RD

Stockstreet

Highfields Farm

Allot Gdns

Paycocke's House

Griggs Bsns Ctr

WEST ST

WEST ST

The Slades

CM77

Grigg's Farm

Garden Ctr

Grange Barn

Grange Farm

Essex Way

Horseshoe Hole

River Blackwater

KELVEDON RD

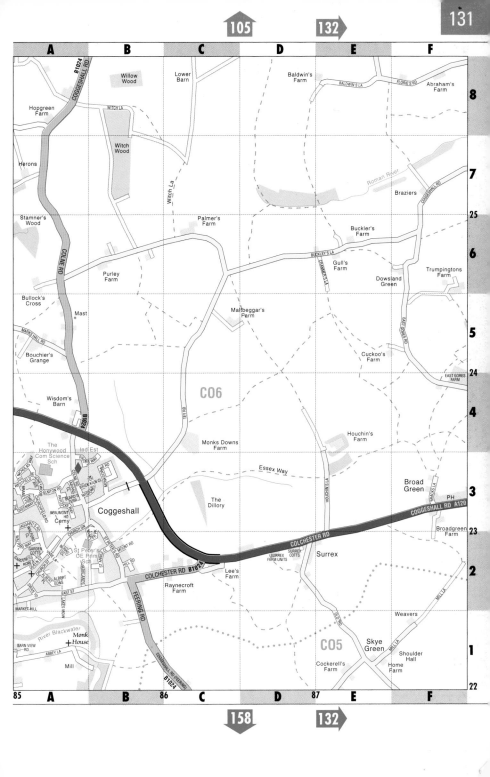

Brookhouse
BROOKHOUSE RD
HARVESTERS WAY
MOOR RD
Great Tey
Moor Farm
Hoe Farm
Walcott's Farm
Brick Kiln Cottage
Warrens Farm
NEW COTTS
PH
WINDMILLS
TAMBOUR CL
Walcott's Hall
COGGESHALL RD
Church House Farm
RECTORY RD
TEY RD
8

Chase Cottage
Tey Brook Centre
Roman River
7
25

Essex Way
Teybrook Farm
Little Tey House
6

Sparrow Grove
Little Tey House Farm
Stonefield Grove
5

East Gores
EAST GORES RD
Knave's Farm
CO6
24
GREAT TEY RD

Uphall Farm
Little Tey
Church Farm
Mott's Farm
Marks Tey
A120
4

SALMON'S LA
CHURCH RD
PH
Roxborough CL
GOODMAN
HAWK MARK END
ASHURST
BURY
Buxton Cotts
SALMON'S CNR
COGGESHALL RD 40
Prim Sch
DOMSEY BANK
PATTEN CL
KINGSBURY CL
STEELE CL
3
A120

Elm Farm
Honeylands Farm
Godbolt's Farm
MANDEVILLE RD
HEYWOOD
PROCTOR
Works
LONDON RD
23
WILSON'S LA
LONG GDN
LC
DOBBES LA
A12

2

ELM LA
Hornigals
CO5
Wishingwell Farm
LONDON RD
A12
1

22

88   89   90

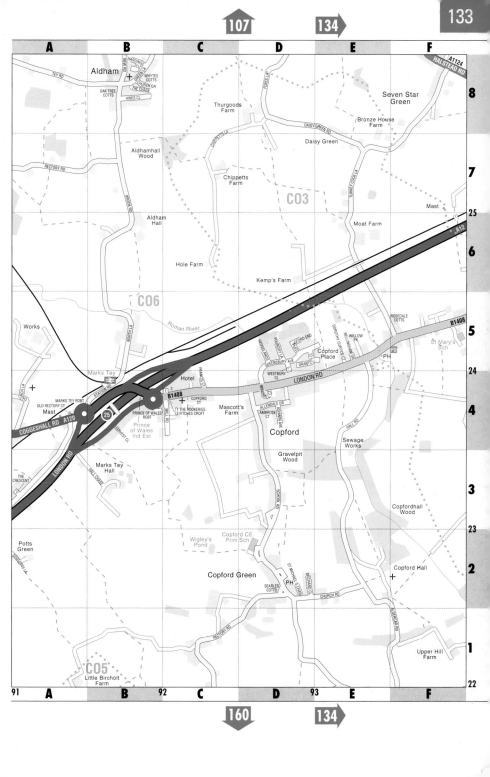

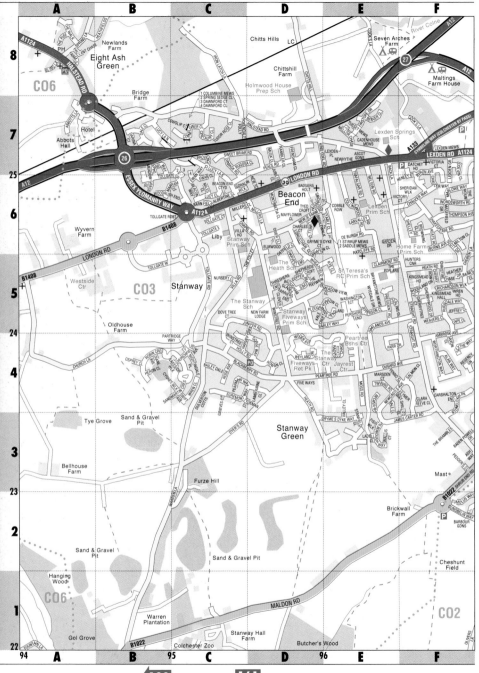

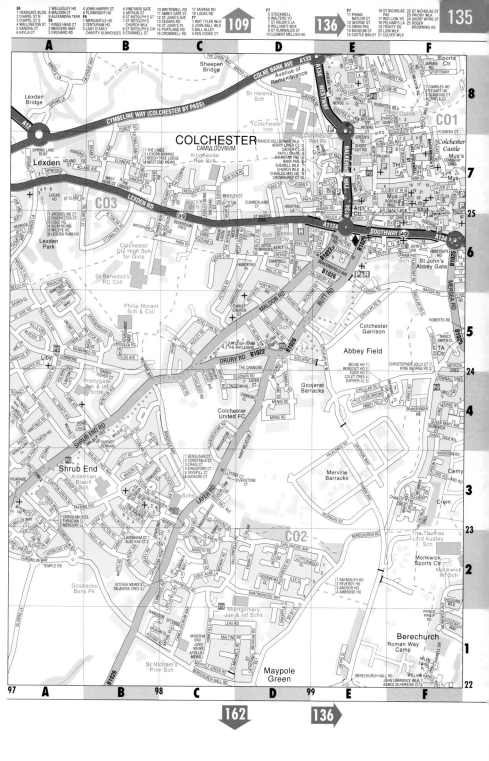

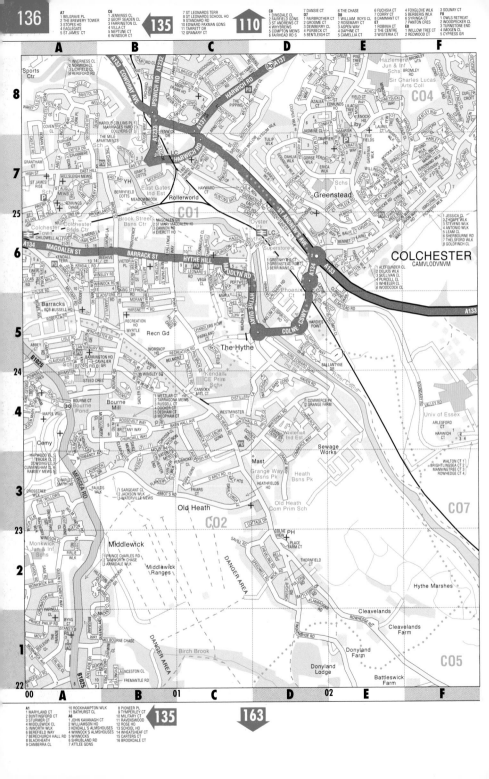

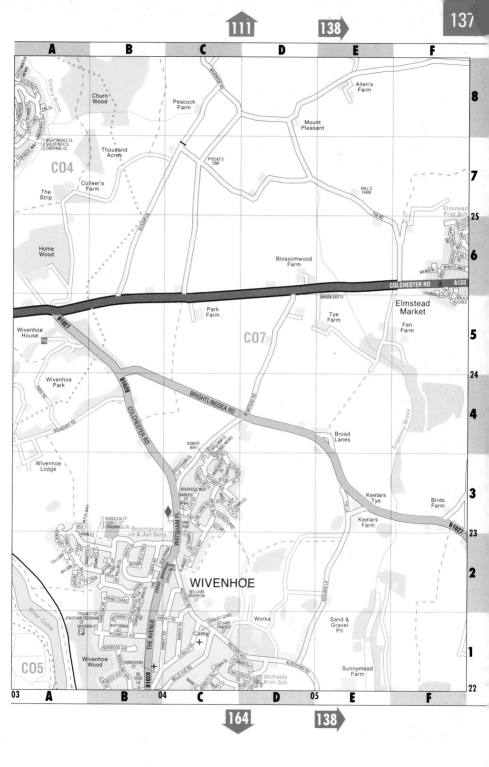

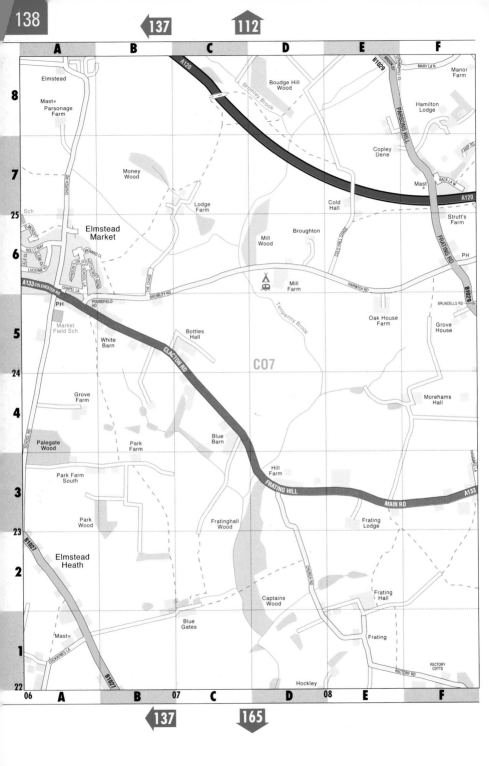

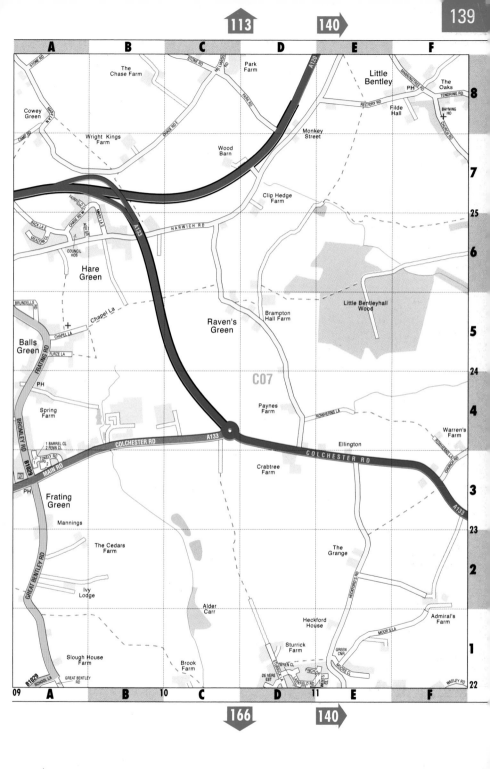

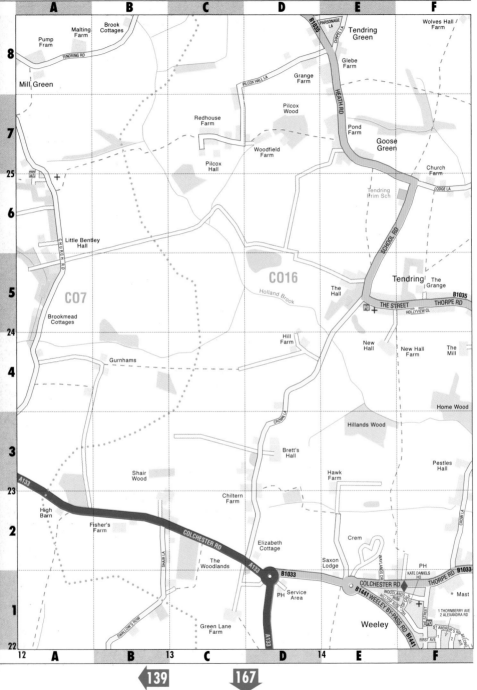

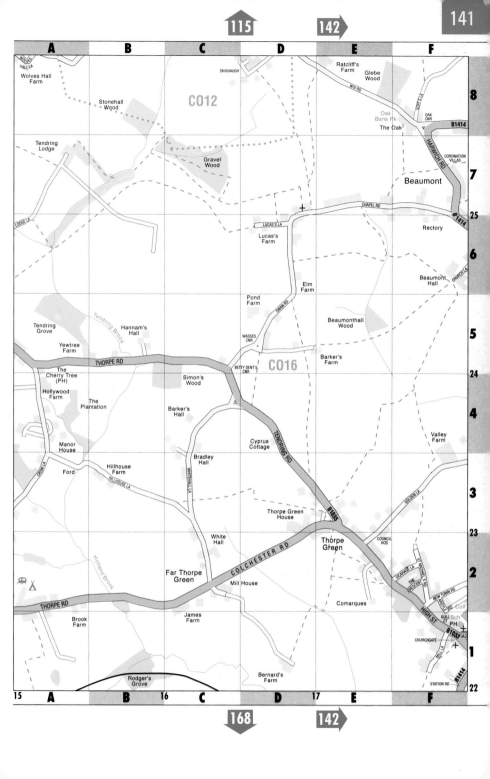

115
142

Wolves Hall
Farm

BROOKS
HALL LA

SKIGHAUGH

CO12

Ratcliff's
Farm

Glebe
Wood

WIX RD

Stonehall
Wood

Oak
Bsns Pk

OAK
CNR

The Oak

OAK
CNR

GOES LA

B1414

8

Tendring
Lodge

Gravel
Wood

CORONATION
VILLAS

HARWICH RD

Beaumont

7

LODGE LA

CHAPEL RD

B1414

25

LUCAS'S LA

Rectory

Lucas's
Farm

6

Tendring
Brook

Elm
Farm

Beaumont
Hall

CHURCH LA

Pond
Farm

SWAN RD

Tendring
Grove

Hannam's
Hall

WASSES
CNR

Beaumonthall
Wood

5

Yewtree
Farm

THORPE RD

BETTY DENT'S
CNR

CO16

Barker's
Farm

24

The
Cherry Tree
(PH)

Simon's
Wood

Hollywood
Farm

The
Plantation

Barker's
Hall

Valley
Farm

4

Manor
House

Cyprus
Cottage

TENDRING RD

Ford

Hillhouse
Farm

Bradley
Hall

WHITEHALL LA

HILLHOUSE LA

CROFT LA

GOLDEN LA

3

Thorpe Green
House

B1035

23

White
Hall

COLCHESTER RD

Thorpe
Green

COUNCIL
HOS

VICARAGE LA

ST MICHAEL'S RD

NEW TOWN RD

2

Far Thorpe
Green

THORPE RD

Mill House

Comarques

HIGH ST

GULL
CT

PH

Coll

Sch

Brook
Farm

James
Farm

B1033

CHURCHGATE

MILL LA

1

Rodger's
Grove

Bernard's
Farm

STATION RD

B1414

22

168
142

15 A B 16 C D 17 E F

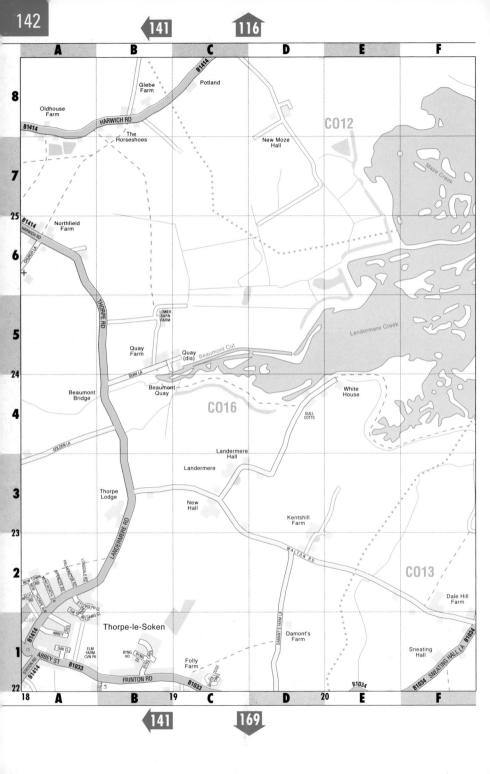

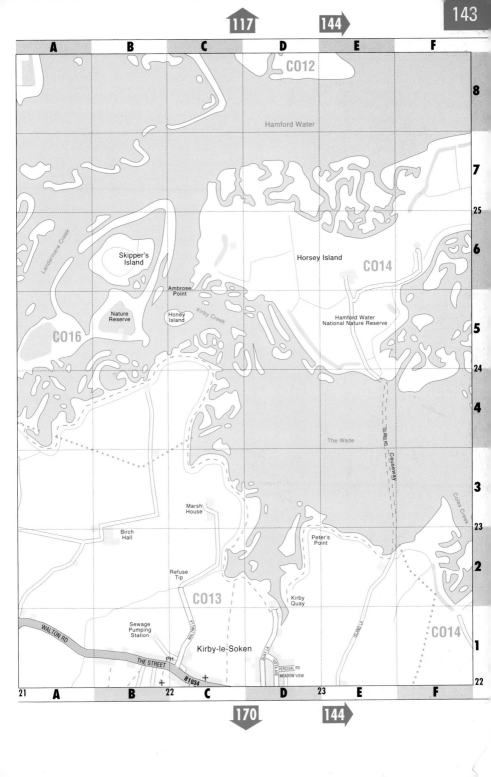

117
144

CO12

Hamford Water

Landermere Creek

Skipper's
Island

Horsey Island

CO14

Ambrose
Point

Nature
Reserve

Honey
Island

Kirby Creek

Hamford Water
National Nature Reserve

CO16

The Wade

ISLAND RD.

Causeway

Coles Creek

Marsh
House

Birch
Hall

Peter's
Point

Refuse
Tip

CO13

Kirby
Quay

Sewage
Pumping
Station

WALTON RD

PH

THE STREET

B1034

Kirby-le-Soken

PUMP HILL RD.

CLOSE AVE

ISLAND LA.

PERCIVAL RD

MEADOW VIEW

CO14

A   B   C   D   E   F

8
7
25
6
5
24
4
3
23
2
1
22

21
22
23

A B C D E F

8

7

25

6

5

24

4

3

23

2

1

22

Stone
Point

Stone
Marsh

Stone Creek

The Dardenelles

Standcreek
Salts

Salt Fleet

Hedge-end
Island

Cormorant Creek

John Weston
Nature Reserve

Sewage
Works

Walton Hall
Marshes

THE NAZE

CREEK
COTTS

The Naze
Nature Trail

CO14

Walton
Hall

The Naze
Tower

Walton Channel

The Twizzle

PH

Titchmarsh
Marina

COLES LA

Sole Creek

Walton
Mere

CH

Martello
Tower

BRIAN BISHOP CL

MELLA

OLD HALL LA

NAZE
CT

EAST
SWOOD LODGE

EL
IZABETH GDNS

SUNNY POINT

P

P

P

Mabel Greville
Breakwater

HIGH TREE LA

STANFORD
CL

FIRST AVE

SECOND AVE

THIRD AVE

NAZE PARK RD

D'ARCY RD 1
RIVERS HO 2

SPENCE

FLORENCE RD

SPENDELLS
HO

2

CL

ROCHFORD
HO

BEATRICE RD

PERCIVAL RD

OLD PIER

Jubilee
Beach

NAZE MARINE
HOLIDAY PK

MANOR LA

WINFIELD
TERR

HALL LA

GREEN LA

BARNETT
REACH

COASTGUARD
COTTS

Walton Maritime
Mus

PENRICE CT 1
EASTCLIFF HO 2
WATERFRONT TERR 3
KINGS REACH 4
HOMELEA 5

EAST TERR

East Terrace
Breakwater

Walton
Prim Sch

SAVILLE ST

P

4
5

STANDLEY RD

EAGLE
AVE

PRINCES ESPL

B1034

26

A B C D E F
25

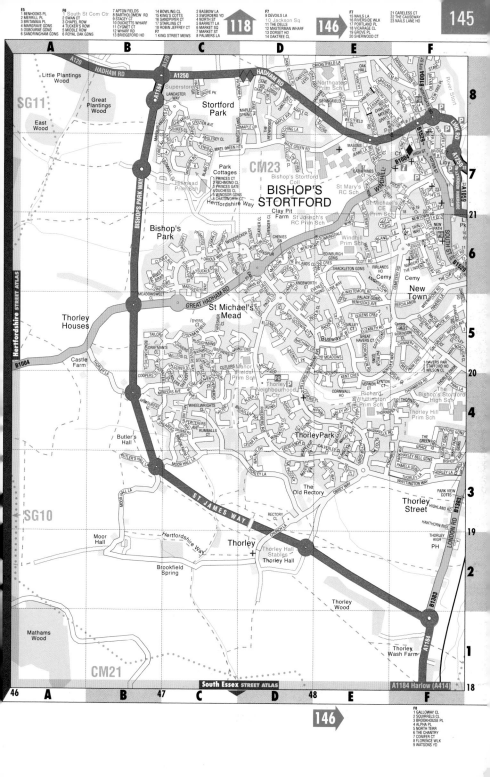

146

A7
1 THE CAUSEWAY
2 THE OLD MALTINGS
3 FULLER CT
4 RED LION CT
5 BAKERS CT
6 HOCKERILL CT

7 HARRINGTON CL
8 PRIORS
9 CLIFFORD CT
10 THOMAS HESKIN CT
11 JOSCELYN'S YD
12 JUBILEE COTT
13 THE PUMP HO

B8
1 BOYD CL
2 HEATH ROW
3 STORTFORD HALL RD
4 GROSVENOR HO
5 EATON HO
6 BELGRAVE HO

145

119

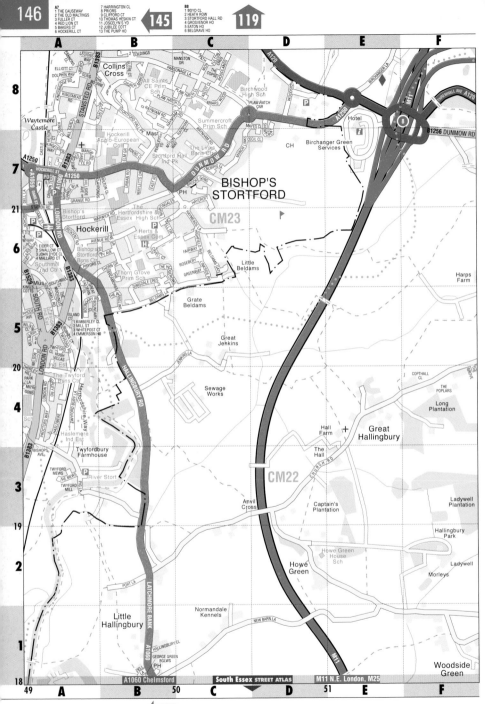

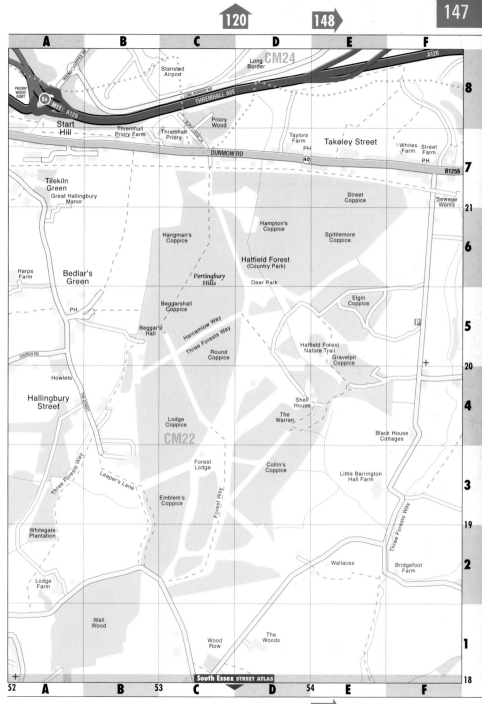

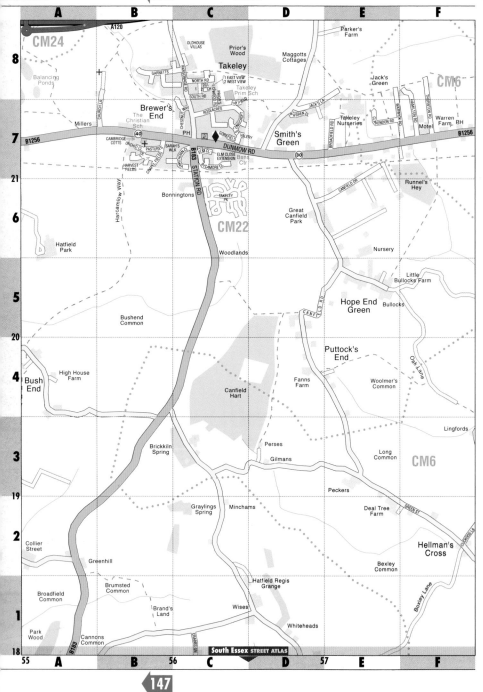

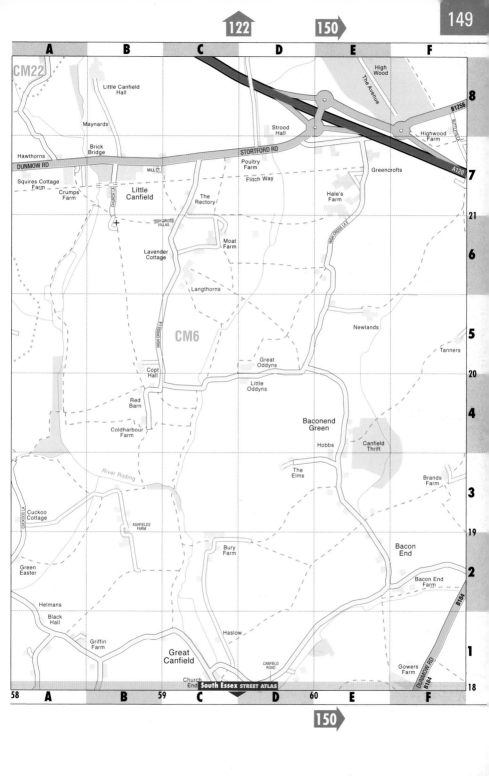

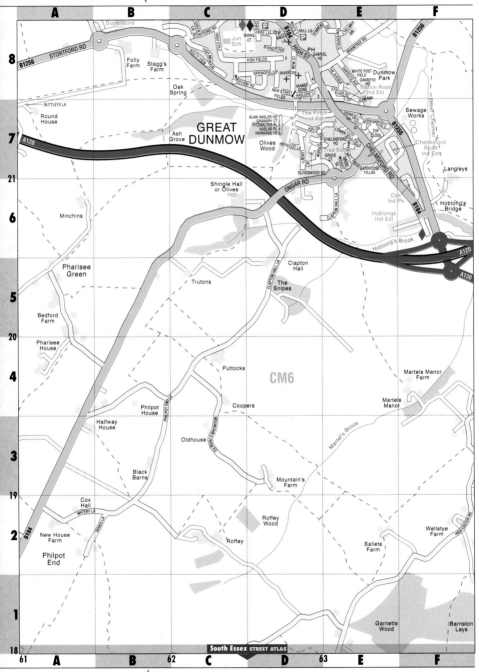

GREAT
DUNMOW

CM6

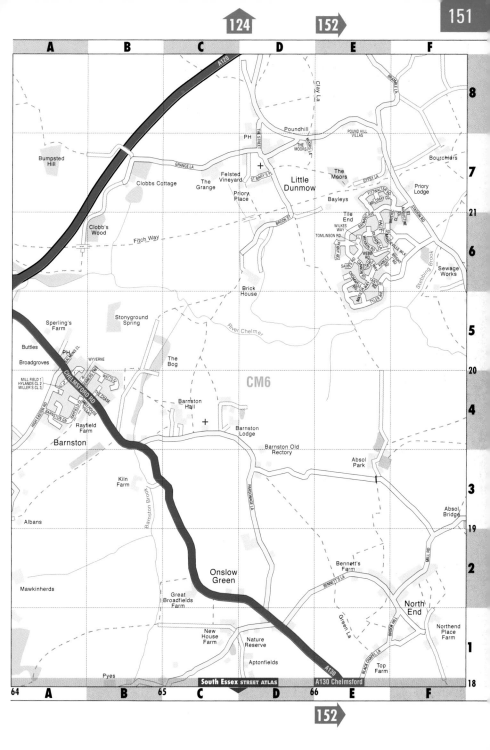

A120

8

Bumpsted Hill

Clay La

Poundhill

PH
THE STREET
THE MOORS

POUND HILL VILLAS

Bourchiers

7

Clobbs Cottage

Grange La

The Grange

Felsted Vineyard

ST MARY'S PL

Priory Place

Little Dunmow

The Moors

GYPSY LA

Bayleys

Priory Lodge

FITZWALTER RD
MILDMAY CL
ST AUGUSTINE
FEDERAL RD

21

Clobb's Wood

Fitch Way

BROOK ST

Tile End

Tomlinson Rd.

Wilkes Way

WEBB RD

Stebbing Brook

Sewage Works

6

Brick House

SAIN

River Chelmer

5

Sperling's Farm

Stonyground Spring

Buttles

Broadgroves

PH
WYVERNE
WATTS CL

The Bog

CM6

20

MILL FIELD 1
HYLANDS CL 2
MILLER S CL 3

THE CHASE

Barnston Hall

Barnston Lodge

4

HIGH CASTER BARNSTON RD

CHELMSFORD RD

Rayfield Farm

Barnston

Barnston Old Rectory

Absol Park

3

Kiln Farm

Barnston Brook

Albans

PARSONAGE LA

MILL RD

Absol Bridge

19

Mawkinherds

Onslow Green

Bennett's Farm

BENNETT S LA

North End

2

Great Broadfields Farm

Green La

Northend Place Farm

New House Farm

Nature Reserve

BLACK CHAPEL LA

1

Aptonfields

A130

Top Farm

Pyes

A130 Chelmsford

18

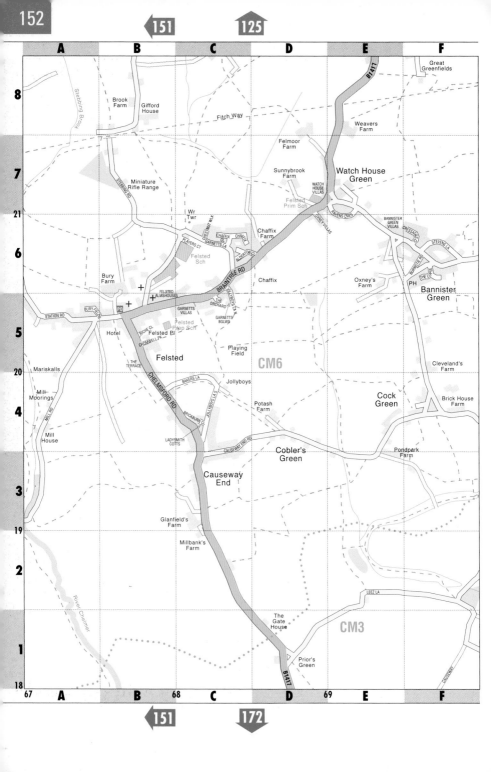

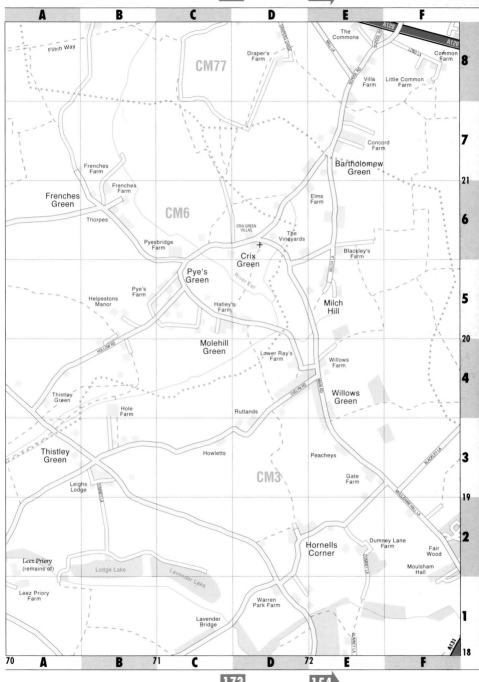

126 154

173 154

A B C D E F

Flitch Way

The Commons

A120

A120

CM77

Draper's Farm

Common Farm

8

School Rd

Mill La

Long La

Villa Farm

Little Common Farm

Concord Farm

7

Frenches Farm

Bartholomew Green

21

Frenches Farm

Elms Farm

Frenches Green

CM6

Thorpes

Crix Green Villas

The Vineyards

6

Blackley's Farm

Pyesbridge Farm

Crix Green

Pye's Green

River Ter

Milch Hill

5

Helpestons Manor

Pye's Farm

Hatley's Farm

Hollow Rd

Molehill Green

Lower Ray's Farm

Willows Farm

20

Evelyn Rd

Main Rd

Willows Green

4

Thistley Green

Hole Farm

Rutlands

Howletts

Peacheys

Blackley La

3

Thistley Green

CM3

Gate Farm

Moulsham Hall La

Leighs Lodge

Dunmow La

19

Leez Priory (remains of)

Lodge Lake

Lavender Lake

Hornells Corner

Dumney Lane Farm

Fair Wood

2

Dunmey La

Moulsham Hall

Leez Priory Farm

Lavender Bridge

Warren Park Farm

Dumney La

1

A131

18

70 A B 71 C D 72 E F

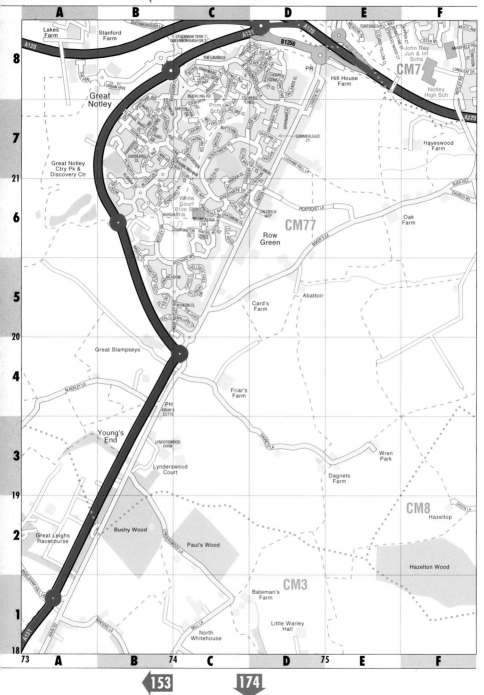

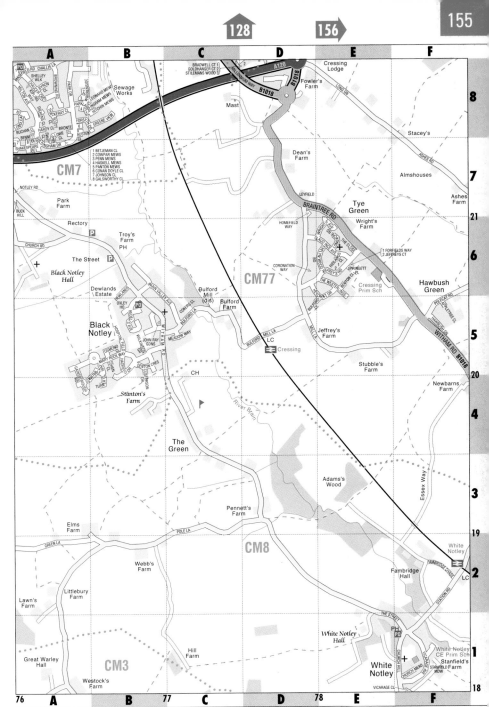

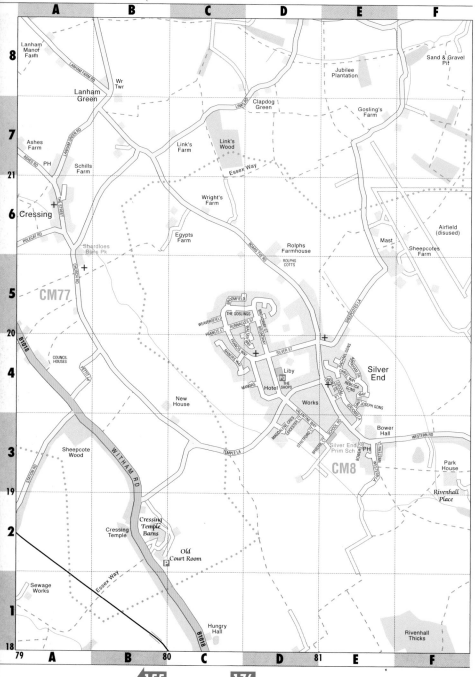

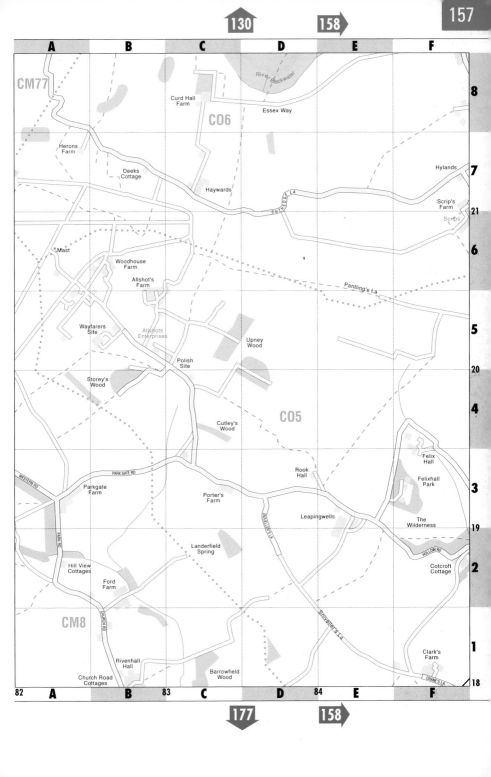

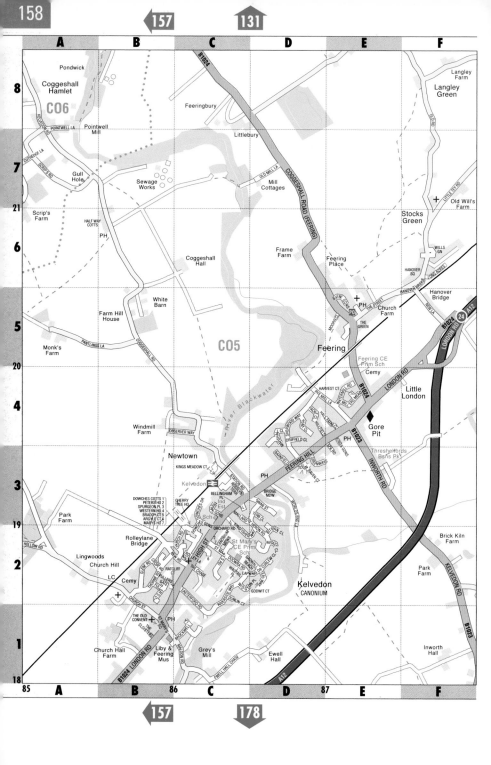

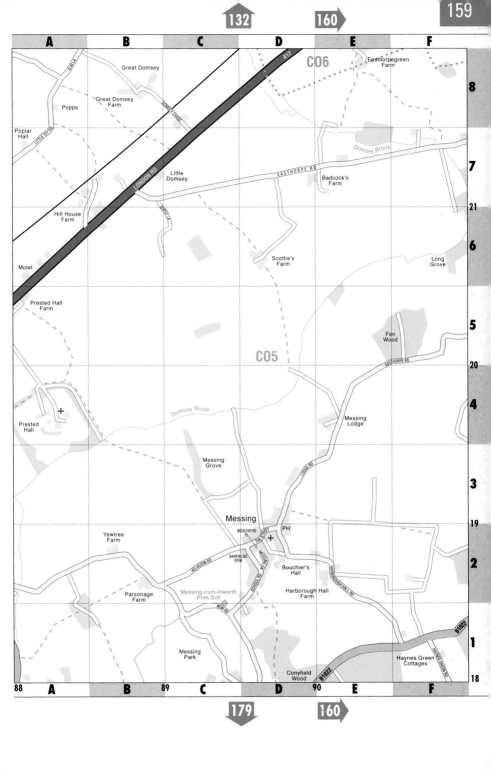

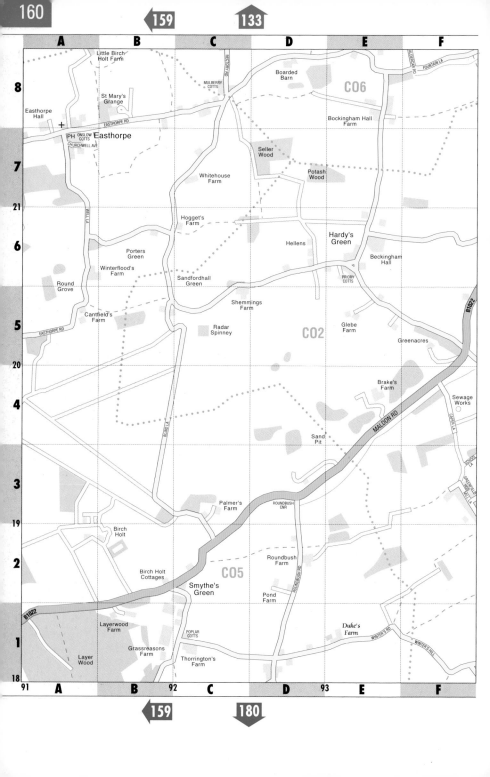

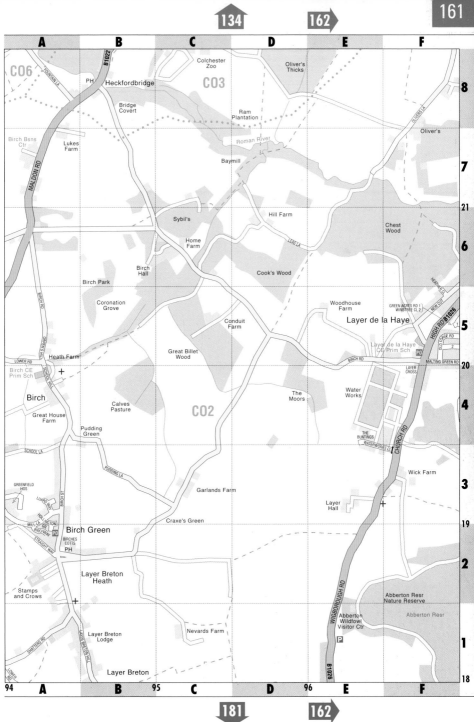

A B C D E F

CO6

B1022

FOUNTAIN LA

PH
Heckfordbridge

Colchester Zoo

CO3

Oliver's Thicks

8

Bridge Covert

Ram Plantation

Oliver's

Birch Bsns Ctr

Lukes Farm

Roman River

Baymill

OLIVERS LA

7

MALDON RD

21

Sybil's

Hill Farm

Chest Wood

6

Home Farm

LEAS LA

BIRCH RD

Birch Park

Birch Hall

Cook's Wood

HEATH RD

Coronation Grove

Conduit Farm

Woodhouse Farm

GREEN ACRES RD 1
WINSTREE CL 2

Layer de la Haye

HIGH RD

NEW CUT

B1026

5

LOWER RD

Heath Farm

Great Billet Wood

Layer de la Haye CE/Prim Sch

PO

OLD FORGE RD

2

GREEN LA

Birch CE Prim Sch

Birch

BIRCH RD

LAYER CROSS

MALTING GREEN RD

20

Great House Farm

Calves Pasture

CO2

The Moors

Water Works

4

Pudding Green

SCHOOL LA

PUDDING LA

THE BUNTINGS

WATERWORKS CL

CHURCH RD

GREENFIELD HOS

LUARD RD

Garlands Farm

Wick Farm

3

MOLLINGTON

MILL LE CR

BIRCHWAY

PO

Craxe's Green

Layer Hall

STRAIGHT WAY

Birch Green

BIRCHES COTTS

PH

19

Layer Breton Heath

2

Stamps and Crows

SPATTERS RD

Layer Breton Lodge

LAYER BRETON HILL

Nevards Farm

Abberton Resr Nature Reserve

Abberton Resr

WIGBOROUGH RD

Abberton Wildfowl Visitor Ctr

P

LOWER RD

Layer Breton

B1026

1

94 A B 95 C D 96 E F 18

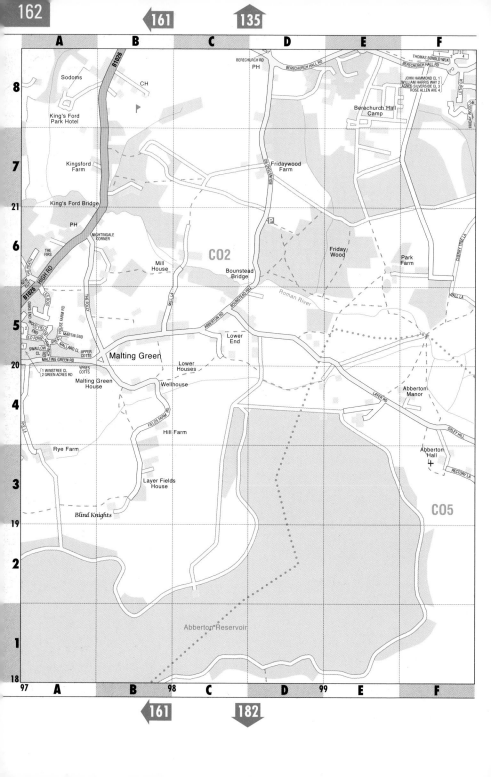

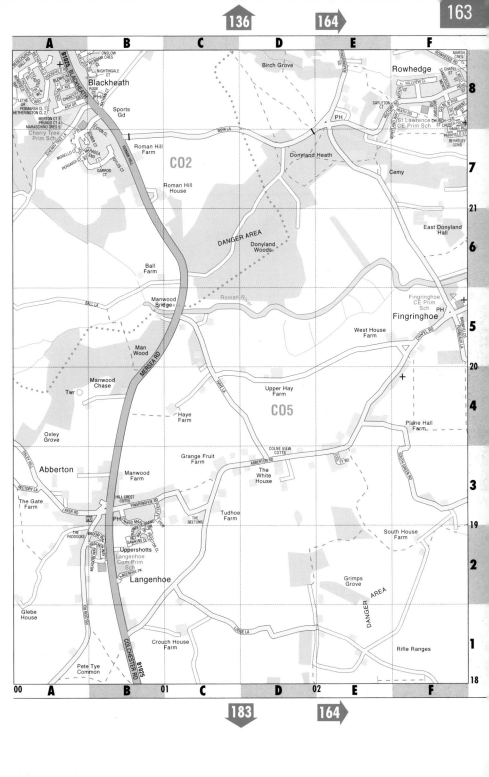

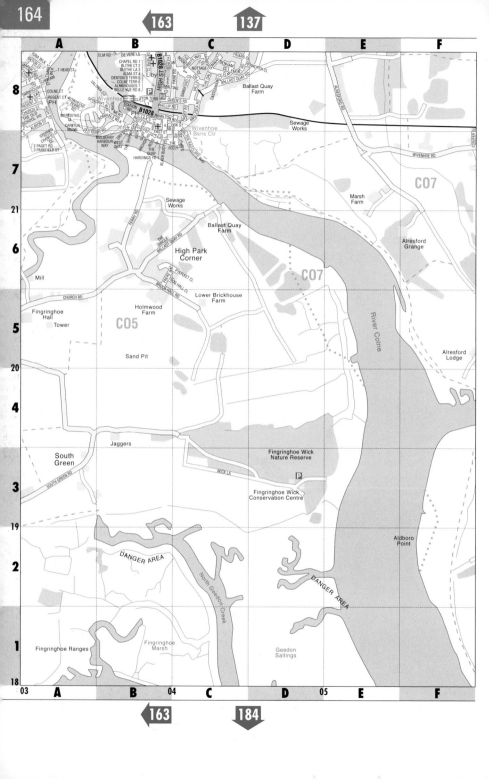

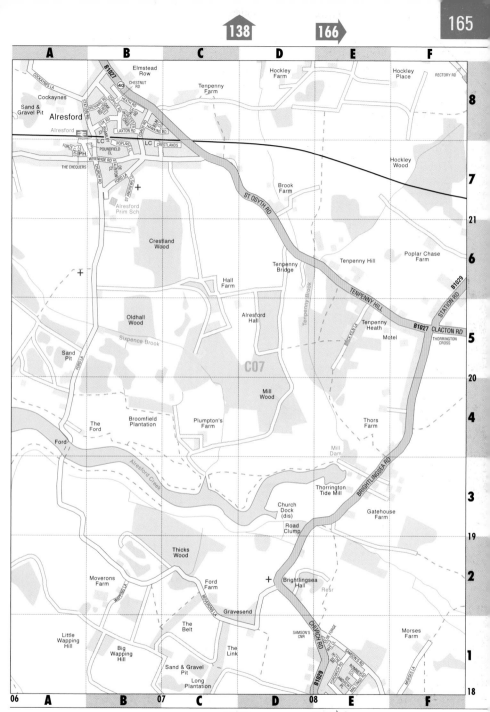

165
139

**A** **B** **C** **D** **E** **F**

SCHOOL LA
B1029
STATION RD
Burr's Farm
GREAT BENTLEY RD
Hill House Farm
THORRINGTON RD
WREN CL
ROBIN CL
LINNET WAY
DE VERE EST
CHERRYWOODS
THE FAITH
Bentley Green
WEELEY RD
LAMBOURNE
SYCAMORE PL
BIRCH AVE
ROWAN CL
CEDAR WAY
ELM CL
THE GREEN
MILL ON THE GREEN
OF ROBBINS
PH
PO
Great Bentley

**8**

Lufkins Farm
FRATING CROSS
GREAT BENTLEY RD
Great Bentley Prim Sch
NEW CUT
MORELLA
Great Bentley Ind Est
LC
NEW STATION RD
HALL VIEW RD
KEEBLE CL

**7**

LC
**21**
Mast
FRATING RD
B1029 STATION RD
The Talbots
Frating Abbey
Bentley Brook
PLOUGH RD
St Mary's Farm

**6**

Whitehouse Farm
FRATING ABBEY FARM RD
CHURCH RD
Lodge Plantation
COUNCIL HOUSES
WEELEY RD
ST MARY'S RD
AINGERS GREEN RD
PH
ST MARY'S RD
THE PADDOCKS
WOOD GREEN EST

Aingers Green

**5**
ACORN WLK 1
THELMA DR 2
B1027
HEATHLANDS
CLOVER CL DN
GUN CELLA
ROSEMARY LA
PH
High Barns
Thicket Grove
Carpenter's Farm
COLLES BACK RD

Thorrington
**20**
VICTORY CL

Glebe Farm
Thorrington Hall
CLACTON RD
The Lodge
Colles Brook

**4**
CO7

Saltwater Brook Cottages
Saltwater Bridge
DIAL RD
STRAIGHT RD
SOUTH HEATH RD

**3**
Thorringtonhall Wood
HOLLYBUSH HILL
DIAL CNR
Lady Wood
Kellands Farm

**19**
MARSH FARM LA
Saltwater Brook

**2**
Crocky Grove
Greatmarsh Farm
Cottage Farm
HILL COTTS
CO16
DEAD LA

**1**
Thorrington Creek
Caravan Site
CH
Hollybush Hill
FLAG HILL
B1027
Dines Farm

**18**
TEE MARELLA
Lowermarsh Farm

**09** **A** **B** **10** **C** **D** **11** **E** **F**

165
186

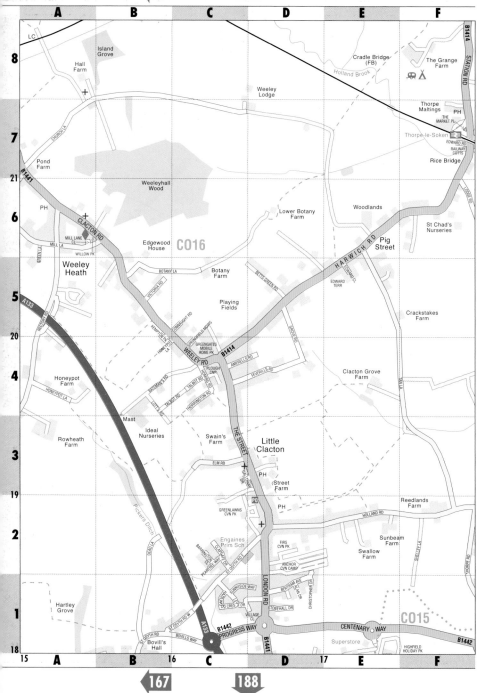

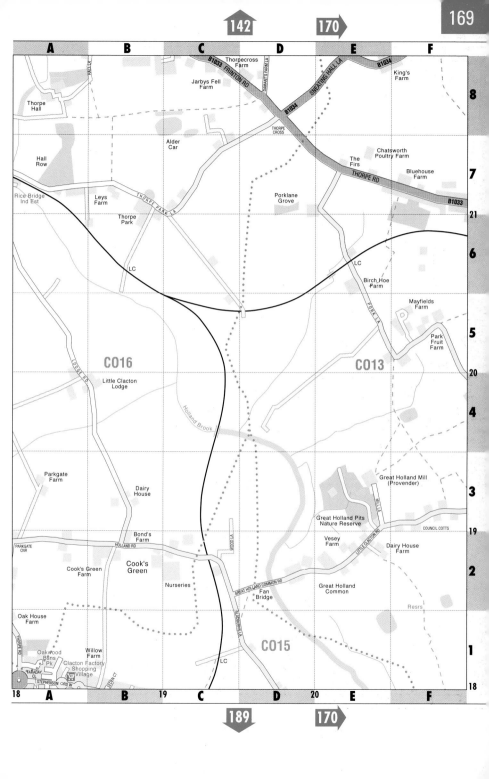

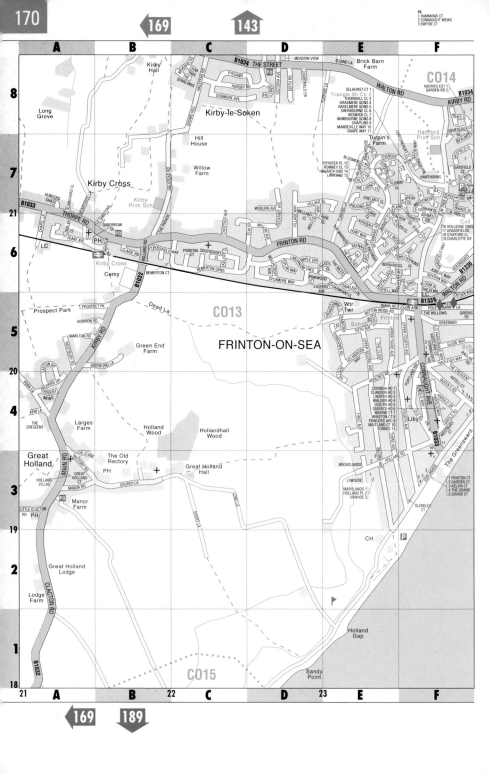

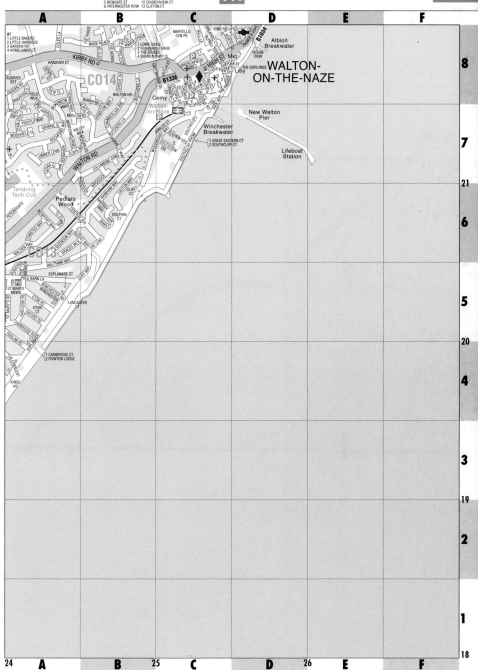

144

**C8**
1 MARINA MEWS
2 VICARAGE LA
3 HAVENCROFT CT
4 STRATFORD PL
5 NEWGATE ST
6 PATERNOSTER ROW

7 NEW PIER ST
8 MARTELLO RD
9 AGAR RD
10 AGAR ROAD APP
11 ST BOTOLPH'S TERR
12 CHURCHVIEW CT
13 CLIFTON CT

14 MARINE BLDGS

**A7**
1 LITTLE BAKERS
2 LITTLE HARBORDS
3 GARDEN RD
4 HOMELANDS CT

**C9**
1 LOWE CHASE
2 HUBBARDS CHASE
3 THE STOKES
4 BRIAN BISHOP CL

WALTON-
ON-THE-NAZE

Albion
Breakwater

OCEAN
VIEW

THE DORLINGS

New Walton
Pier

Winchester
Breakwater

1 GREAT EASTERN CT
2 SOUTHCLIFF CT

Lifeboat
Station

MARTELLO
CVN PK

Walton-
on-Naze

Cemy

Tendring
Tech Coll

Pedlars
Wood

1 CAMBRIDGE CT
2 FRINTON LODGE

KINGS
HO

ST MARY'S
MEWS

POLE BARN LA

LANCASTER
CT

ETON
CT

AUDRIES
EST

HANOVER CT

KIRBY RD

CO14

WALTON RD

CO13

ESPLANADE CT

8
21
7
6
5
20
4
3
19
2
1
18

24 A    B 25 C    D 26 E    F

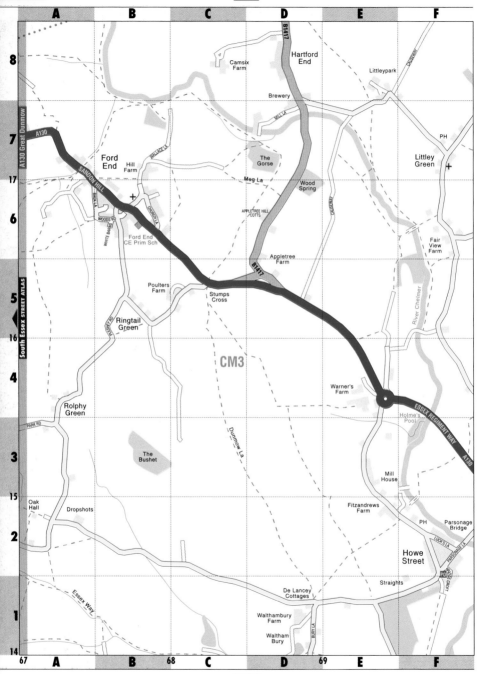

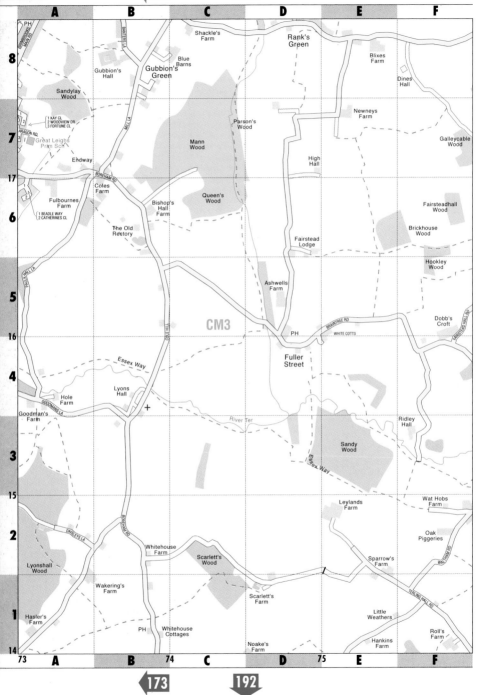

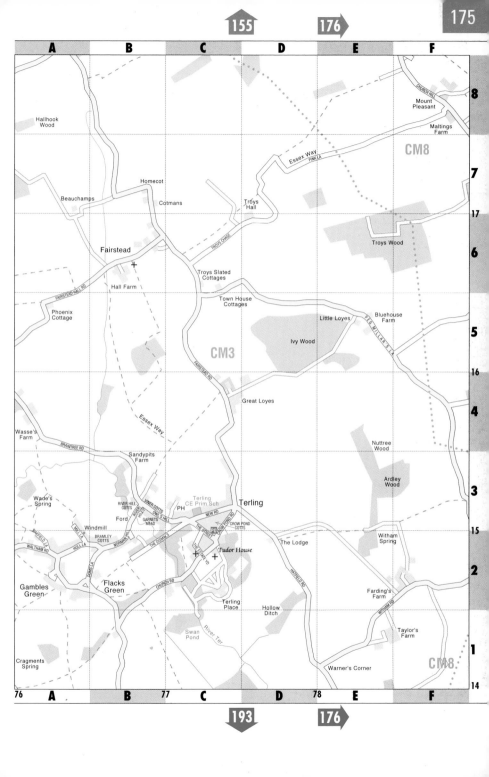

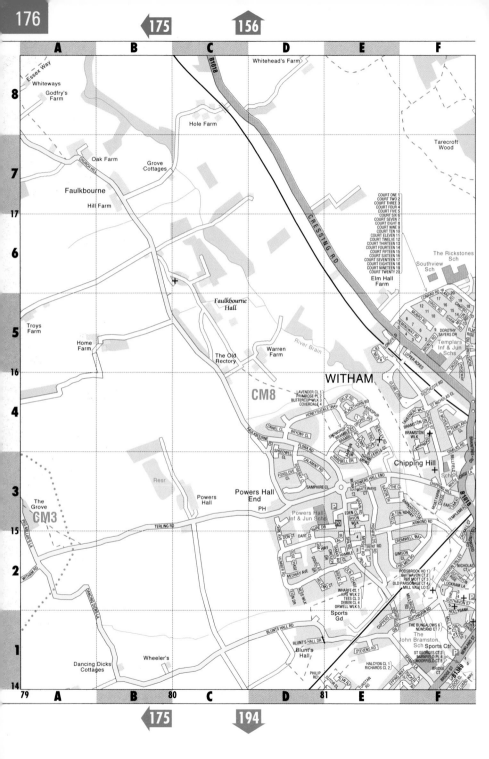

A B C D E F

8

7

17

6

5

16

4

3

15

2

1

14

Essex Way
Whiteways
Godfry's
Farm
Oak Farm
CHURCH HILL
Faulkbourne
Hill Farm
Troys
Farm
Home
Farm
The
Grove
CM3
PEG MILLAR'S LA
WITHAM RD
DANCING DICKS LA
Dancing Dicks
Cottages

Hole Farm
Grove
Cottages

Whitehead's Farm

B1018

CRESSING RD

Tarecroft
Wood

COURT ONE 1
COURT TWO 2
COURT THREE 3
COURT FOUR 4
COURT FIVE 5
COURT SIX 6
COURT SEVEN 7
COURT EIGHT 8
COURT NINE 9
COURT TEN 10
COURT ELEVEN 11
COURT TWELVE 12
COURT THIRTEEN 13
COURT FOURTEEN 14
COURT FIFTEEN 15
COURT SIXTEEN 16
COURT SEVENTEEN 17
COURT EIGHTEEN 18
COURT NINETEEN 19
COURT TWENTY 20
Elm Hall
Farm

The Rickstones
Sch
Southview
Sch

Templars
Inf & Jun
Schs

Faulkbourne
Hall

Warren
Farm
River Brain
The Old
Rectory

WITHAM
CM8

LAVENDER CL 1
PRIMROSE PL 2
BUTTERCUP WLK 3
COVERDALE 4

Chipping Hill

FAULKBOURNE DR

Resr

Powers
Hall

TERLING RD

Powers Hall
End
PH

Powers Hall
Inf & Jun Schs

Sports
Gd

BLUNTS HALL RD

Wheeler's

Blunt's
Hall

The
John Bramston
Sch Sports Ctr

PODSBROOK HO 1
BHITHAVON CT 2
REX MOTT CT 3
OLD PARSONAGE CT 4
MILL VALE LO 5

THE BUNGALOWS 6
NEWLAND CT 7

ST GEORGES CT 3
BARNFIELD PL 4
MOORFIELD CT 5

HALCYON CL 1
RICHARDS CL 2

79 80 81

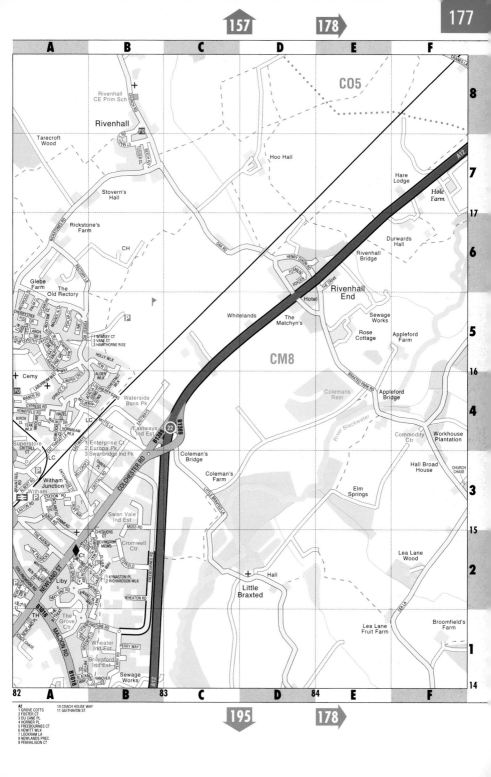

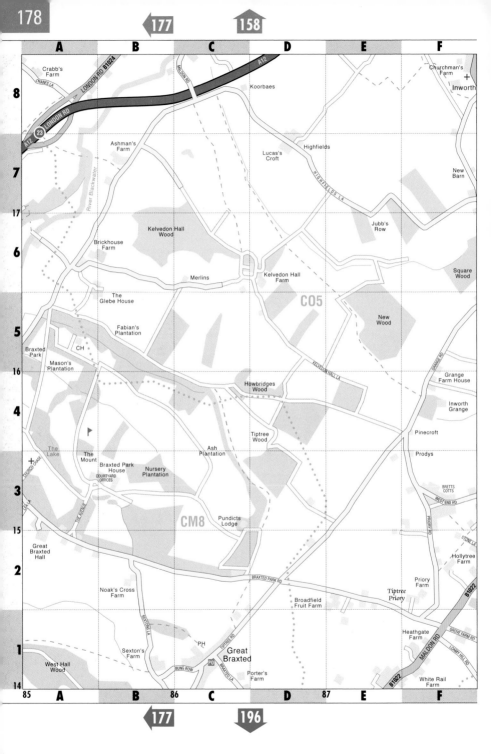

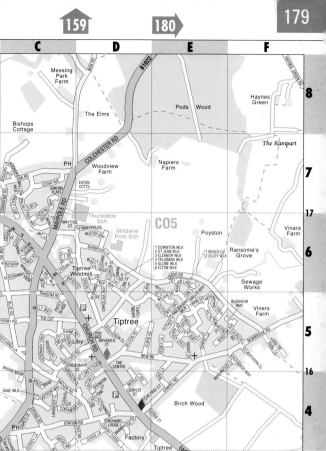

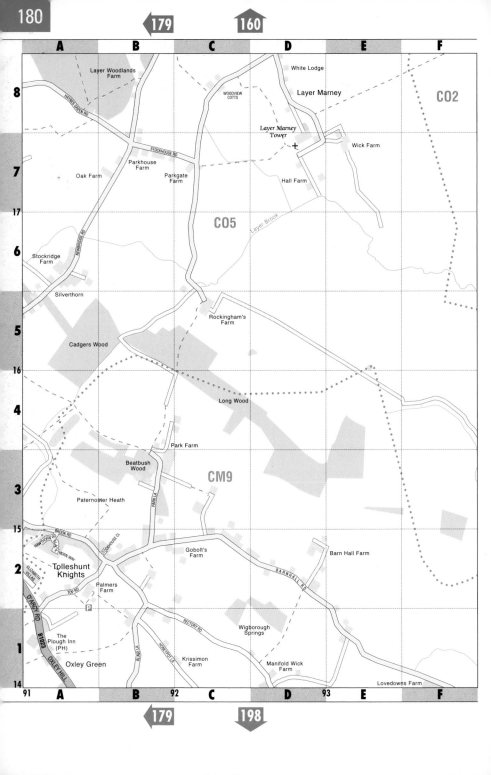

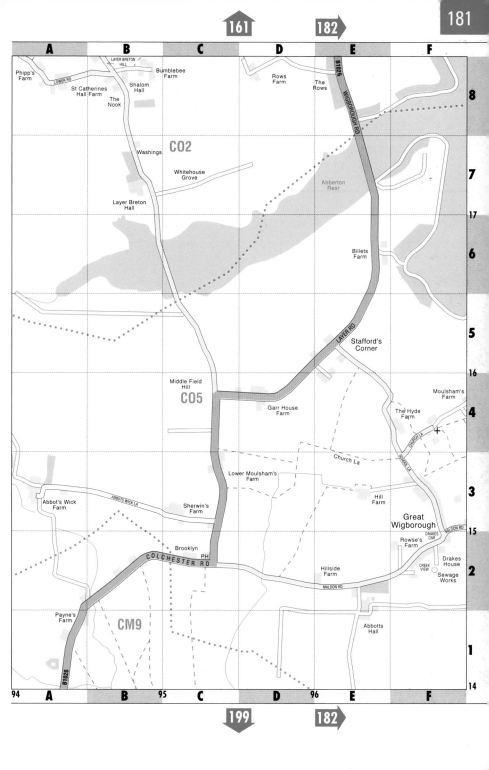

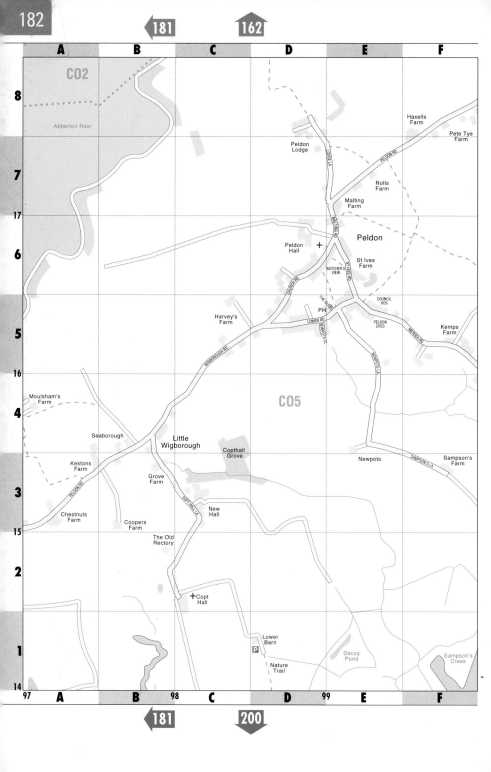

CO2

Abberton Resr

Haxells
Farm

Pete Tye
Farm

Peldon
Lodge

PELDON RD

LODGE LA

Rolls
Farm

Malting
Farm

MALTING RD

Peldon

Peldon
Hall

St Ives
Farm

Peldon

BUTCHER'S
VIEW

CHURCH RD

ST IVES RD

THE GLEBE

PH

COUNCIL
HOS

Harvey's
Farm

LOWER RD

NEWPOTS CL

PELDON
CRES

MESSEA RD

Kemps
Farm

WIGBOROUGH RD

NEWPOTS LA

CO5

Moulsham's
Farm

Seaborough

Little
Wigborough

Copthall
Grove

Newpots

SAMPSONS LA

Sampson's
Farm

Kestons
Farm

Grove
Farm

PELDON RD

Chestnuts
Farm

Coopers
Farm

COPT HALL LA

New
Hall

The Old
Rectory

Copt
Hall

Lower
Barn

P

Decoy
Pond

Sampson's
Creek

Nature
Trail

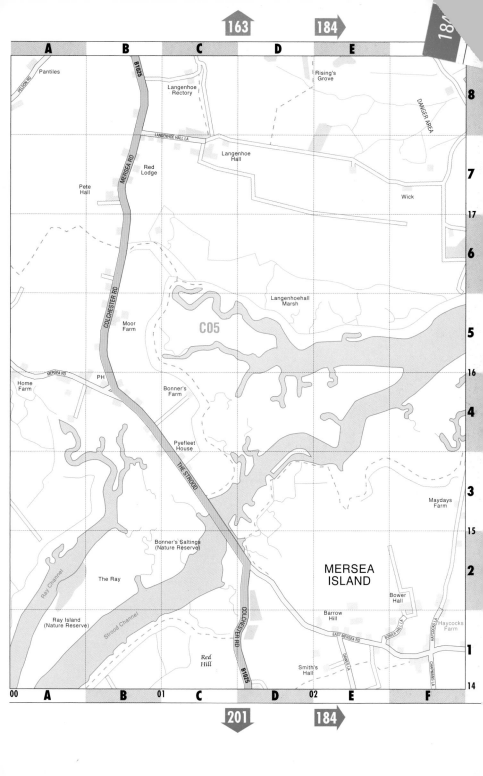

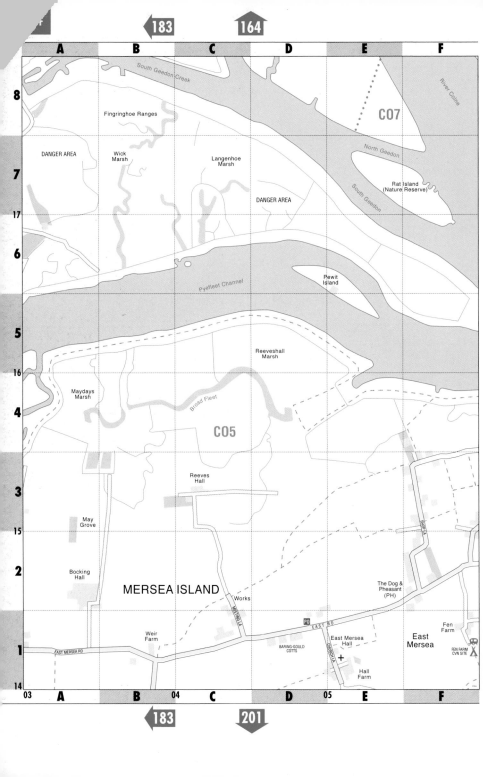

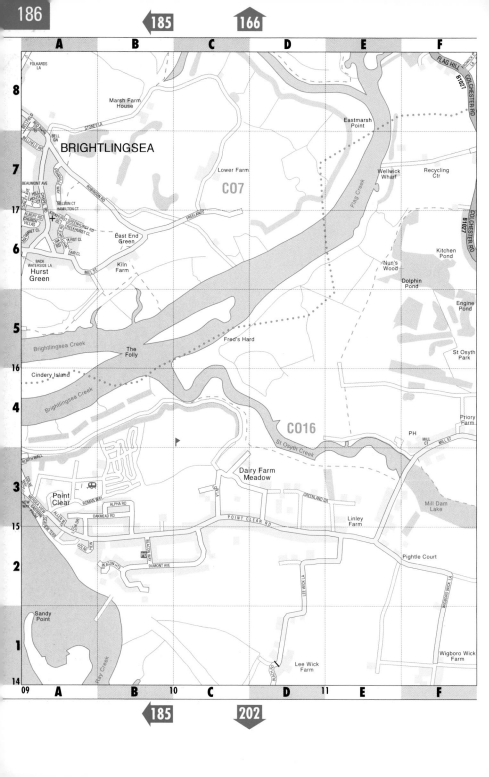

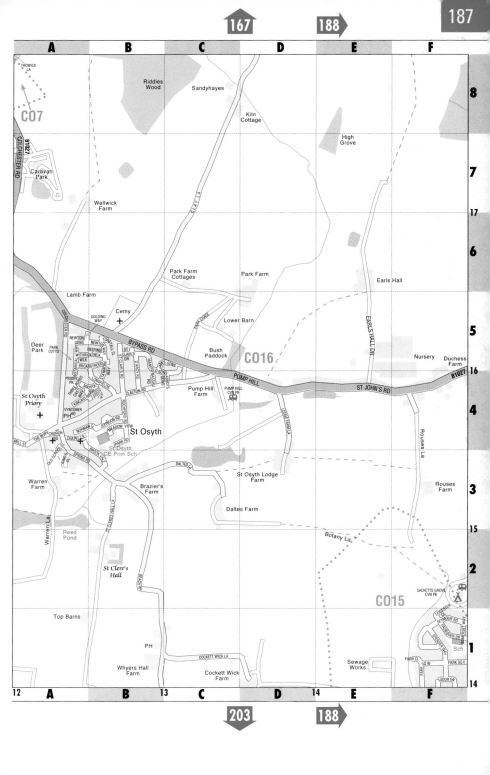

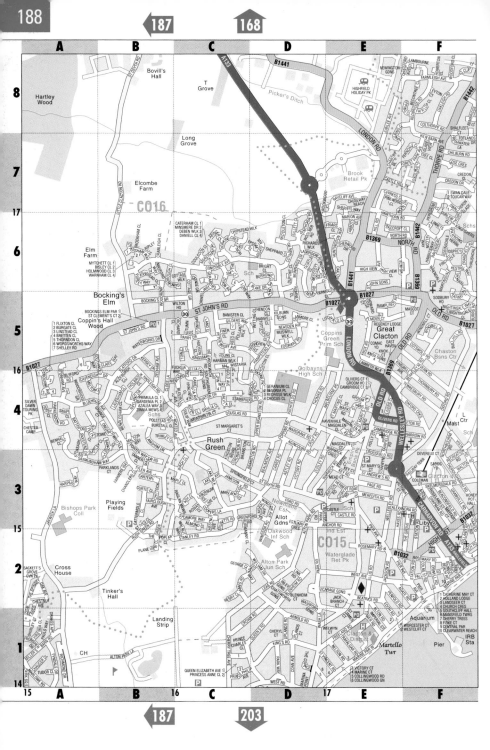

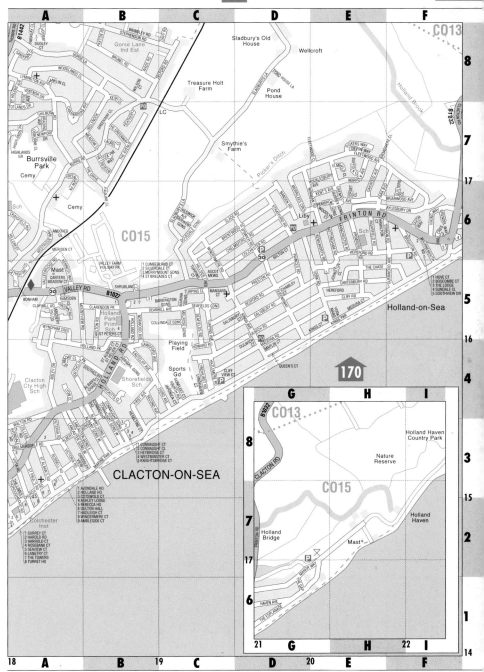

CO13

8

Sladbury's Old House

Wellcroft

Treasure Holt Farm

Holland Brook

Pond House LA

Pond House

B1032

7

Gorse Lane Ind Est

LC

17

Smythie's Farm

Picker's Ditch

CKERS WAY
DEVON WAY
FLEETWOOD
FLEETWOOD AVE

Burrsville Park

Cemy

Cemy

Sch

CO15

Liby

FRINTON RD

BRIARWOOD AVE
AYLESBURY DR

6

Sch

1 CUMBERLAND CT
2 SILVERDALE CT
3 MERRYMOUNT GDNS
4 ST BRELADES CT

VALLEY FARM HOLIDAY PK

SHRUBLAND

ASCOT MEWS

MANSARD CT

30

THE CHASE

CANTERBURY RD

Holland-on-Sea

1 HOVE CT
2 BOSCOMBE CT
3 THE LODGE
4 SUNDALE CL
5 SOUTHVIEW CT

Mast
CANTERS MEADOW CT

VALLEY RD

30

B1022

TURPINS CL

HEREFORD

CLIFF RD

5

BONHAM

RAMSDEN

CLARENDON PK

BARRINGTON GDNS

DEARMILL AVE

SEAFIELDS GDNS

SALISBURY RD

DUNWICH RD

KINGS CT
KINGS PAR

16

Holland Park Prim Sch

ST PETERS CT

COLLINDALE GDNS

HOWARD RD

MEDINA CT
MAPLIN CT

WYNDHAM CRES

HOLLAND PK

Playing Field

Sports Gd

QUEEN'S CT

4

Clacton Cty High Sch

Shorefields Sch

CLIFF VIEW CT

G    H    I

WALTON RD

1 CONNAUGHT CT
2 CONNAUGHT CL
3 HEYBRIDGE CT
4 WESTMINSTER CT
5 KNIGHTSBRIDGE CT

CO13

8

B1022

CLACTON RD

Holland Haven Country Park

SKELMERSDALE RD

MARINE PAR

Nature Reserve

CO15

3

CLACTON-ON-SEA

1 AVONDALE HO
2 HOLLAND HO
3 COTSWOLD CT
4 ASHLEY LODGE
5 REBECCA HO
6 OULTON HALL
7 HADLEIGH CT
8 WINDERMERE CT
9 AMBLESIDE CT

15

Holland Haven

7

Holland Bridge

Mast

Holland Haven

FRINTON RD

17

Colchester Inst

1 SURREY CT
2 HAROLD RD
3 HARROLD CT
4 ROSEBANK CT
5 SEAVIEW CT
6 LANGTRY CT
7 THE TOWERS
8 TURRET HO

MANOR WAY

6

HAVEN AVE

THE ESPLANADE

21    G    H    22    I

14

18    A    B    19    C    D    20    E    F

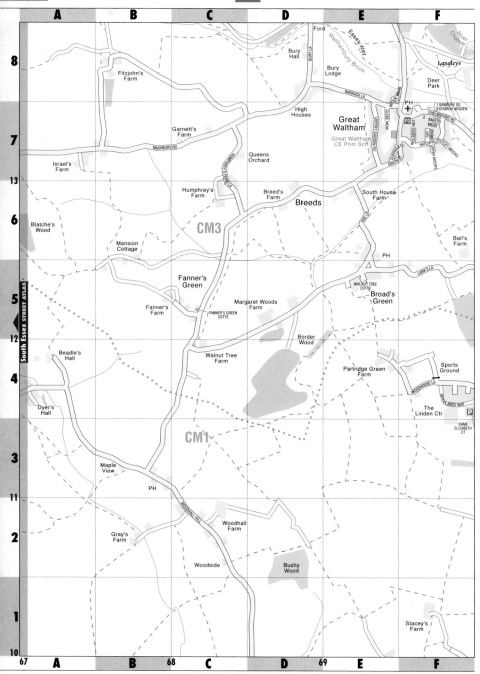

**8**

**7**

**13**

**6**

**5**

**12**

**4**

**3**

**11**

**2**

**1**

**10**

A  B  C  D  E  F

67  A  B  68  C  D  69  E  F

Ford
Bury Hall
Bury Lodge
High Houses
BURY LA
BARRACK LA
Essex Way
Walthambury Brook
River Chelmer
Langleys
Deer Park
Great Waltham
Great Waltham CE Prim Sch
PH
PO
1 BANBURY SQ
2 CHURCH HOUSEN
CHELMSFORD RD
BAKERS MEAD
WALKERS LA
HATCHFIELDS
HICKS MOORS
UPPER MOORS
CHERRY GARDEN RD
QUEENS CL
SOUTH'S
Fitzjohn's Farm
Garnett's Farm
MASHBURY RD
Queens Orchard
Israel's Farm
Humphrey's Farm
Breed's Farm
Breeds
South House Farm
CM3
Blatche's Wood
Mansion Cottage
Ball's Farm
PH
LARKS LA
Fanner's Green
Margaret Woods Farm
WALNUT TREE COTTS
Broad's Green
Fanner's Farm
FANNER'S GREEN COTTS
Border Wood
Beadle's Hall
Walnut Tree Farm
Partridge Green Farm
Sports Ground
WOODHOUSE LA
WOODLANDS WAY
P
The Linden Ctr
DAME ELIZABETH CT
Dyer's Hall
CM1
Maple View
PH
WOODHALL HILL
Gray's Farm
Woodhall Farm
Woodside
Bushy Wood
Stacey's Farm
THOBURN LA

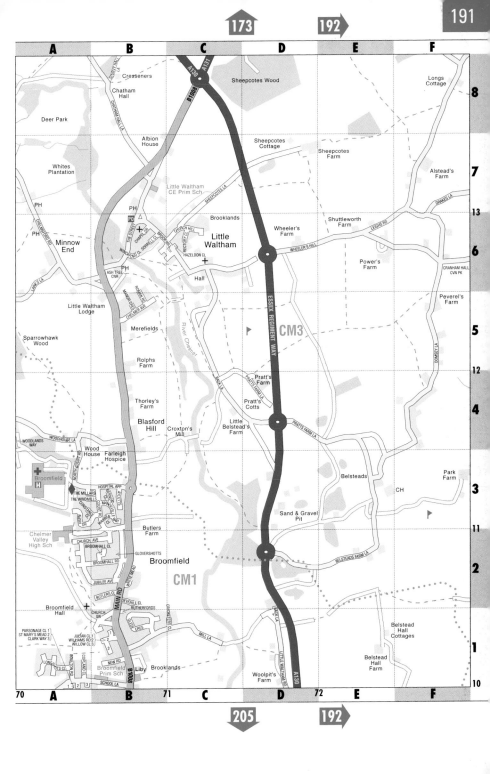

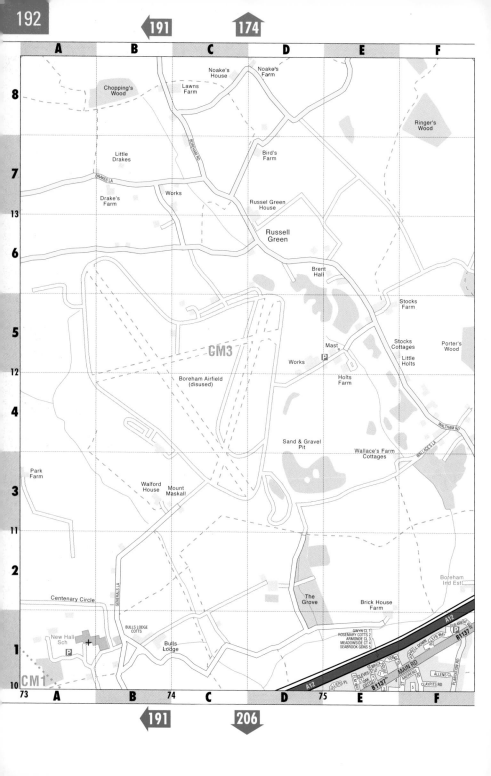

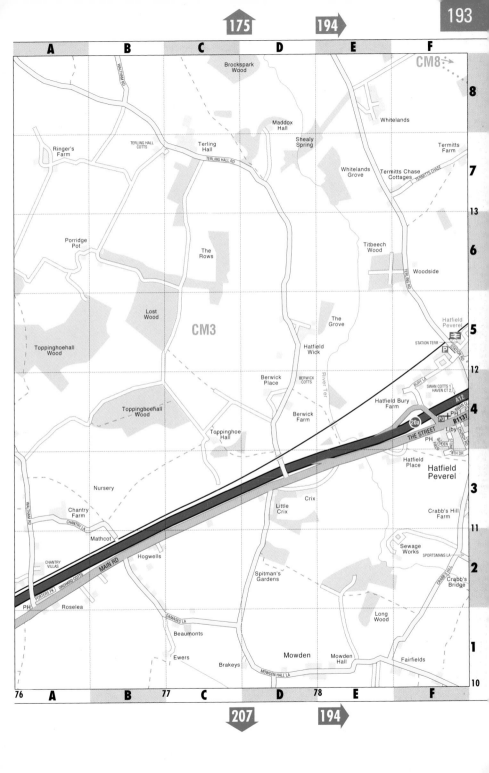

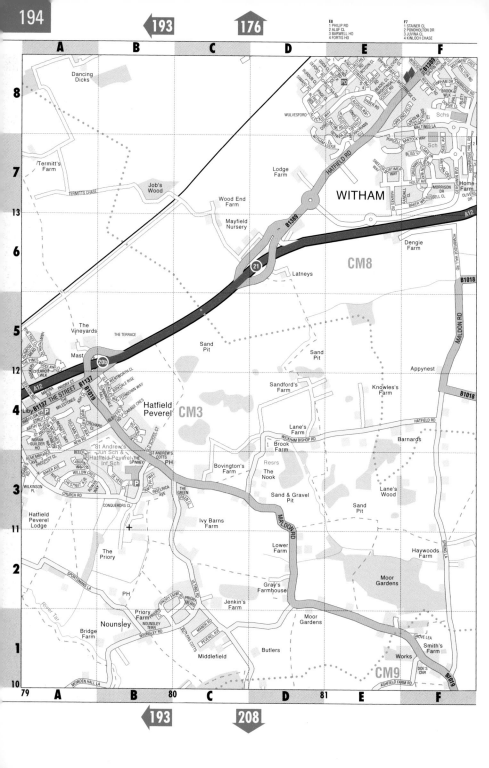

E8
1 PHILIP RD
2 ALUF CL
3 BARWELL HO
4 FORTIS HO

F7
1 STAINER CL
2 PONDHOLTON DR
3 JUVINA CL
4 KINLOCH CHASE

Dancing Dicks

Termitt's Farm

Job's Wood

Lodge Farm

WITHAM

TERMITTS CHASE

Wood End Farm

Mayfield Nursery

WULVESFORD

Schs

Sch

Home Farm

B1389

CM8

Dengie Farm

21

Latneys

The Vineyards

THE TERRACE

Sand Pit

Sand Pit

Appynest

B1018

B1018

20b

Mast

Sandford's Farm

Knowles's Farm

THE STREET

B1137

B1019

Hatfield Peverel

CM3

Lane's Farm

WITCHAM BISHOP RD

Brook Farm

Barnards

HATFIELD RD

A12

B1137

Libly

MILESTONES

St Andrew's Jun Sch & Hatfield Peverel Inf Sch

ST ANDREW'S COTTS

PH

Bovington's Farm

Resrs

The Nook

Lane's Wood

THE SPINNEY

Sand & Gravel Pit

MALDON RD

Sand Pit

WILKINSON PL

CHURCH RD

CONQUERORS CL

THE GREEN

Ivy Barns Farm

Hatfield Peverel Lodge

The Priory

Lower Farm

Haywoods Farm

SPRING LA

SPORTSMANS LA

PH

Gray's Farmhouse

Moor Gardens

River Ter

Priory Farm

NOUNSLEY TERR

NOUNSLEY RD

Jenkin's Farm

Moor Gardens

GROVE LEA

Bridge Farm

Nounsley

MANOR RD

PEVEREL AVE

Middlefield

Butlers

Works

Smith's Farm

DOE'S CNR

CM9

MOYNDEN HALL LA

ASHFIELD FARM RD

B1019

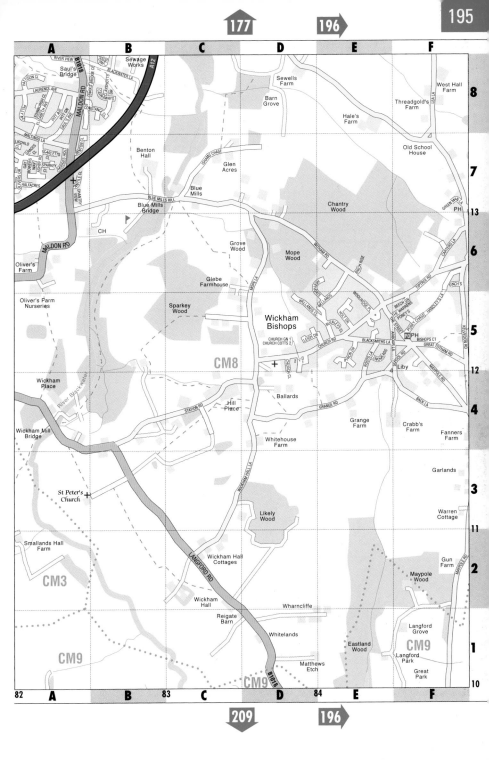

177
196

A B C D E F

8

7

13

6

5

12

4

11

3

2

1

10

209
196

82 A B 83 C D 84 E F

River View
Saul's Bridge
Sewage Works
Blackwater La
West Hall Farm
Threadgold's Farm
Sewells Farm
Barn Grove
Hale's Farm
Old School House
Benton Hall
Shant Chase
Glen Acres
Blue Mills
Chantry Wood
CH
Blue Mills Bridge
Maldon Rd
Oliver's Farm
Grove Wood
Mope Wood
Oliver's Farm Nurseries
Sparkey Wood
Glebe Farmhouse
Wickham Bishops
CHURCH GN 1
CHURCH COTTS 2
Blacksmiths La
Liby
CM8
Wickham Place
Station Rd
Hill Place
Ballards
Grange Rd
Grange Farm
Crabb's Farm
Fanners Farm
Wickham Mill Bridge
Whitehouse Farm
Garlands
St Peter's Church
Langford Rd
Likely Wood
Warren Cottage
Smallands Hall Farm
Wickham Hall Cottages
Gun Farm
CM3
Wickham Hall
Maypole Wood
Reigate Barn
Wharncliffe
Langford Grove
Whitelands
Eastland Wood
Langford Park
CM9
Matthews Etch
Great Park
CM9
CM9

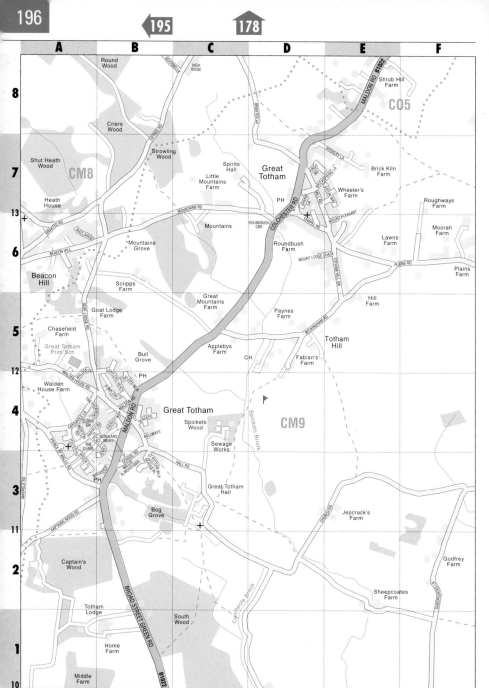

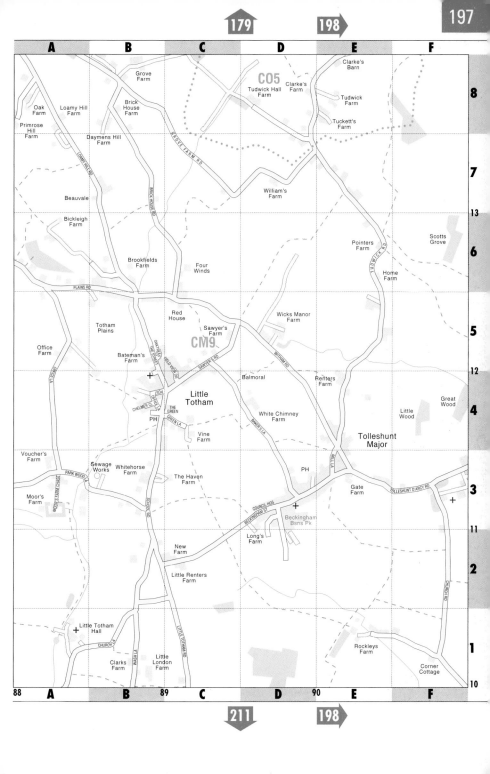

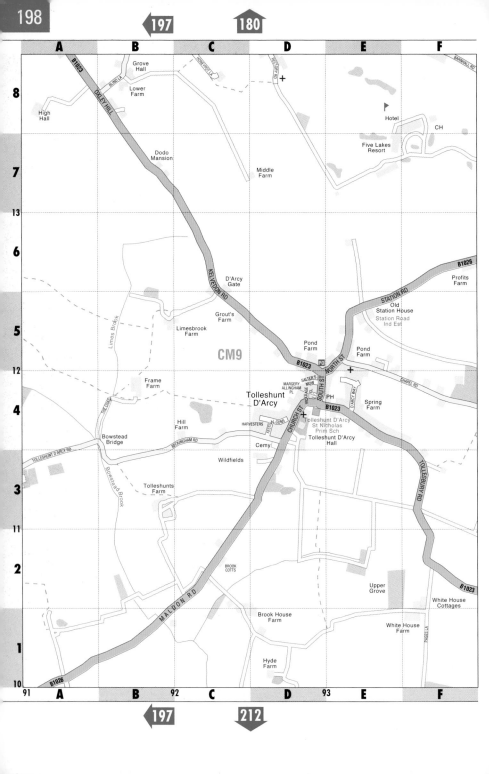

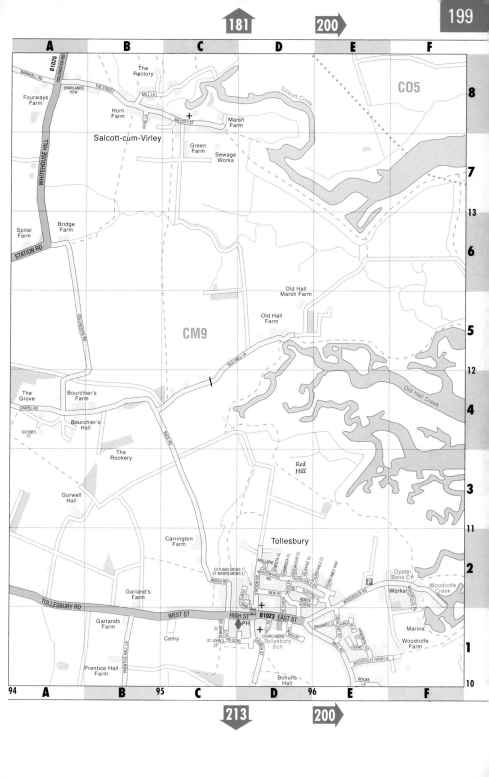

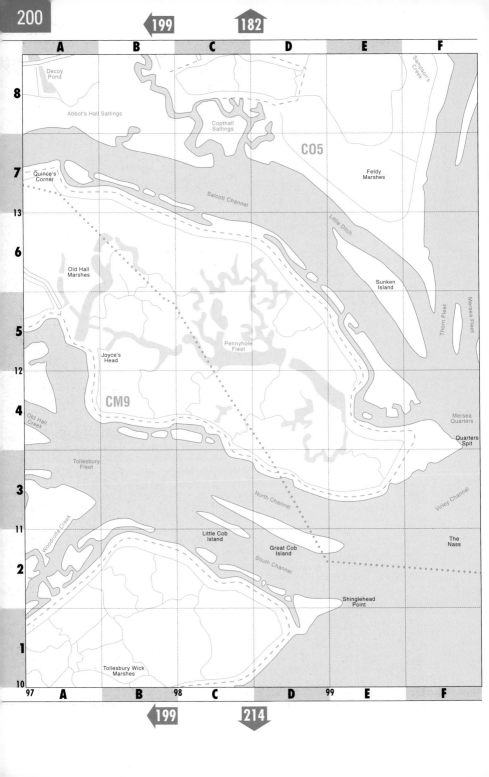

A B C D E F

8

Decoy
Pond

Abbot's Hall Saltings

Copthall
Saltings

Sampson's Creek

CO5

7

Quince's
Corner

Feldy
Marshes

Salcott Channel

13

Little Ditch

6

Old Hall
Marshes

Sunken
Island

Thorn Fleet

Mersea Fleet

5

Pennyhole
Fleet

Joyce's
Head

12

Mersea
Quarters

CM9

4

Old Hall
Creek

Quarters
Spit

Tollesbury
Fleet

Virley Channel

3

North Channel

11

Little Cob
Island

The
Nass

2

Great Cob
Island

South Channel

Woodrolfe Creek

Shinglehead
Point

1

Tollesbury Wick
Marshes

10

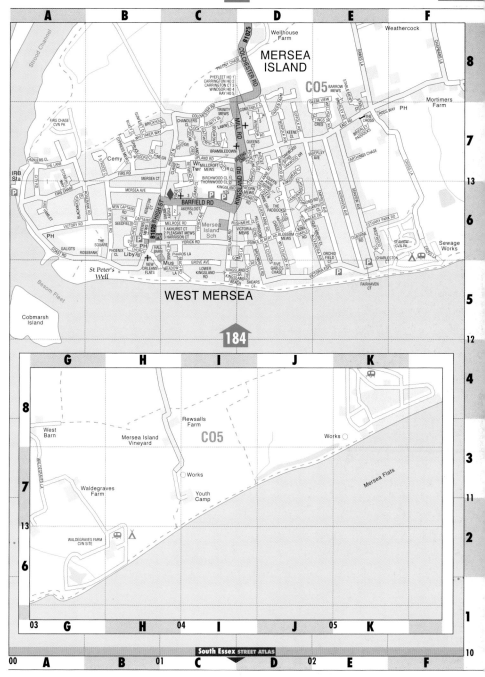

A  B  C  D  E  F

Strod Channel

Weathercock

Wellhouse
Farm

MERSEA
ISLAND

C05

BARROW
MEWS

Mortimers
Farm

B1025

PRECLOT CHASE

PYEFLEET HO 1
CARRINGTON HO 2
CARRINGTON CT 3
WINDSOR HO 4
RAY HO 5

COLCHESTER RD

CHAPMANS LA

DAIRIE LA

CROSS WAY  PH

GLEBE VIEW

THE CROSS

FIRS CHASE
CVN PK

CARRIERS CL

THE LANE

CITY RD

CYPRESS MEWS

WOODFIELD

BRICKHOUSE

WHITTAKER WAY

GUN FLEET RD

BURY CL

CHANDLERS
CL

CLOCK

COLNEVIEW RD

TRINITY
MEWS

TRINITY CT

LAWNS CT

CONSTABLE G

KEENE
DL

QUEENS

SUFFOLK AVE

KINGS AVE

EAST RD

BEVERLEY
AVE

FARTHINGS CHASE

IRB
Sta

FIRS RD

FIRS CHASE

VICTORY RD

FIRS HAMLET

CITY RD

DECELANGE RD

SEEDFIELD

NEW CAPTAINS
RD

CAPTAINS RD

TUDOR

CLAREMONT

UPLAND RD

BRAMBLEDOWN

UPLAND RD

Wm
Twr

MILLCROFT
MEWS

BIRCHWOOD CL 1
THORNWOOD CL 2

ACORN

KINGSLAND RD

RAINTREE
MEWS

OAKWOOD DR

GLENWOOD DR

BARFIELD RD

MELROSE RD

AKERSLOOT
PL

1 AKHURST CT
2 PLEASANT MEWS
3 HARRISON CT

Mersea
Island
Sch

Mersea
Island
Sch

RUSH-MERE CL

VICTORIA
MEWS

HOLLYWOOD

BLOSSOM
MEWS

OSBORNE
RD

ESTUARY PARK RD

WESTCLIFF RD

Sewage
Works

PH

GALIOTS

THE
SQUARE

ROSEBANK

PHOENIX
CL

CHURCH
RD

HALL
BARN

THE CHASE

YORICK RD

PHAROS LA

GROVE AVE

LOWER
KINGSLAND
RD

PRINCE

THE COSWAY

FIVE
GABLES
CHASE

CHARLESTON

FAIRHAVEN
CT

ORCHID
FIELD
CT

SEAVIEW
EVIL PK

Coast Rd

St Peter's
Well

NEW
ORLEANS
FLATS

MEADOW

KINGSLAND
RD

KINGSLAND
BEACH

SHEARS
CT

VICTORIA ESP

WEST MERSEA

Besom Fleet

Cobmarsh
Island

G  H  I  J  K

West
Barn

Rewsalls
Farm

C05

Mersea Island
Vineyard

Works

WALDEGRAVES LA

Waldegraves
Farm

Works

Youth
Camp

Mersea Flats

WALDEGRAVES FARM
CVN SITE

03  G  H  04  I  J  05  K

00  A  B  01  C  D  02  E  F

8  7  13  6  5  12  4  3  11  2  1  10

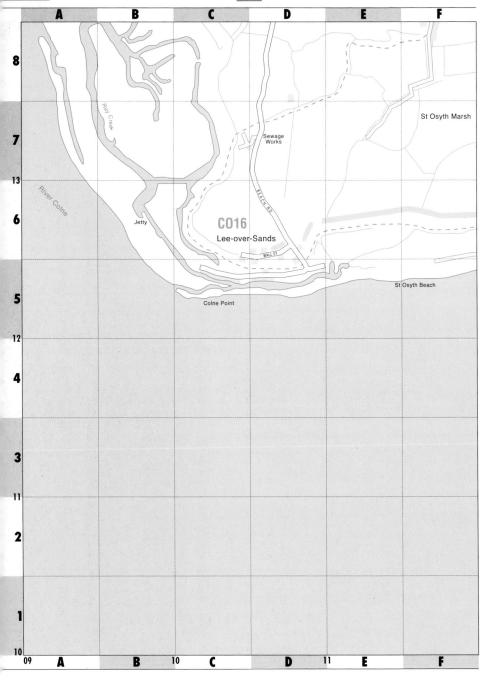

River Colne

Ray Creek

Jetty

Sewage Works

BEACH RD

CO16
Lee-over-Sands

WALL ST

Colne Point

St Osyth Beach

St Osyth Marsh

CO16

Marsh
Cottage

Decoy Pond

CO15

Jaywick

Seawick
Holiday Park

Seawick

THE
GREEN

BISHOPS
GDNS

BEACH
APP

LILAC AVE

SEAVIEW RD

WILLOW AVE

WICK RD

ROSE GDNS

HUNTLEY'S
CVN PK (W)

BEL-AIR
EST

CLUB PAR

MYRTLE AVE

THIRD AVE

SECOND AVE

FIRST AVE

PO

HUNTLEY'S
CVN PK (E)

BEACH RD

BEL-AIR
BEACH
CVN PK.

PH

TOWER
CVN PK

Martello
Tower

PROMENADE

APRILS VIEW 1
STEDMAN CT 2
LANCIA AVE 3

LABBETT'S CHASE

DIANA RD

LINCOLN RD

BEVERLY AVE

CROSSLEY AVE

SINGER AVE

PUMA RD

THIRD AVE

STANDARD AVE

JAGUAR AVE

BENTLEY AVE

MORRIS AVE

WOLSELEY AVE

PALMER AVE

ROYAL AVE

IMPERIAL AVE

BROOKLANDS

TRIUMPH RD

MG RD

LOTUS WAY

GORSE WAY

FERN AVE

BEL-AIR AVE

TAMARISK WAY

BROOME

BEACH WAY

HARVEY CT 1
YEW WAY 2
ELVINA HO 3
BEACH CRES 4

PO

13

8

7

13

6

5

12

4

188

G

H

I

J

3

PARK SQ E

ALLEYNE WAY

CONNIE DR

CROSSWAYS

APPLETON RD

TUDOR
PAR

MARLOWE WAY

The Three Jays
(PH)

WEST RD

P

LULWORTH
CL

CH

PENZANCE

BROXHAM

SHOREHAM RD

PORTSMOUTH CL

KINGS PDE

Slipway
Martello Tower

1 DOVER CL
2 PLYMOUTH RD
3 HYTHE CL
4 SHAMROCK HO
5 AQUILINE HO
6 LITTLE STONE CT
7 WORTHING MEWS

CLACTON-ON-SEA

CO15 ▶

Jaywick

JASMINE WAY

GORSE WAY

MEADOW WAY

GLEBE WAY

CORNFLOWER RD

HERON RD

SPRAY

THE CL

BURNHAM

Martello Tower

ST CHRISTOPHERS WAY

WELLESLEY RD

COLTSFOOT RD

1 BRAMSTON CT
2 BADMINTON CT

8

7

13

6

11

2

1

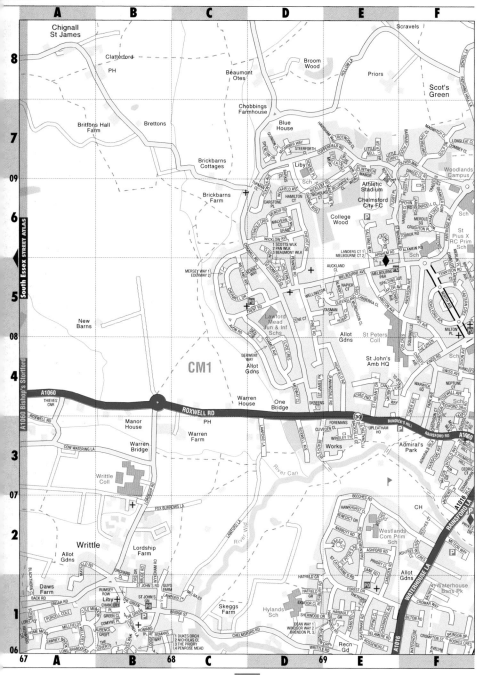

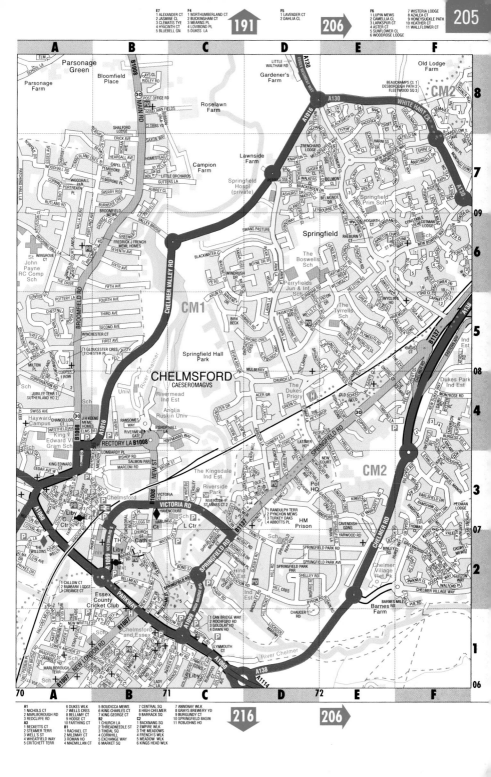

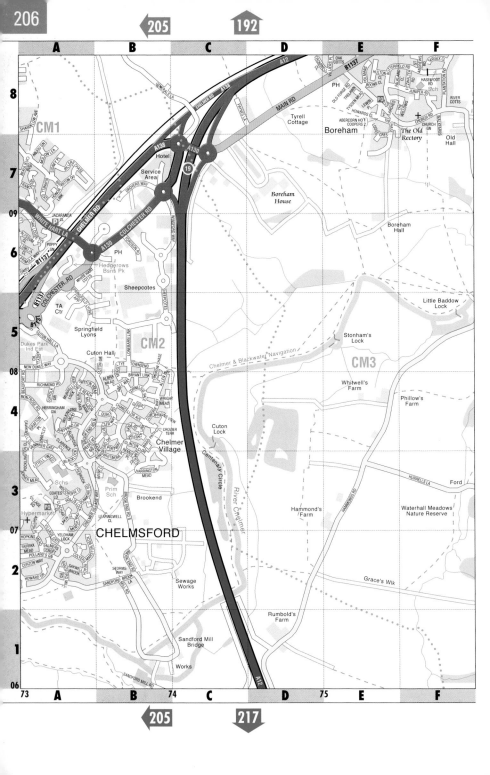

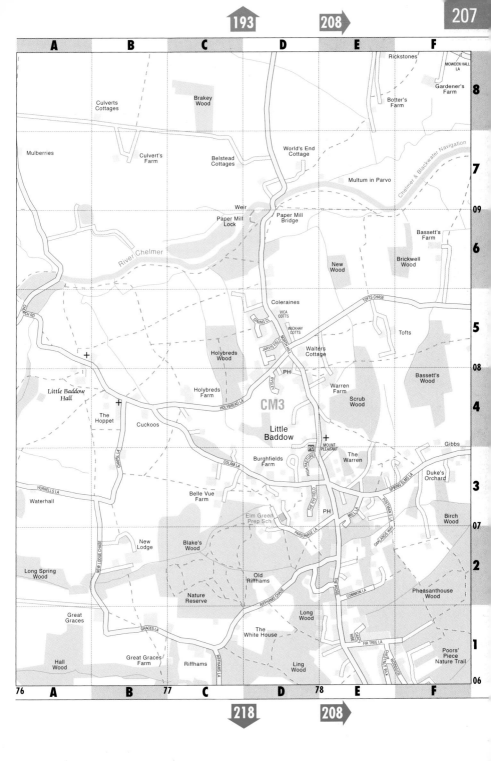

8

Rickstones
MOWDEN HALL LA
Gardener's Farm
Botter's Farm

Culverts Cottages
Brakey Wood

7

Mulberries
Culvert's Farm
Belstead Cottages
World's End Cottage
Multum in Parvo
Chelmer & Blackwater Navigation

09

Bassett's Farm

6

Weir
Paper Mill Lock
Paper Mill Bridge
New Wood
Brickwell Wood

River Chelmer

Coleraines
Toft's Chase

5

VICA COTTS
SPRING CL
WICKHAY COTTS
Tofts

Holybreds Wood
JARVIS FIELD
NORTH HILL
Walters Cottage

08

Holybreds Farm
HOLYBREAD LA
KILN'S LA
PH
Warren Farm
Bassett's Wood

Little Baddow Hall
CM3
Scrub Wood

4

The Hoppet
Cuckoos
Little Baddow
MOUNT PLEASANT
The Warren
Gibbs

CHAPEL LA
COLAM LA
Burghfields Farm
HIGH PASTURES
PO
Duke's Orchard

3

HURRELLS LA
Belle Vue Farm
THE RIDGEFIELD
PH
MILL LA
SPRING ELMS LA
POSTMANS LA
Birch Wood

Waterhall
Elm Green Prep Sch
PARSONAGE LA
ORCHARDS WAY

07

New Lodge
Blake's Wood

2

BELL LODGE CHASE
Long Spring Wood
Old Riffhams
Nature Reserve
RIFFHAMS CHASE
Long Wood
COMMON LA
Pheasanthouse Wood

Great Graces
GRACES LA
The White House
THE RIDGE
FIR TREE LA
CHESTNUT WALK

1

Hall Wood
Great Graces Farm
Riffhams
RIFFHAMS LA
Ling Wood
Poors' Piece Nature Trail

76
77
78
06

A B C D E F

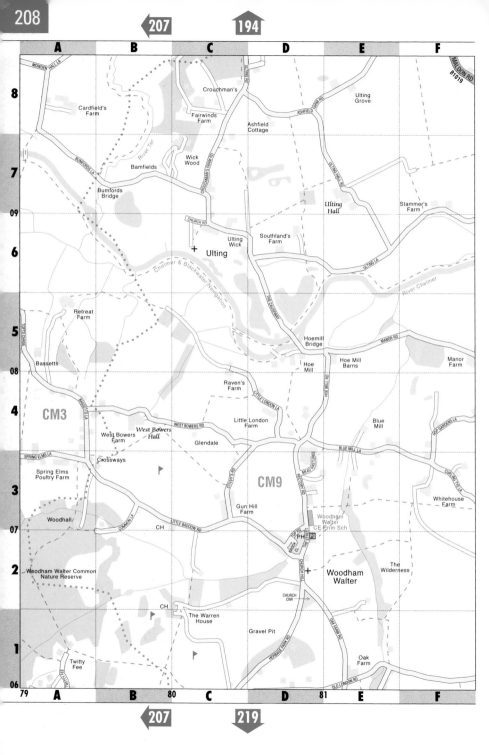

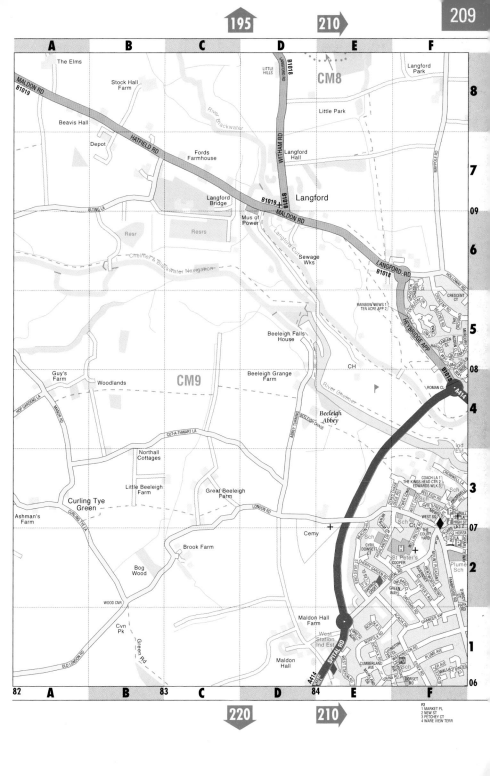

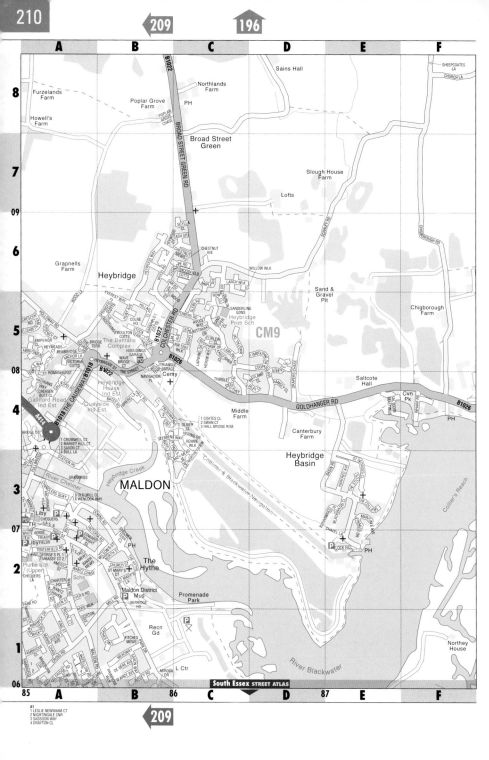

A B C D E F

8

Furzelands Farm

Howell's Farm

Poplar Grove Farm

Northlands Farm

PH

Sains Hall

SHEEPCOATES LA

CHURCH LA

7

POPLAR GROVE CHASE

BROAD STREET GREEN RD

Broad Street Green

Slough House Farm

09

Lofts

SCRAY RD

CHIGBOROUGH RD

6

Grapnells Farm

Heybridge

SCYLLA CL

ASH GR

CHESTNUT MEWS

WOODFIELD COTTS

CHESTNUT AVE

WILLOW WLK

LARCH WLK

MAPLE

Sand & Gravel Pit

Chigborough Farm

5

EVEREST WAY

HILLS

COLNE HO

STOCK

BRIDGE TERR

The Bentalls Complex

HOULDINGS GARAGE

BOULTON CL

AVOCET WAY

CEDAR

FIR TREE

CURLEW

SANDERLING GDNS

Heybridge Prim Sch

LAPWING

DAW CHASE

LARKSPUR

LIMEBURNER

DRAPERS CHASE

CM9

08

CACHOR LA

ANCHOR LA

VICTORIA COTTS

B1022 THE STREET

WAVE BRIDGE CL

B1026

TRIANGLE

Cemy

NAVIGATION PL

THIRSLET

MAYLAND

RAMSEY

SADLER

Saltcote Hall

Cvn Pk

WHARF RD

B1026

PH

4

A414

BRIDGE CT

STATION RD

1 CROMWELL CT
2 MARKET HILL CT
3 SAXON CT
4 BULL LA

B1019 THE CAUSEWAY

Heybridge House Ind Est

Quayside Ind Est

Galliford Road Ind Est

HATFIELD

CREASEN BUTT CL

ROMANHURST

BATES RD

SPRING

PRENTICE

REGINALD

HERON

STEBBENS WAY

OLIVER

HERING DR

RENNIE WLK

Middle Farm

1 COATES CL
2 SWAN CT
3 HALL BRIDGE RISE

GOLDHANGER RD

Canterbury Farm

Heybridge Basin

ST GEORGES

BASIN RD

MAYOR RD

MARY LN

THE COLNE

Collier's Reach

3

River Chelmer

CHARTERS QUAY

GRANARIES

DOWNS RD

5 OLD MILL CL
6 WENLOCK WAY

MALDON

Heybridge Creek

Chelmer & Blackwater Navigation

BUNTING RD

LOCK HILL

CHAPEL

PH

07

Liby

CHEQUERS

WHITE HORSE

FRIARY

Libyfields

TENTERFIELD RD

KING GEORGE'S PL 1
EMBASSY CT 2

EDWARD

BRIGHT

WILLOW'S CT

PH

2

Plume Sch (Upper)

CHEQUERS LA

CHARTER HO

AMERICA

WANTZ CHASE

MARKET

MEADOWS

CHURCH ST

ST MARY'S CT

St Mary's Schs

The Hythe

Maldon District Mus

BERRIDGE RD

MILL RD

Promenade Park

1

FAMBRIDGE

QUEEN'S AVE

MALDON RD

CROSS RD

FITCHES MEWS

PARK DR

MEADWAY

DE VERE AVE

D'ARCY WAY

MIROSA DR

Recn Gd

L Ctr

River Blackwater

Northey House

06

85 A B 86 C D 87 E F

A1
1 LESLIE NEWNHAM CT
2 NIGHTINGALE CNR
3 SASSOON WAY
4 DRAYTON CL

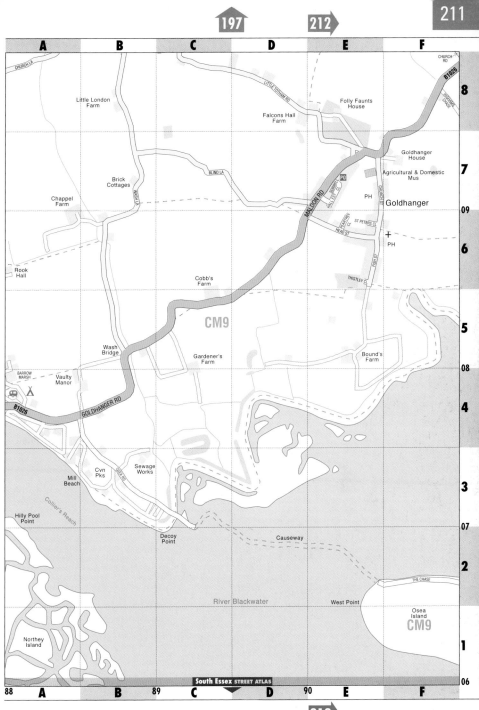

**A**    **B**    **C**    **D**    **E**    **F**

CHURCH LA

LITTLE TOTHAM RD

CHURCH RD

8

Little London
Farm

Folly Faunts
House

Falcons Hall
Farm

B1026

TOTHAM CHASE

Goldhanger
House

7

Brick
Cottages

BLIND LA

Agricultural & Domestic
Mus

WASH LA

Chappel
Farm

MALDON RD

SQUIRES CT

HALL EST

PO

PH

**Goldhanger**

09

Rook
Hall

ST PETERS CL

PLOUGHTREE CL

HEAD ST

FISH ST

6

PH

PH

Cobb's
Farm

THISTLEY CL

CM9

5

Wash
Bridge

Gardener's
Farm

Bound's
Farm

08

BARROW
MARSH

Vaulty
Manor

B1026

GOLDHANGER RD

4

Mill
Beach

Cvn
Pks

DECOY RD

Sewage
Works

3

Collier's Reach

Hilly Pool
Point

Decoy
Point

Causeway

07

River Blackwater

West Point

2

THE CHASE

Osea
Island
CM9

Northey
Island

1

06

88   **A**    **B**   89   **C**    **D**   90   **E**    **F**

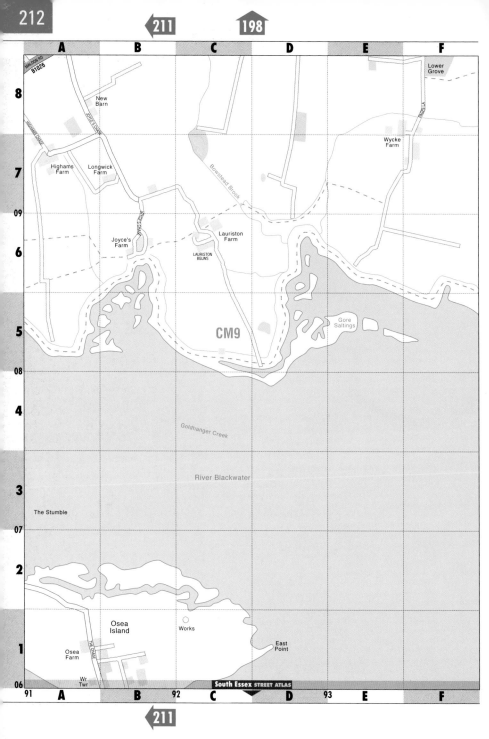

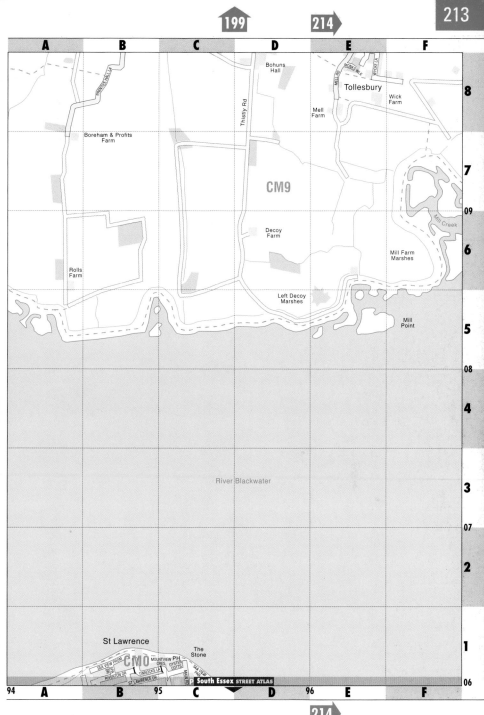

A B C D E F

Bohuns Hall

PRENTICE HALL LA

Tollesbury

MONG WK

WYCKE LA

Mell Farm

Wick Farm

Boreham & Profits Farm

Thistly Rd

CM9

Mill Creek

Decoy Farm

Rolls Farm

Mill Farm Marshes

Left Decoy Marshes

Mill Point

River Blackwater

St Lawrence

The Stone

SEA VIEW PROM

CM0

MOUNTVIEW PH CRES

OYSTER COTTS

TINNOCKS LA

RIVERTON DR

ST LAWRENCE DR

SEA VIEW PROM

MAIN RD

8

7

09

6

5

08

4

3

07

2

1

06

| A | B | C | D | E | F |

CM9

Jetty

River Blackwater

Pewet
Island

Cvn
Pk
SHOEMENDERS
LA
PARKER
CT
Bradwell
Waterside

B1021

OLD
COASTGUARD
COTTS
PH
Mast

Marina

TRUSSES RD

Westwick
Farm

WATERSIDE RD

WOODYARDS

Down
Westwick

CM0

Bradwell Creek

Orplands
ORPLANDS
COTTS

Kennel
Barn

MALDON RD

B1021 MALDON RD

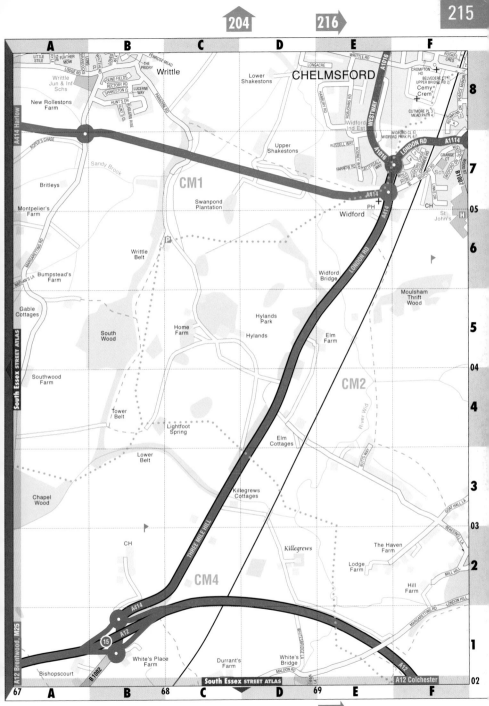

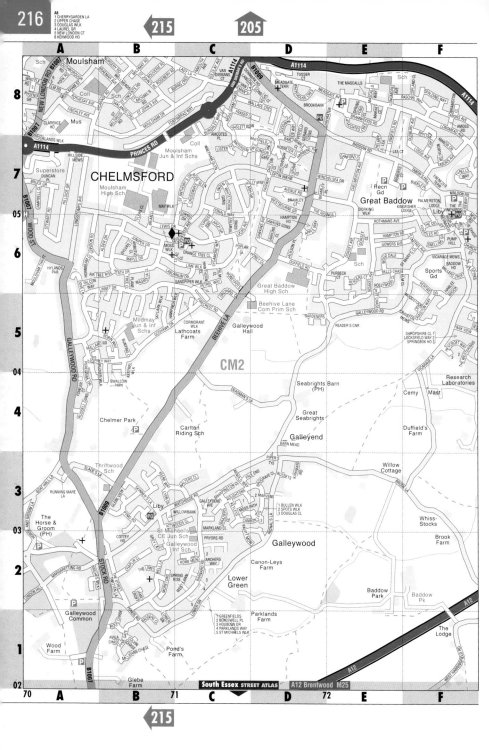

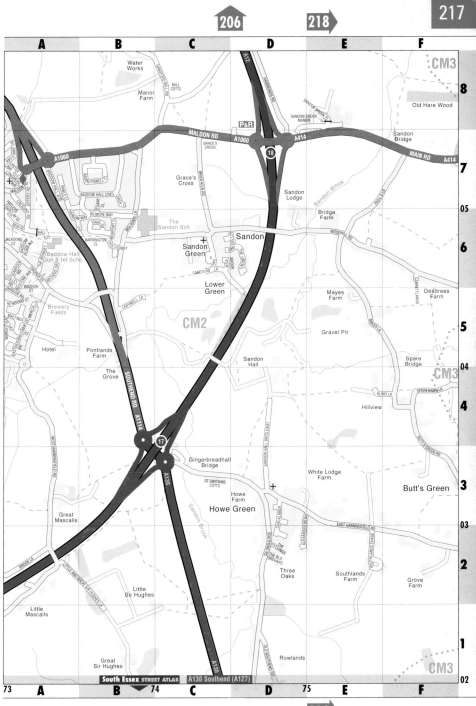

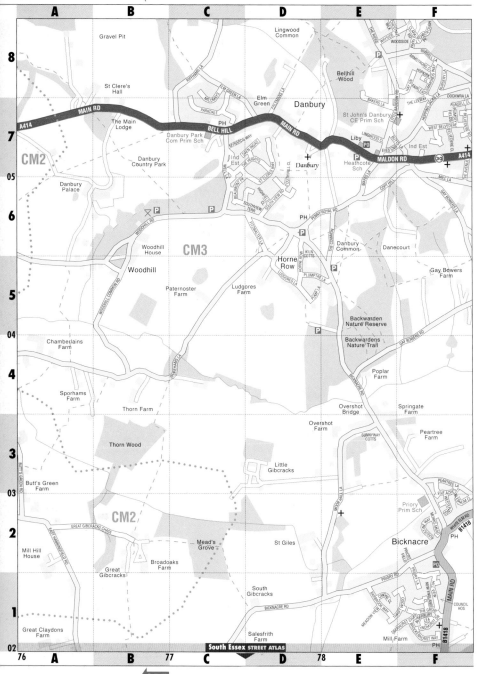

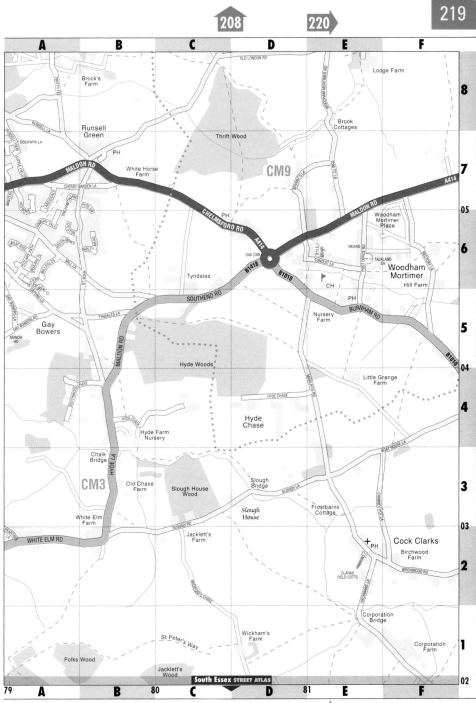

OLD LONDON RD

Brock's
Farm

Lodge Farm

8

Runsell
Green

Thrift Wood

Brook
Cottages

RUNSELL LA

DOCKWRA LA

PH

MALDON RD

CM9

7

White Horse
Farm

CHERRY GARDEN LA

A414

05

CHELMSFORD RD

PH

MALDON RD

Woodham
Mortimer
Place

A414

MEARD

FALKLAND
GN

6

OAK CNR

B1418

B1010

CH

Woodham
Mortimer

Tyndales

B1010

Hill Farm

SOUTHEND RD

PH

BURNHAM RD

Gay
Bowers

TYNDALES LA

Nursery
Farm

5

MANOR
HO

B1010

04

Hyde Woods

Little Grange
Farm

MALDON RD

HYDE CHASE

4

CM3

Hyde
Chase

SOUTHWOOD CHASE

HYDE CHASE

Hyde Farm
Nursery

GOAT HOUSE LA

Chalk
Bridge

HYDE LA

Slough
Bridge

SLOUGH LA

3

Old Chase
Farm

Slough House
Wood

Frostbarns
Cottage

CHIMNEY POTS LA

White Elm
Farm

Slough
House

03

Cock Clarks

PH

CRABTREE CL

WHITE ELM RD

SLOUGH RD

Jacklett's
Farm

Birchwood
Farm

HANNINGFIELD

BIRCHWOOD RD

CLARKS
FIELD COTTS

HACKMANS LA

2

WICKHAM'S CHASE

Wickham's
Farm

Corporation
Bridge

St Peter's Way

Corporation
Farm

1

Folks Wood

Jacklett's
Wood

South Essex STREET ATLAS

02

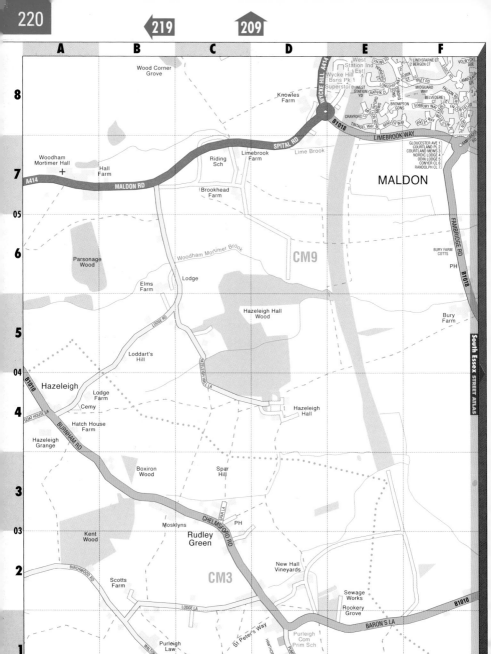

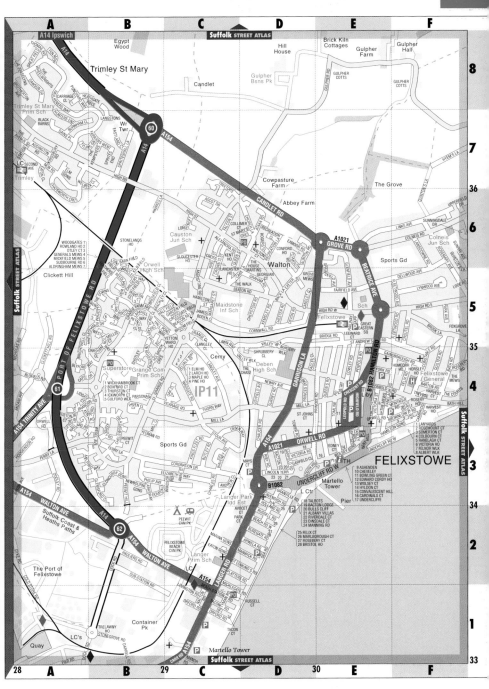

Suffolk STREET ATLAS

Trimley St Mary

Egypt Wood

Candlet

Hill House

Brick Kiln Cottages

Gulpher Farm

Gulpher Hall

Trimley St Mary Prim Sch

Gulpher Bsns Pk

GULPHER COTTS

GULPHER COTTS

Trimley

Cowpasture Farm

The Grove

Candlet Rd

Abbey Farm

Clickett Hill

A1021 GROVE RD

Sports Gd

Colneis Jun Sch

Causton Jun Sch

Walton

BEATRICE AVE

Orwell High Sch

Sch

Felixstowe

Great Eastern Sq

Maidstone Inf Sch

Deben High Sch

FELIXSTOWE

Superstore

Grange Com Prim Sch

IP11

Cemy

GARRISON LA

Felixstowe General

Liby

Sports Gd

ORWELL RD

A1021

Langer Park Ind Est

Martello Tower

L Ctr

Pier

PEEWIT CVN PK

B1082 UNDERCLIFF RD W

Felixstowe Beach CVN PK

Langer Prim Sch

WALTON AVE

The Port of Felixstowe

A154

Container Pk

Quay

Martello Tower

Suffolk STREET ATLAS

# Index

Church Rd **6** Beckenham BR2.........**53** C6

## Abbreviations used in the index

# Index of towns, villages, streets, hospitals, industrial estates, railway stations, schools, shopping centres, universities and places of interest

**222   Abb–All**

## A

Abbas Wlk CO10.........34 C5
ABBERTON ...........163 A3
Abberton Rd
 Fingringhoe CO5 .......163 D3
 Layer de la H CO2 ......162 C5
Abberton Resr Nature
 Reserve★ CO2 .......161 F2
Abberton Wildfowl Visitor
 Ctr★ CO2............161 E1
Abbess Cl CM1.........204 E2
Abbey Cotts CO11 .....115 C7
Abbey Cres CO16 ......142 A1
Abbey Ct
 Colchester CO2 .......136 A5
 **10** Ipswich IP1 .........17 A7
ABBEY FIELD ..........135 E5
Abbey Field View
 CO2..................135 E4
Abbeygate Ho CO2.....135 F6
Abbey Gate St **11** CO2...135 F6
Abbey La
 Coggeshall CO6 ........131 A1
 Saffron Walden CB10....22 D1
Abbey Mdw CO9.........51 D2
Abbey Rd CO10.........15 E1
Abbey St
 Ickleton CB10 ...........3 A4
 Thorpe-le-S CO16 ....142 A1
Abbey Turning CM9 ....209 D4
Abbey View CM6........96 E2
Abbigail Gdns CO15...189 B4
Abbotsbury Cl IP2.....177 A1
Abbots Cl
 Clacton-on-S CO15.....188 E6
 Wix CO11...............115 C5
Abbots Cotts CB9......10 A4
Abbots Gdns CO16 ....187 C4
Abbotsmead CM9......209 F5
Abbot's Rd CO2 .......136 B3
Abbots Wick La CO5...181 B3
Abbott Rd CO12.........90 F2
Abbott's Croft CB9......9 E5
Abbotts Ct CB9..........9 E5
Abbotts La CO4.........134 A7
Abbotts Pl CM2.........205 D3
Abbotts Way CM23....145 E3

Abdy Ave CO12.........90 E2
Abell Way CM2........206 B4
Abels Rd CO9..........103 D8
Abercorn Ct **11** CB9....8 F7
Abercorn Ho CM3 .....206 E8
Abercorn Way CM8 ....177 A2
Aberdare Cl IP2.........17 B2
Abingdon Cl IP2.........17 A1
Abinger Cl CO16.......188 C6
Abington Pl **2** CB9....9 A8
Abraham Dr CM8 ......156 E4
Abram's La SG8 ........19 C4
Acacia Ave CO4........136 E8
Acacia Cl IP3 ...........18 E1
Acacia Ct CO11.........60 D1
Acacia Dr
 Great Dunmow CM6 ....123 C1
 Maldon CM9...........209 F1
Acacia Gdns CM8 .....177 B4
Accommodation Rd
 CO4..................109 D7
Acer Gr
 Chelmsford CM1 .......205 D4
 Ipswich IP8 ............16 C1
Achilles Way CM7 .....128 B5
Achnacone Dr CO4 ....109 C3
Acland Ave CO10......135 B7
Acland Ct CO3.........135 A7
Acorn Ave
 Braintree CM7 .........127 E2
 Halstead CO9............76 D1
Acorn Cl
 Colchester CO4 ........110 D4
 Harwich CO12...........90 F1
 Ipswich IP2 .............16 C2
 Maldon CM9...........209 F5
Acorn Mews CO5 ......108 B6
Acorn Wlk CO7.........166 A5
Acres End CM1........204 E4
Acton Cl CO10...........33 F8
Acton Gn CO10..........33 E7
Acton Sq **4** CO10......33 E7
Adair Rd IP1 ............16 D8
Adams Cl IP2 ...........17 C3
Adams Ct
 Halstead CO9............76 D2
 Saffron Walden CB11....43 C8
Adderley Rd CM23 ....145 F7
Addington Rd IP11 ....221 A7
Addison Rd
 Great Holland CO13....170 B5

Addison Rd continued
 Sudbury CO10 ...........34 B8
Adelaide Dr CO2.......136 A1
Adelaide Rd IP4.........18 D6
Adelaide St CO12.......90 F5
Admiral Rd IP8..........36 E8
Admirals The CO12 .....91 D4
Admirals Wlk
 Chelmsford CM1 .......204 F3
 Wivenhoe CO7.........164 B8
Aerofoil Gr CO4 .......109 D2
Aetheric Rd CM7 ......127 E3
Affleck Rd CO4.........136 E7
Agar Rd **9** CO14......171 C8
Agar Road App **10**
 CO14.................171 C8
Agate Rd CO15........188 F2
Agincourt Rd CO15 ...188 D4
Agnes Silverside Cl
 Beerchurch CO2 .......162 F8
 Colchester CO2 .......135 F1
Agricultural/Domestic
 Mus★ CM9.............211 E7
Ainger Rd CO12........90 E2
AINGERS GREEN .....166 E5
Aingers Green Rd
 CO7..................167 A5
Ainslie Rd IP1...........17 A6
Aire Wlk CM8 ...........176 F2
Airey Hos CO10.........11 D1
Aisne Rd CO2 .........135 D4
Ajax Cl CM7 ...........128 B5
Akersloot Pl CO5 .....201 C6
Akhurst Cl CO5........201 C6
Alamein Rd
 Chelmsford CM1 .......204 F6
 Colchester CO2 .......135 F1
Alanbrooke Rd CO2...136 D2
Alan Dr CO15..........168 D1
Alan Hasler Ho CM6 ..150 D7
Alan Rd
 Ipswich IP3............17 F4
 Witham CM8 ...........176 E1
Alan Way CO3 .........134 F4
Albany Chase CO15...189 B4
Albany Cl
 Chelmsford CM1 .......204 E5
 West Bergholt CO6 ....108 E4
Albany Gdns CO2 .....136 D4
Albany Gdns E CO15 ..189 B3
Albany Gdns W CO15 ..189 B3
Albany Rd CO4.........108 E4
Albany The IP4..........17 E8

Albany Villas IP11 .....221 D3
Albemarle Gdns CM7 ..128 C5
Albemarle Link CM2...205 F8
Albemarle St CO12 .....91 D5
Albert Cotts CO7.......60 C2
Albert Ct CM7 .........128 A3
Albert Gdns
 Clacton-on-S CO15....189 B3
 Coggeshall CO6 .......131 A2
Albert Ho IP2 ..........17 B4
Albertine Cl CO3 ......134 C6
Albert Pl CO6 .........131 A2
Albert Rd
 Braintree CM7 .........128 A3
 Brightlingsea CO7 ....186 A6
 Witham CM8 ...........177 A3
Albert St
 Colchester CO1 .......135 E8
 Harwich CO12...........91 D5
Albert Wlk IP11 .......221 E4
Albion Ct CO5 .........164 A8
Albion Gr CO2 .........136 A5
Albion Hill IP4 ..........17 F7
Albion St CO5 .........164 A8
Albra Mead CM2.......206 B4
Albrighton Croft CO4 ..110 C4
Alconbury CM23 .......119 B3
Alcorns The CM24 ....119 E7
Aldeburgh Cl
 Clacton-on-S CO16....188 B4
 Haverhill CB9 ...........8 E7
Aldeburgh Gdns
 Colchester CO4 .......110 B4
 Ipswich IP4.............18 A6
Aldeburgh Way CM1...205 D5
Alderbury Lea CM3 ...218 F3
Alderbury Rd CM24...119 E8
Alderford Rd CO6......133 F1
Alder Cl CM23 .........145 D4
Alde Rd CM3 ............9 A8
Alder Dr CM2..........216 B6
Alderford Maltings
 CO9....................75 E8
Alderford St CO9 .......75 E8
Alderlee IP2 ............36 F8
Alderman Blaxhill Sch
 CO2..................135 B3
Alderman How Lo
 CO4..................110 B4
Alderman Rd IP1........17 B5
Alderton Cl CM6.......152 C6
Alderton Rd CO4......136 C6
Alder Way CO10.........33 F8

Alder Wlk CM8.........177 B4
ALDHAM .............133 B8
Aldham Ct **10** CB9......8 E7
Aldon Cl CO12...........90 C1
Aldous Cl CO7..........59 C3
Aldridge Cl CM2.......206 A4
Aldringham Mews
 IP11..................221 B5
Alec Kay Ct CO2.......135 C2
Aletha Farm Pl CO9....29 D6
Alexander Ct **11** CM1..205 E7
Alexander Mews CM2..217 D2
Alexander Rd CM7 ....127 E4
Alexandra Ave CO5 ...201 E6
Alexandra Ct CO7.....137 C3
Alexandra Mews **7**
 CM2..................128 A2
Alexandra Rd
 Clacton-on-S CO15....188 F3
 Colchester CO3 .......135 E6
 Felixstowe IP11 .......221 C6
 Harwich CO12...........91 C6
 Ipswich IP4.............17 E6
 Sible Hedingham CO9 ..51 D1
 Sudbury CO10 ..........34 A7
 Weeley CO16 ..........140 F1
Alexandra St CO12......91 D5
Alexandra Terr **9**
 CO3..................135 E6
Alexia Ho CM6.........123 D1
Alfelde Ct CO4.........136 E6
Alfells Rd CO7.........137 F6
Alfred Terr CO14......171 C8
Alfreg Rd CM8.........194 D8
Alienor Ave CM7........72 B1
Allectus Way CM8 ....194 D8
Allenby Rd IP2 .........16 F6
Allen Cotts CO6 .......106 E5
Allendale Dr CO6.....123 A8
Allen Ho CM7..........128 A3
Allens Cl CM3.........192 F1
Allen Way
 Chelmsford CM2 ......206 B4
 Point Clear B CO15 ...186 A3
Alleyne Way CO15 ....203 G8
Allfields CO12 ..........91 A2
All Hallows Ct IP3 ......18 E3
Allington Ct IP4........17 F7
Allington Wlk CO9......8 E8
Allin Cotts CO6........106 C5
All Saints Ave CO3....135 A4
All Saints CE Prim Sch
 Bishop's Stortford
 CM23.................146 B8

**All Saints CE Prim Sch**
continued
Great Oakley CO12 . . . . . . 116 C3
Harwich CO12 . . . . . . . . . . .90 F3
Maldon CM9 . . . . . . . . . . .209 F3
**All Saints Cl**
Ashdon CB10 . . . . . . . . . . .23 F7
Bishop's Stortford
CM23 . . . . . . . . . . . . . . 146 A8
Chelmsford CM1 . . . . . . . .205 E4
**All Saints Maldon CE Prim**
Sch CM9 . . . . . . . . . . . . .209 E2
**All Saints' Rd** IP1 . . . . . . . .17 A8
**Allshots Enterprises**
CO5 . . . . . . . . . . . . . . . .157 B5
**Alma Dr** CM1 . . . . . . . . . .205 A2
**Alma Sq** CO11 . . . . . . . . . .86 D4
**Alma St** CO7 . . . . . . . . . . 164 B8
**Almond Cl**
Clacton-on-S CO15 . . . . . . 188 C3
Tiptree CO5 . . . . . . . . . . 179 C6
Wivenhoe CO7 . . . . . . . . 137 C2
**Almondhayes** IP2 . . . . . . . .17 B3
**Almond Way** CO4 . . . . . . 136 E8
**ALMSHOUSE GREEN** . . . . .74 E7
**Almshouses** CO7 . . . . . . . 164 B8
**Alnesbourn Cres** IP3 . . . . . .38 D7
**Alpe St** IP1 . . . . . . . . . . . .17 B7
**Alpha Cl** CM7 . . . . . . . . . 128 A2
**ALPHAMSTONE** . . . . . . . . .54 F3
**Alphamstone Rd** CO8 . . . .55 B4
**Alpha Pl**
**4** Bishop's Stortford
CM23 . . . . . . . . . . . . . . 145 F8
**2** Saffron Walden CB11 . . .22 E1
**Alpha Rd** CO16 . . . . . . . . 186 B3
**Alpha Terr** IP3 . . . . . . . . . .18 E1
**Alport Ave** CO2 . . . . . . . . 135 C4
**ALRESFORD** . . . . . . . . . . 165 A8
**Alresford Prim Sch**
CO7 . . . . . . . . . . . . . . . 165 B7
**Alresford Rd** CO7 . . . . . . 164 E8
**Alresford Sta** CO7 . . . . . . 165 A8
**Alsa Bsns Pk** CM24 . . . . . .93 F1
**Alsa Gdns** CM22 . . . . . . . .94 C2
**Alsa Leys** CM22 . . . . . . . .94 C2
**Alsa St** CM24 . . . . . . . . . .93 F1
**Alston Cres** CO10 . . . . . . . .2 E6
**Alston Rd** IP3 . . . . . . . . . .17 F4
**Alstons Ct** IP3 . . . . . . . . . .18 D1
**Altbarn Cl** CO4 . . . . . . . . 110 C5
**Altbarn Rd** CO2 . . . . . . . . 136 D5
**Altitude Bsns Pk** IP3 . . . . .18 C1
**Alton Dr** CO3 . . . . . . . . . 135 B6
**Alton Gn** IP9 . . . . . . . . . . .63 A2
**Alton Hall La** IP9 . . . . . . . .61 F3
**Alton Park Jun Sch**
CO15 . . . . . . . . . . . . . . 188 D2
**Alton Park Cl** CO15 . . . . . 188 B1
**Alton Park Rd** CO15 . . . . . 188 D3
**Alton Rd** CO15 . . . . . . . . 188 C1
**Alton Water (Resr)** *
IP9 . . . . . . . . . . . . . . . . .62 A4
**Alton Water Visitor Ctr** *
IP9 . . . . . . . . . . . . . . . . .62 B3
**Aluf Cl** **2** CM8 . . . . . . . 194 E8
**Alverton Cl** CM7 . . . . . . . 154 B6
**Alverton Way** CO4 . . . . . . 110 B3
**Alvis Ave** CO15 . . . . . . . . 203 E6
**Alyssum Cl** CM1 . . . . . . . 206 A6
**Alyssum Wlk** CO4 . . . . . . 136 D8
**Amberley Cl** CO7 . . . . . . . 137 D1
**Ambleside Ct** CO15 . . . . . 189 A3
**Ambridge Rd** CO6 . . . . . . 130 E3
**Ambrose Ave** CO3 . . . . . . 134 F4
**Ambrose Ct** CO6 . . . . . . . 133 D4
**Ambrose Ho** CO2 . . . . . . . 135 D2
**Amcotes Pl** CM2 . . . . . . . 216 C8
**Amerells Rd** CO16 . . . . . . 168 C4
**America Rd** CO6 . . . . . . . 105 C2
**America St** CM9 . . . . . . . 210 A2
**Amos Hill** CO10 . . . . . . . . .54 B8
**Amoss Rd** CM2 . . . . . . . . 216 F8
**Ancaster Rd** CM2 . . . . . . 216 C7
**Anchorage Hill** CM9 . . . . . 210 A3
**Anchorage The** CO12 . . . . .90 F5
**Anchor Cvn Camp**
CO16 . . . . . . . . . . . . . . 168 D2
**Anchor End** CO11 . . . . . . . .87 A4
**Anchor Hill** CO7 . . . . . . . . 164 B7
**Anchor Ho** CO2 . . . . . . . . 135 E2
**Anchor La**
Clacton-on-S CO15 . . . . . . 188 B3
Tiptree CO5 . . . . . . . . . . 179 C4
**Anchor St**
Bishop's Stortford
CM23 . . . . . . . . . . . . . . 146 A6
Chelmsford CM2 . . . . . . . .205 B1
Ipswich IP3 . . . . . . . . . . . .17 E4
**Anderson Ave** CM1 . . . . . 204 F5
**Anderson Cl** CM23 . . . . . . .92 F2
**Andover Cl** CO15 . . . . . . . 189 A6
**Andrew Cl**
Braintree CM7 . . . . . . . . 127 F5
Felixstowe IP11 . . . . . . . . 221 C3
**Andrews Farm La**
CM6 . . . . . . . . . . . . . . . 123 C8
**Andrews Pl** CM2 . . . . . . . 204 F3
**Andros Cl** IP3 . . . . . . . . . .38 A8
**Anemone Ct** CO4 . . . . . . . 109 C2
**Angelgate** CO12 . . . . . . . .91 E6
**Angelgate Cotts** CO12 . . . .91 E6
**Angel La**
Glemsford CO10 . . . . . . . . .2 B4

**Angel La** continued
Great Dunmow CM6 . . . . . 150 D8
**17** Ipswich IP4 . . . . . . . . .17 D5
**Angel Mdw** CO10 . . . . . . . .2 B4
**Anglefield** CO15 . . . . . . . 188 F2
**Anglesea Rd**
Ipswich IP1 . . . . . . . . . . . .17 B7
Wivenhoe CO7 . . . . . . . . 164 C8
**Anglesey Cl** CM23 . . . . . . 145 C7
**Angle Side** CM7 . . . . . . . 128 B2
**Anglia Cl** CO2 . . . . . . . . . 135 B3
**Anglia Ruskin Univ**
Chelmsford CM1 . . . . . . . .205 B2
Chelmsford CM1 . . . . . . . .205 B4
**Anglia Way** CM7 . . . . . . . 128 B2
**Anita Cl** E IP2 . . . . . . . . .16 E5
**Anita Cl** W IP2 . . . . . . . . .16 E5
**Anjou Gn** CM1 . . . . . . . . 206 A7
**Annbrook Rd** IP2 . . . . . . . .16 E1
**Ann Coles Cl** CB9 . . . . . . .27 C6
**Anne Cl** CO7 . . . . . . . . . . 185 F6
**Anne St** IP11 . . . . . . . . . . 221 C3
**Annonay Wlk** CM2 . . . . . 205 C2
**Ann St** IP1 . . . . . . . . . . . .17 B7
**Ansgar Rd** CB11 . . . . . . . .43 E7
**Anson Cl** CO12 . . . . . . . . .91 A2
**Anson Way** CM7 . . . . . . . 128 C4
**Anthony Cl** CO4 . . . . . . . 110 D2
**Antonia Cl** CB9 . . . . . . . . . .9 E7
**Antonio Wlk** CO4 . . . . . . 136 F7
**Antonius Way** CO4 . . . . . 110 B6
**Anvil Way** CM1 . . . . . . . . 205 E7
**Anzani Ave** IP11 . . . . . . . 221 A4
**Anzio Cres** CO2 . . . . . . . . 135 C3
**Apollo Ho** IP2 . . . . . . . . . .16 D1
**Apollo Mews** CO4 . . . . . . 135 C1
**Appleby Cl** IP2 . . . . . . . . .16 D1
**Applegates Mdw** CO9 . . . .29 F2
**Appleton Fields** CM23 . . 145 E4
**Apple Tree Cl** CO9 . . . . . . .77 A2
**Appletree Hill Cotts**
CM3 . . . . . . . . . . . . . . . 172 D6
**Appletree Wlk** CM7 . . . . . 128 A1
**Apple Way** CM2 . . . . . . . 216 D6
**Approach The** CO15 . . . . 203 G8
**Aprils View** CO15 . . . . . . 203 D6
**Apsley Cl** CM23 . . . . . . . 145 F4
**Apsley Ct** **3** IP1 . . . . . . .17 A7
**Apton Cl** CM23 . . . . . . . . 145 F7
**Apton Fields** **7** CM23 . . . 145 F6
**Apton Rd** CM23 . . . . . . . 145 F7
**Aquiline Ho** CO15 . . . . . . 203 J8
**Aragon Cl** CO15 . . . . . . . 203 F8
**Aragon Rd**
Great Leighs CM3 . . . . . . . 173 F7
Haverhill CB9 . . . . . . . . . . .9 D7
**Arakan Cl** CO2 . . . . . . . . 135 B1
**Arbour La**
Chelmsford CM1 . . . . . . . .205 D4
Wickham Bishops CM8 . . . 195 F5
**Arbour Way** CO4 . . . . . . . 110 C4
**Arbutus Cl** CM2 . . . . . . . 216 B6
**Arcade St** **15** IP1 . . . . . . .17 C6
**Arcade The** CO15 . . . . . . 188 F2
**Archangel Gdns** IP2 . . . . . .16 E4
**Archer Cres** CO5 . . . . . . . 179 E5
**Archers Way** CM2 . . . . . . 216 C2
**Archery Fields** CO15 . . . . 189 A5
**Arden Cl** CO4 . . . . . . . . . 110 C3
**Arderne Cl** CO12 . . . . . . . .90 F2
**ARDLEIGH** . . . . . . . . . . . 111 E7
**Ardleigh Ct** CO7 . . . . . . . 111 E8
**ARDLEIGH HEATH** . . . . . .84 D1
**Ardleigh Rd**
Dedham CO7 . . . . . . . . . .84 D3
Great Bromley CO7 . . . . . 112 B4
Little Bromley CO11 . . . . . 112 E5
**Argents La** CO3 . . . . . . . . 108 C2
**Argyle Ct** CO5 . . . . . . . . 158 C2
**Argyle Rd** CO4 . . . . . . . . 141 F2
**Argyle St** IP4 . . . . . . . . . .17 C5
**Argyll Cl** **10** CB9 . . . . . . . .8 F7
**Argyll Rd** CM2 . . . . . . . . 206 A5
**Ariel Cl** CO4 . . . . . . . . . . 136 F7
**ARKESDEN** . . . . . . . . . . . .41 E2
**Arkesden Rd** CB11 . . . . . . .65 E6
**Arkwright Rd** IP2 . . . . . . . .16 E7
**Arlesford Ct** CO4 . . . . . . . 136 F4
**Armidale Wlk** CO2 . . . . . . 136 A2
**ARMIGERS** . . . . . . . . . . . .96 D6
**Armiger Way** CM8 . . . . . . 177 B2
**Armonde Cl** CM3 . . . . . . . 192 E1
**Armond Rd** CM8 . . . . . . . 176 F3
**Armourers Cl** CM23 . . . . 145 B4
**Armoury Rd** CO4 . . . . . . . 108 F4
**Armstrong Cl** CM23 . . . . 218 F8
**Armstrong Way** CO9 . . . . .30 A2
**Arnhem Gr** CM7 . . . . . . . 128 C1
**Arnhem Rd** CM7 . . . . . . . 204 E6
**Arnold Dr** CO4 . . . . . . . . 136 E6
**Arnold Ho** CM2 . . . . . . . 205 A1
**Arnold Rd** CO15 . . . . . . . 188 D1
**Arnold Villas** CO15 . . . . . 179 C6
**Arnold Way** CM2 . . . . . . 216 C3
**Arnstones Cl** CO4 . . . . . . 136 C8
**ARP Shelter Mus*** IP4 . . . .17 F5
**Arras Sq** **12** IP1 . . . . . . . .17 C6
**Arrow Rd** CO4 . . . . . . . . 136 E6
**Arrowsmith Wlk** CO4 . . . . 110 A6
**Arthur Ct** CM1 . . . . . . . . 204 F5
**Arthur St** CO2 . . . . . . . . 135 F6
**Arthur's Terr** IP4 . . . . . . . .17 E6
**Arthy Cl** CM3 . . . . . . . . . 194 A4
**Artillery Dr** CO12 . . . . . . . .90 D1
**Artillery St** CO1 . . . . . . . 136 B6
**Arun Cl** CM1 . . . . . . . . . 205 C5
**Arundel Way** IP3 . . . . . . . .18 E3

**Arundel Wlk** **1** CB9 . . . . .8 E8
**Arwela Rd** IP11 . . . . . . . . 221 D2
**Asbury Ct** CO4 . . . . . . . . 136 D8
**Ascot Cl** CM23 . . . . . . . . 146 C8
**Ascot Dr**
Felixstowe IP11 . . . . . . . . 221 C6
Ipswich IP3 . . . . . . . . . . . .18 B3
**Ascot Gdns** CO3 . . . . . . . 134 E7
**Ascot Mews** CO15 . . . . . . 189 C5
**Ash Bglws** CM7 . . . . . . . . 127 E3
**Ashbury Dr** CO6 . . . . . . . 132 F3
**Ashby Rd** CM8 . . . . . . . . 195 A7
**Ashby Rise** CM3 . . . . . . . 219 B1
**Ash Cl**
Brightlingsea CO7 . . . . . . . 185 E7
Clacton-on-S CO15 . . . . . . 188 C3
Hatfield Peverel CM3 . . . . 194 A4
Ipswich IP3 . . . . . . . . . . . .18 F1
**Ash Ct** CO12 . . . . . . . . . . .90 E2
**Ashdale** CM23 . . . . . . . . 145 D4
**ASHDON** . . . . . . . . . . . . . .6 B1
**Ashdon Mus The*** . . . . . . .6 B1
**Ashdon Prim Sch** CB10 . . . .6 B1
**Ashdon Rd**
Ashdon CB10 . . . . . . . . . .24 E3
Saffron Walden CB10 . . . . .23 C3
**Ashdown Cl** CM7 . . . . . . 154 B8
**Ashdown Way**
Colchester CO4 . . . . . . . . 136 D7
Ipswich IP3 . . . . . . . . . . . .18 E3
**ASHEN** . . . . . . . . . . . . . . .11 D1
**Ashen Cl** CO10 . . . . . . . . .11 D1
**Ashenden** IP11 . . . . . . . . 221 E4
**Ashen Hill** CO10 . . . . . . . .11 C1
**Ashen La** CO10 . . . . . . . . .11 C3
**Ashen Rd**
Ashen CO10 . . . . . . . . . . .12 A1
Clare CO10 . . . . . . . . . . . .12 B5
Ridgewell CO9 . . . . . . . . . .29 B8
**Ashes Cl** CO4 . . . . . . . . . 170 F8
**Ashes Rd** CM77 . . . . . . . . 155 F7
**Ash Fall** CM8 . . . . . . . . . 177 A5
**Ashfield Cl** CM6 . . . . . . . 123 C1
**Ashfield Ct** IP4 . . . . . . . . .18 A6
**Ashfield Farm Rd**
CM9 . . . . . . . . . . . . . . . 208 D8
**Ashfields Farm** CM6 . . . . 149 B3
**Ashford Rd** CM1 . . . . . . . 204 E2
**Ash Gn** CB10 . . . . . . . . . . .3 C1
**Ash Gr**
Blackheath CO2 . . . . . . . . 163 A8
Capel St M IP9 . . . . . . . . . .35 A2
Chelmsford CM2 . . . . . . . 216 D7
Great Cornard CO10 . . . . . .34 C5
Great Dunmow CM6 . . . . . 150 D7
Heybridge CM9 . . . . . . . . 210 C6
Wivenhoe CO7 . . . . . . . . 137 C3
**Ash Ground Cl** CO1 . . . . . .86 D8
**Ash Ho** IP2 . . . . . . . . . . . .16 C2
**Ashlea Cl** CB9 . . . . . . . . . . .9 B6
**Ashlea Rd** CB9 . . . . . . . . . .9 B6
**Ashley Ct** CO12 . . . . . . . . .91 B3
**Ashley Gdns** CO3 . . . . . . . 135 C6
**Ashley Lo** CO15 . . . . . . . . 189 A3
**Ashley Rd** CO12 . . . . . . . . .91 B3
**Ashley St** IP2 . . . . . . . . . .17 A4
**Ashlong Gr** CO9 . . . . . . . . .76 E3
**Ashlyn's Rd** CO13 . . . . . . 170 E4
**Ashmere Gr** IP4 . . . . . . . . .17 F6
**Ashmere Rise** CO10 . . . . . .34 A8
**Ashpole Rd** CM7 . . . . . . . 128 B5
**Ashpole Rd** CM7 . . . . . . . 102 B1
**Ash Rd** CO7 . . . . . . . . . . 165 B8
**Ash Rise** CO9 . . . . . . . . . 103 F8
**Ashstead Cl** CO16 . . . . . . 188 B6
**Ashton Cl** IP2 . . . . . . . . . .16 C2
**Ashton Pl** CM2 . . . . . . . . 206 A3
**Ashtree Cres** CM1 . . . . . . 204 F2
**Ashurst Cl** CO5 . . . . . . . . 163 F8
**Ashurst Dr** CM1 . . . . . . . 205 D7
**Ash Way** CO3 . . . . . . . . . 134 F3
**Ashwells Mdw** CO6 . . . . . 105 B6
**Ashwin Ave** CO6 . . . . . . . 133 D4
**Askins Rd** CO7 . . . . . . . . . .59 C3
**Aspens The** CM23 . . . . . . 119 B3
**Aspen Way**
**8** Colchester CO4 . . . . . . 136 D8
Little Oakley CO12 . . . . . . 117 B7
**Aspin Mews** CO4 . . . . . . . .22 E3
**Asquith Dr** CO4 . . . . . . . . 110 C5
**Astell Ct** CO13 . . . . . . . . 170 F4
**Aster Cl**
Bishop's Stortford
CM23 . . . . . . . . . . . . . . 145 C4
Clacton-on-S CO15 . . . . . . 188 C4
**Aster Ct** **4** CM1 . . . . . . . 205 F6
**Aster Rd** IP2 . . . . . . . . . . .16 E4
**Astley Rd** CO15 . . . . . . . . 188 D3
**Ataka Rd** IP11 . . . . . . . . . 221 D3
**Athelstan Rd** CO3 . . . . . . 135 C5
**Atherton Rd** IP2 . . . . . . . .16 D2
**Atholl Rd** CM2 . . . . . . . . 205 F5
**Atlantic Sq** CM8 . . . . . . . 177 A3
**Atlas Bglws** CO6 . . . . . . . 105 A6
**Atlas Ct** CO6 . . . . . . . . . 105 A6
**Atlas Ho** **3** CM1 . . . . . . . .17 E6
**Atlas Rd** CO6 . . . . . . . . . 105 A6
**Atlas Works** CO6 . . . . . . . 105 A6
**Attlee Gdns** **7** CO1 . . . . . 136 A6
**Attwood Cl** CO4 . . . . . . . . 110 B5
**Attwoods Cl** CM2 . . . . . . 216 C3
**Aubrey Buxton Nature**
Reserve* CM24 . . . . . . . . .94 A1

**Aubrey Cl** CM1 . . . . . . . . 205 B7
**Auckland Cl** CM1 . . . . . . 204 E5
**Audley Cl** CM77 . . . . . . . 154 B7
**Audley Ct** CB11 . . . . . . . . .22 D1
**AUDLEY END** . . . . . . . . . . .42 C7
Castle Hedingham . . . . . . .52 E8
Saffron Walden . . . . . . . . .43 B8
**Audley End House &**
**Gdns**\* CB11 . . . . . . . . . .22 B1
**Audley End Miniature**
Rly\* CB11 . . . . . . . . . . . . .43 A8
**Audley End Rd** CB11 . . . . . .43 C8
**Audley End Sta** CB11 . . . . .42 F5
**Audley Gr** IP4 . . . . . . . . . .18 F5
**Audley Rd**
Colchester CO3 . . . . . . . . 135 C5
Great Leighs CM3 . . . . . . . 173 F7
Saffron Walden CB11 . . . . .22 E1
**Audley Way** CO13 . . . . . . 171 B6
**Audrey Gdns** CM23 . . . . . 145 F4
**Audries Est** CO14 . . . . . . . 171 A8
**Augusta Cl** IP3 . . . . . . . . .38 E7
**Augustine Way** CM3 . . . . 218 F2
**Augustus Cl**
Colchester CO4 . . . . . . . . 110 B6
Haverhill CB9 . . . . . . . . . . .9 D7
**Augustus Mews** CM7 . . . . 127 E2
**Augustus Way** CM8 . . . . . 194 E8
**Austen Cl** CM7 . . . . . . . . 155 A8
**Austin Ave** CO15 . . . . . . . 203 E6
**Austin St** IP2 . . . . . . . . . . .17 C4
**Auton Croft** CB11 . . . . . . .43 D7
**Autoway** CO4 . . . . . . . . . 110 C5
**Autumn Cl** CO16 . . . . . . . 188 C5
**Aveley Way** CM9 . . . . . . . 220 F8
**Aveline Rd** CO7 . . . . . . . . 111 E7
**Avenue Pl** CM23 . . . . . . . 146 A6
**Avenue Rd**
Bishop's Stortford
CM23 . . . . . . . . . . . . . . 146 B6
Chelmsford CM2 . . . . . . . 216 D7
Witham CM8 . . . . . . . . . 177 A3
**Avenue The**
Braintree CM7 . . . . . . . . 127 F3
Clacton-on-S CO15 . . . . . . 189 B7
Colchester CO3 . . . . . . . . 135 C6
Danbury CM3 . . . . . . . . . 218 E7
Great Bardfield CM8 . . . . . 178 A3
Great Dunmow CM6 . . . . . 150 E8
Ipswich IP1 . . . . . . . . . . . .17 C8
Trimley St M IP11 . . . . . . . 221 A7
Washbrook IP8 . . . . . . . . . .35 F7
West Bergholt CO6 . . . . . . 108 D3
Witham CM8 . . . . . . . . . 177 A3
Witham CM8 . . . . . . . . . 137 B1
**Avignon Cl** CO2 . . . . . . . . 136 B4
**Avila Chase** CM2 . . . . . . . 216 B1
**Avitus Way** CO4 . . . . . . . . 110 B5
**Avocet Cl**
Frinton-on-S CO13 . . . . . . 170 E6
Kelvedon CO5 . . . . . . . . . 158 D2
West Mersea CO5 . . . . . . . 201 D7
**Avocet Ct** IP11 . . . . . . . . . 221 C2
**Avocet Way** CM9 . . . . . . . 210 C5
**Avondale Ho** CO15 . . . . . . 189 A3
**Avondale Rd**
Clacton-on-S CO15 . . . . . . 189 A3
Ipswich IP3 . . . . . . . . . . . .18 A2
**Avon Rd** CO4 . . . . . . . . . 204 C5
**Avon Way** CO4 . . . . . . . . 136 F6
**Avon Wlk** CM8 . . . . . . . . 176 E3
**Axial Way** CO4 . . . . . . . . 110 B6
**Aylesbury Dr**
Great Notley CM77 . . . . . . 154 C5
Holland-on-S CO15 . . . . . . 189 F6
**Ayletts** CM1 . . . . . . . . . . 191 B3
**Aylmer Rd** CO4 . . . . . . . . 110 C1
**Ayloffe Rd** CO4 . . . . . . . . 110 C1
**Aynsworth Ave** CM23 . . . . 119 B2
**Azalea Ct**
**6** Chelmsford CM1 . . . . . 205 F6
Colchester CO4 . . . . . . . . 136 D8
**Azalea Way** CO16 . . . . . . 188 C4

**Baburgh Ho** CO10 . . . . . . .33 F7
**Back Hamlet** IP3 . . . . . . . .17 E5
**Back Hill**
Hadstock CB1 . . . . . . . . . . .5 B6
Holbrook IP9 . . . . . . . . . . .62 E4
**Back La**
Broomfield CM1 . . . . . . . . 191 B1
Colchester CO3 . . . . . . . . 134 E7
Felixstowe IP11 . . . . . . . . 221 D5
Ford End CM3 . . . . . . . . . 172 B6
Great Oakley CO12 . . . . . . 116 D7
Ickleton CB10 . . . . . . . . . . .3 A3
Little Waltham CM3 . . . . . 191 C4
Ramsey CO12 . . . . . . . . . .90 A1
Stisted CM77 . . . . . . . . . 129 C7
Tattingstone IP9 . . . . . . . . .61 C6
Washbrook IP8 . . . . . . . . . .35 E8
Wickham Bishops CM8 . . . 195 F4
**Back Rd** CO7 . . . . . . . . . . 139 A6
**Back La W** CO7 . . . . . . . . 138 F7
**Backnang Sq** **1** CM2 . . . . 205 C2
**Back Rd**
Ardleigh CO7 . . . . . . . . . 112 B5
Tollesbury CM9 . . . . . . . . 199 C4
Writtle CM1 . . . . . . . . . . 204 A1
**Backwardens Nature**
Reserve* CM3 . . . . . . . . 218 E4
**Backwardens Nature**
Trail* CM3 . . . . . . . . . . 218 E4

**Back Waterside La**
CO7 . . . . . . . . . . . . . . . 185 F5
**BACON END** . . . . . . . . . . 149 F2
**BACONEND GREEN** . . . . 149 E4
**Bacons Green Cotts**
CO7 . . . . . . . . . . . . . . . . .58 E7
**Bacon's La** CO6 . . . . . . . . 106 C3
**Bacton Lo** IP11 . . . . . . . . 221 D3
**Bacton Rd** IP11 . . . . . . . . 221 D3
**Baddow Ct** CM2 . . . . . . . 217 A6
**Baddow Hall Ave**
CM2 . . . . . . . . . . . . . . . 217 A7
**Baddow Hall Cres**
CM2 . . . . . . . . . . . . . . . 217 B7
**Baddow Hall Inf Sch**
CM2 . . . . . . . . . . . . . . . 217 A6
**Baddow Hall Jun Sch**
CM2 . . . . . . . . . . . . . . . 217 A6
**Baddow Ho** CM2 . . . . . . . 216 F6
**Baddow Pk** CM2 . . . . . . . 216 F2
**Baddow Place Ave**
CM2 . . . . . . . . . . . . . . . 217 A6
**Baddow Rd**
Chelmsford CM2 . . . . . . . 205 C1
Great Baddow CM2 . . . . . 216 F7
**Baden Powell Cl** CM2 . . . . 217 B7
**Baden Powell Dr** CO3 . . . . 135 A4
**Bader Cl** IP3 . . . . . . . . . . .18 C2
**Badger Gr** CM7 . . . . . . . . 128 B3
**Badgers** CM23 . . . . . . . . 145 C5
**Badgers Bank** IP2 . . . . . . .16 E1
**Badgers Cl** CM4 . . . . . . . 215 F6
**Badgers Gn** CO6 . . . . . . . 132 E3
**Badgers Holt** CO10 . . . . . 134 D6
**Badley Hall Rd** CO7 . . . . . 112 F2
**Badminton Cl** CO15 . . . . . 203 G7
**Badminton Rd** CO15 . . . . 203 G7
**Badshah Ave** IP3 . . . . . . . .18 B3
**Bagshaw Rd** CO12 . . . . . . .91 D4
**Bailey Bridge Rd** CM7 . . . 127 E5
**Bailey Cl**
Haverhill CB9 . . . . . . . . . . .9 D7
Ipswich IP2 . . . . . . . . . . . .16 F2
**Bailey Dale** CO3 . . . . . . . 134 C4
**BAILEY HILL** . . . . . . . . . . .28 B5
**Bailey La** CO10 . . . . . . . . .12 C7
**Bainbridge Dr** CO5 . . . . . 179 D4
**Baines Cl** CO3 . . . . . . . . . 135 A5
**Baird Cl** IP2 . . . . . . . . . . .16 F7
**Baker Ave** CM3 . . . . . . . . 194 A3
**Baker Mews** CM9 . . . . . . . 210 A2
**Baker Rd** IP9 . . . . . . . . . . .91 A8
**Bakers Almshouses**
IP9 . . . . . . . . . . . . . . . . .61 F3
**Bakers Ct**
**5** Bishop's Stortford
CM23 . . . . . . . . . . . . . . 146 A2
Colchester CO1 . . . . . . . . 109 E1
**Bakers La**
Danbury CM3 . . . . . . . . . 218 E7
Felsted CM6 . . . . . . . . . . 152 C4
**Baker's La**
Colchester CO4 . . . . . . . . 109 A2
Great Notley CM77 . . . . . . 154 D6
Tolleshunt Major CM9 . . . . 197 D4
**Bakers Mead** CM3 . . . . . . 190 F7
**Baker's Rd** CO10 . . . . . . . .12 F2
**Baker St** CM2 . . . . . . . . . 205 A1
**Baker Way** CM8 . . . . . . . . 194 F7
**Bakery Cl** CM23 . . . . . . . 119 D6
**Baldry Cl** IP8 . . . . . . . . . . .16 C1
**Baldwin's La** CO6 . . . . . . . 131 E8
**Bale Cl** CO3 . . . . . . . . . . 134 E4
**Balfe Cl** CO4 . . . . . . . . . . 136 E6
**Balfour Terr** IP3 . . . . . . . . .38 C8
**Balkerne Gdns** CO1 . . . . . 135 E7
**Balkerne Hill** CO3 . . . . . . 135 E7
**Balkerne Pas** CO1 . . . . . . 135 E7
**Ball Alley** **3** CO1 . . . . . . . 135 F7
**Ballantyne Dr** CO2 . . . . . 136 D5
**Ballast Quay Rd**
Fingringhoe CO5 . . . . . . . 164 B6
Wivenhoe CO7 . . . . . . . . 137 D1
**BALLINGDON** . . . . . . . . . .33 D6
**Ballingdon Gr** CO10 . . . . . .33 D5
**Ballingdon Hill** CO10 . . . . .33 C5
**Ballingdon Hill Ind Est**
CO10 . . . . . . . . . . . . . . . .33 C6
**Ballingdon St** CO10 . . . . . .33 D6
**Ballingdon Trad Est**
CO10 . . . . . . . . . . . . . . . .33 C6
**Ball La**
Abberton CO2 . . . . . . . . . 162 F5
Blackheath CO2 . . . . . . . . 163 B5
**Ball's Chase** CO8 . . . . . . . .79 F2
**Ball's Chase** CO9 . . . . . . . .76 F1
**Ball's Farm** CO7 . . . . . . . 137 E7
**Balmoral Ave** CO15 . . . . . 188 D3
**Balmoral Cl** IP2 . . . . . . . . .16 F1
**Balmoral Ct**
Braintree CM7 . . . . . . . . 128 C4
Chelmsford CM2 . . . . . . . 205 C2
**Balmoral Dr** CM9 . . . . . . . .8 E8
**Balton Way** CO12 . . . . . . . .90 F2
**BAMBER'S GREEN** . . . . . 121 F3
**Bangs Ct** CB21 . . . . . . . . . .7 A7
**Banham Dr** CO10 . . . . . . . .33 F8
**Banister Cl** CO16 . . . . . . . 188 C5
**Bankart La** CM2 . . . . . . . 205 F4
**Bank Pas** CO1 . . . . . . . . . 135 F7
**Bank Rd** IP4 . . . . . . . . . . .17 E6
**Banks Cl** CM6 . . . . . . . . . 150 D8
**Bank St** CM7 . . . . . . . . . 127 F3
**BANNISTER GREEN** . . . . 152 F6

**Bannister Green Villas**
CM6 . . . . . . . . . . . . . . . . .152 E6
**Banters La** CM3 . . . . . . . . .154 B1
**Bantock Way** CM8 . . . . . . .194 F7
**Bantoft Terr** IP3 . . . . . . . . .18 C2
**Barbary Lo** CM2 . . . . . . . .205 A2
**Barbel Rd** CO4 . . . . . . . . . .110 F1
**Barbour Gdns** CO2 . . . . . .134 F2
**Barbrook La** CO5 . . . . . . . .179 D6
**Barbrook Way** CM3 . . . . . .218 E1
**Barclay Cl** CM2 . . . . . . . . .217 A6
**Barclay Sq** CO15 . . . . . . . .203 G7
**Bardell Cl** CM1 . . . . . . . . .204 F6
Bardfield Ctr CM7 . . . . . . . . .72 B1
**BARDFIELD END GREEN**
. . . . . . . . . . . . . . . . . . . . . .70 C2
**Bardfield End Villas**
. . . . . . . . . . . . . . . . . . . . . .70 C2
**Bardfield Rd**
Bardfield Saling CM7 . . . . . .99 F1
Colchester CO2 . . . . . . . . .136 A1
Finchingfield CM7 . . . . . . . .72 C5
Thaxted CM6 . . . . . . . . . . . .70 D2
**BARDFIELD SALING** . . . . .99 C2
Bardfield Way CO13 . . . . . .170 F6
**Bardsley Cl** CM2 . . . . . . . .109 E2
**Bardsley Rd** CM2 . . . . . . . .128 C8
**Barfield Rd** CO5 . . . . . . . .201 C6
**Barfields Row** CO5 . . . . . .159 D2
**Bargate La** CO7 . . . . . . . . . .85 C3
**Baring-Gould Cotts**
CO5 . . . . . . . . . . . . . . . . . .184 D1
**Barker Cl**
Ipswich IP2 . . . . . . . . . . . . . .16 D5
Lawford CO11 . . . . . . . . . . .86 B4
Steeple Bumpstead CB9 . . . .27 B6
**Barker Rd** CO10 . . . . . . . . .15 E2
**Barkers Terr** CO7 . . . . . . . . .85 A5
**Barkis Cl** CM1 . . . . . . . . . .204 D7
**Barkstead Rd** CO4 . . . . . . .110 C1
**Barlee Cl** CB11 . . . . . . . . . .65 C3
**Barley Cl** CO11 . . . . . . . . . .87 A4
**Barley Ct**
Saffron Walden CB11 . . . . . .22 D1
Wivenhoe CO7 . . . . . . . . . .137 C3
**Barleyfields** CM8 . . . . . . .177 A1
**Barleyhayes CL** IP2 . . . . . . .17 B2
**Barley Hills** CM23 . . . . . . .145 E4
**Barley Ho** CO10 . . . . . . . . . .15 B5
**Barley Mead** CM3 . . . . . . .219 B6
**Barley Way** CO3 . . . . . . . .134 E5
**Barlon Rd** CO11 . . . . . . . . .112 F7
**Barlow Road Cotts** CB10 . . .6 B2
**Barlow's Reach** CM2 . . . . .206 A4
**Barnaby Rudge** CM1 . . . . .204 F7
**Barnard Cl** CB11 . . . . . . . . .66 F8
**Barnardiston Rd** CO4 . . . .110 C1
**Barnardiston Way**
CM8 . . . . . . . . . . . . . . . . . .176 F3
**Barnard Rd** CM2 . . . . . . . .216 C2
**Barnards Cl** CB10 . . . . . . . .22 D2
**Barnards Field** CM6 . . . . . .70 B2
**Barnards Orch** CM7 . . . . . .126 F2
**Barnards Yd** CB10 . . . . . . . .22 D1
**Barnby Cl** CB9 . . . . . . . . . . . .8 C8
**Barncroft Cl** CO4 . . . . . . . .110 A5
Barnes Farm Inf Sch
CM2 . . . . . . . . . . . . . . . . . .206 A3
Barnes Farm Jun Sch
CM2 . . . . . . . . . . . . . . . . . .206 A3
**Barnes Mill Rd** CM2 . . . . .205 F2
**Barnett Reach** CO14 . . . . .144 E2
**Barnfield**
Capel St M IP9 . . . . . . . . . . .35 B1
Feering CO5 . . . . . . . . . . . .158 D3
Manningtree CO11 . . . . . . . .86 D4
**Barn Field** IP11 . . . . . . . . .221 B6
**Barnfield Cotts** CM9 . . . . .210 B5
**Barnfield Mews** CM1 . . . . .205 A6
**Barnfield Pl** CM8 . . . . . . . .176 F1
**Barnfield Rd** CO6 . . . . . . . .109 C6
**Barnfields** CO5 . . . . . . . . .163 F5
**Barn Fields** CO3 . . . . . . . .134 C6
**Barn Gn** CM1 . . . . . . . . . .205 E8
**Barn Hall Ave** CO2 . . . . . .136 C4
**Barnhall Rd** CM9 . . . . . . . .180 D2
**Barnham Pl** IP5 . . . . . . . . . .18 F6
**Barn La** CO11 . . . . . . . . . . .112 F7
**Barn Mead**
Braintree CM7 . . . . . . . . . .128 D2
Galleywood CM2 . . . . . . . .216 D4
**BARNSTON** . . . . . . . . . . . .151 A4
**Barnston Gn** CM6 . . . . . . .151 A4
**Barn View Rd** CO6 . . . . . . .131 A1
**Baronia Croft** CO4 . . . . . . .110 C3
**Baron's Ct 5** CB9 . . . . . . . . .8 E7
**Baron's La** CM3 . . . . . . . . .220 E1
**Barons The** CM23 . . . . . . .145 D5
**Baronswood Way**
CO2 . . . . . . . . . . . . . . . . . .135 D2
**Barrack Cnr 5** IP1 . . . . . . . .17 B6
**Barrack La**
Great Waltham CM3 . . . . . .190 E8
Harwich CO12 . . . . . . . . . . .91 E4
Ipswich IP1 . . . . . . . . . . . . . .17 B6
**Barrack Sq 6** CM2 . . . . . . .205 B2
**Barrack St**
Bradfield CO11 . . . . . . . . . .114 C8
Colchester CO1 . . . . . . . . .136 B6
**Barr Cl** CO7 . . . . . . . . . . . .137 C1
**Barrel Cl** CO7 . . . . . . . . . .139 A3
**Barrells Down Rd**
CM23 . . . . . . . . . . . . . . . . .118 E1
**Barrett La 5** CM23 . . . . . .145 F7

**Barrington Cl**
Great Baddow CM2 . . . . . .217 A6
Little Clacton CO16 . . . . . .168 C2
**Barrington Gdns**
CO15 . . . . . . . . . . . . . . . . .189 C5
**Barrington Ho** CO2 . . . . . .136 A5
**Barrington Rd** CO2 . . . . . .136 A5
**Barrow Chase** CM2 . . . . . .206 B4
**Barrow Marsh** CM9 . . . . . .211 A4
**Barrow Mews** CO5 . . . . . .201 E8
**Barryfields** CM7 . . . . . . . . .100 E7
**Bartholomew Cl** CB10 . . . . .3 E2
**Bartholomew Ct** CO4 . . . .109 E3
**BARTHOLOMEW GREEN**
. . . . . . . . . . . . . . . . . . . . .153 E7
**Bartholomew Rd 8**
CM23 . . . . . . . . . . . . . . . . .145 F6
**Bartholomew St** IP4 . . . . . .17 F6
**Bartletts** CB10 . . . . . . . . . . .22 D1
**BARTLOW** . . . . . . . . . . . . . . .6 B7
**Bartlow Rd**
Castle Camps CB21 . . . . . . . .7 D4
Hadstock CB1 . . . . . . . . . . . . .5 D7
**Barton Cl** IP2 . . . . . . . . . . .16 E2
**Barton Rd** IP11 . . . . . . . . .221 F4
**Bartram Ave N** CM7 . . . . .128 C3
**Bartram Ave S** CM7 . . . . . .128 C3
**Barwell Ho 3** CM8 . . . . . . .194 E8
**Barwell Way** CM8 . . . . . . .177 B2
**Basbow La 2** CM23 . . . . . .145 F7
**Basin Rd** CM9 . . . . . . . . . .210 E3
**Bassetts La** CM3, CM9 . . . .208 A4
**Bassingbourn Rd**
CM24 . . . . . . . . . . . . . . . . .121 A3
**Bassingham Cres**
CO5 . . . . . . . . . . . . . . . . . .179 E5
**Bateman Rd** CO7 . . . . . . . .185 E8
**Bateman's Rd** CO16 . . . . .168 B4
**Bates Rd** CM9 . . . . . . . . . .210 B4
**Bath Cl** CB9 . . . . . . . . . . . . .9 F6
**Bath Hill** IP11 . . . . . . . . . .221 F4
**Bath Rd** IP11 . . . . . . . . . .221 F4
**BATH SIDE** . . . . . . . . . . . . .91 D5
**Bath St**
Ipswich IP2 . . . . . . . . . . . . .17 D3
Wivenhoe CO7 . . . . . . . . . .164 B8
**Bathurst Cl 11** CO2 . . . . . .136 A1
**Battery La** IP9 . . . . . . . . . . .91 B8
**Batt Hall** CO10 . . . . . . . . . .33 B6
**Battisford Dr** CO16 . . . . . .188 A4
**Battle Rise** CM9 . . . . . . . . .210 B4
**Battlesbrook Rd** CO2 . . . . .136 D2
**Bawden Way** CM2 . . . . . . .216 D8
**Bawdsey Cl** CO16 . . . . . . .188 B3
**Bawn Cl** CM7 . . . . . . . . . .128 A4
**Bawtree Way** CO3 . . . . . . .135 A5
**Baxters** CM3. . . . . . . . . . . .219 A7
**Bayard Ave** CO7 . . . . . . . .185 F7
**Bay Ct** CO12. . . . . . . . . . . .91 D5
**Bayley St** CO9 . . . . . . . . . . .51 F4
**Baynard Ave** CM6 . . . . . . .151 E6
**Baynard Gn** CO2 . . . . . . . .135 F4
**Baynards Cres** CO13 . . . . .170 E6
Baynard's Prim Sch
CO5 . . . . . . . . . . . . . . . . . .179 B7
**Baynes Pl** CM1 . . . . . . . . . .204 F1
**Bayning Ho** CO7 . . . . . . . .139 F8
**Bay Rd** CO12 . . . . . . . . . . .91 D4
**Bays Dr** CO9. . . . . . . . . . . .76 E2
**Baytree Cl**
Rayne CM77. . . . . . . . . . . .126 F2
Wix CO11. . . . . . . . . . . . . .115 C5
**Bay View Cres**
Harwich CO12. . . . . . . . . . .90 C1
Little Oakley CO12. . . . . . .117 C8
**Beach App** CO16. . . . . . . .203 B6
**Beach Cres** CO15 . . . . . . .203 F6
**Beach Rd**
Clacton-on-S CO15. . . . . . .188 F2
Harwich CO12 . . . . . . . . . . .91 C2
Lee-o-S CO16. . . . . . . . . . .202 D6
St Osyth CO16 . . . . . . . . . .203 C7
West Mersea CO5 . . . . . . .201 C5
**Beach Rd W** IP11. . . . . . . .221 D2
**Beach's Dr** CM1 . . . . . . . . .204 D3
**Beach Station Rd**
IP11. . . . . . . . . . . . . . . . . .221 C1
**Beach Way** CO15 . . . . . . .203 F6
**Beacon Cl** CO7 . . . . . . . . .185 E6
**BEACON END** . . . . . . . . . .134 D6
**Beacon End Ctyd**
CO3 . . . . . . . . . . . . . . . . . .134 C6
**Beacon Field** IP11 . . . . . . .221 C5
**BEACON HILL** . . . . . . . . . .196 A6
**Beacon Hill**
Maldon CM9. . . . . . . . . . . .209 E2
Wickham Bishops CM8 . . . .196 A6
**Beacon Hill Ave** CO12. . . . .91 E4
**Beacon Hill Rd** IP2 . . . . . . .16 F3
**Beacon Hts** CO16 . . . . . . .186 B2
**Beaconsfield Ave**
CO3 . . . . . . . . . . . . . . . . . .135 E6
**Beaconsfield Cl** CO10 . . . . .33 E8
**Beaconsfield Ct 7** CB9 . . . . .8 F7
**Beaconsfield Rd**
Clacton-on-S CO15. . . . . . .188 F3
Ipswich IP1. . . . . . . . . . . . . .16 F7
Sudbury CO10 . . . . . . . . . . .33 E8
**Beacon Way**
Colchester CO3 . . . . . . . . .134 C6
Point Clear B CO16 . . . . . .186 B2
**Beadel Cl** CM23 . . . . . . . . .194 E8
**Beadle Pl** CM9. . . . . . . . . .196 B3
**Beadle Way** CM3 . . . . . . . .174 A6
**Beard's La** CB11 . . . . . . . . .41 A4
**Beardsley Dr** CM1 . . . . . . .205 F7

**Beard's Terr** CO6 . . . . . . .131 A3
**Bear St** CO6. . . . . . . . . . . .56 A1
Bearwalden Bsns Pk
CB11 . . . . . . . . . . . . . . . . . .42 F5
**Beatrice Ave** IP11 . . . . . . .221 E5
**Beatrice Cl** IP3 . . . . . . . . . .18 A3
**Beatrice Rd**
Clacton-on-S CO15. . . . . . .188 E2
Walton-on-t-N CO14 . . . . . .144 D2
**Beatty Gdns** CM7 . . . . . . .128 C4
**Beatty Rd** IP3 . . . . . . . . . . .18 B2
**Beauchamps Cl** CM1 . . . . .205 F8
**Beaufort Ct 5** CB9 . . . . . . . .8 F7
**Beaufort Gdns** CM7 . . . . . .128 B4
**Beaufort Rd** CM2 . . . . . . . .206 A4
**Beaufort St** IP1. . . . . . . . . .17 A7
**Beaulieu Bvd** CM1 . . . . . . .206 A7
**BEAUMONT** . . . . . . . . . . . .141 F7
**Beaumont Ave**
Brightlingsea CO7 . . . . . . . .186 A7
Clacton-on-S CO15. . . . . . .188 D3
**Beaumont Cl**
Colchester CO4 . . . . . . . . .109 F4
Walton-on-t-N CO14 . . . . . .170 F7
**Beaumont Ct** CB9. . . . . . . . .9 B6
**Beaumont Hill** CM6 . . . . . .123 D2
**Beaumont Ho** CO6 . . . . . . .131 A3
**Beaumont Pk** CM3 . . . . . . .218 C6
**Beaumont Pl** CM2 . . . . . . .128 B3
**Beaumont Rd** CO12 . . . . . .116 C3
**Beaumont Vale** CB9. . . . . . . .9 B6
**Beaumont Wlk** CM1 . . . . . .204 D5
**Beaver Cl** CO3 . . . . . . . . . .134 E7
**Beaver Ct** IP4 . . . . . . . . . . .18 B7
**BEAZLEY END** . . . . . . . . .101 C6
**Beche Ho** CO1 . . . . . . . . . .135 E4
**Beche Rd** CO1. . . . . . . . . .136 B5
**Becker Rd** CO3 . . . . . . . . .134 E4
Beckers Green Prim Sch
CM7 . . . . . . . . . . . . . . . . . .128 D2
**Becketts Ct 1** CM1 . . . . . .205 A3
**Becketts La** IP7 . . . . . . . . . .57 D8
**Beckford Rd** CO11 . . . . . . . .87 A4
Beckingham Bsns Pk
CM9 . . . . . . . . . . . . . . . . . .197 D3
**Beckingham Rd**
Great Totham CM9. . . . . . . .196 D5
Tolleshunt D'arcy CM9 . . . .198 C4
Wethersfield CM7 . . . . . . . .73 D8
**Beckingham St** CM9 . . . . . .197 D3
**Beck Rd** CB11 . . . . . . . . . . .22 D1
**Becontree Cl** CO15. . . . . . .188 F8
**Bedells Ave** CM77. . . . . . . .155 B5
**Bedford Cl**
Braintree CM7. . . . . . . . . . .128 B4
Tiptree CO5. . . . . . . . . . . . .179 D5
**Bedford Ct 8** CB9 . . . . . . . . .8 F7
**Bedford Rd**
Colchester CO4 . . . . . . . . .109 F5
Holland-on-S CO15 . . . . . . .189 D5
**Bedford St** IP1 . . . . . . . . . .17 A6
**Bedwell Rd** CM22. . . . . . . . .94 B3
**Beech Ave**
Braintree CM7. . . . . . . . . . .127 F5
Halstead CO9. . . . . . . . . . . .77 A2
Wivenhoe CO7 . . . . . . . . . .137 B1
**Beech Cl**
Sproughton IP8. . . . . . . . . . .16 A6
Takeley CM22 . . . . . . . . . . .148 C8
**Beechcroft Ave** CO13 . . . . .170 D6
**Beeches Cl**
Chelmsford CM1 . . . . . . . . .204 B4
Saffron Walden CB11. . . . . . .43 C7
**Beeches Ct** CM1 . . . . . . . .204 F2
**Beeches Rd**
Chelmsford CM1 . . . . . . . . .204 B4
Heybridge CM9 . . . . . . . . .209 F5
**Beeches The**
Ipswich IP3. . . . . . . . . . . . . .17 F4
Lawford CO11 . . . . . . . . . . .86 C3
Wendens Ambo CB11 . . . . . .42 E6
**Beech Gn** CM8 . . . . . . . . . .195 F5
**Beech Gr**
Fordham Heath CO3 . . . . . .107 F1
Haverhill CB9 . . . . . . . . . . . . .8 F8
Ipswich IP3 . . . . . . . . . . . . .17 F4
Little Oakley CO12. . . . . . . .117 B7
Rushmere St A IP5 . . . . . . . .18 F7
Sible Hedingham CO9 . . . . . .51 D1
**Beech Hill** CO3 . . . . . . . . .135 A6
**Beech Ho**
Ipswich IP2. . . . . . . . . . . . . .16 D2
Saffron Walden CB10. . . . . . .22 E2
**Beechholm 2** CM2 . . . . . . . .17 E6
**Beechlands** CM23. . . . . . . .145 F5
**Beech Rd**
Great Cornard CO10 . . . . . . .34 B6
Rivenhall CM8 . . . . . . . . . .177 B7
**Beech Rise** CM3 . . . . . . . . .194 A3
**Beech Tree Lo** CO3 . . . . . . .135 B7
**Beechwood Cl** CO2 . . . . . . .135 D3
**Beehive Cl** CO7 . . . . . . . . . .59 C3
**Beehive Cnr** CO7 . . . . . . . . .59 C3
**Beehive Ct** CO1. . . . . . . . .136 A6
**Beehive Ho** CM7 . . . . . . . . .127 E4
**Beehive La** CM2 . . . . . . . . .216 C5
Beehive Lane Com Prim
Sch CM2 . . . . . . . . . . . . . .216 C6
**Beeleigh Chase** CM9. . . . . .209 D4
**Beeleigh Cl** CO2. . . . . . . . .136 A1
**Beeleigh Link** CM2 . . . . . . .205 F3
**Beeleigh Rd** CM9 . . . . . . . .209 D5
**BEERCHURCH** . . . . . . . . . .135 F1
**Begonia Cl** CM1 . . . . . . . . .204 E1
**Begonia Pl** CO16. . . . . . . .188 C4
**Bekeswell La** CM2 . . . . . . .215 F2

**Bekeswell Pl** CM2 . . . . . . .216 C2
Bentalls Complex The
CM9 . . . . . . . . . . . . . . . . . .210 B5
**Bel-Air Beach Cvn Pk**
CO15 . . . . . . . . . . . . . . . . .203 C6
**Bel-Air Est** CO16 . . . . . . . .203 A6
**BELCHAMP OTTEN** . . . . . .31 C8
**Belchamp Rd** CO9 . . . . . . . .30 B5
Belchamp St Paul CE Prim
Sch CO10 . . . . . . . . . . . . . .13 A1
**BELCHAMP WALTER** . . . . .31 F5
**Belcham's La** CB11 . . . . . . . .93 E8
**Beldams Cl** CO16 . . . . . . . .142 A1
**Beldams Gate** CM23 . . . . .146 C6
**Beldams La** CM23. . . . . . . .146 B5
**Belgrave Cl** IP3 . . . . . . . . . .38 F7
**Belgrave Cl**
Chelmsford CM2 . . . . . . . . .216 D7
Ipswich IP4. . . . . . . . . . . . . .17 E8
**Belgrave Ho 6** CM2 . . . . . .146 B8
**Belgrave Pl** CO1 . . . . . . . . .136 A7
**Bellamy Cl** CO13 . . . . . . . .170 D6
**Bellamy Ct 8** CM1. . . . . . . .205 A3
**Bellamy Ho 3** CM7 . . . . . .127 F2
**Bell Cl**
Colchester CO2 . . . . . . . . .136 D2
Ipswich IP2 . . . . . . . . . . . . . .17 C4
**Bell Coll** CB11 . . . . . . . . . . .43 E8
**Bellcroft** CM8 . . . . . . . . . .177 A3
**Belle Vue** CM2 . . . . . . . . . .205 A1
**Belle Vue Rd**
Colchester CO1 . . . . . . . . .109 E1
Ipswich IP4. . . . . . . . . . . . . .17 F6
Sudbury CO10 . . . . . . . . . . .33 F7
Wivenhoe CO7 . . . . . . . . . .137 C1
**Bellevue Terr** CO9 . . . . . . . .76 E2
Bell Farm Ind Pk SG8 . . . . . .39 B2
**Bellfield Ave** CO7 . . . . . . . .186 A7
**Bellfield Cl**
Brightlingsea CO7 . . . . . . . .186 A8
Witham CM8 . . . . . . . . . . . .176 F3
**Bell Gn** CO7 . . . . . . . . . . . .186 A7
**Bell Hill**
Danbury CM3. . . . . . . . . . .218 C2
Lamarsh CO8 . . . . . . . . . . . .55 C3
**Bellingham Bldgs**
CB10 . . . . . . . . . . . . . . . . . .22 D2
**Bellingham Dr** CO6 . . . . . .133 E5
**Bellingham Pl** CO5 . . . . . . .158 C3
**Bell La**
Great Bardfield CM7 . . . . . . .72 A2
Ipswich IP2. . . . . . . . . . . . . .17 C4
Nuthampstead SG8 . . . . . . . .39 B2
Panfield CM7 . . . . . . . . . . .127 A7
**2** Thaxted CM6 . . . . . . . . . .70 A3
**Bellmead** CM1. . . . . . . . . .205 B2
**Bells Chase** CM2. . . . . . . . .216 E6
**Bells Cl** CB11 . . . . . . . . . . . .43 E8
**BELL'S CORNER** . . . . . . . . .56 E8
**Bells Hill**
Bishop's Stortford
CM23 . . . . . . . . . . . . . . . . .145 E7
Bures CO8 . . . . . . . . . . . . . .80 A4
**Bells La** CO10 . . . . . . . . . . . .2 C5
**Bell St** CM2 . . . . . . . . . . . .216 F6
**Belmer Rd** CM24. . . . . . . . . .91 A2
**Belmonde Dr** CM1 . . . . . . .205 E7
**Belmont Cl** CM1 . . . . . . . . .205 E7
**Belmont Cres** CO4 . . . . . . .110 C3
**Belmont Ct 6** CB9. . . . . . . . .8 F7
**Belmont Hill** CB11 . . . . . . . .43 A1
**Belmont Pl** CO1 . . . . . . . . .136 C5
**Belmont Rd** IP2 . . . . . . . . . .16 C1
**Belsay Ct** CB9 . . . . . . . . . . . .8 D8
**Belsize Ave** CO15 . . . . . . . .203 D6
**BELSTEAD** . . . . . . . . . . . . . .36 C7
**Belstead Ave** IP2 . . . . . . . . .17 B3
**Belstead Rd** IP2 . . . . . . . . . .17 A4
**Belstead Sch** IP8 . . . . . . . . .16 C2
Belsteads Farm La
CM3 . . . . . . . . . . . . . . . . . .191 E2
**Belvawney Cl** CM1 . . . . . . .204 E6
**Belvedere Cl** CM3 . . . . . . . .218 F7
**Belvedere Ct**
Chelmsford CM2 . . . . . . . . .215 F8
Maldon CM9. . . . . . . . . . . .220 B8
**Belvedere Pl** CM9 . . . . . . . .220 F8
**Belvedere Rd**
Danbury CM3. . . . . . . . . . .218 F7
Ipswich IP4. . . . . . . . . . . . . .17 F7
**Bembridge Cl** CO15 . . . . . .188 F8
**Bemerton Ct** CO13 . . . . . . .170 B6
**Bemerton Gdns** CO13 . . . .170 C6
**Benacre Rd** IP3 . . . . . . . . . . .18 A2
**Benbridge Cl** CM9 . . . . . . .210 A5
Bench Barn Farm
CO10 . . . . . . . . . . . . . . . . . .11 F7
**Bendalls Ct 1** CO11 . . . . . . .86 D4
**Bendlowes Rd** CM7 . . . . . . .72 C8
**Benedict Dr** CM2 . . . . . . . .204 E2
**Benedict Ho** CO2 . . . . . . . .135 E4
**Benezet St** IP1 . . . . . . . . . . .17 B6
**Benfield Way** CM7 . . . . . . .128 B2
**Benhall Cl** CO16 . . . . . . . . .188 A4
**Benhooks Ave** CM23 . . . . .145 E5
**Benhooks Pl 1** CM23 . . . . .145 E5
**Benison Ct** CO4 . . . . . . . . .136 E6
**Bennett Cl**
Braintree CM7. . . . . . . . . . .155 A8
Walton-on-t-N CO14 . . . . . .171 A8
**Bennett Rd** IP1. . . . . . . . . . .16 E8
**Bennett's La** CM6. . . . . . . .151 E2
**Bennett Way** CM3 . . . . . . . .194 A4
**Ben Sainty Ct** CM8 . . . . . . .177 A2
**Benskins Ct** CM23. . . . . . . . .92 A8
**Bensusan Ct** CO2 . . . . . . . .135 B3

**Bentall Cl** CO9. . . . . . . . . .103 F8
Bentalls Complex The
CM9 . . . . . . . . . . . . . . . . . .210 B5
**BENTFIELD BOWER** . . . . .119 C8
**Bentfield End Cswy**
CM24 . . . . . . . . . . . . . . . . .119 D7
**Bentfield Gdns** CM24 . . . . .119 D7
**BENTFIELD GREEN** . . . . . .119 D8
**Bentfield Pl** CM24. . . . . . . .119 D7
Bentfield Prim Sch
CM24 . . . . . . . . . . . . . . . . .119 D8
**Bentfield Rd** CM24. . . . . . .119 D7
**Bent Hill** IP11 . . . . . . . . . .221 E3
**Bent La** IP4 . . . . . . . . . . . . .18 E8
**Bentleigh Ct 5** CO1 . . . . . .136 D7
**BENTLEY** . . . . . . . . . . . . . . .60 E7
**Bentley Ave** CO15. . . . . . . .203 E6
Bentley CE Prim Sch
IP9 . . . . . . . . . . . . . . . . . . . .60 F7
**Bentley Cl** CM23 . . . . . . . .145 F5
**Bentley Ct** CO3 . . . . . . . . .135 C7
**Bentley La**
Belstead IP8 . . . . . . . . . . . . .36 C6
Stutton IP9 . . . . . . . . . . . . . .61 E3
**Bentley Rd**
Little Bromley CM11 . . . . . .113 D3
Weeley Heath CO7,
CO16 . . . . . . . . . . . . . . . . .167 E6
Witham CM8 . . . . . . . . . . . .176 E4
**Benton Cl**
Cressing CM77 . . . . . . . . . .155 E6
Witham CM8 . . . . . . . . . . . .195 A7
**Berberis Wlk 5** CO4 . . . . .136 E7
**Berbice La** CM6 . . . . . . . . .123 D2
**BERDEN** . . . . . . . . . . . . . . . .92 C8
**BERECHURCH** . . . . . . . . . .135 F1
Berechurch Hall Rd
CO2 . . . . . . . . . . . . . . . . . .162 D8
**Berechurch Rd** CO2 . . . . . .135 E2
**Berefield Way 6** CO2 . . . . .136 A1
**Bergamot Rd** CM9 . . . . . . . .8 C8
**Bergen Ct** CM9 . . . . . . . . .220 E8
**Berghoft Rd**
Brantham CO11 . . . . . . . . . .86 B7
Colchester CO4 . . . . . . . . .109 D2
**Beridge Rd** CO9 . . . . . . . . . .76 D2
**Beriffe Pl** CO7 . . . . . . . . . .185 F7
**Berkeley Cl** IP4. . . . . . . . . . .17 E8
**Berkeley Gdns** CO5 . . . . . . .163 F7
**Berkeley Rd** CO15. . . . . . . .188 F5
**Berkely Dr** CM2. . . . . . . . . .205 F2
**Berkley Cl** CO4 . . . . . . . . . .110 C4
**Bermuda Rd** IP3 . . . . . . . . . .38 E7
**Bernard Cl** CO13. . . . . . . . .170 E6
**Bernard Cres** IP3 . . . . . . . . .18 B2
**Berners End** CM6 . . . . . . . .151 B4
**Berners St** IP1 . . . . . . . . . . .17 B6
**Bernside** CM7 . . . . . . . . . .127 F2
**Berrington Cl** CM2 . . . . . . .216 D2
**Berrimans Ct** CO4 . . . . . . .136 D6
**Berry Cl** IP3 . . . . . . . . . . . . .18 F1
**Berryfield Cotts** CO11 . . . . .136 B7
**Berry Terr 19** CO10. . . . . . . .33 E7
**Bertram Ave** CO16 . . . . . . .168 D1
**Berwick Ave** CM1 . . . . . . . .205 B7
**Berwick Cotts** CM3 . . . . . . .193 D4
**Beryl Rd** CO12 . . . . . . . . . . .90 D1
**Beslyns Rd** CM7 . . . . . . . . .127 F3
**Beta Terr** IP3 . . . . . . . . . . . .18 E1
**Betjeman Cl** CM7 . . . . . . . .155 A8
**Betony Wlk** CM7 . . . . . . . . . .8 D8
**Betts Green Rd** CO16 . . . . .168 D5
**Betty Cocker Gr** CO10. . . . . .34 B7
**Betty Dent's Cnr**
CO16 . . . . . . . . . . . . . . . . .141 C5
**Beverley Ave** CO5. . . . . . . .201 E7
**Beverley Ct 5** IP4. . . . . . . . .17 D6
**Beverley Dr** CO13. . . . . . . .170 E7
**Beverley Rd**
Colchester CO3 . . . . . . . . .135 D6
Ipswich IP4. . . . . . . . . . . . . .17 F8
**Bevington Mews** CM8. . . . .177 B2
**Bewick Ct** CO9. . . . . . . . . . .51 E2
**Bexhill Cl** CO15 . . . . . . . . .203 E8
**Bexley Ave** CO12. . . . . . . . . .90 F1
**Bibb Way** IP1 . . . . . . . . . . .17 A5
**BICKNACRE** . . . . . . . . . . . .218 F2
**Bicknacre Rd** CM3 . . . . . . .218 F4
**Bignells Croft** CO4 . . . . . . .110 C4
**Bigods La** CM6 . . . . . . . . . .123 D4
**Bijou Cl** CO15 . . . . . . . . . .179 D6
**Bilberry End** CB1 . . . . . . . . . .5 C7
**Bilbister Way** IP3 . . . . . . . . .38 D7
**Billers Chase** CM1 . . . . . . .206 A7
**Billy's La** CO7 . . . . . . . . . . .58 D2
**Bilsdale Cl** CO4 . . . . . . . . .110 C4
**Bilton Rd** CM1 . . . . . . . . . .204 F1
**Binley Rd** CM2 . . . . . . . . . .205 F2
**BIRCH** . . . . . . . . . . . . . . . .161 A4
**BIRCHALL CORNER** . . . . . . .84 C2
**Birchalls** CM24 . . . . . . . . . .119 E8
**BIRCHANGER** . . . . . . . . . .119 E2
Birchanger CE Prim Sch
CM23 . . . . . . . . . . . . . . . . .119 D2
**Birchanger Ind Est**
CM23 . . . . . . . . . . . . . . . . .119 D2
**Birchanger La** CM23 . . . . .119 D2
**Birch Ave**
Great Bentley CO7. . . . . . . .166 E8
Harwich CO12 . . . . . . . . . . .91 B3
**Birch Bsns Ctr** CO2 . . . . . .161 A7
Birch CE Prim Sch
CO2 . . . . . . . . . . . . . . . . . .161 A4
**Birch Cl**
Braintree CM7. . . . . . . . . . .127 C2
Brightlingsea CO7 . . . . . . . .185 E6
Clacton-on-S CO15. . . . . . .188 C3
Witham CM8 . . . . . . . . . . . .177 A4

**Birch Dr**
Brantham CO11 . . . . . . . . .60 D1
Halstead CO9 . . . . . . . . .77 A2
**Birches Cotts** CO2 . . . . . . 161 A2
**Birches The** CO13 . . . . . . 170 E6
**Birches Wlk** CM7 . . . . . . 216 A2
**BIRCH GREEN** . . . . . . . 161 A2
**Birch Rd**
Birch CO2 . . . . . . . . . . 161 A5
Great Dunmow CM6 . . . . . . 123 B2
Layer de la H CO2 . . . . . . 161 E5
**Birch Rise** CM8 . . . . . . . 195 E6
**Birch St**
Birch CO2 . . . . . . . . . . 161 A3
Nayland CO6 . . . . . . . . . 56 A1
**Birchway** CO2 . . . . . . . . 161 A2
**Birchwood** CM23 . . . . . . 119 D2
**Birchwood Cl**
Tiptree CO5 . . . . . . . . . 179 F5
West Mersea CO5 . . . . . 201 D6
**Birchwood High Sch**
CM23 . . . . . . . . . . . . . 146 C8
**Birchwood Rd**
Cock Clarks CM3 . . . . . . . 219 F2
Dedham CO7 . . . . . . . . . 84 B3
Langham CO4 . . . . . . . . . 84 A4
**Birchwood Way** CO5 . . . . . 179 F5
**BIRDBROOK** . . . . . . . . . 28 B7
**Birdbrook Rd** CO9 . . . . . . 28 A3
**Birdbush Ave** CB11 . . . . . 43 C7
**Bird La** CO5 . . . . . . . . . . 179 E4
**Birds Cl** CB10 . . . . . . . . . 3 A3
**Birk Beck** CM1 . . . . . . . . 205 C5
**Birkdale Rise** CM3 . . . . . . 194 B4
**Birkfield Cl** IP2 . . . . . . . . 17 A4
**Birkfield Dr** IP2 . . . . . . . 16 F2
**Birkin Cl** CO5 . . . . . . . . . 179 C3
**Biscay Cl** CB9 . . . . . . . . . 9 C7
**Bishop Hall La** CM1 . . . . . 205 B4
**Bishop Mews** IP8 . . . . . . 16 B2
**Bishop Rd**
Chelmsford CM1 . . . . . . . 205 B3
Colchester CO2 . . . . . . . 135 A3
**Bishops Ave** CM7 . . . . . . 128 B3
**Bishop's Ave** CM23 . . . . . 145 F3
**Bishops' CE & RC Prim**
Sch The CM1 . . . . . . . . . 205 F6
**Bishop's Ct 8** CB9 . . . . . . 8 E8
**Bishops Court Gdns**
CM2 . . . . . . . . . . . . . . 205 E4
**Bishops Ct** CM8 . . . . . . . 195 F5
**Bishop's Ct 7** CB9 . . . . . . 8 E8
**Bishops Dr** CO16 . . . . . . 203 B6
**Bishopsgarth** IP3 . . . . . . 17 F4
**Bishop's Gdns** CO16 . . . . 203 A6
**Bishop's Hill** IP3 . . . . . . 17 E4
**Bishops La** CO5 . . . . . . . 179 C7
**Bishop's La** CO9 . . . . . . . 54 B3
**BISHOP'S PARK** . . . . . . 145 B6
**Bishops Park Coll**
CO16 . . . . . . . . . . . . . 188 A3
**Bishops Park Way**
CM23 . . . . . . . . . . . . . 145 B7
**BISHOP'S STORTFORD**
. . . . . . . . . . . . . . . . 145 D7
**Bishop's Stortford Bsns**
Ctr CM23 . . . . . . . . . . . 146 A6
**Bishop's Stortford Coll**
CM23 . . . . . . . . . . . . . 145 E7
**Bishop's Stortford High**
Sch The CM23 . . . . . . . . 145 F4
**Bishop's Stortford Mus***
CM23 . . . . . . . . . . . . . 146 A6
**Bishop's Stortford Sta**
CM23 . . . . . . . . . . . . . 146 A6
**Bishop William Ward CE**
Prim Sch The CO6 . . . . . . 109 B7
**Bisley Cl** CO16 . . . . . . . . 188 B6
**Bittern Cl**
Ipswich IP7 . . . . . . . . . . 16 E3
Kelvedon CO5 . . . . . . . . 158 D2
**Bixley Dr** IP4 . . . . . . . . . . 18 E5
**Bixley La** IP4 . . . . . . . . . . 18 D3
**Bixley Rd** IP3 . . . . . . . . . . 18 D3
**Black Arches** IP9 . . . . . . . 36 E8
**Blackberry Rd** CO3 . . . . . . 134 C4
**Black Boy La** CO11 . . . . . . 89 A4
**Black Bread Cl** CM7 . . . . . 128 D3
**Blackbrook Rd** CO6 . . . . . 109 C7
**Black Buoy Hill** CO7 . . . . . 164 B7
**Blackbush La** CB11 . . . . . 111 C1
**Black Chapel La** CM6 . . . . 151 E1
**Blackdown Ave** IP5 . . . . . 18 F6
**Blackfriars** CO10 . . . . . . . 33 D6
**Blackfriars Ct 8** IP4 . . . . . 17 D5
**BLACKHALL** . . . . . . . . . 64 B4
**BLACKHEATH** . . . . . . . . 163 B8
**Blackheath** CO2 . . . . . . . 163 A8
**Black Horse La** IP1 . . . . . . 17 C6
**Blackhouse La** CO10 . . . . . 34 C3
**Black La** CM7 . . . . . . . . . 71 F2
**Blacklands** CB11 . . . . . . . 43 C7
**Blackley La**
Braintree CM6 . . . . . . . . 153 F3
Great Notley CM77 . . . . . 154 A4
**Blacklock** CM2 . . . . . . . . 206 A3
**Blackman Way** CM8 . . . . . 177 A1
**BLACKMORE END** . . . . . . 74 B2
**BLACK NOTLEY** . . . . . . . 155 B5
**Blacksmith Cl** CM1 . . . . . 205 E8
**Blacksmiths Cl** CM23 . . . . 145 B5
**Blacksmith's Cnr** CO6 . . . . 109 B8
**Blacksmith's Cnr** CM7 . . . . 83 D4
**BLACKSMITH'S CORNER**
. . . . . . . . . . . . . . . . 36 C6
**Blacksmiths Hill** CO10 . . . . 11 B4

**Blacksmiths La**
Bulmer Tye CO10 . . . . . . . 32 F2
Shudy Camps CB21 . . . . . . 7 C6
Wickham Bishops CM8 . . . . 195 E5
**Blacksmith's La** CO12 . . . . 90 F2
**Blacksmith's La** CO14 . . . . 136 E7
**Blackthorn Cl**
Ipswich IP3 . . . . . . . . . . 18 E1
Writtle CM1 . . . . . . . . . 204 A1
**Blackthorn Rd**
Harwich CO12 . . . . . . . . . 90 F2
Witham CM8 . . . . . . . . . 176 F3
**Blackthorn Way** CM9 . . . . 180 A2
**Blackwater Cl** CO4 . . . . . . 110 E1
**Blackwater Cl**
Chelmsford CM1 . . . . . . . 205 C6
Heybridge Basin CM9 . . . . 210 E3
**Blackwater Cotts**
CM77 . . . . . . . . . . . . . 129 D3
**Blackwater Dr** CO5 . . . . . . 201 A6
**Blackwater La** CM6 . . . . . . 195 B8
**Blackwater Way** CM7 . . . . . 128 A4
**Blackwell Dr** CM7 . . . . . . . 127 C4
**Bladen Dr** IP4 . . . . . . . . . . 18 F5
**Bladon Cl**
Braintree CM7 . . . . . . . . 127 E2
Tiptree CO5 . . . . . . . . . . 179 E5
**Blaine Dr** CO13 . . . . . . . . 170 F7
**Blair Cl**
Bishop's Stortford
CM23 . . . . . . . . . . . . . 145 C7
Rushmere St A IP4 . . . . . . 18 E5
**Blair Par** CB9 . . . . . . . . . . 8 E8
**Blake Cl** CO11 . . . . . . . . . 86 B4
**Blake Dr**
Braintree CM7 . . . . . . . . 128 C4
Clacton-on-S CO16 . . . . . 188 D6
**BLAKE END** . . . . . . . . . . 126 A2
**Blake Rd** CM8 . . . . . . . . . 176 F5
**Blamsters Cres** CO9 . . . . . . 103 D8
**Blamsters Rise** CM6 . . . . . . 97 A2
**Blanchard Cl** CO13 . . . . . . 170 A7
**Blanche St** IP4 . . . . . . . . . 17 D6
**Blandford Rd** IP3 . . . . . . . . 18 B3
**Blaxhall Ct 17** CB9 . . . . . . . 8 E7
**Blenheim Cl**
Bicknacre CM3 . . . . . . . . 218 F2
Braintree CM7 . . . . . . . . 127 E7
Brantham CO11 . . . . . . . 60 D1
**Blenheim Ct**
Bishop's Stortford
CM23 . . . . . . . . . . . . . 145 C7
Clacton-on-S CO15 . . . . . 188 D2
4 Ipswich IP1 . . . . . . . . . 17 A7
**Blenheim Dr** CO2 . . . . . . . 163 A8
**Blenheim Rd**
Clacton-on-S CO15 . . . . . 188 D2
Ipswich IP1 . . . . . . . . . . 17 A7
**Blenheim Way** CO16 . . . . . 179 F5
**Blickling Cl** IP2 . . . . . . . . . 17 A2
**Blickling Rd** CM77 . . . . . . . 154 C8
**Blind La**
Easthorpe CO2 . . . . . . . . 160 B4
Eight Ash G CO6 . . . . . . . 134 A8
Goldhanger CM9 . . . . . . . 211 C2
Howe Green CM2 . . . . . . 217 F4
Tolleshunt Knights CM9 . . 180 B1
**Bliss Cl** CM8 . . . . . . . . . . 194 F7
**Blithe Ct** CO7 . . . . . . . . . 164 B8
**Blofield Rd** IP11 . . . . . . . . 221 A4
**Blois Meadows Bsns Ctr**
CB9 . . . . . . . . . . . . . . . 27 C8
**Blois Rd**
Steeple Bumpstead
CB9 . . . . . . . . . . . . . . . 27 D8
Sturmer CB9 . . . . . . . . . . 9 F1
**Bloom Cl** CO13 . . . . . . . . 170 F6
**Bloomfield Ave** CO13 . . . . . 170 E7
**Bloomfield Ct** CO10 . . . . . 12 B7
**Bloomfield St** IP4 . . . . . . . 18 B6
**Blooms Hall La** CO10 . . . . . 2 F8
**Blossom Mews** CO5 . . . . . 201 D6
**Blott Rise** CM8 . . . . . . . . 194 F8
**Bloyers Mews** CO1 . . . . . . 109 F1
**Bluebell Ave** CO16 . . . . . . 188 C4
**Bluebell Cl**
Ipswich IP2 . . . . . . . . . . 16 E4
Witham CM8 . . . . . . . . . 176 E3
**Bluebell Gn 5** CM1 . . . . . . 205 E7
**Bluebell Way** CO4 . . . . . . 109 C2
**Bluebridge Cotts** CM7 . . . . 73 A1
**Bluebridge Ind Est**
CO9 . . . . . . . . . . . . . . . 77 B1
**Bluegate La** IP9 . . . . . . . . 60 B7
**Bluehouse Ave** CO16 . . . . . 188 A4
**Blue Mill La** CM9 . . . . . . . 208 E4
**Blue Mills Hill** CM8 . . . . . . 195 B3
**Blue Rd** CO5 . . . . . . . . . . 179 C5
**Bluestem Rd** IP3 . . . . . . . . 38 E8
**Blundens The** CO6 . . . . . . . 56 C6
**Blunt's Hall Dr** CM8 . . . . . . 176 D1
**Blunts Hall Rd** CM8 . . . . . . 176 D1
**Blyford Rd** CO4 . . . . . . . . 188 A4
**Blyford Way** IP11 . . . . . . . 221 A4
**Blyth Cl** IP7 . . . . . . . . . . . 17 A1
**Blyth Ct** CB11 . . . . . . . . . 43 E8
**Blythe La** CO7 . . . . . . . . . 164 B8
**Blyth's Mdw** CM7 . . . . . . . 127 F3
**Blythswood Gdns**
CM24 . . . . . . . . . . . . . 119 D6
**Boadicea Cotts** CO8 . . . . . . 79 F6
**Boadicea Way** CO2 . . . . . . 135 C4
**Boars Tye Rd** CM8 . . . . . . 156 C2
**Boat Ho The** CO7 . . . . . . . 185 E5
**Boat House Mews The**
CO10 . . . . . . . . . . . . . 12 B7
**Boatman Cl** IP8 . . . . . . . . 36 E8

**Bobbits La** IP9 . . . . . . . . . 36 F8
**Bobbits Way** CO7 . . . . . . . 164 C8
**Bober Ct** CO2 . . . . . . . . . 163 B7
**Bob Russell Ho** CO2 . . . . . . 136 A5
**BOCKING** . . . . . . . . . . . . 127 F8
**BOCKING CHURCHSTREET**
. . . . . . . . . . . . . . . . 127 F8
**Bocking Church Street**
Prim Sch CM7 . . . . . . . . 127 F8
**Bocking End** CM7 . . . . . . . 127 F3
**Bocking Pl** CM7 . . . . . . . . 127 F3
**BOCKING'S ELM** . . . . . . . 188 B5
**Bockings Elm Par**
CO16 . . . . . . . . . . . . . 188 B5
**Bocking's Gr** CO16 . . . . . . 188 B5
**Bocking Windmill*** . . . . . . 127 F7
**Bodiam Cl** IP3 . . . . . . . . . 18 D4
**Bodiam Rd** IP3 . . . . . . . . . 18 D4
**Bodiam Wlk 3** CB9 . . . . . . 8 E8
**Bodmin Rd** CM1 . . . . . . . . 205 D5
**Bogmoor Rd** SG8 . . . . . . . 39 A8
**Bohun Cl** CM3 . . . . . . . . . 172 F7
**Bois Field Terr** CO9 . . . . . . 76 E2
**Bois Hall Gdns** CO9 . . . . . . 76 F3
**Boley Dr** CO15 . . . . . . . . . 189 A4
**Boleyns Ave** CM7 . . . . . . . 127 F6
**Boleyn Way**
Boreham CM3 . . . . . . . . 192 F1
Clacton-on-S CO15 . . . . . 203 F8
Haverhill CB9 . . . . . . . . . 8 D7
**Bolingbroke Cl** CM3 . . . . . . 173 F7
**Bolsin Dr** CO4 . . . . . . . . . 109 E4
**Bolton La** IP4 . . . . . . . . . . 17 D6
**Bond St**
Chelmsford CM2 . . . . . . . 205 C2
Ipswich IP4 . . . . . . . . . . 17 D5
**Bonham Cl** CO15 . . . . . . . 189 A5
**Bonington Chase**
CM1 . . . . . . . . . . . . . . 205 E6
**Bonneting La** CM3 . . . . . . . 92 B8
**Bonnington Rd** IP3 . . . . . . 17 F1
**Bonny Cres** IP3 . . . . . . . . . 38 C8
**Boone Pl** CM3 . . . . . . . . . 177 A2
**Boons Cl** CM3 . . . . . . . . . 206 E8
**BOOSE'S GREEN** . . . . . . . 77 F2
**Booth Ave** CO4 . . . . . . . . 136 C8
**Borda Cl** CM3 . . . . . . . . . 206 F8
**BOREHAM** . . . . . . . . . . . 206 E8
**Borehamgate** CO10 . . . . . . 33 F7
**Boreham Ind Est** CM3 . . . . 192 F2
**Boreham Rd** CM3 . . . . . . . 10 B2
**Boreham Prim Sch**
CM3 . . . . . . . . . . . . . . 206 F8
**Boreham Rd**
Great Leighs CM3 . . . . . . 174 B7
Little Waltham CM3 . . . . . 174 B2
**BORLEY** . . . . . . . . . . . . . 14 F3
**BORLEY GREEN** . . . . . . . . 14 D2
**Borley Rd** CO10 . . . . . . . . 15 B4
**Borough La** CB11 . . . . . . . 43 D8
**Borradale Ct** IP4 . . . . . . . . 27 B6
**Borrowdale Ave** IP4 . . . . . 17 E8
**Boscawen Gdns** CM7 . . . . . 128 C4
**Boss Hall Bsns Pk** IP1 . . . . 16 E7
**Boss Hall Rd** IP1 . . . . . . . . 16 E7
**Bostock Rd** IP2 . . . . . . . . . 17 C1
**Boston Rd** IP4 . . . . . . . . . 17 F7
**Boswells Dr** CM2 . . . . . . . 205 C2
**Boswells Sch The**
CM1 . . . . . . . . . . . . . . 205 D6
**Botanical Ave** CM1 . . . . . . 187 A5
**Botany Dr** CM7 . . . . . . . . 128 D3
**Botany La** CO16 . . . . . . . . 168 B5
**Bouchers Mead** CM1 . . . . . 205 F7
**Bouchiers Barn Visitors**
Ctr* CO5 . . . . . . . . . . . 130 D7
**Bouchiers Pl** CO5 . . . . . . . 159 D2
**Boudicca Mews 6**
CM2 . . . . . . . . . . . . . . 205 B1
**Boudicca Wlk** CO7 . . . . . . 137 C3
**Boulton Cotts** CM9 . . . . . . 210 B5
**Boundary Cl** CM23 . . . . . . 146 A5
**Boundary Rd**
Bishop's Stortford
CM23 . . . . . . . . . . . . . 146 A5
Colchester CO4 . . . . . . . 136 F4
Sturmer CB9 . . . . . . . . . . 9 D5
Wivenhoe CO7 . . . . . . . . 137 A4
**Bounderby Gr** CM1 . . . . . . 204 E7
**Bounstead Hill** CO2 . . . . . . 162 C5
**Bounstead Rd** CO2 . . . . . . 162 D7
**Bourchier Ave** CM7 . . . . . . 128 D5
**Bourchier Way** CO9 . . . . . . 103 D8
**Bournebridge Hill**
CO9 . . . . . . . . . . . . . . 103 B6
**Bourne Cl** CO9 . . . . . . . . . 103 D8
**Bourne Ct**
Braintree CM7 . . . . . . . . 128 D1
Colchester CO2 . . . . . . . 136 A4
**Bourne Hill** IP2 . . . . . . . . . 37 B7
**Bourne Mill*** CM2 . . . . . . . 136 B4
**Bournemouth Rd**
CO15 . . . . . . . . . . . . . 189 F6
**Bourne Park Residential**
Pk IP2 . . . . . . . . . . . . . 37 B7
**Bourne Rd**
Colchester CO2 . . . . . . . 136 A4
Haverhill CB9 . . . . . . . . . 8 E4
West Bergholt CO6 . . . . . 108 E2
**Bourne Terr** IP2 . . . . . . . . 37 B7
**Bourne The** CM23 . . . . . . . 146 A8
**Bouverie Rd** CM7 . . . . . . . 216 B8
**Bovills Way** CO16 . . . . . . . 168 C1
**Bovingdon Rd** CM7 . . . . . . 101 D2

**Bowdens La** CO6 . . . . . . . . 80 F7
**Bower Gdns** CM9 . . . . . . . 209 F3
**Bower Hall Dr** CB9 . . . . . . . 27 B6
**Bower Hall La** CO5 . . . . . . 183 F1
**Bower Hall La** CM8 . . . . . . 156 E3
**Bowes Rd** CO7 . . . . . . . . . 137 D1
**Bowland Dr** IP2 . . . . . . . . 16 C1
**Bowling Cl 14** CM23 . . . . . 145 F6
**Bowling Green Ct**
IP11 . . . . . . . . . . . . . . 221 E4
**Bowmans Pk** CO9 . . . . . . . 51 E4
**Bowsers La** CB10 . . . . . . . 5 C3
**Bowthorpe Cl** IP1 . . . . . . . 17 B7
**Boxford Ct**
Felixstowe IP11 . . . . . . . 221 A4
Haverhill CB9 . . . . . . . . . 8 E7
**Boxhouse La** CO7 . . . . . . . 84 C5
**Box Mill La** CO9 . . . . . . . . 76 E3
**BOXTED** . . . . . . . . . . . . . 82 F7
**Boxted Ave** CO16 . . . . . . . 188 C4
**Boxted Church Rd** CO6 . . . . 82 C5
**BOXTED CROSS** . . . . . . . . 83 B5
**Boxted Rd**
Colchester CO4 . . . . . . . 109 E6
Great Horkesley CO6 . . . . 82 C3
**Boxted St Peter's CE Prim**
Sch CO4 . . . . . . . . . . . 82 F7
**Boxted Straight Rd**
CO4 . . . . . . . . . . . . . . 83 A5
**Boyd Cl 1** CM8 . . . . . . . . 146 E8
**Boydell's Dairy Farm***
CM7 . . . . . . . . . . . . . . 100 E8
**Boydin Cl** CM6 . . . . . . . . . 194 E8
**Boydlands** IP9 . . . . . . . . . 35 A1
**Boyes Croft** CM6 . . . . . . . 123 D1
**Boyles Ct** CO2 . . . . . . . . . 163 B7
**Boyne Dr** CM1 . . . . . . . . . 205 D6
**BOYTON END** . . . . . . . . . 70 C5
**Boyton Rd** IP3 . . . . . . . . . 18 B1
**Boytons Acre** CB11 . . . . . . 43 D8
**Boyton's La** CB10 . . . . . . . 26 A1
**Boyton Vineyard***
CO10 . . . . . . . . . . . . . 10 D5
**Brackenbury Cl** IP1 . . . . . . 17 B8
**Brackenden Dr** CM1 . . . . . 205 D7
**Brackenhayes Cl** IP2 . . . . . 17 B3
**Brackens The** CO4 . . . . . . . 110 B3
**Bracken Way** CO15 . . . . . . 163 B2
**Brackley Cl** IP11 . . . . . . . . 221 C5
**Bracks La** CO6 . . . . . . . . . 131 F3
**Bradbrook Cotts** CO6 . . . . . 108 F4
**Bradbury Dr** CM7 . . . . . . . 127 D3
**Braddy Ct** CO5 . . . . . . . . 158 C2
**BRADFIELD** . . . . . . . . . . . 87 F2
**BRADFIELD HEATH** . . . . . . 114 D8
**Bradfield Prim Sch**
CO11 . . . . . . . . . . . . . 86 B7
**Bradfield Rd** CO11 . . . . . . 115 B7
**Bradford Dr** CO4 . . . . . . . 109 E2
**Bradfords Ct** CM7 . . . . . . . 128 A4
**Bradford St**
Braintree CM7 . . . . . . . . 128 A4
Chelmsford CM2 . . . . . . . 205 A1
**Brading Ave** CO15 . . . . . . 189 A7
**Bradley Cl** CM6 . . . . . . . . 123 C2
**Bradley Comm** CM3 . . . . . 119 C3
**Bradley Mews 1** CB10 . . . . 22 F2
**Bradley St 6** IP2 . . . . . . . 17 C4
**BRADWELL** . . . . . . . . . . . 129 D2
**Bradwell Ct** CM77 . . . . . . . 155 C8
**BRADWELL WATERSIDE**
. . . . . . . . . . . . . . . . 214 F4
**Braeburn Dr** CM9 . . . . . . . 210 A1
**Braemar Ave** CM3 . . . . . . 216 B8
**Braemore Cl** CO4 . . . . . . . 110 D3
**Braganza Way** CM2 . . . . . . 205 F8
**Braggon's Hill** IP29 . . . . . . 2 B8
**Braiding Cres** CM7 . . . . . . 128 C3
**Brain Rd** CM8 . . . . . . . . . 176 E3
**BRAINTREE** . . . . . . . . . . . 128 B5
**Braintree Cnr** CO7 . . . . . . . 75 F6
**Braintree Coll** CM7 . . . . . . 128 A5
**Braintree Ent Ctr**
CM7 . . . . . . . . . . . . . . 128 D5
**Braintree Foyer The 7**
CM7 . . . . . . . . . . . . . . 128 F2
**Braintree Mus & Heritage**
Ctr* CM7 . . . . . . . . . . . 127 F3
**Braintree Rd**
Cressing CM77 . . . . . . . . 155 E7
Felsted CM6 . . . . . . . . . 152 C6
Gosfield CO9 . . . . . . . . . 102 E5
Great Bardfield CM7 . . . . 72 B1
Shalford CM7 . . . . . . . . . 100 E6
Terling CM3 . . . . . . . . . 174 E5
Wethersfield CM7 . . . . . . 73 D2
Witham CM8 . . . . . . . . . 176 F4
**Braintree Sta** CM7 . . . . . . 128 A2
**Braintree Town FC**
CM7 . . . . . . . . . . . . . . 128 C2
**Brain Valley Ave**
CM7 . . . . . . . . . . . . . . 155 B6
**BRAISWICK** . . . . . . . . . . . 109 B2
**Braiswick La** CO4 . . . . . . . 109 D4
**Braiswick Pl** CO4 . . . . . . . 109 C3
**Braiswick** CO4 . . . . . . . . . 109 D2
**Bramble Ct** CM7 . . . . . . . . 176 E4
**Bramble Ct** CM6 . . . . . . . . 151 F8
**Bramble Dr** IP3 . . . . . . . . 18 E1
**Bramble La** CM6 . . . . . . . . 151 F8
**Bramble Rd** CM7 . . . . . . . 176 E4
**Brambles** CO14 . . . . . . . . 171 B7
**Brambles The**
Bishop's Stortford
CM23 . . . . . . . . . . . . . 145 C6

**Brambles The** continued
Colchester CM7 . . . . . . . 127 E3
Colchester CO3 . . . . . . . 134 F3
**Bramble Tye** CO12 . . . . . . 90 D1
**Bramblewood 1** IP8 . . . . . . 16 C2
**Bramford La** . . . . . . . . . . 16 F8
**Bramford Rd** IP1 . . . . . . . . 16 E8
**Bramhall Cl** IP2 . . . . . . . . 16 D1
**Bramley Chase** IP4 . . . . . . 18 B7
**Bramley Cl**
Alresford CO7 . . . . . . . . 165 B8
Braintree CM7 . . . . . . . . 128 A1
Colchester CO3 . . . . . . . 135 B7
**Bramley Cotts** CM3 . . . . . . 175 B2
**Bramley Ct** CM2 . . . . . . . . 216 D7
**Bramley Pl** CM2 . . . . . . . . 216 D7
**Bramley Rd** CB9 . . . . . . . . 8 D7
**Bramleys The** CO6 . . . . . . 131 A3
**Bramston Cl** CM2 . . . . . . . 216 F8
**Bramston Gn** CM8 . . . . . . 176 F4
**Bramston Wlk** CM8 . . . . . . 176 F4
**Bramwoods Rd** CM2 . . . . . 216 E8
**Brancaster Dr** CM77 . . . . . 154 C6
**Brand Ct** CM7 . . . . . . . . . 127 F2
**Brand Dr** CO5 . . . . . . . . . 163 B3
**Brandon Rd**
Braintree CM7 . . . . . . . . 127 D2
Felixstowe IP11 . . . . . . . 221 A4
**Brands Cl** CO10 . . . . . . . . 34 C5
**BRAN END** . . . . . . . . . . . 124 D7
**Bran End Fields** CM6 . . . . . 124 D7
**Bransby Gdns** IP4 . . . . . . . 18 A5
**Branscombe Cl** CO13 . . . . . 170 E5
**Branston Cl**
Clacton-on-S, Jaywick
CO15 . . . . . . . . . . . . . 203 G7
Clacton-on-S, Rush Green
CO16 . . . . . . . . . . . . . 188 C4
**Branston Rd** CO15 . . . . . . 188 D3
**BRANTHAM** . . . . . . . . . . . 60 E1
**Brantham Hill** CO11 . . . . . . 86 C8
**Brantham Mill Ind Est**
CO11 . . . . . . . . . . . . . 86 B7
**Braxted La**
Great Braxted CM8 . . . . . 178 C1
Great Totham CM8,
CM9 . . . . . . . . . . . . . . 196 D8
**Braxted Park Rd**
Rivenhall End CM8 . . . . . . 177 E4
Tiptree CO5 . . . . . . . . . . 178 D2
**Braxted Rd** CM8 . . . . . . . 196 A6
**Braybrooke Gdns**
CB11 . . . . . . . . . . . . . 43 D8
**Braziers Cl** CM2 . . . . . . . . 216 C3
**Braziers Quay** CM23 . . . . . 146 A6
**Brazier's Wood Rd** IP3 . . . . 38 B8
**Breach La** CM6 . . . . . . . . . 97 B2
**Bream Ct** CO4 . . . . . . . . . 110 F1
**Brecon Ct** IP2 . . . . . . . . . 17 B2
**Bredfield Cl** IP11 . . . . . . . 221 B5
**Bree Ave** CO6 . . . . . . . . . 132 E3
**Breeze Cl** CO15 . . . . . . . . 179 D4
**Brendon Dr**
Halstead CO9 . . . . . . . . 103 F8
Rushmere St A IP5 . . . . . 18 F6
**Brendon Pl** CM1 . . . . . . . . 204 E1
**Brent Cl**
Frinton-on-S CO13 . . . . . 170 F7
Witham CM8 . . . . . . . . . 176 E2
**Brent Rd** CM7 . . . . . . . . . 72 B6
**BRENT PELHAM** . . . . . . . . 64 B2
**Brentwood Rd** CO15 . . . . . 189 C6
**Brett Cl** IP1 . . . . . . . . . . . 16 E8
**Bretten Cl** CO16 . . . . . . . . 188 A4
**Brettenham Cres** IP4 . . . . . 17 D8
**Bretts Cotts** CO3 . . . . . . . 178 F3
**Brewers Cl** CM23 . . . . . . . 145 C5
**BREWER'S END** . . . . . . . . 148 B7
**Brewery Dr** CO9 . . . . . . . . 103 E8
**Brewery Fields** CM2 . . . . . 217 A5
**Brewery La** CM24 . . . . . . . 119 E7
**Brewery Tower The 2**
CO1 . . . . . . . . . . . . . . 136 A2
**Brewery Yd** CM24 . . . . . . . 119 E2
**Brewster Ct** CO12 . . . . . . . 103 F8
**Brewsters Cl** CO12 . . . . . . 91 D5
**Breydon Way** IP3 . . . . . . . 38 D7
**Brian Bishop Cl** CO14 . . . . 171 B8
**Brian Cl** CM2 . . . . . . . . . . 216 B6
**Briardale Ave** CO13 . . . . . . 90 F3
**Briarfields** CM22 . . . . . . . 148 F8
**Briarhayes Cl** IP2 . . . . . . . 17 B3
**Briar Rd** CO7 . . . . . . . . . . 112 A4
**Briarsford Ind Est**
CM8 . . . . . . . . . . . . . . 177 B1
**Briarswood** CM1 . . . . . . . 205 D7
**Briarwood Ave** CO15 . . . . . 188 D6
**Briarwood End** CO4 . . . . . . 110 B3
**Brices Way** CO10 . . . . . . . 2 B5
**Brickbarns** CM3 . . . . . . . . 173 F7
**Brickburn Cl** CM6 . . . . . . . 152 C4
**Brick Cotts** IP9 . . . . . . . . . 62 F4
**Brick End Villas** CM6 . . . . . 121 E8
**Brick End** CM1 . . . . . . . . . 121 D7
**Brickhouse Cl** IP2 . . . . . . . 201 B7
**BRICK HOUSE END** . . . . . . 92 B5
**Brick House La** CM3 . . . . . 192 E1
**Brickhouse Rd** CO6 . . . . . . 78 A3
**Brick House Rd** CM9 . . . . . 197 B3
**Brick Kiln Cl** CO6 . . . . . . . 131 A3
**BRICKKILN GREEN** . . . . . . 74 A4
**Brick Kiln La**
Great Horkesley CO6 . . . . 109 C7
Rickling Green CB11 . . . . . 66 D1

**Brick Kiln La** *continued*
Stebbing CM6 .......... 124 D7
Thorrington CO7 ........ 165 E5
**Brick Kiln Rd**
Chelmsford CM2 ........ 217 C7
Colchester CO1 .......... 109 E1
Harkstead IP9 .............. 63 C5
**Brick Kiln Way** CM7.... 128 D2
**Brickmakers La** CO4 ..... 109 F2
**Brickman's Hill** CO11 .... 87 D3
**Brick Row** SG8 ............ 19 D3
**Brickspring La** CM9..... 196 D7
**Brick St** CO3 .............. 108 B1
**Brickwall Ct** CO6 ......... 105 B6
**Brickwall Farm** CM77 ... 129 C6
Bridewell Ind Est CO10... 12 C8
Bridewell St CO10 ......... 12 C8
Bridgebrook Ct CO4 ..... 110 D1
**Bridge Cottage*** CO7....85 D7
**Bridge Cotts**
Cavendish CO10 .......... 1 C2
Ridgewell CO9 ............ 29 B7
**Bridge Ct** CM3 .......... 172 F2
**Bridge Ct**
Maldon CM9............ 210 A3
Witham CM8 ............. 176 F1
**BRIDGE END** ............. 72 B3
**Bridge End** CB11 .......... 43 A2
**Bridge End La** CM77 ..... 154 C8
**Bridgefield Cl** CO4..... 136 C7
**Bridge Foot** CO10........ 33 D6
**Bridgeford Ho** 13
CM23 ................... 145 F6
**BRIDGE GREEN** .......... 41 B6
**Bridge Hall Rd** CM77... 129 C3
**Bridge Hill** CO6.......... 107 C7
**Bridge Mdw** CO5 ....... 158 D3
**Bridge Pl** CO11 ........... 86 C7
**Bridge Rd** IP11.......... 221 E5
**Bridge St**
Bishop's Stortford
CM23 ................... 145 F7
Bures CO8 ............... 55 F1
Coggeshall CO6 ......... 130 F1
Finchingfield CM7 ....... 72 C6
Great Bardfield CM7 ..... 72 C2
Great Yeldham CO9 ...... 30 A1
Halstead CO9 ........... 76 E2
Ipswich IP1 ............. 17 C4
Saffron Walden CB10.... 22 D2
Witham CM8 ............. 176 F1
Writtle CM1 ............. 204 C1
**Bridge Terr**
Maldon CM9............ 210 A5
1 Sudbury CO10 ........ 33 F8
**Bridge View** IP3 ......... 17 F1
**Bridgwater Rd** IP2....... 16 D2
**Bridlewalk** CO3.......... 134 D6
**Bridleway The** CO3 ..... 108 A1
**Bridport Ave** IP3 ......... 18 D3
**Bridport Rd** CM1 ....... 205 D5
**Bridport Way** CM7 ..... 128 D4
**Brierley Ave** CO5 ....... 201 E7
**Brierley Paddocks**
CO5 ..................... 201 E7
**Bright Cl** CO16 .......... 188 D6
**BRIGHTLINGSEA** ....... 185 D6
**Brightlingsea Ct** CO7...136 F4
**Brightlingsea Inf Sch**
CO7 ..................... 185 E6
**Brightlingsea Jun Sch**
CO7 ..................... 185 E6
**Brightlingsea Mus**
CO7 ..................... 185 F6
**Brightlingsea Rd**
Thorrington CO7 ........ 165 E3
Wivenhoe CO7 .......... 137 C4
**Brighton Rd** CO15 ...... 189 F6
**Bright Rd** CM6........... 151 F6
**Brightside** CO13 ........ 170 E7
**Brightwell Cl** IP2 ........ 221 A4
**Brimstone Ct** CM7 ...... 154 E8
**Brimstone Rd** IP8 ........ 36 E8
**Brindley Rd** CO15 ....... 189 B8
**Bringey The** CM2 ....... 217 A6
**Brinkley Cres** CO4 ...... 110 D2
**Brinkley Grove Prim Sch**
CO4 ..................... 110 B5
**Brinkley Grove Rd**
CO4 ..................... 110 A5
**Brinkley La** CO4 ......... 110 B5
**Brinkley Pl** CO4 .......... 109 F3
**Brisbane Rd** IP4........... 18 B8
**Brisbane Way** CO2...... 136 A1
**Brise Cl** CM7 ............. 128 A1
**Bristol Cl** CM8........... 156 E3
**Bristol Hill** IP9 ............ 91 B8
**Bristol Ho** IP11.......... 221 D2
**Bristol Rd**
Colchester CO1 .......... 136 A8
Ipswich IP4 ............... 18 A7
**Bristowe Ave** CM2 ...... 217 A6
**Britannia Cres** CO7 ..... 137 B1
**Britannia Ct** CO7 ........ 137 B1
**Britannia Ho** IP4 ......... 18 B5
**Britannia Pl** 3 CM23 ... 145 E5
**Britannia Rd** IP4 ........ 18 B6
**Britric Cl** CM6............ 151 F6
**Brittania Prim Sch** IP4.. 18 B5
**Brittany Way** CO2....... 136 B4
**Britten Cl** CO4........... 136 C6
**Britten Cres**
Great Baddow CM2 ...... 216 F8
Witham CM8 ............. 194 F4
**Brixham Cl** CO15 ....... 203 I8

**Brixton La** CB11, CM23..... 93 B6
**Broadcroft Cres** CB9 ....... 8 F8
**Broadfield** CB11 .......... 118 F2
**Broadfield Rd** CM22...... 148 E7
**Broadfields** CO7 ......... 137 C3
**BROAD GREEN**
Chrishall .................. 19 C4
Coggeshall................ 131 F3
Steeple Bumpstead ....... 27 E8
**Broad La** CO6 ............. 82 C2
**Broadlands** CO13 ........ 170 E3
**Broadlands Way**
Colchester CO4 .......... 110 B1
Rushmere St A IP4 ........ 18 F5
**Broadleaf Ave** CM8...... 195 B2
**Broadmead Rd** CO4..... 110 E1
**Broadmere Cl** CO15..... 189 E7
**Broadmere Rd** IP1....... 16 E8
**Broad Oakes Cl** CB10 .... 44 E2
**Broadoaks Cres** CM7 ... 128 D4
**Broad Oaks Pk** CO4 .... 110 E3
**Broad Oke** IP1 ........... 17 B6
**Broad Rd**
Braintree CM7............ 128 B7
Wickham St P CO9 ....... 53 B8
**BROAD'S GREEN** ........ 190 E5
**Broad St** CB9 ............... 8 F8
**BROAD STREET GREEN** ... 210 C7
**Broad Street Green Rd**
CM9 ................... 210 C7
**Broadstrood** CO16 ...... 187 B5
**Broadwater Gdns** IP9.... 91 A8
**Broadway**
Clacton-on-S CO15...... 203 G7
Glemsford CO10 ........... 2 B5
Silver End CM8 .......... 156 D4
**Broadway Ct** CM6....... 154 D5
**Broadway The** CM6 ..... 123 F3
**Brockenhurst Ct** CO4 .... 110 E1
**Brockenhurst Way**
CM3 ................... 218 F1
**Brockham Cl** CO16...... 188 B6
**Brockley Cres** IP1........ 16 D8
**Brockley Rd** CM2 ........ 205 D2
**Brocks Mead** CM6 ...... 122 E7
**Brockwell La** CO5 ....... 158 C1
**Brograve Cl** CM2 ........ 216 D3
**BROKE HALL** ............. 18 E4
**Broke Hall Com Prim Sch**
IP4........................ 18 E5
**Broke Hall Gdns** IP3...... 18 E4
**Broke Hall Ho** IP3 ........ 18 D3
**Broman's La** CO5 ....... 185 A2
**Bromfield** CB11 ........... 43 E8
**Bromley Cl**
Clacton-on-S CO16...... 188 D4
Ipswich IP2 ............... 17 C3
**Bromley Cnr** CO11....... 86 A2
**BROMLEY CROSS** ....... 112 C3
**Bromley Cross** CO7 ..... 112 B3
**Bromley Hts** CO4 ....... 136 F8
**Bromley La** CB11 ......... 43 B1
**Bromley Rd**
Colchester CO4, CO11 ... 111 C2
Elmstead Market CO7.... 138 B5
Frating Green CO7....... 139 A4
Lawford CO11 ............ 86 B2
**Brompton Gdns** CM9... 220 E8
**Bronte Cl** CM7 ........... 155 A8
**Bronte Rd** CM8 .......... 176 F5
**Bronze Ct** CO9............ 76 F1
**Brookbank** CO4 ......... 216 E8
**Brook Cl**
Braintree CM7............ 127 C2
Great Totham CM9 ....... 196 A3
Tiptree CO5 .............. 179 F3
Woodham Walter CM9... 208 D2
**Brook Cotts**
Boxted CO4 ............... 82 E5
Great Horkesley CO7 .... 137 C5
Stansted Mountfitchet
CM24 ................... 119 E5
Tolleshunt D'arcy CM9 ... 198 C2
**Brookdale Ct** 16 CO1... 136 A6
**Brooke Ave** CB10 ........ 22 E2
**Brooke Gdns** CM23 ..... 146 C7
**BROOKEND** ............. 124 D2
**Brook End Rd** CM2 ...... 206 B2
**Brook End Rd N** CM2 ... 206 A4
**Brook End Rd S** CM2.... 206 B3
**Brookes Nature Reserve***
CM77 .................... 103 E2
**Brooke Sq** CM9 ......... 210 A1
**Brook Farm Cl**
Bishop's Stortford
CM23 ................... 145 C3
Halstead CO9............. 77 A1
**Brook Farm La** IP9 ....... 62 D6
**Brookfield Rd** IP1......... 16 F8
**Brookfields** CM6 ........ 124 D7
**Brook Hall Rd** CO5...... 164 B5
**Brookhampton St** CB10 ... 3 A5
**Brook Hill**
Little Waltham CM3 ...... 191 B6
North End CM6........... 151 F1
**Brookhigh Way** IP4 ..... 18 F4
**Brookhouse Bsns Pk**
IP2........................ 16 F6
**Brookhouse Pl** 3
CM23 ................... 145 F8
**Brookhouse Rd** CO6 .... 132 B8
**Brookhurst** CM2 ........ 205 D3

**Brook La**
Chelmsford CM2 ........ 206 B8
Felixstowe IP11.......... 221 F5
Galleywood CM2 ........ 216 E3
**Brookland** CO5 .......... 179 C4
**Brooklands**
Clacton-on-S CO15...... 203 E6
Colchester CO1 .......... 136 B7
**Brooklands Gdns**
CO15 ................... 203 E6
**Brooklands Prim Sch**
CO15 .................... 86 D8
**Brooklands Rise** CO11 ... 86 D8
**Brooklands Rd** CO11 .... 86 D8
**Brooklands Wlk** CM23 ... 145 C3
**Brook Lo** CO3 ........... 135 C6
**Brooklyn Ct** CO12........ 91 C3
**Brooklyn Mews** CO12 ... 91 C3
**Brooklyn Rd** CO12....... 91 C3
**Brook Mdw** CO5 .......... 51 D1
**Brook Mdws** CO5 ....... 179 C4
**Brook Mead** CM8 ....... 190 E8
**Brook Pl** CO9 ............. 76 E1
**Brook Rd**
Aldham CO6.............. 133 B7
Great Tey CO6 ........... 132 C7
Stansted Mountfitchet
CM24 ................... 119 E6
Tiptree CO5 .............. 179 F3
Tolleshunt Knights CM9,
CO5 ..................... 180 A2
**Brook Retail Pk** CO16 ... 188 E7
**Brook Service Rd** CB9 ..... 8 E7
**Brooks Hall Rd** IP1 ....... 17 A7
**Brookside** CO2.......... 136 B4
**Brooksies** CB11........... 40 F6
**Brooks Malting** 3
CO11 ..................... 86 D4
**Brook St**
Chelmsford CM1 ........ 205 B3
Colchester CO1 .......... 136 B7
Colne Engaine CO6 ....... 77 F1
Dedham CO7 ............. 84 F7
Glemsford CO10 .......... 2 B6
Great Bardfield CM7 ..... 72 B2
Great Bromley CO7 ..... 112 E1
Little Dunmow CM6 ..... 151 D6
Manningtree CO11....... 86 D4
Wivenhoe CO7 .......... 164 C8
**BROOK STREET** ........... 2 B2
**Brook Street Bsns Ctr**
CO1 ..................... 136 B6
**Brook Terr** CO9 ........... 51 E1
**Brook Vale** CO16........ 187 B3
**Brookview** IP2 ............ 36 E8
**Brook View**
Chelmsford CM2 ........ 217 C6
Stansted Mountfitchet
CM24 ................... 119 E5
Thaxted CM6.............. 70 A3
**Brook Wlk** CM8.......... 194 F8
**Broomclose Villas**
CM7 ..................... 100 E5
**Broom Cres** IP3 .......... 17 F1
**Broome Gr** CO7.......... 137 B2
**Broome Way** CO15...... 203 F6
**Broom Farm Rd** CM22 ... 94 C2
**BROOMFIELD** ........... 191 B2
**Broomfield** CM8......... 156 C5
**Broom Field** IP11........ 221 C5
**Broomfield Cres** CO7.... 137 B2
**Broomfield Ctyd** CB9 ..... 8 F8
**Broomfield Hospl**
CM1 ..................... 191 A3
**Broomfield Mews**
CM1 ..................... 205 B6
**Broomfield Prim Sch**
CM1 ..................... 191 B1
**Broomfield Rd** CM1 ..... 205 A5
**Broomgrove Inf & Jun**
Schs CO7 ............... 137 B2
**Broomhall Cl** CM1 ...... 191 B2
**Broomhall Rd** CM1...... 191 B2
**Broomhayes** IP2........ 17 A2
**Broomhill** IP9 ............ 62 D6
**Broom Hill Rd** IP1........ 17 A8
**Broomhills Ind Est**
CM7 ..................... 127 D2
**Broomhills Rd** CO5 ..... 201 D5
**Broom Knoll** CO7......... 60 C2
**Broom St** CO10 ........... 34 B5
**Broom Way**
Abberton CO5 ........... 163 B2
Capel St M IP9 ............ 35 B2
**Brotherton Ave** IP11 .... 221 A8
**Broton Dr** CO9 ........... 76 E2
**Brougham Glades**
CO3 ..................... 134 D5
**Broughton Cl** CO2 ...... 135 C4
**Broughton Rd** IP1........ 17 B7
**Browning Cl** CO3 ....... 134 F6
**Browning Rd**
Braintree CM7............ 155 A8
Chelmsford CM1.......... 86 C7
**Brownings Ave** CM1 .... 205 A5
**Brownlow Rd** IP11....... 221 F4
**Brownsea Way** CO3 ..... 135 A4
**Brown's End Rd** CM6 ... 121 F7
**BROXTED** ................ 95 F2
**Bruce Gr** CM2 ........... 206 A1
**Bruce Rd** CM1 ........... 204 B1
**Bruff Cl** CO4 ............. 109 E2
**Bruff Dr** CO14 ........... 171 A7
**Bruff Rd** IP2 .............. 17 C3
**Bruges Cl** CO12 ........... 91 A1
**Brundells Rd** CO7........ 139 A5
**BRUNDON** ............... 15 C1

**Brundon La** CO10........ 33 C7
**Brunel Ct** CO4 .......... 110 C6
**Brunel Rd**
Braintree CM7............ 128 A1
Clacton-on-S CO15...... 189 B8
Ipswich IP2 ............... 16 F6
**Brunel Way** CO4 ........ 110 C6
**Brunswick House Cut**
CO11 ..................... 87 A3
**Brunswick Rd** IP4 ......... 17 F8
**Brunwin Rd** CM77 ...... 126 F2
**Brussels Cl** CO12 ......... 91 B1
**Bryanita Ct** CO5 ........ 179 D5
**Bryan Rd** CM23 ......... 145 F8
**Bryanstone Mews**
CO3 ..................... 134 E5
**Bryant Link** CM2........ 206 B4
**Bryant's La** CM9 ........ 219 D7
**Bryon Ave** IP11.......... 221 A3
**Bryony Cl** CM8 .......... 176 D4
**Buchan Cl** CM7 ......... 155 A8
**Buckenhoe Rd** CB10 .... 22 E3
**Buckfast Ave** CO13..... 170 D6
**Buckfast Cl** 5 IP2........ 17 A2
**Buck Hill** CM77.......... 154 F6
**Buckingham Ct** 2
CM2 ..................... 205 F4
**Buckingham Dr** CO4 .... 136 E7
**Buckingham Rd** CB9 ...... 8 E6
**Bucklesham Rd** IP3...... 18 E2
**Buckleys** CM2........... 216 F7
**Buckleys La** CM9 ........ 195 E5
**Buckley's La** CO6 ....... 131 E6
**Buck's Horns La** IP8 ..... 36 B6
**Bucks La** CO10 ........... 12 B4
**Buckwoods Rd** CM7..... 128 A1
**Buddleia** CM7 ........... 16 E4
**Buddleia Ct** CO7......... 137 A2
**Buffett Way** CO4........ 136 E6
**Buglers Rise** CM1........ 215 B8
**Buick Ave** CO15 ........ 203 D6
**BUILDING END** ........... 40 B8
**Building End Rd**
Chrishall SG8 ............. 19 C1
Duddenhoe End SG8 ..... 40 B8
**Bulford Cl** CM77 ........ 155 D5
**Bulford La** CM77 ........ 155 D5
**Bulford Mill La** CM77 ... 155 D7
**Bullace Cl** CO4 .......... 110 D3
**Bull Cl** CM7 ............. 127 F3
**Bullen Wlk** CM2 ........ 216 C3
**Bullfields** CB11............ 67 A8
**Bullfinch Cl**
Colchester CO4 .......... 136 F8
Harwich CO12............ 90 E1
**Bullfinch Dr** CO9.......... 77 A1
**Bull Hill Rd** CO15 ....... 188 F5
**Bull La**
Langley CB11............. 40 C2
Long Melford CO10 ....... 15 E8
Maldon CM9............. 210 A3
Tiptree CO5 .............. 179 C3
**Bullocks La** CO10 ......... 33 E6
**Bullocks Terr** CO10 ...... 33 E6
**Bullock Wood Cl** CO4 ... 110 D4
**Bull Rd** IP3 ............... 18 B4
**Bulls Cliff** IP11 .......... 221 D3
**Bulls Lodge Cotts**
CM3 ..................... 192 B1
**BULMER** ................. 32 F5
**Bulmer Rd** CO10 ......... 33 C6
**Bulmer Road Ind Est**
CO10 ..................... 33 C6
**Bulmer St** CO10 .......... 33 D5
**BULMER TYE** ............. 32 F2
**Bulrush Cl** CM7.......... 128 B1
**Bulstrode Rd** IP2 ........ 17 D4
**Bulwer Rd** IP1 ........... 17 A6
**Bumfords La** CM3,
CM9 ..................... 208 A7
**Bumpstead Rd** CB9 ....... 9 B4
**Bundick's Hill** CM3...... 204 F3
**Bungalows The** CM8 ... 176 F1
**Bung Row** CM8 ......... 178 C1
**Bunting Cl** CM2.......... 216 E5
**Buntingford Ct** 2
CO2 ..................... 136 A1
**Bunting Rd** IP2 ........... 16 D3
**BUNTING'S GREEN** ...... 77 D1
**Buntings The** CO2 ...... 161 E4
**Bunyan Rd** CM7 ......... 127 E3
**Burdun Cl** CM8 .......... 194 D8
**Bure Dr** CM8 ............ 176 D3
**Buregate Rd** IP11........ 221 D2
**Bures Cl** CM9 ............ 220 B4
**Burgate Cl** CO16 ........ 188 A4
**Burgate Lane Cotts**
CO7 ...................... 85 B3
**Burgess Field** CM2...... 205 F4
**Burghley Ave** CM23 ..... 145 C7
**Burghley Cl**
Great Notley CM77 ...... 154 B6
4 Ipswich IP2 ............ 17 A2
**Burghley Way** CM2...... 216 D8
**Burgundy Ct** 9 CM2 ... 205 C2
**Burkitts Ct** 8 CO10 ..... 33 E7
**Burkitts La** CO10 ......... 33 E7
**Burley Cl** CM23 ......... 146 A4

**Burlingham Ho** IP2....... 17 B4
**Burlington Rd**
Colchester CO3 .......... 135 E6
Ipswich IP1................ 17 B6
**Burmanny Cl** CO15...... 188 C3
**Burnell Gate** CM1....... 206 A7
**Burnells Way** CM24 ..... 119 E7
**Burnet Cl** IP8 ............. 36 D8
**Burnham Cl**
Ipswich IP4 ............... 17 F7
Trimley St M IP11 ........ 221 A7
Walton-on-t-N CO14 .... 171 B8
**Burnham Ct** CO15....... 203 I8
**Burnham Lo** IP4.......... 18 A6
**Burnham Rd**
Chelmsford CM1 ........ 205 D5
Woodham Mortimer CM9,
CM3 ................... 219 E5
**Burnsall Cl** CB11.......... 43 F8
**Burns Ave** CO3 .......... 134 F6
**Burns Cl** CM9............ 210 A1
**Burns Cres** CM2......... 216 C8
**Burns Gn** CM9 .......... 196 A4
**Burnside Cres** CM1...... 205 B7
**Burnstie Rd** CM6 ....... 152 F6
**Burnt Dick Hill** CO4 ...... 82 D7
**BURNT HEATH** .......... 112 B4
**Burnthouse Rd** CO6 ..... 105 E2
**Burnt Oak Cnr** CO7 ...... 59 D1
**Burr Cl** CO12 .............. 90 C1
**Burrell Rd** IP2 ............. 17 C4
**Burroughs Piece Rd**
CO10 ..................... 33 F7
**Burrows Cl**
Clacton-on-S CO16...... 188 D6
Lawford CO11 ............ 86 B4
**Burrow's Rd** CO6 ....... 105 B7
**Burrow Rd** CO15........ 189 A7
**Burrsville Com Inf Sch**
CO15 ................... 188 F6
**BURRSVILLE PARK** ..... 189 A7
**Burrsward Pl** CM9...... 210 C3
**Burstall Cl** CO16 ........ 188 B4
**Burstall La** IP8........... 16 A6
**Burton Cl** CB9 ............. 8 E7
**BURTON END** ........... 120 C4
**Burton End** CB11 .......... 8 E7
**Burton End Prim Sch**
CB9 ...................... 8 D7
**Burton Pl** CM2.......... 205 F4
**BURTON'S GREEN** ...... 104 B2
**Burton's Green Rd**
CO9 ..................... 104 B4
**Burwood Ct** CM2 ....... 205 C1
**Bury Cl**
Colchester CO1 .......... 136 A8
Marks Tey CO6........... 132 F4
**Bury Farm Cotts** CM9 ... 220 F6
**Bury Fields** CM9......... 152 A5
**Bury Gdns** CB11 .......... 20 A4
**Bury La**
Chrishall SG8 ............. 19 D1
Great Waltham CM3 ..... 190 D8
Hatfield Peverel CM3.... 193 F4
**Bury Lodge La**
Great Hallingbury
CM22 ................... 147 C7
Stansted Mountfitchet
CM24 ................... 120 A2
**Bury Villas** CM22........ 121 E3
**Burywater Cotts** CB11.... 42 F1
**Bury Water La** CB11 ...... 42 E1
**Burywoods** CO4 ........ 109 B3
**Bushell Way** CO13 ...... 170 E6
**BUSH END** .............. 148 A4
**Bushey Cl** IP9 ............. 35 B1
**Bushey Ley** CM7 ........ 128 D3
**Bush Gr** CO10 ............ 33 C6
**Bush Rd** CB10............. 46 E2
**BUSTARD GREEN** ........ 98 B6
**Butcher Row** CB10 ...... 22 D1
**Butcher's Hill** CB10 ....... 3 A4
**Butchers La**
Capel St M IP9 ............ 35 B1
Walton-on-t-N CO14 .... 171 B7
**Butchers Pasture**
CM6 ..................... 122 F5
**Butcher's View** CO5..... 182 E6
**Bute Ct** CB9 ............... 8 F6
**Butler Cl** CB11........... 22 E1
**Butler Rd** CO9 ............ 76 D2
**Butlers Cl** CM1........... 191 B2
**Butlers Cotts** CM3 ...... 204 C1
**Butler's Hall La** CM23 ... 145 B3
**Butlers La** CB10 .......... 23 C5
**Butler's La** CO11 .......... 88 E1
**Butley Cl** IP2............... 36 F8
**Butley Rd** IP11 .......... 221 C3
**Buttcroft La** CM6......... 16 C2
**Buttercup Wlk** CM6 ..... 176 E4
**Butterfield Rd** CM3 ..... 206 E8
**Butterfly Gdns** IP4....... 18 E5
**Butter Market** IP1......... 17 C5
**Buttermarket Sh Ctr** 3
IP1........................ 17 C5
**Buttermere** CM77 ...... 154 C7
**Butt La**
Maldon CM9............. 210 A3
Manuden CM23 ........... 92 E2
**Buttleys La** CM6 ........ 149 F8
**Butt Rd**
Colchester CO3 .......... 135 C5
Great Cornard CO10 ..... 34 B6
Stoke-by-N CO6 .......... 56 C5
**BUTTS GREEN** ........... 68 E8

Butt's Green Rd CM2 ....217 F3
Butts La CM3..........218 F7
Butts Way CM2.........215 E3
Buxey Cl CO5..........201 B7
Buxton Cotts CO6......132 A3
Buxton Rd
  Coggeshall CO6......130 F3
  Colchester CO2......136 A3
Bylam La IP9..........63 C6
Byland Cl IP2.........17 A2
Bylands Cl CM23.......145 D6
Byng Cl CO16.........142 B1
Byng Cres CO16......142 B1
Byng Gdns CM7........128 C4
Byng Ho CO16........142 B1
Bypass Rd CO16.......187 B5
Byrd's Farm La CB10....22 E3
Byron Ave CO3........134 F7
Byron Cl CM7.........155 A8
Byron Dr CM8.........195 E5
Byron Rd CM2.........205 D2

## C

Cadenhouse Mews
  CO3...............134 E7
Caelum Dr CO2.......136 D5
Caernarvon Wlk CB9.....8 E8
Cage La
  Boxted CO4..........83 B4
  Felixstowe IP11.....221 D5
Cairns Rd CO2........136 B2
Caithness Cl IP4......18 B8
Calamint Rd CM8......176 D3
Caldbeck Way CM7.....154 C6
Calford Dr CB9........8 C8
CALFORD GREEN........9 F7
CALIFORNIA..........18 A6
California Cl CO4.....110 B4
California Rd CO11.....87 A4
Callis Ct CO10........12 C8
Callis St CO10........12 B8
Callisto Ct IP1.......16 D7
Callow Ct CM2........205 A2
Callowood Croft CM3...220 D1
Calverley Cl CM23.....145 E4
Calves La CO6.........56 B8
Camberley Rd IP4......18 D7
Camberton Rd CM7.....127 E6
Cambie Cres CO4......109 E4
Camborne Cl CM1......205 E5
Cambrai Rd CO2.......135 D4
Cambria Cl CO11.......87 B3
Cambridge Ave CO9.....75 E8
Cambridge Cotts
  CM2...............148 B7
Cambridge Cl
  Clacton-on-S CO15...188 E4
  Frinton-on-S CO13...171 A5
Cambridge Dr IP2......16 F1
Cambridge Ho CO9......9 B6
Cambridge Rd
  Clacton-on-S CO15...188 E4
  Colchester CO13.....135 C5
  Felixstowe IP11.....221 F4
  Frinton-on-S CO13...171 A5
  Littlebury CB11......21 F4
  Newport CB11........43 A2
  Stansted Mountfitchet
  CM24..............119 E8
Cambridge Way CO8.....79 F8
Camden Rd IP3........18 B8
Camellia Ave CO16....188 C4
Camellia Cl 2 CM1....205 F6
Camellia Cres CO16...188 C5
Camellia Cl 5 CO4....136 D8
Camelot Cl CM1.......204 F5
Camelot Mews CM7.....127 E2
Cameron Cl
  Braintree CM7.......127 F8
  Long Melford CO10....15 C6
Camoise Cl CO9.......50 B7
Camomile Way CO4.....109 C2
Campbell Cl CM2......216 A7
Campbell Cl CO3......135 D6
Campbell Dr CO4......110 E2
Campbell Rd
  Ipswich IP3.........18 C1
  Witham CM8.........176 F5
Campernell Cl CO7....185 F8
Campion Rd
  Colchester CO2......136 A5
  Ipswich IP2.........16 F4
Campions Hill CO6.....81 D8
Campions The CM24....119 E8
Campion Way CM8.....176 E3
Camp Rd CO7.........139 A7
CAMPS END..........7 A1
Camps Rd
  Bartlow CB21........6 B7
  Haverhill CB9........8 F7
  Helions Bumpstead CB9.8 B1
Camulodunum Way
  CO2...............135 C1
Camulus Cl
  1 Braintree CM7....128 A2
  Colchester CO2......135 A2
Cam Way CM8.........176 D2
Camwood Gdns IP3....18 B4
Canberra Cl
  Chelmsford CM1.....204 E5
  9 Colchester CM2...136 A1
  Ipswich IP4.........18 D6
Can Bridge Way CM2...205 C1
Candlet Gr IP11......221 D5

Candlet Rd IP11......221 D6
Candytuft Rd CM1.....205 F6
Canes Hill CO4.......128 A5
Canfield CM23........145 E8
Canfield Dr CM22.....148 E6
Canfield Rd
  Great Canfield CM6..149 D1
  Takeley CM22.......148 D5
Canford Cl CM2.......216 E7
Cangle Junc CB9.......9 A8
Canhams Rd CO10.....34 C5
Canham St 8 IP1.....17 B6
Cann Cl CO10.........15 D7
  Cann Hall Prim Sch
  CO16..............188 D6
Canning St CO12......91 D5
Cannock Mill Ct CO2..136 C4
Cannon Circ CM7......73 D6
Cannon Leys CM2.....216 D3
Cannon Rd
  Colchester CO1......136 B6
  Little Dunmow CM6...151 E6
Cannons Cl
  Bishop's Stortford
  CM23.............119 A1
  Colchester CO2.....119 D7
Cannons Mead CM24...119 D7
Cannons Mill La
  CM23.............119 A1
Cannon St CO1.......136 B6
Cannons The CO2.....135 D8
Cansey La CO11.......114 E6
Canterbury Cl IP2.....36 F8
Canterbury Grange
  CM7..............127 F8
Canterbury Rd
  Colchester CO2.....136 A5
  Holland-on-S CO15..189 E5
  Sudbury CO10......15 C2
Canterbury Way CM1..204 E4
Canters Meadow Ct
  CO15.............189 A5
Cant Way CM7........128 C1
Canuden Rd CM1.....204 E2
Canvey Wlk CM1.....205 E6
Canwick Gr CO2......136 C4
Capel Cl CO3.........134 F5
Capel Cl
  Chelmsford CM1.....205 B7
  Rayne CM7.........126 F2
Capel Dr IP11........221 A4
Capel Ho CO4........109 F4
Capel Pk CO13.......170 E7
Capel Rd
  Colchester CO3.....135 C5
  Rayne CM7.........126 F2
CAPEL ST MARY.......35 A2
  Capel St Mary CE Prim
  Sch IP9...........35 A1
Caper La CO2........160 F4
Capons La CM3.......219 A5
Cap Pillar Cl CO7.....137 B2
Capstan Pl CO4......136 D5
Captains Rd CO5.....201 B6
Captains Wood Rd CM8,
  CM9..............196 A3
Caracalla Way CO4....110 B6
Cardiff Ave IP2......17 B2
Cardigan St IP1......17 B7
Cardinal Cl CO4......137 A7
Cardinal Pk IP1......17 C5
Cardinals Cl IP11....221 E3
Cardinal St IP1......17 C5
Card's Rd CM7.......127 E8
Careless Ct 2 CM23..145 F7
Carisbrooke Ave
  CO15.............189 A7
Carleton Ct CO3.....163 E8
Carlford Ct IP4......18 B5
Carlisle Cl CO1......136 A8
Carlton Cl CO9.......30 A2
Carlton Mews CO7....164 A8
Carlton Rd CO15.....189 B5
Carlton Way IP4......17 E8
Carmarthen Cl IP2....17 A2
Carmelite Way CM9...209 F7
Carmel St CB10.......3 D2
Carmen St CB10......3 D3
Carnarvon Rd CO15...188 F3
Carnation Cl CM1....205 F5
Carnation Ct CB10....22 F2
Carolbrook Rd IP2....16 E1
Carolina Way CO5....179 D5
Caroline Cl CO7......137 C3
Carpenters Dr CM7....154 B7
Carpenters The CM23..145 B5
Carraways CM8.......195 B8
Carriage Cl IP11.....221 A8
Carriage Dr CM1.....205 F7
Carriers Cl CO5......201 A1
Carriers Ct CO7......59 D3
Carrigans CM23......145 E6
Carrington Cl CO5...201 D7
Carrington Ho CO5...201 D7
Carrington Rd CO7...112 D4
Carrington Way CM7..127 F8
Carr Rd IP11........221 C1
Carrs Rd CO15.......188 B3
Carr St IP4..........17 D6
Carsey Hill CO11.....85 A4
Carshalton End CO3..134 F4
Carsons Dr CO3......34 D1
Carstone Pl CM1.....204 F2
Cartbridge Cl CO14...171 B8
Carters Cl CO16.....188 B3
Carters Croft CB10....6 B1

Carters Cl 15 CO1....136 A6
Carters Hill
  Boxted CO4.........83 A6
  Manuden CM23......93 A1
Carters La
  Henham CM22......94 F5
  Wickham Bishops CM8..195 F6
Carters Leys CM23...145 D8
Carters Vineyard*
  CO4..............82 E5
Cartwright Wlk CM2..205 F2
Carus Cres CO4......110 B5
Case La IP9.........60 D7
Cassino Rd
  Chelmsford CM1.....204 E6
  Colchester CO2.....135 C3
Castings The CO6....105 A6
Castle Ave CB9.......8 E7
Castle Bailey 15 CO1..135 F7
CASTLE CAMPS........7 E3
  Castle Camps CE Prim Sch
  CB21.............7 E3
Castle Cl
  Castle Hedingham CO9.51 E4
  Great Leighs CM3....173 F6
Castle Cross CB10....22 E2
Castle Ct
  Clacton-on-S CO15..188 E3
  Colchester CO1.....135 F8
Castleden Way CM6...123 D2
Castlefields CM3.....173 F7
Castlegate St CO12...91 E6
CASTLE HEDINGHAM....51 E4
Castle Hill
  Dedham CO7........84 F4
  Saffron Walden CB10..22 D2
Castle Hill Mid Sch CB9..8 D7
Castle Hill Pk CO16..188 E7
Castle Ho* CO7......85 A5
Castle La
  Castle Hedingham CO9.51 E4
  Haverhill CB9.......8 F8
Castle Manor Bsns &
  Enterprise Coll CB9..8 E8
Castle Mdw CO2......51 D2
Castle Rd
  Clacton-on-S CO15..188 E3
  Colchester CO1.....136 A7
Castle St
  Bishop's Stortford
  CM23.............145 F6
  Saffron Walden CB10..22 D2
Castle View CM23....146 A7
Castleward Cl CO7....164 C8
Castle Way CO16.....187 A4
Castle Wlk
  Colchester CO1......8 E8
  Stansted Mountfitchet
  CM24.............119 E6
Caswell Mews CM2....205 F2
Catchpole Ct 12 CO10..33 E7
Catchpole La CM9....196 A4
Catchpool Rd CO1....135 F8
Caterham Cl CO16....188 C6
Cates Cnr CB10......22 E1
Cathedral CE Prim Sch
  The CM1..........205 C4
Cathedral Wlk CM1...205 B3
Catherine Cl CO15...189 A5
Catherine Hunt Way
  CO2.............135 C2
Catherine May Ct
  CO15............188 F3
Catherines Cl CM3...174 A6
CATMERE END.......21 A3
Catons La CO10.....22 D2
Cat's La CO10......34 A7
Cattawade St CO11..86 C7
Cattermole Ct CO16..188 B3
Catts Ct CO11......61 F2
Cattsfield IP7......61 F2
Cauldwell Ave IP4...17 F6
Cauldwell Hall Rd IP4..18 A6
Causeway
  Felsted CM3........152 F1
  Ford End CM3.......172 E6
Causeway Cl CO10....2 C5
CAUSEWAY END......152 C3
Causeway End Rd CO11..86 B5
Causeway End Rd
  CM6.............152 C3
Causeway Reach
  CO15............188 E7
Causeway The
  1 Bishop's Stortford
  CM23............146 A7
  Braintree CM7......127 F4
  Brent Pelham SG9...64 B1
  Colchester CO4.....110 C1
  Finchingfield CM7...72 D6
  Great Baddow CM2...216 F7
  Great Dunmow CM6..123 D2
  Great Horkesley CO6..82 B2
  Halstead CO9.......76 E1
  Henham CB11.......40 A8
  Langley SG11......40 C3
  Maldon CM9........210 A4
  Ridgewell CO9......28 F8
  Toppesfield CO9....47 C7
  Ulting CM9........208 D5
Causton Jun Sch
  IP11............221 C6
Causton Rd CO1......135 E8
Caustons Cl CO10....34 C5
Cavalier Cl CO2.....236 A5

Cavell Ct CM23......146 B6
Cavell Dr CM23......146 B6
CAVENDISH..........1 C1
Cavendish Ave CO2...136 C3
Cavendish CE Prim Sch
  CO10............1 C2
Cavendish Cl
  2 Haverhill CB9.....8 E6
  8 Saffron Walden CB10.22 F2
Cavendish Dr
  Clacton-on-S CO16..188 A4
  Lawford CO11......86 B3
Cavendish Gdns
  Braintree CM7......128 C5
  Chelmsford CM2....205 E3
Cavendish Ho CB9....8 F7
Cavendish La CO10...1 F3
Cavendish Rd
  Clare CO10........12 D7
  Felixstowe IP11....221 D3
Cavendish St IP3....17 F5
Cavendish Way CO10..33 F7
Cawkell Cl CM7......124 E4
Cawkwell Ct CM2....206 A4
Caxton Cl CO5.......179 D4
Caxton Ct CO9.......110 C6
Caxton Pl CO9......76 E2
Cecil Cl CM23.......146 D7
Cecilia St IP1.......17 C5
Cecil Rd IP1........17 B7
Cedar Ave
  Brightlingsea CO7...185 E7
  Chelmsford CM1....205 A3
  Tiptree CO5.......179 C7
Cedar Ave W CM1....205 A3
Cedar Chase CM9....210 C5
Cedar Cl
  Brantham CO11.....60 D1
  Great Dunmow CM6..123 A1
  Walton-on-t-N CO14..171 A7
Cedar Cres CO11.....86 C3
Cedar Ct
  Bishop's Stortford
  CM23............118 F1
  West Bergholt CO6..108 D5
Cedar Dr CM8.......177 A5
Cedar Ho IP2.......17 A3
Cedar Pk CM23......145 D4
Cedar Rd 15 CO2....135 F6
Cedars The
  Chelmsford CM2....205 F4
  Gosfield CO9......102 E7
  CM24...........119 D6
Cedar Way CO7......166 E8
Cedric Ct CM1......204 F3
Celandine Ct CO4....109 C2
Celestion Dr IP3....18 B4
Cemetery La
  East Bergholt CO7...59 B2
  Ipswich IP4.......17 E8
Cemetery Rd
  Bishop's Stortford
  CM23............145 F6
  Ipswich IP4.......17 E6
Centaury Cl CO3.....134 C7
Centenary Way CO15,
  CO16...........168 E1
Central Arc CB10....22 D1
Central Ave
  Frinton-on-S CO13..171 A6
  Ipswich IP4.......38 E8
Central Ho CO12.....42 E7
Central Maltings The 5
  CO11...........86 D4
Central Par CO15....188 F2
Chalkners Cl 8 IP9..35 A1
Central Sq 7 CM1...205 B2
Centre The
  2 Colchester CO4...136 E7
  Halstead CO9......76 E2
Centre The IP2......17 A1
Centre The CO5.....179 F8
Centrum Ct IP7.....17 B4
Centurion Ho 2 CO2..135 F6
Centurion Way CO2...135 A3
Century Dr CM7.....128 B2
Chadburn Rd CO10...15 D8
Chadwick Dr CM7....127 E3
Chaffinch Dr CO12...90 E1
Chaffinch Gdns CO4..136 F8
Chaffinch Way CO9...77 A1
Chaffix CM6........152 C6
Chaffix Cl CM6......152 C6
Chainey Pieces 12 CB9..8 A7
Chalfont Pl CO4.....110 C3
Chalfont Sq 18 IP4..17 D6
Chalklands
  Howe Green CM2....217 D3
  Saffron Walden CB10..22 E3
Chalkners Cl 8 IP9..35 A1
Chalks Rd CM8......176 F4
Chalkstone Mid Sch
  CB9.............9 A8
Chalkstone Way CB9...9 D7
Chalky La SG8......19 D2
Challenge Way CO1...136 B6
Challis La CM7......155 A8
Chalon St IP1......17 B5
Chamberlain Way IP8..16 C2
Chamley Ct CO15....189 D5
Chancellor Ave CM2..206 B4
Chancellor Park Prim Sch
  CM2............206 A5
Chancery Gr CO2....163 A8
Chancery Pl CM1....204 E4

Chancery Rd IP1.....17 B5
Chandlers Cl
  Bishop's Stortford
  CM23...........145 C4
  Clacton-on-S CO16..188 B3
  West Mersea CO5...201 C7
Chandlers Quay CM9..210 C3
Chandlers Row CO1..136 C5
Chaney Rd CO7.....137 A2
Chant Ct CO4.......110 D3
Chantlcefe CO4.....110 B3
CHANTRY..........16 E3
Chantry Cl
  Bishop's Stortford
  CM23...........145 E8
  Clacton-on-S CO16..188 E7
Chantry Dr CO6.....80 E4
Chantry Gn IP2.....16 D3
Chantry High Sch & Sixth
  Form Ctr IP2......16 F3
Chantry Home Farm Pk
  IP2............16 E5
Chantry La CM3.....193 A3
Chantry Mount CM8..145 E8
Chantry Rd CM23....145 E8
Chantry The
  6 Bishop's Stortford
  CM23...........145 F8
  Colchester CO3.....135 C7
Chantry View CM8...195 A7
Chantry Villas CM3..193 A3
Chanute Ave CM7....73 D7
Chapel Cl IP9......35 A1
Chapel Cnr CO6.....80 F4
Chapel Croft CO7...111 E7
Chapel Cut CO11....87 A4
Chapel Dr CM3.....191 B6
CHAPELEND........23 A8
CHAPEL END.......121 C7
CHAPELEND WAY....28 B2
Chapel End Way CO9..28 B2
Chapelfields CO13...170 E6
Chapel Fields CM22..148 E7
Chapel Hill
  Belchamp Walter CO10.31 D4
  Braintree CM7......128 A2
  Halstead CO9......76 D2
  Stansted Mountfitchet
  CM24...........119 E6
Chapel Hill Bsns & Ret Pk
  CM7...........128 C1
Chapel La
  Belstead IP8......36 C7
  Colchester CO4.....83 A3
  Colchester CO7....111 B1
  Elmstead Market CO7..138 A6
  Great Bromley CO7..139 A5
  Heybridge Basin CM9..210 E2
  Kirby Cross CO13...170 A6
  Little Baddow CM3..207 B3
  Newport CB11......67 A8
  St Osyth CO16.....187 A4
  Tendring CO16.....166 B5
  Thorington Street CO6.57 D6
  Thorrington CO7....166 B5
  Tiptree CO5.......179 C5
  Washbrook IP8.....16 A1
  West Bergholt CO6..108 A3
Chapel Mews 18 IP4..17 D6
Chapel Rd
  Beaumont CO16....141 E8
  Boxted CO4........83 A3
  Brightlingsea CO7...186 A7
  Colchester CO4.....134 C6
  Great Totham CM9..196 D6
  Langham CO4......83 D4
  Ridgewell CO9.....28 F8
  Tiptree CO5.......179 E4
Chapel Rise CM7....129 D2
Chapel Row 3 CM23..145 F6
Chapel St N 2 CO2..135 E6
Chapel St S 3 CO2..135 E6
Chapel St
  Halstead CO9......76 E2
  Rowhedge CO5.....164 A8
  Steeple Bumpstead CB9.27 C7
  Stoke by C CO10....11 A3
Chaplin Cl CM2.....216 B2
Chaplin Dr CO4.....110 D1
Chaplin Rd CO7.....59 D3
Chaplins CO13......170 F6
Chaplin Wlk CO10...34 D5
Chapman Cl IP11....17 B6
Chapman La CO4....110 B6
Chapman Rd CO15...188 F3
Chapmans La CO5...201 F8
CHAPPEL..........106 C5
Chappel CE Prim Sch
  CO6...........106 D5
Chappel Cnr CO6....106 C5
Chappel Hill CO6...106 C5
Chappel Rd
  Bures CO6, CO8.....79 E3
  Fordham CO6......107 D7
  Great Tey CO6.....106 F5
Chappel & Wakes Colne
  Sta CO6.........106 C4
Chariot Dr CO2.....135 F3
Charlecote Rd CM7...154 C7
Charles Ct
  Colchester CO3.....134 D6

**Charles Ct** continued
Wivenhoe CO7 . . . . . . . . . 137 C3
**Charles Cvn Pk** CO16 . . . . 167 E8
**Charles Hall** CO4 . . . . . . . 109 F4
**Charles Ho** CO1 . . . . . . . . 135 F8
**Charles Pell Rd** CO4 . . . . 136 E7
**Charles Rd**
Brightlingsea CO7 . . . . . . 185 F6
Felixstowe IP11 . . . . . . . . 221 C3
**Charles Smith Ho**
CO2 . . . . . . . . . . . . . . . . 136 A3
**Charles St**
Colchester CO1 . . . . . . . . 136 A6
Ipswich IP1 . . . . . . . . . . . .17 C6
**Charleston Ct** CO5 . . . . . . 201 E6
**Charlotte Dr** CO13 . . . . . . 170 E6
**Charlotte Way** CM8 . . . . . 177 B2
**Charnock Cl** CO13 . . . . . . 170 E6
**Charnwood Ave** CM1 . . . . 204 E1
**Charnwood Ct** IP2 . . . . . . .17 B4
**Charrington Cl** CB9 . . . . . . .9 C6
**Charter Ct** CO4 . . . . . . . . 110 C6
**Charter Ho** CM9 . . . . . . . 210 A2
**Charters The** CM6 . . . . . . 123 D2
**Charter Way**
Braintree CM77 . . . . . . . . 128 C1
Colchester CO4 . . . . . . . . 109 F4
**Chartfield Dr** CO13 . . . . . 170 D8
**Chartwell Cl**
Braintree CM7 . . . . . . . . . 127 E7
Ipswich IP4 . . . . . . . . . . . .18 A5
**Chartwell Pl** CM23 . . . . . 119 B1
**Chase Ct**
Colchester CO4 . . . . . . . . 136 D7
Harwich CO12 . . . . . . . . . .90 E2
**Chase La** CO12 . . . . . . . . . .90 E2
**Chase Lane Prim Sch**
CO12 . . . . . . . . . . . . . . . . .90 E2
**Chaser Cl** IP3 . . . . . . . . . . .38 C8
**Chase Rd E** CO7 . . . . . . . 139 C8
**Chase Rd W** CO7 . . . . . . . 139 A6
**Chase The**
Aldham CO6 . . . . . . . . . . 133 B8
Barnston CM6 . . . . . . . . . 151 B4
Bishop's Stortford
CM23 . . . . . . . . . . . . . . 145 F6
Boreham CM3 . . . . . . . . . 206 E8
Braintree CM7 . . . . . . . . . 128 A7
Brantham CO11 . . . . . . . . .60 F1
Colchester CO1 . . . . . . . . 136 B7
**6** Colchester, Greenstead
CO1 . . . . . . . . . . . . . . . 136 D7
Elmstead Market CO7 . . . . 138 B6
Felixstowe IP11 . . . . . . . . 221 D4
Foxearth CO10 . . . . . . . . .14 C6
Goldhanger CM9 . . . . . . . 212 A1
Great Baddow CM2 . . . . . 216 F6
Great Notley CM77 . . . . . 154 C5
Great Tey CO6 . . . . . . . . 132 C8
Great Totham CM9 . . . . . . 196 A4
Henham CM22 . . . . . . . . . .94 F6
Holland-on-S CO15 . . . . . 189 E5
Kelvedon CO5 . . . . . . . . . 158 C2
Manningtree CO11 . . . . . . .86 D3
Steeple Bumpstead CB9 . . .27 B7
Thaxted CM6 . . . . . . . . . . .70 A2
Tollesbury CM9 . . . . . . . . 199 D2
Tolleshunt D'arcy CM9 . . . 198 B4
West Mersea CO5 . . . . . . 201 C6
**Chaseway** CM8 . . . . . . . . 176 F5
**Chaseway The** CM7 . . . . . 128 C2
**Chase Way The**
Colchester CO3 . . . . . . . . 109 C1
Colchester, Lexden CO3 . . 109 B1
**Chaston Bsns Ctr**
CO15 . . . . . . . . . . . . . . . 188 F5
**Chaters Hill** CB10 . . . . . . .22 E2
**Chatham Gn** CM3 . . . . . . 173 D3
**Chatham Hall La** CM3 . . . 191 B8
**Chatley Rd** CM3 . . . . . . . 173 F7
**Chatsworth Ave** CM77 . . . 154 B7
**Chatsworth Cl** CM23 . . . . 145 C7
**Chatsworth Cres**
Ipswich IP2 . . . . . . . . . . . .17 B2
Trimley St M IP11 . . . . . . 221 A6
**Chatsworth Dr** IP4 . . . . . . .18 E5
**Chatsworth Gdns**
CO5 . . . . . . . . . . . . . . . . 188 D2
**Chatsworth Rd** CO5 . . . . . 201 C7
**CHATTER END** . . . . . . . . 118 C7
**Chattisham Rd** IP8 . . . . . . .35 C8
**Chaucer Cl** CO15 . . . . . . . 188 A1
**Chaucer Cres** CM7 . . . . . . 155 A8
**Chaucer Rd**
Chelmsford CM2 . . . . . . . 205 D1
Felixstowe IP11 . . . . . . . . 221 D3
Sudbury CO10 . . . . . . . . . .33 D2
**Chaucer Way** CO3 . . . . . . 134 F6
**Chauntry Rd** CB9 . . . . . . . .8 F7
**Chauntry The** **2** CB9 . . . . .9 A7
**Chedburgh Pl** **3** CB9 . . . . .9 A8
**Chedworth Pl** IP9 . . . . . . . .61 D7
**Chelmer Ave** CM3 . . . . . . 191 B5
**Chelmer Cl**
Kirby Cross CO13 . . . . . . 170 E7
Little Totham CM9 . . . . . . 197 B4
**Chelmer Dr** CM6 . . . . . . . 150 E8
**Chelmer Lea** CM2 . . . . . . 216 E7
**Chelmer Pl** CM2 . . . . . . . 205 D3
**Chelmer Rd**
Braintree CM7 . . . . . . . . . 128 D1
Chelmsford CM2 . . . . . . . 205 D4
Haverhill CB9 . . . . . . . . . . .9 B8
Witham CM8 . . . . . . . . . . 176 F2
**Chelmer Terr** CM9 . . . . . . 210 B2

**Chelmerton Ave** CM2 . . . . 216 E7
**Chelmer Valley High Sch**
CM1 . . . . . . . . . . . . . . . . 191 A2
**Chelmer Valley Rd**
CM1 . . . . . . . . . . . . . . . . 205 B5
**CHELMER VILLAGE** . . . . . 206 B4
**Chelmer Village Ret Pk**
CM2 . . . . . . . . . . . . . . . . 205 E2
**Chelmer Village Way**
CM2 . . . . . . . . . . . . . . . . 206 A3
**CHELMONDISTON** . . . . . . . .63 E8
**Chelmondiston CE Prim**
**Sch** IP9 . . . . . . . . . . . . . . .63 E7
**CHELMSFORD** . . . . . . . . . 205 C4
**Chelmsford Coll**
Chelmsford CM2 . . . . . . . 216 A8
Chelmsford CM2 . . . . . . . 216 C7
**Chelmsford Cty High Sch**
**for Girls** CM1 . . . . . . . . 205 A4
**Chelmsford & Essex Ctr**
CM2 . . . . . . . . . . . . . . . . 205 B1
**Chelmsford & Essex**
**Regiment Mus** *
CM2 . . . . . . . . . . . . . . . . 216 A8
**Chelmsford Ho** CM6 . . . . . 150 E7
**Chelmsford New Model**
**Specl Sch, Hayward**
Campus The CM1 . . . . . . 205 A4
**Chelmsford New Model**
**Specl Sch, Woodlands**
Campus The CM1 . . . . . . 204 F6
**Chelmsford Rd**
Barnston CM6 . . . . . . . . . 151 A4
Felsted CM6 . . . . . . . . . . 152 B4
Great Dunmow CM6 . . . . 150 E7
Great Waltham CM3 . . . . . 191 A6
Holland-on-S CO15 . . . . . 189 D6
Purleigh CM3 . . . . . . . . . 220 C3
Woodham Mortimer
CM9 . . . . . . . . . . . . . . 219 C6
Writtle CM1 . . . . . . . . . . 204 C1
**Chelmsford Road Ind Est**
CM6 . . . . . . . . . . . . . . . . 150 E7
**Chelmsford Sta** CM1 . . . . . 205 B3
**Chelsea Ct** CO10 . . . . . . . .33 F7
**Chelsea Mews** **12**
CM7 . . . . . . . . . . . . . . . . 127 F2
**Chelsea Rd** CO10 . . . . . . . .33 F7
**Chelsworth Ave** CO10 . . . . .34 B7
**Chelsworth Rd** IP11 . . . . . 221 B3
**Chelwater** CM2 . . . . . . . . 216 D8
**Chenies Gn** CM23 . . . . . . 145 D6
**Chepstow Rd** IP11 . . . . . . 221 D5
**Chequers** CM23 . . . . . . . . 145 C8
**Chequers Ct** CM8 . . . . . . . 177 B2
**Chequers La**
Glemsford CO10 . . . . . . . . .2 C6
Great Dunmow CM6 . . . . 150 D8
Maldon CM9 . . . . . . . . . . 210 A2
**Chequers Rd** CO11 . . . . . . 113 C6
**Chequers The** CO7 . . . . . . 165 A7
**Cheriton Rd** CM7 . . . . . . . 128 C1
**Cherry Bglws** **1** CM7 . . . . 127 F3
**Cherry Blossom Cl** IP8 . . . .16 A2
**Cherry Chase** CO5 . . . . . . 179 D4
**Cherry Cres** CM6 . . . . . . . 123 C1
**Cherrygarden La** **1**
CM7 . . . . . . . . . . . . . . . . 216 A8
**Cherry Garden La**
Danbury CM3 . . . . . . . . . 219 B7
Newport CB11 . . . . . . . . . .66 F8
**Cherry Garden Rd**
Great Waltham CM3 . . . . . 190 E7
Maldon CM9 . . . . . . . . . . 209 E2
**Cherry Gdns**
Bishop's Stortford
CM23 . . . . . . . . . . . . . . 146 A8
Great Notley CM77 . . . . . 154 D8
Haverhill CB9 . . . . . . . . . . .9 B5
**CHERRY GREEN**
**(CHAURETH GREEN)** . . . . .95 E7
**Cherry La** CO9 . . . . . . . . . .51 A8
**Cherry Lane Gdns** IP4 . . . .18 A7
**Cherry Row** CO3 . . . . . . . 134 F5
**Cherry Tree Ave**
CO15 . . . . . . . . . . . . . . . 188 C1
**Cherry Tree Cl**
Halstead CO9 . . . . . . . . . .77 A2
Little Oakley CO12 . . . . . 117 B7
**Cherrytree Ct** CO3 . . . . . . 134 F5
**Cherry Tree Ho** CO5 . . . . . 158 C3
**Cherry Tree La**
Abberton CO2 . . . . . . . . . 162 F6
Blackheath CO2 . . . . . . . 163 A7
**Cherry Tree Prim Sch**
CO2 . . . . . . . . . . . . . . . . 163 A8
**Cherrytree Rd** CO10 . . . . . .34 B7
**Cherrytree Rise** CM8 . . . . 177 A5
**Cherry Trees** CO15 . . . . . . 188 F2
**Cherrywood Dr** CO13 . . . . 170 E8
**Cherrywoods** CO7 . . . . . . 166 D8
**Chervil Cl** CO5 . . . . . . . . . 179 C4
**Cherwell Dr** CM1 . . . . . . . 204 C5
**Cheryl Ct** CO15 . . . . . . . . 188 D1
**Chesapeake Cl** IP9 . . . . . . .63 F7
**Chesapeake Rd** IP3 . . . . . . .38 A8
**Chesfield Ct** CM23 . . . . . . 145 F5
**Cheshunt Rd** IP2 . . . . . . . .17 B4
**Chessington Gdns** IP1 . . . .16 F8
**Chess La** CM8 . . . . . . . . . 177 A2
**Chester Camp** CO10 . . . . . 188 A4
**Chester Ct** **4** CB9 . . . . . . . .8 E6
**Chester Pl** CM1 . . . . . . . . 205 A5
**Chester Rd** IP11 . . . . . . . . 221 D5
**Chesterton Ct** IP2 . . . . . . .16 F1
**Chesterwall Mews**
CO4 . . . . . . . . . . . . . . . . 109 D6

**Chestnut Ave**
Blackheath CO2 . . . . . . . 163 A8
Clacton-on-S CO15 . . . . . 188 C3
Gosfield CO9 . . . . . . . . . 102 E8
Great Notley CM77 . . . . . 154 C7
Hatfield Peverel CM3 . . . . 194 A3
Heybridge CM9 . . . . . . . 210 C6
Jaywick CO16 . . . . . . . . 188 A2
Kirby Cross CO13 . . . . . . 170 C6
Littlebury CB11 . . . . . . . . .21 C1
**Chestnut Cl**
Bishop's Stortford
CM23 . . . . . . . . . . . . . . 145 E6
Colchester CO6 . . . . . . . 109 D5
Haverhill CB9 . . . . . . . . . . .8 F8
**Chestnut Ct** CM3 . . . . . . . 217 A8
**Chestnut Gr** CM2 . . . . . . . 127 E2
**Chestnut Mews** CM9 . . . . 210 C6
**Chestnut Rd**
Alresford CO7 . . . . . . . . 165 B8
Glemsford CO10 . . . . . . . . .2 B5
**Chestnuts The** IP2 . . . . . . .16 C2
**Chestnut Terr** CO10 . . . . . .15 C8
**Chestnut View** CM6 . . . . . 123 C1
**Chestnut Way**
Brightlingsea CO7 . . . . . . 185 E7
Takeley CM22 . . . . . . . . . 148 C7
Tiptree CO5 . . . . . . . . . . 179 C7
**Chestnut Wlk**
Chelmsford CM1 . . . . . . . 205 A5
Felsted CM6 . . . . . . . . . . 152 C6
Little Baddow CM3 . . . . . 207 E1
Witham CM8 . . . . . . . . . . 177 B4
**Chevalier Rd** IP11 . . . . . . 221 F4
**Chevallier St** IP1 . . . . . . . .17 A7
**Cheveley** IP11 . . . . . . . . . . 221 E4
**Cheveling Rd** CO2 . . . . . . 136 D2
**Cheviot Dr** CM1 . . . . . . . 204 D6
**Chevy Ct** CO10 . . . . . . . . . .90 C2
**Cheyne Ct** CO10 . . . . . . . . .33 C7
**Chichester Ct** CO3 . . . . . . 135 A7
**Chichester Dr** CM1 . . . . . . 205 C4
**Chichester Rd** CB11 . . . . . .43 E8
**CHICKNEY** . . . . . . . . . . . . .95 F4
**Chickney Rd** CM22 . . . . . . .95 C7
**Chigborough Rd** CM9 . . . . 210 F6
**Chignall Rd** CM1 . . . . . . . 204 D5
**CHIGNALL ST JAMES** . . . . 204 A8
**Chilburn Rd** CO15 . . . . . . 189 A7
**Childers Field** IP11 . . . . . . 221 B5
**Childwell Alley** CO1 . . . . . 136 A6
**Chilford Ct** CM7 . . . . . . . 127 D3
**Chiltern Cl**
Chelmsford CM1 . . . . . . . 204 D5
Colchester CO1 . . . . . . . 109 E1
**Chilton Cl**
Chelmsford CM2 . . . . . . . 216 D7
Great Horkesley CO6 . . . . 109 B7
**Chilton Cotts** CO6 . . . . . . .80 E4
**Chilton Ct**
Ipswich IP2 . . . . . . . . . . . .17 B3
Sudbury CO10 . . . . . . . . . .34 A6
Chilton Ind Est CO10 . . . . .34 B8
**Chilton Lodge Rd**
CO10 . . . . . . . . . . . . . . . .34 A7
**Chilton Rd** IP3 . . . . . . . . . .18 C4
Chilton Rd Ind Est
CO10 . . . . . . . . . . . . . . . .34 B8
**Chimney Pot La** CM3 . . . . 219 E3
**Chimswell Way** CB9 . . . . . .8 C8
**Chinery Cl** CM1 . . . . . . . . 205 D4
**Chingford Ave** CO15 . . . . . 188 F8
**Chinnel La** CB11 . . . . . . . . .42 D5
**Chinnery Hill** CM23 . . . . . 145 F5
**Chinook** CO4 . . . . . . . . . . 110 B4
**Chippetts La** CO3 . . . . . . . 133 C7
**Chippingdell** CM8 . . . . . . 176 F4
**CHIPPING HILL** . . . . . . . . 176 F3
**Chipping Hill**
**3** Halstead CO9 . . . . . . . .76 F2
Witham CM8 . . . . . . . . . . 176 F3
**Chipping Hill Inf Sch**
CM8 . . . . . . . . . . . . . . . . 176 F3
**Chipstead Wlk** CO9 . . . . . 188 C6
**Chishill Rd** SG8 . . . . . . . . .19 A4
**Chislett Row** CM2 . . . . . . 216 C8
**Chittock Ct** CO16 . . . . . . 188 B3
**Chitts Hill** CO3 . . . . . . . . 108 D1
**Chivers Rd** CB9 . . . . . . . . . .8 D7
**Choat's Cotts** CO6 . . . . . . 107 E1
**Choats Wood** CO3 . . . . . . 107 F1
**CHRISHALL** . . . . . . . . . . . .19 D3
**Chrismund Way** CO6 . . . . 106 C1
**Christchurch Ct** **4**
IP4 . . . . . . . . . . . . . . . . . .17 D6
**Christ Church Ct** CO3 . . . . 135 D5
**Christchurch Mansion**
**(Mus)** * IP4 . . . . . . . . . . .17 D6
**Christchurch St** IP4 . . . . . .17 D6
**Christian Sch The**
CM22 . . . . . . . . . . . . . . . 148 B7
**Christina Rd** CM6 . . . . . . 194 E8
**Christine Chase** CO3 . . . . 134 F5
**Christmas Field** CO9 . . . . . .51 D2
**Christopher Cl** **9**
CO10 . . . . . . . . . . . . . . . .33 E7
**Christopher Dr** CO16 . . . . 168 D1
**Christopher Jolly Ct**
CO2 . . . . . . . . . . . . . . . . 135 F4
**Christopher La** CO10 . . . . .33 E7
**Christy Ave** CM1 . . . . . . . 204 F4
**Churcharce** CM9 . . . . . . . 199 D1
**Church Ave** CM1 . . . . . . . 191 A2
**Church Chase** CM8 . . . . . . 178 A3
**Church Cl**
Cavendish CO10 . . . . . . . . .1 D2
Sproughton IP8 . . . . . . . . .16 A6

**Church Cl** continued
West Bergholt CO6 . . . . . 108 E4
Wickham Bishops CM8 . . 195 D5
**Church Cnr** CM9 . . . . . . . 208 D2
**Church Cotts** CM8 . . . . . . 195 D5
**Church Cres**
Clacton-on-S CO15 . . . . . 188 F2
Sproughton IP8 . . . . . . . . .16 A6
**Church Dr** CM23 . . . . . . . .92 B8
**CHURCHEND** . . . . . . . . . . 123 E2
**CHURCH END**
Ashdon . . . . . . . . . . . . . . .24 A7
Elsenham . . . . . . . . . . . . . .95 F3
**Church End**
Great Dunmow CM6 . . . . 123 E2
Panfield CM7 . . . . . . . . . 127 B8
**CHURCH END**
Shalford . . . . . . . . . . . . . 100 A4
Stebbing . . . . . . . . . . . . . 124 F4
**Church End Villas**
CM6 . . . . . . . . . . . . . . . . 123 E2
**Church Farm Way**
CM4 . . . . . . . . . . . . . . . . 109 E4
**Church Field**
Ashdon CB10 . . . . . . . . . .23 F7
Saffron Walden CB11 . . . . .43 E7
**Churchfield Rd**
Coggeshall CO6 . . . . . . . 131 A3
Walton-on-t-N CO14 . . . . 171 C8
**Church Field Rd**
Stutton IP9 . . . . . . . . . . . .62 B2
Sudbury CO10 . . . . . . . . . .34 C8
**Churchfields**
Stansted Mountfitchet
CM24 . . . . . . . . . . . . . . 119 F6
West Mersea CO5 . . . . . . 201 B6
**Church Fields** CM9 . . . . . . .29 F2
**Churchfields Ave**
CO3 . . . . . . . . . . . . . . . . 134 C4
**Churchfields Dr** CB9 . . . . . .27 B6
**Churchfields Wlk** CB9 . . . . .27 B6
**Churchgate**
Glemsford CO10 . . . . . . . . .2 C5
Thorpe-le-S CO16 . . . . . . 141 F1
**Church Gdns** CM6 . . . . . . 123 D2
**Church Gn**
Boreham CM3 . . . . . . . . . 206 F8
Broomfield CM1 . . . . . . . 191 B1
Coggeshall CO6 . . . . . . . 131 A3
Hinxton CB10 . . . . . . . . . . .3 E2
Little Yeldham CO9 . . . . . .30 D4
Wickham Bishops CM8 . . 195 D5
**Church Gr** CO6 . . . . . . . . 133 B8
**Church Hill**
Ashdon CB10 . . . . . . . . . .24 A8
Earls Colne CO6 . . . . . . . 105 C6
Finchingfield CM7 . . . . . . .72 D6
Harwich CO12 . . . . . . . . . .90 B1
Helions Bumpstead CB9 . . .26 C8
Hobrook IP9 . . . . . . . . . . .62 D5
Lawford CO11 . . . . . . . . . .85 F3
Little Waltham CM3 . . . . . 191 C6
Purleigh CM3 . . . . . . . . . 220 E1
Radwinter CB10 . . . . . . . . .45 F7
Rowhedge CO5 . . . . . . . . 163 F8
White Notley CM8 . . . . . . 155 F5
Wormingford CO6 . . . . . . 208 D2
**Church Housen** CM3 . . . . 190 F7
**Churchill Ave**
Halstead CO9 . . . . . . . . . .77 A3
Ipswich IP4 . . . . . . . . . . . .18 B5
**Churchill Cl** CO7 . . . . . . . 185 E8
**Churchill Cnr** CM24 . . . . . 119 F5
**Churchill Ct** CO12 . . . . . . .91 A4
**Churchill Rd**
Braintree CM7 . . . . . . . . . 127 E7
Tiptree CO5 . . . . . . . . . . 179 F5
**Churchill Rise** CM1 . . . . . 205 E7
**Churchill Terr** CM7 . . . . . . 127 E6
**Churchill Way** CO2 . . . . . 136 B4
**Church La**
Beaumont CO16 . . . . . . . 142 A6
Belstead IP8 . . . . . . . . . . .36 A7
Bishop's Stortford
CM23 . . . . . . . . . . . . . . 145 D3
Braintree CM7 . . . . . . . . . 127 F6
Brantham CO11 . . . . . . . . .60 E1
Castle Camps CB21 . . . . . . .7 E3
Castle Hedingham CO9 . . . .51 E4
**1** Chelmsford, Moulsham
CM1 . . . . . . . . . . . . . . 205 B2
Chrishall, Springfield
CM1 . . . . . . . . . . . . . . 205 D4
Clare CO10 . . . . . . . . . . . .12 B7
Colchester, Lexden
CO3 . . . . . . . . . . . . . . 135 A6
Colchester, Stanway
CO3 . . . . . . . . . . . . . . 134 A4
Copdock IP8 . . . . . . . . . . .35 F7
Debden CB11 . . . . . . . . . .66 C7
East Mersea CO5 . . . . . . 184 E1
Elsenham CM22 . . . . . . . 120 D8
Felixstowe IP11 . . . . . . . . 221 D6
Ford End CM3 . . . . . . . . . 172 B6
Great Henny CO10 . . . . . .54 D8
Great Holland CO13 . . . . 170 B3
Great Leighs CM3 . . . . . . 173 D7
Great Tey CO6 . . . . . . . . 132 C4
Great Wigborough CO5 . . 181 F4
Harkstead IP9 . . . . . . . . . .63 B3
Harwich CO12 . . . . . . . . . .91 B5
Little Totham CM9 . . . . . . 197 B1
Marks Tey CO6 . . . . . . . . 133 A4
Mistley CO11 . . . . . . . . . .86 E4
Nayland CO6 . . . . . . . . . . .56 E1
Ridgewell CO9 . . . . . . . . .29 B6
Sproughton IP8 . . . . . . . . .16 B6

**Church La** continued
Takeley, Brewer's End
CM22 . . . . . . . . . . . . . . 148 B7
Takeley, Little Canfield
CM6 . . . . . . . . . . . . . . . 149 B7
Toppesfield CO9 . . . . . . . .50 B7
Washbrook IP8 . . . . . . . . .35 B8
Weeley Heath CO16 . . . . . 168 A7
Widdington CB11 . . . . . . . .67 D4
Writtle CM1 . . . . . . . . . . 204 B1
**Church Manor** CM23 . . . . 146 B8
**Churchmans Ho** IP1 . . . . . .17 B5
**Church Mdw** CO10 . . . . . . .32 E5
**Church Mdws** CM7 . . . . . . 127 F6
**Church Mead** CM8 . . . . . . 155 F1
**Church Mews** CO6 . . . . . . .56 B1
**Church Path**
Hadstock CB1 . . . . . . . . . . .5 B6
Saffron Walden CB10 . . . . .22 D2
**Church Pk** CO10 . . . . . . . . .11 C3
**Churchponds** CO9 . . . . . . .51 E4
**Church Rd**
Alphamstone CO10 . . . . . .54 C6
Boxted CO4 . . . . . . . . . . 165 B7
Bentley IP9 . . . . . . . . . . . .60 F7
Black Notley CM77 . . . . . 155 A6
Boxted CO4 . . . . . . . . . . .82 E6
Bradwell CM7 . . . . . . . . . 129 E1
Brightlingsea CO7 . . . . . . 185 E8
Bulmer CO10 . . . . . . . . . .32 F4
Capel St M IP9 . . . . . . . . .35 F1
Chrishall SG8 . . . . . . . . . .19 D3
Clacton-on-S CO15 . . . . . 189 A3
Copford CO6 . . . . . . . . . 133 C2
Cressing CM77 . . . . . . . . 156 A5
Elmstead Market CO7 . . . . 138 A7
Fingringhoe CO5 . . . . . . . 164 A5
Fordham CO6 . . . . . . . . . 107 D5
Frating Green CO7 . . . . . . 138 D2
Gosfield CO9 . . . . . . . . . 102 E8
Great Cornard CO10 . . . . . .34 A5
Great Hallingbury
CM22 . . . . . . . . . . . . . . 146 D3
Great Notley CM77 . . . . . 154 F6
Great Totham CM9 . . . . . . 196 E3
Great Yeldham CO9 . . . . . .29 F2
Greenstead Green CO9 . . 104 A5
Hatfield Peverel CM3 . . . . 194 A3
Hempstead CB10 . . . . . . . .46 F8
Holland-on-S CO15 . . . . . 189 A6
Layer de la H CO2 . . . . . . 161 F4
Little Baddow CM3 . . . . . 207 A5
Little Bentley CO7 . . . . . . 140 A5
Little Bromley CO11 . . . . . 113 B4
Pattiswick CM77 . . . . . . . 129 F5
Peldon CO5 . . . . . . . . . . 182 D6
Rivenhall CM8 . . . . . . . . . 157 B1
Study Camps CB21 . . . . . . .7 C5
Stambourne CO9 . . . . . . . .28 D2
Stansted Mountfitchet
CM24 . . . . . . . . . . . . . . 119 F5
Stutton IP9 . . . . . . . . . . . .62 A2
Tattingstone IP9 . . . . . . . .61 C7
Terling CM3 . . . . . . . . . . 175 B2
Thorrington CO7 . . . . . . . 166 A6
Tiptree CO5 . . . . . . . . . . 179 D5
Tolleshunt Major CM9 . . . 197 F2
Ulting CM9 . . . . . . . . . . . 208 C6
Walton-on-t-N CO14 . . . . 171 C8
West Mersea CO5 . . . . . . 201 B6
Wickham Bishops CM8 . . 195 E5
Wickham St P CO9 . . . . . . .53 B6
Wormingford CO6 . . . . . . .80 E5
Wrabness CO11 . . . . . . . . .88 F4
**Church Rise** CM9 . . . . . . . .26 C8
**Church Row** CM6 . . . . . . . 122 E3
**Church So**
Bures CO8 . . . . . . . . . . . . .55 F1
St Osyth CO16 . . . . . . . . 187 A4
**Church St**
Belchamp St P CO10 . . . . .13 B3
Bishop's Stortford
CM23 . . . . . . . . . . . . . . 145 F7
Boxted CO4 . . . . . . . . . . .82 F7
Braintree CM7 . . . . . . . . . 102 B1
Chelmondiston IP9 . . . . . . .63 E7
Chelmsford CM1 . . . . . . . 205 B2
Clare CO10 . . . . . . . . . . . .12 B7
Colchester CO1 . . . . . . . 135 C7
Colne Engaine CO6 . . . . . .78 A1
Gestingthorpe CO9 . . . . . .31 E1
Goldhanger CM9 . . . . . . . 211 B2
Great Baddow CM2 . . . . . 217 A6
Great Chesterford CB10 . . . .3 D2
Great Dunmow CM6 . . . . 123 D2
Great Maplestead CO9 . . . .52 D1
Harwich CO12 . . . . . . . . . .91 E6
Henham CM22 . . . . . . . . . .94 F6
Ickleton CB10 . . . . . . . . . . .3 B4
Kelvedon CO5 . . . . . . . . . 158 B2
Maldon CM9 . . . . . . . . . . 209 E1
Newport CB11 . . . . . . . . . .43 A1
Rowhedge CO5 . . . . . . . . 164 A8
Saffron Walden CB10 . . . . .22 D2
Sible Hedingham CO9 . . . .51 D1
Steeple Bumpstead CB9 . . .27 B7
Stoke-by-N CO6 . . . . . . . .56 D5
Sudbury CO10 . . . . . . . . . .33 D6
Tollesbury CM9 . . . . . . . . 199 D4
Tolleshunt D'arcy CM9 . . . 198 D4
Wendens Ambo CB11 . . . . .42 E5
Witham CM8 . . . . . . . . . . 176 F4
**CHURCH STREET** . . . . . . . .13 B3
**Church Terr**
Bures CO8 . . . . . . . . . . . . .55 F1
Stoke by C CO10 . . . . . . . .10 D2

**Church View**
Ardleigh CO7 . . . . . . . . . . .111 E7
Colne Engaine CO6 . . . . . . .77 F1
Dedham CO7 . . . . . . . . . . .84 F3
Stoke by C CO10 . . . . . . . . .10 D3
**Churchview Ct 12**
CO14 . . . . . . . . . . . . . . . .171 C8
**Church Villas** CO4 . . . . . . .186 A6
**Churchwell Ave** CO5 . . . . . .160 A7
**Church Wlk**
Colchester CO1 . . . . . . . . .135 E7
Littlebury CB11 . . . . . . . . . .21 F4
Maldon CM9 . . . . . . . . . . .209 F3
Sturmer CB9 . . . . . . . . . . . .9 E8
5 Sudbury CO10 . . . . . . . .33 E7
**Churnwood Cl** CO4 . . . . . . .110 D1
**Churnwood Rd** CO4 . . . . . .110 D1
**Chuzzlewit Dr** CM1 . . . . . . .204 E7
**Cinnabar Cl** IP8 . . . . . . . . . .36 E8
**Cinque Port Rd** CO7 . . . . . .185 F7
**Circular Rd E** CO2 . . . . . . .135 F5
**Circular Rd N** CO2 . . . . . . .135 E5
**Circular Rd S** CO2 . . . . . . .135 E5
**Circular Rd W** CO2 . . . . . . .135 E5
**Circus Sq** CO2 . . . . . . . . . .135 F3
**City Rd** CO5 . . . . . . . . . . .201 A6
**Civic Dr** IP1 . . . . . . . . . . . .17 B6
**Civic Ind Est** CB9 . . . . . . . . .8 F5
**Clachar Cl** CM2 . . . . . . . . .206 A3
**Clacton Com** CO15 . . . . . . .169 A1
**Clacton Cty High Sch**
CO15 . . . . . . . . . . . . . . . .189 A4
**Clacton & District Hospl**
CO15 . . . . . . . . . . . . . . . .188 E1
**Clacton Factory Shopping**
Village CO15 . . . . . . . . . . .169 A1
**CLACTON-ON-SEA** . . . . . .189 B3
**Clacton Rd**
Bradfield CO11 . . . . . . . . .114 A6
Elmstead Market CO7 . . . .138 C5
Great Holland CO13 . . . . . .170 A2
Holland-on-S CO15 . . . . . .189 F7
Little Oakley CO12 . . . . . . .117 B5
Mistley CO11 . . . . . . . . . . .86 E2
St Osyth CO16 . . . . . . . . .187 B4
Thorrington CO7 . . . . . . . .166 C4
Weeley Heath CO16 . . . . . .168 A6
Wivenhoe CO7 . . . . . . . . .137 C5
Wix CO11 . . . . . . . . . . . . .115 C5
Wix, Stones Green
CO12 . . . . . . . . . . . . . . . .115 D1
**Clacton Sta** CO15 . . . . . . .188 F3
**Claire Ct** CO5 . . . . . . . . . .201 C7
**Claire Rd** CO13 . . . . . . . . .170 B6
**Clairmont Cl** CM7 . . . . . . .127 F2
**Clairmont Rd** CO3 . . . . . . .134 E5
**Clandon Ho** CO13 . . . . . . .170 F4
**Clapgate Dr** CO16 . . . . . . .168 C2
**Clapgate La** IP3 . . . . . . . . .18 A2
**Clapton Hall La**
Great Dunmow CM6 . . . . . .150 D5
Great Dunmow CM6 . . . . . .150 E6
**Clara Reeve Cl** CO3 . . . . . .134 F4
**CLARE** . . . . . . . . . . . . . . .12 C8
**Clare Ancient House**
Mus* CO10 . . . . . . . . . . .12 B7
**Clare Castle Ctry Pk***
CO10 . . . . . . . . . . . . . . . .12 C7
**Clare Cl** CO9 . . . . . . . . . . .103 D7
**Clare Com Prim Sch**
CO10 . . . . . . . . . . . . . . . .12 B8
**Clare Ct** CM6 . . . . . . . . . . .69 F3
**Clare Mid Sch** CO10 . . . . . .12 C8
**Claremont Hts** CO1 . . . . . .109 E1
**Claremont Rd** CO7 . . . . . . .164 C8
**Clarence Cl** CM2 . . . . . . . .206 A4
**Clarence Ho** CM2 . . . . . . . .216 A8
**Clarence Rd**
Clare CO10 . . . . . . . . . . . .12 B8
Ipswich IP3 . . . . . . . . . . . .18 B1
Stansted Mountfitchet
CM24 . . . . . . . . . . . . . . . .119 E7
Sudbury CO10 . . . . . . . . . .15 E1
**Clarendon Pk** CO15 . . . . . .189 B5
**Clarendon Rd**
Haverhill CB9 . . . . . . . . . . .8 F6
Takeley CM6 . . . . . . . . . . .148 E7
**Clarendon Way** CO1 . . . . . .109 E1
**Clare Rd**
Braintree CM7 . . . . . . . . . .127 E2
Ipswich IP4 . . . . . . . . . . . .17 F8
**Clare Way** CO16 . . . . . . . .188 B5
**Clarkesmead** CO5 . . . . . . .179 C4
**Clarke's Rd** CO1 . . . . . . . . .90 F3
**Clarkia Wlk** CO4 . . . . . . . .136 D7
**Clarks Farm Rd** CM3 . . . . .218 F8
**Clarks Field Cotts**
CM3 . . . . . . . . . . . . . . . . .219 E2
**Clarkson St** IP1 . . . . . . . . . .17 B6
**Clarks Wood Dr** CM7 . . . . .128 D3
**Clark Way** CM1 . . . . . . . . .191 A1
**Clatterbury La**
Arkesden CB11 . . . . . . . . . .41 E1
Clavering CB11 . . . . . . . . . .65 D5
**Claude Oliver Cl** CO11 . . . . .86 A2
**Claude St** IP1 . . . . . . . . . . .17 C6
**Claudian Cl** CB9 . . . . . . . . .9 D7
**Claud Ince Ave** CM7 . . . . . .155 E6
**Claudius Ct** CO1 . . . . . . . .135 F8
**Claudius Rd** CO2 . . . . . . . .136 A5
**Claudius Way** CM8 . . . . . . .194 E8
**CLAVERING** . . . . . . . . . . . .65 C5
**Clavering Prim Sch**
CB11 . . . . . . . . . . . . . . . . .65 C4
**Clavering Rd** CM7 . . . . . . .127 F6
**Claverton Way** IP4 . . . . . . .18 E4
**Claydon Cl** CB21 . . . . . . . . .7 E4

**Clayhall Rd** CO15 . . . . . . . .189 A5
**Clay Hill** CO10 . . . . . . . . . . .54 C8
**Clay Hills** CO9 . . . . . . . . . . .77 F8
**Clayhive Dr** CB9 . . . . . . . . .8 F7
**Clay La**
Stebbing CM6 . . . . . . . . . .124 D7
St Osyth CO16 . . . . . . . . .187 C7
**Clay Lane Gr** CO4 . . . . . . .110 D4
**Claypit Hill** CM22 . . . . . . . .120 E5
**Clay Pit Piece** CB11 . . . . . . .43 E6
**Clay Pits** CM7 . . . . . . . . . .128 D3
**Claypits Ave** CO8 . . . . . . . .80 A8
**Claypits La** CO10 . . . . . . . .14 D5
**Claypits La** CM6 . . . . . . . .192 F1
**Claypits Villas** CM6 . . . . . . .70 B2
**Clay Pits Way** CM7 . . . . . . .128 D3
**Clayponds** CM23 . . . . . . . .146 B7
**Clayshotts Dr** CM8 . . . . . . .195 B8
**Clays Mdw** CB11 . . . . . . . . .21 F4
**Clays Rd**
Walton-on-t-N CO14 . . . . .171 A7
Walton-on-t-N CO14 . . . . .171 B7
**Clayton Rd** CO12 . . . . . . . .90 C2
**Claywall Bridge** CB9 . . . . . .27 C7
**Claywall Cotts** CB9 . . . . . . .27 C7
**Clear Springs Chalet Site**
CO12 . . . . . . . . . . . . . . . . .91 A1
**Clearwater** CO2 . . . . . . . . .136 B3
**Clearwater Reach**
CO15 . . . . . . . . . . . . . . . .188 F2
**Clearwing Cl** IP8 . . . . . . . . .36 E8
**Clees Hall** CO8 . . . . . . . . . .55 A1
**Clematis Tye 3** CM1 . . . . .205 E7
**Clematis Way** CO4 . . . . . . .136 E7
**Clementine Gdns** IP4 . . . . . .18 B5
**Clement Mellish Ho 10**
CO1 . . . . . . . . . . . . . . . . .135 F7
**Clements Cl**
Chelmsford CM2 . . . . . . . .206 B3
Haverhill CB9 . . . . . . . . . . .8 F7
**Clements Com Prim Sch**
CB9 . . . . . . . . . . . . . . . . . .8 F7
**Clements Dr** CB9 . . . . . . . . .8 F7
**Clement's La** CB9 . . . . . . . . .8 F7
**Clench Cl 8** IP4 . . . . . . . . .17 D6
**Clench Rd** IP9 . . . . . . . . . . .62 D7
**Clermont Ave** CO10 . . . . . . .15 E2
**Clevedon Cl** CM7 . . . . . . . .154 C7
**Cleveland Cl** CO4 . . . . . . . .110 C4
**Cleves Ct** CM1 . . . . . . . . . .192 E1
**Cleves Rd** CO9 . . . . . . . . . .77 A8
**Clibbon Ho** CO10 . . . . . . . .34 B6
**Clicket Hill** CO8 . . . . . . . . . .80 B8
**Clickett Hill Rd** IP11 . . . . . .221 A4
**Cliff Cres** CM7 . . . . . . . . . .100 E7
**Cliff Ct**
Frinton-on-S CO13 . . . . . . .171 B6
Harwich CO12 . . . . . . . . . .91 D3
**Cliffield** CM7 . . . . . . . . . . .100 F7
**Cliff La** IP3 . . . . . . . . . . . . .17 F3
**Cliff Lane Prim Sch**
IP3 . . . . . . . . . . . . . . . . . .17 E3
**Clifford Cl 9** CM23 . . . . . .146 A4
**Clifford Rd** IP4 . . . . . . . . . .17 F5
**Clifford Road Air Raid**
Shelter Mus* IP4 . . . . . . .17 F5
**Clifford Road Prim Sch**
IP4 . . . . . . . . . . . . . . . . . .17 F5
**Cliff Par** CO14 . . . . . . . . . .144 E2
**Cliff Rd**
Harwich CO12 . . . . . . . . . .91 D3
Holland-on-S CO15 . . . . . .189 E5
Ipswich IP3 . . . . . . . . . . . .17 F3
**Cliff View Ct** CO15 . . . . . . .189 C4
**Clifton Cl** CO15 . . . . . . . . .171 B5
**Clifton Ct 13** CO11 . . . . . . .171 C8
**Cliftons Farm Dr** CO10 . . . .12 B7
**Clifton Terr** CO7 . . . . . . . . .164 B8
**Clifton Way** IP2 . . . . . . . . . .16 D2
**Clifton Wood** IP9 . . . . . . . . .62 D6
**Clingoe Ct** CO4 . . . . . . . . .136 E5
**Cliveden Cl** CM1 . . . . . . . .204 E3
**Clive Rd** CO1, CO2 . . . . . . .136 A6
**Clobbs Yd** CM1 . . . . . . . . .205 B8
**Clockhouse Way** CM7 . . . . .128 C2
**CLODMORE HILL** . . . . . . . .41 C3
**Cloes La** CO16 . . . . . . . . . .188 B4
**Cloisters The**
Braintree CM7 . . . . . . . . . .128 A5
Kelvedon CO5 . . . . . . . . . .158 B1
**Cloncurry Gdns** IP11 . . . . . .221 F3
**Clopton Dr** CO10 . . . . . . . . .15 C6
**Close The**
Clacton-on-S CO15 . . . . . .203 H7
Cressing CM77 . . . . . . . . . .155 E6
Debden CB11 . . . . . . . . . . .68 B7
Frinton-on-S CO13 . . . . . . .170 E5
Great Dunmow CM6 . . . . . .122 A1
Great Holland CO13 . . . . . .170 A3
Nayland CO10 . . . . . . . . . .33 F8
Sudbury CO10 . . . . . . . . . .15 D1
Tattingstone IP9 . . . . . . . . .61 D7
**Clouded Yellow Cl**
CM7 . . . . . . . . . . . . . . . . .154 E8
**Clough Rd** CO4 . . . . . . . . .110 D6
**Clovelly Cl** IP4 . . . . . . . . . . .18 F4
**Clover Ave** CM23 . . . . . . . .145 B6
**Clover Cl** IP8 . . . . . . . . . . . .16 F4
**Clover Ct**
Colchester CO3 . . . . . . . . .134 D5
Great Cornard CO10 . . . . . .34 C6
**Clover Dr** CO7 . . . . . . . . . .166 A5
**Clover Field** CB9 . . . . . . . . .8 D8
**Cloverlands** CO4 . . . . . . . .110 C2
**Clovers 5** CO9 . . . . . . . . . .76 D1
**Clover Way** CO7 . . . . . . . . .111 B5
**Cluanie Orch** CO10 . . . . . . .1 E1
**Club Par** CO16 . . . . . . . . . .203 B6

**Clump Field** IP2 . . . . . . . . . .16 F2
**Clunford Pl** CM1 . . . . . . . . .205 F7
**Clyde Cres** CM1 . . . . . . . . .204 D4
**Clydesdale Rd** CM7 . . . . . . .127 E2
**Coach Ho The** CO6 . . . . . . .105 A7
**Coach House Way 10**
CM6 . . . . . . . . . . . . . . . . .177 A2
**Coach La** CM9 . . . . . . . . . .209 F3
**Coachmans Ct 6** IP4 . . . . . .17 C5
**Coachmans Mead** CM7 . . . .72 C6
**Coachman's Paddock**
IP9 . . . . . . . . . . . . . . . . . .62 D6
**Coach Rd**
Alresford CO7 . . . . . . . . . .165 B8
Great Horkesley CO6 . . . . .109 A7
Hempstead CB10 . . . . . . . .25 F2
**Coan Ave** CO15 . . . . . . . . .188 D1
**Coastguard Cotts**
CO14 . . . . . . . . . . . . . . . .144 D1
**Coast Rd** CO5 . . . . . . . . . .201 A6
**Coates Cl** CM9 . . . . . . . . . .210 B4
**Coates Lo** CM2 . . . . . . . . .206 A3
**Coates Quay** CM2 . . . . . . .205 C2
**Coats Hutton Rd** CO2 . . . . .135 B3
**Cobble Row** CO3 . . . . . . . .134 E6
**Cobbold Mews 16** IP4 . . . . .17 D6
**Cobbold Rd** IP11 . . . . . . . .221 E4
**Cobbold St** IP4 . . . . . . . . . .17 D6
**COBBS FENN** . . . . . . . . . . .75 D7
**Cobbs La** CM22 . . . . . . . . .121 F3
**Cobbs Rd** CM22 . . . . . . . . .121 E3
**Cobden Pl** IP4 . . . . . . . . . . .17 D6
**Cobham Rd** IP3 . . . . . . . . . .18 C2
**COBLER'S GREEN** . . . . . . .152 D4
**Cockaynes La** CO7 . . . . . . .138 A1
**Cock & Bell La** CO10 . . . . . .15 C8
**COCK CLARKS** . . . . . . . . .219 F2
**Cockett Wick La**
CO16 . . . . . . . . . . . . . . . .187 C1
**COCK GREEN** . . . . . . . . . .152 E4
**Cock La** CB11 . . . . . . . . . . .64 F3
**Cock Rd** CO9 . . . . . . . . . . .53 B1
**Cockrell's Rd** CO6 . . . . . . . .81 B4
**Codham Little Park Dr**
CM7 . . . . . . . . . . . . . . . . .101 C6
**Cody Rd** IP3 . . . . . . . . . . . .18 C1
**Coeur De Lion** CO4 . . . . . . .109 F2
**COGGESHALL** . . . . . . . . . .131 B3
**COGGESHALL HAMLET** . . .158 A8
**Coggeshall Rd**
Ardleigh CO7 . . . . . . . . . . .84 F2
Braintree CM7 . . . . . . . . . .128 C3
Coggeshall CO6 . . . . . . . . .131 F3
Earls Colne CO6 . . . . . . . .105 B3
Great Tey CO6 . . . . . . . . . .132 B7
Kelvedon CO5 . . . . . . . . . .158 A1
Marks Tey CO6 . . . . . . . . .132 C3
**Coggeshall Rd (Feering)**
CO5 . . . . . . . . . . . . . . . . .158 D7
**Coggeshall Road**
(Feering) CO6 . . . . . . . . .131 B1
**Coggeshall Way** CO9 . . . . . .77 A2
Clacton-on-S CO15 . . . . . .188 D1
**Cohen Cl** CM77 . . . . . . . . .155 B5
**Cohort Dr** CO2 . . . . . . . . . .136 B5
**Cokers Cl** CM77 . . . . . . . . .155 C5
**Coke St** CO12 . . . . . . . . . . .91 D5
**Colam La** CO6 . . . . . . . . . .207 C3
**Colbayns High Sch**
CO15 . . . . . . . . . . . . . . . .188 D4
**Colbourn Ct** IP11 . . . . . . . .221 E4
**COLCHESTER** . . . . . . . . . .135 C7
**Colchester Bsns Ctr**
CO1 . . . . . . . . . . . . . . . . .136 A6
**Colchester Bsns Pk**
CO4 . . . . . . . . . . . . . . . . .110 C6
**Colchester Castle*** CO1 . . .135 F7
**Colchester Castle Mus***
CO1 . . . . . . . . . . . . . . . . .135 F7
**Colchester Cty High Sch**
for Girls CO3 . . . . . . . . . .135 B6
**Colchester General Hospl**
CO4 . . . . . . . . . . . . . . . . .109 E3
**Colchester High Sch**
CO3 . . . . . . . . . . . . . . . . .135 C6
**Colchester Inst**
Clacton-on-S CO15 . . . . . .189 A2
Colchester CO3 . . . . . . . . .135 D8
**Colchester Natural History**
Mus* CO1 . . . . . . . . . . . .135 F7
**Colchester Rd**
Abberton CO5 . . . . . . . . . .163 B1
Ardleigh CO7 . . . . . . . . . . .111 C6
Bures CO8 . . . . . . . . . . . . .79 F8
Chappel CO6 . . . . . . . . . . .106 E5
Chelmsford CM2 . . . . . . . .206 A6
Coggeshall CO6 . . . . . . . . .131 D2
Dedham CO7 . . . . . . . . . . .84 B5
Elmstead Market CO7 . . . .137 F6
Frating Green CO7 . . . . . . .139 E3
Great Bentley CO7,
CO16 . . . . . . . . . . . . . . . .186 F8
Great Bromley CO7 . . . . . .112 A3
Great Totham CM9 . . . . . . .196 D7
Great Wigborough CM9,
CO5 . . . . . . . . . . . . . . . . .181 C2
Harwich CO12 . . . . . . . . . .91 A1
Heybridge CM9 . . . . . . . . .210 B5
Holland-on-S CO15 . . . . . .189 D6
Ipswich IP4 . . . . . . . . . . . .18 D6
Lawford CO11 . . . . . . . . . .86 C3
Little Horkesley CO6 . . . . . .81 B1
Peldon CO5 . . . . . . . . . . . .183 B5
Salcott-c-V CM9 . . . . . . . . .199 A5
St Osyth CO16 . . . . . . . . .187 A5
Thorpe-le-S CO16 . . . . . . .141 D2

**Colchester Rd** continued
Tiptree CO5 . . . . . . . . . . . .179 D7
Weeley CO16 . . . . . . . . . . .140 C2
West Bergholt CO6 . . . . . . .108 E4
West Mersea CO5 . . . . . . . .201 C7
White Colne CO6 . . . . . . . .105 E6
Wivenhoe CO7 . . . . . . . . . .137 B3
Wix CO12 . . . . . . . . . . . . .115 B3
Wix, Goose Green
CO11 . . . . . . . . . . . . . . . .114 E4
Wormingford CO8 . . . . . . . .80 A6
**Colchester Ret Pk**
CO3 . . . . . . . . . . . . . . . . .135 E7
**Colchester Royal Gram**
Sch CO3 . . . . . . . . . . . . .135 D6
**Colchester Sta** CO1 . . . . . .109 E1
**Colchester Town Sta**
CO1 . . . . . . . . . . . . . . . . .136 A6
**Colchester Zoo*** CO3 . . . . .134 C1
**Cold Hall Chase** CO7 . . . . .138 E6
**Coldnailhurst Ave**
CM7 . . . . . . . . . . . . . . . . .127 F5
**Cold Store Rd** IP11 . . . . . .221 A1
**COLE END** . . . . . . . . . . . . .44 D6
**Cole End La** CB10 . . . . . . . .44 D5
**Cole Hill** CO3 . . . . . . . . . . .13 A1
**Cole Hill** CM3 . . . . . . . . . .174 B5
**Colehills** CB11 . . . . . . . . . . .65 C4
**Colehills Cl** CB11 . . . . . . . . .65 C4
**Coleman Ct** CO3 . . . . . . . .188 F3
**Colemans La** CM3 . . . . . . .218 D7
**Cole Ness Rd** IP3 . . . . . . . .38 A8
**Coleridge Rd** CM9 . . . . . . .210 A1
**COLES GREEN** . . . . . . . . . .35 C8
**Coles La** CO10 . . . . . . . . . .144 A1
**Coles Oak La** CO7 . . . . . . . .84 C6
**Colet Cres** CO2 . . . . . . . . .135 F4
**College Cl** CM23 . . . . . . . .145 D7
**College Ct** CO11 . . . . . . . . .86 C4
**College Rd** CM7 . . . . . . . . .127 E2
**College Rd**
Braintree CM7 . . . . . . . . . .127 E2
Clacton-on-S CO15 . . . . . .189 A3
**College St** IP4 . . . . . . . . . . .17 C5
**Coller Rd** CO12 . . . . . . . . . .90 F5
**Colles Brook Rd** CO7 . . . . .164 F8
**Colletts Chase** CO6 . . . . . . .80 F4
**Colley Rd** CM2 . . . . . . . . . .217 A6
**Collier Row** CB10 . . . . . . . . .6 B1
**Colliers The** CM9 . . . . . . . .210 E3
**Collimer Cl** IP3 . . . . . . . . . .63 E7
**Collimer Ct** IP11 . . . . . . . .221 C6
**Collindale Gdns** CO15 . . . . .189 C5
**Collingwood Ave** IP3 . . . . . .18 B3
**Collingwood Cl** CM7 . . . . . .128 C5
**Collingwood Fields**
CO7 . . . . . . . . . . . . . . . . .59 B4
**Collingwood Gn**
CO15 . . . . . . . . . . . . . . . .188 D1
**Collingwood Rd**
Clacton-on-S CO15 . . . . . .188 D1
Witham CM8 . . . . . . . . . . .177 A2
**Collingwood Ho**
Clacton-on-S CO15 . . . . . .188 D1
Frinton-on-S CO13 . . . . . . .170 F5
**Collins Cross** CM23 . . . . . .119 B1
**Collins Rd** CO9 . . . . . . . . . .53 D1
**Collops Villas** CM6 . . . . . . .125 A4
**Collyers Ct** CO1 . . . . . . . . .136 B7
**Colne Bank Ave** CO3 . . . . .135 D8
**Colne Chase** CM8 . . . . . . .176 E2
**Colne Com Sch & Coll The**
CO7 . . . . . . . . . . . . . . . . .185 E8
**Colne Cswy** CO2 . . . . . . . .136 D5
**Colne Ct**
Braintree CM7 . . . . . . . . . .128 C1
Rowhedge CO5 . . . . . . . . .164 A8
**COLNE ENGAINE** . . . . . . . .77 F2
**Colne Engaine CE Prim**
Sch CO6 . . . . . . . . . . . . .78 A2
**Colneford Hill** CO6 . . . . . . .105 D7
**Colne Ho** IP9 . . . . . . . . . . .210 B5
**Colneis Jun Sch** IP11 . . . . .221 F6
**Colneis Rd** IP11 . . . . . . . . .221 F6
**Colne Park Rd** CO6 . . . . . .105 D7
**Colne Rd**
Brightlingsea CO7 . . . . . . .185 E6
Bures CO8 . . . . . . . . . . . . .79 E8
Clacton-on-S CO15 . . . . . .188 F2
Coggeshall CO6 . . . . . . . . .131 A6
Halstead CO9 . . . . . . . . . . .77 A2
Sible Hedingham CO9 . . . . .75 E8
**Colne Rise** CO5 . . . . . . . . .163 F8
**Colne Springs** CO9 . . . . . . .29 B6
**Colne The** CO7 . . . . . . . . . .185 E5
**Colne Terr** CO7 . . . . . . . . .164 B8
**Colne Valley Cl** CO9 . . . . . .76 D2
**Colne Valley Farm Pk***
CO9 . . . . . . . . . . . . . . . . .51 D5
**Colne Valley Rly*** CO9 . . . . .51 C5
**Colne View**
Colchester CO2 . . . . . . . . .136 D2
Point Clear B CO16 . . . . . .186 A2
**Colne View Cotts**
CO5 . . . . . . . . . . . . . . . . .163 D3
**Colne View Ret Pk**
CO1 . . . . . . . . . . . . . . . . .110 A1
**Colne Wlk** CM7 . . . . . . . . .128 D1
**Colneys Cl** CO10 . . . . . . . . .15 D1
**Colthorpe Rd** CO15 . . . . . .188 F8
**Coltsfield Ct** CO4 . . . . . . . .119 E8
**Coltsfoot Cl** CO4 . . . . . . . .109 C2
**Coltsfoot Rd** IP2 . . . . . . . . .16 E4

**Colts The** CM23 . . . . . . . . .145 E4
**Columbine Gdns**
Ipswich IP1 . . . . . . . . . . . .16 E5
Walton-on-t-N CO14 . . . . .171 B7
**Columbine Mews**
CO3 . . . . . . . . . . . . . . . . .134 C7
**Columbines The** CO10 . . . . .1 E2
**Colville Cl** CM77 . . . . . . . . .154 C7
**Colvin Chase** CM2 . . . . . . .216 B1
**Colvin Cl** CO3 . . . . . . . . . .134 F7
**Colyers Reach** CM2 . . . . . .206 A2
**Colyn Dr** IP3 . . . . . . . . . . . .18 D1
**Comac Yd** CO15 . . . . . . . .188 E5
**Comma Cl** CM7 . . . . . . . . .127 E1
**Commerce Pk** CO2 . . . . . . .136 D4
**Commerce Way**
Colchester CO2 . . . . . . . . .136 D4
Lawford CO11 . . . . . . . . . .86 C3
**Commercial Rd** IP1 . . . . . . .17 B4
**Commodity Ctr** CM8 . . . . . .177 F4
**Common Hill** CB10 . . . . . . .22 D2
**Common La**
Duddenhoe End SG8 . . . . .40 B7
Little Baddow CM3 . . . . . .207 E3
Woodham Walter CM9 . . . .208 E3
**Common Quay** IP1 . . . . . . .17 D5
**Common St** CO10 . . . . . . . .12 B8
**Common The** CM3 . . . . . . .135 A5
**Common The** CM3 . . . . . . .218 E6
**Compass Ct 16** CO11 . . . . .86 D4
**Compasses Rd** CM77 . . . . .129 F5
**Compton Mews 5**
CO4 . . . . . . . . . . . . . . . . .136 C8
**Compton Rd** CO4 . . . . . . . .110 A6
**Comyns Cl** CO4 . . . . . . . . .110 A6
**Comyns Pl** CM1 . . . . . . . . .204 B1
**Conan Doyle Cl** CM7 . . . . .155 A8
**Conder Way** CO2 . . . . . . . .136 D4
**Conduit La** CM9 . . . . . . . . .219 E6
**Coney Acre** CB11 . . . . . . . . .93 D8
**Conford Ho** IP11 . . . . . . . .221 D6
**Congregation Ho 6**
CO9 . . . . . . . . . . . . . . . . .76 F2
**Conies Rd** CO9 . . . . . . . . .103 D7
**Conifer Cl**
Alresford CO7 . . . . . . . . . .164 F7
Colchester CO4 . . . . . . . . .136 E8
**Conifer Ct 7** CM23 . . . . . .145 F8
**Conifer The** CM23 . . . . . . .123 C1
**Coniston Cl** CM77 . . . . . . .154 D6
**Coniston Rd** IP3 . . . . . . . . .18 B2
**Coniston Sq** IP3 . . . . . . . . .18 B2
**Connaught Ave** CO13 . . . . .170 F4
**Connaught Cl**
Clacton-on-S CO15 . . . . . .189 B3
Colchester CO1 . . . . . . . . .136 C6
**Connaught Ct** CO15 . . . . . .189 B4
**Connaught Gdns** CM7 . . . .128 B4
**Connaught Gdns E**
CO15 . . . . . . . . . . . . . . . .189 B4
**Connaught Gdns W**
CO15 . . . . . . . . . . . . . . . .189 B3
**Connaught Ho**
Clacton-on-S CO15 . . . . . .189 B4
Frinton-on-S CO13 . . . . . . .170 F5
**Connaught Mews 2**
CO13 . . . . . . . . . . . . . . . .170 F5
**Connaught Rd**
Haverhill CB9 . . . . . . . . . . .8 E7
Little Clacton CO16 . . . . . .168 C5
**Conquerors Cl** CM3 . . . . . .194 B3
**Conrad Rd** CM8 . . . . . . . . .176 F5
**Constable Ave** CO16 . . . . . .188 C6
**Constable Cl**
Lawford CO11 . . . . . . . . . .86 B4
West Mersea CO5 . . . . . . . .201 D7
**Constable Ct**
Brightlingsea CO7 . . . . . . .185 F7
Colchester CO2 . . . . . . . . .135 B3
**Constable Ho** CM7 . . . . . . .127 E3
**Constable Rd**
Felixstowe IP11 . . . . . . . .221 F4
Ipswich IP4 . . . . . . . . . . . .17 D8
Sudbury CO10 . . . . . . . . . .33 F8
**Constable View** CM1 . . . . . .205 F6
**Constable Way** CM77 . . . . .155 B5
**Constance Cl**
Broomfield CM1 . . . . . . . . .191 A3
Witham CM8 . . . . . . . . . . .195 B8
**Constantine Rd**
Colchester CO3 . . . . . . . . .135 D5
Ipswich IP1 . . . . . . . . . . . .17 B5
Witham CM8 . . . . . . . . . . .194 E8
**Constitution Hill**
Ipswich IP1 . . . . . . . . . . . .17 B8
Sudbury CO10 . . . . . . . . . .33 F8
**Convalescent Hill**
IP11 . . . . . . . . . . . . . . . . .221 E3
**Convent Hill** CM7 . . . . . . . .128 A5
**Convent La** CM7 . . . . . . . . .128 A5
**Conway Cl**
Halstead CO9 . . . . . . . . . . .103 D8
Haverhill CB9 . . . . . . . . . . .8 E8
Ipswich IP2 . . . . . . . . . . . .16 D2
Wivenhoe CO7 . . . . . . . . .137 D8
**Conyer Cl** CM9 . . . . . . . . . .220 F8
**Cook Cl** CO12 . . . . . . . . . . .90 F1
**Cook Cres** CO4 . . . . . . . . .136 C6
**Cook Pl** CM2 . . . . . . . . . . .205 F3
**Cooks Cl** CO15 . . . . . . . . . .103 F8
**Cook's Cnr** CO11 . . . . . . . . .55 B1
**Cook's Gn** CO8 . . . . . . . . . .55 B1
**COOK'S GREEN** . . . . . . . .169 B2
**Cook's Hall Rd** CO6 . . . . . .108 C3
**Cooks Hill** CO6 . . . . . . . . . .83 B6

Cook's La
  Colchester CO3 . . . . . . . .134 F7
  Great Bardfield CM7 . . . . . .71 E4
  West Bergholt CO3 . . . . . .134 E8
Coolyne Way CO15. . . . . .189 B7
Coombe Lo CO6 . . . . . . . . .105 B6
Coombe Rise CM4. . . . . .205 B7
Cooper Ct CM9 . . . . . . . . .209 F2
Cooper Dr CM7 . . . . . . . . .127 D4
Cooper Pk CM7. . . . . . . . .127 D4
Coopers CM3. . . . . . . . . . . .206 E8
Coopers Ave CM9. . . . . . .210 D5
Coopers Cl CM23 . . . . . .145 B4
Coopers Cres
  Great Notley CM77 . . . . . .154 C8
  West Bergholt CO6 . . . . . .108 F4
COOPER'S END . . . . . . . . . . .41 A5
Coopers End Rd
  CM24 . . . . . . . . . . . . . . . . .121 A2
Coopers End Rdbt
  CM24 . . . . . . . . . . . . . . . . .121 B3
Coopers La
  Clacton-on-S CO15. . . . .188 C3
  Great Leighs CM3 . . . . . .173 F7
Cooper's La CO7. . . . . . . . .84 F5
Coopers Villas CM22 . . . .121 B2
Cooper Wlk CO4. . . . . . . . .136 D8
COPDOCK . . . . . . . . . . . . . . . .35 F7
Copdock Prim Sch IP8. . . .35 F8
COPFORD . . . . . . . . . . . . . .133 D4
Copford CE Prim Sch
  CO6 . . . . . . . . . . . . . . . . . .133 D2
Copford Ct CO6. . . . . . . . .133 C4
COPFORD GREEN . . . . . . . . .133 C2
Copingford End CO6 . . . .133 D5
Copland Cl
  Broomfield CM1. . . . . . . . .191 A1
  Great Baddow CM2. . . . . .216 F8
Copleston High Sch
  IP4. . . . . . . . . . . . . . . . . . .18 C5
Copleston Rd IP4. . . . . . . . .18 B5
Coploe Ho CO10 . . . . . . . . . .3 A2
Coploe Rise CB10. . . . . . . . .3 A3
Coppas Rd CO7. . . . . . . . .185 F5
Copper Beeches CO3 . . . .134 D5
Copper Ct CM7 . . . . . . . . .127 E1
Copperfield Rd
  Chelmsford CM1. . . . . . . . .204 E7
  Ipswich IP2. . . . . . . . . . . . .18 C8
Copperfields CB11. . . . . . .43 C8
Copper Gr IP8. . . . . . . . . . .36 E8
Coppice Cl CM6 . . . . . . . .123 D1
Coppice End CO4 . . . . . . .110 B3
Coppice Rd CO7. . . . . . . . .165 B8
Coppice The
  Bishop's Stortford
    CM23 . . . . . . . . . . . . . . .145 D5
  Clacton-on-S CO15. . . . . .188 D1
Coppins Cl CM2. . . . . . . .205 E4
Coppins Green Prim Sch
  CO15 . . . . . . . . . . . . . . . . .188 E5
Coppins Rd CO15 . . . . . . .188 D4
Coprolite St IP3. . . . . . . . .17 E5
Copse The
  Bishop's Stortford
    CM23 . . . . . . . . . . . . . . .146 C8
  Colchester CO4 . . . . . . . .109 F3
  Felsted CM6. . . . . . . . . . . .152 F6
Copthall Cl CM22. . . . . . .146 F4
Copthall La CM6 . . . . . . . .70 B3
Copt Hall La CO5 . . . . . . .182 C3
Copt Hill CM3 . . . . . . . . .218 E6
Copy Hill CB9 . . . . . . . . . . .8 E3
Coral Dr IP1 . . . . . . . . . . .16 D8
Coralin Wlk CO3 . . . . . . .134 C6
Cordell Cl CO10 . . . . . . . . .15 D8
Cordell Pl CO10 . . . . . . . . .15 D8
Cordell Rd CO10 . . . . . . . .15 D8
Corder Rd IP4. . . . . . . . . . .17 D8
Cordwinders CO7. . . . . . .59 F1
Coriander Rd CO5 . . . . . .179 C4
Corinda Ho CO13. . . . . . . .170 F4
Coriolanus Cl CO2 . . . . .135 A3
Cormorant Wlk CM2. . . .216 C6
Cornard Mere Nature
  Trail* CO10. . . . . . . . . . .34 B3
Cornard Rd CO10 . . . . . . .33 F7
CORNARD TYE . . . . . . . . . . .34 E7
Cornel Cl CM8. . . . . . . . . .176 E4
Cornelius Vale CM2. . . . .206 B4
Cornells La CB11 . . . . . . . .67 E3
Corner Pk CB10 . . . . . . . . .22 E3
Cornerth Cres CO10 . . . . .34 B6
Cornflower Cl
  Colchester CO3 . . . . . . . .134 C7
  Ipswich IP2. . . . . . . . . . . . .16 E4
Cornflower Dr CM1. . . . .205 F6
Cornflower Rd CO15 . . . .203 G7
Cornford Way CO11. . . . . .86 B4
Cornhill
  4 Chelmsford CM1 . . . . .205 B7
  16 Ipswich IP1. . . . . . . . .17 C6
Corniche The CM7. . . . . . . .72 B1
Cornish Ct CO10 . . . . . . . . .34 A7
CORNISH HALL END . . . . . . .48 C5
Cornish Hall End Rd
  Stambourne CO9. . . . . . . .28 A1
  Steeple Bumpstead CM7,
    CO9. . . . . . . . . . . . . . . . .48 E8
Corn Mill Ct CB11 . . . . . . .43 E8
Cornwall Cl CO11. . . . . . . .86 B3
Cornwall Cres CM1 . . . . .205 A4
Cornwall Gdns CM7. . . .128 B4
Cornwall Ho CM23 . . . . .145 E4

Cornwallis Dr CO6 . . . . . .132 F3
Cornwallis Pl CB10 . . . . . .22 E3
Cornwallis Rd CB9. . . . . . . .8 F6
Cornwallis Terr IP4. . . . . .17 F6
Cornwall Rd IP11. . . . . .221 D5
Coronation Ave
  Braintree CM7. . . . . . . . .127 F2
  Colchester CO2 . . . . . . . .136 A2
Coronation Dr IP11. . . .221 C3
Coronation Rd
  Bishop's Stortford
    CM23 . . . . . . . . . . . . . . .145 E5
  Clacton-on-S CO15. . . . . .188 C3
  Ipswich IP4. . . . . . . . . . . .18 B5
Coronation Villas
  CO16 . . . . . . . . . . . . . . . . .141 F7
Coronation Way
  CM77 . . . . . . . . . . . . . . . . .155 D6
Corporal Lillie Cl CO10. . .33 E6
Corporation Ave IP2. . . .37 A8
Corporation Rd CM1. . . .205 A4
Corriander Dr CM22 . . . .94 D2
Corry Ct 7 CO2 . . . . . . . .136 D8
Corsellis Ho CO7. . . . . . . .137 B1
Cortoncroft Cl CO13 . . . .170 F7
Corton Rd IP3. . . . . . . . . . .18 B1
Cotman Ave CO11. . . . . . . .86 B4
Cotman Lo CM1. . . . . . . .205 F6
Cotman Rd
  Clacton-on-S CO16. . . . .188 D6
  Colchester CO3 . . . . . . . .135 A5
  Ipswich IP3. . . . . . . . . . . .18 A1
Cotswold Cres CM1. . . . .204 D6
Cotswold Ct
  Clacton-on-S CO15. . . . . .189 A3
  Colchester CO4 . . . . . . . .110 C4
Cotswold Dr CO10 . . . . . .15 C6
Cotswold Rd CO15. . . . . .188 F5
Cottage Dr CO2. . . . . . . . .136 D3
Cottage Gn CO16. . . . . . .188 C6
Cottage Gr CO16. . . . . . .188 C6
Cottage Pl
  Chelmsford CM1. . . . . . . .205 B3
  3 Ipswich IP1. . . . . . . . . .17 B6
Cottage Wlk CO16 . . . . .188 C6
Cottey Ho CM2. . . . . . . . .216 B2
Cottingham Rd IP8. . . . . .16 B1
Cottonwood Cl CO2 . . . .135 D2
Coulsdon Cl CO16 . . . . . .188 C6
Council Bglws CM7. . . . .127 F7
Council Cotts
  Great Holland CO13. . . .169 F3
  Helions Bumpstead CB9 . . .8 E1
Council Hos
  Bicknacre CM3. . . . . . . . .218 F1
  Finchingfield CM7 . . . . . . .72 C6
  Great Bromley CO7 . . . . .139 A6
  Hadstock CB1 . . . . . . . . . .49 B4
  Holbrook IP9. . . . . . . . . . . .62 D6
  Peldon CO5 . . . . . . . . . . .182 E5
  Shudy Camps CB21 . . . . . .7 B6
  Thorington Street CO6. . .57 B3
  Thorpe-le-S CO16 . . . . .141 E2
  Tolleshunt Major CM9 . . .197 D3
  Wakes Colne CO6 . . . . . . .79 C1
  Wix CO11. . . . . . . . . . . . .115 B5
  Wrabness CO11. . . . . . . . .88 F2
Council Houses
  Cressing CM77 . . . . . . . . .156 A4
  Great Bentley CO7. . . . . .166 F5
COUNTESS CROSS . . . . . . .78 D3
Counting House La
  CM6 . . . . . . . . . . . . . . . . .123 D1
County Pl CM2 . . . . . . . . .205 B1
Coupals Cl CB9. . . . . . . . . . .9 C6
Coupals Com Prim Sch
  CB9 . . . . . . . . . . . . . . . . . . .9 D7
Coupals Ct CB9. . . . . . . . . .9 C6
Coupals Rd CB9 . . . . . . . . .9 E6
Courtauld Cl CO9. . . . . . . .76 F1
Courtauld Homes of Rest
  CO9 . . . . . . . . . . . . . . . . . .76 E3
Courtauld Mews 1
  CM7 . . . . . . . . . . . . . . . . .127 F2
Courtauld Rd CM7 . . . . . .128 A4
Court Cl CM23. . . . . . . . . .145 E5
Court Eight CM8. . . . . . . .176 F5
Court Eighteen CM8 . . . .176 F5
Court Eleven CM8 . . . . . .176 F5
Courtenay Cl CO10. . . . . .15 D2
Court Farm CO11. . . . . . . .61 A1
Court Fifteen CM8 . . . . . .176 F5
Court Five CM8 . . . . . . . . .176 F5
Court Four CM8 . . . . . . . . .176 F5
Court Fourteen CM8 . . . .176 F5
Court Ind Est CM2 . . . . . .205 C2
Courtland Mews CM9 . . .220 F8
Courtland Pl CM9. . . . . .220 F8
Courtlands
  Chelmsford CM1 . . . . . . .205 A6
  Halstead CO9. . . . . . . . . .103 D8
Court Nine CM8 . . . . . . . .176 F5
Court Nineteen CM8 . . . .176 F5
Court One CM8 . . . . . . . . .176 F5
Court Rd CM1 . . . . . . . . .191 B3
Court Seven CM8 . . . . . . .176 F5
Court Seventeen CM8. . .176 F5
Court Sixteen CM8. . . . . .176 F5
Court St CO6. . . . . . . . . . . .56 A1
Courts The IP11. . . . . . . .221 F4
Court Ten CM8 . . . . . . . . .176 F5
Court The CO7. . . . . . . . . .59 B2
Court Thirteen CM8 . . . .176 F5
Court Three CM8 . . . . . . .176 F5
Court Twelve CM8 . . . . .176 F5
Court Twenty CM8 . . . . .176 F5
Court Two CM8 . . . . . . . .176 F5

Courtyard Offices
  CM8 . . . . . . . . . . . . . . . . .178 B3
Courtyard The
  Braintree CM7. . . . . . . . .128 A4
  Ipswich IP1. . . . . . . . . . . .17 B7
Coval Ave CM1. . . . . . . . .205 A3
Coval La CM1. . . . . . . . . . .205 A2
Coval Wells CM1. . . . . . . .205 A2
Covehite Ct 3 CB9 . . . . . .8 E6
Coventry Cl CO1 . . . . . . . .136 A8
Coverdale CM8. . . . . . . . .176 E4
Coverts The
  West Mersea CO5. . . . . . .201 D6
  Writtle CM1. . . . . . . . . . . .204 B1
Cowdray Ave CO1. . . . . .109 F1
Cowdray Cres CO1. . . . . .135 F7
Cowdray Ctr The CO1 . . .110 A1
Cowdrie Way CM2. . . . . .206 B4
Cowell Ave CM1. . . . . . . .204 E5
Cowell St IP2. . . . . . . . . . .17 C3
Cowels Farm La CM6. . . .97 E5
Cow La
  Great Chesterford CB10 . . .4 A5
  Point Clear B CO16 . . . . .186 C3
Cowley Rd CM1. . . . . . . . .221 E4
Cowpar Mews CM7. . . . .155 A8
Cowper St IP4. . . . . . . . . . .18 B6
Cowslip Cl IP2. . . . . . . . . .16 E4
Cowslip Ct CO13 . . . . . . .134 C7
Coxhall Rd IP9. . . . . . . . . .36 E1
Cox La IP4. . . . . . . . . . . . .17 D5
Cox Rd CO7. . . . . . . . . . . .165 B8
Coxs Cl CB9. . . . . . . . . . . . .8 D7
Cox's Ct CO12 . . . . . . . . . .91 E5
Cox's Gdns CM23 . . . . . .145 E5
Cox's Hill CO11 . . . . . . . . .86 B4
Coytes Gdns 2 IP1. . . . .17 C5
Crabbe St IP4. . . . . . . . . . .18 A6
Crabbs Gn CM22 . . . . . . .119 E8
Crabb's Hill CM3 . . . . . . .193 F2
Crabs Croft CM7 . . . . . . .128 D3
Crabtree CO13. . . . . . . . . .170 C8
Crabtree Hill CB11. . . . . .67 C3
Crabtree La CM3 . . . . . . . .81 C1
Crabtrees CB11. . . . . . . . . .43 E8
Cracknell Cl CO7 . . . . . . .137 B2
Crafton Gn CM24 . . . . . .119 E7
Craig Ct CO2. . . . . . . . . . .135 B3
Craigfield Ave CO15 . . . .189 A6
Craig Ho CM7 . . . . . . . . . .128 A3
CRAIG'S END . . . . . . . . . . . .49 D8
Craig's Hill CO8. . . . . . . . .79 E6
Craigs La CO8. . . . . . . . . . .79 E6
Craiston Mews CM2 . . . .216 F5
Craiston Way CM2. . . . . .216 F5
Cramphorn Wlk CM1. . .204 F3
Cramswell Cl CB9 . . . . . . . .9 D6
Cranberry Sq IP3. . . . . . . .38 C7
Cranborne Cl CO4 . . . . . .109 F2
Cranbrook La CO10 . . . . . .2 F1
Crane Ave CO3 . . . . . . . . .134 B4
Crane Hill IP2. . . . . . . . . . .16 E4
Crane's La CO5 . . . . . . . . .157 F1
Cranford Cl CO13 . . . . . .170 E5
Cranham Hall Cvn Pk
  CM3 . . . . . . . . . . . . . . . . .191 F6
Cranham Rd CM6. . . . . . . .95 F3
Cranleigh Cl CO16 . . . . .188 B6
Cranmere Ct CO1. . . . . . .136 A7
Cranmer Ho CM2 . . . . . .215 F7
Cranmer's La CO6 . . . . . .131 E6
Cranmore Ct CM22 . . . . .94 C2
Cranmoregreen La
  CO10 . . . . . . . . . . . . . . . . . .2 F3
Cranwell Cres IP3 . . . . . .18 C1
Cranwell Gdns CM23. . .119 C1
Craven Dr CO4 . . . . . . . . .110 C3
CRAWLEY END . . . . . . . . . . .19 D4
Crawley End SG8 . . . . . . .19 D4
Crayfields CM8. . . . . . . . .123 E1
Crayford Cl CM9 . . . . . . .220 E8
Crayford Rd CO10. . . . . .15 D2
Creance Ct CM2. . . . . . . . .205 A2
Creasen Butt Cl CM9. . . .210 A4
Credon Cl CO15 . . . . . . . .188 F7
Credon Dr CO15 . . . . . . .188 F7
Creek Cotts CO14. . . . . .144 E4
Creekhurst Cl CO7. . . . . .186 A6
Creek View CO5. . . . . . . .181 F2
Creffield Rd CO3 . . . . . . .135 D6
Crepping Hall Dr IP9. . . .61 F1
Crescent Ct CM9 . . . . . . .209 F5
Crescent Rd
  Bishop's Stortford
    CM23 . . . . . . . . . . . . . . .146 A6
  Felixstowe IP11. . . . . . . .221 E4
  Great Baddow CM2. . . . .217 A7
  Heybridge CM9. . . . . . . . .209 F5
  Ipswich IP11. . . . . . . . . . .17 B6
  Tollesbury CM9. . . . . . . .199 E1
  Walton-on-t-N CO14 . . .171 C8
Crescent The
  Clacton-on-S CO15. . . . . .189 B7
  Colchester CO4 . . . . . . . .110 C7
  Frinton-on-S CO13. . . . . .170 F4
  Gestingthorpe CO9 . . . . . .31 F2
  Great Holland CO13. . . . .170 A4
  Great Horkesley CO6. . . .82 D8
  Great Leighs CM3 . . . . . .173 E5
  Marks Tey CO6 . . . . . . . .133 A3
  Steeple Bumpstead CB9. . .27 B7
  Thorpe-le-S CO16. . . . . .141 F2
  West Bergholt CO6 . . . . .108 D5
Cressages Cl CM6 . . . . . .152 F6
Cress Croft CM7 . . . . . . . .128 D1
CRESSING . . . . . . . . . . . . . .156 A6

Cressing Prim Sch
  CM77 . . . . . . . . . . . . . . . . .155 E6
Cressing Rd
  Braintree CM7. . . . . . . . .128 C2
  Witham CM8 . . . . . . . . . .176 D6
  Cressing Sta CM77. . . . .155 D5
Cressing Temple Barns*
  CM77 . . . . . . . . . . . . . . . . .156 B2
Crestlands CO2. . . . . . . . .165 B7
Cricketers Cl
  Broomfield CM1. . . . . . . .191 C1
  Sudbury CO10 . . . . . . . . . .33 E6
Cricketfield La CM23. . .145 E8
Cricket Hill Rd IP11 . . . .221 B5
CRIPPLE CORNER . . . . . . . . .54 B2
Crispin Cl CO9 . . . . . . . . . .8 D7
Critchett Terr 5 CM1. . .205 A3
Crittall Cl CM8 . . . . . . . . .156 E4
Crittall Ct CM8 . . . . . . . . .177 A3
Crittall Dr CM7 . . . . . . . .127 D4
Crittall Rd CM8 . . . . . . . .177 B3
CRIX GREEN . . . . . . . . . . .153 D6
Crix Green Villas
  CM6 . . . . . . . . . . . . . . . . .153 D6
Croasdaile Rd CM24 . . . .119 E8
Croasdale Cl CM24. . . . . .119 E8
Crocklands CO9 . . . . . . .104 A5
CROCKLEFORD HEATH
  . . . . . . . . . . . . . . . . . . . . . .111 C2
Crocus Cl
  Clacton-on-S CO16. . . . .188 C3
  Ipswich IP2. . . . . . . . . . . .16 E4
Crocus Fields CB10 . . . . .22 E3
Crocus Way CM1 . . . . . . .205 E7
Croft Cl CM7 . . . . . . . . . .128 A3
Croft Ct
  Chelmsford CM1 . . . . . . .205 A8
  20 Sudbury CO10 . . . . . . .33 E7
Crofters Wlk CM7. . . . . .154 D8
Crofton Cl CO4 . . . . . . . . .76 F2
Crofton La CB9 . . . . . . . . . .9 B6
Crofton Cl IP4. . . . . . . . . .18 B7
Crofton Ho 6 CO10. . . . . .33 E8
Crofton Rd IP4 . . . . . . . . .18 B7
Croft Rd
  Clacton-on-S CO15. . . . . .188 D4
  Kelvedon CO5 . . . . . . . . .158 B2
  Sudbury CO10 . . . . . . . . . .33 E8
Croftside CO8 . . . . . . . . . .55 F1
Croft St IP2. . . . . . . . . . . .17 C3
Croft The
  Bures CO8 . . . . . . . . . . . . .55 F1
  Earls Colne CO6. . . . . . . .105 A6
  Elsenham CM22 . . . . . . . .94 C1
  Glemsford CO10 . . . . . . . . .2 C4
  Great Yeldham CO9 . . . . .30 A2
Croft Villas CO10 . . . . . . . .2 C3
Croft Way CM3. . . . . . . . .177 A3
Cromarty Rd IP4 . . . . . . . .18 B8
Cromar Way CM1. . . . . .204 F1
Crome Cl CO3 . . . . . . . . .135 A5
Crome Rd CO16 . . . . . . .188 D5
Cromer Mews CO4. . . . .109 E3
Cromer Rd IP1. . . . . . . . . .18 B8
Crompton Ho CM1. . . . .215 F8
Crompton St CM1. . . . . . .16 F7
Crompton St CM1. . . . . .205 A1
Cromwell Cl
  Bishop's Stortford
    CM23 . . . . . . . . . . . . . . .145 B7
  Boreham CM3 . . . . . . . . . .206 D8
Cromwell Ct
  11 Ipswich IP1 . . . . . . . . .17 C5
Cromwell Ho CM8 . . . . .210 A3
Cromwell Ctr CM8 . . . . .177 B2
Cromwell Hill CM9. . . . .209 F3
Cromwell Ho CM9. . . . . .209 F4
Cromwell La CM9. . . . . . .209 F3
Cromwell Pk CM6 . . . . .152 B5
Cromwell Rd
  16 Colchester CO2 . . . . .135 F6
  Little Oakham CM6 . . . .151 E6
  Saffron Walden CB11. . . .43 E7
Cromwell Sq 8 IP1. . . . . .17 C5
Cromwell Way CM8 . . . .176 F2
Croquet Gdns CO7. . . . . .137 C1
Cross Cotts CO4. . . . . . . . .83 B6
CROSS END . . . . . . . . . . . . . .78 C8
Crossfield Rd CO15 . . . .188 E3
Crossfields
  Halstead CO9. . . . . . . . . .103 F8
  Stoke-by-N CO6. . . . . . . .56 C5
Crossfield Way CO13. . .170 B6
Cross Field Way CO4. . . .83 B5
Cross Hill CO12. . . . . . . . .116 D1
Cross La CO5. . . . . . . . . . .201 F7
Crossley Ave CO15 . . . .203 E4
Crossley View CO15. . . .189 B3
Cross Rd
  Maldon CM9 . . . . . . . . . .210 A1
  Witham CM8 . . . . . . . . . .176 A1
Crossroads CO9 . . . . . . . . .31 E2
Cross St
  Felixstowe IP11. . . . . . . .221 C6
  Wivenhoe CO7. . . . . . . . .137 B2
Crosstree Wlk CO4 . . . . .83 A7
Cross Way CO5 . . . . . . . .201 E7
Crossways
  Chelmsford CM2 . . . . . . .216 C7
  Clacton-on-S CO15. . . . .203 G8
  Colne Engaine CO6. . . . . .77 F1
Crotchets Cl IP9. . . . . . . . .35 A1

Crouch Ct CM7 . . . . . . . .128 D1
Crouch Dr CM8. . . . . . . . .176 E2
CROUCH GREEN . . . . . . . . . .51 C4
Crouchman's Farm Rd
  CM9 . . . . . . . . . . . . . . . . .208 C7
Crouch St CO3 . . . . . . . . .135 E6
Croutel Rd IP11. . . . . . . .221 F5
Crowe Hall La IP9. . . . . . .62 A1
Crowhall La CO11. . . . . . .87 E1
Crowhurst Ct CO3 . . . . .135 E7
Crowhurst Rd CO3 . . . .135 E7
Crow La CO16. . . . . . . . . .141 A3
Crowland Cl 7 IP2. . . . . .17 A2
Crowland Rd CB9. . . . . . . .8 F8
Crown Bays Rd CO4. . . .136 C8
Crownfield Rd CO10 . . . . .2 B6
Crownfields CO7. . . . . . . .84 F6
Crown Gate CO4 . . . . . . .110 D6
Crown Hill CB10. . . . . . . . .6 B1
Crown La
  Harwich CO12 . . . . . . . . . .91 D4
  Tendring CO16. . . . . . . . .140 D3
Crown La N CO7 . . . . . . .110 F7
Crown La S CO7 . . . . . . .111 A4
Crown Mdw CM7. . . . . .128 C4
Crown Rd CO15 . . . . . . .188 C1
Crown St
  Castle Hedingham CO9. . .51 E4
  Dedham CO7. . . . . . . . . . .84 F6
  Felixstowe IP11. . . . . . . .221 C6
  Great Bardfield CM7 . . . .72 B2
  Ipswich IP1. . . . . . . . . . . .17 C6
Crown Terr CM23 . . . . . .146 A7
Crow Pond Cotts
  CM3 . . . . . . . . . . . . . . . . .175 C3
Crow Pond Rd CM3 . . . .175 C3
CROW'S GREEN . . . . . . . . .125 E8
Crow St CM22 . . . . . . . . . .94 F5
Croxall Ct CM8 . . . . . . . .176 F2
Crozier Ave CM23. . . . . .145 E8
Crozier Mews CM9 . . . . . .18 B6
Crozier Terr CM2 . . . . . .206 B4
Cruce Way CO16. . . . . . . .185 F3
Crummock Ct CM7. . . . .154 C6
Crunch Croft CB9. . . . . . . .9 E5
Crusader Way CM7 . . . .128 D2
Crushton Pl CM1 . . . . . . .204 F6
Cuckfield Ave IP3. . . . . . .18 E3
Cuckoo Farm Bsns Pk
  CO4 . . . . . . . . . . . . . . . . .110 A7
Cuckoo Hill
  Bures CO8 . . . . . . . . . . . . .55 F1
  Sible Hedingham CO9 . . .75 B8
Cuckoos La
  Great Canfield CM6. . . . .149 A3
  Takeley CM6. . . . . . . . . . .148 F2
Cuckoo Way CM7. . . . . . .154 C7
Cudmore Grow Cntry Pk*
  CO5 . . . . . . . . . . . . . . . . .185 A1
Culford IP3. . . . . . . . . . . .17 F4
Culford Wlk IP11. . . . . .221 G6
Cullingham Rd IP1. . . . .17 A5
Culver St E CO1 . . . . . . . .135 F7
Culver St W CO1. . . . . . . .135 F7
Culvert Cl CO6. . . . . . . . .130 F1
Culver Wlk CM7 . . . . . . .128 D2
Cumberland Ave CO9. . .209 E1
Cumberland Cl CM7. . . .128 B4
Cumberland Cres
  CM1 . . . . . . . . . . . . . . . . .205 A7
Cumberland Ct
  Clacton-on-S CO15. . . . .189 B5
  Colchester CO3 . . . . . . . .135 D6
Cumberland St IP1. . . . . .17 B7
Cumberland Twrs 9
  IP1 . . . . . . . . . . . . . . . . . .17 C6
Cunningham Cl CO2. . . .136 A4
Cunnington Rd CM7 . . .128 C3
Cunobelin Way CO2. . . .135 A2
Cuppers Cl CM8 . . . . . . .176 E1
Curds Rd CO6 . . . . . . . . .105 A4
Curlew Cl
  Clacton-on-S CO15. . . . .188 F6
  Kelvedon CO5 . . . . . . . . .210 C5
  Kelvedon CO5 . . . . . . . . .158 D2
Curlew Croft CO4. . . . . .136 F8
Curlew Rd IP2. . . . . . . . . .16 D4
CURLING TYE GREEN
  . . . . . . . . . . . . . . . . . . . . . .209 A3
Curling Tye La
  Maldon CM9 . . . . . . . . . .209 A3
  Woodham Walter CM9. . .208 F3
Currents Farm Rd
  CM7 . . . . . . . . . . . . . . . . .127 E5
Currents La CO12. . . . . . . .91 E6
Curriers' La IP1. . . . . . . . .17 C5
Curtis Cl
  Clacton-on-S CO16. . . . .188 B3
  Ipswich IP8. . . . . . . . . . . .16 C1
Curzon Rd CO10 . . . . . . . .34 B8
Curzon Way CM2. . . . . .206 A2
Cusak Rd CM2. . . . . . . . .205 F3
Custerson Ct CB11. . . . . .22 D1
Custerson Dr CM7 . . . . .155 B5
Custom House La
  CO12 . . . . . . . . . . . . . . . . . .91 D6
Cut-A-Thwart La
  Maldon CM9 . . . . . . . . . .209 C4
Cut Hedge CM7. . . . . . . . .154 C6
Cuthedge La CO6. . . . . . .105 C5
Cutlers Cl CM23 . . . . . . .145 C5
CUTLERS GREEN . . . . . . . . .69 D2
Cutler St IP1. . . . . . . . . . .17 C5
Cutmore Pl CM2. . . . . . .215 F8
Cuton Gr CM2 . . . . . . . . .206 B5
Cuton Hall La CM2. . . . .206 A4
Cut The CO5. . . . . . . . . . .179 C5

Cut Throat La CM8...... 177 A4
Cutting Dr CO9.........76 E1
Cygnet Ct
[11] Bishop's Stortford
　CM23.............145 F6
　Sible Hedingham CO9 ....51 E1
Cygnet Wlk CO3.......134 C4
Cymbeline Way
(Colchester By Pass)
　CO3................135 B8
Cypress Cl CO15.......188 E7
Cypress Ct CM6.........123 B1
Cypress Dr CM2.......216 C6
Cypress Gr [5] CO4....136 F8
Cypress Mews CO5 ....201 B7
Cypress Rd CM8.......177 A4
Cyril Child Cl CO4 ....136 E7
Cyril Dowsett Cl CM9 ..209 E2

**D**

Daen Ingas CM3.......218 D7
Daffodil Cl IP2.........16 E3
Daffodil Way CM1.....205 E7
Dagnets La CM77......154 D3
Dahlia Cl
[2] Chelmsford CM1 ...205 F5
　Clacton-on-S CO16....188 C4
Dahlia Wlk CO4.......136 D7
Daimler Ave CO15.....203 D6
Dains Pl IP11.........221 A7
DAIRY FARM MEADOW
　.................186 C3
Dairyhouse La CO11 ..114 F7
Dairy Rd CM2.........205 F4
Daisleys La CM3.......137 A2
Daisy Cl La CO6.......206 A6
Daisy Green Rd CO3 ..133 E8
Daisyley Rd CM6.......98 B4
Dale Cl
　Colchester CO3.......134 B7
　Elmstead Market CO7 ..138 A6
Dale Ct CO12.........91 A4
Dale Ho CM7.........127 E4
Dales Tne CO12........90 F1
Dales View IP8.........35 E8
Dales View Rd [1] IP1 ..17 A8
Dale The CO7.........164 C8
Daleview Ave CO11 ...115 C5
Dalham Pl [4] CB9......9 A8
Dalhams CO10.........1 C1
Dallwood Way CM7 ...208 D3
Dalrymple Cl CM1.....205 D3
Dattes La CO16.......187 C3
Dalton Gdns CM23 ....145 E4
Dalton Rd IP1.........17 B6
Damant's Farm La
　CO16...............142 D1
Damases La CM3......193 C1
Damask Mews [9]
　CM7...............128 A2
Damask Rd CO3.......134 C7
Dame Elizabeth Ct
　CM1...............190 F3
Dame Johane Bradbury's
　Sch CB10............22 F2
Dammant Ct [8] CO4 ..136 D8
Dampier Rd CO6......130 F3
Damselfly Rd IP3.......38 C8
DANBURY.............218 D7
Danbury Ctry Pk★
　CM3...............218 B7
Danbury Park Com Prim
　Sch CM3............218 C7
Danbury Vale CM7....219 A6
Dancing Dicks La
　CM8...............176 A2
Dandalan Cl IP1.......16 E8
Dane Acres CM23.....145 D8
Dane Ho CM23........145 D8
Dane O'Coys Rd CM23 ..118 E1
Dane Pk CM23........145 D8
Dane Rd CM1.........204 E2
Danes Ct CO10........34 B4
Dane St CM23........146 A7
Daneum Holt CO10 ....12 A4
Daniel Cole Rd CO2 ...135 F4
Daniell Cl CO16.......188 C6
Daniell Dr CO2........135 B2
Daniells Ho CO6.......108 F4
Daniel Way CM6.......156 E4
Dansie Ct [7] CO4.....136 C8
Daphne Cl CM77......154 C7
Daphne Ct [4] CO4....136 D8
Daphne Ct CO3........135 F4
Dapifer Dr CM7.......128 D3
D'arcy Ave CM9.......210 B1
D'arcy Cl CO13.......170 F6
D'arcy Ct CM9........209 F2
D'arcy Hts CO2.......136 C3
D'arcy Rd
　Colchester CO2.......136 C3
　St Osyth CO16.......187 B5
　Tiptree CO5..........179 F2
Darcy Rise CM3.......207 E1
D'arcy Way
　Brightlingsea CO7 ....185 E7
　Tolleshunt D'arcy CM9 ..198 E4
Darina Ct CO3.........134 B7
Darkhouse La CO5.....164 A8
Darnay Rise CM1......204 D6
Darnel Way CO3.......134 D7
Darnet Rd CM9.......199 E1
Darrell Cl CM1........205 B6

Darrell Rd IP11.......221 B1
Darsham Cl IP11......221 B4
Dart Ct CM8..........176 D2
Darter Cl IP3..........38 C8
Dartmouth Rd CM1 ...205 E6
Darwin Cl
[5] Braintree CM7 ....127 F1
　Colchester CO2.......136 B1
Darwin Rd IP4.........17 F5
Dashwood Cl IP8......16 D1
Datchet Ho CO3......134 F7
Daundy Cl CM2........16 D5
Davall Cl CO12........90 C1
Davey Cl
　Colchester CO1.......136 D6
　Ipswich IP3...........17 F1
Davidson Cl CM1......205 A6
David Wright Cl CM6 ..150 E7
Davies Ct CM7........128 A2
Davies Way CM6......151 E6
Davy Rd CO15........189 C8
Dawes La CO5........201 E8
Dawlish Rd CO15.....203 I8
Dawnbrook Cl [1] IP2 ..16 F1
Dawnford Cl CO3.....134 C7
Dawnford Ct CO3.....134 C7
Daws Ho CM2.........205 C1
Daws Cross CO8........78 F6
Daw's Hall (Wildfowl
　Farm)★ CO8...........55 B6
Dawson Cl CB10.......22 F2
Dawson Dr IP11......221 A8
Dawson Way CM8.....194 F7
Daw St
　Birdbrook CO9.........28 B7
　Finchingfield CM7.....72 E4
Days Cl CM1..........205 B8
Dazeley's La CO7.......85 F8
Dead La
　Ardleigh CO7.........111 C8
　Great Bentley CO7....166 F2
　Lawford CO11.........86 C2
　Little Clacton CO16 ..168 B2
Deadman's La CM2 ...216 C4
Deal Cl
　Braintree CM7........127 E6
　Clacton-on-S CO15 ..203 J8
Deal Way CO7........185 E8
Deanery Gdns CM7 ...127 F7
Deanery Hill CM7.....127 E7
Deane's Cl CO12......91 A2
Deanes Ct CO12......91 A2
Deane's La CO12......90 E1
Deanhall Ave CO15...189 C5
Dean Rogers Pl CM7 ..127 F7
Dean St CO7..........185 E7
Deans Wlk CM7.......127 F8
Dean Way CM1.......204 E1
DEBDEN..............68 B7
Debden CE Prim Sch
　CB11...............68 F5
Debden Dr CB10......44 E2
DEBDEN GREEN.......68 F5
Debden Rd
　Newport CB11........67 C8
　Saffron Walden CB11...43 D8
　Saffron Walden CB11...43 E6
Deben Cl CM8........176 E2
Debden Ct CM7.......128 D1
Deben Dr CO10.......34 A8
Deben High Sch IP11 ..221 D4
Deben Rd
　Colchester CO4.......110 F1
　Haverhill CB9..........9 B8
Deben Way IP11.......221 C3
Deben Wlk CO16.....188 C6
De Burgh Rd CO4....134 E6
DEDHAM.............84 F7
Dedham Ave CO16...188 B5
Dedham CE Prim Sch
　CO7...............85 A6
Dedham Cl CO2.......136 B4
Dedham Hall Bsns Ctr
　CO7...............84 F7
DEDHAM HEATH......84 F4
Dedham Meade CO7 ..84 F3
Dedham Pl [7] IP4....17 D5
Dedham Rd
　Ardleigh CO7.........84 D1
　Boxted CO4...........83 B6
　Langham CO4.........84 A7
　Lawford CO11.........84 B2
　Stratford St M CO7....58 E1
Deepdale Rd CO2.....91 A4
Deeping Wlk CO16...187 B7
Deerhurst Chase CM3 ..218 F1
Deerleap Way CM7 ...128 D4
Deer Park Cl CO9......51 F3
DEER'S GREEN........65 A4
Defoe Cres CO4......109 E4
Deford Rd CM8.......194 D8
De Greys Cl CO10......34 C5
Delamere Rd
　Chelmsford CM1......204 E1
　Colchester CO4.......110 D3
Delius Wlk CO4......136 E6
Dell La
　Bishop's Stortford, Hockerill
　　CM23...............146 A7
　Little Hallingbury CM22 ..146 B1
Dellows La CM22......94 A2
Dells The [11] CM23 ..145 F7
Dell The
　Colchester CO1.......136 A6
　Great Baddow CM2 ..216 F6
　Great Cornard CO10 ..34 A6

Dell The continued
　Great Dunmow CM6 ..123 E1
Dellwood Ave IP11 ...221 F5
DELVIN END...........50 F3
Delvyn's La CO9........52 C6
De Mandeville Rd
　CM22...............94 C2
De-Marci Ct CM7......128 D3
Demoiselle Cres IP3 ...38 C8
Dene Ct CM1.........204 D5
Dengie Ct CM1.......194 F8
Denghams Ct CM3....164 C8
Denholm Ct CM6.....194 F8
Denmark Gdns IP9 ....62 D6
Denmark Rd CM2.....216 D8
Denny Ct CM23......119 B2
Denton Cl IP2.........16 D2
Denton Cres CM77 ...155 B5
Denton's Terr CO7....164 B8
Derby Cl IP4..........18 A5
Derby Rd IP3..........18 A5
Derby Road Sta IP3 ...18 A4
Dereham Ave IP3......17 F3
Dereham Ct CO2......135 C3
Derwent Gdns CO15 ..189 C6
Derwent Rd
　Colchester CO4.......110 C4
　Ipswich IP3...........17 F3
Derwent Way
　Chelmsford CM1......204 D4
　Great Notley CM77 ...154 C7
Desborough Path
　CM2...............205 F8
De Staunton Cl CO7 ..165 B7
Devereaux Cl CO14 ..170 F8
Devereaux Cl CO7....164 B8
Devereaux Ct [7] IP4 ..17 D6
Devereaux Pl CO4....109 C3
De Vere Ave CM9.....210 B1
De Vere Cl
　Hatfield Peverel CM3 ..194 B3
　Wivenhoe CO7.......164 B8
De Vere Est CO7......166 D8
De Vere La CO7.......164 B8
De Vere Prim Sch CO9 ..51 E4
De Vere Rd
　Colchester CO3.......135 A5
　Earls Colne CO6......104 F7
De Veres Rd [7] CO9 ..76 D1
Devereux Ct CO15....188 F3
Devereux Pl CO4......109 C3
De Vere Way CO12 ....90 F2
Deverill Cl CM1.......191 B2
De Vigier Ave CB10 ...23 A2
Devlin Rd IP8..........16 B1
Devoils La [5] CM23 ..145 F7
Devon Rd
　Colchester CO2.......135 B3
　Felixstowe IP11......221 D5
Devonshire Gdns
　CM7...............128 B4
Devonshire Rd IP3 ....17 F5
Devon Way
　Harwich CO12........90 D2
　Holland-on-S CO15 ..189 E7
Dewberry Cl [3] CO4 ..136 D7
DEWES GREEN........64 F1
Dewes Green Rd
　Berden CM23.........92 A8
　Clavering CM23.......64 F1
Dewlands CM77......155 B6
Deynes Rd CM11......68 B7
Dhobi Pl IP1..........16 C7
Dial Cnr CO7.........166 E3
Dial La IP1...........17 C6
Dial Rd CO7..........166 E3
Diana Ho CO13.......170 E5
Diana Way CO15.....188 C2
Dickens Cl CM7......155 A8
Dickenson Rd CO4....109 E3
Dickens Pl CM1.......204 D7
Dickens Rd CO15....189 E7
Dickett's Hill CO9......51 B6
Dicksons Cnr IP1......16 C7
Dicky Moors CM3....190 F7
Didsbury Cl IP2.......16 D2
Digby Mews CO5.....201 C6
Digby Rd IP4..........18 C7
Dilbridge Rd E CO4 ..136 C8
Dilbridge Rd W CO4 ..136 C8
Dilestone Ct CB9.......9 E5
Dillwyn St W IP1......17 B2
Dillwyn St IP1........17 A6
Dilston CO7..........219 A6
Dimsdale Cres CM3 ..146 B6
Dinants Cres CO6.....132 E3
Dingle The CO5.......164 B6
Dinsdale Cl [1] CM3 ..136 C8
Dinsdale Cl IP11......221 C3
Dismals The CM3.....175 B2
Distillery La CO2......136 C4
Ditchingham Gr IP5 ..18 F6
Ditton Way IP3........18 A4
Dixon Ave
　Clacton-on-S CO16 ..188 C6
　Clacton-on-S CO16...86 B4
Dixon Way CO7.......164 C8
Dobbies La CO6.......132 F3
Docker Ct CO2.......136 B4
Dockfield Ave CO12 ..90 F3
Dock La CO12........117 A4
Dock Rd IP11.........221 B2
Dock St IP2...........17 C4
Dockwra La CM3......219 A7
Doctor's La CO10.....112 D7
Docwra Rd CO5......158 C2
Doddenhill Cl CB10 ..22 E3
Dodmans [7] IP9......35 A1

Doe's Cnr
　Halstead CO9..........76 D5
　Hatfield Peverel CM9 ..194 F1
Dog Chase CM7........73 C3
Dogden La CM23......92 E2
Doggetts La CO6.....132 F2
Doghouse Rd CM77 ..129 F4
Dogs Head St [4] IP4 ..17 C5
Dogwood Cl IP3.......18 D2
Dolby Rise CM2......205 F2
Dolphin Ct CO13.....171 B6
Dolphin Way CM23 ..146 A6
Dombey Cl CM1......204 F7
Dombey Rd IP2........16 F5
Domitian Cl CO4......110 B6
Domsey Bank CO6 ...132 E3
Domsey Chase CO5 ..159 C6
Domsey La CM3.....191 F5
Doms La CM3........175 B2
Donald Way CM2......216 C7
Donne Dr CO15......203 G8
Donyland Way CO5 ..163 F8
Dooley Rd
　Felixstowe IP11......221 A3
　Halstead CO9..........76 D1
Dorchester End CO2 ..136 B3
Dorchester Rd IP3....18 D3
Dordell Cl CO7.......154 C7
Dorewards Ave CM7 ..127 F7
Dorking Cres CO16 ..188 C6
Dorking Wlk CM2....216 E7
Dorlings The CO14 ...171 C8
Dorothy Curtice Ct
　CO6...............133 E5
Dorothy Sayers Dr
　CM8...............177 A5
Dorset Ave CM2......216 E6
Dorset Cl
　Great Baddow CM2 ..216 E6
　Halstead CO9..........76 E1
　Holland-on-S CO15 ..189 E6
Dorset Ho [1] CM23 ..145 F7
Dorset Rd CM9.......209 F2
Dorvis La CB10........6 B1
Doubleday Cnr CO6 ..130 F2
Doubleday Dr CM9 ..209 F5
Doubleday Gdns CM8 ..128 B5
Doucecroft Sch CO5 ..158 C3
Douglas Cl CM2......216 D3
Douglas Gr CM8......176 D2
Douglas Rd
　Clacton-on-S CO15 ..188 C4
　Harwich CO12........91 B3
Douglas Wlk [3] CM2 ..216 A8
Dove Cl
　Bishop's Stortford
　　CM23...............145 E3
　Stansted Mountfitchet
　　CM24...............119 E8
Dove Cotts CM22......93 F3
Dove Cres CM9.......209 D2
Dovedale IP11........221 B3
Dovedale Gdns CO15 ..189 C6
Dove House Rd CB9 ....9 A8
Dove La CM2.........216 A6
Dover Cl
　Braintree CM7........127 E6
　Clacton-on-S CO15 ..203 J8
DOVERCOURT.........91 C4
Dovercourt Cvn Pk
　CO12..............91 A1
Dovercourt Sta CO12 ..91 D4
Dover Rd
　Brightlingsea CO7 ...185 F8
　Ipswich IP3...........18 B4
Doves Ct CO7.........185 F6
Dowches La CM6......150 B2
Dove St IP4...........17 E5
Dove Tree Ct CO3....134 C5
Dowches Cotts CO5 ..158 C2
Dowches Dr CO5......158 C3
Dowding Cl CO2......136 A4
Dowling Rd CO8.......79 F3
Downham Bvd IP3....38 C8
Downham Cl IP2......16 E2
Downs Cres
　Great Dunmow CM6 ..123 C1
　Haverhill CB9.........18 C3
Downside Cl IP2.......36 F8
Downs Pl [2] CB9......8 B8
Downs Cnr CO5......181 F2
Downsway CM1.......205 D6
Downton Dr CB9.......8 E8
Downton Wlk CO5 ...179 D6
Dragon's Gn CB10.....23 D1
Drake Ave IP3.........17 D3
Drake Gdns CM7......128 C4
Drakes App CO15.....188 A1
Drakes Cnr CO5......181 F2
Drakes La
　Boreham CM3.......192 B7
　Little Waltham CM3 ..191 F7
Drake Sq N IP3.......18 B2
Drake Sq S IP3........18 B2
Drake's Yd CB9.........9 A8
Drapers Chase
　Heybridge CM9.......210 D4
　Rayne CM7...........153 D8
Drapers La CB9.........8 B2
Drapery Comm CO10 ..2 B4

Dray Ct CO6.........108 F4
Drayman's Cl CM23 ..145 B5
Drayman Gr CM7.....154 C8
Draymans Way IP3 ....17 E3
Drays The CO10........15 B5
Drayton Cl [4] CM9 ..210 A1
Dreys The CB10........44 D8
Driberg Way CM7.....128 A1
Driffield Cl CO5......158 D4
Drift The
　Dedham CO7..........84 F7
　East Bergholt CO7.....60 C2
　Great Cornard CO10 ..34 C5
　Ipswich, California IP4 ..18 A6
　Ipswich, Priory Heath
　　IP3................18 C1
　Stutton IP9...........62 C2
Driftway The CM4......18 B6
Drive The
　Chelmsford CM1......205 A6
　Clacton-on-S CO15...189 B7
　Harwich CO12.........91 B2
　Rivenhall End CM8 ...177 E6
　Thaxted CM6..........69 F3
Drood Cl CM1........204 F7
Drovers Way
　Bishop's Stortford
　　CM23...............145 C5
　Chelmsford CM2.....206 B7
Druce The CB11.......65 D4
Drum Field CO7.......58 D1
Drury Dr CO10........15 F2
Drury La
[5] Braintree CM7 ....127 F3
　Ridgewell CO9........29 A6
Dry Dock CO7........164 B8
Du Cane Pl [3] CM8 ..177 A2
Duchess Cl CM23 ....145 C7
DUCK END
　Bishop's Stortford
　　CM23...............119 E1
　Finchingfield..........72 E7
　Stansted..............98 D1
Duckend Farm La CM6 ..97 F6
DUCKEND GREEN.....126 F3
Ducketts Wharf [10]
　CM23...............145 F6
Duck St
　Little Easton CM6....122 F5
　Wendens Ambo CB11 ..42 E5
DUDDENHOE END....41 A6
Duddery Cl CB9........9 B7
Duddery Hill CB9.......9 A7
Duddery Rd CB9.......9 A7
Dudley Cl
　Boreham CM3.......192 E1
　Colchester CO4.......136 A4
Dudley Ct CO15......189 A8
Dudley Rd
　Clacton-on-S CO15 ..188 D3
　Earls Colne CO6......104 F7
　Fingringhoe CO5.....163 E3
Duffield Dr CO4......136 E7
Duffield Rd CM2.....216 D6
Duffries Cl CM3......190 E7
Duffs Hill CO10........2 E1
Dugard Ave CO3......134 E4
Duggers La CM7......128 E4
Dugmore Ave CO13 ..170 C8
Dukes Cl CM7........205 F4
Dukes Orch CM1.....204 B1
Dukes Park Ind Est
　CM2...............205 F4
Dukes Priory Hospl The
　CM1...............205 D4
Dukes Rd CM7.......127 F6
Dukes Ride CM23....145 C7
Duke St
　Brightlingsea CO7 ...185 E6
　Chelmsford CM1.....205 B2
　Ipswich IP3...........17 E4
Dukes Wlk [6] CM1 ..205 A3
Dulverton Cotts CO3 ..134 C4
Dulwich Cl CO15.....189 D4
Dulwich Rd CO15....189 D5
Dumbarton Rd IP4 ....18 C8
Dumfries Rd IP4......18 C8
Dumney La
　Braintree, Hornells Corner
　　CM3...............153 E2
　Braintree, Thistley Green
　　CM6...............153 B3
　Great Leighs CM3 ...173 E8
　Great Bardfield CM7 ..98 F8
　Great Canfield CM6 ..149 F1
　Great Hallingbury
　　CM22...............147 C2
　Rayne CM7...........126 B2
　Takeley CM22........148 C7
　Thaxted CM6..........97 A7

Dunmow St Mary's Prim
 Sch CM6 . . . . . . . 150 C8
Dunning Cl CO11 . . . . 114 C8
Dunnock Way CO4 . . . 137 A7
Dunoon Cl CM7 . . . . . 128 D4
Dunstable Dr CM7 . . . 128 D3
Dunster Dr CB9 . . . . . . 8 E8
Dunthorne Rd CO4 . . . 110 C2
Dunthorpe Rd CO16 . . 188 D6
Duntons Almshouses
 CO7 . . . . . . . . . . . 84 F6
Dunwich Ct
 Colchester CO2 . . . . 135 F4
 Haverhill CB9 . . . . . . 8 C8
 Ipswich IP1 . . . . . . 16 E8
Dupont Cl CO16 . . . . . 188 D6
Durand La CM6 . . . . . 151 E6
Durham Cl CM7 . . . . . 72 A1
Durham Sq CO1 . . . . . 136 A7
DUTON HILL . . . . . . . 96 E3
Duxford Rd CB10 . . . . . 3 A7
Dyehouse Mdw CO10 . . 15 B7
Dyers Ct CM23 . . . . . 145 C5
DYER'S END . . . . . . . 28 E1
Dyers Rd CO9 . . . . . . 28 E1
Dyer's Rd
 Colchester CO3 . . . . 134 C3
 Maldon CM9 . . . . . 210 A2
Dyke Rd IP11 . . . . . . 221 A2
Dykes Chase CM9 . . . . 209 F3
Dyke St IP1 . . . . . . . 17 C7
Dyne's Hall Rd CO9 . . . 76 C8

**E**

Eagle Ave CO14 . . . . . 144 D1
Eaglegate [4] CO1 . . . . 136 A7
Eagle La CM7 . . . . . . 127 F6
Eagles Cl IP11 . . . . . . 221 D4
Eagle St [3] IP4 . . . . . 17 D5
Earlhams Cl CO12 . . . . 90 F1
Earlhams Mews CO12 . . 90 D1
Earls Cl CM23 . . . . . . 145 D6
EARLS COLNE . . . . . 105 C6
 Bishop's Stortford
Earls Colne Rd CO6 . . . 106 A1
Earlsfield Dr CM2 . . . . 205 F3
Earls Gn CB9 . . . . . . . 8 C8
Earls Hall Dr CO16 . . . 187 E5
Earlsmead CM8 . . . . . 176 F3
Earlswood Way CO2 . . . 135 D2
Eastacre CB10 . . . . . . 22 E2
East Anglian Rly Mus*
 CO6 . . . . . . . . . . . 106 D6
East Area IP1 . . . . . . . 16 C7
East Bay CO1 . . . . . . 136 B7
EAST BERGHOLT . . . . 59 C2
East Bergholt CE Prim Sch
 CO7 . . . . . . . . . . . . 59 B3
East Bergholt High Sch
 CO7 . . . . . . . . . . . . 59 D3
East Bergholt Place Gdn*
 CO7 . . . . . . . . . . . . 59 F1
Eastby Cl CB11 . . . . . 43 F8
Eastcliff Ave CO15 . . . 189 B4
Eastcliff Ho CO14 . . . . 144 D1
East Court Ho CO14 . . . 136 C7
East Dock Rd CO12 . . . 90 F6
EAST END . . . . . . . . 60 C2
Eastend La CM6, CM22 . 121 C8
East End La CO7 . . . . . 60 A3
East End Rd CO7 . . . . . 60 A3
Easten Greene CO6 . . . 80 E4
Easterford Rd CO5 . . . 158 C2
Easterling Cl CO12 . . . . 91 A4
Eastern App CM2 . . . . 205 F5
Eastern Ave CB9 . . . . . 8 F8
Eastern Cres CM1 . . . . 204 F5
Eastern Prom CO16 . . . 185 F3
Eastern Rd CO7 . . . . . 185 E6
East Essex Aviation Mus*
 CO16 . . . . . . . . . . 185 E4
Eastgate CB10 . . . . . . . 3 D2
Eastgate St [7] IP4 . . . . 17 D6
East Gates Ind Est
 CO1 . . . . . . . . . . . 136 B7
Eastgate St CO12 . . . . 91 D6
EAST GORES . . . . . . 132 A4
East Gores Farm CO6 . . 131 F4
East Gores Rd CO6 . . . 131 F5
East Hanningfield Rd
 CM2 . . . . . . . . . . . 217 E2
East Haven CO15 . . . . 188 E5
East Hill CO11 . . . . . . 136 A7
EASTHORPE . . . . . . . 160 B7
Easthorpe Rd
 Feering CO5 . . . . . . 159 D2
 Messing CO5 . . . . . 159 F5
East La CO7 . . . . . . . 85 B5
Eastland Ct IP11 . . . . . 221 B7
East Lawn IP4 . . . . . . 18 C8
EAST MERSEA . . . . . 184 F1
East Mersea Rd CO5 . . 183 E1
East Mill CO7 . . . . . . . 76 F2
East Mill Gn IP9 . . . . . 60 E6
Easton Farm CM6 . . . . 122 E6
Easton Rd CM8 . . . . . 177 A3
Easton Way CO13 . . . . 171 B6
East Rd
 Bishop's Stortford
  CM23 . . . . . . . . 146 B7

East Rd *continued*
 East Mersea CO5 . . . . 184 D1
 West Mersea CO5 . . . 201 E7
East Row IP9 . . . . . . . 62 D6
East Side CO4 . . . . . . 83 A4
East St
 Braintree CM7 . . . . . 128 A3
 Coggeshall CO6 . . . . 131 A2
 Colchester CO1 . . . . 136 B7
 Harwich CO12 . . . . . 91 D4
 Saffron Walden CB10 . . 22 E1
 Sudbury CO10 . . . . . 33 F8
 Tollesbury CM9 . . . . 199 D1
 Wivenhoe CO7 . . . . 164 B7
East Stockwell St
 CO1 . . . . . . . . . . . 135 F7
East Terr CO14 . . . . . 144 D1
East View CM22 . . . . . 148 C8
East View Cl CB10 . . . . 45 F8
East Ward Mews CO1 . . 136 C7
Eastway Ind Ctr IP1 . . . 16 D8
Eastways CM8 . . . . . . 177 B4
Eastways Ind Est CM8 . 177 B4
Eastwood Dr CO4 . . . . 110 B3
Eastwood Pk CM2 . . . . 217 A5
Eaton Cl IP11 . . . . . . 221 A7
Eaton Cotts CO5 . . . . . 179 D7
Eaton Gdns IP11 . . . . . 221 C2
Eaton Ho [5] . . . . . . . 146 B8
Eaton Mews CO2 . . . . 136 B3
Eaton Way CM9 . . . . . 196 E7
Ebenezer Cl CM8 . . . . 176 E5
Ebenezer Terr CM2 . . . 216 F7
Ebony Cl CO2 . . . . . . 135 D2
Eccles Rd IP2 . . . . . . . 16 D1
Eckersley Rd CM1 . . . . 205 C3
Eden Cl CM8 . . . . . . . 176 E3
Eden Rd
 Haverhill CB9 . . . . . . 9 A7
 Ipswich IP4 . . . . . . 18 B5
Edens Cl CM23 . . . . . 146 B7
Edenside CO13 . . . . . 170 E7
Edenway CM1 . . . . . . 204 C5
Edgefield Ave CO11 . . . 86 B3
Edgeworth Rd IP2 . . . . 16 E2
Edgware Rd CO16 . . . . 188 D5
Edgworth Rd CO10 . . . 33 E7
Edinburgh Cl CM8 . . . . 195 A8
Edinburgh Gdns
 Bishop's Stortford
  CM23 . . . . . . . . 145 E6
 Braintree CM7 . . . . . 128 C4
Edison Cl [3] CM7 . . . . 127 F1
Edison Gdns CO1 . . . . 110 C1
Edison Rd CO15 . . . . . 189 F6
Edith Borthwick Sch The
 CM7 . . . . . . . . . . . 127 F8
Edith Cavell Way CB9 . . 27 C6
Edith Rd
 Clacton-on-S CO15 . . 188 E2
 Kirby-le-S CO13 . . . . 170 D8
Edmund Cl CM8 . . . . . 195 A8
Edmund Gn CO9 . . . . . 102 E8
Edmund Rd CM8 . . . . . 194 E8
Edney Ct IP11 . . . . . . 221 E3
Edward Ave CO7 . . . . . 185 F7
Edward Bowden Ct
 CB10 . . . . . . . . . . . 22 D1
Edward Bright Cl
 CM9 . . . . . . . . . . . 210 A2
Edward Cl
 Ipswich IP1 . . . . . . 16 F8
 Little Clacton CO16 . . 168 E5
Edward Cordy Ho
 CO1 . . . . . . . . . . . 221 E3
Edward Dr CM1 . . . . . 216 C7
Edward Ho CB10 . . . . . 22 C2
Edward Marke Dr
 CO5 . . . . . . . . . . . 163 B3
Edward Paxman Gdns [10]
 CO1 . . . . . . . . . . . 136 C6
Edward Rd CO16 . . . . . 168 F7
Edward St CO12 . . . . . 90 E5
Edwards Wlk CM9 . . . . 209 F3
Edward Terr CO16 . . . . 168 E5
Egerton Green Rd
 CO2 . . . . . . . . . . . 135 A3
Egglestone Cl IP2 . . . . 16 F1
Eggshall La CM7 . . . . . 27 E2
Eglinton Dr CM2 . . . . . 206 B4
Egremont St CO10 . . . . 2 B3
Egremont Way CO3 . . . 134 C4
Egret Cres CO4 . . . . . 137 A8
Ehringshausen Way CB9 . 9 B7
Eider Cl CM23 . . . . . . 146 A6
Eight Acre La CO2 . . . . 135 C2
EIGHT ASH GREEN . . . 134 B8
Eight Ash Green & Aldham
 CE Prim Sch CO3 . . . 107 F1
Elderberry Gdns CM8 . . 177 B4
Elder Field CM7 . . . . . 154 B5
ELDER STREET . . . . . 44 E1
Eld La CO1 . . . . . . . . 135 F7
Eldon Cl CO4 . . . . . . . 110 C1
Eldred Ave CO2 . . . . . 135 B3
Eldred Cl IP1 . . . . . . . 16 D8
Eldred Ct CO10 . . . . . 34 C4
Eldred Dr CO10 . . . . . 34 C4
Eleanor Cl CO5 . . . . . 179 D6
Eleanor Wlk CO5 . . . . . 179 D6
Eleventh Ave CM24 . . . 120 B2
Elfrida Ho CO2 . . . . . . 135 B3
Elgar Dr CM8 . . . . . . . 194 F7
Elgin Ave CM1 . . . . . . 205 A2
Elianore Rd CO3 . . . . . 135 B7
Eliot Way CM9 . . . . . . 210 A1
Elizabeth Ave CM8 . . . 195 A8

Elizabeth Cl
 Colchester CO4 . . . . 110 C4
 Saffron Walden CB10 . . 22 F2
Elizabeth Ct
 Harwich CO12 . . . . . 91 A3
 Ipswich IP3 . . . . . . 17 F5
 [4] Sudbury CO10 . . . 33 F8
 Walton-on-N CO14 . . 144 E3
Elizabeth Rd
 Bishop's Stortford
  CM23 . . . . . . . . 145 E5
 Harwich CO12 . . . . . 91 A3
Elizabeth Villas CO5 . . . 180 A2
Elizabeth Way
 Brightlingsea CO7 . . . 185 F6
 Felixstowe IP11 . . . . 221 C3
 Halstead CO9 . . . . . 76 E2
 Hatfield Peverel CM3 . . 194 A4
 Heybridge CM9 . . . . 210 A5
 Saffron Walden CB10 . . 22 F2
 Sudbury CO10 . . . . . 33 C5
 Wivenhoe CO7 . . . . 137 C3
Ellenborough Cl
 CM23 . . . . . . . . . . 145 D5
Ellenbrook Gn IP2 . . . . 16 D1
Ellenbrook Rd IP2 . . . . 16 D1
Ellen Way CM77 . . . . . 154 D7
Elliot Pl CM7 . . . . . . . 128 C3
Elliots Dr CO14 . . . . . 171 B8
Elliott Cl CM23 . . . . . 146 A8
Elliott St IP1 . . . . . . . 17 A6
Ellis Rd
 Boxted CO4 . . . . . . 82 F3
 Bradfield CO11 . . . . 114 D8
 Clacton-on-S CO15 . . 188 E2
Elm Ave CM9 . . . . . . . 210 C5
Elm Bglws CM7 . . . . . 127 D4
Elmbrook Dr CM23 . . . 145 E3
Elm Cl
 Alresford CO7 . . . . . 165 B8
 Brantham CO11 . . . . 60 D1
 Chelmsford CM1 . . . . 205 A8
 Elsenham CM22 . . . . 94 C2
 Great Baddow CM2 . . 216 F6
 Great Bentley CO7 . . . 166 E8
 Haverhill CB9 . . . . . . 8 F8
 Sible Hedingham CO9 . . 51 D2
 Takeley CM22 . . . . . 148 C7
 Tiptree CO5 . . . . . . 179 C7
Elm Close Extension
 CM22 . . . . . . . . . . 148 C7
Elm Cres CO5 . . . . . . 136 D7
Elmcroft CO7 . . . . . . . 138 A6
Elm Ct
 Elmdon CB11 . . . . . 20 B4
 Sturmer CB9 . . . . . . 9 E5
Elmdale Dr CO11 . . . . 86 D3
Elmden Ct CO15 . . . . . 188 E5
ELMDON . . . . . . . . . 20 A4
Elmdon Pl [1] . . . . . . . 9 B8
Elm Dr
 Brightlingsea CO7 . . . 185 D7
 Halstead CO9 . . . . . 76 F1
 Harwich CO12 . . . . . 91 B3
Elm Est CO7 . . . . . . . 59 C3
Elm Farm Cvn Pk
 CO16 . . . . . . . . . . . 142 A1
Elmfield Cl CO15 . . . . . 189 E7
Elm Gdns IP11 . . . . . . 221 A7
Elm Gr
 Bishop's Stortford
  CM23 . . . . . . . . 146 B7
 Chelmsford CM2 . . . . 216 A8
 East Bergholt CO7 . . . 59 C2
 Kirby Cross CO13 . . . 170 D6
 Saffron Walden CB10 . . 22 D1
 Wivenhoe CO7 . . . . 137 B1
Elm Green La CM3 . . . . 218 C8
Elm Green Prep Sch
 CM3 . . . . . . . . . . . 207 D3
Elm Ho IP11 . . . . . . . 221 C4
Elmhurst Cl CB9 . . . . . 9 B7
Elmhurst Dr IP3 . . . . . 17 F3
Elmhurst Rd CO12 . . . . 91 C3
Elm La
 Capel St M IP9 . . . . . 35 A1
 Marks Tey CO5 . . . . . 132 B2
 Washbrook IP8 . . . . . 35 E8
Elm Rd
 Bishop's Stortford
  CM23 . . . . . . . . 145 E6
 Chelmsford CM2 . . . . 216 A8
 East Bergholt CO7 . . . 59 C2
 Great Dunmow CM6 . . 123 D2
 Little Clacton CO16 . . 168 C3
 Rushmere St A IP5 . . . 18 F7
 Sudbury CO10 . . . . . 34 A7
Elm Rise CM8 . . . . . . 177 A5
Elms Dr CM1 . . . . . . . 205 A4
Elms Hall Rd CO6 . . . . 104 E8
Elms The
 East Bergholt CO7 . . . 60 C3
 Frinton-on-S CO13 . . 170 F2
 Great Chesterford CB10 . 3 E3
Elm Tree Ave CO13 . . . 170 F7
Elm Tree Cl CO13 . . . . 170 F7
Elm Way CM3 . . . . . . 192 E1
Elm Wlk CM77 . . . . . . 126 F2
Elmwood CO3 . . . . . . 134 D6
Elmwood Ave CO2 . . . . 135 B2
Elmwood Dr CO5 . . . . . 201 D7

ELSENHAM . . . . . . . . 94 C1
Elsenham CE Prim Sch
 CM22 . . . . . . . . . . 94 D1
Elsenham Cross CM22 . . 94 D1
Elsenham Hall CM22 . . 120 C8
Elsenham Sta CM22 . . . 94 B6
Elsham Dr CM7 . . . . . 154 B6
Elsmere Rd IP1 . . . . . 17 C8
Elstar La CO6 . . . . . . . 109 B8
Elthorne Pk CO16 . . . . 188 D4
Elton Park Bsns Ctr
 IP2 . . . . . . . . . . . . 16 D6
Elton Pk IP2 . . . . . . . 16 D6
Elton Wlk CO5 . . . . . . 179 D6
Elvina Ho CO15 . . . . . 203 F6
Elves Cl CO4 . . . . . . . 110 D1
Elwin Rd CO5 . . . . . . 179 D6
Ely Gdns CO1 . . . . . . 136 A7
Elysian Gdns CM9 . . . . 199 C1
Embassy Ct CM9 . . . . . 210 A2
Emberson Ct CM7 . . . . 205 F4
Emblems CM6 . . . . . . 123 C1
Embra Ct CO2 . . . . . . 136 B5
Emily Bray Ho IP4 . . . . 17 F7
Emily May Ct CO2 . . . . 91 A3
Emlen St IP1 . . . . . . . 17 A6
Emmanuel Cl IP2 . . . . 16 F3
Emmerson Ho CM23 . . 146 A5
Emmett Acre CO5 . . . . 209 E1
Emperor Circ IP3 . . . . . 38 C8
Emperor Cl CM9 . . . . . 210 A5
Empire Bsns Pk CO15 . . 188 E3
Empire Ct
 Clacton-on-S CO15 . . 188 E3
 [3] Frinton-on-S CO13 . 170 F5
Empire Rd CO12 . . . . . 91 D3
Empire Wlk [2] CM7 . . . 128 A3
Empress Ave CO5 . . . . 201 E6
Empress Dr CO5 . . . . . 201 D6
Emson Cl CB10 . . . . . . 22 D2
Endean Ct CO7 . . . . . 137 A2
Endeavour Cl CM9 . . . . 199 D2
Endsleigh Ct CO3 . . . . 135 C7
Endway The
 Great Easton CM6 . . . 122 F7
 Steeple Bumpstead CB9 . 27 C8
Engaines Prim Sch
 CO16 . . . . . . . . . . . 168 C2
Engineers Sq CO4 . . . . 109 D2
Engleric SG8 . . . . . . . 19 D5
Enid Way CO9 . . . . . . 109 D2
Ennerdale Ave CM77 . . 154 C6
Enoch Ho CO1 . . . . . . 136 E8
Enterprise Ct CM7 . . . . 128 B2
Enterprise Ctr CM7 . . . 177 A3
Enterprise Ho CO9 . . . . 51 E2
Enville Way CO4 . . . . . 110 B4
Epping Cl
 Chelmsford CM1 . . . . 204 E1
 Clacton-on-S CO15 . . 188 F8
Epping Way CM8 . . . . . 176 E1
Epsom Cl CO16 . . . . . 188 D6
Erbury Pl CO10 . . . . . 12 B8
Erica Wlk CO4 . . . . . . 136 D7
Erick Ave CM1 . . . . . . 205 B7
Eridge Cl CM1 . . . . . . 205 B7
Eriswell Rd CB9 . . . . . 9 B8
Erle Havard Rd CO6 . . . 108 E4
Ernalds Cl CO6 . . . . . 105 B7
Ernest Rd CO7 . . . . . . 137 C1
Ernleigh Rd IP4 . . . . . 18 B6
Errington Rd CO3 . . . . 135 D5
Erskine Rd CO11 . . . . . 86 D4
Esplanade
 Frinton-on-S CO13 . . 170 F3
 Harwich CO12 . . . . . 91 E4
Esplanade Ct
 Frinton-on-S CO13 . . 171 A5
 Harwich CO12 . . . . . 91 E6
Esplanade The CO15 . . 189 G6
Essex Ave
 Chelmsford CM1 . . . . 205 A7
 Clacton-on-S CO15 . . 203 A7
 Sudbury CO10 . . . . . 15 F2
Essex County Cricket
 Club* CM2 . . . . . . . 205 B2
Essex Cty Hospl CO3 . . 135 D6
Essex Hall Rd CO1 . . . . 109 E1
Essex Knowle CO8 . . . . 55 F1
Essex Rd
 Braintree CM7 . . . . . 128 B4
 Maldon CM9 . . . . . . 209 F1
Essex Regiment Way
 CM3 . . . . . . . . . . . 191 D5
Essex Way IP1 . . . . . . 18 E1
Essex Yeomanry Way
 CO3 . . . . . . . . . . . 134 B7
Estate Yd The CM3 . . . . 175 C2
Estella Mead CM1 . . . . 204 E7
Estuary Cl CO14 . . . . . 109 E4
Estuary Cres
 Clacton-on-S CO15 . . 188 D3
 Shotley Gate IP9 . . . 91 B8
Estuary Mews CM9 . . . 199 D2
Estuary Park Rd CO5 . . 201 E6
Eton Ct CO13 . . . . . . 171 A5
Eton Rd
 Clacton-on-S CO15 . . 188 F4
 Frinton-on-S CO13 . . 171 A5
Eudo Ho CO1 . . . . . . . 135 F4
Eudo Rd CO2 . . . . . . . 135 F4
Europa Pk CM8 . . . . . 177 A3
Europa Way
 Harwich CO12 . . . . . 90 F4
 Ipswich IP1 . . . . . . 16 D7
Eustace Rd IP1 . . . . . 16 E8

Euston Ave IP4 . . . . . 18 F6
Euston Ct IP11 . . . . . 221 A4
Evabrook Cl IP2 . . . . . 16 E1
Evelyn Pl CM1 . . . . . . 204 F1
Evelyn Rd CM3 . . . . . 153 D4
Evelyn Wood Rd
 CM7 . . . . . . . . . . . 155 E6
Everest Gdns CM23 . . . 145 E6
Everest Way CM9 . . . . 210 B5
Everett Ho CO1 . . . . . 136 B6
Evergreen Dr CO4 . . . . 110 D4
Everitt Rd CO10 . . . . . 22 F2
Everitt Way CO9 . . . . . 51 E2
Eves Cnr CM3 . . . . . . 218 E7
Eves Cres CM1 . . . . . . 205 A5
Eves Ct CO12 . . . . . . . 90 D1
Evesham Cl IP2 . . . . . 17 A2
Eves Orch CO8 . . . . . . 55 F1
Ewan Cl CO3 . . . . . . . 134 C6
Ewan Way CO3 . . . . . 134 C7
Ewell Hall Chase CO5 . . 158 C1
Ewer Ct CO1 . . . . . . . 136 A6
Exchange Way [5]
 CM1 . . . . . . . . . . . 205 B2
Exeter Cl
 Braintree CM7 . . . . . 128 B5
 Great Horkesley CO6 . . 109 C7
Exeter Ct [6] CB9 . . . . 8 E6
Exeter Dr CO1 . . . . . . 136 A7
Exeter Rd
 Chelmsford CM1 . . . . 205 E5
 Felixstowe IP11 . . . . 221 A4
 Ipswich IP3 . . . . . . 18 B4
Exmoor Cl CM1 . . . . . 204 D1
Exmoor Rd IP11 . . . . . 221 D6

**F**

Faber Rd CM8 . . . . . . 194 E8
Fabians Cl CO6 . . . . . 131 A3
Factory Hill CO5 . . . . . 179 E3
Factory La CO11 . . . . . 86 C7
Factory La E CO9 . . . . 76 E1
Factory La W CO9 . . . . 76 E1
Factory Terr CO9 . . . . . 76 E2
Faggot Yd CM7 . . . . . 127 F5
Fairbrother Ct [1]
 CO4 . . . . . . . . . . . 136 D7
Fair Cl CO7 . . . . . . . . 186 A6
Fairclough Ave CO16 . . 188 B3
Fairfax Hall CO4 . . . . . 109 F4
Fairfax Mead CM2 . . . . 206 A2
Fairfield Ho [7] CO2 . . . 135 F6
Fairfield Ave IP11 . . . . 221 E5
Fairfield Cl CO7 . . . . . 139 A7
Fairfield Gdns [2]
 CO4 . . . . . . . . . . . 136 C8
Fairfield Inf Sch IP11 . . 221 E5
Fairfield Rd
 Braintree CM7 . . . . . 127 F2
 Chelmsford CM1 . . . . 205 A3
 Clacton-on-S CO15 . . 188 E4
 Ipswich IP3 . . . . . . 18 A2
Fairfields CM23 . . . . . 220 D1
Fairhaven Ave CO5 . . . 201 E6
Fairhaven Ct CO5 . . . . 201 E5
Fairhead Rd N CO4 . . . 136 C8
Fairhead Rd S [6] CO4 . 136 C8
Fairleads CM3 . . . . . . 218 F8
Fair Leas CB10 . . . . . . 22 E3
Fairlop Cl CO15 . . . . . 188 F8
FAIRSTEAD . . . . . . . . 175 B6
Fairstead Hall Rd
 CM3 . . . . . . . . . . . 175 A5
Fairstead Rd CM3 . . . . 175 C6
Fairway
 Bishop's Stortford
  CM23 . . . . . . . . 146 A3
 Chelmsford CM2 . . . . 216 D7
Fairways CO4 . . . . . . 109 B3
Fairways The IP4 . . . . . 18 E5
Faircycroft Rd CO16 . . . 22 E1
Fairy Hall La CM77 . . . 127 A1
Falcon Cl CB9 . . . . . . 9 C8
Falcon Cres CO1 . . . . . 136 B5
Falconer Rd CO9 . . . . . 9 C5
Falcon St CM23 . . . . . 145 C5
Falcon Fields CM6 . . . . 220 F8
Falcon Mews CM9 . . . . 220 F8
Falcons Mead CM2 . . . 205 A1
Falcon Sq CO9 . . . . . . 51 F4
Falcon St
 Felixstowe IP11 . . . . 221 C6
 Ipswich IP1 . . . . . . 17 C5
Falcon Way
 Chelmsford CM2 . . . . 216 A6
 Clacton-on-S CO15 . . 188 F6
Falkland Ct CM1 . . . . . 206 E8
Falkland Ct CM7 . . . . . 128 B4
Falkland Gn CM9 . . . . . 219 E6
Falklands Dr [8] CO11 . . 86 D4
Falklands Rd CO2 . . . . 135 E3
Fallowden La CB10 . . . 23 F4
Fallowfield Cl CO12 . . . 90 F3
Fallowfield Ct [4] CB9 . . 8 E7
Fallowfields CM8 . . . . . 176 E5
Falmouth Rd CM1 . . . . 205 E5
Falstaff Cotts IP9 . . . . . 60 F8
Fambridge Chase
 CM8 . . . . . . . . . . . 155 F2
Fambridge Cl CM9 . . . . 210 A1
Fambridge Rd CM9 . . . 209 F2
FANNER'S GREEN . . . . 190 C5

Fanner's Green Cotts
CM3 . . . . . . . . . . . . . . . . 190 C5
Fanny's La CO16 . . . . . . . 167 D2
Faraday Cl
Braintree CM7 . . . . . . . . . 127 F1
Clacton-on-S CO15 . . . . . 169 A1
Faraday Rd IP4 . . . . . . . . . . 17 F5
Farford Field CO10 . . . . . . 34 C5
Farina Cl IP1 . . . . . . . . . . . 16 F7
Farmadine CB11 . . . . . . . . 22 E1
Farmadine Ct **4** CB11 . . 22 E1
Farmadine Gr CB11 . . . . . 22 E1
Farmadine Ho **6** CB11 . . 22 E1
Farm Dr CO6 . . . . . . . . . . 134 A8
Farmers Way CO16 . . . . . 188 B3
Farmfield Rd CO6 . . . . . . 106 B1
Farmleigh Ave CO15 . . . . 188 F8
Farm Rd CO12 . . . . . . . . . 116 D3
Farm Wlk CO7 . . . . . . . . . 185 E8
FARNHAM . . . . . . . . . . . . 118 D6
Farnham CE Prim Sch
CM23 . . . . . . . . . . . . . . . 118 D6
FARNHAM GREEN . . . . . . 118 B7
Farriers Chase CO5 . . . . . 201 D6
Farriers End CO3 . . . . . . . 134 D5
Farriers Way CM7 . . . . . . 154 B7
Farrington Cl **3** CO1 . . 136 C6
Farrow Rd CM4 . . . . . . . . 215 E7
Farthing Cl CM7 . . . . . . . 128 D4
Farthing Ct **10** CM1 . . . 205 A3
Farthing Rd IP1 . . . . . . . . . 16 C7
Farthing Road Ind Est
IP1 . . . . . . . . . . . . . . . . . . 16 C7
Farthings Chase CO5 . . . . 201 E7
Farthings Went IP9 . . . . . . 35 B2
FAR THORPE GREEN
. . . . . . . . . . . . . . . . . . . . 141 C2
Fastnet Cl CB9 . . . . . . . . . . 9 D8
Faulds Wlk CO2 . . . . . . . . 136 A3
FAULKBOURNE . . . . . . . . 176 A7
Faulkbourne Rd CM8 . . . 176 D4
Faulkeners Way IP11 . . . . 221 A8
Fawkner Cl CM2 . . . . . . . 205 F2
Fawley Cl IP4 . . . . . . . . . . . 18 C7
Fayrewood Dr CM3 . . . . . 173 F7
Feather Cl CM7 . . . . . . . . 128 D3
Feathers Field IP11 . . . . . . 221 B5
Feedhams Cl CO7 . . . . . . 137 C3
FEERING . . . . . . . . . . . . . 158 E5
Feering CE Prim Sch
CO5 . . . . . . . . . . . . . . . . 158 E4
Feering Hill CO5 . . . . . . . 158 D3
Feering Rd CO6 . . . . . . . . 131 B1
Felaw St IP2 . . . . . . . . . . . . 17 D4
Felbrigg Cl CM7 . . . . . . . 154 B7
Felix Ct IP11 . . . . . . . . . . . 221 D2
Felix Rd
Felixstowe IP11 . . . . . . . . 221 F4
Ipswich IP3 . . . . . . . . . . . . 18 C2
FELIXSTOWE . . . . . . . . . . 221 F3
Felixstowe Beach Cvn Pk
IP11 . . . . . . . . . . . . . . . . 221 C2
Felixstowe CO16 . . . . . . . 188 A4
Felixstowe General Hospl
IP11 . . . . . . . . . . . . . . . . 221 F4
Felixstowe Rd IP3 . . . . . . . 18 B3
Felixstowe Sta IP11 . . . . . 221 E5
Fellbrigg Ave IP5 . . . . . . . 18 F6
Fell Christy CM1 . . . . . . . 205 B5
Fellowes Cl CO4 . . . . . . . 109 F2
Fell Rd CO9 . . . . . . . . . . . . 28 B8
Felnor Wlk IP11 . . . . . . . . 221 E4
Felstead Cl CO2 . . . . . . . 163 A8
FELSTED . . . . . . . . . . . . . 152 B5
Felsted Almshouses
CM6 . . . . . . . . . . . . . . . . 152 B6
Felsted Prep Sch
CM6 . . . . . . . . . . . . . . . . 152 B5
Felsted Prim Sch
CM6 . . . . . . . . . . . . . . . . 152 D7
Felsted Sch CM6 . . . . . . . 152 C6
Felsted Vineyard *
CM6 . . . . . . . . . . . . . . . . 151 C7
Feltwell Pl **2** CB9 . . . . . . 9 B8
Fen Bight Circ IP3 . . . . . . . 38 C7
Fenbridge La CO7 . . . . . . . 59 B1
Fen Farm Cvn Site
CO5 . . . . . . . . . . . . . . . . 184 F1
Fen Field Units CO9 . . . . . . 8 F5
Fen La CO7 . . . . . . . . . . . . 84 D1
Fenman Ct CM22 . . . . . . . 94 C2
Fen Mdw IP11 . . . . . . . . . 221 A8
Fenn Cl CO7 . . . . . . . . . . 139 A3
Fennel Cl CO15 . . . . . . . . 179 C5
Fennels Cl CB9 . . . . . . . . . . 9 A7
Fennes Rd CM7 . . . . . . . . 128 B6
Fennings Chase CO1 . . . . 136 A7
Fenno Cl CO13 . . . . . . . . 134 F4
Fenn Rd CO9 . . . . . . . . . . . 77 A1
Fen St CO6 . . . . . . . . . . . . 56 B1
Fenton Rd CO9 . . . . . . . . . . 9 B8
Fen View IP8 . . . . . . . . . . . 35 E8
Fenwick Dr CO1 . . . . . . . 136 B8
Ferdinand Wlk CO4 . . . . . 136 F7
Ferguson Cl CB11 . . . . . . . 23 A2
Ferndale Cl CO15 . . . . . . 188 F7
Ferndale Rd CO12 . . . . . . . 91 D5
Ferndown Rd CO13 . . . . . 170 E5
Ferndown Way CM3 . . . . 194 B4
Fern Gr CB9 . . . . . . . . . . . . 8 E8
Fernhayes Cl IP2 . . . . . . . . 17 A2
Fern Hill CO10 . . . . . . . . . 12 C6
Fernie Rd CM7 . . . . . . . . 127 D2
Fernlea CO6 . . . . . . . . . . 109 C2
Fernlea Rd CO12 . . . . . . . 91 D5
Fern Way CO15 . . . . . . . . 203 F7

Fernwood Ave CO15 . . . . 189 F5
Ferry La IP11 . . . . . . . . . . 221 A3
Ferry Rd CO5 . . . . . . . . . . 164 B6
Festival Gdns CM1 . . . . . 205 B3
Feverills Rd CO16 . . . . . . 168 D4
Fiat Ave CO15 . . . . . . . . . 203 D6
Fiddlers Folly CO3 . . . . . . 107 E1
Fiddlers Hill CO3 . . . . . . . 107 E2
Fiddlers La CO7 . . . . . . . . . 59 C3
Field Ct CO4 . . . . . . . . . . 136 E8
Fieldgate Dock CO7 . . . . 185 E5
Field Gate La CM7 . . . . . . 22 A3
Fields Cl CO16 . . . . . . . . . 167 F6
Fields Farm Rd CO2 . . . . 162 B4
Fieldside CB11 . . . . . . . . . 43 E7
Field View CO10 . . . . . . . . 33 F8
Fieldview Cl CO4 . . . . . . . 109 F4
Field View Dr CM9 . . . . . 197 C4
Field Way CO7 . . . . . . . . . 137 C2
Field Wlk CO14 . . . . . . . . 171 A8
Fifth Ave
Chelmsford CM1 . . . . . . . 205 B6
Frinton-on-S CO13 . . . . . 170 E5
Halstead CO9 . . . . . . . . . . 77 B1
Stansted Mountfitchet
CM24 . . . . . . . . . . . . . . . 120 B2
Finbars Wlk IP4 . . . . . . . . . 17 F5
Finborough Cl IP4 . . . . . . . 18 F6
Finchdale CO15 . . . . . . . . 188 F6
Finch Dr
Braintree CM7 . . . . . . . . . 127 D4
Great Bentley CO7 . . . . . . 139 D1
Finch Hill CO10 . . . . . . . . . 33 A7
FINCHINGFIELD . . . . . . . . 72 C5
Finchingfield CE Prim Sch
CM7 . . . . . . . . . . . . . . . . . 72 D6
Finchingfield Guildhall
Mus * CM7 . . . . . . . . . . . 72 D6
Finchingfield Rd
Stambourne CO9 . . . . . . . 49 C2
Steeple Bumpstead CB9 . . 27 C6
Finchingfield Way
CO2 . . . . . . . . . . . . . . . . 163 A8
Finchley Ave CM2 . . . . . . 216 A8
Finchley Rd IP4 . . . . . . . . . 17 E6
Finch's CM8 . . . . . . . . . . 195 F6
Findley Cl IP9 . . . . . . . . . . . 61 F2
Finer Cl CO16 . . . . . . . . . 188 C5
FINGRINGHOE . . . . . . . . 163 F5
Fingringhoe CE Prim Sch
CO5 . . . . . . . . . . . . . . . . 163 F5
Fingringhoe Rd
Abberton CO5 . . . . . . . . . 163 B3
Colchester CO2, CO5 . . . . 136 D1
Fingringhoe Wick
Conservation Ctr*
CO5 . . . . . . . . . . . . . . . . 164 D3
Finham Cl CO4 . . . . . . . . 136 F7
FINKLE GREEN . . . . . . . . . 28 A5
Finsbury Pl CO9 . . . . . . . . 76 F2
Firebronds Rd IP9 . . . . . . . 62 D5
Firecrest Rd CM2 . . . . . . 216 C5
Firefly Way IP3 . . . . . . . . . 38 B8
Firlands CM23 . . . . . . . . . 145 E6
Firlands Ho CM23 . . . . . . 145 E6
Firlie Wlk CO2 . . . . . . . . . 136 A3
Firmin Cl IP1 . . . . . . . . . . . 17 A6
Firs Chase CO5 . . . . . . . . 108 D4
Firs Chase CO5 . . . . . . . . 201 A6
Firs Chase Cvn Pk
CO5 . . . . . . . . . . . . . . . . 201 A7
Firs Cvn Pk CO16 . . . . . . 168 D2
Firs Dr CM1 . . . . . . . . . . . 204 B1
Firs Hamlet CO16 . . . . . . 201 A6
Firs Rd
Tiptree CO5 . . . . . . . . . . 179 D4
West Mersea CO5 . . . . . . 201 B7
First Ave
Chelmsford CM1 . . . . . . . 205 B5
Clacton-on-S CO15 . . . . . 189 B4
Frinton-on-S CO13 . . . . . 170 E4
Glemsford CO10 . . . . . . . . 2 C6
Halstead CO9 . . . . . . . . . . 77 B1
Harwich CO12 . . . . . . . . . 91 C3
Seawick CO16 . . . . . . . . . 203 C6
Stansted Mountfitchet
CM24 . . . . . . . . . . . . . . . 120 B2
Walton-on-t-N CO14 . . . . 144 E3
Weeley CO16 . . . . . . . . . 140 F1
Firs The
Gosfield CO9 . . . . . . . . . . 102 E8
Layer de la H CO2 . . . . . . 162 A6
Firstore Dr CO3 . . . . . . . . 134 E7
Fir Tree Cl CO4 . . . . . . . . 110 B4
Fir Tree Hill IP9 . . . . . . . . . 62 E4
Fir Tree La CM3 . . . . . . . . 207 E1
Fir Tree Rise
Chelmsford CM2 . . . . . . . 216 B6
Ipswich IP8 . . . . . . . . . . . . 16 C2
Fir Tree Wlk CM9 . . . . . . 210 C5
Fir Way CO15 . . . . . . . . . 203 G6
Firwood's Rd CO9 . . . . . . 103 E8
Fisbhane Cl IP3 . . . . . . . . . 38 B8
Fisher Cl CO9 . . . . . . . . . . . 9 D8
Fisher's La CO7 . . . . . . . . . 60 C3
Fisher Way CM7 . . . . . . . 128 C4
Fishmarket St CM6 . . . . . . 70 A2
Fish Pond Hill IP9 . . . . . . . 63 C3
Fishponds Hill CO6 . . . . . . 81 F4
Fishponds La IP9 . . . . . . . . 62 E5
Fish St CM9 . . . . . . . . . . . 211 E6
Fisin Wlk CO3 . . . . . . . . . 134 E8
Fiske Ct CO15 . . . . . . . . . 188 E2
Fitches Cres CM9 . . . . . . 210 B1
Fitches Croft CO6 . . . . . . 133 C4

Fitches Mews CM9 . . . . . 210 B1
Fitzgerald Cl CO11 . . . . . . 86 B4
Fitzgerald Cotts CO12 . . . . 90 F2
Fitzgerald Ct IP4 . . . . . . . . 18 A5
Fitzgilbert Rd CO2 . . . . . . 135 C4
Fitzmaurice Rd IP3 . . . . . . 18 B3
Fitzpiers CB10 . . . . . . . . . . 22 E2
Fitzroy St **2** IP1 . . . . . . . 17 C6
Fitzwalter La CM3 . . . . . . 218 D6
Fitzwalter Pl
Chelmsford CM1 . . . . . . . 204 D3
Great Dunmow CM6 . . . . 150 D8
Fitzwalter Rd
Boreham CM3 . . . . . . . . . 206 F8
Colchester CO3 . . . . . . . . 135 B6
Little Dunmow CM6 . . . . . 151 E7
Fitzwilliam Cl IP2 . . . . . . . 16 F2
Fitzwilliam Rd CO3 . . . . . 135 B7
Five Acres
Bicknacre CM3 . . . . . . . . 218 F3
Writtle IP9 . . . . . . . . . . . . 62 D5
Stansted Mountfitchet
CM24 . . . . . . . . . . . . . . . 119 E8
Walton-on-t-N CO14 . . . . 171 B8
Fiveash La CM7 . . . . . . . . 129 E1
Five Elms CO6 . . . . . . . . . 136 E7
Five Gables Chase
CO5 . . . . . . . . . . . . . . . . 201 D5
Five Ways CO3 . . . . . . . . 134 D4
Fiveways Ret Pk CO3 . . . . 134 D4
FLACKS GREEN . . . . . . . . 175 B2
Flag Hill CO7 . . . . . . . . . . 186 F8
Flagstaff Rd CO2 . . . . . . . 135 F6
Flail Cl CO7 . . . . . . . . . . . 137 F6
Flanders Cl CM7 . . . . . . . 127 E5
Flanders Field CO2 . . . . . 136 B3
Flatford Dr CO16 . . . . . . . 188 B5
Flatford La CM7 . . . . . . . . . 85 D7
Flatford Mill (Field Ctr)*
CO7 . . . . . . . . . . . . . . . . . 85 D7
Flatford Rd
East Bergholt CO7 . . . . . . . 85 C8
Haverhill CB9 . . . . . . . . . . . 8 C4
Flavian Cl CB9 . . . . . . . . . . 9 D7
Flavius Way CO4 . . . . . . . 110 A6
Flax La CO10 . . . . . . . . . . . 2 C3
Fleetwood Ave
Felixstowe IP11 . . . . . . . . 221 F5
Holland-on-S CO15 . . . . . 189 E7
Fleetwood Cl CO15 . . . . . 189 E7
Fleetwood Rd IP11 . . . . . 221 F5
Fleetwood Sq CM2 . . . . . 205 F8
Fleming Cl **7** CM7 . . . . 127 F1
Flemish Cotts The CO7 . . . 84 F6
Fletcher Cl CO1 . . . . . . . . 135 F8
Fletcher Rd IP3 . . . . . . . . . 18 B3
Flint Cl IP2 . . . . . . . . . . . . 17 B2
Flintwich Manor CM1 . . . 204 E7
Flitch Ind Est The
CM6 . . . . . . . . . . . . . . . . 150 D7
Flitch La CM6 . . . . . . . . . 150 E7
Flixton Cl CO16 . . . . . . . . 188 A4
Flood La CO4 . . . . . . . . . . 110 C6
Florence Cl IP4 . . . . . . . . . 18 A5
Florence Cotts CO7 . . . . . 185 F6
Florence Rd CO14 . . . . . . 144 E2
Florence Wlk **8**
CM23 . . . . . . . . . . . . . . . 145 F8
Florie's Rd CO6 . . . . . . . . 131 F8
Flowers Way CO15 . . . . . 203 G7
Foley Cotts CM7 . . . . . . . 102 D3
Folkards La CO7 . . . . . . . . 85 D8
Folley The CO3 . . . . . . . . 134 D5
FOLLY GREEN CO5 . . . . . 103 D1
Folly Mill La CM6 . . . . . . . 96 E6
Folly The
Layer de la H CO2 . . . . . . 162 A5
Tiptree CO5 . . . . . . . . . . 179 F2
Wivenhoe CO7 . . . . . . . . 164 C7
Fonnereau Rd IP1 . . . . . . . 17 C6
FORD END
Clavering . . . . . . . . . . . . . 64 E4
Felsted . . . . . . . . . . . . . . 172 B7
Ford End CE Prim Sch
CM3 . . . . . . . . . . . . . . . . 172 B6
Ford La CO7 . . . . . . . . . . 165 A5
Ford Rd CO15 . . . . . . . . . 188 D3
Fords La CO4 . . . . . . . . . . 109 D5
Ford St CO6 . . . . . . . . . . 108 D5
Ford St CO6 . . . . . . . . . . 107 C2
FORDSTREET . . . . . . . . . 107 C3
Fordstreet Hill CO6 . . . . . 107 C2
Fordwater Cl CO9 . . . . . . . 10 B3
Fordwater Rd CO7 . . . . . . 165 E1
Fordwich Rd CO7 . . . . . . 165 E1
Fore Field CM7 . . . . . . . . 128 D3
Forefield Gn CM1 . . . . . . 205 F7
Fore Hamlet IP3 . . . . . . . . 17 E5
Foremans CM1 . . . . . . . . 205 F7
Foresight Rd CO2 . . . . . . 136 D2
Fore St IP4 . . . . . . . . . . . . 17 D5
Forest Dr CM1 . . . . . . . . . 204 E1
Forest Gdns CO3 . . . . . . . 135 B6
Foresters Ct CO7 . . . . . . . 137 B1
Foresthall Rd CM24 . . . . . 119 E4
Forest Park Ave CO15 . . . 188 F7
Forest Rd
Colchester CO4 . . . . . . . . 136 D7
Witham CM8 . . . . . . . . . . 177 A5
Forfar Cl IP4 . . . . . . . . . . . 18 B8

Forfields Way CM77 . . . . 155 E6
Forge Cotts CO10 . . . . . . . 13 E6
Forge Cres CM77 . . . . . . 129 D3
Forge Ct CO7 . . . . . . . . . 113 E7
Forges Cnr CO10 . . . . . . . 13 E6
Forge St CO7 . . . . . . . . . . . 85 A6
Former Horsehair Factory
CO10 . . . . . . . . . . . . . . . . 2 C5
Fornham Ho IP4 . . . . . . . . 18 B6
Forres CO13 . . . . . . . . . . 170 F4
Forrest Ct IP4 . . . . . . . . . . 18 A7
FORRY'S GREEN . . . . . . . 75 B6
Forsyth Dr CM7 . . . . . . . . 155 A8
Forsythia Cl CM1 . . . . . . . 205 E7
Fortescue Rd CM3 . . . . . . 173 E5
Fortinbras Way CM2 . . . . 216 B8
Fortis CM8 . . . . . . . . . . . 194 E8
Fortis Ho **4** CM8 . . . . . 194 E8
Fortune Cl CM3 . . . . . . . . 174 A7
Fossetts La CO6 . . . . . . . . 107 F4
Foster Ct **2** CM8 . . . . . 177 A2
Foster Rd
Great Totham CM9 . . . . . 196 A4
Harwich CO12 . . . . . . . . . 90 E5
Foster's Cotts CM77 . . . . 129 D2
Foundation St **13** IP4 . . 17 C5
Foundry La
Copford CO6 . . . . . . . . . 133 D5
Earls Colne CO6 . . . . . . . 105 B6
Ipswich IP2 . . . . . . . . . . . 17 C5
Fountain Cl
Harwich CO12 . . . . . . . . . 91 E5
West Mersea CO5 . . . . . . 201 D7
Fountain La
Fordham CO6 . . . . . . . . . 134 A1
Easthorpe CO6 . . . . . . . . 160 F8
Fountains Rd IP2 . . . . . . . . 16 F1
Four Acres
Great Chesterford CB10 . . . 3 E3
Saffron Walden CB11 . . . . 22 E1
Four Ashes CM7 . . . . . . . . 74 C1
Four Ash Hill CO9 . . . . . . . 10 E1
Four Sisters CO7 . . . . . . . . 59 B5
Fourth Ave
Chelmsford CM1 . . . . . . . 205 B5
Clacton-on-S CO15 . . . . . 189 C4
Frinton-on-S CO13 . . . . . 170 F4
Glemsford CO10 . . . . . . . . 2 B5
Halstead CO9 . . . . . . . . . . 77 B1
Seawick CO16 . . . . . . . . . 203 B6
Stansted Mountfitchet
CM24 . . . . . . . . . . . . . . . 120 B2
Fourways CM22 . . . . . . . . 94 C1
Fowe's La CO10 . . . . . . . . 31 B8
Fowler Cl CM7 . . . . . . . . 127 C4
Fowlers Arc CO13 . . . . . . 170 F4
Fowlmere Rd Sg8 . . . . . . . 19 A6
Foxberry Gdns IP3 . . . . . . 18 D5
Foxburrow Rd IP3 . . . . . . . 18 F1
Fox Burrows La CM1 . . . . 204 B2
Fox Cres CM1 . . . . . . . . . 204 F4
Foxdells La CM23 . . . . . . 118 F2
Foxden CM8 . . . . . . . . . . 177 D6
FOXEARTH . . . . . . . . . . . . 14 C6
Foxendale Folly CO3 . . . . 134 C7
Foxes Cnr CO7 . . . . . . . . 107 D1
Foxes La
Aldham CO3, CO6 . . . . . . 133 D8
Ashen CO10 . . . . . . . . . . . 11 D1
Foxes Rd CO10 . . . . . . . . . 11 E1
Foxglove Cl
Bishop's Stortford
CM23 . . . . . . . . . . . . . . . 145 C6
Clacton-on-S CO15 . . . . . 188 F7
Witham CM8 . . . . . . . . . . 176 D3
Foxglove Cres IP3 . . . . . . . 18 E1
Foxglove Way CM1 . . . . . 205 F6
Foxglove Wlk **4** CO4 . . 136 E7
Foxgrove La IP11 . . . . . . . 221 F5
Foxhall Cl CO7 . . . . . . . . . 59 C4
Foxhall Fields CO7 . . . . . . 59 C3
Foxhall Rd IP3, IP4 . . . . . . 18 D5
Foxholes Rd CM2 . . . . . . 216 F6
Foxley Cl IP3 . . . . . . . . . . . 18 A4
Foxmead CM8 . . . . . . . . . 177 D6
Fox St CO7 . . . . . . . . . . . 110 F4
FOX STREET . . . . . . . . . . 110 F4
Foxtail Rd IP3 . . . . . . . . . . 38 E8
Foxwood Cl CO11 . . . . . . 86 C2
Foxwood Cres IP4 . . . . . . . 18 F5
Fox Yd CO9 . . . . . . . . . . . 53 C5
Frambury La CB11 . . . . . . 66 F8
Framlingham Ct **5**
IP1 . . . . . . . . . . . . . . . . . 17 A8
Framlingham Way
CM77 . . . . . . . . . . . . . . . 154 C7
Frampton Rd IP3 . . . . . . . 38 A8
Frances Cl CO7 . . . . . . . . 137 B2
Franciscan Way IP1 . . . . . 17 C5
Francis Cl
Haverhill CB9 . . . . . . . . . . 8 F8
Tiptree CO5 . . . . . . . . . . 179 C4
Francis Ct
Copford CO6 . . . . . . . . . 133 C4
Silver End CM8 . . . . . . . . 156 C5
Francis Kellerman Wlk
CO3 . . . . . . . . . . . . . . . . 135 E7
Francis Rd
Braintree CM7 . . . . . . . . . 127 D2
**14** Sudbury CO10 . . . . . 33 E7
Francis St CO7 . . . . . . . . 185 F5
Francis Way
Colchester CO4 . . . . . . . . 110 D1
Silver End CM8 . . . . . . . . 156 C4
Frank Clater Cl CO4 . . . . 136 C8
Franklin Rd IP3 . . . . . . . . . 18 B2

Frank Naylor Ct **11**
CO1 . . . . . . . . . . . . . . . . 135 F7
Fraser Cl CM2 . . . . . . . . . 216 C8
Fraser Rd IP1 . . . . . . . . . . 16 F7
Frating Abbey Farm Rd
CO7 . . . . . . . . . . . . . . . . 166 C6
Frating Cross CO7 . . . . . . 166 B7
Frating Ct CM7 . . . . . . . . 128 D1
FRATING GREEN . . . . . . . 139 A3
Frating Hill CO7 . . . . . . . . 138 D3
Frating Rd
Ardleigh CO7 . . . . . . . . . 111 F6
Great Bromley CO7 . . . . . 138 F6
Thorrington CO7 . . . . . . . 166 A7
Fredrick J French Meml
Homes CM1 . . . . . . . . . . 205 B6
Fredricks Cl CO11 . . . . . . 115 C5
Freebournes Ct **5**
CM8 . . . . . . . . . . . . . . . . 177 A2
Freebournes Rd CM8 . . . 177 B2
Freehold Rd IP4 . . . . . . . . 18 A6
Freeland Ct CO15 . . . . . . 188 E1
Freelands
Brightlingsea CO7 . . . . . . 186 C6
Ipswich IP4 . . . . . . . . . . . 18 B6
Freeman Cl CO4 . . . . . . . 110 A6
Freeport Designer Outlet
CM7 . . . . . . . . . . . . . . . . 128 C1
Freeport Office Village
CM7 . . . . . . . . . . . . . . . . 128 B1
Freeport Sta CM77 . . . . . 128 B1
Free Rodwell Ho CO11 . . . 86 F4
Freewood La CB11 . . . . . . 20 B3
Freezes Barns CB9 . . . . . . 27 B7
Fremantle Rd CO2 . . . . . . 136 B1
FRENCHES GREEN . . . . . 153 A6
French's Wlk **4** CM2 . . 205 C2
Frensham Cl CO3 . . . . . . 134 D7
Frere Ct CM23 . . . . . . . . . 118 F1
Frere Way CO5 . . . . . . . . 164 B6
Freshfields CO12 . . . . . . . 90 F1
Freshfields Rd CO12 . . . . . 91 A4
Freshwater Cres CM9 . . . 210 B4
Freshwater La CO15 . . . . 188 F7
Freshwell Gdns CB10 . . . . 22 D2
Freshwell St CB10 . . . . . . 22 D2
FRESTON . . . . . . . . . . . . . 37 E3
Freston Hill IP9 . . . . . . . . . 37 E4
Freston St IP3 . . . . . . . . . . 38 C8
Freston St IP9 . . . . . . . . . . 37 E2
Friars IP9 . . . . . . . . . . . . . . 60 B8
Friars Bridge Rd IP1 . . . . . 17 B5
Friars Cl
Clacton-on-S CO15 . . . . . 188 E6
Colchester CO4 . . . . . . . . 110 C2
Sible Hedingham CO9 . . . . 51 D2
Wivenhoe CO7 . . . . . . . . 164 C8
Friar's Cotts CM77 . . . . . 154 B4
Friars Ct
Colchester CO2 . . . . . . . . 136 C3
**15** Sudbury CO10 . . . . . 33 E7
Friars Ctyd **1** IP1 . . . . . 17 C5
Friars Grove Jun & Inf
Schs CO4 . . . . . . . . . . . . 110 C2
Friars La
Braintree CM7 . . . . . . . . . 127 F4
Maldon CM9 . . . . . . . . . . 209 F2
Friars Mead CB9 . . . . . . . . 9 F4
Friars St
Ipswich IP1 . . . . . . . . . . . 17 C5
Sudbury CO10 . . . . . . . . . 33 E7
Friars Wlk CM2 . . . . . . . . 205 B3
Friars Wood CO3 . . . . . . . 146 C8
Friary Fields CM9 . . . . . . 210 A2
Friday Wood Gn CO2 . . . 162 F8
Friedberg Ave CM23 . . . . 145 D4
Friends Field CO8 . . . . . . . 55 F1
Friends Cl CB11 . . . . . . . . 43 D8
Friends Wlk CB11 . . . . . . . 43 D7
Friesian Cl CM7 . . . . . . . . 127 D2
Frietuna Rd CO13 . . . . . . 170 A5
Frinton Cl CO13 . . . . . . . 170 F3
Frinton Lo CO13 . . . . . . . 171 A4
FRINTON-ON-SEA . . . . . 170 D5
Frinton-on-Sea Prim Sch
CO13 . . . . . . . . . . . . . . . 170 E5
Frinton Rd
Holland-on-S CO15 . . . . . 189 D6
Kirby Cross CO13 . . . . . . 170 D6
Thorpe-le-S CO16 . . . . . . 142 B1
Frinton Sta CO13 . . . . . . 170 F5
Fritillary Cl IP8 . . . . . . . . . 36 E8
Fritton Cl IP2 . . . . . . . . . . 17 A1
Fritton Ct **16** CB9 . . . . . . 8 E7
Frobisher Dr CO15 . . . . . 188 C7
Frobisher Prim Sch
CO15 . . . . . . . . . . . . . . . 187 F1
Frobisher Rd
Harwich CO12 . . . . . . . . . 90 F1
Ipswich IP1 . . . . . . . . . . . 17 E1
Frobisher Way CM23 . . . 128 C4
Frogge St CB10 . . . . . . . . . 3 B3
Frog Hall Cl CO5 . . . . . . . 164 B6
Frog Mdw CO7 . . . . . . . . . 84 F7
Fronks Ave CO12 . . . . . . . 91 C2
Fronk's Rd CO12 . . . . . . . 91 B2
Front Rd IP3 . . . . . . . . . . . 38 D8
Frowick La CO16 . . . . . . . 167 B2
Fryatt Ave CO12 . . . . . . . . 91 A3
Fryatt Hospl CO12 . . . . . . 91 A3
Fuchsia Cl **6** CO4 . . . . . 136 D8
Fuchsia La IP4 . . . . . . . . . . 18 A5
Fuchsia Way CO16 . . . . . 188 C3
Fulcher Ave CM2 . . . . . . . 205 F3
Fulfen CB11 . . . . . . . . . . . 43 D7

Fullbridge CM9 . . . . . . . . 210 A3
Fuller Ct **5** CM23 . . . . . . 146 A7
Fuller's Almshouses
CM24 . . . . . . . . . . . . . . 119 F6
Fuller's Cl CO5 . . . . . . . . 158 B2
Fullers Ct CM7 . . . . . . . . 128 A3
FULLER'S END . . . . . . . . 120 D8
Fullers Gate CO5 . . . . . . 158 B2
Fullers Rd CO2 . . . . . . . . 136 D2
FULLER STREET . . . . . . . 174 D4
Fulmar Cl CO4 . . . . . . . . 137 A8
Fulton Cres CM23 . . . . . . 146 C8
Furneaux La CO5 . . . . . . 163 F5
Furness Cl IP2 . . . . . . . . . .36 F8
Furriers Cl CM23 . . . . . . 145 C5
Furrow Cl CO3 . . . . . . . . 134 E5
FURTHER FORD END . . . . .64 D6
Further Mdw CM1 . . . . . . 215 A8
Furze Cres CO7 . . . . . . . . 165 A7
Furze La CO7 . . . . . . . . . 139 A5

## G

Gablefields CM2 . . . . . . . 217 D6
Gable Ho IP4 . . . . . . . . . . .17 F6
Gables The CO6 . . . . . . . . . .9 F4
Gabriel Ho CM6 . . . . . . . 150 D8
Gaces Acre CB11 . . . . . . . .43 A1
Gadwall Reach CO5 . . . . 158 D2
Gager Dr CO5 . . . . . . . . . 179 E5
Gage's Rd
Belcham St P CO10 . . . . . .13 A1
Little Yeldham CO10 . . . . . .30 F8
Gaiger Cl CM1 . . . . . . . . 205 D7
GAINSBOROUGH . . . . . . .38 B8
Gainsborough Cl
Clacton-on-S CO16 . . . . . 188 B6
West Mersea CO5 . . . . . . 201 D6
Gainsborough Cres
CM2 . . . . . . . . . . . . . . 205 E3
Gainsborough Ct **17**
CO10 . . . . . . . . . . . . . . .33 E7
Gainsborough Dr CO11 . . .86 C4
Gainsborough La IP3 . . . . .37 F7
Gainsborough Rd
Black Notley CM77 . . . . . 155 A4
Colchester CO3 . . . . . . . . 135 B5
Felixstowe IP11 . . . . . . . 221 F4
Ipswich IP4 . . . . . . . . . . .17 D8
Sudbury CO10 . . . . . . . . . .33 E8
Gainsborough's House
Mus* CO10 . . . . . . . . . . .33 E7
Gainsborough St CO10 . . .33 E7
Gainsford Ave CO15 . . . . 189 B4
GAINSFORD END . . . . . . .49 F4
Gainsford End Rd CO9 . . . .50 B6
Galiots CO5 . . . . . . . . . . 201 A6
Gall End La CM24 . . . . . . 119 F7
Galleydene Ave CM2 . . . . 216 C3
GALLEYEND . . . . . . . . . . 216 D4
GALLEYWOOD . . . . . . . . 216 D2
Galleywood Inf Sch
CM2 . . . . . . . . . . . . . . 216 C2
Galleywood Rd
Chelmsford CM2 . . . . . . . 216 A5
Great Baddow CM2 . . . . . 216 E5
Galliford Rd CM9 . . . . . . 210 A4
Galliford Road Ind Est
CM9 . . . . . . . . . . . . . . 210 A4
Galloway Cl **1** CM23 . . 145 F8
Galloway Dr CO16 . . . . . 168 D3
Galloway Rd CM23 . . . . . 118 F1
GALLOWS GREEN
Fordham Heath . . . . . . . . 107 C1
Great Easton . . . . . . . . . . .97 F2
Gallows Green Rd CM6 . . . .97 F2
Gallows Hill CB11 . . . . . . .43 C7
Galpin Ho CM8 . . . . . . . . 194 F8
Galsworthy Cl CM7 . . . . . 155 A7
GAMBLES GREEN . . . . . . 175 A2
Gamma Terr IP3 . . . . . . . .18 E1
Gandish Cl CO7 . . . . . . . . .59 D1
Gandish Rd CO7 . . . . . . . .59 E2
Ganges Rd IP9 . . . . . . . . .91 B8
Gannet Cl IP3 . . . . . . . . . . .9 C8
Gannet Rd IP2 . . . . . . . . .16 E3
Ganymede Cl IP1 . . . . . . .16 D7
Gaol La CO10 . . . . . . . . . .33 E7
Gap The
Arkesden CB11 . . . . . . . . .41 F1
Holland-on-S CO15 . . . . . 189 G6
Garden Cotts CO6 . . . . . . 131 A2
Garden Ct CO13 . . . . . . . 170 F3
Garden Dr CO3 . . . . . . . . 134 E6
Gardeners CM29 . . . . . . . 216 D5
Gardeners Rd CO9 . . . . . . .76 F1
Gardeners Row CO6 . . . . 131 A2
Garden Farm CM8,
CM9 . . . . . . . . . . . . . . 196 A5
Garden Field
Felixstowe IP11 . . . . . . . 221 C5
Hatfield Peverel CM3 . . . . 193 F4
Garden Field Cotts
CO6 . . . . . . . . . . . . . . . .81 C5
Garden Fields
Great Tey CO6 . . . . . . . . 132 C8
Stebbing CM6 . . . . . . . . 124 D6
Gardenia Pl CO16 . . . . . . 188 B4
Gardenia Wlk CO4 . . . . . 136 C1
Garden Pl CO10 . . . . . . . . .33 D7
Garden Rd
Clacton-on-S CO15 . . . . . 203 G7
Walton-on-t-N CO14 . . . . 171 A7
Garden Terr . . . . . . . . . . .76 F2
Garfield Pl IP11 . . . . . . . 221 D3

Garfield Rd IP11 . . . . . . . 221 D3
Garland Rd CO12 . . . . . . . .90 F5
Garlands Wlk CO6 . . . . . . 108 E3
Garnets Mead CM3 . . . . . 175 B3
Garnetts CM22 . . . . . . . . 148 B8
Garnetts Bglws CM6 . . . . 152 C5
Garnetts La CM6 . . . . . . . 152 C6
Garnetts Villas CM6 . . . . 152 C5
Garnons Chase CO6 . . . . . .81 A5
Garret Pl CO6 . . . . . . . . . 108 F4
Garrettlands CM2 . . . . . . 217 F6
Garrison La IP11 . . . . . . . 221 D4
Garrod Ct CO2 . . . . . . . . 163 B7
Garrods IP9 . . . . . . . . . . .35 B1
Garthwood Cl CO6 . . . . . 108 E4
Gascoigne Rd CO4 . . . . . 136 C8
Gasfield **14** CO11 . . . . . .86 D4
Gasgoine Ho CO4 . . . . . . 109 F4
Gaston End CO7 . . . . . . . .59 C3
Gaston St CO7 . . . . . . . . .59 C3
Gatacre Ct CO2 . . . . . . . 135 B3
Gatacre Rd IP1 . . . . . . . . .17 A7
Gatefield Cl CO14 . . . . . . 170 F7
Gatefield Ct CO14 . . . . . . 170 F7
Gatehouse Villas CM6 . . . 150 E7
Gatekeeper Cl
**8** Braintree CM7 . . . . . 127 F1
Ipswich IP8 . . . . . . . . . . .36 E8
Gate St CM9 . . . . . . . . . . 209 F3
Gate Street Mews
CM7 . . . . . . . . . . . . . . 209 F3
Gatwick Ct CM23 . . . . . . 119 B1
Gaucho Rd CM7 . . . . . . . 127 F7
GAUNT'S END . . . . . . . . 120 F7
Gavin Way CO4 . . . . . . . . 110 B6
Gawlers CM23 . . . . . . . . . .92 B8
GAY BOWERS . . . . . . . . 219 A5
Gay Bowers La CM3 . . . . 218 F6
Gay Bowers Rd CM3 . . . . 218 F4
Gay Bowers Way CM8 . . . 195 A5
Gaye St **18** IP1 . . . . . . . .17 B6
Gazelle Cl CO4 . . . . . . . . 110 C4
Geetons The CO5 . . . . . . 163 C3
Generals La CM3 . . . . . . . 192 B2
Generals Mews IP11 . . . . 221 B5
Genesta Cl CM9 . . . . . . . 199 D2
Geneva Rd IP1 . . . . . . . . .17 B7
Genevyll Cl CO10 . . . . . . . .1 D2
Gentian Ct CO4 . . . . . . . 109 C2
Geoff Seaden Cl **2**
CO1 . . . . . . . . . . . . . . 136 C6
George Ave CO7 . . . . . . . 185 F7
George Cl CO15 . . . . . . . 188 C2
George Ct CM2 . . . . . . . . 205 B1
George Cut CO7 . . . . . . . 185 F6
George Frost Cl IP4 . . . . . .17 D7
George Gent **29** CB9 . . .27 B6
George Green Bglws
CM22 . . . . . . . . . . . . . 146 B1
George La CO10 . . . . . . . . .2 B3
George Rd CM7 . . . . . . . . 127 D2
George St
Chelmsford CM2 . . . . . . . 205 B1
**12** Colchester CO1 . . . 135 F7
Harwich CO12 . . . . . . . . .91 D6
Saffron Walden CB10 . . . . .22 D1
George Williams Way
CO1 . . . . . . . . . . . . . . 136 A6
George Yard Sh Ctr **8**
CM7 . . . . . . . . . . . . . . 127 F3
Georgian Cl IP11 . . . . . . 221 D5
Georgian Ho CM7 . . . . . . 128 A4
Gepp Pl CM2 . . . . . . . . . 206 B4
Geralds Ave IP4 . . . . . . . .18 A5
Geranium Cl CO16 . . . . . 188 C4
Geranium Wlk CO4 . . . . . 136 D7
Gerard Ave CM23 . . . . . . 145 E4
Gerard Gdns CM23 . . . . . 216 D8
Gernon Cl CM1 . . . . . . . . 191 B3
Gernon Rd CO7 . . . . . . . . 111 E7
Gershwin Bvd CM8 . . . . . 194 F7
GESTINGTHORPE . . . . . . .31 E1
Gestingthorpe Rd
CO10 . . . . . . . . . . . . . . .31 F4
Gibbons Ct CM6 . . . . . . . 123 D1
Gibson Cl **3** IP1 . . . . . . .17 A6
Gibbs Field CM23 . . . . . . 145 D5
Gibson Cl
Ipswich IP3 . . . . . . . . . . .18 C2
Saffron Walden CB10 . . . . .22 D1
Gibson Gdns CB10 . . . . . . .22 D1
Gibson Rd CO9 . . . . . . . . .51 D1
Gibson Vale CM1 . . . . . . 205 B8
Gibson Way CB10 . . . . . . .22 D1
Gifford Cl IP9 . . . . . . . . . .62 D5
Giffords Pl IP4 . . . . . . . . .18 F6
Gilbard Ct CO4 . . . . . . . . 110 C6
Gilbert Cl CO4 . . . . . . . . 188 C4
Gilberd Rd CO2 . . . . . . . . 136 B4
Gilberd Sch The CO4 . . . . 110 B5
Gilbert Rd CO10 . . . . . . . .12 B8
Gilbert Way CM7 . . . . . . 128 C5
Gilbey Ave CM23 . . . . . . 146 B6
Gilbey Cotts CM22 . . . . . .94 C1
Gilbey Cres CM24 . . . . . . 119 E8
Gilbey Gn CB11 . . . . . . . . .42 F1
Gilchrist Way CM7 . . . . . 127 F4
Gilda Terr CM7 . . . . . . . . 127 B2
Gilderdale Cl CO4 . . . . . . 110 D3
Gilders Way CO16 . . . . . . 188 C5
Gill Cl CM9 . . . . . . . . . . 209 F6
Gilmore Way CM2 . . . . . . 217 B6
Gilson Cl CM2 . . . . . . . . 205 F2
Gilwell Park CI CO3 . . . . . 135 A4
Gimson Cl CM8 . . . . . . . . 176 F2

Gippeswyk Ave IP2 . . . . . .17 A4
Gippeswyk Rd IP2 . . . . . . .17 B4
Gipping Cl CB9 . . . . . . . . . .8 E6
Gipping Way IP8 . . . . . . . .16 B6
Gipsy La CM23, CM24 . . . 119 C4
Girling St CO10 . . . . . . . . .33 E8
Girton Rd CB9 . . . . . . . . . .9 B7
Girton Way IP2 . . . . . . . . .16 F1
Glade The CO4 . . . . . . . . 110 F2
Gladiole CO15 . . . . . . . . 188 F7
Gladiator Way CO2 . . . . . 135 A2
Gladstone Ct CM2 . . . . . 205 B1
Gladstone Rd
Colchester CO1 . . . . . . . . 136 B5
Ipswich IP5 . . . . . . . . . . .17 F5
Tiptree CO5 . . . . . . . . . . 179 D4
Gladwin Rd CO2 . . . . . . . 135 D4
Glamis Cl CB9 . . . . . . . . . .8 D8
Glamorgan Rd IP2 . . . . . . .17 B1
Glastonbury Cl IP2 . . . . . .16 F1
Glebe Ave CM7 . . . . . . . . 127 F6
Glebe Cl
Elmstead Market CO7 . . . . 138 A6
Sproughton IP8 . . . . . . . . .16 B6
Tattingstone IP9 . . . . . . . .61 C7
Wix CO11 . . . . . . . . . . . 115 C5
Glebe Cres
Broomfield CM1 . . . . . . . 191 B1
Witham CM8 . . . . . . . . . 176 E4
Glebe Ct CM23 . . . . . . . . 146 B8
Glebe End
Capel St M IP9 . . . . . . . . .35 B2
Elsenham CM22 . . . . . . . .94 D1
Glebe Gdns CO5 . . . . . . . 158 E5
Glebe La
Chelmondiston IP9 . . . . . . .63 A8
Little Easton CM6 . . . . . . 122 F5
Woolverstone IP9 . . . . . . .38 B1
Glebelands CO6 . . . . . . . .82 B1
Glebe Mdw CM3 . . . . . . . 190 E7
Glebe Rd
Chelmsford CM1 . . . . . . . 205 B3
Colchester CO2 . . . . . . . . 135 C2
Heybridge CM9 . . . . . . . . 210 C5
Kelvedon CO5 . . . . . . . . 158 B2
Tiptree CO5 . . . . . . . . . . 179 C5
Glebe The
Elmdon CB11 . . . . . . . . . .20 A4
Elsenham CM22 . . . . . . . .94 C1
Peldon CO5 . . . . . . . . . . 182 E5
Purleigh CM3 . . . . . . . . . 220 D1
Saffron Walden CB11 . . . . .43 E7
Glebe View
Galleywood CM2 . . . . . . . 216 A3
West Mersea CO5 . . . . . . 201 E8
Glebe Way
Clacton-on-S CO15 . . . . . 203 G2
Frinton-on-S CO13 . . . . . 170 F5
Glemham Dr IP4 . . . . . . . .18 F4
GLEMSFORD . . . . . . . . . . .2 C4
Glemsford Cl IP11 . . . . . . 221 B3
Glemsford Com Prim Sch
CO10 . . . . . . . . . . . . . . .2 B5
Glemsford Pl **3** CB9 . . . .9 B8
Glen Ave CO5 . . . . . . . . . 135 B7
Glenavon Rd IP4 . . . . . . . .18 D7
Glencoe Rd IP4 . . . . . . . . .18 C8
Glendale Gr CO4 . . . . . . . 110 C3
Gleneagles Dr IP4 . . . . . . .18 D5
Gleneley Ct CO13 . . . . . . 170 F3
Glenfield Ave IP11 . . . . . 221 E5
Glenhurst Ave CM4 . . . . . 158 E5
Glenside CO4 . . . . . . . . . .34 A6
Glentress Ct CO4 . . . . . . 110 D3
Glenway Cl CO6 . . . . . . . .82 B1
Glenway Ct CO6 . . . . . . . .82 B1
Glisson Sq CO2 . . . . . . . . 135 B4
Globe Cl CO5 . . . . . . . . . 179 D6
Globe Cres CM3 . . . . . . . 118 D6
Globe Wlk CO5 . . . . . . . . 179 D6
Globe Yd **8** CO10 . . . . . .33 E8
Gloucester Ave
Chelmsford CM2 . . . . . . . 216 C6
Colchester CM2 . . . . . . . 135 C3
Maldon CM9 . . . . . . . . . 209 F1
Gloucester Cres CM1 . . . . 205 A5
Gloucester Gdns CM7 . . . 128 B4
Gloucester Ho IP11 . . . . . 221 C6
Gloucester Rd
Haverhill CB9 . . . . . . . . . . .8 F6
Ipswich IP1 . . . . . . . . . . .18 B2
Gloucester Way CO10 . . . .15 D2
Glovers CM3 . . . . . . . . . 173 F7
Glovershotts CM1 . . . . . . 191 B2
Goat Hall La
Chelmsford CM2 . . . . . . . 215 F3
Galleywood CM2 . . . . . . . 216 A3
Goat House La CM3 . . . . . 219 F4
Goat Lodge Rd CM8,
CM9 . . . . . . . . . . . . . . 196 A5
Goda Cl CM8 . . . . . . . . . 194 D8
Goddard Way
Chelmsford CM2 . . . . . . . 205 F2
Saffron Walden CB10 . . . . .22 E3
Godfreys Mews CM3 . . . . 205 B1
Godfrey Way CM3 . . . . . . 206 A1
Godings Way CM7 . . . . . . 127 F2
Godmans La CO6 . . . . . . 132 E3
Godric Pl CM7 . . . . . . . . 127 E3
Godric Rd CM8 . . . . . . . . 194 E8
Godwin Cl CO9 . . . . . . . . .76 D1
Godwit Ct CO5 . . . . . . . . 158 D2
Goff's La CO16 . . . . . . . . 141 F8
Goings La CO5 . . . . . . . . 201 D6
Gold Cl CM22 . . . . . . . . . .94 B3
Goldcrest CO4 . . . . . . . . 137 A8

Goldcrest Ct IP2 . . . . . . . .16 D3
Goldcrest Rd IP2 . . . . . . . .16 C3
Goldenacres CM1 . . . . . . 205 F8
Golden Dawn Way
CO4 . . . . . . . . . . . . . . 109 E2
Golden La
Radwinter CB10 . . . . . . . . .25 A2
Thorpe-le-S CO16 . . . . . . 141 F3
Golden Lion La CO12 . . . . .91 E6
Goldenlonds CO6 . . . . . . .56 A6
Golden Noble Hill
CO1 . . . . . . . . . . . . . . 136 A6
Goldfinch Cl CO4 . . . . . . 136 F7
St Osyth CO16 . . . . . . . . 187 A5
Goldhanger Cl CM7 . . . . . 128 D1
Goldhanger Rd CM9 . . . . 210 D4
Goldingham Dr CM7 . . . . 155 A7
Goldings CM23 . . . . . . . . 146 B8
Golding Thoroughfare
CM2 . . . . . . . . . . . . . . 205 F3
Golding Way
Glemsford CO10 . . . . . . . . .2 B4
**3** Colchester CO4 . . . . 137 A8
Golds Nursery Bsns Pk
CM22 . . . . . . . . . . . . . .94 C3
Gold St CB10 . . . . . . . . . .22 D1
Golf Green Rd CO15 . . . . 203 G8
Goodchild Way CO9 . . . . . .30 A2
Goodey Cl CO1 . . . . . . . . 136 A6
Goodier Rd CM1 . . . . . . . 204 F4
Goodlake Cl CO12 . . . . . . .90 F2
Goodliffe Pk CM23 . . . . . 119 B2
Goodmans La CM3 . . . . . 173 F4
Goodwin Cl CM2 . . . . . . . 216 D8
Goodwin Stile CM23 . . . . 145 D5
Goodwins News CO7 . . . . 166 E8
Goojerat Rd CO2 . . . . . . . 135 D5
GOOSE GREEN
Tendring Green . . . . . . . . 140 E7
Wix . . . . . . . . . . . . . . . 114 E3
Gordian Wlk CO4 . . . . . . 110 D5
Gordon Dr CO4 . . . . . . . . 110 B6
Gordon Rd
Chelmsford CM2 . . . . . . . 216 A6
Harwich CO12 . . . . . . . . .91 B2
Ipswich IP4 . . . . . . . . . . .18 A7
Gordon Way IP2 . . . . . . . .91 B2
Gorefield CM22 . . . . . . . . 148 C7
Gorefield Rd CM22,
CM24 . . . . . . . . . . . . . 121 B5
Gorefield Rdbt CM24 . . . . 121 B5
Gore La CM7 . . . . . . . . . 172 B8
GORE PIT . . . . . . . . . . . 158 E4
Gore Rd CM7 . . . . . . . . . 127 A2
Gore Terr CM7 . . . . . . . . 127 A2
Goring Ho CO4 . . . . . . . . 109 E4
Goring Rd
Colchester CO4 . . . . . . . . 110 C1
Ipswich IP4 . . . . . . . . . . .18 C6
Gorse La
Clacton-on-S CO15 . . . . . 189 A8
Tiptree CO5 . . . . . . . . . . 179 D4
Gorse Lane Ind Est
CO15 . . . . . . . . . . . . . 189 B8
Gorse Way
Clacton-on-S CO15 . . . . . 203 F7
Colchester CO3 . . . . . . . . 134 D4
Gorse Wlk CO4 . . . . . . . . 136 D7
Gosbecks Bsns Pk
CO2 . . . . . . . . . . . . . . 135 B2
Gosbecks Prim Sch
CO2 . . . . . . . . . . . . . . 135 A2
Gosbecks Rd CO2 . . . . . . 135 A2
Gosbecks View CO2 . . . . . 135 A2
GOSFIELD . . . . . . . . . . . 102 E7
Gosfield Com Prim Sch
CO9 . . . . . . . . . . . . . . 102 C8
Gosfield Hall* CO9 . . . . . 102 C8
Gosfield Rd
Blackheath CO2 . . . . . . . . 163 A8
Braintree CM7 . . . . . . . . 102 D3
Gosfield Sch CO9 . . . . . . . .75 F2
Gosford Ct CO10 . . . . . . . .12 B8
Goshawk Dr CM2 . . . . . . 216 B5
Goslings The CM8 . . . . . . 156 C5
Gouldings Ave CO14 . . . . 171 B8
Goulds Rd CO8 . . . . . . . . .54 F2
Goul La CB10 . . . . . . . . . .22 D1
Goulton Rd CM1 . . . . . . . 191 A1
Government Ct CO12 . . . . .91 E5
Gowers Ave CO10 . . . . . . . .2 C5
Gowers End CO10 . . . . . . . .2 C5
Gower St IP2 . . . . . . . . . .17 C4
Gowrie Cl IP11 . . . . . . . . 221 D4
Grace Gdns CM23 . . . . . . 145 F4
Graces Cl CM8 . . . . . . . . 195 A3
Grace's Cross CM7 . . . . . 217 C2
Graces La CM3 . . . . . . . . 207 B1
Graces Wlk CO13 . . . . . . 171 A6
Grafton Pl CM23 . . . . . . . 206 A4
Grafton Rd CO12 . . . . . . . .91 A4
Grafton Way CM7 . . . . . . .17 C5
Graham Ave IP11 . . . . . . 221 D4
Graham Rd
Felixstowe IP11 . . . . . . . 221 D5
Ipswich IP1 . . . . . . . . . . .17 B7
Grailands CM23 . . . . . . . 145 D5
Grammar School Pl **11**
CO10 . . . . . . . . . . . . . . .33 D7
Grampian Gr CM1 . . . . . . 204 D6
Granaries CM9 . . . . . . . . 210 A3

Granary Ct
**12** Colchester CO1 . . . 136 C6
Great Dunmow CM6 . . . . 150 D7
Granary The
Bures CO8 . . . . . . . . . . . .55 F1
Clare CO10 . . . . . . . . . . .12 B6
Granchester Ct CO4 . . . . 110 C4
Grand Ct CO13 . . . . . . . . 170 F3
Grand The CO13 . . . . . . . 170 F3
Grange Cl
Felixstowe IP11 . . . . . . . 221 C5
Halstead CO9 . . . . . . . . . 103 E7
Walton-on-t-N CO14 . . . . 171 A7
Grange Com Prim Sch
IP11 . . . . . . . . . . . . . . 221 B4
Grange Ct
Chelmsford CM2 . . . . . . . 215 F7
Clacton-on-S CO16 . . . . . 188 A4
Grange Farm CO2 . . . . . . 136 C4
Grange Farm Ave
IP11 . . . . . . . . . . . . . . 221 B5
Grange Farm Rd CO2 . . . 136 D4
Grange Hill CO6 . . . . . . . 130 F1
Grange La CM6 . . . . . . . . 151 C7
Grange Mill CO6 . . . . . . . 130 F1
Grange Pk CM23 . . . . . . . 118 F1
Granger Ave CM9 . . . . . . 209 F1
Bishop's Stortford
CM23 . . . . . . . . . . . . . 146 A7
Felixstowe IP11 . . . . . . . 221 B4
Great Horkesley CO6 . . . . 109 B7
Harwich CO12 . . . . . . . . .91 A3
Ickleton CB10 . . . . . . . . . .20 A8
Ipswich IP4 . . . . . . . . . . .17 E6
Lawford CO11 . . . . . . . . .85 F1
Little Bromley CO11 . . . . 112 E7
Tiptree CO5 . . . . . . . . . . 179 A6
Wickham Bishops CM8 . . . 195 E4
Granger Row CM1 . . . . . . 204 F6
Grangeside CM3 . . . . . . . 218 A2
Grange The CM23 . . . . . . 118 F1
Grange Way CO2 . . . . . . . 136 D3
Grange Way Bsns Pk
CO2 . . . . . . . . . . . . . . 136 D3
Grange Wlk CM23 . . . . . . 146 A7
GRANSMORE GREEN . . . . 125 F1
Granta Cl CB10 . . . . . . . . . .3 D1
Granta Cotts CB10 . . . . . . .3 C2
Grantham Ave CM7 . . . . . 154 B7
Grantham Cres CM7 . . . . .17 A4
Grantham Ct CM1 . . . . . . 136 A7
Grantham Rd CO6 . . . . . . 109 B7
Grantley Cl CO6 . . . . . . . 133 D5
Grants Ct CO14 . . . . . . . . 171 C8
Grantwood CO16 . . . . . . 108 E3
Granville Cl
Clacton-on-S CO15 . . . . . 188 F3
Colchester CO1 . . . . . . . . 136 B5
Felixstowe IP11 . . . . . . . 221 D3
Granville St **2** IP1 . . . . . .17 B6
Granville Way CO7 . . . . . 186 A7
Grasby Cl CO7 . . . . . . . . . 137 B2
Grasmere Cl
Braintree CM7 . . . . . . . . 154 C6
Ipswich IP1 . . . . . . . . . . .18 B1
Grasmere Gdns CO13 . . . 170 F7
Grassfields CO13 . . . . . . 170 E6
GRASS GREEN . . . . . . . . .29 B1
Grassmere CO4 . . . . . . . . 110 B5
Gratian Cl CO4 . . . . . . . . 110 D5
Gravel Ct CO6 . . . . . . . . . 130 F2
Gravel Hill CO6 . . . . . . . . .56 A2
Gravel Hill Way CO12 . . . .90 F1
Gravel Pit La CO11 . . . . . .60 E2
Gravel The CO6 . . . . . . . . 130 F2
Grayling Cl CM7 . . . . . . . 127 E1
Grayling Dr CO4 . . . . . . . 110 F1
Grayling Rd IP8 . . . . . . . . .36 E8
Gray Rd CO3 . . . . . . . . . 135 D6
Grays Brewery Yd **8**
CM2 . . . . . . . . . . . . . . 205 C2
Grays Cotts CO5 . . . . . . . 201 C6
Gray's Cotts CO1 . . . . . . 136 B7
Grays Cl CM23 . . . . . . . . 145 C6
Gray's La CM7 . . . . . . . . . .73 E4
Grays Mead CO9 . . . . . . . .51 D2
GREAT BADDOW . . . . . . 205 B1
Great Baddow High Sch
CM2 . . . . . . . . . . . . . . 216 B6
GREAT BARDFIELD . . . . . .72 C1
Great Bardfield Cage*
CM7 . . . . . . . . . . . . . . .72 B2
Great Bardfield Cottage
Mus* CM7 . . . . . . . . . . .72 A1
Great Bardfield Prim Sch
CM7 . . . . . . . . . . . . . . .72 B2
GREAT BENTLEY . . . . . . 166 D8
Great Bentley Rd
CO7 . . . . . . . . . . . . . . 166 A8
Great Bentley Sta
CO7 . . . . . . . . . . . . . . 166 E8
Great Bradfords Jun & Inf
Schs CM7 . . . . . . . . . . 128 B4
GREAT BRAXTED . . . . . . 178 C1
Great Bromley CE Prim
Sch CB10 . . . . . . . . . . . .3 D2
GREAT BROMLEY . . . . . . 112 F7
GREAT CANFIELD . . . . . . 149 C1
GREAT CHESTERFORD . . . .3 D2
Great Chesterford CE Prim
Sch CB10 . . . . . . . . . . . .3 D2
Great Chesterford Ct
CB10 . . . . . . . . . . . . . . .3 C2
Great Chesterford Sta
CB10 . . . . . . . . . . . . . . .3 C1
GREAT CLACTON . . . . . . 188 E6

Great Clacton CE Jun Sch CO15 188 F6
Great Cob CM1 205 E5
Great Colman St 14 IP4 17 D6
GREAT CORNARD 34 B5
Great Cornard Ctry Pk* CO10 34 C3
Great Cornard Mid Sch CO10 34 C4
Great Cornard Upper Sch & Tech Coll CO10 34 B4
GREAT DAWKINS 25 F4
GREAT DUNMOW 150 C7
Great Dunmow Mus* CM6 123 D1
Great Dunmow Prim Sch CM6 123 B1
Great Eastern Cl CM23 146 A6
Great Eastern Ct CO14 171 C7
Great Eastern Rd CO10 33 F7
Great Eastern Sq IP11 221 E5
GREAT EASTON 122 F7
Great Easton CE Prim Sch CM6 123 A8
Greate House Farm Rd CO2 162 A5
Great Field IP11 221 A8
Great Gibcracks Chase CM2 218 A2
Great Gipping St IP1 17 B5
Great Hadham Rd CM23 145 C5
GREAT HALLINGBURY 146 E4
Great Harrods CO14 171 A7
Great Havers Ct CM23 145 E5
GREAT HENNY 54 C8
GREAT HOLLAND 170 A3
Great Holland Common Rd CO13 169 D2
Great Holland Ct CO13 170 A3
GREAT HORKESLEY 82 A1
GREAT LEIGHS 173 E7
Great Leighs Prim Sch CM3 174 A7
GREAT MAPLESTEAD 52 D2
GREAT NOTLEY 154 B8
Great Notley Ave CM77 154 C5
Great Notley Country Park & Doscovery Ctr* CM77 154 A7
Great Oak Ct CO9 30 A1
GREAT OAKLEY 116 C4
Great Pitchers CO6 105 A7
Great Priory Cotts CM7 127 C8
GREAT SALING 126 A8
GREAT SAMPFORD 47 B4
Great Sampford Prim Sch CB10 47 A3
Great Sq 10 CM7 127 F3
GREAT TEY 132 C8
Great Tey CE Prim Sch CO6 106 C1
Great Tey Rd CO6 132 C4
GREAT TOTHAM 196 C4
Great Totham Prim Sch CM9 196 A5
Great Totham Rd CM8 195 F5
Great Tufts IP9 35 B1
GREAT WALTHAM 190 E7
Great Waltham CE Prim Sch CM3 190 E7
Great Whip St IP2 17 C4
GREAT WIGBOROUGH 181 F3
GREAT YELDHAM 30 A1
Great Yeldham Rd CO9 50 D7
Grebe Cl IP2 16 E2
Greenacres
Clacton-on-S CO15 189 A5
Coggeshall CO6 130 F1
Colchester CO4 109 E3
Greenacres Cvn Pk CO12 91 A1
Green Acres Rd CO2 162 A5
Green Cl
Chelmsford CM1 205 D4
Hatfield Peverel CM3 194 C3
Writtle CM1 204 B1
Green Cnr CO7 139 E1
Green Ct CO6 104 F7
Green End La CO13 170 B5
Greene View CM7 155 B8
Green Farm Rd CO6 78 B2
Greenfield CM8 177 A1
Greenfield Cotts CO4 82 E6
Greenfield Dr CO6 106 B1
Greenfield Hos
Birch CO2 161 A3
Birch Green CO2 160 F3
Greenfields
Galleywood CM2 216 C2
Gosfield CO9 102 F7
Stansted Mountfitchet CM24 119 E7
Greenfields Way CB9 8 E6
Greenfinch Ave IP2 16 D3
Greenfinch End CO4 136 F8
Greenford Rd CO15 188 C3
Greengates Mobile Home Pk CO16 168 C4
Greenhill Pk CM23 145 D5
Greenhurst Rd CO7 186 A6
Greenhythe Ct CO4 136 D6
Green La
Aldham CO6 107 C1
Ardleigh CO7 111 D6
Black Notley CM8 155 A2
Boxted CO4 82 D5
Colchester CO4 110 E2
Colchester, Crockleford Heath CO7 111 C1
Great Dunmow CM6 150 C8
Great Horkesley CO6 109 C6
Great Notley CM8 154 F2
Little Totham CM9 197 C4
Stratford St M CO7 58 C4
Tattingstone IP9 61 D7
Tiptree CO5 179 D6
Tolleshunt Knights CO5 179 E1
Walton-on-t-N CO14 144 D2
Weeley Heath CO16 168 A6
Greenland Gr CO16 186 D3
Greenlawns Cvn Pk CO16 168 C2
Green Man La CM8 195 F7
Green Mdws CM3 219 A6
Green Oak Glade IP8 36 D8
Greensmill CO11 86 C5
Greenspire Gr IP8 16 B2
Green St CM6 148 F2
GREENSTEAD 136 E7
Greenstead Ct CO1 136 D6
GREENSTEAD GREEN 104 A5
Greenstead Rd CO1 136 D7
Greenstead Rdbt CO4 136 D6
Greens The IP4 18 F4
Greens Yd CO13 170 F5
Green's Yd CO1 135 E7
GREEN THE 155 C4
Green The
Bishop's Stortford CM23 145 F4
Chelmsford CM1 204 F4
Chrishall SG8 19 D3
Clacton-on-S CO16 188 B2
Colne Engaine CO6 78 A2
Feering CO5 158 E5
Great Bentley CO7 166 D8
Hatfield Peverel CM3 194 C3
Little Totham CM9 197 C4
Mistley CO11 86 F4
Saffron Walden CB10 22 D3
Seawick CO16 203 B6
Stanstead CO10 2 E7
Wickham St P CO9 53 C5
Writtle CM1 204 B1
Greenview Pk CO15 189 A7
Greenway
Bishop's Stortford CM23 146 C6
Frinton-on-S CO13 170 F5
Green Way CO6 78 A2
Greenway Cl CO15 189 B7
Greenway Gdns CM77 154 D7
Greenways
Chelmsford CM1 205 B6
Feering CO5 158 D3
Gosfield CO9 102 F7
Maldon CM9 209 F2
Saffron Walden CB11 43 E7
Greenways Cl IP1 17 B8
Greenways The CO6 131 A3
Greenway The CO15 189 B7
Greenwell Rd CM8 194 F7
GREENWICH 17 E1
Greenwich Bsns Pk IP3 17 E2
Greenwich Cl IP3 17 E2
Greenwich Rd IP3 17 E2
Greenwood Cl
Chelmsford CM2 205 F2
Haverhill CB9 8 E7
Greenwood Gr CO4 110 C3
Gregory St CO10 33 E7
Grenadier Rd CB9 8 C8
Grendel Way CO15 189 F6
Grenfell Ave CO15 189 E6
Grenfell Cl CO4 110 C1
Grenville Rd
Braintree CM7 127 E2
Sudbury CO10 15 F2
Gresham Ct IP1 17 B8
Gresham Pl CM7 127 F4
Gresley Cl CO4 109 F2
Gresley Dr 2 CM7 128 A2
Gresley Gdns IP2 17 C3
Gretna Gdns IP4 18 B8
Greville Cl CO14 144 E2
Grey Friars Rd 10 IP1 17 C5
Greyhound Hill CO4 83 E5
Greyhound Rd CO10 2 B3
Grey Ladys CM2 216 B2
Greys Cl CO10 1 C1
Greys Hollow CB11 93 D8
Greystones Cl CO3 135 A3
Grieves Ct CO3 134 C4
Griffin Ct IP2 17 D3
Griggs Bsns Ctr CO6 130 E1
Grimston Rd CO2 136 A4
Grimston Way CO14 171 B7
Grimwade Cl CO11 86 D7
Grimwade St IP4 17 D5
Grimwood Cnr 18 CO10 33 E7
Grindle The IP8 16 A7
Groome Ct 2 CO4 136 D7
Groom Ho CO15 188 E4
Groom Pk CO15 188 E4
Groomside 5 CM7 128 A2
Grooms La CM8 156 E4
Grosvenor Cl
Bishop's Stortford CM23 145 D4
Chelmsford CM2 216 D7
Ipswich IP4 17 E8
Tiptree CO5 179 D5
Grosvenor Ct IP3 18 B1
Grosvenor Ho 4 CM23 146 B8
Grosvenor Pl CO1 136 B7
Grosvenor Rd CO10 15 D2
Grove Ave
Walton-on-t-N CO14 171 B8
West Mersea CO5 201 C5
Grove Cotts 1 CM8 177 A2
Grove Ct CM6 150 E7
Grove Ctr The CM8 177 A1
Grove Farm Rd
Little Totham CM9 197 C7
Tiptree CO5, CM9 179 A1
Grove Field CM7 102 C1
Grove Hill
Belstead IP8 36 C7
Dedham CO7 84 D4
Langham CO4 83 F5
Stansted Mountfitchet CM24 119 F7
Grove La
Chelmondiston IP9 63 E5
Ipswich IP4 17 E5
Grove Lea CM9 194 F1
Grove Mews IP11 221 D5
Grove Orch CM7 102 C1
Grove Pk CM23 145 C8
Grove Pl 19 CM23 145 F7
Grove Rd
Bentley IP9 60 E6
Brantham CO11 86 D8
Chelmsford CM2 205 B1
Felixstowe IP11 221 E6
Little Clacton CO16 168 D5
Tiptree CO5 179 E6
Groves Cl CO4 109 E2
Grove The
Bicknacre CM3 218 F1
Clacton-on-S CO15 188 F2
Earls Colne CO6 105 B6
Great Hallingbury CM22 146 F4
Witham CM8 177 A2
Grove Villas CM7 126 A8
Grove Wlk IP8 36 D8
Gryme's Dyke Ct CO3 134 D6
Gryme's Dyke Way CO3 134 E3
Gryphon Way CO2 135 E3
Gryps Cl CO2 135 E1
GUBBION'S GREEN 174 B8
Guelph's La CM6 70 A3
Guernsey Ct CM9 209 F2
Guernsey Way CM7 127 D2
Guildford Rd CO1 136 A8
Guildhall Way CB10 24 A7
Guinea Cl CM7 128 D4
Guisnes Ct CM9 199 A4
Guithavon Ct CM8 176 F2
Guithavon Rd CM8 176 F1
Guithavon Rise CM8 176 F2
Guithavon St CM8 176 F2
Guithavon Valley CM8 176 F2
Gull Cotts CO16 142 D4
Gull Ct CO16 141 F1
Gulls Croft CM7 128 D3
Gull's La CO7 85 A3
Gulpher Bsns Pk IP11 221 D8
Gulpher Cotts IP11 221 E8
Gulpher Rd IP11 221 E8
Gunfleet Cl CO5 201 B7
Gunfleet Ct CO15 189 C4
Gun Hill CO7 84 C7
Gunson Gate CM2 216 D7
Gurdon Rd CO2 135 F3
Gurney Benham Cl CO2 135 B4
Gurton Rd CO6 131 A3
Gusford Com Prim Sch IP2 16 D1
Gutteridge Hall La CO16 167 E7
Gutters La CM1 205 C7
Guy Cook Cl CO10 34 C4
Guys Farm CM1 204 B1
Gwendoline Cl IP4 18 F4
Gwent Ho IP2 17 B3
Gwyn Cl CM3 192 E1
Gwynne Rd CO12 91 D4
Gymnasium St IP1 17 B7
Gypsy La
Feering CO5 159 C6
Little Dunmow CM6 151 E7
Sudbury CO10 33 C6


## H


Hackmans La CM3 219 E2
Haddon Pk CO1 136 C6
Hadfelda Sq CM3 194 A4
Hadfield Dr CM77 155 B5
Hadham Ct CM23 145 E8
Hadham Gr CM23 145 C8
Hadham Rd CM23 145 D8
Hadleigh Ct
Clacton-on-S CO15 189 A3
4 Saffron Walden CB10 22 F2
Hadleigh Rd
Clacton-on-S CO16 188 B4
East Bergholt CO7 59 B3
Frinton-on-S CO13 171 A5
Ipswich IP2 16 D5
Stratford St M CO7 58 A6
Hadleigh Road Ind Est IP2 16 F7
Hadleigh Way CO13 170 F5
Hadley Cl CM7 102 B1
Hadrian Cl
Colchester CO4 110 B6
Haverhill CB9 9 D7
Hadrians Cl CM8 194 E8
Hadrians Way CM9 210 A4
HADSTOCK 5 C6
Hadstock Rd CB1 5 B8
Haggars La CO7 138 F3
Haggers Cl CB10 3 D2
Haig Ct CM2 205 A1
Hailes Wood CM22 94 D1
Hailes Wood Cl CM22 94 D1
Hainault Gr CM1 204 E1
Hakewill Way CO4 109 E3
Halcyon Cl CM8 176 F1
Hale Cl IP2 16 D2
Halesowen Cl IP2 36 F8
Hale Way CO4 110 B6
Halfacres CM8 195 A7
Half Acres CM23 145 F8
Half Moon Yd CO10 12 B7
Halford Ct 6 IP8 16 C2
Halfway Cotts CO5 158 B6
Half Way Cotts CO5 158 B6
Halifax Prim Sch IP2 17 B2
Halifax Rd IP2 17 B2
Halifax Way CO6 104 F2
Hall Barn CO5 201 B6
Hall Barns CM24 119 D7
Hall Bridge Rise CM9 210 C4
Hall Chase CO6 133 B3
Hall Cl
Great Baddow CM2 217 A6
Henham CM22 94 F5
Hall Cres CO15 189 F6
Hallcroft Chase CO4 110 C4
Hall Cut CO7 185 F6
Hall Dr CO9 102 D8
Hall Est CM9 211 E7
Hallett Rd CM6 151 E6
Hall Farm Cl CO5 158 E4
Hallfield CB11 66 E1
Hall Field IP11 221 C5
Hallingbury Cl CM22 146 B1
Hallingbury Rd CM22, CM23 146 B4
HALLINGBURY STREET 147 A4
Halliwell Rd IP4 18 B6
Hall La
Chelmsford CM2 217 C6
Harwich CO12 91 A2
Ridgewell CO9 29 B6
Thorpe-le-S CO16 169 B8
Walton-on-t-N CO14 144 D2
Hall Pond Way IP11 221 C5
Hall Rd
Belchamp Walter CO10 32 A6
Borley CO10 15 A3
Bures CO8 79 E5
Copford CO6 133 E4
Elsenham CM22 94 D1
Fordham CO6 107 D5
Great Bromley CO7 112 C2
Great Totham CM9 196 C3
Maldon CM9 210 B4
Panfield CM7 127 A6
Tiptree CO5 179 C3
Tollesbury CM9 199 D1
West Bergholt CO6 108 D5
Hall Rise
Sudbury CO10 33 C6
Witham CM8 194 F8
Hall Road Cotts CO6 108 D6
Hall St
Chelmsford CM2 205 B1
Long Melford CO10 15 C8
Hall View Rd CO7 166 E7
Hall Villas CM7 72 B1
HALSTEAD 76 D2
Halstead Bsns Ctr CO9 76 E1
Halstead Hospl CO9 76 E3
Halstead Rd
Braintree CM7 102 E3
Colchester CO3 134 D7
Earls Colne CO6 104 F7
Eight Ash G CO6 134 A8
Fordham CO6 107 B3
Fordham Heath CO6 107 E1
Gosfield CO9 75 F1
Kirby Cross CO13 170 B7
Kirby-le-S CO13 170 C8
Sible Hedingham CO9 76 B6
Halston Pl CM9 220 F8
Halton Cres IP3 18 C1
Hamble Cl CM8 176 E2
Hamel Way CB11 67 D4
Hamford Cl CO14 144 D2
Hamford Dr CO12 116 C3
Hamford Prim Sch CO14 170 F7
Hamilton Ct
Brightlingsea CO7 186 A7
Chelmsford CM1 204 D6
Clacton-on-S CO15 189 E6
Hamilton Gdns IP11 221 F3
Hamilton Ho IP4 18 A7
Hamilton Mews 3 CB10 22 F2
Hamilton Prim Sch CO3 135 D5
Hamilton Rd
Colchester CO3 135 D5
Felixstowe IP11 221 E4
Great Holland CO13 170 A5
Ipswich IP3 18 B3
Sudbury CO10 33 E7
Takeley CM6 148 F7
Wivenhoe CO7 164 B8
Hamilton St
Felixstowe IP11 221 C5
Harwich CO12 90 F5
Hamlet Ct CO8 79 E8
Hamlet Dr CO4 136 F7
Hamlet Rd
Chelmsford CM2 205 B1
Haverhill CB9 9 B7
Hammond Ct 1 CO13 170 F5
Hammonds Rd CM3 206 E3
HAMPERDEN END 68 D3
Hampit Rd CB11 41 D2
HAMPITS 41 D2
Hampstead Ave CO16 188 D5
Hampton Ho CM2 216 D6
Hampton Rd
Great Baddow CM2 216 E6
Ipswich IP1 16 F7
Hamsters Cl CO9 77 F8
Hanbury Gdns CO4 110 B5
Hanbury Rd CM1 215 E8
Hance La CM77 126 F2
Hanchetts Orch CM6 70 A3
HANCHETT VILLAGE 8 B8
Handel Wlk CO4 136 E6
Handford Cut IP1 17 A6
Handford Hall Prim Sch IP1 17 A6
Handford Pl CO3 135 D6
Handford Rd IP1 17 A6
Handley's La CM8 195 F5
Handy Fisher Ct CO3 135 B4
Hankin Ave CO12 90 C1
Hanlee Brook CM2 216 F6
Hanningfield Way CO4 110 B5
Hanover Bridge CO5 158 F5
Hanover Ct
Braintree CM7 127 F8
Harwich CO12 91 C3
Ipswich IP4 17 E6
Sudbury CO10 33 D6
Walton-on-t-N CO14 171 A8
Witham CM8 177 B1
Hanover Pl CB10 22 C1
Hanover Sq CO5 158 F6
Hanwell Cl CO16 188 D5
Ha'penny Dr IP9 62 D5
Ha'penny Field IP9 62 D5
Ha'penny Pier Visitor Ctr* CO12 91 D6
Happy Gdns CO5 179 A8
Harberd Tye CM2 216 D7
Harborough Hall Rd CO5 159 E2
Harbour Cres CO12 91 E5
Harcourt Ave CO12 91 A4
Hardies Point CO2 136 D5
Hardings Cl CO6 133 B8
Hardings Yd CO7 164 B7
Hard The CO7 185 F5
Hardwick Cl
Great Notley CM77 154 B7
Rushmere St A IP4 18 E5
Hardwick Rd CB9 9 B8
Hardy Cl
Braintree CM7 155 A8
Brantham CO11 86 C7
Hardy Ct CO10 15 F2
HARDY'S GREEN 160 E6
Harebell Cl CO4 110 B3
Harebell Dr CM8 176 E3
Harebell Rd IP2 16 F4
HARE GREEN 139 A6
Hares Wlk CO10 33 F8
Harewood Rd CM1 204 E1
Harewood Terr 20 CB9 8 E7
Harfred Ave CM9 210 E3
Hargrave Cl CM24 119 E8
Harkilees Way CM7 127 F5
HARKSTEAD 63 B2
Harkstead La
Chelmondiston IP9 63 A7
Woolverstone IP9 38 A1
Harkstead Rd IP9 62 F3
Harland St IP2 17 C3
Harlings Gr CM1 205 C3
Harmans Yd CM6 150 D8
Harman Wlk CO16 188 C5
Harness Cl CM1 205 E7
Harnham Dr CM77 154 C7

Harold Cl CO9 . . . . . . . . . . . .76 F1
Harold Collins Pl CO1 . . .136 B7
Harold Gr CO13 . . . . . . . . . .170 F4
**Harold Rd**
  Braintree CM7 . . . . . . . . . .127 E2
  Clacton-on-S CO15 . . . . . .188 F3
  Frinton-on-S CO13 . . . . . .170 F4
Harold Rise CM9 . . . . . . . .209 F5
Harold Sims Ho CO6 . . . .105 B7
Harold Way CO11 . . . . . . . .170 F4
Harp Close Rd CO10 . . . .33 F8
Harpers Way CO16 . . . . . .188 A3
Harp La CO10 . . . . . . . . . .12 C8
**Harp Meadow La**
  CO2 . . . . . . . . . . . . . . . . . .135 D4
Harpur's Rd CO10 . . . . . . . .2 B4
Harrier Cl IP3 . . . . . . . . . . . .18 B1
**Harrington Cl**
  **7** Bishop's Stortford
  CM23 . . . . . . . . . . . . . . .146 A7
  Tiptree CO5 . . . . . . . . . . .179 B5
**Harrington Mead**
  CM2 . . . . . . . . . . . . . . . .206 B3
Harris Gn CM6 . . . . . . . . . .150 E7
**Harrison Ct**
  Chelmsford CM1 . . . . . . .204 F3
  West Mersea CO5 . . . . . .201 C6
Harrison Dr CM7 . . . . . . .128 A1
Harrison Ho CO12 . . . . . . .91 D4
Harrison Rd CO2 . . . . . . .153 E3
Harrisons CM23 . . . . . . . .119 D2
Harris Yd CO10 . . . . . . . . .22 F1
Harrold Ct CO15 . . . . . . . .189 A2
Harrow Cl CM4 . . . . . . . . .18 B5
HARROWCROSS . . . . . . . . .75 C8
Harrow Hill CO9 . . . . . . . .49 F6
**Harrow Rd**
  Clacton-on-S CO15 . . . . . .188 F4
  Haverhill CB9 . . . . . . . . . . . .8 E7
Harrow Way CM2 . . . . . . .217 A6
Harsnett Rd CO1 . . . . . . .136 B5
Hartest Way CO10 . . . . . . .34 B6
HARTFORD END . . . . . . . .172 D8
Hartley Cl CM2 . . . . . . . .206 A4
Hartley St IP7 . . . . . . . . . . .17 C4
Hart's La CO7 . . . . . . . . . . .84 B2
Hart St CM2 . . . . . . . . . . .205 A1
Harvard Ct CO4 . . . . . . . .110 B4
Harvest Cl CO6 . . . . . . . . .133 B4
**Harvest Ct**
  Feering CO5 . . . . . . . . . . .158 E4
  Felixstowe IP11 . . . . . . . .221 F4
Harvest End CO3 . . . . . . .134 D5
Harvesters CM9 . . . . . . . .199 D4
Harvesters' Way CO6 . . . .132 B8
Harvest Fields CM22 . . . .148 B7
Harvest Ho IP11 . . . . . . . .221 F4
**Harvest Way**
  Elmstead Market CO7 . . .137 F6
  Maldon CM9 . . . . . . . . . .209 F5
Harvey Cl CO11 . . . . . . . . .86 C4
Harvey Cres CO3 . . . . . . .134 C4
Harvey Ct CO15 . . . . . . . .203 F6
**Harvey Rd**
  Colchester CO2 . . . . . . . .135 B2
  Great Totham CM9 . . . . . .196 A4
  Wivenhoe CO7 . . . . . . . .137 C1
Harvey St CO9 . . . . . . . . . .76 F1
**Harvey Way**
  Hempstead CB10 . . . . . . .25 F1
  Saffron Walden CB10 . . . .22 F2
Harwich Cl CM7 . . . . . . . .128 D4
**HARWICH** . . . . . . . . . . . . .91 E5
Harwich Com Prim Sch
  CO12 . . . . . . . . . . . . . . . .91 A4
Harwich Crane The*
  CO12 . . . . . . . . . . . . . . . .91 E5
Harwich Ct CO4 . . . . . . . .136 F4
Harwich Gateway Retail
  Pk CO12 . . . . . . . . . . . . .91 A4
Harwich Ind Est CO12 . . . .90 F5
Harwich International Port
  CO12 . . . . . . . . . . . . . . . .90 F6
Harwich Parkeston Quay
  Sta CO12 . . . . . . . . . . . . .90 F6
**Harwich Rd**
  Ardleigh CO7 . . . . . . . . . .111 F8
  Beaumont CO16 . . . . . . . .141 F7
  Bradfield CO11 . . . . . . . . .87 F2
  Colchester CO7 . . . . . . . .110 F3
  Colchester, Greenstead
  CO1 . . . . . . . . . . . . . . . .136 C2
  Dedham CO7 . . . . . . . . . .84 F1
  Great Bromley CO7 . . . . .139 C6
  Great Oakley CO12 . . . . .116 D5
  Lawford CO11 . . . . . . . . . .85 C2
  Little Bentley CO7 . . . . . .113 E1
  Little Clacton CO16 . . . . .168 E6
  Little Oakley CO12 . . . . . .117 C7
  New Mistley CO11 . . . . . . .87 B3
  Wix CO11, CO12 . . . . . . .116 A7
  Wix, Wix Green CO11 . . . .115 D5
  Wrabness CO11 . . . . . . . .88 D2
Harwich Sch The CO12 . . .91 A2
Harwich Town Sta
  CO12 . . . . . . . . . . . . . . . .91 D5
Harwood Cl CO2 . . . . . . .136 A4
Haselfoot Rd CM3 . . . . . .206 F8
**Haselmere Gdns**
  CO13 . . . . . . . . . . . . . . .170 F7
Haskell Mews CM7 . . . . . .155 A8
Haslar Pl CM7 . . . . . . . . . .150 D8
Haslemere CM23 . . . . . . . .119 A2
Haslemere Dr IP4 . . . . . . . .17 C2

Haslemere Ind Est
  CM23 . . . . . . . . . . . . . . .146 A4
Hasler Rd CM9 . . . . . . . . .199 D2
Haslers La CM6 . . . . . . . . .150 D8
Hastings Ave CO15 . . . . . .203 A8
Hastings Pl CO7 . . . . . . . .185 F8
Hastings Rd CO3 . . . . . . .135 A4
Hatchcroft Gdns CO7 . . . .138 A6
Hatcher Cres CO2 . . . . . .136 C5
Hatchfields CM3 . . . . . . . .190 F7
Hatfield Forest (Ctry Pk)*
  CM22 . . . . . . . . . . . . . . .147 D6
Hatfield Forest Nature
  Trail* CM22 . . . . . . . . . . .147 E5
Hatfield Gr CM1 . . . . . . . .204 D1
HATFIELD PEVEREL . . . .194 B4
Hatfield Peverel Inf Sch
  CM3 . . . . . . . . . . . . . . . .194 B3
Hatfield Peverel St
  Andrew's Jun Sch
  CM3 . . . . . . . . . . . . . . . .194 A3
Hatfield Peverel Sta
  CM3 . . . . . . . . . . . . . . . .193 F5
**Hatfield Rd**
  Hatfield Peverel CM8 . . . .194 F4
  Ipswich IP3 . . . . . . . . . . . .18 A3
  Langford CM9 . . . . . . . . .209 B7
  Terling CM3 . . . . . . . . . . .175 D2
  Witham CM8 . . . . . . . . . .194 E7
Hatherley Ct CB10 . . . . . . .22 E2
Hatleys CM2 . . . . . . . . . . .217 A4
Haubourdin Ct CO9 . . . . . .77 A2
Haughley Dr IP4 . . . . . . . .18 F6
Hauliers Rd IP11 . . . . . . . .221 B2
Havelock Rd CM1 . . . . . . .205 B3
Havencroft Ct **5**
  CO14 . . . . . . . . . . . . . . .171 C8
Haven Ct CM3 . . . . . . . . .193 F4
Havengore CM1 . . . . . . . .205 F5
Haven Rd CO2 . . . . . . . . .136 D4
Havens The IP3 . . . . . . . . .38 E7
Haven The CO12 . . . . . . . .90 F3
Havenvale CO15 . . . . . . . .188 E4
Havergate Rd IP3 . . . . . . .38 D8
HAVERHILL . . . . . . . . . . . . .9 C7
Haverhill Rd
  Castle Camps CB21 . . . . . .7 E5
  Helions Bumpstead CB9 . . .8 D1
  Steeple Bumpstead CB9 . . .27 C8
**Havering Cl**
  Clacton-on-S CO15 . . . . . .188 E7
  Colchester CO4 . . . . . . . .110 B1
Havers La CM23 . . . . . . . .145 F5
Havers Par CM23 . . . . . . .145 F5
Havisham Way CM1 . . . . .204 E7
Hawbridge IP9 . . . . . . . . . .35 A2
Hawbush Gn CM7 . . . . . . .127 F5
HAWBUSH GREEN . . . . . .155 F6
Hawes St IP2 . . . . . . . . . . .17 D3
Hawfinch Rd CO2 . . . . . . .162 A5
Hawfinch Wlk CM7 . . . . . .216 B5
Hawkendon Rd CO16 . . . .188 A4
Hawke Rd IP3 . . . . . . . . . . .17 E1
Hawkes La IP11 . . . . . . . . .221 B6
**Hawkes Rd**
  Coggeshall CO6 . . . . . . . .130 F3
  Witham CM8 . . . . . . . . . .194 E7
Hawkeswey CO15 . . . . . . .188 F6
Hawkhurst Cl CM1 . . . . . .204 E2
Hawkins Cl CM3 . . . . . . . .219 E2
Hawkins Ct CO10 . . . . . . . .15 F2
HAWKIN'S HILL . . . . . . . . .71 E7
**Hawkins Rd**
  Alresford CO7 . . . . . . . . .165 B8
  Colchester CO2 . . . . . . . .136 D5
Hawkins Way CM7 . . . . . .128 C4
Hawks Cl CM3 . . . . . . . . .219 A6
Hawkwood Rd CO9 . . . . . .75 D8
Hawlmark End CO6 . . . . . .132 E3
Hawthorn Ave CO4 . . . . . .136 E7
**Hawthorn Cl**
  Chelmsford CM2 . . . . . . .216 C6
  Halstead CO9 . . . . . . . . . .77 A2
  Takeley CM22 . . . . . . . . .148 C7
Hawthorn Dr IP2 . . . . . . . .16 E3
Hawthorn Rise CM8 . . . . .177 A5
Hawthornes CM3 . . . . . . .220 D1
**Hawthorn Rd**
  Clacton-on-S CO15 . . . . . .188 E6
  Great Cornard CO10 . . . . .34 B7
  Hatfield Peverel CM3 . . . .194 A5
  Tolleshunt Knights
  CM9 . . . . . . . . . . . . . . . .180 A2
Hawthorn Rise CM23 . . . .145 F3
**Hawthorns**
  Kirby Cross CO13 . . . . . . .170 F7
  Sible Hedingham CO9 . . . .51 D2
Hawthorns The CM3 . . . . .220 B1
Haycocks Farm CO5 . . . . .183 F1
Haycocks La CO5 . . . . . . .183 F1
Haycroft CM23 . . . . . . . . .146 C7
Haye La CO5 . . . . . . . . . . .163 C4
Hayes Cl CM3 . . . . . . . . . .205 B1
Hayes Rd CO15 . . . . . . . . .188 E3
Hay Gn CM3 . . . . . . . . . . .218 F8
Hayhill Rd IP4 . . . . . . . . . . .17 E7
Hayhouse Rd CO6 . . . . . . .105 A6
Hay La N CM7 . . . . . . . . . .128 C3
Hay La S CM7 . . . . . . . . . .128 C3
Hayley Bell Gdns
  CM23 . . . . . . . . . . . . . . .145 F3
Hayman Rd IP3 . . . . . . . . . .17 F1
Haymeads La CM23 . . . . . .146 C6
**Haynes Green Rd**
  CO5 . . . . . . . . . . . . . . . .180 A8

Haytor Cl CM7 . . . . . . . . .128 C2
Haywain The CO3 . . . . . . .134 D5
Hayward Ct CO1 . . . . . . . .136 C7
**Hazel Cl**
  Great Dunmow CM6 . . . .123 C1
  Haverhill CB9 . . . . . . . . . . . .8 E7
  Thorrington CO7 . . . . . . .166 A5
  Witham CM8 . . . . . . . . . .177 A4
Hazeldon Cl CM3 . . . . . . .191 C6
Hazel Dr IP3 . . . . . . . . . . . .18 F1
HAZELEIGH . . . . . . . . . . . .220 A4
Hazeleigh Hall La
  CM3 . . . . . . . . . . . . . . . .220 A4
HAZEL END . . . . . . . . . . . .119 A6
Hazelend Rd CM23 . . . . . .119 B4
Hazel Gr CM7 . . . . . . . . . .127 E1
Hazell Ave CO2 . . . . . . . . .135 B2
Hazel Mews CO7 . . . . . . . .185 E7
HAZEL STUB . . . . . . . . . . . .8 C7
Hazelton Rd CO4 . . . . . . . .110 D1
Hazelville Cl CO2 . . . . . . . .90 E1
**Hazelwood Cres**
  CO6 . . . . . . . . . . . . . . . .168 C1
Hazelwood Ct CO4 . . . . . .210 B6
Hazlemere Jun & Inf Schs
  CO4 . . . . . . . . . . . . . . . .136 E8
Hazlemere Rd CO15 . . . . .189 C4
**Headgate** CO1 . . . . . . . . .135 E6
Headgate Bldg **1**
  CO2 . . . . . . . . . . . . . . . .135 E6
Headingham Cl **3** IP2 . . .17 A2
Head La CO10 . . . . . . . . . . .34 B5
Headland Ave CB9 . . . . . . . .8 E7
**Head St**
  Colchester CO1 . . . . . . . .135 E7
  Goldhanger CM9 . . . . . . .211 E6
  Halstead CO9 . . . . . . . . . .76 F2
  Rowhedge CO5 . . . . . . . .163 F8
Head Way CO10 . . . . . . . . .15 C2
**Heards La**
  Cornish Hall End CM7 . . . .48 C6
  Cornish Hall End CM7 . . . .48 D5
Hearsall Ave CM1 . . . . . . .205 B7
Heath Bsns Pk CO2 . . . . . .136 D3
Heath Cl CO3 . . . . . . . . . . .59 D3
Heathcote Sch CM3 . . . . .218 E7
Heath Cotts CO3 . . . . . . . .107 F1
Heath Dr CM2 . . . . . . . . . .216 B6
Heather Ave IP3 . . . . . . . . .18 C3
**Heather Cl**
  Bishop's Stortford
  CM23 . . . . . . . . . . . . . . .145 D6
  Clacton-on-S CO15 . . . . . .189 B7
  Layer de la H CO2 . . . . . .161 F5
Heather Ct **10** CM1 . . . . .205 F6
Heather Dr CO3 . . . . . . . .134 F5
Heatherhayes IP2 . . . . . . . .17 A3
**Heathfield Rd**
  Chelmsford CM1 . . . . . . .205 B7
  Holbrook IP9 . . . . . . . . . .62 D5
Heathfields CO6 . . . . . . . .134 B8
Heathfields Ho CO2 . . . . .136 C3
**Heathgate** CM8 . . . . . . . .195 D6
**Heathgate Piece**
  IP11 . . . . . . . . . . . . . . . .221 A8
Heath La IP4 . . . . . . . . . . . .18 C5
Heathlands CO7 . . . . . . . .166 A5
Heathlands CE Prim Sch
  CO6 . . . . . . . . . . . . . . . .108 E4
Heathlands IP4 . . . . . . . . . .18 E4
**Heath Rd**
  Alresford CO7 . . . . . . . . .165 B8
  Bradfield CO11 . . . . . . . .114 D8
  Colchester CO3 . . . . . . . .134 F5
  Colchester, Stanway Green
  CO3 . . . . . . . . . . . . . . . .134 D4
  East Bergholt CO7 . . . . . .59 D3
  Fordham Heath CO3 . . . .108 A1
  Ipswich IP4 . . . . . . . . . . . .18 D6
  New Mistley CO11 . . . . . . .87 B2
  Rowhedge CO5 . . . . . . . .163 F8
  St Osyth Heath CO16 . . . .167 E1
  Tendring CO16 . . . . . . . . .140 E7
  Wivenhoe CO7 . . . . . . . .137 B2
Heath Row CM23 . . . . . . .119 B1
Heath Sch The CO3 . . . . . .134 D5
Heathside CO6 . . . . . . . . .108 E4
Heathside Sch IP4 . . . . . . .18 D6
**Heath The**
  Dedham CO7 . . . . . . . . . .85 A4
  Layer de la H CO2 . . . . . .162 A6
Heatley Way CO3 . . . . . . .136 F8
Heaton Way CO5 . . . . . . .179 D6
HECKFORDBRIDGE . . . . . .161 B8
Heckford's Rd CO7 . . . . . .139 E2
Heckworth Cl CO4 . . . . . .110 C6
Hedge Dr CO2 . . . . . . . . . .135 B3
Hedgelands CO6 . . . . . . . .133 D5
Hedgerows CO3 . . . . . . . .134 D6
**Hedgerows Bsns Pk**
  CM2 . . . . . . . . . . . . . . . .206 A6
Hedgerows The CM3 . . . . .146 B6
Hedingham Castle*
  CO9 . . . . . . . . . . . . . . . . .51 F4
Hedingham Pl CO9 . . . . . . .51 E1
**Hedingham Rd**
  Bulmer Tye CO10 . . . . . . .32 C1
  Gosfield CO9 . . . . . . . . . . .75 E3
  Halstead CO9 . . . . . . . . . .76 E3
  Wickham St P CO9 . . . . . .53 A7
Hedingham Sch CO9 . . . . .51 F3
Heights The CM3 . . . . . . .218 D7
Helena Rd IP3 . . . . . . . . . . .17 E3
Helena Romanes Sch &
  Sixth Form Ctr CM6 . . . .123 C1
Helen Ewing Pl CO2 . . . . .135 F1
Helen How CO2 . . . . . . . .173 F7
Helford Ct CM8 . . . . . . . . .176 D2

**HELIONS BUMPSTEAD**
  . . . . . . . . . . . . . . . . . . . .26 C8
Helions Bumpstead Rd
  CB9 . . . . . . . . . . . . . . . . . .9 A5
Helions Park Ave CB9 . . . . .9 A7
Helions Park Gdns CB9 . . . .9 A7
Helions Park Gr CB9 . . . . . .9 A7
Helions Rd CB9 . . . . . . . . . .9 A7
Helions Service Rd CB9 . . . .9 A7
Helions Wlk CB9 . . . . . . . . .9 A7
**HELLMAN'S CROSS** . . . . .148 F2
Helm Cl CO6 . . . . . . . . . . .109 C7
Helston Rd CM1 . . . . . . . .205 E6
Hemingway Rd CM8 . . . . .176 F5
Hemlock Cl CM8 . . . . . . . .177 A4
Hemmings CM9 . . . . . . . .220 E8
HEMPSTEAD . . . . . . . . . . . .25 F1
Hendon Cl CO16 . . . . . . . .188 D5
Hengrave Cl IP2 . . . . . . . . .17 A2
HENHAM . . . . . . . . . . . . . . .94 F6
**Henham Rd**
  Debden CB11 . . . . . . . . . .68 E3
  Elsenham CM22 . . . . . . . .94 E2
Henham & Ugley Prim Sch
  CM22 . . . . . . . . . . . . . . . .94 F5
Hening Ave IP3 . . . . . . . . . .38 D8
Hening Ho IP3 . . . . . . . . . .38 D8
**Henley Ct**
  Colchester CO3 . . . . . . . .134 F6
  Manningtree CO11 . . . . . . .86 C4
Henley Rd IP1 . . . . . . . . . . .17 C8
Henniker Gate CM2 . . . . .206 A4
Henniker Rd IP1 . . . . . . . . .16 D8
Henny Back Rd CO8 . . . . . .54 E4
Henny Rd CO8 . . . . . . . . . .55 B5
HENNY STREET . . . . . . . . .33 F1
Henrietta Cl CO7 . . . . . . .137 C3
**Henry Cl**
  Clacton-on-S CO15 . . . . . .188 C2
  Haverhill CB9 . . . . . . . . . . . .8 D6
Henry Dixon Rd CM8 . . . .177 D6
Henry Laver Ct CO3 . . . . .135 E7
**Henry Rd**
  Chelmsford CM1 . . . . . . .205 B4
  Ipswich IP3 . . . . . . . . . . . .18 B1
Henslow Rd IP4 . . . . . . . . .18 B5
Henstead Gdns IP3 . . . . . .18 A2
Herald Cl CM23 . . . . . . . .145 D6
**Herbage Park Rd**
  CM9 . . . . . . . . . . . . . . . .208 D1
Herbert Rd CO15 . . . . . . .188 E3
**Hereford Ct**
  Clacton-on-S CO15 . . . . . .189 E5
  Great Baddow CM2 . . . . .217 A5
Hereford Dr CM7 . . . . . . .128 D5
**Hereford Rd**
  Colchester CO1 . . . . . . . .136 A8
  Holland-on-S CO15 . . . . . .189 E6
Hereward Cl CO7 . . . . . . .137 C3
Hereward Way CM7 . . . . . .73 C3
Hering Dr CM7 . . . . . . . . .210 C4
Heriot Way CM9 . . . . . . . .196 B4
**Heritage Mus The***
  CO6 . . . . . . . . . . . . . . . .105 A6
Hermitage Ct CM24 . . . . .119 D7
Hermitage Ho CM24 . . . . .119 D7
Heron Cl CM3 . . . . . . . . . .134 B4
Heron Ct CM23 . . . . . . . . .146 A7
Heron Glade CO15 . . . . . .188 F7
**Heron Rd**
  Ipswich IP2 . . . . . . . . . . . .16 E3
  Kelvedon IP3 . . . . . . . . . .158 D2
Heronsgate CO13 . . . . . . .170 F6
**Heron Way**
  Frinton-on-S CO13 . . . . . .170 E6
  Heybridge CM9 . . . . . . . .210 C5
Herrick Pl CO3 . . . . . . . . .135 A6
Herringham Gn CM2 . . . . .206 A4
Herring's Way CO6 . . . . . .107 D6
Hertford La SG8, CB11 . . . .19 E5
Hertfordshire & Essex
  High Sch The CM23 . . . . .146 B7
Herts & Essex Com Hospl
  CM23 . . . . . . . . . . . . . . .146 B6
Hervey St IP1 . . . . . . . . . . .17 D7
Hervilly Way CO14 . . . . . .171 B7
Heseltine Ct CO15 . . . . . .189 B3
Hesper Rd CO2 . . . . . . . . .136 C5
Hetherington Cl CO2 . . . .163 A8
Hewes Cl CO4 . . . . . . . . . .136 F7
Hewitt Rd CO12 . . . . . . . . .90 C1
Hewitt Wlk **6** CM8 . . . . .177 A2
Hexham Cl **3** IP2 . . . . . . .17 A2
HEYBRIDGE . . . . . . . . . . . .210 B6
Heybridge App CM9 . . . . .209 F5
HEYBRIDGE BASIN . . . . . .210 F3
Heybridge Cl CO15 . . . . . .189 B3
Heybridge House Ind Est
  CM9 . . . . . . . . . . . . . . . .210 B4
Heybridge Prim Sch
  CM9 . . . . . . . . . . . . . . . .210 C5
Heybridge St CM9 . . . . . . .210 C5
Heycroft Dr CM7 . . . . . . . .155 E5
**Heycroft Way**
  Great Baddow CM2 . . . . .216 F5
  Tiptree CO5 . . . . . . . . . . .179 D6
HEYDON . . . . . . . . . . . . . . . .19 A5
Heydon La
  Chrishall SG8 . . . . . . . . . . .19 A5
  Elmdon CB11 . . . . . . . . . .19 A7
Heywood Cl CO15 . . . . . . .210 A5
Heywood Ct CM3 . . . . . . .205 D4
Heywthrop The CM2 . . . . .205 D4
Heywood Cl IP2 . . . . . . . . .16 E1
Heywood Ct CM3 . . . . . . .205 D4
Heywood La CM6 . . . . . . . .150 D7
Heywood Way CM9 . . . . . .210 A5
Hickford Hill CO10 . . . . . . .12 D6
Hickory Ave CO4 . . . . . . . .136 D7

Hicks Way CB9 . . . . . . . . . . .9 E5
Hidcote Way CM77 . . . . . .154 B7
**HIGHAM** . . . . . . . . . . . . . . .58 B4
Higham Hill CO7, IP7 . . . . .58 A8
**Higham Lodge Cotts**
  CO7 . . . . . . . . . . . . . . . . .58 B5
Higham Rd CO7 . . . . . . . . .58 C3
Highams Chase CM24 . . . .212 A8
Highbank CO12 . . . . . . . . .91 B3
Highbirch Rd CO16 . . . . . .167 D3
High Bridge Rd CM2 . . . . .205 C1
Highbury Terr **1** CO9 . . . . .76 F2
Highbury Way CO10 . . . . . .34 B5
High Chelmer **8** CM1 . . . .205 B2
High Cl SG8 . . . . . . . . . . . .19 A5
**Highclere Rd**
  Colchester CO4 . . . . . . . .110 B4
  Great Notley CM77 . . . . . .154 B6
High Croft CO6 . . . . . . . . . .78 A2
High Cross La CM6 . . . . . .149 B5
High Cross La E CM6 . . . . .149 E6
**Highfield**
  CM6 . . . . . . . . . . . . . . . .149 C6
High Easter Rd CM6 . . . . .150 F2
Highfield CO10 . . . . . . . . . .12 D7
**Highfield Ave**
  Bishop's Stortford
  CM23 . . . . . . . . . . . . . . .146 C6
  Harwich CO12 . . . . . . . . .91 B3
**Highfield Cl**
  Braintree CM7 . . . . . . . . .128 A6
  Danbury CM3 . . . . . . . . . .218 D6
  Highfield Dr CO12 . . . . . .91 B3
Highfield Dr CO3 . . . . . . . .135 C7
**Highfield Holiday Pk**
  Clacton-on-S CO16 . . . . . .188 E8
  Little Clacton CO15 . . . . .168 F1
**Highfield Rd**
  Chelmsford CM1 . . . . . . .204 E4
  Felixstowe IP11 . . . . . . . .221 E4
  Sudbury CO10 . . . . . . . . . .34 A8
**Highfields**
  Bentley IP9 . . . . . . . . . . . .60 E6
  Debden CB11 . . . . . . . . . .68 B7
  Great Yeldham CO9 . . . . . .30 A3
  Halstead CO9 . . . . . . . . . .103 F8
  Henham CM22 . . . . . . . . .94 F6
  Langley CB11 . . . . . . . . . .40 D2
  Saffron Walden CB10 . . . .22 E2
High Fields CM6 . . . . . . . .150 D8
Highfields La CO5 . . . . . . .178 E7
Highfields Prim Sch
  CO11 . . . . . . . . . . . . . . . .86 C4
Highfields Rd CM8 . . . . . .176 E1
Highfield Stile Rd
  CM7 . . . . . . . . . . . . . . . .128 A6
HIGH GARRETT . . . . . . . . .102 D2
High Garrett CM7 . . . . . . .102 C2
Highgates CO9 . . . . . . . . .102 E8
High La CM24 . . . . . . . . . .119 E7
Highland Rd CM23 . . . . . .145 F3
**Highlands** CO9 . . . . . . . . . .75 E1
Highlands Dr CM9 . . . . . . .209 E2
Highlands Gr CO15 . . . . . .189 A7
Highlands Pk CO15 . . . . . .189 A7
High Lift Villas CO4 . . . . . .83 D8
High Mdw CM6 . . . . . . . . .150 C8
Highmead CM24 . . . . . . . .119 E8
High Oaks CO15 . . . . . . . . .90 B2
**HIGH PARK CORNER**
  . . . . . . . . . . . . . . . . . . . .164 C6
High Pastures CM3 . . . . . .207 D3
**High Rd**
  Layer de la H CO2 . . . . . .161 F5
  Trimley St M IP11 . . . . . .221 B7
High Rd E IP11 . . . . . . . . .221 F5
High Rd W IP11 . . . . . . . . .221 D5
High Ridge CM6 . . . . . . . .196 C8
High St N CO5 . . . . . . . . . .201 C7
**High St**
  Bishop's Stortford
  CM23 . . . . . . . . . . . . . . .145 F7
  Braintree CM7 . . . . . . . . .127 F3
  Brightlingsea CO7 . . . . . .185 F6
  Bures CO8 . . . . . . . . . . . .55 F1
  Castle Camps CB21 . . . . . .1 D2
  Cavendish CO10 . . . . . . . . .1 B1
  Chelmsford CM1 . . . . . . .205 B2
  Chrishall SG8 . . . . . . . . . .19 D3
  Clacton-on-S CO15 . . . . . .188 F3
  Clare CO10 . . . . . . . . . . . .12 B7
  Clavering CB11 . . . . . . . . .65 D4
  Colchester CO1 . . . . . . . .135 F7
  Debden CB11 . . . . . . . . . .68 B7
  Dedham CO7 . . . . . . . . . .84 F6
  Earls Colne CO6 . . . . . . . .105 B6
  Elsenham CM22 . . . . . . . .94 D1
  Felixstowe IP11 . . . . . . . .221 C6
  Great Baddow CM2 . . . . .216 F6
  Great Bardfield CM7 . . . . .72 A1
  Great Chesterford CB10 . . .3 E2
  Great Dunmow CM6 . . . .150 D8
  Great Oakley CO12 . . . . .116 C4
  Great Yeldham CO9 . . . . . .30 A1
  Halstead CO9 . . . . . . . . . .76 E2
  Harwich CO12 . . . . . . . . .91 D4
  Haverhill CB9 . . . . . . . . . . .9 A7
  Hempstead CB10 . . . . . . .25 F1
  Henham CM22 . . . . . . . . .94 F5
  Hinxton CB10 . . . . . . . . . . .3 B7
  Ickleton CB10 . . . . . . . . . . .3 F8
  Kelvedon CO5 . . . . . . . . .158 C2
  Langham CO4 . . . . . . . . . .83 D4
  Littlebury CB11 . . . . . . . . .21 F4
  Little Chesterford CB10 . . .21 F8
  Maldon CM9 . . . . . . . . . .210 A2
  Manningtree CO11 . . . . . . .86 D4
  Mistley CO11 . . . . . . . . . .86 F4

**High St** continued
Nayland C06 . . . . . . . . . . . .56 B1
Newport CB11 . . . . . . . . . . . .67 A8
Rowhedge CO5 . . . . . . . . . .164 A8
Saffron Walden CB10. . . . . .22 D1
Sproughton IP8 . . . . . . . . . .16 A6
Stebbing CM6 . . . . . . . . . .124 E5
Thorpe-le-S CO16 . . . . . . .141 F1
Tollesbury CM9 . . . . . . . . .199 D1
Walton-on-t-N CO14 . . . . .171 C8
West Mersea CO5 . . . . . . .201 B6
Wethersfield CM7 . . . . . . . .73 C3
Widdington CB11. . . . . . . . .67 D4
Wivenhoe CO7 . . . . . . . . . .164 B8
**High Stile** CM6 . . . . . . . .150 C8
**HIGHSTREET GREEN** . . . .51 A2
**High Tree La** CO14 . . . . . .144 D2
**High View** CM23 . . . . . . . .119 D3
**High View Ave** CO15 . . . . .188 E6
**Highview Cl** CO10. . . . . . . .15 E2
**High View Cl** CO15 . . . . . .188 E6
**High View Rd** IP1 . . . . . . .16 D8
**Highwoods App** CO4. . . . .110 D4
**Highwoods Com Prim Sch**
CO4 . . . . . . . . . . . . . . . . . . .110 B4
**High Woods Country Park**
Visitor Ctr★ CO4 . . . . . .109 F3
**High Woods Ctry Pk★**
CO4 . . . . . . . . . . . . . . . . . . .110 A3
**Highwoods Sq** CO4 . . . . . .110 B4
**Hildabrook Cl** ☑ IP2 . . . . .16 E1
**Hillary Cl**
Bradwell CM77 . . . . . . . . .129 D2
Chelmsford CM1 . . . . . . . .205 D4
Heybridge CM9 . . . . . . . . .210 B5
Ipswich IP4 . . . . . . . . . . . . .18 A5
**Hill Cl** CO10 . . . . . . . . . . . . .15 D8
**Hill Cotts** CO7 . . . . . . . . . .166 E1
**Hill Cres** CM2 . . . . . . . . . .205 D2
**Hillcrest**
Clacton-on-S CO15. . . . . .189 A6
Kirby-le-S CO13 . . . . . . . .170 D8
**Hill Crest Cotts** CO4 . . . . .83 E6
**Hill Crest Cotts** CO3 . . . . .163 B3
**Hillcrest Rd** CO12 . . . . . . . .91 C3
**Hillcrest Rd** CO10. . . . . . . .15 D8
**Hill Farm La** IP9 . . . . . . . .63 F7
**Hillfield** CO5 . . . . . . . . . . .158 D4
**HILL GREEN** . . . . . . . . . . . .65 E6
**Hill House** CO7 . . . . . . . . .186 A7
**Hillhouse La** CO16 . . . . . .141 B3
**Hill House Rd** IP3 . . . . . . .17 E5
**Hilliards Rd** CO7 . . . . . . . .113 C2
**Hillie Bunnies** CO6. . . . . .105 B7
**Hill La** CB9 . . . . . . . . . . . . . .9 F4
**Hillman Ave** CO15 . . . . . .203 E6
**Hillmead Prim Sch**
CM23 . . . . . . . . . . . . . . . . .145 C7
**Hill Rd**
Chelmsford CM2 . . . . . . . .205 D2
Clacton-on-S CO15. . . . . .188 E6
Coggeshall CO6 . . . . . . . .131 B2
Harwich CO12 . . . . . . . . . . .91 C4
Hempstead CB10. . . . . . . .46 D8
Ramsey CO12 . . . . . . . . . .116 E8
**Hill Rd S** CM2 . . . . . . . . . .205 D2
**Hillridge** CO4. . . . . . . . . . .110 B3
**Hills Cl** CM7 . . . . . . . . . . . .127 F4
**Hills Cres** CO3 . . . . . . . . . .135 A5
**Hillside Ave** CM3 . . . . . . .146 A7
**Hillside Com Prim Sch**
IP2. . . . . . . . . . . . . . . . . . . . .17 C3
**Hillside Cotts**
Birchanger CM23. . . . . . . .119 C3
Ipswich IP9 . . . . . . . . . . . . .37 E4
Sudbury CO10 . . . . . . . . . . .34 A7
**Hillside Cres**
Holland-on-S CO15 . . . . .189 C5
Ipswich IP3 . . . . . . . . . . . . .18 C3
**Hillside End** CM23 . . . . . .119 C3
**Hillside Gdns** CM7. . . . . . .127 E4
**Hillside Gr** CM2. . . . . . . . .216 A7
**Hillside Ho** ☑ CM7 . . . . . .127 F1
**Hillside Mews** CM4 . . . . . .216 A7
**Hillside Rd** CO10. . . . . . . . .34 A7
**Hillside Specl Sch**
CO10 . . . . . . . . . . . . . . . . . . .15 F1
**Hillside Terr** ☑ CM7 . . . . .127 F1
**Hillsleigh Mews** CO1. . . . .136 A7
**Hills Rd** CO9. . . . . . . . . . . . .75 D8
**Hill St** CB10 . . . . . . . . . . . . .22 D1
**Hillston Cl** CO12 . . . . . . . .136 B2
**Hill Terr** CO10 . . . . . . . . . . .12 C8
**Hilltop** CO2 . . . . . . . . . . . . .136 D4
**Hilltop Cres** CO16. . . . . . .140 F1
**Hill Top La** CB11 . . . . . . . . .43 E7
**Hilltop Rise** CO16. . . . . . .140 E1
**Hill View** CM3 . . . . . . . . . . .18 B3
**HillView Cl** CO15 . . . . . . . .163 F8
**Hill View Rd** CM1 . . . . . . .205 C4
**Hillybroom Gdns** CO5. . . .201 D6
**Hilton Cl** CO11. . . . . . . . . . .86 D4
**Hilton Rd** IP3 . . . . . . . . . . . .18 C1
**Hilton Way** CO9. . . . . . . . . .75 E8
**Hilton Wlk** CO9. . . . . . . . . .75 E8
**Hines Cl** CO6 . . . . . . . . . . .133 B8
**Hines Rd** IP3 . . . . . . . . . . . .18 A4
**Hintlesham Cl** IP4. . . . . . . .18 F5
**Hintlesham Dr** IP11. . . . . .221 B5
**HINXTON** . . . . . . . . . . . . . . . .3 B7
Hinxton Mill★ CB10. . . . . . .3 A7
**Hinxton Rd** CB10 . . . . . . . . .3 A7
**Hipkins** CM23. . . . . . . . . . .145 E4
**Histon Cl** IP5. . . . . . . . . . . .18 F7
**Hitcham Rd** CO6. . . . . . . .130 F3
**Hitchcock Pl** CO10. . . . . . . .15 F1

**Hitch Common Rd**
CB11 . . . . . . . . . . . . . . . . . . .66 F8
**Hitchin Mews** CM7 . . . . . .155 B8
**HMS Ganges Assoc Mus★**
CO12. . . . . . . . . . . . . . . . . . .91 C8
**Hobart Cl** CM1. . . . . . . . . .204 E5
**Hobbs Dr** CO4. . . . . . . . . . .83 A5
**Hobbs La** CO10 . . . . . . . . . . .2 D2
**Hoblongs Ind Est**
CM6. . . . . . . . . . . . . . . . . . .150 E6
**HOCKERILL** . . . . . . . . . . . .146 A6
**Hockerill Anglo-European**
Coll CM23. . . . . . . . . . . . .146 B7
**Hockerill Cl** ☑ CM23. . . . .146 A7
**Hockerill St** CM23. . . . . . .146 A7
**Hockley Cl** CB21. . . . . . . . . .7 B5
**Hockney Gdns** IP3. . . . . . . .38 A8
**Hodge Cl** ☑ CM1. . . . . . . .205 A3
**Hodges Holt** CM5 . . . . . . .195 A7
**Hodgkinson Rd** IP11. . . . .221 A3
**Hoe Dr** CO3 . . . . . . . . . . . .135 A5
**Hoe La**
Great Waltham CM3. . . . . .190 E6
Pentlow CO10 . . . . . . . . . . .13 F8
**Hoe Mill Rd** CM9 . . . . . . . .208 E4
**Hoffmanns Way** CM1. . . . .205 B4
**Hogarth Cl** CO5. . . . . . . . .201 D6
**Hogarth Cl** CM4. . . . . . . . .205 E6
**Hogarth End** CO13. . . . . . .170 E7
**Hogarth Rd** IP3. . . . . . . . . .18 A1
**Hogarth Sq** IP3. . . . . . . . . .18 A1
**Hog's La** SG8. . . . . . . . . . . .19 D3
**Holborough Cl** CO4 . . . . . .136 F7
**HOLBROOK**. . . . . . . . . . . . .62 D5
**Holbrook Cl** CO6. . . . . . . . .86 A5
**Holbrook Cres** IP11. . . . . .221 B4
**Holbrook Wlk** CO5. . . . . . .179 E5
**Holbrook High Sch**
IP9. . . . . . . . . . . . . . . . . . . . .62 D6
**Holbrook Prim Sch**
IP9. . . . . . . . . . . . . . . . . . . . .62 D6
**Holbrook Rd**
Harkstead IP9 . . . . . . . . . . .63 A2
Haverhill CB9. . . . . . . . . . . . .8 E6
Ipswich IP3 . . . . . . . . . . . . .17 F1
Stutton IP9 . . . . . . . . . . . . .62 A2
**Holcombe Cres** IP2. . . . . . .16 D2
**Holden Cl**
Braintree CM7 . . . . . . . . . .128 A2
Ipswich IP2. . . . . . . . . . . . . .17 D3
**HOLDEN END** . . . . . . . . . . . .6 B2
**Holden Rd** CO4 . . . . . . . . .109 F2
**HOLDER'S GREEN** . . . . . . .97 E6
**Holdsworth Cl** CO10 . . . . . .2 B3
**Holkham Cl** IP4 . . . . . . . . . .18 F3
**Holland Haven Ctry Pk★**
CO15. . . . . . . . . . . . . . . . . .189 I8
**Holland Haven Prim Sch**
CO15 . . . . . . . . . . . . . . . . . .189 E6
**Holland Ho** CO15. . . . . . . .189 A3
**Holland Lo** CO15. . . . . . . . .188 F3
**HOLLAND-ON-SAND**
. . . . . . . . . . . . . . . . . . . . . . .189 F5
**Holland Park Prim Sch**
CO15 . . . . . . . . . . . . . . . . . .189 B5
**Holland Pk** CO15 . . . . . . . .189 B5
**Holland Pl** CO13 . . . . . . . .170 E3
**Holland Rd**
Clacton-on-S, Rush Green
CO15. . . . . . . . . . . . . . . . .188 F2
Felixstowe IP11. . . . . . . . .221 D3
Frinton-on-S CO13. . . . . .170 E3
Ipswich IP4. . . . . . . . . . . . . .17 F6
Kirby Cross CO13 . . . . . . .170 B6
Little Clacton CO16 . . . . .168 E2
**Hollands Rd** CB9 . . . . . . . . .9 A6
**Holland Villas** CO15 . . . . .170 A3
**Holledge Cres** CO13 . . . . .170 E6
**Hollesley Ave** CB9 . . . . . . . .8 E8
**Hollies Rd** CM77. . . . . . . . .129 C3
**Holland Croft** CO6. . . . . . .132 C8
**Hollington Gr** CO2 . . . . . .161 A3
**Hollis Lock** CM2 . . . . . . . .206 A3
**Holliwell Cl** CO3 . . . . . . . .134 D6
**Holloway Rd** CM9. . . . . . . .210 A5
**Hollow La**
Broomfield CM1. . . . . . . . .204 E8
Bures CO8 . . . . . . . . . . . . . .55 F3
Chelmondiston IP9 . . . . . . .63 F7
**Hollow Rd**
Ashen CO10. . . . . . . . . . . . .11 E3
Braintree CM6 . . . . . . . . . .153 E4
Chrishall SG8 . . . . . . . . . . .19 D2
Elmdon CB11 . . . . . . . . . . .20 C4
Kelvedon CO5 . . . . . . . . . .157 E8
Washbrook IP8 . . . . . . . . . .35 D8
Widdington CB11. . . . . . . .67 C3
**Hollybank** CM6. . . . . . . . . .176 F1
**Holly Blue Cl** IP8. . . . . . . . .36 E8
**Holly Brook** CM7 . . . . . . . .128 A4
**Holly Bush Cnr** CO7. . . . . . .58 C5
**HOLLYBUSH HILL** . . . . . . .166 F1
**Hollybush Hill** CO7 . . . . . .166 F1
**Holly Cl**
Colchester CO2 . . . . . . . . .135 C2
Great Dunmow CM6 . . . . .123 C1
Ipswich IP3. . . . . . . . . . . . . .18 F1
**Holly Cotts** CO2 . . . . . . . . . .60 C2
**Hollycroft** CM7 . . . . . . . . .217 B6
**Holly Ct** CO15. . . . . . . . . . .188 E4
**Hollyhock Rd** CB10 . . . . . . .22 E2
**Holly La**
Belstead IP8 . . . . . . . . . . . .36 C7
Great Horkesley CO6. . . . . .82 C4
**Hollymead Cl** CO4 . . . . . . .109 F3
**Holly Oaks** CO6. . . . . . . . . .80 E4

**Holly Rd**
Colchester CO3 . . . . . . . . .134 C4
Ipswich IP1 . . . . . . . . . . . . . .17 B7
Rushmere St A IP5 . . . . . . .18 F7
**Hollytree Cl** CO2 . . . . . . . .135 C3
**Hollytrees Mus★** CO1 . . . .135 F7
**Hollyview Cl** CO16 . . . . . . .140 F5
**Holly Way**
Chelmsford CM2 . . . . . . . .216 D1
Elmstead Market CO7 . . . .138 A6
Tiptree CO5 . . . . . . . . . . . .179 C5
**Holly Wlk** CM3 . . . . . . . . . .177 B5
**Hollywood Cl** CM2 . . . . . .216 E6
**Holman Cres** CO3 . . . . . . .135 A4
**Holman Rd** CO9 . . . . . . . . .103 E8
**Holmans** CM3 . . . . . . . . . .206 E8
**Holmbrook Way** CO13. . . .170 E5
**Holm Dr** CM6. . . . . . . . . . .123 B1
**Holme Oaks Ct** IP3 . . . . . . .17 F3
**Holmes Rd** CO9 . . . . . . . . .103 E8
**Holmook** IP9 . . . . . . . . . . . .62 D6
**Holm Oak** CO2. . . . . . . . . .136 A3
**Holmwood Cl** CO16. . . . . .188 B6
**Holmwood Ho** IP4 . . . . . . .17 F6
**Holmwood House Prep**
Sch CO3 . . . . . . . . . . . . . . .134 D8
**Holst Ave** CM8. . . . . . . . . .194 F7
**Holt Dr**
Blackheath CO2 . . . . . . . . .163 A7
Wickham Bishops CM8 . . .195 E5
**HOLTON ST MARY** . . . . . . .58 F6
**Holt's Rd** CO6 . . . . . . . . . . .81 B3
**Holybread La** CM3 . . . . . . .207 C4
**Holy Family RC Prim Sch**
CM8 . . . . . . . . . . . . . . . . . . .194 F7
**Holyrood** CO12 . . . . . . . . . .90 F2
**Holyrood** CO10 . . . . . . . . . .33 E5
**Holy Trinity CE Prim Sch**
CO9 . . . . . . . . . . . . . . . . . . . .76 D2
**Holy Trinity & St Nicholas**
CE Prim Sch SG8. . . . . . . .19 C3
**Holywells Cl** IP3. . . . . . . . . .17 E4
**Holywells Cl** IP3 . . . . . . . . .18 B1
**Holywells High Sch**
IP3. . . . . . . . . . . . . . . . . . . . .18 C1
**Holywells Rd** IP3 . . . . . . . . .17 E3
**Homebridge** CB10 . . . . . . .47 A3
**Home Cl** CB9 . . . . . . . . . . . .27 C7
**Homedale Cotts** CO4. . . . . .83 B6
**Home Farm La**
Ardleigh CO7 . . . . . . . . . . .112 A8
Dedham CO7 . . . . . . . . . . . .85 A1
**Home Farm Prim Sch**
CO3 . . . . . . . . . . . . . . . . . . .134 F6
**Homefield** IP9. . . . . . . . . . . .35 B1
**Homefield Cl** CM1 . . . . . . .204 D5
**Homefield Rd**
Colchester CO2 . . . . . . . . .135 C1
Haverhill CB9 . . . . . . . . . . . .8 F5
Witham CM8 . . . . . . . . . . .177 A4
**Homefield Road Units**
CB9 . . . . . . . . . . . . . . . . . . . . .9 A4
**Homefield Way**
Cressing CM77 . . . . . . . . .155 D7
Earls Colne CO6. . . . . . . . .105 B7
**Homelands Ct** CO14 . . . . .171 A7
**Homelea** CO14. . . . . . . . . .144 D1
**Homelye Chase** CM6. . . . .124 B1
**Home Mead**
Galleywood CM2 . . . . . . . .216 C2
Writtle CM1. . . . . . . . . . . . .204 A1
**Homeorr Ho** IP11. . . . . . . .221 F4
**Homerton Cl** CO15. . . . . . .188 F8
**Homestead** CM6 . . . . . . . .205 B7
**Homestead Sch** CO4. . . . . .83 E4
**Homeweave Ho** CO6 . . . . . .56 C8
**Homey Bridge Rd** CO6. . . .56 C8
**Homing Rd** CO16 . . . . . . . .168 C4
**Honeybourne** CM23. . . . . .145 E4
**Honey Cl** CM2 . . . . . . . . . .216 D6
**Honeycroft** CO11. . . . . . . . .86 B3
**Honey Hill** CM8 . . . . . . . . .176 D4
**Honeyman Rd** CO9 . . . . . . .76 E4
**Honeywood Rd** CO9. . . . . .76 E4
**Honorius Dr** CO4 . . . . . . . .110 B6
**Honor Link** CM1 . . . . . . . .206 A7
**Honywood Cl** CM3 . . . . . . .132 E3
**Honywood Com Science**
Sch The CO6 . . . . . . . . . .131 A3
**Honywood Rd** CO3 . . . . . .135 D6
**Honywood Way** CO13 . . . .170 F7
**Hood Cl** CM7 . . . . . . . . . . .128 C4
**Hood Rd** IP3. . . . . . . . . . . . .57 B5
**Hope Ct** IP3 . . . . . . . . . . . . .17 E4
**HOPE END GREEN** . . . . . .148 E5
**Hop Fields** CB11. . . . . . . . .43 E8
**Hop Gardens La** CM9 . . . .208 F4
**Hopgrounds The** CM7. . . . .72 D6
**Hopkins Cl**
Chelmsford CM2 . . . . . . . .206 A3
Clacton-on-S CO13 . . . . .170 F6
**Hopkin's La** CO12. . . . . . . . .91 D6
**Hopkins Mead** CM2 . . . . .206 A2

**Hopkirk Cl** CM3. . . . . . . . .218 F8
**Hop Mdw** CO7 . . . . . . . . . . .59 B2
**Hopping Jacks La**
CM3 . . . . . . . . . . . . . . . . . . .218 F7
**Hoppit Mead** CM7. . . . . . .127 F1
**Hopton Rise** CB9 . . . . . . . . .8 B8
**Horace Eves Cl** ☑ CB9. . . . .8 F8
**Hordle Cl** CO12. . . . . . . . . .91 D4
**Hordle Pl** CO12 . . . . . . . . . .91 D4
**Hordle St** CO12. . . . . . . . . .91 D4
**HORKESLEY HEATH** . . . . .109 B7
**Horkesley Hill** CO6. . . . . . .82 A7
**Horkesley Rd**
Great Horkesley CO4 . . . . .109 E8
Nayland CO6. . . . . . . . . . . .56 A1
**Horley** IP2 . . . . . . . . . . . . . . .16 E4
**Horley Cl** CO16 . . . . . . . . . .188 C6
**Hornbeam Cl**
Chelmsford CM2 . . . . . . . .216 A6
Colchester CO2 . . . . . . . . .135 D2
**Hornbeam Dr** CM6 . . . . . . .117 B7
**Hornbeam Wlk** CM8 . . . . .177 A4
**Horn Book** CO10 . . . . . . . . .22 F1
**HORNELLS CORNER** . . . . .153 E2
**HORNE ROW** . . . . . . . . . . .218 D5
**Horne Row** CM3 . . . . . . . . .218 D5
**Horner Pl** ☑ CM8. . . . . . . .177 A2
**HORNESTREET** . . . . . . . . . .83 D5
**Horn Hill** CO9 . . . . . . . . . . .75 C5
**Hornsea Villas** CM6 . . . . . .124 D7
**Horrocks Cl** CO2. . . . . . . . .136 A4
**Horse & Groom La**
CM2 . . . . . . . . . . . . . . . . . . .216 A3
**Horse Pond Cl** CO10 . . . . . .34 C4
**Horseshoe Cl** CB11 . . . . . . .20 B4
**Horseshoe La** CB9 . . . . . . . .8 E7
**Horsey Rd** CO13 . . . . . . . .170 C8
**Horsham Ave** IP3 . . . . . . . .18 D3
**Horsley Cross** CO11 . . . . .114 A3
**HORSLEYCROSS STREET**
. . . . . . . . . . . . . . . . . . . . . . .114 A6
**Horsley Ho** IP11. . . . . . . . .221 F4
**Horton Cl** CM9 . . . . . . . . . .210 A1
**Hospital App** CM1 . . . . . . .191 B3
**Hospital Field** CM77 . . . . .155 B5
**Hospital La** CO3 . . . . . . . . .135 D6
**Hospital La** CO4 . . . . . . . . .136 C8
**Hossack Rd** IP3 . . . . . . . . . .38 A8
**Houblon Dr** CM2. . . . . . . . .216 C2
**Houchin's La** CO6 . . . . . . . .131 E3
**Houghton Pl** IP4 . . . . . . . . .18 F5
**Houldings Garage**
CM9. . . . . . . . . . . . . . . . . . .210 B5
**House Martins The**
IP11. . . . . . . . . . . . . . . . . . .221 D6
**House on the Hill Toy Mus**
The★ CM24 . . . . . . . . . . .119 F7
**Hove Cl** CO15 . . . . . . . . . . .189 F6
**Howard Ave** CO12. . . . . . . .90 F2
**Howard Cl**
Braintree CM7 . . . . . . . . . .128 C3
Haverhill CB9 . . . . . . . . . . . .8 D7
**Howard Dr** CM2 . . . . . . . . .206 A2
**Howard Ho** IP2 . . . . . . . . . .17 A4
**Howard Rd**
Holland-on-S CO15 . . . . .189 C4
Saffron Walden CB10. . . . .22 E2
**Howards Cl** CM3 . . . . . . . .206 E8
**Howards Croft** CO4 . . . . . .109 D5
**Howard Vyse Ct** CO15. . . .188 E5
**Howbridge CE Jun Sch**
CM8 . . . . . . . . . . . . . . . . . . .194 F8
**Howbridge Hall Rd**
Witham CM8 . . . . . . . . . . .194 F6
Witham CM8 . . . . . . . . . . .194 F7
**Howbridge Inf Sch The**
CM8 . . . . . . . . . . . . . . . . . . .194 F8
**Howbridge Rd** CM8 . . . . . .194 F8
**Howe Ave** IP3 . . . . . . . . . . .18 C3
**Howe Chase** CO9 . . . . . . . .76 E4
**Howe Cl** CO4 . . . . . . . . . . .136 D7
**HOWE GREEN**
Bishop's Stortford . . . . . .146 D2
Chelmsford . . . . . . . . . . . .217 D3
**Howe Green House Sch**
CM22 . . . . . . . . . . . . . . . . .146 D2
**Howe La** CB10. . . . . . . . . . .47 A5
**HOWE STREET**
Finchingfield . . . . . . . . . . . .48 F1
Great Waltham . . . . . . . . .172 F2
**Howlett Terr** IP9 . . . . . . . . .63 E2
**HOWLETT END** . . . . . . . . . .45 B2
**Hoxter Way** CO10 . . . . . . . .15 E2
**Hoxton Cl** CO16 . . . . . . . . .188 D5
**Hoynors** CM3 . . . . . . . . . . .219 A7
**Hubbards Chase**
CO14 . . . . . . . . . . . . . . . . . .171 B8
**Hubert Rd** CO3 . . . . . . . . . .135 B8
**Hub The** CM7 . . . . . . . . . . .154 A8
**Huckleberry Cres** CO4 . . . .38 C7
**Hucklesbury Ave**
CO15. . . . . . . . . . . . . . . . . .189 E7
**Hudson Cl**
Clacton-on-S CO16. . . . . .188 C5
Harwich CO12 . . . . . . . . . . .91 A1
Haverhill CB9. . . . . . . . . . . . .8 D7
**Hudson's Hill** CM7 . . . . . . .73 D4
**Hudson Way** CO16 . . . . . . .188 B6
**Hugh Dickson Rd** CM8 . . .109 E2
**Hughes Cnr** CO7. . . . . . . . . .59 A4
**Hughes Rd** CO7. . . . . . . . . . .59 A4
**Hughes Stanton Way**
CO11. . . . . . . . . . . . . . . . . . . .86 B4
**Hugh Villas** CM23 . . . . . . .145 F6
**Hull La** CM3. . . . . . . . . . . . .175 A2
**Hull's La** CM3 . . . . . . . . . . .217 E7
**Hulton Cl** CM3 . . . . . . . . . .206 E8
**Hulver Ct** IP3 . . . . . . . . . . . .38 B2

**Humber Ave** CO15 . . . . . . .203 E6
**Humber Doucy La** IP4 . . . .18 D8
**Humber Rd**
Chelmsford CM1 . . . . . . . .205 C5
Witham CM8 . . . . . . . . . . .176 D2
**Humphrey's Farm La**
CM3 . . . . . . . . . . . . . . . . . . .190 C7
**Humphry Rd** CO10 . . . . . . .33 E8
**Hundon Pl** ☑ CB9. . . . . . . .9 B8
**Hundred La** CO4 . . . . . . . . .83 C4
**Hungerdown La** CO11. . . . .85 E1
**Hunnable Ind Est** CO9 . . . .50 F8
**Hunnable Rd** CM7 . . . . . . .127 C2
**Hunt Ave** CM9 . . . . . . . . . . .210 B5
**Hunt Cl** CO5. . . . . . . . . . . . .158 D4
**Hunt Dr** CO16 . . . . . . . . . . .188 D6
**Hunter Dr**
Braintree CM7 . . . . . . . . . .128 C2
Lawford CO11. . . . . . . . . . .86 A3
**Hunter Rd** IP3. . . . . . . . . . . .38 C8
**Hunters Chase** CO13. . . . .170 E4
**Hunters Ridge** CO4. . . . . . .110 B4
**Hunters Way**
Chelmsford CM5 . . . . . . . .205 F7
Saffron Walden CB11. . . . .43 D7
**Huntingdon Way**
CO15. . . . . . . . . . . . . . . . . .188 E6
**Hunting Gate** CO1 . . . . . . .136 A8
**Huntley's Cvn Pk (E)**
CO16 . . . . . . . . . . . . . . . . . .203 C6
**Huntley's Cvn Pk (W)**
CO16. . . . . . . . . . . . . . . . . .203 B6
**Hunt Rd** CO6 . . . . . . . . . . .105 A6
**Hunt's Cl** CM1. . . . . . . . . . .215 B8
**Hunt's Dr** CM1. . . . . . . . . . .215 B8
**Hunts Farm Cl** CM9 . . . . . .199 D2
**Hunts Hill** CO10 . . . . . . . . . .3 B7
**Hunts La** CB10. . . . . . . . . . . .3 B7
**Hunts Yd** CO6 . . . . . . . . . . .105 B6
**Hunt Way** CO13 . . . . . . . . .170 E6
**Hunwicke Rd** CO4 . . . . . . .136 E7
**Hurnard Dr** CO3 . . . . . . . . .135 A7
**Hurn Gr** CM23. . . . . . . . . . .119 C1
**Hurrell Down**
Boreham CM3 . . . . . . . . . .192 F1
Colchester CO4 . . . . . . . . .110 A4
**Hurrells La** CM3 . . . . . . . . .206 F3
**Hurricane Pl** IP3 . . . . . . . . .18 C1
**Hurst Cl**
Bishop's Stortford
CM23 . . . . . . . . . . . . . . . . .145 E2
Brightlingsea CO7 . . . . . . .186 A6
**HURST GREEN** . . . . . . . . . .186 A6
**Hurst Way** CM22 . . . . . . . .205 E4
**Hutchinson Cl** CO5 . . . . . .179 D4
**Hutley Dr** IP4 . . . . . . . . . . . .17 F7
**Hutley Br** ☑ CO4 . . . . . . . .109 E2
**Huxtables La** CO3. . . . . . . .108 A1
**Hyacinth Cl**
Clacton-on-S CO15 . . . . .188 C4
Tollesbury CM9 . . . . . . . . .199 E1
**Hyacinth Ct** ☑ CM1. . . . . .205 E7
**Hyams La** IP9 . . . . . . . . . . . .62 D5
**Hyam's La** IP9. . . . . . . . . . . .61 F1
**HYDE CHASE** . . . . . . . . . . .219 D4
**Hyde Chase**
Danbury CM3. . . . . . . . . . .219 B4
Woodham Mortimer
CM9 . . . . . . . . . . . . . . . . . .219 D4
**Hyde Gn** CM3 . . . . . . . . . . .219 B4
**Hyde La**
Blackmore End CM7 . . . . . .74 B2
Danbury CM3. . . . . . . . . . .219 B6
**Hyde Park Cnr** CO10 . . . . . .1 D2
**Hyde Rd** CO10 . . . . . . . . . . .33 E7
**Hyde The** CB11 . . . . . . . . . .65 C4
**Hyde Sta** CO4 . . . . . . . . . . .136 D6
**Hyde Station Rd**
CO2 . . . . . . . . . . . . . . . . . . .136 D6
**HYTHE THE**
Colchester . . . . . . . . . . . . .136 C4
Maldon. . . . . . . . . . . . . . . .210 B2
**Hythe The** CM9 . . . . . . . . .210 B2

# I

**Iceni Way** CO2. . . . . . . . . .135 B3
**ICKLETON** . . . . . . . . . . . . . . . .3 A4
**Ickleton Pl** ☑ CB9 . . . . . . . .9 B8
**Ickleton Rd**
Elmdon CB11 . . . . . . . . . . .20 A4
Great Chesterford CB10 . . .3 C2
Hinxton CB10. . . . . . . . . . . .3 B6
**Icknield Cl** CB10. . . . . . . . . .3 A3
**Icknield Way** CB10 . . . . . . . .3 A3
**Ickworth Cl** CM77. . . . . . . .154 C7

**James St** *continued*
Colchester CO1 . . . . . . . . . 136 A6
James Wicks Ct CO3 . . . . . 135 E7
Jamebrook Rd IP2 . . . . . . . . .16 A1
JANKE'S GREEN . . . . . . . . . 106 E8
Janmead CM8 . . . . . . . . . . . 177 A3
Janus CI CB9 . . . . . . . . . . . . . .9 C6
Japonica CI CO15 . . . . . . . . 189 C4
Jaques CI CO10 . . . . . . . . . . . .2 C5
Jarmin Rd CO1 . . . . . . . . . . 135 F8
Jarndyce CM1 . . . . . . . . . . . 204 F6
Jarvis Field CM3 . . . . . . . . . 207 D5
Jasmin CI CM23 . . . . . . . . . 145 C6
Jasmine CI
  ☑ Chelmsford CM1 . . . . . 205 E7
  Colchester CO4 . . . . . . . . 136 E8
  Ipswich IP2 . . . . . . . . . . . .16 F3
Jasmine Way CO15 . . . . . . . 203 G7
JASPER'S GREEN . . . . . . . . 100 E2
Jay CI
  Great Notley CM77 . . . . . 154 D8
  Haverhill CB9 . . . . . . . . . . .9 C7
Jaymar Ct ☑ CM7 . . . . . . . 127 F2
Jayrest Cnr CO3 . . . . . . . . . 134 E4
Jays La CO6 . . . . . . . . . . . . 132 F3
Jays The CO4 . . . . . . . . . . . 110 C3
JAYWICK . . . . . . . . . . . . . . 203 F7
Jaywick La CO15,
  CO16 . . . . . . . . . . . . . . . 188 A3
Jaywick Rd CB9 . . . . . . . . . . .9 A8
Jeans La CM23 . . . . . . . . . . 145 E7
Jeffcut Rd CM2 . . . . . . . . . . 205 E2
Jefferies Rd IP4 . . . . . . . . . . .17 E6
Jefferson CI CO3 . . . . . . . . 134 E5
Jeffery Rd CM2 . . . . . . . . . 217 A7
Jeffrey CI CO3 . . . . . . . . . . 134 F5
Jeffreys Ct CM7 . . . . . . . . . 155 E6
Jeffrey's Rd CM77 . . . . . . . 155 E6
Jekylls La CM7 . . . . . . . . . . .48 D4
Jellicoe Way CM7 . . . . . . . . 128 C4
Jenkins Dr CM22 . . . . . . . . .94 C3
Jenkins Hill CO11 . . . . . . . . .87 C3
Jenkins La CM22 . . . . . . . . 146 C5
Jenner CI CM7 . . . . . . . . . . 127 F1
Jenner Mead CM7 . . . . . . . 206 A3
Jennings CI ☑ CO1 . . . . . . 136 C6
Jermyns CI IP9 . . . . . . . . . . .35 B2
Jersey Rd CM9 . . . . . . . . . . 210 B1
Jersey Way CM7 . . . . . . . . . 127 D2
Jervis CI IP9 . . . . . . . . . . . . .62 D5
Jervis Rd CM23 . . . . . . . . . 145 F6
Jessica CI CM7 . . . . . . . . . . 136 F7
Jessop CI CO15 . . . . . . . . . 189 A8
Jimmy's La CO14 . . . . . . . . 171 A6
Joes Rd CO10 . . . . . . . . . . . .34 F6
John Ball Wlk ☑ CO1 . . . . 135 F7
John Barr Ho CM7 . . . . . . . 127 B7
John Bird Ct CO1 . . . . . . . . 109 F1
John Bramston Sch The
  CM8 . . . . . . . . . . . . . . . . 176 F1
John Bunyan Inf Sch
  CM7 . . . . . . . . . . . . . . . . 127 E4
John Bunyan Jun Sch
  CM7 . . . . . . . . . . . . . . . . 127 E4
John Crouch Ct CO12 . . . . . .91 C3
John Dane Player Ct ☑
  CB10 . . . . . . . . . . . . . . . . .22 E1
John Dyde CI CM23 . . . . . . 146 A6
John English Ave
  CM7 . . . . . . . . . . . . . . . . 127 E4
John Hammond CI
  CM7 . . . . . . . . . . . . . . . . 127 E4
John Harper St ☑
  CO1 . . . . . . . . . . . . . . . . 135 E8
John Henry Keene Meml
  Homes CM7 . . . . . . . . . . 205 A4
John Kavanagh Ct ☑
  CO1 . . . . . . . . . . . . . . . . 136 A6
John Kent Ave CM23 . . . . . 135 B2
John King Ct CO7 . . . . . . . . 185 F6
John Lawrence Wlk
  CO2 . . . . . . . . . . . . . . . . 135 F1
John Raven Ct CO5 . . . . . . 158 D3
John Ray Gdns CM77 . . . . . 155 B5
John Ray Inf Sch
  CM7 . . . . . . . . . . . . . . . . 154 F8
John Ray Jun Sch
  CM7 . . . . . . . . . . . . . . . . 154 F8
John Ray St CM7 . . . . . . . . 128 A3
Johnson CI
  Braintree CM7 . . . . . . . . 155 A4
  Ipswich IP2 . . . . . . . . . . . .17 C3
Johnson Rd
  Great Baddow CM2 . . . . . 217 A5
  St Osyth CO16 . . . . . . . . 187 B4
Johnson's Dr CO7 . . . . . . . 138 A6
Johnsons Yd CB11 . . . . . . . .22 D2
Kelvin Ct CO13 . . . . . . . . . 170 F3
Kemball St IP4 . . . . . . . . . . .18 A5
Kempe Rd CM7 . . . . . . . . . .72 D6
Kempson Dr CO10 . . . . . . . .34 C5
Kempsters The IP11 . . . . . . 221 B7
Kempton Pk CO16 . . . . . . . 168 B5
Kemsley Rd
  Earls Colne CO6 . . . . . . . 105 A6
  Felixstowe IP11 . . . . . . . 221 D5
Ken Cooke Ct CO1 . . . . . . . 135 F7
Kendall CE Prim Sch
  CO1 . . . . . . . . . . . . . . . . 136 C4
Kendall Rd CO1 . . . . . . . . . 136 A6
Kendall Terr CO1 . . . . . . . . 136 A6
Kenilworth Gr CO15 . . . . . 142 A2
Kenilworth Rd CO15 . . . . . 189 E6
Kennedy CI IP4 . . . . . . . . . . .18 A6
Kennedy Way CO15 . . . . . . 189 A5
Kennels The CO6 . . . . . . . . 104 F6
John Weston Nature
  Reserve* CO14 . . . . . . . . 144 D6
Jollyboys La M CO16 . . . . . 152 C6
Jollyboys La S CM6 . . . . . . 152 C4
Jonathan Feedham Ct
  CO7 . . . . . . . . . . . . . . . . 137 B1
Jonquil Way CO4 . . . . . . . . 109 C2
Jordan CI CB11 . . . . . . . . . .43 E8
Joscelyn's Yd ☑
  CM23 . . . . . . . . . . . . . . . 146 A7
Joseph Gdns CM8 . . . . . . . 156 E4
Josselin CI CO9 . . . . . . . . . 105 B7
Josselyns The IP11 . . . . . . . 221 A8

**Jovian Way**
Colchester CO4 . . . . . . . . . 110 B6
Ipswich IP1 . . . . . . . . . . . . .16 D7
Joyce Brooks Ho
  CO3 . . . . . . . . . . . . . . . . 135 D6
Joyce's Chase CM9 . . . . . . 212 A8
Jubilee Ave
  Broomfield CM1 . . . . . . . 191 B2
  Clacton-on-S CO16 . . . . . 188 E8
Jubilee CI
  Colchester CO3 . . . . . . . . 134 D6
  Harwich CO12 . . . . . . . . . .90 E2
Jubilee Cott ☑ CM23 . . . . 146 A7
Jubilee Ct
  Great Dunmow CM6 . . . . 123 C1
  Sible Hedingham CO9 . . . . .75 E8
  Tiptree CO5 . . . . . . . . . . 179 D4
  Walton-on-t-N CO14 . . . . 171 C7
Jubilee End CO15 . . . . . . . . .86 C5
Jubilee La CO7 . . . . . . . . . 111 C3
Jubilee Rd CM1 . . . . . . . . . .33 F6
Jubilee Rise CM3 . . . . . . . . 219 A6
Jubilee Terr CM1 . . . . . . . . 205 A4
Jubilee Way CO13 . . . . . . . 170 F6
Jubilee Wks CB11 . . . . . . . . .65 E6
Jubilee Wlk ☑ CB9 . . . . . . .9 A7
Judge Rd CM2 . . . . . . . . . . 206 B4
Julian Ave CO4 . . . . . . . . . . 110 A5
Julian CI
  Broomfield CM1 . . . . . . . 191 B1
  Haverhill CB9 . . . . . . . . . . .9 D7
Julien Court Rd CM7 . . . . . 128 A4
Juniper CI CO9 . . . . . . . . . 103 D8
Juniper Cres CM8 . . . . . . . 177 A4
Juniper Ct CM8 . . . . . . . . . 176 E1
Juniper CI CM3 . . . . . . . . . 123 B1
Juniper Dr CM2 . . . . . . . . . 216 B6
Juniper Rd
  Boreham CM3 . . . . . . . . . 206 F8
  Colchester CO3 . . . . . . . . 134 D5
Juniper Way CO4 . . . . . . . . 136 D8
Juno Mews CO2 . . . . . . . . . 135 C1
Jupes Hill CO7 . . . . . . . . . . .85 C4
Jupe's Hill CO6 . . . . . . . . . . .79 D1
Jupiter CI CB9 . . . . . . . . . . . .9 D6
Jupiter Rd IP4 . . . . . . . . . . .18 B7
Justinian CI CB9 . . . . . . . . . .9 D6
Jutland Ct CO10 . . . . . . . . . .33 F7
Juvina CI ☑ CM8 . . . . . . . . 194 F7

**K**

Kale Croft CO3 . . . . . . . . . 134 D5
Kangels The CB11 . . . . . . . . .40 D2
Kate Daniels Ho CO16 . . . . 140 F1
Kate's La CB10 . . . . . . . . . . .24 C8
Katherine Semar Inf Sch
  CB11 . . . . . . . . . . . . . . . . .43 E6
Katherine Semar Jun Sch
  CB11 . . . . . . . . . . . . . . . . .43 E6
Kay CI CM3 . . . . . . . . . . . . 174 A7
Kayla Ct ☑ CO3 . . . . . . . . 135 E6
Keable Rd CO4 . . . . . . . . . . 132 E3
Keary Cl CO11 . . . . . . . . . . .86 B4
Keats Ave CM7 . . . . . . . . . 154 F8
Keats Rd CO3 . . . . . . . . . . . 134 F6
Kebbles CO10 . . . . . . . . . . . .2 B6
Keble CI CO3 . . . . . . . . . . . 135 D6
Kedington Hill CO10 . . . . . .34 B2
Keeble CI CO5 . . . . . . . . . . 179 E5
Keeble Ct CO7 . . . . . . . . . . 166 E7
Keeble Way CM7 . . . . . . . . 206 F8
Keeble's Yd ☑ CB9 . . . . . . . .9 A8
Keeble Way CM7 . . . . . . . . 128 A3
Keelars La CO7 . . . . . . . . . 137 E2
Keelers Way CO6 . . . . . . . . 109 B7
Keene CI CO5 . . . . . . . . . . 201 D7
Keene Way CM2 . . . . . . . . 216 B3
Keepers Gn CO4 . . . . . . . . 109 B3
Keep The ☑ CB9 . . . . . . . . .8 E7
Keith CI CO15 . . . . . . . . . . 188 F8
Kelly Rd IP2 . . . . . . . . . . . . .16 E5
Kelso CI CO6 . . . . . . . . . . . 109 C6
KELVEDON . . . . . . . . . . . . 158 C2
Kelvedon CI CM1 . . . . . . . . 205 A6
Kelvedon Dr IP4 . . . . . . . . . .18 F5
Kelvedon Hall La CO5 . . . . 178 E5
Kelvedon Rd
  Coggeshall CO6 . . . . . . . . 158 A8
  Kelvedon CO5 . . . . . . . . . 158 F2
  Messing CO5 . . . . . . . . . . 159 C2
  Tiptree CO5 . . . . . . . . . . 179 B7
  Tolleshunt D'arcy CM9 . . . 198 C6
  Wickham Bishops CM8 . . . 195 F5
Kelvedon St Mary's CE
  Prim Sch CO5 . . . . . . . . . 158 C2
Kelvedon Sta CO5 . . . . . . . 158 C3
Kelvin CI CO13 . . . . . . . . . 170 F3

**Kennet Way** CM1 . . . . . . 204 D5
Kensington Rd IP1 . . . . . . . .17 A8
Kenston Ct CO5 . . . . . . . . . 201 B6
Kent CI CO7 . . . . . . . . . . . . 185 F7
Kent Cres CM23 . . . . . . . . 145 E4
Kentford Rd IP11 . . . . . . . . 221 A4
Kent Gdns CM7 . . . . . . . . . 128 B4
Kent Ho IP11 . . . . . . . . . . . 221 C6
Kentings The CM7 . . . . . . . 127 E2
Kentmere Ct CO4 . . . . . . . . 110 E2
Kent's Ave CO15 . . . . . . . . 189 E6
Kents Grass CM7 . . . . . . . . 199 D2
Kents Yd CB11 . . . . . . . . . . .21 F4
Kentwell CI IP4 . . . . . . . . . .18 F4
Kenwood Ho ☑ CM7 . . . . 216 A8
Kenworthy Rd CM7 . . . . . . 127 F2
Kenyon CI CO17 . . . . . . . . . .58 D1
Kenyon St IP2 . . . . . . . . . . . .17 C4
Kerby Rise CM2 . . . . . . . . . 205 F3
Kerridge's Cut CO11 . . . . . .87 A4
Kerry Ct CO1 . . . . . . . . . . . 136 C7
Kersey Ave CO10 . . . . . . . . .34 B6
Kersey Ct CO2 . . . . . . . . . . 135 C3
Kersey Dr CO16 . . . . . . . . . 188 B5
Kersey Rd IP11 . . . . . . . . . 221 B3
Kessler Ave CM7 . . . . . . . . .73 D7
Kesteven Rd IP2 . . . . . . . . . .17 B4
Kestrel Gdns CM23 . . . . . . 145 C6
Kestrel Rd
  Haverhill CB9 . . . . . . . . . . .9 C7
  Ipswich IP2 . . . . . . . . . . . .16 E1
Kestrel Rise CO9 . . . . . . . . .76 F1
Kestrel Way CO15 . . . . . . . 188 F6
Kestrel Wlk CM7 . . . . . . . . 216 B5
Keswick Ave CO15 . . . . . . . 189 C6
Keswick CI CO13 . . . . . . . . 170 F7
Ketley CI CO5 . . . . . . . . . . 179 E5
Ketleys CM23 . . . . . . . . . . 216 C3
Ketleys View CM7 . . . . . . . 127 A7
Kettlebaston Way IP4 . . . . . .17 D8
Kew La CO10 . . . . . . . . . . . 170 A4
Key Ct CO15 . . . . . . . . . . . 188 E3
Keyes Way CM7 . . . . . . . . . 128 C4
Keymer Way CO3 . . . . . . . . 134 F4
Keynes Way CO12 . . . . . . . .90 F1
Khartoum Rd IP4 . . . . . . . . .17 F7
Khartoum Villas CO7 . . . . . 111 B8
Kidder Rd CM77 . . . . . . . . 126 F1
Kilburn Gdns CO4 . . . . . . . 110 B3
Kildermorie CI CO4 . . . . . . 110 D3
KILLEM'S GREEN . . . . . . . . .40 A4
Kilmaine Rd CO2 . . . . . . . . .90 F2
Kiln Barn Ave CO15 . . . . . . 188 F7
Kiln Cotts
  Danbury CM3 . . . . . . . . . 218 D6
  Dedham CO7 . . . . . . . . . . .84 F5
Kiln Dr CO10 . . . . . . . . . . . .34 B6
Kiln Field IP11 . . . . . . . . . . 221 B5
Kiln La CO11 . . . . . . . . . . . .86 D4
Kilns Hill CO6 . . . . . . . . . . 130 F5
Kiltie Rd CO5 . . . . . . . . . . 179 E5
Kimberley CI CM23 . . . . . . 146 A5
Kimberley Rd CO1 . . . . . . . 136 B5
Kincaid Rd CO16 . . . . . . . . 187 A4
King Charles Ct ☑
  CM2 . . . . . . . . . . . . . . . . 205 B1
King Charles Rd CO5 . . . . . 201 D6
King Coel Rd CO3 . . . . . . . 134 D7
King Edward Ct CM1 . . . . . 205 A3
King Edward Ind Pk
  CO2 . . . . . . . . . . . . . . . . 135 D5
King Edward Quay
  CO2 . . . . . . . . . . . . . . . . 136 D5
King Edward Rd IP3 . . . . . . .18 B3
King Edward VI Gram Sch
  CM1 . . . . . . . . . . . . . . . . 205 A3
King Edward VII Dr
  IP9 . . . . . . . . . . . . . . . . . .35 B2
King Edward VI's
  Almshouses CB11 . . . . . . .22 D1
King Edward Way
  CM8 . . . . . . . . . . . . . . . . 194 E8
Kingfisher Ave IP2 . . . . . . . .16 E3
Kingfisher CI
  Colchester CO4 . . . . . . . . 136 F8
  Haverhill CB9 . . . . . . . . . . .9 C8
  Heybridge CM9 . . . . . . . . 210 C5
Kingfisher Dr CO12 . . . . . . .90 E1
Kingfisher Gate CM7 . . . . . 128 A5
Kingfisher Lo CM2 . . . . . . . 216 F7
Kingfisher Mdws CO9 . . . . .76 F1
Kingfishers CO15 . . . . . . . . 188 F6
Kingfisher Way
  Bishop's Stortford
  CM23 . . . . . . . . . . . . . . . 146 A2
  Kelvedon CO5 . . . . . . . . . 158 C2
King George Ct ☑
  CM2 . . . . . . . . . . . . . . . . 205 B1
King George Rd CO2 . . . . . 135 F4
King George's Ave
  CO12 . . . . . . . . . . . . . . . . .91 B4
King George's PI
  CM9 . . . . . . . . . . . . . . . . 210 A2
King Georges View
  CM7 . . . . . . . . . . . . . . . . 128 D2
King George V Meml
  Homes IP3 . . . . . . . . . . . . .17 F3
Kings Acre CO6 . . . . . . . . . 130 F2
Kings Ave
  Clacton-on-S CO15 . . . . . 189 D5
  Ipswich IP1 . . . . . . . . . . . .17 B1
Kingsbridge CI CM7 . . . . . . 127 F8
Kingsbridge Rd CO4 . . . . . 110 A2
Kingsbury CI CO6 . . . . . . . 132 F3
Kingsbury Rd IP11 . . . . . . . 221 A7

**Kingsbury Wlk** CO10 . . . . .34 C5
Kings Chase CM8 . . . . . . . . 177 A1
Kings CI CO11 . . . . . . . . . . .86 C4
King's CI CO16 . . . . . . . . . 187 A3
King's Cotts CM23 . . . . . . . 146 A6
Kings Ct CM23 . . . . . . . . . 146 A8
Kings Ct CO4 . . . . . . . . . . . 110 B6
Kings Ct
  Harwich CO12 . . . . . . . . . .91 B3
  Holland-on-S CO15 . . . . . 189 E5
King's Ct CM6 . . . . . . . . . . 123 D1
Kingsdale Ind Est The
  CM1 . . . . . . . . . . . . . . . . 205 C3
Kingsfield Ave IP1 . . . . . . . .17 D8
Kings Fleet Rd IP11 . . . . . . 221 C3
Kingsford Ct CO2 . . . . . . . . 135 B3
Kingsford Dr CM2 . . . . . . . 206 B4
Kings Gdns CO2 . . . . . . . . . 135 C3
Kingsgate Dr IP4 . . . . . . . . .17 E8
Kings Gdns CO5 . . . . . . . . . 158 E4
Kings Head Ct ☑ . . . . . . . 135 E8
Kings Head Ctr The
  CM9 . . . . . . . . . . . . . . . . 209 F3
King's Head St ☑ CO12 . . . .91 E6
Kings Head Wlk ☑
  CM2 . . . . . . . . . . . . . . . . 205 C2
Kings Hill CO10 . . . . . . . . . .34 A6
Kings Ho CO13 . . . . . . . . . 171 A4
Kings La CM77 . . . . . . . . . 129 A6
King's
  Elmdon CB11 . . . . . . . . . .20 A3
  Long Melford CO10 . . . . . .15 F7
Kingsland Beach CO5 . . . . . 201 C5
Kingsland CI CO5 . . . . . . . . 201 C5
Kingsland Hts CO5 . . . . . . . 201 C6
Kingsland Rd CO5 . . . . . . . 201 D6
Kingsman Dr CO16 . . . . . . 188 C5
Kings Mdw CO10 . . . . . . . . .34 A6
Kings Mead CO9 . . . . . . . . .78 A7
Kingsmead Hall CO3 . . . . . 134 F5
Kingsmead Rd CO3 . . . . . . 134 F5
Kings Meadow Ct
  CO5 . . . . . . . . . . . . . . . . 158 C3
Kings Meadow Rd
  CO1 . . . . . . . . . . . . . . . . 135 F8
Kingsmead Pk CM7 . . . . . . 128 C4
Kingsmead Rd CM23 . . . . . 146 A8
Kingsmere CI CO5 . . . . . . . 201 D7
Kings Mews CO7 . . . . . . . . 137 C4
Kings Par CO15 . . . . . . . . . 189 E5
Kings Prom CO15 . . . . . . . 203 J8
King's Quay St CO12 . . . . . .91 E6
King's Quay St CO12 . . . . . .91 E6
Kings Rd
  Braintree CM7 . . . . . . . . 127 E6
  Chelmsford CM1 . . . . . . . 204 F4
  Glemsford CO10 . . . . . . . . .2 B5
  Great Totham CM9 . . . . . 196 D7
  Halstead CO9 . . . . . . . . . .76 E1
King's Rd
  Clacton-on-S CO15 . . . . . 188 D1
  Harwich CO12 . . . . . . . . . .91 B3
Kings Reach CO14 . . . . . . . 144 D1
Kings Road Prim Sch
  CM1 . . . . . . . . . . . . . . . . 204 F4
King St
  Bishop's Stortford
  CM23 . . . . . . . . . . . . . . . 145 F7
  Bradfield CO11 . . . . . . . . 114 C8
  Castle Hedingham CO9 . . . .51 F4
  Felixstowe IP11 . . . . . . . 221 C6
  ☑ Ipswich IP1 . . . . . . . . .17 C6
  Maldon CM9 . . . . . . . . . . 210 A1
  Saffron Walden CB10 . . . . .22 D1
  Sudbury CO10 . . . . . . . . . .33 E7
Kings Stephen Rd CO1 . . . . 136 B6
Kingston Ave CM2 . . . . . . . 205 E3
Kingston Chase CM9 . . . . . 209 F5
Kingston Cres CM2 . . . . . . 205 E3
Kingston Mews CO15 . . . . . 188 C3
Kingston Rd IP1 . . . . . . . . . .17 A1
King Street Mews ☑
  CM23 . . . . . . . . . . . . . . . 145 F7
Kingsway
  Harwich CO12 . . . . . . . . . .91 D4
  Tiptree CO5 . . . . . . . . . . 179 C6
King's Way IP3 . . . . . . . . . . .18 C2
King's Way CM9 . . . . . . . . . 199 E1
Kingswode Hoe Sch
  CO3 . . . . . . . . . . . . . . . . 135 C2
Kingswood Rd CO4 . . . . . . 109 F4
Kingwell Ave CO15 . . . . . . 188 E5
Kinlett CI CO4 . . . . . . . . . . 110 B4
Kinloch Chase ☑
  CM8 . . . . . . . . . . . . . . . . 194 F7
Kino Rd CO14 . . . . . . . . . . 171 D8
Kipling CI CM1 . . . . . . . . . 205 A5
Kipling Way CM7 . . . . . . . . 155 A8
Kirby Ct IP4 . . . . . . . . . . . . .17 D7
KIRBY CROSS . . . . . . . . . . 170 B7
Kirby Cross Sta CO13 . . . . . 170 B6
Kirby Hall Rd CO9 . . . . . . . .51 D5
KIRBY-LE-SOKEN . . . . . . . 170 C8
Kirby Rd
  Great Holland CO13 . . . . . 170 B5
  Walton-on-t-N CO14 . . . . 171 B8
Kirby St IP4 . . . . . . . . . . . . .17 B6
Kirkbaye CO13 . . . . . . . . . . 170 E6
Kirkham CI IP2 . . . . . . . . . . .17 A2
Kirkhurst CI CO7 . . . . . . . . 186 A6
Kirklees CM1 . . . . . . . . . . . 204 F4
Kirkley Ct CB9 . . . . . . . . . . . .8 C8
Kirkmans Rd CM2 . . . . . . . 216 D3
Kirk PI CM2 . . . . . . . . . . . . 205 F3
Kirkton CI IP9 . . . . . . . . . . . .91 A8
Kirtling PI ☑ CB9 . . . . . . . . .9 B8

**Ickworth Cres** IP4 . . . . . . .18 F5
Ickworth Ct IP11 . . . . . . . . 221 A3
Iconfield Pk CO12 . . . . . . . .91 A4
Ilex CI CO2 . . . . . . . . . . . . 135 D2
Imogen CI ☑ CO4 . . . . . . . 136 F8
Imperial Ct CO15 . . . . . . . . 188 E1
Imphal CI CO2 . . . . . . . . . . 135 C1
Ingarfield Rd CO15 . . . . . . 189 E6
Ingelow Gdns IP4 . . . . . . . . .18 B6
Ingelrica Ave CM3 . . . . . . . 194 B3
Ingestre St CO12 . . . . . . . . .91 D4
Ingham Rd IP2 . . . . . . . . . . . .9 B8
Inglenook CO15 . . . . . . . . . 189 D7
Ingleside Ct CB10 . . . . . . . . .22 D1
Inglis Rd CO3 . . . . . . . . . . 135 D6
Ingram Mews CM7 . . . . . . . 155 B8
Ingram's Piece CO7 . . . . . . 111 E8
Ingram's Well CO10 . . . . . . .33 F7
Ingram's Well Rd CO10 . . . .33 F7
Inkerman Row ☑ CO10 . . . .33 E8
Inkerpole PI CM2 . . . . . . . . 205 F4
Innes End ☑ IP8 . . . . . . . . .16 C2
Innham Hill CO9 . . . . . . . . . .75 C6
Inverness CI CO1 . . . . . . . . 136 A8
INWORTH . . . . . . . . . . . . . 178 F8
Inworth La CO6 . . . . . . . . . .79 D2
Inworth Rd CO5 . . . . . . . . . 158 E3
Inworth Wlk ☑ CO2 . . . . . 136 A1
Iona Wlk CO5 . . . . . . . . . . 164 A8
IP Central ☑ IP4 . . . . . . . . .17 C5
Ipswich Cres . . . . . . . . . . . .18 F5
Ipswich High Sch IP9 . . . . . .38 C2
Ipswich Hospl IP4 . . . . . . . .18 C6
Ipswich Mus* IP1 . . . . . . . . .17 C6
Ipswich Prep Sch IP1 . . . . . .17 B7
Ipswich Rd
  Ardleigh CO7 . . . . . . . . . .83 F1
  Brantham CO11 . . . . . . . . .60 E2
  Colchester CO4 . . . . . . . . 110 C3
  Dedham CO7 . . . . . . . . . . .84 B6
  Harkstead IP9 . . . . . . . . . .63 B3
  Holbrook IP9 . . . . . . . . . . .62 E6
  Holland-on-S CO15 . . . . . 189 D6
  Ipswich IP10 . . . . . . . . . . .38 B6
  Stratford St M CO7 . . . . . .58 E2
Ipswich Sch IP1 . . . . . . . . . .17 C7
Ipswich Sta IP2 . . . . . . . . . .17 B4
Ipswich Transport Mus*
  IP3 . . . . . . . . . . . . . . . . . .18 C2
Ireland Rd IP3 . . . . . . . . . . .17 F1
Ireton Ho CO4 . . . . . . . . . . 109 F4
Ireton Rd CO3 . . . . . . . . . . 135 D5
Iris CI
  Chelmsford CM1 . . . . . . . 205 F5
  Ipswich IP2 . . . . . . . . . . . .16 F1
Irlam Rd IP2 . . . . . . . . . . . . .16 D1
Iron Latch La CO3 . . . . . . . 134 C8
Ironside Wlk CO11 . . . . . . . .86 C4
Iron View CM7 . . . . . . . . . . 128 C2
Irvine Rd CO3 . . . . . . . . . . 135 C5
Irving CI CM23 . . . . . . . . . 145 D4
Isaac Sq CM2 . . . . . . . . . . 217 B6
Isbourne Rd CO4 . . . . . . . . 136 F7
Isham PI IP3 . . . . . . . . . . . . .17 E4
Ishams Chase CM8 . . . . . . 195 C2
Island Ct CM23 . . . . . . . . . 145 A5
Island La CO13 . . . . . . . . . 143 E1
Island Rd CO14 . . . . . . . . . 143 E4
Ivanhoe CO13 . . . . . . . . . . 170 E3
Ivor Brown Ct CO4 . . . . . . 110 B4
Ivry St IP1 . . . . . . . . . . . . . .17 B7
Ivy Cotts CM6 . . . . . . . . . . 123 B4
Ivy La CO5 . . . . . . . . . . . . 185 B3
Ivy Lodge Rd CO6 . . . . . . . 109 C8
Ivy Todd Hill CB11 . . . . . . . .68 A8
Ixworth Rd CB9 . . . . . . . . . . .8 E6

**J**

Jacaranda CI CM1 . . . . . . . 206 A6
Jack Andrews Dr
  CO4 . . . . . . . . . . . . . . . . 110 C5
Jack Branch Ct CO15 . . . . . 188 E2
Jack Hatch Way CO7 . . . . . 137 A3
Jack's La CM22 . . . . . . . . . 148 D7
Jackson Ho CO4 . . . . . . . . 110 B6
Jackson PI CM2 . . . . . . . . . 216 D6
Jackson Rd CO15 . . . . . . . . 188 E2
Jacksons Ct CM2 . . . . . . . . 217 A6
Jackson's La CB10 . . . . . . . . .3 D3
Jackson's Sq CB10 . . . . . . . . .3 D3
Jackson Wlk CO2 . . . . . . . . 136 B3
Jacobs Ct CO10 . . . . . . . . . .34 B5
Jacobs Ct CO7 . . . . . . . . . . 185 F6
Jacquard Way ☑
  CM7 . . . . . . . . . . . . . . . . 128 A2
Jacqueline Ct CO3 . . . . . . . 135 A7
Jacques Hall Sch
  CO11 . . . . . . . . . . . . . . . . .88 A3
Jaggard's Rd CO4 . . . . . . . 110 A6
James Boden CI IP11 . . . . . 221 C5
James Carter Rd CO3 . . . . . 134 F3
James CI CO7 . . . . . . . . . . 137 C3
James Croft CM2 . . . . . . . . 216 B2
James Gdns CO16 . . . . . . . 187 B5
James Hatfield Ho IP2 . . . . .17 A1
Jameson PI ☑ CO10 . . . . . 133 E8
Jameson Rd CO15 . . . . . . . 188 C3
James Parnell Dr
  CO2 . . . . . . . . . . . . . . . . 135 F1
James Rd CO15 . . . . . . . . . 188 C2
James St
  Brightlingsea CO7 . . . . . . 185 F6

Kitchener Rd IP1 . . . . . . . .16 F8
Kitchener Way IP9 . . . . . . .91 A8
Kitchen Field CM7 . . . . .128 D3
Kitchen Hill CO10 . . . . . . .33 B6
Kittiwake Cl IP2 . . . . . . . . .16 E3
Kittiwake Dr CM9 . . . . . .210 C5
Knapton Cl CM1 . . . . . . . .205 D7
Knebworth Ct CM23 . . . . .145 D6
Knevett Cl CO4 . . . . . . . . .109 E3
Knightsbridge Cl CO2 . . .135 C3
Knightsbridge Ct
CO15 . . . . . . . . . . . . . . .189 B3
Knights Cl
Bishop's Stortford
CM23 . . . . . . . . . . . . .145 C8
Lawford CO11 . . . . . . . . .86 C4
Tiptree CO5 . . . . . . . . . .179 F3
Knight's Ct **2** CB9 . . . . . . .8 E7
Knights Field CO2 . . . . . .136 A5
Knights Rd
Braintree CM7 . . . . . . . .128 D1
Coggeshall CO6 . . . . . . .130 F2
Knights Row CM23 . . . . . .145 E6
Knights Way CM6 . . . . . .123 D1
Knole La CB11 . . . . . . . . . . .41 A7
Knowles Cl CO9 . . . . . . . . .76 E1
KNOWL GREEN . . . . . . . . .30 E8
Knox Ct CO15 . . . . . . . . . .188 E5
Knox Gdns CO15 . . . . . . .188 E5
Knox Rd CO15 . . . . . . . . .188 E5
Knutsford Cl IP4 . . . . . . . .16 C1
Kohima Rd CO2 . . . . . . . .135 B1
Kreswell Gr CO12 . . . . . . . .91 B2
Kynaston Pl CM8 . . . . . . .177 B2
Kynaston Rd CM7 . . . . . .127 A7

**L**

Laburnum Cl
Clacton-on-S CO15 . . . . .188 C3
Great Bentley CO7 . . . . .166 F8
**2** Ipswich, Chantry IP8 . .16 C2
Ipswich, Warren Heath
IP3 . . . . . . . . . . . . . . . . . .18 E2
Laburnum Cres CO13 . . . .170 D6
Laburnum Dr CO2 . . . . . .216 C6
Laburnum Gr CO4 . . . . . .136 E8
Laburnum Rd CM6 . . . . . .123 B1
Laburnum Way
Hatfield Peverel CM3 . . . .194 A3
Witham CM8 . . . . . . . . .177 A5
Lacewing Cl IP8 . . . . . . . . .36 E8
Lacey St IP4 . . . . . . . . . . . .17 C6
Lackford Pl IP3 . . . . . . . . . .38 C8
Ladbrook Dr CO2 . . . . . . .136 A3
Ladbrooke Rd CO16 . . . . .188 D6
Ladell Cl CO3 . . . . . . . . . .134 E3
Lady D'Arcy Charity
Almhouses **3** CO1 . . . . .135 F6
Ladygate CB9 . . . . . . . . . . .8 E6
Lady La
Chelmsford CM2 . . . . . .216 C8
**6** Ipswich IP1 . . . . . . . . .17 B6
Ladysmith Ave CO7 . . . . .185 E6
Ladysmith Cotts CM6 . . . .152 C4
Ladywell La CO2 . . . . . . .217 B5
Ladywood Rd IP4 . . . . . . . .18 C7
Laing Rd CO4 . . . . . . . . . .136 E6
Lake Ave CO15 . . . . . . . .188 C3
Lake Mead CM9 . . . . . . . .210 C3
Lakeside Cl IP2 . . . . . . . . .16 E2
Lakeside Rd IP2 . . . . . . . . .16 E2
Lakeside Wlk CO3 . . . . . .134 C4
Lakes End Ind Pk CM7 . . . .128 B2
Lakewood CO7 . . . . . . . . .112 C1
Lakforth CO10 . . . . . . . . . .15 D8
Lakin Cl CM2 . . . . . . . . . .206 A3
LAMARSH . . . . . . . . . . . . .55 B4
Lamarsh Hill
Bures CO8 . . . . . . . . . . .55 C1
Lamarsh CO8 . . . . . . . . . .55 B6
Lamarsh Rd CO8 . . . . . . . .55 A4
LAMB CORNER . . . . . . . .84 D4
Lambert Cross CB10 . . . . .22 E3
Lamberts Orch CM7 . . . . .127 D4
Lambert's Rd CO6 . . . . . .105 F3
Lambeth Cl IP11 . . . . . . . . .16 F8
Lambeth Wlk CO15 . . . . . .188 E5
Lamb La CO9 . . . . . . . . . . .75 D7
Lambourne Cl
Clacton-on-S CO15 . . . . .188 F8
Colchester CO3 . . . . . . .134 D4
Lambourne Gr CM9 . . . . . .220 F8
Lammas Dr CM7 . . . . . . .128 D3
Lammas Way CO7 . . . . . .137 C2
Lancaster Ct
**5** Braintree CM7 . . . . .128 B2
Frinton-on-S CO13 . . . . .171 A5
Lancaster Gdns E
CO15 . . . . . . . . . . . . . . .189 A3
Lancaster Gdns W
CO15 . . . . . . . . . . . . . . .189 A3
Lancaster Ho IP11 . . . . . .221 C5
Lancaster Rd
**5** Ipswich IP4 . . . . . . . .17 E6
Sudbury CO10 . . . . . . . . .15 D2
Lancaster Way
Bishop's Stortford
CM23 . . . . . . . . . . . . .145 C8
Braintree CM7 . . . . . . . .127 E4
Earls Colne CO6 . . . . . . .104 F2
Lanchester Ave CO15 . . . .203 D6
Lancia Ave CO15 . . . . . . .203 D6

Lancing Ave IP4 . . . . . . . .18 A8
Land Cl CO16 . . . . . . . . . .188 C5
Landermere Rd CO16 . . . .142 B2
Landers Ct CM1 . . . . . . . .204 D5
Landisdale CM3 . . . . . . . .219 A7
Land La CO1 . . . . . . . . . . . .17 C5
Landscape View CB11 . . . . .43 D6
Landsdown Rd CO10 . . . . .34 A8
Landseer Cl IP3 . . . . . . . . . .18 A1
Landseer Ct
Clacton-on-S CO15 . . . . .188 F2
Haverhill CB9 . . . . . . . . . .8 F6
Landseer Rd
Colchester CO3 . . . . . . .135 B5
Ipswich IP3 . . . . . . . . . . .17 E2
Lanercost Way IP2 . . . . . . .17 A1
Lane Rd CO6 . . . . . . . . . .106 B7
Lane The
Mistley CO11 . . . . . . . . . .86 F4
West Mersea CO5 . . . . . .201 A7
Langdale CM7 . . . . . . . . . .154 C7
Langdale Dr CO4 . . . . . . .141 B6
Langdale Gdns CM2 . . . . .216 D8
LANGENHOE . . . . . . . . . .163 B2
Langenhoe Com Prim Sch
CO5 . . . . . . . . . . . . . . .163 B2
Langenhoe Hall La
CO5 . . . . . . . . . . . . . . .183 C7
Langenhoe Pk CO5 . . . . . .163 B2
Langer Park Ind Est
IP11 . . . . . . . . . . . . . . .221 D3
Langer Prim Sch
IP11 . . . . . . . . . . . . . . .221 C2
Langer Rd IP11 . . . . . . . .221 C2
LANGFORD . . . . . . . . . . .209 D7
Langford Rd
Heybridge CM9 . . . . . . .209 F6
Wickham Bishops CM8,
CM9 . . . . . . . . . . . . . .195 C2
LANGHAM . . . . . . . . . . . .83 F4
Langham Dr CO16 . . . . . .188 B4
Langham La CO4 . . . . . . . .83 B2
LANGHAM MOOR . . . . . . .83 C4
Langham Pl CO4 . . . . . . . .110 B3
Langham Prim Sch
CO4 . . . . . . . . . . . . . . . .83 F4
Langham Rd CO4 . . . . . . . .82 F1
LANGLEY . . . . . . . . . . . . .40 C2
Langley Ave
Felixstowe IP11 . . . . . . .221 C4
Wethersfield CM7 . . . . . . .73 D7
Langley Cl
Felixstowe IP11 . . . . . . .221 C5
Harwich CO12 . . . . . . . . .91 C3
LANGLEY GREEN . . . . . . .158 F8
Langley Hill CO8 . . . . . . . .55 C3
Langleys CO6 . . . . . . . . . .106 C1
Langstons IP1 . . . . . . . . . .221 B7
Langton Ave CM1 . . . . . . .204 E5
Langtry Ct CO15 . . . . . . . .189 A2
Languidic Cl CO10 . . . . . . .34 C6
Langwood CO5 . . . . . . . . .201 C7
Lanham Farm Rd
CM7 . . . . . . . . . . . . . . .156 A8
LANHAM GREEN . . . . . . .156 A8
Lanham Green Rd
CM7 . . . . . . . . . . . . . . .156 A7
Lansdowne Cl CO5 . . . . . .179 C6
Lansdowne Rd
Felixstowe IP11 . . . . . . .221 A6
Ipswich IP3 . . . . . . . . . . .18 A5
Lanvalley Rd CO3 . . . . . . .134 E6
Lanyards IP11 . . . . . . . . . .221 F4
Lapwing Dr
Heybridge CM9 . . . . . . .210 C5
Kelvedon CO5 . . . . . . . .158 D2
Lapwing Rd IP2 . . . . . . . . .16 D3
Larch Cl CO4 . . . . . . . . . .136 D8
Larches The CM3 . . . . . . .206 E8
Larch Gr
Chelmsford CM2 . . . . . .216 C6
Witham CM8 . . . . . . . . .177 A5
Larch Ho IP11 . . . . . . . . .221 C4
Larch Way CM6 . . . . . . . .123 B1
Larch Wlk
Hatfield Peverel CM3 . . . .194 A4
Heybridge CM9 . . . . . . .210 C6
Larchwood CM23 . . . . . . .145 D5
Larchwood Cl IP2 . . . . . . .16 C5
Larkfield Rd CO7 . . . . . . .139 D1
Larkhill Rise IP4 . . . . . . . . .18 E5
Larkhill Way IP11 . . . . . . .221 B5
Lark Rise CO10 . . . . . . . . .33 D5
Larkrise Prim Sch
CM2 . . . . . . . . . . . . . . .216 E6
Larks Cl CB9 . . . . . . . . . . . .9 C7
Larksfield Cres CO12 . . . . .91 B4
Larksfield Rd IP9 . . . . . . . .62 A2
Lark's La
Broomfield CM3 . . . . . . .191 A6
Great Waltham CM3 . . . . .190 F5
Larkspur Cl
Bishop's Stortford
CM23 . . . . . . . . . . . . .145 D6
Witham CM8 . . . . . . . . .176 E4
Larkspur Ct **3** CM3 . . . . .205 F6
Larkspur Rd IP2 . . . . . . . . .16 F3
Larks Rise CO9 . . . . . . . . .77 A1
Larksway
Bishop's Stortford
CM23 . . . . . . . . . . . . .145 C8
Felixstowe IP11 . . . . . . .221 B3
Larkway CO13 . . . . . . . . .170 E7
Larman Ct CO11 . . . . . . . .86 C7
Larneys The CO14 . . . . . .170 E7
La Salle Cl IP2 . . . . . . . . . .16 F3
Latchmore Bank
CM22 . . . . . . . . . . . . . .146 B2

Lathcoates Cres CM2 . . . .216 E8
Lathe Ct CO4 . . . . . . . . . .136 D6
Latimer Ho CM1 . . . . . . . .205 D3
Lattice Ave IP4 . . . . . . . . . .18 C6
LATTINFORD HILL . . . . . . .59 D6
Laud Mews IP3 . . . . . . . . .18 A2
Launceston Cl CO2 . . . . . .136 B1
Laundry Gdns CO10 . . . . . .33 D6
Laurel Ave CO12 . . . . . . . .90 F2
Laurel Cl CO15 . . . . . . . . .189 B7
Laurel Ct CO4 . . . . . . . . . .136 E8
Laurel Dr
Great Dunmow CM6 . . . .123 B1
Long Melford CO10 . . . . .15 C7
Laurel Gr **4** CM2 . . . . . .216 A8
Laurelhayes IP2 . . . . . . . . .17 A3
Laurels The
Braintree CM7 . . . . . . . .128 A3
Great Notley CM7 . . . . . .154 C8
Laurence Ave CM8 . . . . . .195 A8
Laurence Cl CO7 . . . . . . . .137 F6
Laurence Croft CM1 . . . . .204 B1
Lauriston Bglws CM9 . . . .212 C6
Lavender Cl
Bishop's Stortford
CM23 . . . . . . . . . . . . .145 D6
Tiptree CO5 . . . . . . . . . .179 C4
Lavender Ct CM8 . . . . . . .176 E4
Lavender Ct **1** CM1 . . . .205 F5
Lavender Field
Haverhill CB9 . . . . . . . . . .8 D8
**6** Saffron Walden CB10 . .22 F2
Lavender Hill IP2 . . . . . . . .16 F4
Lavender Way CO4 . . . . . .109 C2
Lavenham Cl CO16 . . . . . .188 B4
Lavenham Ct CO2 . . . . . . .135 C2
Lavenham Rd IP2 . . . . . . . .16 E5
Lawford Pl CM7 . . . . . . . . .86 B3
LAWFORD . . . . . . . . . . . . .86 B2
Lawford CE Prim Sch
CO11 . . . . . . . . . . . . . . .86 B2
Lawford La
Chelmsford CM1 . . . . . .204 D3
Writtle CM1 . . . . . . . . . .204 C1
Lawford Mead Inf Sch
CM1 . . . . . . . . . . . . . . .204 D5
Lawford Mead Jun Sch
CM1 . . . . . . . . . . . . . . .204 D5
Lawford Rd
Lawford CO11 . . . . . . . . .86 A3
Rushmere St A IP4 . . . . . .18 F5
Lawling Ave CM9 . . . . . . .210 C5
Lawn Chase CM8 . . . . . . .176 F1
Lawn La CM1 . . . . . . . . . .205 D6
Lawns Cl CO5 . . . . . . . . . .201 C7
Lawns The
Chelmsford CM2 . . . . . .205 D5
Ipswich IP4 . . . . . . . . . . .18 C8
Lawn Way IP11 . . . . . . . .221 C5
Lawshall's Hill CM1 . . . . .43 D7
Lawshall's Hill . . . . . . . . . .78 D1
Laxton Ave CM1 . . . . . . . .204 E5
Laxton Cl IP3 . . . . . . . . . . .38 D8
Laxton Gr CM23 . . . . . . . .170 A5
Laxton Rd CO7 . . . . . . . . .165 B8
LAYER BRETON . . . . . . . .161 B1
Layer Breton Hill CO2 . . . .161 B1
Layer Cross CO2 . . . . . . . .161 F5
Layer Ct CM2 . . . . . . . . . .135 D4
LAYER DE LA HAYE . . . . . .161 D5
Layer de la Haye CE Prim
Sch CO2 . . . . . . . . . . . .161 F5
LAYER MARNEY . . . . . . . .180 D8
Layer Marney Twr* . . . . . .
CO5 . . . . . . . . . . . . . . .180 D8
Layer Rd
Abberton CO5 . . . . . . . .163 A3
Colchester CO2 . . . . . . .135 C3
Great Wigborough CO5 . .181 E5
Layer Ct CM7 . . . . . . . . . .126 F1
Layzell Croft CO10 . . . . . .34 C4
Leach Cl CM2 . . . . . . . . . .217 B7
Lea Cl
Bishop's Stortford
CM23 . . . . . . . . . . . . .119 B1
Braintree CM7 . . . . . . . .128 D1
Lea Gr CM23 . . . . . . . . . .216 E7
Lea La CM8 . . . . . . . . . . .177 F2
Leam Cl CO4 . . . . . . . . . .136 F7
Leapingwell CM2 . . . . . . .206 A3
Leas Cl CO5 . . . . . . . . . . .201 D6
Leas La CO2 . . . . . . . . . . .161 D6
Leas Rd
Clacton-on-S CO15 . . . . .188 D2
Colchester CO3 . . . . . . .135 C1
Leas The CO15 . . . . . . . . .171 B6
Leather La
**6** Braintree CM7 . . . . .127 F3
Great Yeldham CO9 . . . . .30 A1
Haverhill CB9 . . . . . . . . . .8 E7
Le Cateau Rd CM2 . . . . . .135 C6
Leech's La CO4 . . . . . . . . .109 D4
Ledford Cl CM1 . . . . . . . .204 F6
LEE-OVER-SANDS . . . . . . .202 C6
Lee Rd
Harwich CO12 . . . . . . . . .91 C3
Ipswich IP3 . . . . . . . . . . .17 F3
Lees Ct CO10 . . . . . . . . . . .2 B4
Lees The CM6 . . . . . . . . . .70 A3
Leeward Ct IP11 . . . . . . . .221 E5
Leeway The CM3 . . . . . . .218 F7
Lee Wick La CO16 . . . . . .186 E3
Leez Priory* CM3 . . . . . . .153 A2
Legerton Cotts CO6 . . . . . .79 C1
Legg St CM1 . . . . . . . . . .205 B3
Legions Way CM23 . . . . . .146 A8

Leicester Cl
Colchester CO1 . . . . . . . .136 A8
Ipswich IP1 . . . . . . . . . . .16 F1
Jaywick CO15 . . . . . . . .187 F1
Leicester Ct CM8 . . . . . . .156 D3
Leigh Dr
Elsenham CM22 . . . . . . . .94 C1
Wickham Bishops CM8 . .195 D5
Leighs Rd CM3 . . . . . . . .191 E6
Leighton Rd IP3 . . . . . . . . .38 A8
Leighton Sq IP3 . . . . . . . . .38 A8
Leiston Rd CB9 . . . . . . . . . .8 E7
Lely Rd IP3 . . . . . . . . . . . .37 F8
Lemons Hill IP9 . . . . . . . . .61 D8
Leonard Mews CM7 . . . . .155 B8
Leopold Gdns IP4 . . . . . . .18 B8
Leopold Rd
Felixstowe IP11 . . . . . . .221 C4
Ipswich IP4 . . . . . . . . . . .18 A8
Les Bois CO2 . . . . . . . . . .162 A5
Leslie Newnham Ct **1**
CM9 . . . . . . . . . . . . . . .210 A1
Leslie Rd IP3 . . . . . . . . . . .18 D1
Lethe Gr
Blackheath CO2 . . . . . . .163 A8
Colchester CO2 . . . . . . .162 F8
Letton Cl IP9 . . . . . . . . . . .62 A5
Leval St IP11 . . . . . . . . . . .221 C4
Levens Way CM77 . . . . . .154 C6
Levington Rd
Felixstowe IP11 . . . . . . .221 C1
Ipswich IP3 . . . . . . . . . . .18 A3
Lewes Cl IP3 . . . . . . . . . . .18 E3
Lewin Pl CM3 . . . . . . . . . .206 E8
Lewis Dr CM2 . . . . . . . . . .216 B6
Lewis La IP9 . . . . . . . . . . . .61 E2
LEXDEN . . . . . . . . . . . . . .135 A7
Lexden Ct CO3 . . . . . . . . .135 C2
Lexden Gr CO3 . . . . . . . . .134 F7
Lexden Mews CO3 . . . . . .134 F7
Lexden Park Ho CO3 . . . . .135 A7
Lexden Prim Sch CO3 . . . .134 E6
Lexden Rd
Colchester CO3 . . . . . . .135 B7
West Bergholt CO6 . . . . .108 C4
Lexden Springs Sch
CO3 . . . . . . . . . . . . . . .134 E7
Leybourne Dr CM1 . . . . . .205 E7
Leyfield CM77 . . . . . . . . . .155 D7
Ley Field
Marks Tey CO6 . . . . . . . .132 E3
Takeley CM22 . . . . . . . .148 C7
Leyfields CM77 . . . . . . . . .126 F1
Leys Dr CO16 . . . . . . . . . .168 C1
Leys Rd CO7 . . . . . . . . . . .137 C3
Leys The
Chelmsford CM2 . . . . . .205 F5
Wimbish CB10 . . . . . . . .45 C3
Ley The CM7 . . . . . . . . . .128 D1
Leyton Ct CO15 . . . . . . . .188 F8
Leywood Cl CM7 . . . . . . . .128 D2
Libius Dr CO4 . . . . . . . . . .110 A5
Lichfield Cl
Chelmsford CM1 . . . . . .204 E4
Colchester CO1 . . . . . . .136 A8
Lidgate Ct IP11 . . . . . . . .221 A4
Lie Field Cl CM7 . . . . . . .128 D3
Lichild Cl CM8 . . . . . . . . .195 A7
Lightship Way CO2 . . . . . .136 D5
Lilac Ave CO16 . . . . . . . . .203 B6
Lilac Cl CM2 . . . . . . . . . . .216 C6
Lilac Cl CO7 . . . . . . . . . . .137 A2
Lilac Tree Ct CO4 . . . . . . .136 E8
Lilian Impey Dr CO4 . . . . .110 B5
Lilley's La CO7 . . . . . . . . . .112 D4
Lilley Cres CM7 . . . . . . . . .102 B1
Lilly Cnr CM9 . . . . . . . . . . .27 A6
Lily Cl CM1 . . . . . . . . . . . .205 F6
Limbourne Dr CM9 . . . . . .210 D5
Lime Ave
Colchester CO4 . . . . . . .136 D8
Harwich CO12 . . . . . . . . .91 B3
Limebrook Way CM9 . . . . .220 F7
Lime Cl
Clacton-on-S CO15 . . . . .188 C3
Witham CM8 . . . . . . . . .177 A5
Limefields CB10 . . . . . . . . .22 D4
Lime Gr CO10 . . . . . . . . . .33 C5
Limekiln La CM24 . . . . . . .119 C5
Limes Cres CM23 . . . . . . .146 A7
Lime St CO7 . . . . . . . . . . .185 F5
Limes The
Ardleigh CO7 . . . . . . . . .111 F7
Clacton-on-S CO15 . . . . .189 A3
Galleywood CM2 . . . . . .216 B2
Gosfield CO9 . . . . . . . . .102 E7
Long Melford CO10 . . . . .15 C7
Limetree Dr IP3 . . . . . . . . .18 D2
Lime Tree Hill CM6 . . . . . .123 D2
Lime Tree Pl IP1 . . . . . . . .16 E7
Lime Wlk CO15 . . . . . . . .216 C6
Limington Ct IP3 . . . . . . . .17 E5
Lincoln Ave CO15 . . . . . . .203 D6
Lincoln Cl CM2 . . . . . . . . .145 D5
Lincoln La CO6 . . . . . . . . .82 C1
Lincoln Terr CM12 . . . . . .18 F5
Lincoln Way CO1 . . . . . . .136 A8
Lindbergh Rd IP3 . . . . . . . .18 C2
Linden Cl
Chelmsford CM2 . . . . . .216 C7
Colchester CO4 . . . . . . .110 E1
Lawford CO11 . . . . . . . . .86 B3

Linden Dr CO15 . . . . . . . .188 E7
Lindens The
Bishop's Stortford
CM23 . . . . . . . . . . . . .145 F6
Braintree CM7 . . . . . . . .128 A1
Colchester CO3 . . . . . . .135 B7
Halstead CO9 . . . . . . . . .103 F8
Lindisfarne Cl IP2 . . . . . . .17 A1
Lindisfarne Ct CO4 . . . . . .220 E8
LINDSELL . . . . . . . . . . . . .98 A3
Lindsell La CM6 . . . . . . . . .98 B2
Lindsey Ave CO10 . . . . . . .34 B6
Lindsey Cl CM23 . . . . . . . .118 F1
Lindsey Ct CO10 . . . . . . . .34 B6
Lindsey Rd
Bishop's Stortford
CM23 . . . . . . . . . . . . .118 F1
Ipswich IP4 . . . . . . . . . . .18 C7
Line Cotts CO4 . . . . . . . . .83 A4
Linfold Cl CM7 . . . . . . . . .128 D4
Linford Mews CM9 . . . . . .220 E8
Ling's La IP9 . . . . . . . . . . . .63 D5
Lingwood Cl CM3 . . . . . . .218 E2
Link Cl CO4 . . . . . . . . . . .109 E4
Link Rd
Bishop's Stortford
CM23 . . . . . . . . . . . . .145 F8
Brightlingsea CO7 . . . . . .186 A6
Capel St M IP9 . . . . . . . .35 A1
Clacton-on-S CO15 . . . . .188 D2
Colchester CO4 . . . . . . .103 D8
Witham CM8 . . . . . . . . .177 A5
Links Ave IP11 . . . . . . . . .221 F6
Links Bsns Ctr The
CM23 . . . . . . . . . . . . . .146 C7
Links Cl CO10 . . . . . . . . . . .2 C5
Links Dr CM2 . . . . . . . . . .215 F7
Linksfield IP5 . . . . . . . . . . .18 E7
Linksfield Gdns IP5 . . . . . .18 F7
Linkside CO13 . . . . . . . . . .170 E3
Link Side CM23 . . . . . . . .146 C6
Links Rd
Cressing CM77 . . . . . . . .156 C7
Seawick CO16 . . . . . . . .203 B6
Link The IP9 . . . . . . . . . . . .60 D6
Link Way CM23 . . . . . . . .145 E6
Linley Gdns CO15 . . . . . . .188 D2
Linnet Dr CM2 . . . . . . . . .216 B6
Linnet Rd IP2 . . . . . . . . . . .16 D4
Linnets CO15 . . . . . . . . . .188 F6
Linnetts La CB9 . . . . . . . . .10 A4
Linnet Way CO7 . . . . . . . .166 D8
Linstead Cl CO16 . . . . . . .188 A4
Linton Cl CB11 . . . . . . . . . .43 F8
Linton Pl **13** CB9 . . . . . . . . .9 B8
Linton Rd CB1 . . . . . . . . . . .5 B7
Lintons The CM2 . . . . . . .217 D6
Lionel Hurst Cl CO10 . . . . .34 C5
Lionfield Terr CM1 . . . . . .205 D7
Lion Mdw CB9 . . . . . . . . . .27 B7
Lion Rd CO10 . . . . . . . . . . .2 B5
Lion St IP1 . . . . . . . . . . . . .17 C5
Lion Wlk **20** CO15 . . . . . . .135 F7
Lisle Ho
Colchester, Lexden
CO3 . . . . . . . . . . . . . .135 A7
Colchester, Mile End
CO4 . . . . . . . . . . . . . .109 E4
Lisle Rd CO2 . . . . . . . . . . .136 A5
Lister Rd CM7 . . . . . . . . . .154 F8
Lister Tye CM2 . . . . . . . . .216 C2
List Ho CO10 . . . . . . . . . . .15 C8
LISTON . . . . . . . . . . . . . . .15 A6
LISTON GARDENS . . . . . . .14 E8
Listonhall Chase CO9 . . . . .75 B5
Liston La CO10 . . . . . . . . . .15 B6
Litchborough Pk CM3 . . . .218 F4
Litchfield CO12 . . . . . . . . .90 E2
Litchfield Cl CO15 . . . . . .188 E5
Littell Tweed CM2 . . . . . . .206 A3
LITTLE BADDOW . . . . . . .207 D4
Little Baddow Rd
Danbury CM3 . . . . . . . . .218 E7
Woodham Walter CM9 . . .208 C3
Little Bakers CO14 . . . . . .171 A7
LITTLE BENTLEY . . . . . . .139 E8
Little Bentley Rd
CO16 . . . . . . . . . . . . . . .114 B1
Little Bradfords CM7 . . . . .128 A4
LITTLE BRAISWICK . . . . . .109 C4
Little Bramford La IP1 . . . .17 A7
LITTLE BRAXTED . . . . . . .177 D2
Little Braxted La CM8 . . . .177 C3
LITTLE BROMLEY . . . . . . .113 B6
Little Bromley Rd
Ardleigh CO7 . . . . . . . . .112 B7
Great Bromley CO7 . . . . .112 F3
Little Bentley CO7 . . . . . .113 E1
LITTLEBURY . . . . . . . . . . .21 E4
LITTLE CAMBRIDGE . . . . .97 B3
LITTLE CANFIELD . . . . . . .121 E8
Littlebury Green Rd
CB11 . . . . . . . . . . . . . . .21 A3
LITTLE CAMBRIDGE . . . . .97 B3
LITTLE CHESTERFORD . . . .21 F8
LITTLE CHISHILL . . . . . . . .39 E7
Little Chishill Rd SG8 . . . . .39 C8
LITTLE CLACTON . . . . . . .168 D3
Little Clacton Rd
Clacton-on-S CO16 . . . . .188 B4
Great Holland CO13 . . . . .169 E2
LITTLE CORNARD . . . . . . .34 E3

Littlecotes CO4 . . . . . . . . .109 D4
Little Croft St IP2 . . . . . . . .17 C3
Little Dorrit CM1 . . . . . . . .204 E7
LITTLE DUNMOW . . . . . . . .151 D7
LITTLE EASTON . . . . . . . . .122 F5
Littlefield CO7 . . . . . . . . . . .137 C1
Littlefield Rd CO2 . . . . . . .135 C2
Little Fields CM3 . . . . . . . .219 A7
Little Foxburrows
CO2 . . . . . . . . . . . . . . . . . .135 E4
Littlegarth Sch CO6 . . . . . . .82 B7
Little Gipping St **7**
IP1 . . . . . . . . . . . . . . . . . . . .17 B6
Little Gr **4** IP9 . . . . . . . . . .35 A1
Little & Great Sir Hughes
La CM2 . . . . . . . . . . . . . . .217 B2
Little Gulls **6** IP9 . . . . . . .35 A1
LITTLE HALLINGBURY . . . .146 B1
Little Harrods CO14 . . . . . .171 A7
LITTLE HENHAM . . . . . . . . .67 C1
Little Hills CM9 . . . . . . . . .209 D8
LITTLE HORKESLEY . . . . . . .81 E3
Little Horkesley Rd
CO6 . . . . . . . . . . . . . . . . . . .81 A4
Little Hyde Cl CO9 . . . . . . . .30 A2
Little Hyde Rd CO9 . . . . . . .30 A2
Little Larchmount
CB11 . . . . . . . . . . . . . . . . . .43 D8
LITTLE LEIGHS . . . . . . . . .173 E6
LITTLE LONDON
Berden . . . . . . . . . . . . . . . . .92 D7
Feering . . . . . . . . . . . . . . .158 F4
Finchingfield . . . . . . . . . . . .48 C3
Little London Hill CM7 . . . . .72 D8
Little London La CM9 . . . . .208 D4
LITTLE MAPLESTEAD . . . . . .53 B1
Little Mdw CM1 . . . . . . . . .204 A1
Little Mdws CM9 . . . . . . . .219 E6
Little Nell CM1 . . . . . . . . . .204 E2
LITTLE OAKLEY . . . . . . . . .117 B7
Little Orch IP9 . . . . . . . . . . .62 D5
Little Orchards CM1 . . . . . .205 B7
Little Paddocks CM77 . . . .126 F1
Little Pasture CM7 . . . . . . .127 D4
Little St Mary's CO10 . . . . .15 C7
LITTLE SAMPFORD . . . . . . . .71 D8
Little's Cres IP2 . . . . . . . . . .17 C4
Little Stile CM1 . . . . . . . . .215 A8
Little Stone Ct CO15 . . . . .203 J8
LITTLE TEY . . . . . . . . . . . . .132 C4
Little Tey Rd CO5 . . . . . . . .132 A5
LITTLE TOTHAM . . . . . . . . .197 C4
Little Totham Rd
CM9 . . . . . . . . . . . . . . . . .211 D8
Little Tufts IP9 . . . . . . . . . . .35 B1
LITTLE WALDEN . . . . . . . . .22 F8
Little Walden Rd CB10 . . . . .22 E5
LITTLE WALTHAM . . . . . . . .191 C6
Little Waltham CE Prim
Sch CM3 . . . . . . . . . . . . . .191 B7
Little Waltham Rd
CM1 . . . . . . . . . . . . . . . . . .191 D1
Little Whip St **8** IP2 . . . . .17 C4
LITTLE WIGBOROUGH
. . . . . . . . . . . . . . . . . . . . . .182 B4
Little Wood CO13 . . . . . . . .170 E6
Little Wood Mews
CO4 . . . . . . . . . . . . . . . . . .109 D2
LITTLE YELDHAM . . . . . . . . .30 E4
Little Yeldham Rd CO9 . . . . .30 C3
LITTLEY GREEN . . . . . . . . .172 F7
Livery Mews CM6 . . . . . . . .124 E5
Llewellyn Cl CM1 . . . . . . . .205 D3
Lloyd Rd IP9 . . . . . . . . . . . . .91 A8
Lloyds Ave **4** IP1 . . . . . . .17 C6
Loamy Hill Rd
Little Totham CM9 . . . . . .197 A7
Tiptree CO5 . . . . . . . . . . .178 F1
Loates Pasture CM24 . . . . .119 D8
Lobelia Cl CM1 . . . . . . . . . .206 A6
Locarno Rd IP3 . . . . . . . . . . .18 B3
Lockhart Ave CO3 . . . . . . . .135 C7
Lock Hill CM9 . . . . . . . . . . .210 E2
Lockram La
Witham CM8 . . . . . . . . . . .176 F2
**7** Witham CM8 . . . . . . .177 A2
Lock Rd CO9 . . . . . . . . . . . .103 E8
Lockside Marina CO2 . . . . .205 D1
Lodge Ave CM2 . . . . . . . . . .216 F7
Lodge Cl
Clacton-on-S CO15 . . . . . .188 E4
Great Oakley CO12 . . . . . .117 C8
Lodge Cres CM3 . . . . . . . . .206 E7
Lodge Ct CO6 . . . . . . . . . . .108 F4
Lodge Farm La CO16 . . . . .187 D4
Lodge Farm Rd CO10 . . . . . .2 C3
Lodge La
Abberton CO5 . . . . . . . . . .163 D1
Ardleigh CO7 . . . . . . . . . . .111 B6
Ardleigh CO7 . . . . . . . . . . .111 C6
Brightlingsea CO7 . . . . . . .185 E7
Langham CO4 . . . . . . . . . . .110 D8
Peldon CO5 . . . . . . . . . . . .182 E7
Purleigh CM3 . . . . . . . . . .220 C2
Tendring CO16 . . . . . . . . .140 F6
Lodge Rd
Braintree CM7 . . . . . . . . . .127 F1
Brightlingsea CO7 . . . . . . .185 E8
Little Clacton CO16 . . . . .169 A5
Little Oakley CO12 . . . . . .117 C8
Maldon CM9 . . . . . . . . . . .209 F3
Messing CO5 . . . . . . . . . . .159 D3
Thorpe-le-S CO16 . . . . . . .168 F6

Lodge Rd continued
Woodham Mortimer CM3,
CM9 . . . . . . . . . . . . . . . . .220 B5
Writtle CM1 . . . . . . . . . . . .215 A8
Lodge The CO15 . . . . . . . . .189 F6
Loftin Way CM2 . . . . . . . . .216 D7
Loganberry Rd IP3 . . . . . . . .38 C7
Lombard Ct IP4 . . . . . . . . . .17 F7
Lombardy Pk IP2 . . . . . . . . .17 B1
Lombardy Pl CM1 . . . . . . . .205 B3
Lombardy Rd CO10 . . . . . . .15 D2
Lonbarn Hill CO11 . . . . . . . .88 A2
London Hill
Chelmsford CM2 . . . . . . . .215 F2
Galleywood CM2 . . . . . . . .216 A2
London Land Cotts
CO6 . . . . . . . . . . . . . . . . . . .80 E4
London Rd
Bishop's Stortford
CM23 . . . . . . . . . . . . . . . .146 A5
Braintree CM7 . . . . . . . . . .127 E1
Capel St M IP9 . . . . . . . . . .35 B1
Chelmsford CM2 . . . . . . . .215 E6
Clacton-on-S CO15 . . . . . .188 E7
Colchester CO3 . . . . . . . . .134 D6
Copford CO3, CO6 . . . . . . .133 D4
Feering CO5 . . . . . . . . . . . .159 B7
Great Chesterford CB10 . . . .3 D2
Great Horkesley CO6 . . . . . .81 F2
Great Notley CM77 . . . . . .154 D6
Ipswich, Chantry IP2 . . . . .16 C3
Ipswich, Chantry IP2 . . . . .16 F5
Ipswich IP1 . . . . . . . . . . . . .17 A6
Kelvedon CO5 . . . . . . . . . .158 B1
Littlebury CB11 . . . . . . . . . .22 A1
Maldon CM9 . . . . . . . . . . .209 D3
Marks Tey CO6 . . . . . . . . .133 A3
Newport CB11 . . . . . . . . . . .67 A6
Saffron Walden CB11 . . . . .43 D8
Washbrook IP8 . . . . . . . . . .15 C4
Wendens Ambo CB11 . . . . .42 F4
London Stansted Airport
CM24 . . . . . . . . . . . . . . . .121 A4
Lone Barn Ct IP1 . . . . . . . . .16 D8
Lonebarn Link CM2 . . . . . .206 B5
Longacre
Chelmsford CM1 . . . . . . . .215 E8
Colchester CO4 . . . . . . . . .109 E2
Longacre Rd CM77 . . . . . . .155 E6
Longacres CM1 . . . . . . . . . .128 A1
Long Acres CO5 . . . . . . . . .158 F6
Long Border Rd
Great Hallingbury CM22,
CM24 . . . . . . . . . . . . . . . .147 C8
Takeley CM24 . . . . . . . . . .120 E1
Long Brandocks CM1 . . . . .204 A1
Long Comm CM9 . . . . . . . .209 F5
Longcroft
Felixstowe IP11 . . . . . . . . .221 C6
Hempstead CB10 . . . . . . . . .46 E8
Takeley CM22 . . . . . . . . . .148 C7
Long Croft CM1 . . . . . . . . .119 D8
Longcroft Rd CO4 . . . . . . . .136 C8
Longedryve CO2 . . . . . . . . .135 C3
Longfellow Rd CM9 . . . . . . .210 A1
Longfield CM8 . . . . . . . . . . .176 E5
Long Field IP11 . . . . . . . . .221 B6
Longfield Rd
Capel St M IP9 . . . . . . . . . .35 B2
Great Baddow CM2 . . . . . .216 E8
Longfields CO16 . . . . . . . . .187 B4
Long Gdns CO9 . . . . . . . . . .53 F5
Long Gn
Braintree CM77 . . . . . . . . .155 E8
Marks Tey CO6 . . . . . . . . .132 E3
Long Green La CM7 . . . . . . .99 C2
Longhedges CB11 . . . . . . . .22 E1
Long Horse Croft CB11 . . . .43 F7
Long La
Arkesden CB11 . . . . . . . . . .41 E5
Great Holland CO13 . . . . .170 C3
Rayne CM7 . . . . . . . . . . . .153 F8
Longleaf Dr CM7 . . . . . . . . .155 A8
Longleat Cl CM1 . . . . . . . . .204 F7
Long Ley CB11 . . . . . . . . . . .40 D2
Long Mdw
Bishop's Stortford
CM23 . . . . . . . . . . . . . . . .145 D6
Great Notley CM77 . . . . . .154 B5
Long Mdws CO12 . . . . . . . . .90 F2
Longmead Ave CM6 . . . . . .216 F8
Longmeads CM8 . . . . . . . . .195 E5
Longmeads Cl CM1 . . . . . . .204 A1
LONG MELFORD . . . . . . . . . .15 D7
Long Melford CE Prim Sch
CO10 . . . . . . . . . . . . . . . . . .15 C7
Longmore Ave CM2 . . . . . . .216 E8
Long Pastures CO10 . . . . . . .2 C3
Long Perry IP5 . . . . . . . . . . .35 B1
Long Rd CO11 . . . . . . . . . . .86 C3
Long Rd E CO7 . . . . . . . . . . .85 B3
Long Rd W CO7 . . . . . . . . . .84 E3
Longridge CO4 . . . . . . . . . .136 F8
Longship Way CM9 . . . . . . .220 E8
Longshots Cl CM1 . . . . . . . .191 A1
Longs La CM3 . . . . . . . . . . .173 F1
Long St IP3 . . . . . . . . . . . . .17 E5
Longstomps Ave CM2 . . . . .216 A7
Longstraw Cl CO3 . . . . . . . .134 D6
Long Wyre St CO1 . . . . . . . .135 F7
Lonsdale **4** IP2 . . . . . . . . .17 C4
Lonsdale Cl IP2 . . . . . . . . . .17 F7
Lonsdale Rd CO16 . . . . . . . .142 A2
Looe Rd IP11 . . . . . . . . . . . .221 F5
Loompits Way CB11 . . . . . . .43 D7
Loppys Hill **11** CM24 . . .119 E6
Loraine Way IP8 . . . . . . . . . .16 A6
Lord Holland Rd CO2 . . . . .135 F3

Lords Ave CM23 . . . . . . . . .145 B7
Lords Cl CB10 . . . . . . . . . . .23 D1
Lord's Croft La CB9 . . . . . . .9 A8
Lordship Rd CM1 . . . . . . . .204 B3
Lordsland La CM7 . . . . . . . .103 C1
Lordswood Rd CO2 . . . . . . .135 C2
Lorkin's La CO10 . . . . . . . . .54 C4
Lorkin Way CO6 . . . . . . . . .108 F4
Lott's Rd CO16 . . . . . . . . . .168 B4
Lotus Way CO15 . . . . . . . . .203 E7
Louise Cl CO14 . . . . . . . . . .144 E3
Louse La CO7 . . . . . . . . . . . .84 E4
Louvain Dr CM1 . . . . . . . . .205 F7
Louvain Rd CO12 . . . . . . . . .91 A1
Loveday Cl SG8 . . . . . . . . . .19 D3
Love La CO7 . . . . . . . . . . . .185 F8
Lovers La IP9 . . . . . . . . . . . .63 C4
Lover's La CO7 . . . . . . . . . .167 A7
Loves Wlk CM1 . . . . . . . . . .204 B1
Love Way CO16 . . . . . . . . . .188 C6
Lovibond Pl **4** CM2 . . . . .205 F4
Lowe Chase CO14 . . . . . . . .171 B8
Lowefields CO6 . . . . . . . . . .105 D5
Lower Anchor St
CM2 . . . . . . . . . . . . . . . . . .205 A1
Lower Barn Farm
CO16 . . . . . . . . . . . . . . . . .142 B5
Lower Brook Mews **14**
IP1 . . . . . . . . . . . . . . . . . . . .17 C5
Lower Brook St IP4 . . . . . . .17 C5
Lower Cotts SG9 . . . . . . . . .64 A2
Lower Dales View Rd **3**
IP1 . . . . . . . . . . . . . . . . . . . .17 A8
Lower Downs Slade
CB9 . . . . . . . . . . . . . . . . . . . .9 A8
Lower Farm Rd CO4,
CO6 . . . . . . . . . . . . . . . . . . .57 B1
Lower Gn
Galleywood CM2 . . . . . . . .216 C2
Stoke by C CO10 . . . . . . . . .11 C4
Wakes Colne CO6 . . . . . . . .79 C1
LOWER GREEN
Blackmore End . . . . . . . . . .74 B3
Galleywood . . . . . . . . . . . .216 C2
Great Baddow . . . . . . . . . .217 C6
Langley . . . . . . . . . . . . . . . .40 B1
Radwinter . . . . . . . . . . . . . .45 E2
Lower Green Ho CO7 . . . . .185 F6
Lower Harlings IP9 . . . . . . . .91 A8
Lower Holt St CO6 . . . . . . .105 D6
Lower Houses Rd IP9 . . . . . .63 D2
Lower King CM7 . . . . . . . . .128 D1
Lower Kingsland Rd
CO5 . . . . . . . . . . . . . . . . . .201 C5
Lower Langley CO6 . . . . . . .106 C1
Lower Marine Par
CO12 . . . . . . . . . . . . . . . . . .91 C3
Lower Mill Field CM6 . . . . .150 E7
Lower Orwell St IP4 . . . . . . .17 D5
Lower Park Cres
CM23 . . . . . . . . . . . . . . . .145 F5
Lower Park Rd CO2 . . . . . . .185 E6
LOWER POND STREET
. . . . . . . . . . . . . . . . . . . . . . .40 F8
Lower Rd
Birch CO2 . . . . . . . . . . . . .161 A5
Birch Green CO2 . . . . . . . .181 A8
Borley CO10 . . . . . . . . . . . . .15 B3
Glemsford CO10 . . . . . . . . . .2 B2
Peldon CO5 . . . . . . . . . . . .182 D5
Wormingford CO8, CO6 . . .80 B5
Lower Sq CO10 . . . . . . . . . . .22 D2
Lower St
Cavendish CO10 . . . . . . . . . .1 D1
Sproughton IP8 . . . . . . . . . .16 A7
Stanstead CO10 . . . . . . . . . .2 E6
Stansted Mountfitchet
CM24 . . . . . . . . . . . . . . . .119 F7
Stutton IP9 . . . . . . . . . . . . .62 A2
LOWER STREET . . . . . . . . . .62 A1
Low Lighthouse Maritime
Mus* CO12 . . . . . . . . . . . .91 E5
Low Rd CO12 . . . . . . . . . . . .90 E1
Lowry Gdns CM1 . . . . . . . . .38 A8
Low St CO10 . . . . . . . . . . . . .2 C6
Luard Way
Birch CO2 . . . . . . . . . . . . .161 A3
Witham CM8 . . . . . . . . . . .176 F1
Lubberhedges La
CM6 . . . . . . . . . . . . . . . . . .125 B8
Lucas Ave
Chelmsford CM2 . . . . . . . .216 C6
Fordham CO6 . . . . . . . . . . .107 D5
Lucas Hall CO4 . . . . . . . . . .109 F4
Lucas Ho CO3 . . . . . . . . . . .135 A7
Lucas Rd
**18** Colchester CO2 . . . . .135 F6
Sudbury CO10 . . . . . . . . . . .33 F7
Lucas's La CO16 . . . . . . . . .141 D6
Lucerne Rd CO7 . . . . . . . . .138 A6
Lucerne Way CM1 . . . . . . . .215 B8
Luces La CO9 . . . . . . . . . . . .51 F4
Lucius Cres CO4 . . . . . . . . .110 B6
Lucksfield Way CM2 . . . . . .216 F5
Luck's La CM3 . . . . . . . . . . .172 F2
Lucy Cl CO3 . . . . . . . . . . . . .134 D4
Lucy La N CO3 . . . . . . . . . .134 B7
Lucy La S CO3 . . . . . . . . . . .134 C7
Ludgores La CM3 . . . . . . . .218 D5
Ludham Hall La
CM7 . . . . . . . . . . . . . . . . . .154 D7
Luff Way CO13 . . . . . . . . . .170 F7
Lufkin Rd CO4 . . . . . . . . . . .109 F3
Lugar Ct CO4 . . . . . . . . . . .136 E6
Lukin's Dr CM6 . . . . . . . . . .150 D7
Lulworth Ave IP3 . . . . . . . . .18 D3
Lulworth Cl CO15 . . . . . . . .203 I8

Lulworth Dr CB9 . . . . . . . . . .8 E8
Lumber Leys CO14 . . . . . . .171 A7
Lundy Cl CB9 . . . . . . . . . . . . .9 D7
Lunnish Hill CO12 . . . . . . . .89 F2
Lupin Dr CM1 . . . . . . . . . . .205 F6
Lupin Mews **1** CM1 . . . .205 F6
Lupin Rd IP2 . . . . . . . . . . . . .16 E5
Lupin Way CO16 . . . . . . . . .168 C4
Lushington Ave CO13 . . . . .170 E6
Lushington Rd CO11 . . . . . .86 C4
Luther Dr CO5 . . . . . . . . . . .179 E5
Luther Rd IP2 . . . . . . . . . . . .17 C4
Lutus Cl CO10 . . . . . . . . . . .12 A6
Lydgate Cl CO11 . . . . . . . . .86 B4
Lydia Dr CO16 . . . . . . . . . . .186 A2
Lymington Ave CO15 . . . . .189 A8
Lyndenswood Farm
CM77 . . . . . . . . . . . . . . . . .154 B3
Lyndenswood La CM77,
CM3 . . . . . . . . . . . . . . . . . .154 B2
Lyndhaven Ct CO15 . . . . . .189 C4
Lyndhurst Ave CM77 . . . . . .18 D5
Lyndhurst Dr CM3 . . . . . . .218 F1
Lyndhurst Rd CO15 . . . . . .189 C4
Lynmouth Ave CM2 . . . . . .205 C1
Lynmouth Ct CM2 . . . . . . .205 C1
Lynmouth Gdns CM2 . . . . .205 C1
Lynnbrook Cl IP2 . . . . . . . . .16 E1
Lynne Cl CO13 . . . . . . . . . .170 E6
Lynton Cl CM12 . . . . . . . . . .91 B4
Lynton Ct CM23 . . . . . . . . .145 E4
Lynton Dr CM1 . . . . . . . . . .205 E5
Lynwood Ave IP11 . . . . . . . .221 F5
Lyon Cl
Clacton-on-S CO15 . . . . . .189 A4
Galleywood CM2 . . . . . . . .216 B3
Lyons Hall Prim Sch
CM7 . . . . . . . . . . . . . . . . . .128 D4
Lyons Hall Rd CM7 . . . . . . .128 D8
Lysander Rd IP3 . . . . . . . . . .38 C8
Lyster Ave CM2 . . . . . . . . . .217 A7

**M**

Mabbitt Way CO4 . . . . . . . .110 B5
Maberly Ct CB10 . . . . . . . . .22 D2
Macbeth Cl CO4 . . . . . . . . .136 F7
MacDonough Cotts
CO12 . . . . . . . . . . . . . . . . . .91 E5
MACE GREEN . . . . . . . . . . . .35 C7
Mace Wlk CM1 . . . . . . . . . .204 F3
Mackay Ct CO2 . . . . . . . . . .136 B1
Maclarens CM8 . . . . . . . . . .196 A6
Macmillan Ct **4** CM2 . . .205 B1
McNamara Cl **4** IP4 . . . . .17 E6
McWilliamsRd CO15 . . . . . .189 D4
Madeline Pl CM1 . . . . . . . .204 E6
Madgements Rd
CM77 . . . . . . . . . . . . . . . . .129 C8
Magazine Farm Way
CO3 . . . . . . . . . . . . . . . . . .135 A6
Magdalen Cl CO15 . . . . . . .188 E4
Magdalen Ct CO15 . . . . . . .188 E4
Magdalene Cl IP2 . . . . . . . . .16 F2
Magdalen Gn
Colchester CO1 . . . . . . . . .136 B6
Thaxted CM6 . . . . . . . . . . . .70 B2
Magdalen Rd CO15 . . . . . . .188 E4
Magdalen St CO1 . . . . . . . .136 A6
MAGGOTS END . . . . . . . . . .92 D4
Magingley Cres IP5 . . . . . . . .18 F6
Magnolia Cl CM23 . . . . . . .145 A4
Magnolia Cl
Chelmsford CM2 . . . . . . . .216 B6
Witham CM8 . . . . . . . . . . .177 A5
Magnolia Dr CO4 . . . . . . . .136 F8
Magnus Dr CO4 . . . . . . . . .110 B6
Magpie Cl
Harwich CO12 . . . . . . . . . . .90 E1
Ipswich IP8 . . . . . . . . . . . . .16 C2
Magwitch Cl CM1 . . . . . . . .204 F7
Maidenburgh St CO1 . . . . .135 F7
MAIDENHALL . . . . . . . . . . . .17 B2
Maidenhall App IP2 . . . . . . .17 B3
Maidenhall Gn IP2 . . . . . . . .17 B2
Maidment Cres CM8 . . . . . .194 F4
Maidstone Inf Sch
IP11 . . . . . . . . . . . . . . . . . .221 C5
Maidstone Rd IP11 . . . . . . .221 C5
Mailers La CM23 . . . . . . . . .92 F2
Main Rd
Boreham CM3 . . . . . . . . . .192 F1
Braintree CM3 . . . . . . . . . .153 D4
Broomfield CM1 . . . . . . . .191 B2
Chelmondiston IP9 . . . . . . .63 D7
Chelmsford CM2 . . . . . . . .217 F7
Danbury CM3 . . . . . . . . . .218 A4
Danbury CM3 . . . . . . . . . .218 A1
Frating Green CO7 . . . . . . .138 C3
Great Holland CO13 . . . . .170 A3
Great Leighs CM3 . . . . . . .173 F7
Harwich, Bath Side CO12 . .91 E5
Harwich, Dovercourt
CO12 . . . . . . . . . . . . . . . . .91 B3
Ramsey CO12 . . . . . . . . . . .90 A1
Rushmere St A IP5 . . . . . . .18 F8
Woolverstone IP9 . . . . . . . .62 E5
Wormingford CO6 . . . . . . . .80 F4
Main St CB21 . . . . . . . . . . . . .6 F6
Mais Ct IP2 . . . . . . . . . . . . . .16 F2
Maitland Ct CO13 . . . . . . . .170 F4
Maitland Rd CO4 . . . . . . . . .136 B8
Majendie La CO9 . . . . . . . . .51 F4
Makemores CM7 . . . . . . . . .128 B4
Makins Rd CO12 . . . . . . . . . .90 F5
MALDON . . . . . . . . . . . . . . .210 B3

Maldon Court Prep Sch
CM9 . . . . . . . . . . . . . . . . .209 F3
Maldon Ct
**8** Colchester CO3 . . . . .135 C6
Great Cornard CO10 . . . . . .34 B7
Maldon & District
Agricultural & Domestic
Mus* CM9 . . . . . . . . . . .211 C7
Maldon District Mus*
CM9 . . . . . . . . . . . . . . . . .210 B2
Maldon Prim Sch
CM9 . . . . . . . . . . . . . . . . .210 A2
Maldon Rd
Birch Green CO2 . . . . . . . .160 E4
Bradwell Waterside
CM0 . . . . . . . . . . . . . . . . .214 F1
Colchester, Abbey Field
CO3 . . . . . . . . . . . . . . . . .135 D5
Colchester, Stanway Green
CO3 . . . . . . . . . . . . . . . . .134 D1
Danbury, Gay Bowers
CM3 . . . . . . . . . . . . . . . . .219 B5
Danbury, Runsell Green
CM3 . . . . . . . . . . . . . . . . .219 B7
Goldhanger CM9 . . . . . . . .211 E7
Great Baddow CM2 . . . . . .217 C2
Great Totham CM9 . . . . . .196 B4
Great Wigborough CO5 . . .181 E2
Hatfield Peverel CM3,
CM9 . . . . . . . . . . . . . . . . .194 D3
Kelvedon CO5 . . . . . . . . . .158 C1
Langford CM9 . . . . . . . . . .209 D6
Maldon CM9 . . . . . . . . . . .210 A1
Tiptree CO5 . . . . . . . . . . . .179 B3
Witham CM8 . . . . . . . . . . .195 A6
Woodham Mortimer
CM9 . . . . . . . . . . . . . . . . .219 E6
Maldon Way CO16 . . . . . . .188 B4
Malin Cl CM7 . . . . . . . . . . . . .9 D7
Mallard Cl
Great Cornard CO10 . . . . . .34 C5
Kelvedon CO5 . . . . . . . . . .158 C3
Layer de la H CO2 . . . . . . .162 A5
Tollesbury CM9 . . . . . . . . .199 D2
Mallard Ct
Bishop's Stortford
CM23 . . . . . . . . . . . . . . . .146 A6
Ipswich IP2 . . . . . . . . . . . . .16 F3
Mallard Rd CM2 . . . . . . . . .216 A5
Mallard Way
Great Cornard CO10 . . . . . .34 C5
Ipswich IP2 . . . . . . . . . . . . .16 E3
Mallowhayes Cl IP2 . . . . . . .17 B3
Mallows Field CO9 . . . . . . . .76 F2
MALLOWS GREEN . . . . . . . .92 D2
Mallows Green Rd
CM23 . . . . . . . . . . . . . . . . .92 D1
Mallow Wlk CB9 . . . . . . . . . .8 D8
Malmesbury Cl IP2 . . . . . . .17 A1
Maltese Rd CM1 . . . . . . . . .205 A4
Malthouse Rd CO11 . . . . . . .86 D4
Malthouse The CO10 . . . . . .15 B5
Malting Cotts CB9 . . . . . . . . .9 F4
Malting Farm La CO7 . . . . . .84 D2
MALTING GREEN . . . . . . . .162 B5
Malting Green Rd
CO2 . . . . . . . . . . . . . . . . . .162 A5
Malting La
Clare CO10 . . . . . . . . . . . . .12 B7
Kirby-le-S CO13 . . . . . . . . .143 C1
Malting Rd
Colchester CO2 . . . . . . . . .135 C1
Peldon CO5 . . . . . . . . . . . .182 E6
Maltings Cl CO8 . . . . . . . . . .55 E1
Maltings Ct CM8 . . . . . . . . .194 F8
Maltings La CM8 . . . . . . . . .194 F8
Maltings Rd
Brightlingsea CO7 . . . . . . .165 E1
Great Baddow CM2 . . . . . .217 A5
Maltings The
Cavendish CO10 . . . . . . . . . .1 D2
Great Dunmow CM6 . . . . .123 D1
Great Easton CM6 . . . . . . . .96 F2
Ramsey CO12 . . . . . . . . . .116 E8
Rayne CM77 . . . . . . . . . . .127 A2
Saffron Walden CB10 . . . . .22 D1
Thaxted CM6 . . . . . . . . . . . .70 A2
Maltings View CM7 . . . . . . .128 A3
Maltings Wharf CO11 . . . . . .86 D4
Malting Terr IP7 . . . . . . . . . .17 D4
Malting Yd CO7 . . . . . . . . . .164 B8
Maltings Park Rd
CO6 . . . . . . . . . . . . . . . . . .108 F2
Malvern Cl
Chelmsford CM1 . . . . . . . .204 D6
Ipswich IP3 . . . . . . . . . . . . .18 B4
Rushmere St A IP5 . . . . . . .18 F7
Malvern Way CO4 . . . . . . . .109 B7
Manchester Rd
Holland-on-S CO15 . . . . . .189 E6
Ipswich IP2 . . . . . . . . . . . . .16 D2
Mandeville Rd
Marks Tey CO6 . . . . . . . . .132 C3
Saffron Walden CB11 . . . . .43 D8
Mandeville Way
Chelmsford CM1 . . . . . . . .191 B3
Kirby Cross CO13 . . . . . . . .170 F6
Mandeville Wlk CM6 . . . . . .151 E6
Mandy Cl IP4 . . . . . . . . . . . .18 A6
Manfield **2** CO9 . . . . . . . .76 F2
Manfield Gdns CO16 . . . . .187 B5
Manning Rd IP11 . . . . . . . . .221 D3
Mannings Cl CB11 . . . . . . . .43 E7
Mannings La IP9 . . . . . . . . . .38 A2
Mannington Cl IP4 . . . . . . . .18 F5

MANNINGTREE
Manningtree Ct CO7 . . . . . 136 F4
Manningtree High Sch
CO11 . . . . . . . . . . . . . . . . 86 B3
Manningtree Mus*
CO11 . . . . . . . . . . . . . . . . 86 D4
Manningtree Rd
Brantham CO11 . . . . . . . . . 86 A8
Dedham CO7 . . . . . . . . . . . 85 B6
East Bergholt CO7 . . . . . . . 59 F1
Little Bentley CO7 . . . . . . 139 F8
Stutton IP9 . . . . . . . . . . . . 61 F2
Manningtree Sta CO11 . . . 86 A5
Manor Cl
Cavendish CO10 . . . . . . . . . 1 C2
Great Horkesley CO6 . . . . 109 C7
Manor Cres CM3 . . . . . . . 191 B5
Manor Dr CM2 . . . . . . . . . 216 F7
Manor Farm Cl CB9 . . . . . . 9 B6
Manor Fields Prim Sch
CM23 . . . . . . . . . . . . . . 145 D5
Manor Ho CM3 . . . . . . . . 219 A5
Manor House Way
CO7 . . . . . . . . . . . . . . . . 185 E8
Manor La
Great Chesterford CB10 . . . 3 D2
Harwich CO12 . . . . . . . . . . 91 B2
Stutton IP9 . . . . . . . . . . . . 61 E2
Manor Links CM23 . . . . . 146 C2
Manor Mews CO7 . . . . . . 185 E7
Manor Pl CM7 . . . . . . . . . 185 E7
Manor Pl CM7 . . . . . . . . . 128 A3
Manor Rd
Bishop's Stortford
CM23 . . . . . . . . . . . . . . 146 A7
Chelmsford CM2 . . . . . . . 205 C1
Colchester CO3 . . . . . . . . 135 E7
Felixstowe IP11 . . . . . . . 221 C1
Great Holland CO13 . . . . . 170 A3
Harwich CO12 . . . . . . . . . . 91 B3
Hatfield Peverel CM3 . . . 194 C1
Haverhill CB9 . . . . . . . . . . . 9 B7
Ipswich IP4 . . . . . . . . . . . . 17 D8
Little Easton CM6 . . . . . . 122 F5
Maldon CM9 . . . . . . . . . . 209 A4
Stansted Mountfitchet
CM24 . . . . . . . . . . . . . . 119 E5
Sudbury CO10 . . . . . . . . . . 15 E1
West Bergholt CO6 . . . . . 108 E5
Witham CM8 . . . . . . . . . . 177 A4
Wivenhoe CO7 . . . . . . . . . 137 C1
Woodham Walter CM9 . . 208 E5
Manors CM8 . . . . . . . . . . 156 D4
Manor St CM7 . . . . . . . . . 128 A3
Manors Way CM8 . . . . . . 156 C4
Manor Way CO15 . . . . . . 189 G6
Mansard Ct CO15 . . . . . . 189 C5
Mansbrook Blvd IP3 . . . . . 38 D7
Man's Cross . . . . . . . . . . . . 29 E2
Manse Chase CM9 . . . . . 210 A1
Manse Gdns CM6 . . . . . . 150 D8
Mansfield Twrs CO15 . . . 188 F2
Manston Dr CM23 . . . . . . 119 B1
MANUDEN . . . . . . . . . . . . 92 F2
Manuden Prim Sch
CM23 . . . . . . . . . . . . . . . 93 A2
Manwick Rd IP11 . . . . . . 221 D2
Maple Ave
Bishop's Stortford
CM23 . . . . . . . . . . . . . . 145 D8
Braintree CM7 . . . . . . . . 127 D2
Heybridge CM9 . . . . . . . . 210 C6
Maple Cl
Bishop's Stortford
CM23 . . . . . . . . . . . . . . 145 D8
Clacton-on-S CO15 . . . . . 188 C3
Halstead CO9 . . . . . . . . . . 77 A2
Harwich CO12 . . . . . . . . . . 91 B3
Ipswich IP2 . . . . . . . . . . . . 17 A3
Maple Dr
Chelmsford CM2 . . . . . . . 216 B6
Kirby Cross CO13 . . . . . . 170 C6
Witham CM8 . . . . . . . . . . 177 A5
MAPLE END . . . . . . . . . . . 45 D7
Maple Gr CM23 . . . . . . . 145 D8
Maple La CB10 . . . . . . . . . 45 C5
Maple Ho IP11 . . . . . . . . 221 C4
Maple Leaf CO5 . . . . . . . 179 C7
Maple Rd CO10 . . . . . . . . . 34 B5
Maple Spring CM23 . . . . 145 D8
Maplestead Ct CO9 . . . . . 53 D2
Maples The IP4 . . . . . . . . . 18 E8
Maple Way
Colchester CO2 . . . . . . . . 136 A4
Great Dunmow CM6 . . . . 123 B1
Maplin Ct CO15 . . . . . . . 189 D4
Marasca End CO2 . . . . . . 163 A7
Maraschino Cres CO2 . . 163 A7
Marbled White Dr IP8 . . . 36 E8
Marconi Rd CM1 . . . . . . . 205 B3
Marcus Cl
Colchester CO4 . . . . . . . . 110 B6
Haverhill CB9 . . . . . . . . . . . 9 D7
Marennes Cres CO7 . . . . 185 E7
Mareth Rd CO2 . . . . . . . . 135 C2
Margaret Rd CO1 . . . . . . 135 F8
Margaret St
Felixstowe IP11 . . . . . . . 221 C5
Thaxted CM6 . . . . . . . . . . 70 A3
Margaret Way CB10 . . . . . 22 D1
Margate Rd IP3 . . . . . . . . 18 C3
Margery Allingham Pl
CM9 . . . . . . . . . . . . . . . 198 D4

Margrave Gdns 4
CM23 . . . . . . . . . . . . . . 145 E5
Marguerite Way
CM23 . . . . . . . . . . . . . . 145 C6
Maria Cl CO2 . . . . . . . . . 136 C5
Maria St CO12 . . . . . . . . . 91 D5
Marigold Ave
Clacton-on-S CO16 . . . . . 188 C4
Ipswich IP2 . . . . . . . . . . . . 16 E3
Marigold Cl
Chelmsford CM1 . . . . . . . 205 F6
Colchester CO4 . . . . . . . . 136 E8
Marina Gdns
Clacton-on-S CO15 . . . . . 189 C5
Felixstowe IP11 . . . . . . . 221 C2
Marina Mews 1
CO14 . . . . . . . . . . . . . . . 171 C8
Marina Point CO15 . . . . . 188 D1
Marina Rd CM3 . . . . . . . . 194 A4
Marine Bldgs 14
CO14 . . . . . . . . . . . . . . . 171 C8
Marine Ct
Clacton-on-S CO15 . . . . . 188 E1
Frinton-on-S CO13 . . . . . 170 F4
Marine Par CO12 . . . . . . . 91 D3
Marine Par E CO15 . . . . . 189 B3
Marine Par W CO15 . . . . 188 E1
Mariners The CO12 . . . . . . 91 C3
Marion Ave CO15 . . . . . . 188 E6
Mario Way CO2 . . . . . . . . 135 F3
Maritime Ave CM9 . . . . . 210 E3
Maritime Ct 12 IP4 . . . . . . 17 D5
Market Cl CO1 . . . . . . . . . 135 E8
Market End CO6 . . . . . . . 130 F2
Market Field Sch
CO7 . . . . . . . . . . . . . . . . 138 A5
Market Gr CO9 . . . . . . . . . 30 A1
Market Hill
Clare CO10 . . . . . . . . . . . . 12 B7
Coggeshall CO6 . . . . . . . 131 A2
Halstead CO9 . . . . . . . . . . 76 E2
Haverhill CB9 . . . . . . . . . . . 9 A8
Maldon CM9 . . . . . . . . . . 210 A3
Saffron Walden CB10 . . . . 22 D2
Sudbury CO10 . . . . . . . . . . 33 E7
Market Hill Ct CM9 . . . . 210 A3
Market Pl
2 Braintree CM7 . . . . . . 127 F3
Great Dunmow CM6 . . . . 123 D1
1 Maldon CM9 . . . . . . . 209 F2
Saffron Walden CB10 . . . . 22 D2
Market Pl The CO16 . . . . 168 F7
Market Rd CM1 . . . . . . . . 205 B2
Market Row CB10 . . . . . . . 22 D1
Market Sq
6 Bishop's Stortford
CM23 . . . . . . . . . . . . . . 145 F7
13 Chelmsford CM1 . . . 205 B2
Market St
7 Bishop's Stortford
CM23 . . . . . . . . . . . . . . 145 F7
11 Braintree CM7 . . . . . 127 F3
Harwich CO12 . . . . . . . . . . 91 E6
Saffron Walden CB10 . . . . 22 D2
Market Wlk CB10 . . . . . . . 22 D1
Marking's Field CB10 . . . . 22 E2
Markland Cl CO2 . . . . . . . 216 C3
Markland Dr CM9 . . . . . . 209 E1
Marks Gdns CM7 . . . . . . 128 C3
Marks Hall Ctry Est*
CO6 . . . . . . . . . . . . . . . . 130 E6
Marks Hall Rd CO6 . . . . . 130 E6
MARKS TEY . . . . . . . . . . 133 A4
Marks Tey Sta CO6 . . . . . 133 A4
Marks Tey Sta CO6 . . . . . 133 A4
Markwells CM22 . . . . . . . . 94 D2
Marlborough Cl
Bishop's Stortford
CM23 . . . . . . . . . . . . . . 145 F5
Clacton-on-S CO15 . . . . . 188 C3
Marlborough Ct
Felixstowe IP11 . . . . . . . 221 D2
Haverhill CB9 . . . . . . . . . . . 8 E7
Marlborough Dr CO10 . . . 33 F8
Marlborough Rd
Braintree CM7 . . . . . . . . 128 A4
2 Chelmsford CM2 . . . . 205 A1
Ipswich IP4 . . . . . . . . . . . . 18 A6
Marlborough Terr
CM2 . . . . . . . . . . . . . . . 205 A1
Marlowe Cl CM7 . . . . . . . 155 A8
Marlowe Rd
Clacton-on-S CO15 . . . . . 203 G8
Jaywick CO15 . . . . . . . . . 188 A1
Marlowe Way CO3 . . . . . 134 F6
Marlpits Rd CM3, CM9 . . 219 E4
Marney Cl CM2 . . . . . . . . 216 E8
Marney Way CO13 . . . . . 171 B6
Marquis Cl CM7 . . . . . . . 155 B7
Marram Cl CO3 . . . . . . . . 134 B6
Marriages Yd CO1 . . . . . 136 B7
Marsden Ct CO3 . . . . . . . 134 E4
Marshall Cl CO5 . . . . . . . 158 D4
Marshalls Piece CM6 . . . 124 D6
Marshalls Rd CM7 . . . . . 127 E5
Marshbarns CM23 . . . . . 145 C8
Marsh Cres CO5 . . . . . . . 164 A8
Marsh Farm La CO7 . . . . 166 D3
Marsh Rd CO6, CO7 . . . . . 57 E6
Marsh Way CO7 . . . . . . . 185 E6
Marston Beck CM2 . . . . . 206 A2
Martello Cvn Pk
CO14 . . . . . . . . . . . . . . . 171 C8
Martello Rd 8 CO14 . . . . 171 C8
Marten's La CO7 . . . . . . . . 56 F8
Martens Mdw CM7 . . . . 128 B2
Martin End CO2 . . . . . . . 162 A5
Martinet Gn IP3 . . . . . . . . 18 C1

Martingale Dr CM1 . . . . . 205 F7
Martin Rd IP2 . . . . . . . . . . 17 C4
Martinsdale CO15 . . . . . . 188 F6
Martins Mews CB9 . . . . . . 8 C8
Martins Rise CO10 . . . . . . 15 C5
Marvens . . . . . . . . . . . . . 216 D3
Marvens The IP8 . . . . . . . . 16 A1
Maryborough Gr CO2 . . . 136 B2
Mary Frank Ho CO4 . . . . 136 C8
Mary La N CO7 . . . . . . . . 139 A8
Maryland Ct 1 CO2 . . . . 136 A1
Marylands CO13 . . . . . . . 170 E3
Mary La S CO7 . . . . . . . . 139 B6
Mary McArthur Pl
CM24 . . . . . . . . . . . . . . 119 E8
Maryon Rd IP3 . . . . . . . . . 18 B1
Mary Park Gdns
CM23 . . . . . . . . . . . . . . 145 F4
Marys Ho CO5 . . . . . . . . . 158 C2
Mary Warner Rd CO7 . . . 137 B8
Mascalls The CM2 . . . . . . 216 E8
Mascalls Way CM2 . . . . . 216 E8
Mascot Ct CO15 . . . . . . . 188 F5
Mascot Sq CO4 . . . . . . . . 136 D5
Masefield Dr CO3 . . . . . . 134 F6
Masefield Rd CM7 . . . . . 155 A8
Mashay Rd CO9 . . . . . . . . . 30 D5
Mashbury Rd CM3 . . . . . 190 B7
Mason Cl CO2 . . . . . . . . . 135 B3
Mason Rd
Clacton-on-S CO16 . . . . . 188 B3
Colchester CO1 . . . . . . . . 109 F1
Masons Cl IP4 . . . . . . . . . . 17 F6
Masons Ct
Bishop's Stortford
CM23 . . . . . . . . . . . . . . 145 F7
Stansted Mountfitchet
CM24 . . . . . . . . . . . . . . 119 D6
Massingham Dr CO6 . . . 105 A6
Masterlord Bsns Pk
IP3 . . . . . . . . . . . . . . . . . 18 E1
Masterman Wharf 12
CM23 . . . . . . . . . . . . . . 145 F7
Matchett Dr CO4 . . . . . . . 110 B6
Matching La CM23 . . . . . 145 A5
Matfield Cl CM1 . . . . . . . 205 D7
Mathams Dr CM23 . . . . . 145 D5
Mather Way IP2 . . . . . . . . 17 D4
Mathews Cl CO9 . . . . . . . . 77 A3
Matilda Way CM6 . . . . . . 151 E6
Matlock Cl 8 IP2 . . . . . . . 16 C2
Matson Rd IP1 . . . . . . . . . 16 F8
Matthews Cl CO7 . . . . . . . 58 C1
Maude St IP3 . . . . . . . . . . 17 F4
Maudlyn Rd CO1, CO4 . . 136 C6
Maurice Cl CB10 . . . . . . . . 45 B1
Maximus Dr CO4 . . . . . . . 110 B6
Mayberry Wlk CO2 . . . . . 136 A3
Maybury Cl CO6 . . . . . . . 132 F3
Maybury Rd IP3 . . . . . . . . 18 B4
Mayda Cl CO9 . . . . . . . . . . 76 D1
Mayes Cl CM23 . . . . . . . 146 D8
Mayes La
Chelmsford CM2 . . . . . . . 217 E5
Danbury CM3 . . . . . . . . . 218 E6
Harwich CO12 . . . . . . . . . . 90 C1
Mayes Rd CM6 . . . . . . . . . 97 A6
Mayfair Ct CO15 . . . . . . . 188 F3
Mayfield Cl CO4 . . . . . . . 110 C2
Mayfield Pk CM23 . . . . . 145 D3
Mayfield Rd
Ipswich IP4 . . . . . . . . . . . . 18 C7
Writtle CM1 . . . . . . . . . . 204 A2
Mayflower Ave CO12 . . . . 91 E5
Mayflower Cl CO3 . . . . . . 134 D6
Mayflower Gdns
CM23 . . . . . . . . . . . . . . 145 B6
Mayflower Ho CO12 . . . . . 91 D6
Mayflower Prim Sch The
CO12 . . . . . . . . . . . . . . . 91 B4
Mayflower Way CO10 . . . 15 F2
Mayfly Cl IP8 . . . . . . . . . . . 36 E8
Mayford Way CO16 . . . . . 188 B6
Mayland Cl CM9 . . . . . . . 210 D4
Mayland Cl CM8 . . . . . . . 177 A2
Maylands Dr CM7 . . . . . . 154 D8
Maynard Cl CM6 . . . . . . . 123 D1
Maynards Villas CM6 . . . 123 D1
Mayne Crest CM1 . . . . . . 205 E6
Maypole Cl CB11 . . . . . . . 43 C7
Maypole Dr CO16 . . . . . . 187 B4
MAYPOLE GREEN . . . . . 135 D1
Maypole Green Rd
CO2 . . . . . . . . . . . . . . . 135 C1
Maypole Rd
Tiptree CO5 . . . . . . . . . . 179 C6
Wickham Bishops CM8,
CO9 . . . . . . . . . . . . . . . 195 F2
Maypole Terr CB9 . . . . . . . 9 A7
Maypole The CM6 . . . . . . 69 F3
May Rd IP3 . . . . . . . . . . . . 18 C4
Mays Ct IP11 . . . . . . . . . . 221 D3
Maysent Ave CM7 . . . . . 127 F5
May's La CO7 . . . . . . . . . . 84 E4
May Wlk
Chelmsford CM2 . . . . . . . 216 C7
Elsenham CM24 . . . . . . . . 94 A1
Maze Green Hts
CM23 . . . . . . . . . . . . . . 145 C7
Maze Green Rd CM23 . . 145 B7
Mazers Ct 14 CM7 . . . . . 127 F2
Mazoe Cl CM23 . . . . . . . 145 F5
Mazoe Rd CM23 . . . . . . . 145 F5
Meachen Rd CO2 . . . . . . 136 C5

Mead Ct
Clacton-on-S CO15 . . . . . 188 E3
Stansted Mountfitchet
CM24 . . . . . . . . . . . . . . 119 D7
Meadgate Ave CM2 . . . . 216 D8
Meadgate Prim Sch
CM2 . . . . . . . . . . . . . . . 216 E8
Meadgate Terr CM2 . . . . 216 D8
Meadowbrook Ct
CO1 . . . . . . . . . . . . . . . 136 B7
Meadow Brown Ct
CM7 . . . . . . . . . . . . . . . 127 E1
Meadow Cl
Chelmondiston IP9 . . . . . . 63 F7
Clacton-on-S CO15 . . . . . 189 B7
Elmstead Market CO7 . . . 137 F6
Great Bromley CO7 . . . . . 139 A6
Halstead CO9 . . . . . . . . . 103 F8
Panfield CM7 . . . . . . . . . 127 A7
Meadow Cres IP3 . . . . . . . 18 F1
Meadowcroft CM24 . . . . 119 E7
Meadowcroft Way
CO13 . . . . . . . . . . . . . . 170 F7
MEADOWEND . . . . . . . . . 29 C5
Meadowford CB11 . . . . . . 42 F1
Meadow Grass Cl
CO3 . . . . . . . . . . . . . . . 134 B6
Meadow La
Sudbury CO10 . . . . . . . . . 33 E7
West Mersea CO5 . . . . . . 201 C5
Meadowlands CM23 . . . 119 A2
Meadow Pk CM7 . . . . . . 154 E8
Meadow Pl CO10 . . . . . . . 33 E6
Meadow Rd
Colchester CO2 . . . . . . . . 135 D1
Great Chesterford CB10 . . . 3 D3
Meadowside
Braintree CM7 . . . . . . . . 127 E5
Chelmsford CM2 . . . . . . . 205 C3
Meadow Side CM1 . . . . . 205 B3
Meadowside CM3 . . . . . . 192 E1
Meadows The
Bishop's Stortford
CM23 . . . . . . . . . . . . . . 145 E5
3 Chelmsford CM2 . . . . 205 C2
Meadowsweet Cl
CM23 . . . . . . . . . . . . . . 145 C6
Meadowvale Cl IP4 . . . . . 17 F7
Meadow View
Bicknacre CM3 . . . . . . . . 218 E1
Great Bardfield CM7 . . . . . 72 B2
Kirby-le-S CO13 . . . . . . . 143 D1
St Osyth CO16 . . . . . . . . 187 B4
Tiptree CO5 . . . . . . . . . . 179 B5
Meadow View Cl CO3 . . 134 E5
Meadow View Rd
CO10 . . . . . . . . . . . . . . . 33 D5
Meadow Way
Abberton CO5 . . . . . . . . . 163 B2
Black Notley CM77 . . . . . 155 C5
Clacton-on-S CO15 . . . . . 203 G7
Meadow Wlk 5 CM2 . . . 205 C2
Mead Pastures CM9 . . . . 208 D3
Mead Path CM2 . . . . . . . 215 F8
Meadside CM7 . . . . . . . . . 73 B3
Meads The
Chelmsford CM2 . . . . . . . 205 A1
Stansted Mountfitchet
CM24 . . . . . . . . . . . . . . 119 F6
Wicken Bonhunt CB11 . . . 66 A7
Mead The
Bishop's Stortford CM23 . 185 F8
Great Cornard CO10 . . . . . 34 B4
Great Dunmow CM6 . . . . 123 C2
Thaxted CM6 . . . . . . . . . . 70 A3
Meadway
Gosfield CO9 . . . . . . . . . 102 E8
Lawford CO11 . . . . . . . . . . 86 B3
Maldon CM9 . . . . . . . . . . 210 B1
Meard CM23 . . . . . . . . . . 119 A2
Meares Pl 3 CM2 . . . . . . 205 F4
Mede Way CO7 . . . . . . . . 137 C3
Medina Bsns Ctr CB11 . . . 22 F1
Medlar Cl CM4 . . . . . . . . 177 A4
Medley Rd CM77 . . . . . . 126 F2
Medusa Ct
Harwich CO12 . . . . . . . . . . 91 B2
Holland-on-S CO15 . . . . . 189 E5
Medway Ave CM8 . . . . . . 176 D2
Medway Cl CM1 . . . . . . . 204 D4
Medway Rd IP3 . . . . . . . . 17 F2
Meekings Rd CO10 . . . . . 34 B8
Meers The CO13 . . . . . . . 170 E6
MEESDEN . . . . . . . . . . . . 64 A6
Meeson Mdws CM9 . . . . 220 E8
Meeting Field CO10 . . . . . 15 C7
Meeting La
East Mersea CO5 . . . . . . 184 C1
Ridgewell CO9 . . . . . . . . . 29 B7
Meeting Wlk CB9 . . . . . . . 9 A5
Meggy Tye CM2 . . . . . . . 206 B5
Megs Way CM7 . . . . . . . 128 B2
Melba Ct CM1 . . . . . . . . . 204 E1
Melbourne Chase
CO2 . . . . . . . . . . . . . . . 136 B1
Melbourne Par CM1 . . . . 204 F4
Melbourne Park Prim Sch
CM1 . . . . . . . . . . . . . . . 204 F6
Melbourne Rd
Clacton-on-S CO15 . . . . . 188 E4
Ipswich IP2 . . . . . . . . . . . . 17 D7
Melford Cl IP4 . . . . . . . . . 18 F1
Melford Ct CM77 . . . . . . 154 B7
Melford Rd
Cavendish CO10 . . . . . . . . 1 E2

Melford Rd continued
Sudbury CO10 . . . . . . . . . 15 D2
Melford Way IP11 . . . . . . 221 A3
Mellings CO6 . . . . . . . . . 130 F3
Mellis Ct IP11 . . . . . . . . . 221 B5
Mellor Chase CO3 . . . . . 134 E7
Mell Rd CM9 . . . . . . . . . 199 E1
Melplash Cl IP3 . . . . . . . . 18 E4
Melplash Rd IP3 . . . . . . . . 18 E4
Melrose Gdns
Clacton-on-S CO15 . . . . . 189 C5
Ipswich IP1 . . . . . . . . . . . . 18 B8
Melrose Rd CO5 . . . . . . . 201 C6
Melso Cl CO10 . . . . . . . . . 34 A5
Melton Cl CO16 . . . . . . . 188 A4
Melville Rd IP4 . . . . . . . . . 17 F5
Memnon Ct CO2 . . . . . . 135 F3
Menai Ct IP1 . . . . . . . . . . 17 B2
Mendip Dr IP5 . . . . . . . . . 18 F6
Mendip Rd CM1 . . . . . . . 204 D6
Mendlesham Cl CO16 . . 188 B4
Menin Rd CO2 . . . . . . . . 135 D4
Menish Way CM2 . . . . . . 206 A3
Meon Cl CM1 . . . . . . . . . 205 C6
Meopham Ct CO2 . . . . . . 136 C2
Mercantile Ho 1 CO1 . . 135 E6
Mercers Ave CM23 . . . . . 145 C4
Mercers Row CO10 . . . . . 22 D1
Mercers Way 2 CO1 . . . 135 E8
Mercia Cl CM2 . . . . . . . . 217 A5
Mercia Rd CO3 . . . . . . . . 135 A3
Mercury Pl CM9 . . . . . . . 209 F5
Merdle Sq CM1 . . . . . . . 204 F6
Meredith Rd CO15 . . . . . 188 E3
Merediths Cl CO7 . . . . . . 164 B8
Mere Gdns IP4 . . . . . . . . . 18 F4
Meriden Ct CO15 . . . . . . 189 A5
Merivale Cl CO11 . . . . . . . 86 C3
Merivale Rd CO11 . . . . . . 86 B3
Merlin Ct IP2 . . . . . . . . . . 17 B4
Merlin End CO4 . . . . . . . 110 F1
Merlin Pl CM2 . . . . . . . . 204 F5
Merlin Rd IP2 . . . . . . . . . . 16 C3
Merriam Cl CO11 . . . . . . . 86 D8
Merrielees Ct CO15 . . . . 189 D6
Merrill Hts IP2 . . . . . . . . . 17 C3
Merrill Rd 2 CM23 . . . . . 145 E5
Merrion Cl 7 IP2 . . . . . . . 16 C2
Merrymount Gdns
CO15 . . . . . . . . . . . . . . 189 B5
Mersea Ave CO5 . . . . . . . 201 B6
Mersea Ct CO5 . . . . . . . . 201 B7
Mersea Fleet Way
CM7 . . . . . . . . . . . . . . . 128 C1
Mersea Island Mus*
CO5 . . . . . . . . . . . . . . . 201 B6
Mersea Island Sch
CO5 . . . . . . . . . . . . . . . 201 C6
Mersea Island Vineyard*
CO5 . . . . . . . . . . . . . . . 201 H8
Mersea Point Nature
Reserve* CO5 . . . . . . . 185 C3
Mersea Rd
Abberton CO2, CO5 . . . . 163 B5
Colchester CO2 . . . . . . . . 136 A3
Peldon CO5 . . . . . . . . . . 182 F5
Mersea View CO16 . . . . . 186 A3
Mersey Rd
Ipswich IP3 . . . . . . . . . . . . 17 F2
Witham CM8 . . . . . . . . . . 176 E2
Mersey Way CM1 . . . . . . 204 C5
Merstham Dr CO16 . . . . . 188 C6
Merton Ct CO2 . . . . . . . . 163 A7
Merton Pl CB11 . . . . . . . . 21 E4
Messines Rd CO2 . . . . . . 135 D5
MESSING . . . . . . . . . . . . 159 D3
Messing-cum-Inworth
Prim Sch CO5 . . . . . . . 159 C2
Messing Gn CO5 . . . . . . 159 D2
Meteor Way CM1 . . . . . . 204 F2
Mews Ct CM2 . . . . . . . . . 205 B1
Mews The
Bishop's Stortford
CM22 . . . . . . . . . . . . . . 146 A3
Felixstowe IP11 . . . . . . . 221 E4
Felixstowe IP11 . . . . . . . 221 F4
Frinton-on-S CO13 . . . . . 171 A3
Harwich CO12 . . . . . . . . . . 91 C3
Panfield CM7 . . . . . . . . . 126 A7
Stansted Mountfitchet
CM24 . . . . . . . . . . . . . . 119 F7
Meyrick Cres CO2 . . . . . . 135 F5
Micawber Way CM1 . . . . 204 D7
Michaels Rd CM23 . . . . . 119 B2
Michaelstowe Cl CO12 . . . 90 F2
Michaelstowe Dr CO12 . . 90 C2
Mickfield Mews IP11 . . . 221 B5
Micklegate Rd IP11 . . . . 221 C2
Middleborough CO1 . . . . 135 E8
Middlefield CO9 . . . . . . . . 76 F1
Middlefield Rd CO11 . . . . 87 A3
Middle Gn CO6 . . . . . . . . 106 A8
Middle King CM7 . . . . . . 128 D1
Middle Mill Rd CO1 . . . . 135 F6
Middle Row 5 CM3 . . . . 145 F6
Middleside Cvn Pk
CM24 . . . . . . . . . . . . . . 120 A4
Middle St CB11 . . . . . . . . 65 C4
MIDDLETON . . . . . . . . . . 33 E4
Middleton Cl
Clacton-on-S CO16 . . . . . 188 D6
Ipswich IP2 . . . . . . . . . . . . 16 D2
Middleton Rd CO10 . . . . . 33 D5
Middle Way CO15 . . . . . . 188 D8
MIDDLEWICK . . . . . . . . . 136 B2

**Middlewick Cl 4**
CO2 . . . . . . . . . . . . . . . 136 A1
**Midguard Way** CM9 . . . . . . 220 F8
**Midland Cl** CO2 . . . . . . . .135 F4
**Midland Ho** CO12 . . . . . . . .91 C4
**Midway** CO15 . . . . . . . . . .203 E6
**Midway Rd** CO2 . . . . . . . . 135 C2
**Milbank** CM2 . . . . . . . . . .206 B4
**Milburn Cres** CM1 . . . . . . 204 D1
**MILCH HILL** . . . . . . . . . . .153 E5
**Milch La** CM7 . . . . . . . . . .153 E6
**Mildenhall Pl** 1 CB9 . . . . . .9 B8
**Milden Rd** IP2 . . . . . . . . . . .16 E5
**Mildmay Cl** CM6 . . . . . . . .151 E7
**Mildmay Ct** 2 CM2 . . . . . .205 B1
**Mildmay Inf Sch** CM2 . . . .216 B5
**Mildmay Jun Sch**
CM2 . . . . . . . . . . . . . . . .216 B5
**Mildmay Rd**
Chelmsford CM2 . . . . . . .205 B1
Ipswich IP3 . . . . . . . . . . . .18 B1
**Mildmays** CM3 . . . . . . . . 218 C7
**MILE END** . . . . . . . . . . . .109 E3
**Mile End Rd** CO4 . . . . . . .109 E3
**Miles Cl** CO3 . . . . . . . . . .134 C6
**Milestones The** CM3 . . . . 194 A4
**Milford Cl** CO7 . . . . . . . . .137 D1
**Military Ct** 10 CO1 . . . . . .136 A6
**Military Rd** CO1 . . . . . . . .136 A5
**Military Way** CO12 . . . . . . .90 C1
**Mill Apartments The**
CO1 . . . . . . . . . . . . . . . .136 B7
**Millars The** CM1 . . . . . . . 191 A3
**Millbridge Rd** CM8 . . . . . .176 F2
**Mill Chase**
Halstead CO9 . . . . . . . . . .76 F2
Steeple Bumpstead CB9 . . .27 C5
**Mill Cl**
Elsenham CM22 . . . . . . . . .94 C1
Felixstowe IP11 . . . . . . . . .221 B4
Great Bardfield CM7 . . . . . .72 B2
Harwich CO12 . . . . . . . . . .91 C4
Tiptree CO5 . . . . . . . . . . . .179 C6
**Mill Cotts** CM2 . . . . . . . . .217 C8
**Millcroft** CM23 . . . . . . . . 119 A1
**Millcroft Mews** CO5 . . . . . .201 C7
**Mill Cswy** SG8 . . . . . . . . . .19 C5
**Mill Ct**
Braintree CM7 . . . . . . . . .128 B2
St Osyth CO16 . . . . . . . . .186 F4
Takeley CM6 . . . . . . . . . .149 B7
**Milldene Prim Sch**
CO5 . . . . . . . . . . . . . . . .179 D6
**MILL END** . . . . . . . . . . . .123 B4
**Mill End** CM6 . . . . . . . . . . .70 A2
**MILLEND GREEN** . . . . . . . .97 B1
**Millennium Way** CM7 . . . . 155 D8
**Miller's Barn Rd**
CO15 . . . . . . . . . . . . . . . 188 A1
**Millers Cl**
Bishop's Stortford
CM23 . . . . . . . . . . . . . 145 C5
Braintree CM7 . . . . . . . . .128 A8
Colchester CO3 . . . . . . . .134 C6
Great Horkesley CO6 . . . . .109 B7
**Miller's Cl** CM6 . . . . . . . . .151 A4
**Millers Croft**
Great Baddow CM2 . . . . . .216 F6
Great Dunmow CM6 . . . . .123 E1
**Millers Dr** CM7 . . . . . . . . 154 C7
**Millers La** CO3 . . . . . . . . .134 D6
**Millers Mead** CO5 . . . . . . 158 E4
**Millers Reach** CO11 . . . . . .87 A4
**Millers Row** CM7 . . . . . . . .48 C6
**Millers View** IP1 . . . . . . . . .16 F7
**Mill Field**
Barnston CM6 . . . . . . . . .151 A4
Chelmondiston IP9 . . . . . . .63 E8
**Millfield Gdns** IP4 . . . . . . . .18 A6
**Millfields**
Danbury CM3 . . . . . . . . 219 A6
Stansted Mountfitchet
CM24 . . . . . . . . . . . . . 119 C6
Tiptree CO5 . . . . . . . . . .179 C6
Writtle CM1 . . . . . . . . . .204 A1
**Millfields Prim Sch**
CO7 . . . . . . . . . . . . . . . 137 D1
**Millfields Way** CB9 . . . . . . . .9 B8
**MILL GREEN**
Haverhill . . . . . . . . . . . . . .7 D7
Little Bentley . . . . . . . . . 140 A8
**Mill Hill**
Braintree CM7 . . . . . . . . .128 B2
Chelmsford CM2 . . . . . . .215 F2
Farnham CM23 . . . . . . . . 118 E5
Harwich CO12 . . . . . . . . . .91 C3
Haverhill CB9 . . . . . . . . . . .9 A7
Lawford CO11 . . . . . . . . . .85 D4
Manningtree CO11 . . . . . . .86 C4
Purleigh CM3 . . . . . . . . . 220 C1
Stansted Mountfitchet
CM24 . . . . . . . . . . . . . 119 C6
Sudbury CO10 . . . . . . . . . .33 D7
Wormingford CO6 . . . . . . .80 E6
**Mill House Cotts**
CO12 . . . . . . . . . . . . . . . 116 B7
**Millhouse Villas** CM6 . . . . 151 A4
**Milligans Chase** CM2 . . . . 216 B1
**Milliners Way** CM23 . . . . . 145 C4
**Mill La**
Ardleigh CO7 . . . . . . . . . .112 B4
Birch CO2 . . . . . . . . . . . .161 A3
Bradfield CO11 . . . . . . . . . .87 D2
Brent Pelham SG9 . . . . . . .64 A5

**Mill La** _continued_
Broomfield CM1 . . . . . . . . 191 C1
Chelmondiston IP9 . . . . . . .13 B8
Clavering CB11 . . . . . . . . . .65 B6
Coggeshall CO5 . . . . . . . . .131 F1
Colne Engaine CO6 . . . . . .105 B8
Cressing CM77 . . . . . . . . .155 D5
Danbury CM3 . . . . . . . . . 219 A6
Dedham CO7 . . . . . . . . . . .84 F7
Felixstowe IP11 . . . . . . . .221 C4
Finchingfield CM7 . . . . . . . .48 F3
Ford End CM3 . . . . . . . . .172 D7
Great Dunmow CM6 . . . . .123 D1
Great Holland CO13 . . . . . .169 E3
Great Leighs CM3 . . . . . . .174 B7
Great Leighs CM7 . . . . . . .154 C1
Great Maplestead CO9 . . . . .76 E8
Great Yeldham CO9 . . . . . . .30 A3
Harwich CO12 . . . . . . . . . .91 D3
Hinxton CB10 . . . . . . . . . . .3 A7
Ickleton CB10 . . . . . . . . . . .3 B4
Layer de la H CO2 . . . . . . .162 B5
Little Baddow CM3 . . . . . .207 E3
Littlebury CB11 . . . . . . . . . .21 F4
Maldon CM9 . . . . . . . . . . 210 A3
Manningtree CO11 . . . . . . .86 D4
Pebmarsh CO9 . . . . . . . . . .78 A7
Purleigh CM3 . . . . . . . . . 220 C1
Rayne CM7 . . . . . . . . . . .153 E8
Saffron Walden CB10 . . . . . .22 F2
Salcott-c-V CM9 . . . . . . . .199 B8
Stebbing CM6 . . . . . . . . . .124 E5
Stoke-by-N CO6 . . . . . . . . .56 D7
Sudbury CO10 . . . . . . . . . .33 D7
Terling CM3 . . . . . . . . . . .175 A3
Thorpe-le-S CO16 . . . . . . . .57 C4
Thorington St CO6 . . . . . . .57 C4
Tollesbury CM9 . . . . . . . . .141 F1
Tolleshunt Major CM9 . . . .197 E3
Walton-on-t-N CO14 . . . . . .171 C8
Washbrook IP8 . . . . . . . . . .16 A1
Weeley Heath CO16 . . . . . .168 A6
Witham CM8 . . . . . . . . . . .176 F1
**Mill Lane Cl** CO16 . . . . . . .168 A6
**Mill on the Gn** CO7 . . . . . .166 E8
**Mill Park Dr** CM7 . . . . . . .128 B1
**Mill Rd**
Birdbrook CO9 . . . . . . . . . .10 E2
Boxted CO4 . . . . . . . . . . . .82 F4
Clare CO10 . . . . . . . . . . . .12 C7
Colchester CO4 . . . . . . . . .109 F4
Debden CB11 . . . . . . . . . . .68 B8
East Bergholt CO7 . . . . . . . .59 E2
Elder Street CB10 . . . . . . . .45 B3
Fingringhoe CO5 . . . . . . . .152 A4
Finchingfield CM7 . . . . . . . .72 D8
Fordham CO6 . . . . . . . . . .107 D4
Foxearth CO10 . . . . . . . . . .14 C5
Great Bardfield CM7 . . . . . .72 B2
Great Totham CM9 . . . . . .196 D7
Haverhill CB9 . . . . . . . . . . .9 A7
Helions Bumpstead CB9 . . . .26 D8
Henham CM22 . . . . . . . . . .94 E4
Maldon CM9 . . . . . . . . . . 210 B2
Marks Tey CO6 . . . . . . . . .133 C4
North End CM6 . . . . . . . . .151 F2
Ridgewell CO9 . . . . . . . . . .29 B6
Stambourne CO9 . . . . . . . .28 C3
West Mersea CO5 . . . . . . .201 D7
**Mill Rise** IP9 . . . . . . . . . . .62 D5
**Mill Road Cotts** CB10 . . . . .45 B3
**Mill Road Dr** IP3 . . . . . . . . .18 E2
**Mill Side** CM24 . . . . . . . . .119 E6
**Millside Ind Est** CM23 . . . .146 A5
**Mills La** CO15 . . . . . . . . . . .15 C4
**Maldon Bank** CM2 . . . . . . .206 A4
**Mills Rd** CO10 . . . . . . . . . . .34 A8
**Mill St**
Bishop's Stortford
CM23 . . . . . . . . . . . . . 146 A5
Brightlingsea CO7 . . . . . . .186 A6
Colchester CO1 . . . . . . . . .136 A6
Nayland CO6 . . . . . . . . . . .56 B1
Stoke-by-N CO6 . . . . . . . . .56 D8
St Osyth CO16 . . . . . . . . .186 F4
**Mills The** IP4 . . . . . . . . . . .18 E8
**MILL STREET** . . . . . . . . . . .56 D7
**Mill Tye** CO10 . . . . . . . . . . .34 A4
**Mill Vale** Lo CM8 . . . . . . . .176 F2
**Mill View**
Bradwell CM77 . . . . . . . . .129 D3
Great Chesterford CB10 . . . . .3 D2
**Mill Vue Rd** CM2 . . . . . . . .205 F2
**Millways** CM9 . . . . . . . . . .196 B4
**Mill Wlk** CO5 . . . . . . . . . . .179 C6
**Millwrights** CO5 . . . . . . . .179 C6
**Milner Rd** CO15 . . . . . . . . .188 C2
**Milner St** IP4 . . . . . . . . . . .17 E5
**Milnrow** IP2 . . . . . . . . . . . .16 C2
**Milton Ave** CM7 . . . . . . . . .155 A8
**Milton Cl** CO3 . . . . . . . . . .134 F6
**Milton Ct** CO15 . . . . . . . . .189 E6
**Milton Pl** CM1 . . . . . . . . . .205 A5
**Milton Rd**
Harwich CO12 . . . . . . . . . .91 D4
Lawford CO11 . . . . . . . . . .86 D4
Witham CM8 . . . . . . . . . . .176 F5
**Milton St** IP4 . . . . . . . . . . .18 B6
**Mimosa Cl** CM1 . . . . . . . . .205 F6
**Mimosa Ct** CO4 . . . . . . . . .136 E8
**Minden Rd** CO10 . . . . . . . . .33 F7
**Minerva Cl**
Harwich CO12 . . . . . . . . . .90 F1
Haverhill CB9 . . . . . . . . . . .9 D6
**Minerva Rd** CO2 . . . . . . . .135 C1
**MINNOW END** . . . . . . . . . .174 A8
**Minos Way** IP1 . . . . . . . . . .16 D8
**Minsmere Dr** CO16 . . . . . . 188 C6

**Minsmere Rd** IP3 . . . . . . . .38 D8
**Minsmere Way** CO10 . . . . . .34 C6
**Minster Way** CM9 . . . . . . .220 E8
**Minters Cotts** CO11 . . . . . . 115 C5
**Miranda Wlk** CO4 . . . . . . .136 E7
**Mirosa Dr** CM9 . . . . . . . . .210 B1
**Mission La** CO7 . . . . . . . . . .60 B3
**MISTLEY** . . . . . . . . . . . . . .86 F4
**MISTLEY HEATH** . . . . . . . .87 B2
**Mistley Norman CE Prim**
Sch CO11 . . . . . . . . . . . . .87 A4
**Mistley Place Pk** * . . . . . . . .
CO11 . . . . . . . . . . . . . . . .86 E4
**Mistley Sta** CO11 . . . . . . . . .86 F4
**Mistley Twrs** * CO11 . . . . . . .86 F5
**Mitchell Ave** CO9 . . . . . . . .76 E1
**Mitchell Circ** CM7 . . . . . . . .73 C6
**Mitre Gdns** CM23 . . . . . . .146 A4
**Mitre Way** IP3 . . . . . . . . . . .17 F4
**Mitton Vale** CM2 . . . . . . . .205 F2
**Moat Farm** CO9 . . . . . . . . .28 B7
**Moat Farm Chase**
CM8 . . . . . . . . . . . . . . . .176 F3
**Moat Farm La** IP4 . . . . . . . .17 F8
**Moat Fields** CO6 . . . . . . . .107 D6
**Moat La** CO8 . . . . . . . . . . . .55 A4
**Moat Rd**
Birdbrook CO9 . . . . . . . . . .28 C7
Fordham CO6 . . . . . . . . . .107 D6
**Moat Wlk** CB9 . . . . . . . . . . .8 E8
**Modlen Rd** CO14 . . . . . . . .171 B7
**Moffat Ave** IP4 . . . . . . . . . .18 B8
**Mole Hall La** CB11 . . . . . . . .67 F3
**Mole Hall Wildlife Pk** *
CB11 . . . . . . . . . . . . . . . .67 D6
**MOLEHILL GREEN**
Elsenham . . . . . . . . . . . . 121 D6
Great Notley . . . . . . . . . . 153 C4
**Molehill Green Cotts**
CM22 . . . . . . . . . . . . . . . 121 C5
**Molehill Green Rdbt**
CM22 . . . . . . . . . . . . . . . 121 C5
**Molrams La** CM2 . . . . . . . .217 B6
**Monarch Cl** CB9 . . . . . . . . . .8 C8
**Monarch Way** IP8 . . . . . . . .36 D8
**Monkdowns Rd** CO6 . . . . . .105 B7
**Monken Hadley** CM7 . . . . .128 B8
**Monklands** 2 2 CO9 . . . . . .76 D1
**Monk's Cnr** CB10 . . . . . . . . .47 B4
**Monks Ct** CM8 . . . . . . . . . .176 E3
**Monks Gate** IP8 . . . . . . . . .16 A6
**Monks Hill** CB11 . . . . . . . . .43 F8
**Monk's La** CO7 . . . . . . . . . .84 D4
**Monks Lodge Rd** CO9 . . . . .52 D2
**Monks Mead** CM3 . . . . . . .218 F2
**Monks Rd** CO8 . . . . . . . . . .105 B7
**MONK STREET** . . . . . . . . . .97 B6
**Monks Wlk** CM7 . . . . . . . . .213 E8
**Monkswood Dr** CM23 . . . . .145 D6
**Monkwick Ave** CO2 . . . . . .135 F1
**Monkwick Jun & Inf Schs**
CO2 . . . . . . . . . . . . . . . .136 A2
**Monmouth Cl** IP2 . . . . . . . . .17 B1
**Mons Rd** CO2 . . . . . . . . . . .135 E5
**Montague Rd** IP11 . . . . . . .221 F4
**Montagu Gdns** CM1 . . . . . .205 F7
**Montbretia Cl** CO3 . . . . . . .134 D6
**Montbretia Ct** CO16 . . . . . .188 C4
**Montfort Ct** 8 CM7 . . . . . . . .8 F7
**Montgomery Cl**
Chelmsford CM1 . . . . . . .205 E7
Colchester CO2 . . . . . . . .136 B4
**Montgomery Ave** and Inf
Schs CO2 . . . . . . . . . . . .135 D2
**Montgomery Rd** IP2 . . . . . . .17 B1
**Monton Rise** IP2 . . . . . . . . .16 D2
**Montrose Ct** IP3 . . . . . . . . .17 F4
**Montrose Rd** CM2 . . . . . . . .206 A4
**Moonhall Bsns Pk** CB9 . . . . . .9 A5
**Moon Hall La** CB9 . . . . . . . . .9 A6
**Moorfield Ct** CM8 . . . . . . . .176 F1
**Moor Hall La**
Bishop's Stortford
CM23 . . . . . . . . . . . . . 145 C3
Bishop's Stortford, Thorley
CM23 . . . . . . . . . . . . . 145 B3
Danbury CM3 . . . . . . . . . 218 E2
**Moorhouse Gn** CO7 . . . . . . 111 E8
**Moorside** CO3 . . . . . . . . . .136 B7
**Moors La**
Little Dunmow CM6 . . . . . .151 D7
Rayne CM77 . . . . . . . . . . .126 D3
**Moor's La** CO7 . . . . . . . . . .139 E1
**Moors The** CM6 . . . . . . . . .151 D7
**Mope La** CM8 . . . . . . . . . .195 D6
**Moorcroft** CM7 . . . . . . . . . .128 D3
**Moor's Farm Chase**
CM6 . . . . . . . . . . . . . . . .197 A3
**Mooring Cl** CM9 . . . . . . . . .220 E8
**Morant Rd** CO1 . . . . . . . . .136 B5
**Morebarn Rd** CO7 . . . . . . . .112 E2
**Morecombe Ct** CM7 . . . . . . .18 A7
**Morella Cl** CO4 . . . . . . . . . .166 E8
**Morello Ct** CM7 . . . . . . . . .163 A7
**Moretons** CM2 . . . . . . . . . .216 B2
**Morland Ct** CO6 . . . . . . . . . .82 B1
**Morland Prim Sch** IP3 . . . . .38 A8
**Morland Rd** IP3 . . . . . . . . . .37 F8
**Morley Rd**
Halstead CO9 . . . . . . . . . .76 F2

**Morley Rd** _continued_
Tiptree CO5 . . . . . . . . . . .179 D4
**Morleys Rd** CO6 . . . . . . . . .105 A6
**Mornington Ave** 2
IP1 . . . . . . . . . . . . . . . . .17 A8
**Morris Ave** CO15 . . . . . . . .203 E6
**MORRIS GREEN** . . . . . . . . .74 C8
**Morris Harp** CB10 . . . . . . . .22 E3
**Morrison Dr** CM8 . . . . . . . .194 F7
**Morris Rd** CM2 . . . . . . . . .205 D2
**Morrow La** CO7 . . . . . . . . .112 A6
**Mors End** CO7 . . . . . . . . . . .58 D2
**Morses La** CO7 . . . . . . . . .165 F1
**Morten Rd** CO1 . . . . . . . . .135 E8
**Mortimer Gdns** CO4 . . . . . .110 B6
**Mortimer Rd** CM3 . . . . . . .194 A4
**Mortimer Way** CM8 . . . . . .194 F7
**Morton Rd** CM9 . . . . . . . . .196 A4
**Morton Way** CO9 . . . . . . . . .77 A3
**Mossfield Cl** CO3 . . . . . . . .135 C6
**Moss Path** CM2 . . . . . . . . .216 C3
**Moss Rd**
Colchester CO3 . . . . . . . .134 E4
Witham CM8 . . . . . . . . . .177 B3
**Moss Way** CO6 . . . . . . . . . .108 E3
**Moss Wlk** CM2 . . . . . . . . .216 B6
**Mottram Cl** IP9 . . . . . . . . . .16 C2
**Motts Cl** CM7 . . . . . . . . . .127 E4
**Motts La** CM8 . . . . . . . . . .177 B4
**Mott's Cl** CO4 . . . . . . . . . .132 D4
**Mott's La** CM6 . . . . . . . . . .124 E5
**Moules La** CB1 . . . . . . . . . . .5 C6
**MOULSHAM** . . . . . . . . . . .216 A8
**Moulsham Chase**
CM2 . . . . . . . . . . . . . . . .216 C8
**Moulsham Dr** CM2 . . . . . . .216 B8
**Moulsham Hall La**
Braintree CM3 . . . . . . . . .153 F2
Great Leighs CM3 . . . . . . .154 A1
**Moulsham High Sch**
CM2 . . . . . . . . . . . . . . . .216 B7
**Moulsham Inf Sch**
CM2 . . . . . . . . . . . . . . . .216 B7
**Moulsham Jun Sch**
CM2 . . . . . . . . . . . . . . . .216 B7
**Moulsham St**
Chelmsford CM1 . . . . . . .205 B2
Chelmsford, Moulsham
CM2 . . . . . . . . . . . . . . . .216 A8
**Moulsham Thrift** CM2 . . . . .216 A6
**Moulton Cl** CO3 . . . . . . . . . .33 F8
**Mountain Ash Cl** CO4 . . . . .110 C2
**Mountain's Farm Rd**
CM6 . . . . . . . . . . . . . . . .150 C3
**Mountbatten Cl** CO10 . . . . . .15 F2
**Mountbatten Ct**
Braintree CM7 . . . . . . . . .128 B4
7 Ipswich IP1 . . . . . . . . . .17 A7
**Mountbatten Dr** CO2 . . . . .136 B4
**Mountbatten Rd**
Braintree CM7 . . . . . . . . .128 C4
Chelmsford CM2 . . . . . . .205 E7
**Mountbatten Way**
CM1 . . . . . . . . . . . . . . . .205 E7
**MOUNT BURES** . . . . . . . . . .79 F5
**Mount Dr**
Ipswich IP3 . . . . . . . . . . . .18 F1
Stansted Mountfitchet
CM24 . . . . . . . . . . . . . 119 F6
**Mountfitchet Castle &**
**Norman Village** *
CM24 . . . . . . . . . . . . . . . 119 F6
**Mountfitchet Mathematics**
**& Computing Coll The**
CM24 . . . . . . . . . . . . . . . 119 F4
**Mountfitchet Rd**
CM24 . . . . . . . . . . . . . . . 119 E5
**Mount Hill** CO9 . . . . . . . . . .76 D1
**Mounthill Ave** CM2 . . . . . . .205 D3
**Mount Lodge Chase**
CM9 . . . . . . . . . . . . . . . .196 B6
**Mount Pleasant**
Great Totham CM9 . . . . . .196 E6
Halstead CO9 . . . . . . . . . .76 E1
Little Baddow CM3 . . . . . .207 E4
Maldon CM9 . . . . . . . . . .209 F2
**Mount Pleasant Cotts**
CB11 . . . . . . . . . . . . . . . .43 D8
**Mount Pleasant Rd**
CB11 . . . . . . . . . . . . . . . .43 D8
**Mount Rd**
Braintree CM7 . . . . . . . . .128 A2
Coggeshall CO6 . . . . . . . .131 B2
Haverhill CB9 . . . . . . . . . . .9 B7
**Mount Rise** 4 CO9 . . . . . . . .76 D1
**Mount The**
Colchester CO3 . . . . . . . .134 F6
Tollesbury CM9 . . . . . . . .199 D1
**Mountview Rd** CO5 . . . . . . .189 A5
**Moverons La** CO7 . . . . . . . .165 C2
**MOWDEN** . . . . . . . . . . . . .193 D1
**Mowden Hall La**
Hatfield Peverel CM3 . . . . .193 D1
Ulting CM3 . . . . . . . . . . .208 A8
**Mowlands** IP9 . . . . . . . . . . .35 B1
**Moy Rd** CO2 . . . . . . . . . . . .135 A1
**Moze Cross** CO12 . . . . . . . .116 D1
**Mulberries The** 8
CM7 . . . . . . . . . . . . . . . .128 A2
**Mulberry Ave** CO2 . . . . . . .135 B8
**Mulberry Cotts** CO6 . . . . . .160 C8
**Mulberry Gdns** CM8 . . . . . .177 A4
**Mulberry Harbour Way**
CO2 . . . . . . . . . . . . . . . .164 B8
**Mulberry Rd** IP3 . . . . . . . . . .38 C7

**Mulberry Way** CM1 . . . . . . .205 D4
**Mullins Rd** CM7 . . . . . . . . .127 F6
**Multon Lea** CM1 . . . . . . . . .206 A7
**Mumford Cl** CO6 . . . . . . . .108 E4
**Mumford Rd**
Ipswich IP1 . . . . . . . . . . . .16 E8
West Bergholt CO6 . . . . . .108 D4
**Mumfords La** CO13 . . . . . . .170 A7
**Mundon Rd** CM7 . . . . . . . . .128 D1
**Munnings Cl** IP3 . . . . . . . . . .38 B8
**Munnings Dr** CO16 . . . . . . .188 D6
**Munnings Rd** CO3 . . . . . . . .135 A5
**Munro Rd** CM8 . . . . . . . . . .176 F5
**Murchison Cl** CM1 . . . . . . . .204 E5
**Murray Cl** CM7 . . . . . . . . . .127 F6
**Murrayfield Com Prim Sch**
IP3 . . . . . . . . . . . . . . . . .18 A2
**Murray Rd** IP3 . . . . . . . . . . .18 A3
**Murrell Lock** CM2 . . . . . . . .206 A4
**Murrills Rd** IP3 . . . . . . . . . .38 A1
**Murton Slade** 6 CB9 . . . . . . . .9 A8
**Muscade Cl** CO5 . . . . . . . . .179 D6
**Museum St**
14 Colchester CO1 . . . . . .135 F7
Ipswich IP1 . . . . . . . . . . . .17 C6
Saffron Walden CB10 . . . . .22 D2
**Musgrave Cl** CO12 . . . . . . . .90 F1
**Musk Cl** CO3 . . . . . . . . . . .134 D7
**Mus of Power** * CM6 . . . . . .209 D6
**Mustard Gapp** CB9 . . . . . . . .9 C7
**Muswell Wlk** CO16 . . . . . . .188 D5
**Mutlow Cl** CB11 . . . . . . . . . .42 F5
**Mutlow Hill** CB11 . . . . . . . . .42 F5
**Myddylton Pl** CB10 . . . . . . . .22 D2
**Myland Hall Chase**
CO4 . . . . . . . . . . . . . . . . 110 C3
**Myland Prim Sch**
CO4 . . . . . . . . . . . . . . . .109 E4
**Mynards Way** CM4 . . . . . . .218 C2
**Myneer Pk** CO6 . . . . . . . . . .131 B2
**Myrtle Gr** CO2 . . . . . . . . . .136 B5
**Myrtle Rd** IP3 . . . . . . . . . . .17 E4
**Myson Way** CM23 . . . . . . . .146 B7
**Mytchett Cl** CO16 . . . . . . . .188 B6

**N**

**Nabbott Rd** CM1 . . . . . . . . .204 D5
**Nacton Cres** IP3 . . . . . . . . . .18 B2
**Nacton Rd**
Felixstowe IP11 . . . . . . . .221 C1
Ipswich, Racecourse IP3 . . . .18 B2
Ipswich, Rose Hill IP3 . . . . .18 A3
**Nails La** CM23 . . . . . . . . . . .145 F7
**Nails Lane Ho** 20
CM23 . . . . . . . . . . . . . . . .145 F7
**Nalla Gdns** CM1 . . . . . . . . .205 A6
**Nancy Smith Cl** CO2 . . . . . .135 F5
**Nansen Rd**
Holland-on-S CO15 . . . . . .189 D6
Ipswich IP3 . . . . . . . . . . . .18 B2
**Napier Ave** CO15 . . . . . . . .203 D6
**Napier Ct** CM1 . . . . . . . . . .205 F6
**Napier Rd** CO2 . . . . . . . . . .135 F6
**Narvik Cl** CM9 . . . . . . . . . .220 E8
**Nash Cl**
Colchester CO3 . . . . . . . .135 B5
Lawford CO11 . . . . . . . . . .86 B5
**Nash Ct** CO9 . . . . . . . . . . . .76 F1
**Nash Dr** CM1 . . . . . . . . . . .191 A3
**Nash Gdns** IP3 . . . . . . . . . .38 B8
**Nassau Rd** CO16 . . . . . . . . .187 B4
**Nathan Ct** CO2 . . . . . . . . . .163 B8
**National Wireless &**
**Televion Mus The** *
CO12 . . . . . . . . . . . . . . . .91 E5
**Nats La** CB11 . . . . . . . . . . . .42 F5
**Navarre St** 4 IP1 . . . . . . . . .17 C6
**Navarre Rd** CM9 . . . . . . . . .210 B4
**Navigation Rd** CM2 . . . . . . .205 C2
**NAYLAND** . . . . . . . . . . . . . .56 B1
**Nayland Dr** CO16 . . . . . . . .188 B4
**Nayland Prim Sch** CO6 . . . . .56 A1
**Nayland Rd**
Bures CO8 . . . . . . . . . . . .79 F8
Colchester CO6 . . . . . . . .109 D6
Felixstowe IP11 . . . . . . . .221 A4
Great Horkesley CO6 . . . . . .82 B4
Haverhill CB9 . . . . . . . . . . .9 D6
West Bergholt CO6 . . . . . .108 D7
**Nayling Rd** CM7 . . . . . . . . .127 C2
**Nazecliff Gdns** CO14 . . . . . .144 E3
**Naze Ct** CO14 . . . . . . . . . . .144 E3
**Naze Marine Holiday Pk**
CO14 . . . . . . . . . . . . . . . .144 D2
**Naze Nature Trail The** *
CO14 . . . . . . . . . . . . . . . .144 D2
**Naze Park Rd** CO14 . . . . . . .144 E2
**Naze Rd** CO14 . . . . . . . . . . .76 E1
**Neale St** IP1 . . . . . . . . . . . .17 C6
**Neasden Ave** CO16 . . . . . . .188 D5
**Neath Dr** IP2 . . . . . . . . . . . .17 A1
**Needle Cnr** IP9 . . . . . . . . . .63 D1
**Nelson Cl** CO7 . . . . . . . . . .186 A7
**Nelson Ct** CM4 . . . . . . . . . .128 C4
**Nelson Gr** CM2 . . . . . . . . . .204 F3
**Nelson Ho** IP3 . . . . . . . . . . .38 D4
**Nelson Rd**
Bishop's Stortford
CM23 . . . . . . . . . . . . . 146 A5
Clacton-on-S CO15 . . . . . .188 E1
Colchester CO3 . . . . . . . .134 E6
Harwich CO12 . . . . . . . . . .91 D4
Ipswich IP4 . . . . . . . . . . . .18 A7
**Nelson's Ave** IP9 . . . . . . . . .35 C1
**Nelson St** CO7 . . . . . . . . . .185 F6

Nene Dr IP3 38 D7
Neptune Ct
Chelmsford CM1 204 F4
5 Colchester CO1 136 C6
Neptune Quay IP4 17 D5
Neptune Sq IP4 17 D5
Ness Wlk CM8 176 D2
Nether Ct CO9 77 A1
Nethergate St CO10 12 B7
Nether Hill CO9, CO10 31 D3
Nether Rd CO10 1 D2
Netley Cl IP2 36 F8
Nettleditch CB11 21 E4
Neville Rd CB10 22 E2
Newark Cl IP2 16 F1
New Barn La CM22 146 D1
Newbarn Rd CO6 106 B1
Newbiggen St CM6 69 F3
Newbourne Gdns IP11 221 B3
New Bowers Way CM1 205 F6
Newbridge Hill CO6 108 D2
Newbridge Rd
Birch CO5 180 A6
Tiptree CO5 179 F5
Newbury Cl CM23 145 E8
Newbury Ho IP4 18 B6
Newbury Rd IP4 18 C6
Newby Dr IP4 18 F5
New Captains Rd CO5 201 B6
New Cardinal St IP1 17 B5
Newcastle Ave CO3 134 F4
New Church Rd CO6 108 E4
Newcomen Way CO4 110 C6
New Cotts
Great Tey CO6 132 C8
Wakes Colne CO6 106 C6
New Court Pl CM2 205 E3
Newcourt Rd CM2 205 D3
Newcroft 1 CB10 22 E1
New Cut
Bures CO8 79 E8
Glemsford CO10 2 B3
Great Bentley CO7 166 E8
Layer de la H CO2 161 F5
New Cut E IP2, IP3 17 D4
New Cut W IP2 17 D4
New Dukes Way CM2 205 F4
New England Cl CM3 218 F1
New Farm Lo CO3 134 D5
New Farm Rd CO3 134 D6
Newgate St 5 CO14 171 C8
New Hall Cotts CO7 58 F7
New Hall Sch CM3 192 A1
New Hall Vineyards* CM3 220 D2
Newhaven La CO12 91 D6
New House La CB10 24 C3
Newhouse Rd CO6 104 F5
Newhythe CO3 134 E7
Newington Gdns CO15 188 F8
New Kiln Rd CO3 135 C7
New La
Feering CO5 158 F5
Holbrook IP9 63 A5
Newland Ave CM7 72 B1
Newland Ct CM8 176 F1
Newland Pl CM8 177 A1
Newlands Dr CM8 177 A2
Newlands La CO6 56 B1
Newlands Prec 8 CM8 177 A2
Newlands Spring Prim Sch CM1 204 D7
Newland St CM8 177 A2
New Lodge Chase CM3 207 B2
New London Ct 5 CM2 216 A8
New London Rd CM2 205 A1
Newmain Rd CO2 135 E3
Newman Dr CO4 83 A4
Newmans Est CO15 188 D3
Newman's Rd CO10 33 F8
Newmarket Rd CB10 3 C3
Newmill La
Brantham CO11 61 A1
Stutton CO11 87 A8
NEW MISTLEY 87 B4
New Nabbotts Way CM1 205 E7
Newnham Cl CM7 127 E2
Newnham Ct IP2 16 E2
Newnham Gn CM9 209 E3
New Orleans Flats CO5 201 B5
New Park Gdns CO7 185 F7
New Park St CO1 136 B6
Newpasture La CM6 125 C5
New Path CM23 145 F6
New Pier St 7 CO14 171 C8
New Pk CO9 51 F3
New Place Ho IP2 17 A4
New Pond La CB10 22 C2
NEWPORT 43 A1
Newport Cl
Great Baddow CM2 217 B6
Harwich CO12 91 A1
Newport Dr
Clacton-on-S CO15 189 A7
Rickling Green CB11 66 F4
Newport Free Gram Sch CB11 42 F1
NEWPORT POND 67 A7
Newport Prim Sch CB11 66 F7
Newport Rd CB11 43 C7
Newport Sta CB11 67 A8
Newport Way CO13 171 A6
Newpots Cl CO5 182 D5
Newpots La CO5 182 E5
Newquay Cl IP5 18 F6
New Queens Rd CO10 15 E1
New Rd
Aldham CO6 107 B2
Broomfield CM1 191 B1
Colchester CO3 134 D6
Elsenham CM22 94 C2
Gosfield CO9 102 E5
Great Baddow CM2 217 A6
Hatfield Peverel CM3 194 A4
Hinxton CB10 3 B6
Kelvedon CO5 158 C2
Long Melford CO10 15 C7
Messing CO5 159 C1
Mistley CO11 86 E4
Rayne CM77 127 A1
Saffron Walden CB10 22 E1
Shudy Camps CB21 7 C7
Terling CM3 175 C3
Tiptree CO5 179 D5
Tollesbury CM9 199 D2
Trimley St M IP11 221 A7
New Road Terr CM77 126 F1
New Row CB21 7 E4
Newry Ave IP11 221 D4
Newson St IP1 17 B7
New St
Braintree CM7 127 F2
Brightlingsea CO7 185 F6
Chelmsford CM1 205 B3
Glemsford CO10 2 A5
Great Dunmow CM6 150 D8
Halstead CO9 76 E1
2 Maldon CM9 209 F2
Sudbury CO10 33 E8
New Street Fields CM6 150 D8
New Thorpe Ave CO16 142 A2
Newton Cl 4 CM7 127 F1
Newton Croft CO10 34 A7
Newton Gdns CO16 187 A5
Newton Gn CM6 123 C1
Newton Hall CM6 123 B2
Newton Pl 15 CB9 9 B8
Newton Rd
Harwich CO12 91 A3
Ipswich IP3 18 A4
Sudbury CO10 34 A7
Newton St 10 IP4 17 D6
Newton Way CO16 187 B5
NEWTOWN 158 C3
NEW TOWN 145 F6
Newtown Rd CM23 145 F6
New Town Rd
Colchester CO1 136 A6
Thorpe-le-S CO16 141 F2
New Village CO11 86 C7
New Way
Ipswich IP2 16 F6
Point Clear B CO16 185 F3
New Writtle St CM2 205 B1
Nexus The CO1 135 E8
Nicholas Cl CM1 204 B1
Nicholas Ct
Chelmsford, Scot's Green CM1 204 D6
Witham CM8 176 F2
Nicholas Rd IP11 221 A4
Nichols Cl CO11 86 B3
Nichols Cnr CO7 112 A5
Nichols Ct 1 CM2 205 A1
Nichols Gr CM7 128 C3
Nicholsons Gr CO1 136 A6
Nickleby Rd CM1 204 D6
Nien-Oord CO16 188 C4
Nightingale Cl
Clacton-on-S CO15 188 F5
Colchester CO4 137 A8
Harwich CO12 90 F1
Witham CM8 194 E8
Nightingale Cnr
Layer de la H CO2 162 A6
2 Maldon CM9 210 A1
Nightingale Ct CO2 163 A8
Nightingale Hill CO4 83 F6
Nightingale Mews 2 CB10 22 F2
Nightingale Pl CO3 134 C4
Nightingale Rd IP3 38 A8
Nightingales CM23 146 B7
Nightingale Sq IP3 38 A8
Nightingale Way CO15 188 F5
Nineacres CM7 128 A1
Nine Acres IP2 16 D5
Ninth Ave CM24 120 B2
Noah's Ark La CO10 33 D7
Noakes Ave CM2 216 E6
Noaks Rd IP7 58 D8
Nobles The CM23 145 D6
Nonancourt Way CO6 105 A6
Nonesuch Mdw CO10 33 E6
Nonsuch Mdw CO10 33 E7
Nook The CO7 164 C8
Norah Guilder Ho CM3 194 A4
Norbury Cl CO6 132 F3
Norbury Rd IP4 18 B8
Nordic Lo CM9 220 F8
Norfolk Ave
Clacton-on-S CO15 189 E7
West Mersea CO5 201 D7
Norfolk Cl CM9 209 E1
Norfolk Cres CO4 110 B1
Norfolk Dr CM1 205 A7
Norfolk Gdns CM7 128 B4
Norfolk Rd
Ipswich IP4 17 D6
Maldon CM9 209 E1
Norfolk Way CM23 145 F5
Norman Ave CM23 145 D6
Norman Cl
Marks Tey CO6 132 E3
St Osyth CO16 187 A4
Norman Cres IP3 18 A2
Norman Ct CM24 119 E7
Normandie Way CO8 79 E8
Normandy Ave CO2 136 A3
Norman Hill CM3 175 B2
Norman Rd
Clacton-on-S CO15 189 E6
Manningtree CO11 86 D4
Normansfield CM6 150 E7
Norman's Way CM24 119 E7
Norman Way
Colchester, Lexden CO3 135 B6
Colchester, Shrub End CO3 135 B4
Point Clear B CO16 185 F3
Norris Cl
Bishop's Stortford CM23 146 C7
Braintree CM7 128 C5
Northampton Cl CM7 128 D5
Northampton Mdw CM7 72 B2
North Ave
Chelmsford CM1 204 F5
Haverhill CB9 8 E8
Northbourne Rd CO15 188 F4
North Cl IP4 17 E8
North Court Rd CM1 191 A3
North Cres CB9 27 B7
Northcroft CO10 33 E7
North Dell CM1 205 E7
North Dr CM2 216 F7
NORTHEND 22 A3
NORTH END
Felsted 151 F2
Great Yeldham 30 F3
North End Rd
Gestingthorpe CO9, CO10 31 C2
Hinxton CB10 3 B8
Little Yeldham CO9 30 E2
Northern App CO4 109 E3
Northern Rd CO10 34 B8
Northey View CM9 210 C3
Northfield CM7 72 B3
Northfield Gdns CO4 110 A4
Northfield Rd CB11 43 E8
Northfields CM24 119 E7
Northgate End CM23 145 F8
Northgate Prim Sch CM23 145 E8
Northgate St
Colchester CO1 135 F8
Ipswich IP1 17 C6
North Hall Rd
Henham CM22 94 B7
Rickling Green CB11 67 A2
North Hill
Colchester CO1 135 E7
Little Baddow CM3 207 D5
North Hill Gdns 1 IP4 17 E6
North Hill Rd IP4 17 E6
North Ho CO13 170 F4
North La CO6 133 B5
North Lawn IP4 18 C8
North Mill Pl CO9 76 E3
Northolt Ave CM23 119 B1
North Prim Sch CO1 135 E8
North Rd
Belchamp Walter CO10 31 F6
Brightlingsea CO7 185 F7
Clacton-on-S CO15 188 F6
Great Yeldham CO9 30 A2
Takeley CM22 148 C8
Tollesbury CM9 199 C2
North Rise CO10 34 A6
North Sea View CO12 90 F2
North St
4 Bishop's Stortford CM23 145 F7
Great Dunmow CM6 123 D1
Maldon CM9 210 B2
Manningtree CO11 86 D4
Steeple Bumpstead CB9 27 B7
Sudbury CO10 33 E8
Tolleshunt D'arcy CM9 198 E5
Walton-on-t-N CO14 171 C8
North Station Rd CO1 135 E8
North Street Par 1 CO10 33 E7
North Terr 5 CM23 145 F8
Northumberland Cl CM7 128 B4
Northumberland Ct 1 CM2 205 F4
North View Cotts CO6 109 B7
North Wall CO16 186 A3
NORTON END 42 E4
Norton Rd
Chelmsford CM1 205 A3
Haverhill CB9 8 E6
Norway Cres CO12 90 F3
Norwich Cl
Clacton-on-S CO16 188 E6
Colchester CO1 136 A8
Norwich Ct 2 IP1 17 A7
Norwich Rd IP1 17 A7
Norwood Ave CO15 189 B5
Norwood Way CO14 171 A7
NOSTERFIELD END 7 F5
Notcutts CO7 59 E1
Notley Gn CM77 154 B6
Notley Green Prim Sch CM77 154 C8
Notley High Sch CM7 154 F8
Notley Rd CM7 154 F8
Nottage Cl CO7 164 C8
Nottage Cres CM7 127 E3
Nottidge Rd IP4 17 E6
Nottingham Rd CO15 189 E6
NOUNSLEY 194 B1
Nounsley Rd CM3 194 B1
Nounsley Terr CM3 194 B1
Nunnery St CO9 51 D4
Nunns Cl CO6 131 A2
Nunn's Rd CO1 135 E7
Nun's Mdw CO9 102 E7
Nuns Wlk CO9 29 F1
Nunty's La
Greenstead Green CO9 104 A1
Pattiswick CM77 129 F8
Nursery Cl
Bishop's Stortford CM23 145 F6
Colchester CO3 134 C5
Nursery Dr CM7 128 A5
Nursery La CM3 218 F8
Nursery Rd
Bishop's Stortford CM23 145 F6
Chelmsford CM2 216 B8
Great Cornard CO10 34 B5
Nursery Rise CM6 150 D7
Nursery Wlk IP11 221 D5
NUTHAMPSTEAD 39 A2

## O

Oakapple Cl CO2 135 D1
Oak Ave CO16 188 A2
Oak Bglws CM7 127 E3
Oak Bsns Pk CO16 141 F8
Oak Cl
Clacton-on-S CO15 188 E6
Felixstowe IP11 221 C4
Rushmere St A IP4 18 E7
Thorpe-le-S CO16 142 A1
West Bergholt CO6 108 E4
Oak Cnr
Beaumont CO16 141 F8
Woodham Mortimer CM9 219 D6
Oak Cotts CM3 206 E8
Oak Eggar Chase IP8 36 D8
Oak Fall CM8 177 A5
Oak Farm Rd CM9 208 E1
Oakfield CM6 125 A4
Oakfield Dr CO4 83 A5
Oakfield La CM3 175 A2
Oakfield Rd
Belstead IP8 36 A7
Washbrook IP8 35 F6
Oakfield Wood Nature Reserve* CO11 88 D4
Oak Gr IP8 16 A6
Oak Hall CM23 145 E8
Oakhaven CO12 90 F1
Oak Hill
Beazley End CM7 101 A8
Wethersfield CM7 73 F1
Oak Hill La IP2 17 B3
Oak Ho
Ipswich IP2 16 D2
Stutton IP9 61 F2
Oak Ind Pk CM6 150 F6
Oakland Rd CO12 91 C3
Oaklands Ave CO3 134 E5
Oaklands Cl
Bishop's Stortford CM23 119 B2
Great Notley CM77 154 D8
Oaklands Cres CM2 216 B8
Oaklands Dr CM23 119 B2
Oaklands Inf Sch CM2 216 B8
Oaklands Pk CM23 119 B2
Oaklands Way CM3 207 E2
Oaklea Ave CM2 205 E3
Oaklee IP2 17 A1
Oakleigh Ct CM23 145 D8
Oakleigh Rd CO15 188 F8
Oakley Cross CO12 117 B7
Oakley Rd
Braintree CM7 127 F7
Harwich CO12 90 D1
Wix CO11 115 E5
Oak Lodge Tye CM1 206 A6
Oak Manor View CM3 173 F7
Oakmead Rd CO16 186 B3
Oak Rd
Chappel CO6 106 B3
Great Cornard CO10 34 B6
Halstead CO9 103 D7
Heybridge CM9 210 B6
Little Maplestead CO9 77 A8
Pebmarsh CO9 77 F8
Rivenhall CM8 177 C6
Tiptree CO5 179 C7
Oak Ridge CO12 117 B7
Oakroyd Ave CM6 150 E8
Oakroyd Ho CM6 150 E8
Oaks Com Prim Sch The IP2 16 E3
Oaks Dr CO3 135 D7
Oaks End CO2 162 A5
Oaks Hospl The CO4 109 E3
Oaksmere Gdns IP2 17 A2
Oaks Pl CO4 109 E2
Oak St CM23 145 F6
Oakstead Cl IP4 18 A6
Oaks The CO13 170 F6
Oaktree Cl 14 CM23 145 F7
Oak Tree Cotts CO6 133 B8
Oak Tree Rd CO7 165 B8
Oaktrees CM9 197 B5
Oakview CO12 90 F1
Oak View Cvn Pk CM24 120 A4
Oak Wlk CO9 51 D2
Oakwood Ave
Clacton-on-S CO15 189 E7
West Mersea CO5 201 D7
Oakwood Bsns Pk CO15 169 A1
Oakwood Cl CO13 170 E6
Oakwood Dr CO5 201 D7
Oakwood Gdns CO5 201 D7
Oakwood Inf Sch CO15 188 D2
Oak Yd CO9 76 E2
Oasis Ct CM1 205 F5
Oasthouse Ct CB10 22 D1
Oast House Spinney CM7 127 F6
Oatfield Cl CO3 134 D6
Oatlands CO7 137 F6
Oban St IP1 17 B7
Oberon Cl CO4 136 F7
Obrey Way CM23 145 E3
Observation Ct IP1 17 B5
Observer Way CO5 158 C4
Ocean View CO14 171 D8
Ockelford Ave CM1 204 F5
Ockendon Way CO14 171 A8
Octavia Dr CM8 194 E7
Oddcroft CO6 77 F1
Odin Lo CM9 220 F8
Office La CM9 197 A4
Old Barn Rd CO8 80 A6
Old Bell Cl CM24 119 D6
Oldbury Ave CM2 216 F8
Old Burylodge La CM24 120 A4
Old Camps Castle CB21 7 E3
Old Cattle Market 5 IP4 17 C5
Old Church La
Bulmer CO10 32 F3
Bulmer Tye CO10 32 F2
West Bergholt CO6 108 D5
Old Clements La CB9 8 F7
Old Coach Rd CO1 136 B7
Old Coastguard Cotts CM0 214 E4
Old Convent The CO5 158 B1
Old Court Ho 2 CM24 119 E6
Old Court Rd CM2 205 D3
Old Ct
Chelmsford CM2 205 D3
Long Melford CO10 15 D8
Olde Forge CO7 165 E1
Old Ferry Rd CO7 164 B8
Oldfield Rd IP8 16 B1
Old Forge CO7 137 C2
Old Forge Rd
Boreham CM3 206 E8
Layer de la H CO2 161 F5
Old Foundry Rd IP4 17 D6
Old Hall Cl CB9 27 C7
Old Hall La
Capel St M IP9 35 F3
Tollesbury CM9 199 C5
Walton-on-t-N CO14 144 E3
OLD HEATH 136 C3
Old Heath Com Prim Sch CO2 136 D3
Old Heath Rd CO1, CO2 136 C4
Old House La CO4 83 B2
Old House Rd CO6 109 A8
Oldhouse Villas CM22 148 C8
Old Ipswich Rd CO7 110 E7
Old Library The 15 CO11 86 D4
Old London Rd
Capel St M IP9 59 F7
Woodham Walter CM9 208 E1
Old Maltings The 2 CM23 146 A7
Old Market Ct 3 CO10 33 E7
Old Market Pl 2 CO10 33 E7
OLD MEAD 94 D4
Old Mead La CM22 94 D4
Old Mead Rd CM22 94 C5
Old Mill Chase CM7 73 C3
Old Mill Cl CM9 210 A3
Old Mill La CO5 158 D7
Old Mill Rd
Langham CO4 83 D5
Saffron Walden CB11 43 E8
Old Moors CM3 173 F7

**Old Orchard The** CM2 217 D2
**Old Parsonage Ct** CM8 176 F2
**Old Parsonage Way** CO13 170 F5
**Old Pier St** CO14 171 C8
**Old Rd**
Clacton-on-S CO15 188 E4
Coggeshall CO6, CO5 131 E1
Frinton-on-S CO13 170 F4
Pattiswick CM77 129 F5
Wickham St P CO9 53 D5
**Old Rectory Ct** CO6 133 A4
**Old River La** CM23 145 F7
**Old Rope Wlk** CB9 8 E7
**Old Rose Gdns** CO4 109 D4
**Old St The** IP9 35 B1
**Old School Cl** CO16 187 A4
**Old School Ct**
Brightlingsea CO7 185 E6
Hatfield Peverel CM3 194 B3
**Old School Field** CM1 205 E4
**Old School Ho** IP9 91 B8
**Old School Ho The** CO5 164 A8
**Old School La** CO7 138 A6
**Old School Yd** CB11 43 D8
**Old Southend Rd** CM2 217 D1
**Old Vicarage Rd** CO12 91 C3
**Old Vicarage The** CM7 72 D6
**Old Way** CO13 170 F4
**Olive Gr** CO2 135 D2
**Oliver Cl** CM9 210 B4
**Oliver Pl** CM8 177 B2
**Olivers Cl**
Clacton-on-S CO15 188 E4
Long Melford CO10 15 D7
**Olivers Ct** CO15 188 E4
**Olivers Dr** CM8 195 A7
**Olivers La** CO2 135 A1
**Olivers Rd** CO15 188 E4
**Oliver Way** CM1 204 F7
**Oliveswood Rd** CM6 150 D7
**Olley Wlk** CO5 179 E6
**OLMSTEAD GREEN** 25 E7
**Ongar Cl** CO16 188 B4
**Ongar Rd**
Great Dunmow CM6 150 D6
Writtle CM1 204 B1
Ongar Road Trad Est CM6 150 E7
**Onslow Cotts** CO5 160 A7
**Onslow Cres** CO2 136 B1
**ONSLOW GREEN** 151 C2
**Opal Ave** IP1 16 D8
**Ophir Rd** CO7 185 F5
**Orange St** CM6 70 A2
**Orange Tree Cl** CM2 216 C6
**Orchard Ave** CO9 76 D2
**Orchard Cl**
Chelmsford CM2 216 C6
Clacton-on-S CO16 188 C5
Copford CO6 133 D2
Elmstead Market CO7 138 A6
Great Oakley CO12 116 C3
Hatfield Peverel CM3 194 A4
Haverhill CB9 8 F7
Maldon CM9 209 F2
Newport CB11 66 F8
Ramsey CO12 90 A2
Ridgewell CO9 29 B6
Saffron Walden CB11 43 D7
Thaxted CM6 70 A3
Tollesbury CM9 199 E1
Writtle CM1 204 B1
**Orchard Cotts**
Boreham CM3 193 A2
Langham CO4 83 F3
Little Horkesley CO6 81 E5
**Orchard Ct** CO3 135 C7
**Orchard Dr**
Braintree CM7 128 A1
Great Holland CO13 170 A4
**Orchard Gate** IP2 16 C5
**Orchard Gdns** CO4 136 B8
**Orchard Gr** IP5 18 F7
**Orchard Lo** CO5 179 D4
**Orchard Mews** CO5 179 C4
**Orchard Pightle** CB1 5 C6
**Orchard Pl**
Colchester CO4 109 F4
Sudbury CO10 33 D6
**Orchard Rd**
Alresford CO7 165 B8
Bishop's Stortford CM23 119 B1
[3] Colchester CO1 135 E8
Kelvedon CO5 158 C3
Maldon CM9 209 F2
**Orchards** CM8 176 F1
**Orchard St**
Chelmsford CM2 205 B1
[9] Ipswich IP4 17 D6
**Orchard The**
Felsted CM6 152 C5
Maldon CM9 209 F5
**Orchard Way** CO10 2 B3
**Orchid Ave** CM8 176 E4
**Orchid Cl**
Ipswich IP2 16 E4
Takeley CM22 148 B7
**Orchid Field Ct** CO5 201 E6
**Orford Cres** CM1 205 D5
**Orford Ho** CM22 93 F3
**Orford Rd**
Felixstowe IP11 221 C1
Haverhill CB9 8 F6
**Orford St** IP1 17 B7
**Oriel Cl** CO10 34 B6
**Oriole Way** CM23 145 C6
**Orion Way** CM7 128 B4
**Orkney Cl** CB9 9 D7
**Orlando Ct** CO14 171 C8
**Ormonde Cl** CO6 108 E4
**Orpen Cl** CO6 108 D4
**Orpen's Hill** CO2 161 A5
**Orplands Cotts** CM0 214 F1
**Orrin Wlk** [6] CO4 109 E2
**Orsino Wlk** CO4 136 F7
**Orvis La** CO7 59 E1
Orwell Bsns Ctr IP3 17 E2
**Orwell Cl** CO4 110 E1
Orwell Country Pk* IP10 38 B6
**Orwell Ct** [1] IP4 17 D5
Orwell Ctry Pk* IP3 37 F8
**Orwell Gdns** IP2 17 A3
Orwell High Sch IP11 221 C5
**Orwell Ho** IP11 221 A4
**Orwell Hts** IP2 16 E2
**Orwell Pl**
Chelmondiston IP9 63 F7
[2] Ipswich IP4 17 D5
**Orwell Rd**
Clacton-on-S CO15 188 F2
Felixstowe IP11 221 D3
Harwich CO12 91 D4
Ipswich IP3 18 A4
Orwell Ret Pk IP2 16 F5
**Orwell Rise** IP9 63 F8
**Orwell Way** CO16 188 C6
**Orwell Wlk** CM8 176 E3
**Osbert Rd** CM8 194 E8
**Osborne Cl** CO15 189 A7
**Osborne Rd**
Ipswich IP3 18 A4
West Mersea CO5 201 E6
**Osbornes Ct** CO7 185 F6
**Osborne St** CO2 135 F6
**Osbourne Gdns** [5] CM23 145 E5
**Osea Rd** CM9 211 B3
**Osea Way** CM1 205 F5
**Osier Cl** CO3 134 D6
**Osier Pl** [3] CB9 8 F8
**Osmond Cl** CM77 155 B5
**Osprey Cl** CO3 134 B4
**Osprey Rd** CB9 9 C7
**Ospreys** CO15 188 F6
**Osprey Way** CM2 216 A5
**Ostler Cl** CM23 145 C4
**Ostler's Gn** CB11 41 B5
**Othello Cl** CO4 136 F8
**Otho Dr** CO4 110 A6
**Otley Ct** IP11 221 B5
**Otten Rd** CO10 13 B1
**Ottershaw Way** CO16 188 B6
**Oulton Cl** CO12 90 F3
**Oulton Hall** CO15 189 A3
**Oulton Rd** IP3 17 E2
Our Lady Immaculate RC Prim Sch CM2 205 A1
**Ouse Chase** CM8 176 D2
**OUTER PART OF TOWN EASTWARD** 91 E6
**OUTER PART OF TOWN WESTWARD** 91 D6
**Outpart Eastward** CO12 91 E6
**Overchurch Cl** CB9 8 F7
**Overhall Hill** CO6 78 C2
**Over Hall La** CB10 6 D2
**Overstone Ct** CO2 135 C3
**OVINGTON** 12 B1
**Ovington Pl** [16] CB9 9 B8
**Owen Ward Cl** CO2 135 A3
**Owl's Hill** CM3 175 B3
**Owls Retreat** [1] CO4 136 F8
**Oxborrow Cl** CO13 170 A6
**Oxcroft** CM23 145 F3
**OXEN END** 98 E6
**Oxenford Cl** CO12 90 F1
**Oxford Cl** CO10 34 A6
**Oxford Cres** CO15 188 F4
**Oxford Ct**
Chelmsford CM2 205 E4
Colchester CO3 135 D6
Earls Colne CO6 105 B6
**Oxford Ho** CB9 9 B6
Oxford House Sch CO3 135 D6
**Oxford La** CO9 51 D2
**Oxford Mdw** CO9 51 D2
**Oxford Pl** CO6 105 B6
**Oxford Rd**
Clacton-on-S CO15 188 F4
Colchester CO3 135 D6
Frinton-on-S CO13 171 A5
Halstead CO9 76 D1
Ipswich IP4 17 E5
Manningtree CO11 86 D4
**OXLEY GREEN** 180 A1
**Oxley Hill**
Abberton CO5 163 A3
Tolleshunt D'arcy CM9 198 B8
Tolleshunt Knights CM9 180 A1
**Oxley Ho** CM77 155 B5
**Oxley Parker Dr** CO4 110 A6
**Oxleys Cl** CB11 65 C3
**Oxlip Rd** CM8 176 E4
**Oxney Villas** CM6 152 D6
**Oxton Cl** CO5 164 A8
**Ox Yd** CO9 102 E7
Oyster Bsns Ctr CM9 199 F2
**Oyster Cl** CO5 201 C7
**Oyster Cotts** CM0 213 C1
Oyster Pk CO1 136 D6
**Oyster Pl** CM2 205 F4
**Oyster Tank Rd** CO7 185 E5
**Ozier Ct** CB11 43 E7
**Ozier Fields** CO9 103 F8
**Oziers** CM22 94 C2


## P


**Packard Ave** IP3 18 B2
**Packards La** CO6 80 F1
**Packe Cl** CO5 158 D4
**Padbrook Ct** IP3 17 F5
**Paddock Cl** CO12 91 C4
**Paddock Dr** CM1 205 E8
**Paddocks The**
Abberton CO5 163 A2
Ashen CO10 11 D1
Bures CO8 79 E8
Great Bentley CO7 166 F5
Great Totham CM9 196 A4
West Mersea CO5 201 D6
Witham CM8 177 A2
**Paddock The** CM23 145 D3
**Paddock Way** CO7 137 C3
**Padua Ho** IP4 17 F6
**Paeony Chase** CO5 201 C8
**Page Cl** CM8 194 D8
**Page Rd** CO15 188 E3
**Pages Cl** CM23 145 D5
**Pages La** CM9 198 F1
**Paget Ct** CM22 94 C1
**Paget Rd**
Ipswich IP1 17 B7
Rowhedge CO5 163 F8
Wivenhoe CO7 164 C8
**Paignton Ave** CM1 205 D5
**Pakenham Pl** [18] CB9 9 B8
**Palace Gdns** CM23 145 E5
**PALE GREEN** 8 D1
**Palfrey Hts** CO11 86 D8
**Pallant Chase** CO6 134 A8
**Pallister Rd** CO15 188 F2
**Palm Cl**
Chelmsford CM2 216 C6
Witham CM8 177 A5
**Palmers Croft** CM2 206 A2
**Palmers La**
[8] Bishop's Stortford CM23 145 F7
Chrishall SG8 19 C3
**Palmerston Ct** [7] IP4 17 E6
**Palmerston Lo** CM2 216 F7
**Palmerston Rd**
Ipswich IP4 17 E6
Thorpe-le-S CO16 142 A2
**Palmerswent Cl** CO10 15 D8
**Pamela Gdns** CM23 145 F3
**Pampas Cl** CO4 110 A4
**PANFIELD** 127 B7
**Panfield La** CM7 127 E5
**Pannells Ash** CO10 11 D1
**Pannels Cl** CO10 2 B4
**Pantile Cl** CM8 195 A7
**Pantlings La** CO5 158 A5
**Panton Cres** [7] CO4 136 E7
**Panton Mews** CM7 155 A8
**Pan Wlk** CM1 204 D5
**Papermill Cotts** CO9 76 E2
**Papillon Ho** CO1 135 E7
**Papillon Rd** CO3 135 E7
**Parade Dr** CO12 90 C1
**Parade Rd** IP4 17 F7
**Parade The**
Colchester CO2 136 A1
Kirby Cross CO13 170 B6
Walton-on-t-N CO14 171 C8
**Paradise Rd** CM1 215 B8
**Pardoe Pl** IP4 18 E5
**Park Ave**
Bishop's Stortford CM23 145 F3
Chelmsford CM1 204 F4
Felixstowe IP11 221 F5
**Park Bvd** CO15 189 E6
**Park Chase** CO16 187 C5
**Park Cl** CO10 34 A8
**Park Cotts**
Gosfield CO9 102 E8
Manningtree CO11 86 D3
St Osyth CO16 187 A5
**Park Ct**
Felixstowe IP11 221 D2
Harwich CO12 91 D4
Sible Hedingham CO9 51 D1
**Parkdale** CM3 218 C7
**Park Dr**
Braintree CM7 155 A8
Brightlingsea CO7 185 E7
Halstead CO9 76 E1
Maldon CM9 210 B1
Tiptree CO5 179 F5
**Parker Ct** CM0 214 F4
**Parker Rd**
Chelmsford CM2 205 C1
Colchester CO4 110 B6
**Parker's Way** CO6 56 A1
**Parker Way** CO9 103 E8
**PARKESTON** 90 E5
**Parkeston Rd**
Felixstowe IP11 221 B4
**Parkeston Rd** *continued*
Harwich CO12 90 F4
Harwich, Upper Dovercourt CO12 91 A4
**Park Farm** CB10 3 F6
Park Farm Ind Est SG8 39 C2
**Park Farm La** SG8 39 C2
**Parkfields** CO9 51 D1
**Parkfield St** CO5 163 F7
**Parkgate Cnr** CO16 169 A2
**Park Gate Rd** CM8 157 B3
**PARK GREEN** 92 B6
**Parkhall Rd**
Beazley End CM7 101 E7
Gosfield CO9 102 B7
**Parkinson Dr** CM1 204 F1
**Parkins The** IP9 35 C2
**Park La**
Bishop's Stortford CM23 145 F4
Bulmer Tye CO10 32 F2
Castle Camps CB21 7 F3
Earls Colne CO6 105 B6
Glemsford CO10 2 D4
Gosfield CO9 102 F7
Langham CO4 83 E3
Langley CB11 40 A3
Saffron Walden CB10 22 D1
Tiptree CO5 179 F5
Tolleshunt Knights CM9 180 B3
Toppesfield CO9 50 B7
**Parkland Ct** CO1 136 C5
**Parklands**
Braintree CM7 155 A8
Coggeshall CO6 131 A2
**Parklands Cl** CO10 2 C5
**Parklands Ct** CO16 188 B3
**Parklands Dr** CM1 205 D3
**Parklands Way** CM2 216 C2
**Park Lane Cl** CO6 105 B6
**Park N** IP4 17 D8
**Park Rd**
Ardleigh CO7 111 F3
Chelmsford CM1 205 B2
Clacton-on-S CO15 188 D2
Colchester CO3 135 C6
East Bergholt CO7 60 B2
Elsenham CM22 94 D1
Ford End CM3 172 A3
Great Chesterford CB10 3 E5
Harwich CO12 91 D4
Haverhill CB9 8 D8
Ipswich IP1 17 C8
Little Bentley CO7 139 D8
Little Easton CM6 122 F3
Little Horkesley CO6 82 B8
Maldon CM9 209 F2
Rivenhall CM8 157 A2
Stansted Mountfitchet CM24 119 E6
Stoke-by-N CO6 56 E4
St Osyth CO16 187 B4
Sudbury CO10 34 A8
Wivenhoe CO7 164 C8
Wivenhoe, Wivenhoe Park CO4 137 A4
**Parkside**
Haverhill CB9 8 F6
Saffron Walden CB10 22 C1
**Park Side** CM6 124 D6
**Parkside Ave** IP4 17 D7
**Parkside Quarter** CO1 135 E8
**Park Sq E**
Clacton-on-S CO15 203 G8
Jaywick CO15 188 A1
**Park Sq W**
Clacton-on-S CO15 203 F8
Jaywick CO15 187 F1
**Park St**
Stoke-by-N CO6 56 D5
Thaxted CM6 70 A2
**Parkstone Rdbt** CO12 90 F4
**Park Terr**
Harwich CO12 91 D4
Long Melford CO10 15 C7
**Park The** CO11 86 D3
**Park Vale Cl** CO9 51 E4
**Park View** CO10 12 C7
**Park View Cres** CM2 216 F5
**Park View Rd** IP1 17 B8
**Parkway**
Chelmsford CM1 CM2 205 B2
Shudy Camps CB21 7 C6
**Park Way** CO15 188 D1
Parkway Mid Sch CB9 8 D8
**Parkwood** IP1 17 C7
**Parkwood Ave** CO7 137 B1
**Parkwood Dr** CO10 15 E2
**Park Wood La** CM9 197 A3
**Parley Beams Cotts** CO9 104 D7
**Parliament Rd** IP4 18 B5
**Parmenter Dr** CO10 34 C5
**Parnell Cl** CO2 136 A2
**PARNEY HEATH** 84 B4
**Parnham Pl** IP4 18 F5
**Parr Cl**
Braintree CM7 128 D4
Jaywick CO15 187 F1
**Parr Dr** CO3 134 E4
**Parrington Way** CO11 86 A3
**Parr Rd** CB9 8 D6
**Parry Dr** CO16 188 C5
**Parsonage Cl**
Broomfield CM1 191 A1
Felixstowe IP11 221 B4
**Parsonage Downs** CM6 123 C3
**Parsonage Farm La** CB10 47 B4
Parsonage Farm Trad Est CM24 119 F3
**Parsonage Gdns** [6] CB9 8 E7
**Parsonage Gr** CO8 79 E8
**PARSONAGE GREEN** 205 A8
**Parsonage La**
Barnston CM6 151 D3
Bishop's Stortford CM23 146 C8
Clavering CB11 65 B3
Elder Street CB10 44 F3
Howe Street CM3 172 F2
Little Baddow CM3 207 D2
Stansted Mountfitchet CM24 119 F4
Tendring CO16 140 E8
**Parsonage Rd** CM22 148 C8
**Parsonage St** CO9 76 F1
**Parsonage Terr** CM7 72 D6
**Parsons Ct** [7] CO9 76 F2
**Parson's Field** CO7 85 A6
**PARSON'S HEATH** 110 D1
**Parson's Heath** CO4 110 E2
Parsons Heath CE Prim Sch CO4 110 E2
**Parsons Hill** CO7 138 F8
**Parson's Hill** CO3 135 A6
**Parsons La** CO1 136 C6
**Parsonson Ct** CO4 110 D1
**Parsons Yd** [10] CO11 86 D4
**Partridge Ave** CM1 204 F6
**Partridge Cl** CO12 116 D4
**Partridge Dr** CO6 107 D5
**Partridge Rd** IP2 16 E3
**Partridge Way** CO3 134 C4
**Paschal Way** CM2 216 F8
**Pashford Pl** IP3 38 C8
**Pashlers Alley** CO10 12 B7
**Paske Ave** CB9 8 F7
**Pasture Rd** CM8 177 B1
**Pastures The**
Rushmere St A IP4 18 F5
Takeley CM22 148 B7
**Patching Hall La** CM1 205 A6
**Paternoster Row** [6] CO14 171 C8
**Pathfields Rd** CO15 188 D4
**Path The** CO7 166 E8
**Pathway The** CO13 170 E6
**Patmore Cl** CM23 145 C8
**Patmore Fields** CM22 93 E6
**Patmore Rd** CO4 110 D1
**Patricia Gdns** CM23 145 E5
**Patten Cl** CO6 132 F3
**Pattern Bush Cl** CO11 86 D8
**Patteson Rd** IP3 17 E4
**Patticroft** CO10 2 B6
**Pattinson Wlk** CO6 109 B8
**Pattison Cl** CM8 195 A8
**PATTISWICK** 129 F5
**Pattock's La** CO6 106 C2
**Pattrick's La** CO12 91 C4
**Pauline Cl** CO15 189 B6
**Pauline St** [7] IP2 17 C4
**Paulk Hall La** CM3 174 A5
**Pauls Cres** CO7 137 F6
**Paul Spendlove Ct** CO4 110 E1
**Paul's Rd** IP2 16 F5
**Pauls Way** CO15 188 A1
**Pavilion Ct** CB9 9 B7
**Pavitt Mdw** CM2 216 C2
**Pawle Cl** CM2 217 A7
**Paxman Ave** CO2 135 A3
**Paxton Rd** CO15 189 B8
Paycocke's Ho* CO6 130 F1
**Paycocke Way** CO6 131 A3
**Paynes La** CM3 206 C8
**Payne's La** CO11 113 C3
**Peacehaven** CO13 171 A5
**Peace Rd** CO3 134 D7
**Peacock Cl**
Braintree CM7 127 F1
[5] Ipswich IP8 16 C2
**Peacocks Cl** CO10 1 C2
**Peacocks Rd** CO10 1 C2
**Peake Ave** CO13 170 A6
**Peakes Cl** CO5 179 B4
**Peal Rd** CB11 43 F7
**Pearce Manor** CM2 215 F8
**Pearce Rd** IP3 18 A5
**Pearl Dr** CM7 128 C3
**Pearl Rd** IP1 16 D8
**Pearmains** CM3 173 F7
**Pearmain Way** CO3 134 C4
**Pearmain Wlk** CB9 8 C8
**Pearse Way** IP3 18 E1
**Pearson Rd** IP3 18 C5
**Pearsons** CO10 2 B4
Peartree Bsns Ctr CO3 134 E4
**Peartree Cl**
Braintree CM7 128 A1
Goldhanger CM9 211 E6
**Pear Tree Cl** CO9 77 A3
**Pear Tree Ct** CO5 179 D4
**Peartree Hill** CO8 80 A5
**Peartree La** CM3 218 F3
**Peartree Rd** CO3 134 E4
**Peartree Way** CO16 168 C2
**Peaslands Rd** CB11 43 E8
**Peasleys Yd** CM23 146 B7
**PEBMARSH** 78 B7
**Pebmarsh Cl** CO2 163 A8

**Pebmarsh Rd**
Alphamstone CO8 .........54 E2
Colne Engaine CO6 .......77 F2
Pecockes CI CO10 .........34 C5
Peddars Ct CO10 ...........1 C5
Pedder's CI CO3 ..........134 F3
Pedlars CI CM3 ...........219 A6
Pedlars Path CM3 .........219 A6
Pedler's Cnr CO11 .........86 D2
Peek's Cnr CO6 ...........105 D5
Peel Cres CM7 ............127 E3
Peel Rd CM2 ..............205 F4
Peel St **5** IP1 .............17 C8
Peers Sq CM2 .............206 A4
Peerswood Rd CO2 ........135 D2
Peewit Ct IP11 ...........221 B3
Peewit Cnr Pk IP11 ......221 C2
Peewit Hill IP11 ..........221 B3
Peewit Rd IP2 .............16 C3
**Pegasus Way**
Braintree CM7 ..........127 E5
Colchester CO4 .........110 C1
Peggotty CI CM1 .........204 F6
Peggy's Wlk C8L1 ..........21 E3
Peg Millar's La CM3 ......175 E5
**PELDON** ..................182 E6
Peldon Cres CO5 .........182 E5
**Peldon Rd**
Abberton CO5 ..........182 E7
Great Wigborough CO5 ...182 A3
Pelham CI CO12 ...........90 F2
Pelham Rd CB11 ...........65 C4
Pelham's La **16** CO1 .......135 F7
Pelican CI IP2 ............16 E3
Pelly Ave CM8 ............195 A8
Pembroke Ave CM9 ........209 F1
**Pembroke CI**
Colchester CO2 .........136 C3
Ipswich IP2 ..............17 B3
Pembroke Gdns CO15 .....189 E6
**Pembroke PI**
Chelmsford CM1 ........205 B7
Sudbury CO10 ...........15 D2
Pendleton Rd IP2 .........16 D1
**Penfold Rd**
Clacton-on-S CO15.....188 D3
Felixstowe IP11.........221 E4
**Penhaligon Ct** **9**
CM8 ...................177 A2
**Peninsula Bsns Ctr The**
IP9 .....................37 B5
Penlan Hall La CO6 ......107 B5
Penn CI IP9 ..............35 B2
Pennine Rd CM1...........204 D5
**Pennington La** CM22,
CM24 ...................93 D2
Penningtons CM23 .......145 C5
Penn Mews CM7...........155 A8
Pennsylvania La CO15 ....179 C5
Penny Cnr IP1 ...........16 C8
Penny La IP3 .............18 F1
Penny Mdw IP7 ...........35 A1
Pennypot Cnr CO9 .......103 B6
Pennypot Cotts CO9 ......103 B5
Pennyroyal Cres CM8 ....176 E4
Pennyroyal Gdns IP2 ......16 C9
Penny Royal Rd CM3......218 D6
Pennystone Rd CB11......43 E8
Penrice CI CO14 ..........136 E6
Penrice Ct CO14 ..........144 D1
Penrose Mead CM1 .......215 B8
Penryn Rd IP5 ...........18 F7
Penshurst PI CM77 ......154 B6
Penshurst Rd IP3 ........18 D4
Penticton Rd CM7 .......127 D2
Pentland Ave CM1 .......205 A6
**PENTLOW** ...............13 F6
Pentlow Dr CO10 ........1 E1
Pentlow Hawke CI CB9....9 B7
Pentlow Hill CO10 .......14 A8
Pentlow La CO10 ........1 E1
Pentlow Ridge CO10 .....13 F6
**PENTLOW STREET** ......14 A8
**Penzance CI**
Chelmsford CM1 .......205 E5
Clacton-on-S CO15.....203 I8
Penzance Rd IP3 .........18 F6
Peppercorn CI CO4 ......109 F2
Peppercorn Way IP2 ......17 D3
Pepper's Rd CO4 .........82 E1
**Pepples La**
Debden CB10 ..........69 A8
Elder Street CB10 ......45 A1
Pepys St CO7 ...........91 D5
**Percival Rd**
Kirby-le-S CO13 ........143 D1
Walton-on-t-N CO14 ....144 D2
Percy Ruse CI CO10......34 B7
**Peregrine CI**
Bishop's Stortford
CM23 .................145 D6
Clacton-on-S CO15....188 F7
Peregrine Ct CO4 ........136 E8
Peregrine Dr CM2 .......216 A4
Perkins Way IP3 ..........17 F1
Perriclose CM1 ..........205 D7
Perrin PI CM2 ...........205 A1
Perryfields CO10.........34 B4
**Perryfields Jun & Inf Sch**
CM1 ..................205 D6
**PERRY GREEN** ..........129 D1
Perry La CO4 ............84 A4
**Perry Rd**
Little Dunmow CM6......151 E8
Tiptree CO5 ...........179 C5
Witham CM8 ...........177 B1
Perry Way CM8...........177 B1

Persardi Ct CO2 ..........163 A7
Pershore End CO3 ........134 E5
Perth CI CO2 ............136 A1
Pertwee Ct CO7 ..........185 E8
Pertwee Dr CM2 .........216 F6
Pertwee Cres CO1 .......136 C6
Pertwee Way CO5 ........163 B2
Pesthouse La CO12 ......116 D3
Petchey Ct **3** CM7.......209 F2
Peter Bruff Ave CO16 ....188 C5
Peterfield's La CO9 ......102 F5
Peterhouse CI IP2 ........16 F2
Petersfield CM1 ..........205 B7
Peter's Gr IP9 ...........35 A1
Peters Ho CO5 ..........158 C2
Petlands CB10 ...........22 F8
Peto Ave CO14 ...........109 F2
Petrebrook CM2 .........206 A3
Petrel Way CM2 .........216 C6
Petrolea CI CO4 .........109 F1
Petronius Way CO4 ......110 B5
Pettit La CM7 ...........156 A4
Petts La CB10 ...........4 E1
Pettwood Gdns IP9........62 D6
Petunia Cres CM1 .......205 F6
**Petworth CI**
Great Notley CM77 .....154 B7
Wivenhoe CO7 .........164 C8
Pevensey Dr CO15 .......203 I8
Peverel Ave CM3 ........194 C1
Peverells Rd CB10 ......44 D1
Pewterers Ave CM23 ....145 C4
**PHARISEE GREEN** .......150 A5
Pharos La CO5 ...........201 C6
Pheasant Rd IP2 .........16 E3
Pheasant Rise IP8 ........35 F8
Philbrick CI CO1 ........136 C5
Philip Ave IP11 ..........221 B3
Philip CI CO14 ..........171 A8
**Philip Morant Sch & Coll**
CO3 ..................135 B5
**Philip Rd**
Ipswich IP2 .............17 C4
**1** Witham CM8..........194 E8
Philips CI CM77 .........126 F2
Philips Rd CM77 .........126 F2
Phillip Rd CO7...........164 B8
Phillips Chase CM7 ......128 A5
Phillips Field Rd CO10 ...34 A5
**PHILPOT END** ...........150 A2
Philpot End La CM6......150 B8
Phoenix Ct CO5..........201 B6
Phoenix Gr CM2 .........216 A8
Phoenix CI **21** CO10......33 E7
Phoenix Ind Pk CO12 ....91 A4
**Phoenix Pavilions**
CO12 ..................91 C2
Phoenix Rd IP4 ..........18 A7
Phoenix Sq CO4 .........126 B8
Piccotts La CM7 .........126 B8
Pickers Way CO15 .......189 E7
Pickford Wlk CO4........136 F7
Pickpocket La CM77 .....154 D6
Pickwick Ave CO11 ......16 E5
Pickwick Rd CO10 ......16 E5
Pier App CO14 ..........171 C8
Pier Ave CO15 ..........188 E2
Pierce Glade CO5 ........179 C5
Pier Gap CO15 ..........188 F2
Pier Rd IP11 ............221 A1
Pierrefitte Way CM7 .....127 E3
Pigeon's La IP8 ..........16 A3
**Pightle The**
Capel St M IP9 .........35 B2
Finchingfield CM7 ......72 D6
Haverhill CB9............9 A8
Pightle Way CO14 .......171 A7
Pig La CM22 .............146 A3
Pigotts Way CM23 .......145 C5
**PIG STREET** .............168 E6
Pilborough Way CO3.....134 E3
Pilcox Hall La CO16......140 D8
Pilgrim CI CM7 ..........127 F5
Pilgrims CI CB10 ........3 D2
Pilgrims Ct CB10 ........55 F1
Pimblett Row CM22 ......94 F5
Pimpernel Rd IP2 ........16 F3
Pincey Rd CM4 ..........120 F3
Pincey Rdbt CM24 .......121 A3
Pinchpools Rd CM23.....93 A3
**Pine Ave**
Great Dunmow CM6 .....123 B1
Ipswich IP1 .............17 B8
**Pine CI**
Brantham CO11.........86 D8
Great Bentley CO7......166 F8
Pinecroft Gdns CO4.....110 B3
Pinecroft Rise CO10 .....33 D5
Pine Gr IP11 ............18 F1
**Pine Gr**
Bishop's Stortford
CM23 .................146 B6
West Mersea CO5.......201 B7
Witham CM8 ...........194 E8
Pine Ho IP11 ............221 A4
Pinelands CM23 ..........146 A3
Pines Hill CM24 .........119 D5
Pines Rd CM1 ...........204 D5
Pines The CM3 ..........194 A5
Pinetree CI IP5 ..........18 F7
Pine Tree Ct CO4 .......136 E8
Pine View Rd IP1 ........17 A8
**Pinewood CI**
Clacton-on-S CO15....188 E7
Kirby Cross CO13 ......170 D6
Pinhoe Dr CB9 ..........8 C8
Pinkeneys SG8 ..........19 D5

Pinkham Dr CM8 ........194 F8
Pink La CM3...............175 D7
Pinkney CI CO10 ..........44 E2
Pinkuah La CO10 .........13 F6
Pin Mill CI IP2 ...........16 C1
Pinmill Rd IP9 ...........63 F8
Pinner's Cross SG8 ......39 A7
Pintail CI IP2 ............16 E3
Pintail Cres CM77.......154 C6
Pioneer PI **8** CO1 ........136 A6
Pipchin Rd CM1 .........204 F6
Piperell Way CB9 ........9 A5
Piperell Way Units CB9 ...9 A5
Pipers Rd CO3 ...........135 B7
Pipers CI CB9 ...........9 C6
Piper's Tye CM2 .........216 D3
Pipers Vale CI IP3 ........17 E1
**Piper's Vale Com Prim Sch**
IP3 ....................17 F1
**Pippins The**
Colchester CO4 ........136 C8
Glemsford CO10 ........2 C4
Halstead CO9 ...........76 D2
Pirie Rd CO6 ............108 E3
Pitcairn Rd IP1 ..........16 E8
Pitfield CM2 .............216 D8
Pitfield Ho CM7 .........127 D4
Pit La CO5 ..............179 C6
Pitmire La CO8 ..........95 B8
Pitt Ave CM8 ............195 A8
Pitt Chase CM2 .........216 E5
Pitt Gn CM8 ............195 A8
Pitts End CO7 ...........59 D3
**Place Farm Com Prim Sch**
CB9 ...................148 C8
Place Farm Ct CO2 ......136 D2
Plains Farm CI CO7 ......110 D6
Plains Field CM7 .........128 D1
**Plains Rd**
Great Totham CM9......196 F6
Little Totham CM9 ......197 A6
**PLAISTOW GREEN** ......103 D5
**Plaistow Green Rd**
CO9 ...................103 C5
Plaiters Way CM23 ......128 D3
Plane Tree CI CM2 ......216 B6
Plane View CI CO16 .....188 B2
Plantation CI CB11 .......43 E6
Plantation Rd CM3.......192 F1
Planton Way CO7 ........185 E6
Platters CI IP3 ..........38 B7
Platters Rd IP11 .........221 C2
Plaw Hatch CM23 .......146 B8
**Plaw Hatch Cnr**
CM23 .................146 D8
Players Ct CM6 ..........152 C6
Playfield Rd IP9 .........35 B1
Playford Ct **2** CO16......18 E8
Playford Rd IP4 .........18 E8
Playle Chase CM9 ........196 B4
Pleasant Mews CO5 .....201 C6
Pleasant Rd CM23 .......145 A8
Pleasant Row **13** IP4 .....17 D5
Pleasant Valley CB11.....43 D7
Pleasant Way CM7.......154 B6
**PLEDGDON GREEN** ......95 C3
Pleshey Rd CM3 .........172 B5
Plough Cnr CO16 ........168 C4
Plough Dr CO3 ..........135 A5
Plough La CO10 .........13 E6
Ploughmans CI CM23 ....145 C5
**Ploughmans Headland**
CO3 ...................134 E5
Ploughmans La CM77 ...154 C8
Plough Rd CO7 ..........166 E6
Plough St IP3 ...........17 E4
Plover CI CO13 ..........170 E6
Plover Rd IP2............16 E2
Plover Wlk CM7 .........128 A5
Plowright Ho **6** CO1......135 E8
**Plume Ave**
Colchester CO3 .........135 A4
Maldon CM9.............209 F1
Plume Sch CM9 ..........209 F2
**Plume Sch (Lower)**
CM9 ...................210 A2
Plummers Rd CO6 .......107 E7
Plumptre La CM3 ........218 D5
Plums La CM7 ...........99 E4
Plum St CO10 ...........2 A6
Plumtree Ave CM2 .......216 F6
**Plymouth Rd**
Chelmsford CM1 .......205 E5
Clacton-on-S CO15....203 A4
Felixstowe IP11.........221 D6
Pochard Way CM77 .....154 C5
Pocklington Ct CM2 .....206 A3
Podsbrook Ho CM8 .....176 F2
Pod's Brook Rd CM7 ....127 D2
Pods La CM77 ...........126 D2
**POINT CLEAR** ...........186 A3
**POINT CLEAR BAY** ......185 F3
**Point Clear Bay Holiday**
Cvn Pk CO16 ..........185 F3
Point Clear Rd CO16 ....186 D3
Pointwell La CO6 .......158 A4
Pole Barn La CO13 ......170 F5
Polecat Rd CM77 ........155 F5
Pole La CM8 ............113 C5
Pollard Ct IP2 ..........16 D2
Pollard's Gn CM2 .......205 D2
Pollards Villas CM7......99 D2
Pollard Wlk CO16 .......188 C5
Polley CI CO13...........170 E7
Polstead St CO6 ........56 D5
Polstead Way CO16......188 B4
Pond Chase CO13 .......170 E7
Pond CI IP11 ............221 B5
Pond Cotts IP9 ..........61 E2

Pond Cross Cotts CB11...67 A8
Pond Cross Farm CB11...67 A8
Pond Cross Way CB11....67 A8
Ponders Rd CO6 ........107 C4
Pondfield Rd CO4 .......110 D1
Pondfields CM6 .........123 D1
**Pondholton Dr** **2**
CM8 ...................194 F7
Pond House La CO15 ....189 D8
Pond La CM24 ..........119 D7
Ponds Rd CM2 ..........119 D7
Pondtail CI CO13 ........170 C6
Poney Chase CM8 .......195 F5
Poney's CM8 ............195 F5
**Pontisbright Cotts**
CO6 ...................106 E6
Poole CI IP3 ............18 D3
**Poole St**
Cavendish CO10 .........1 C1
Great Yeldham CO9 .....51 B6
Pooley's Yd IP2 ..........17 B4
Poore St CB11 ...........65 F8
Poperinghe Rd CO2......135 F4
Popes Ct CB9 ...........9 E5
Pope's La CO3 ..........135 E7
Pope's Rd CO6 ..........106 D4
**Poplar CI**
Chelmsford CM2 .......216 C6
Clacton-on-S CO15.....188 B2
Great Yeldham CO9 ....30 A1
Poplar Dr CM9 ..........103 F8
Poplar Hall CI CO11 .....109 E1
Poplar La CM23 .........16 B3
Poplar Rd CO10 .........34 B7
Poplars CI CO7 ..........165 B7
**Poplars The**
Brantham CO11........60 D2
Colchester CO3 ........134 E5
Great Dunmow CM6 ...123 C2
CM22 .................146 F4
Poplar Way CO13 .......170 D6
Poppy CI IP2 ...........16 F4
Poppy Gdns CO13 .......136 C3
Poppy Gn CM23 .........206 A6
Pork La CO13 ...........169 E5
Portal Prec CO1 .........135 F7
Porter Rd IP3 ...........18 F1
**Porters Brook Wlk**
CO4 ...................110 C2
Porter's CI CO3 .........107 F2
Porter's Cotts CO3 ......107 F1
Porters Field CM7 .......127 D4
Porter's La CO3 .........107 F2
Porters Pk CM3 .........193 A2
Porter Way CO16 .......188 B3
**Port La**
Bishop's Stortford
CM22 .................146 B2
Colchester CO3 .........136 B5
Portland Ave CO12......91 C3
Portland CI CM7 ........128 B3
Portland Cres CO12......91 C3
Portland Ho CO13 .......170 F5
Portland Rd CO13 .......170 F5
Portland Rd **17** CM23....145 F7
Portman Rd IP1 ..........17 B5
**Portman Road (Ipswich**
Town FC) IP1 ...........17 B5
**Portmans Walk Ind Ctr**
IP11 ...................17 A5
Portman's Wlk IP1 .......17 A5
Portobello Rd CO14 .....171 C8
**Port Of Felixstowe Rd**
IP11 ...................221 A4
Portreath PI CM1........205 A7
Portsmouth Rd CO15 ....203 J8
Portway CM2 ............206 B4
Portway Ct CO9 .........76 F3
Posford Ct CO4 .........109 F4
Postman's La CO10 .....207 E3
Post Mill CI IP4 .........17 F6
Post Office Cnr IP9......61 F2
**Post Office La**
Glemsford CO10 ........2 B5
Little Totham CM9 ......197 B4
**Post Office Rd**
Chelmsford CM1 ........205 B8
Potash Rd IP9 ..........60 E8
Potash La IP9 ...........60 E8
Pot Kiln Chase CO9......31 F2
**Pot Kiln Prim Sch**
CO10 .................34 B6
Pot Kiln Rd CO10 ......34 B6
Pot Kilns The CO10 .....34 B6
Potters CI CM23 ........219 A6
**Potter St**
Bishop's Stortford
CM23 .................145 F7
Sible Hedingham CO9 ...75 E7
**Pottery La**
Castle Hedingham CO9...51 F3
Chelmsford CM1 .......205 A5
Poulteney Rd CM24......119 E8

Pound Farm Dr CO12....91 A3
Poundfield CI CO7 .......165 B7
Poundfield Ho CO7 ......138 A5
Pound Fields CM1 .......215 B8
Pound Gate CM6 ........213 B8
Pound Hill Villas CM6 ...151 E8
Pound La IP9 ...........59 F8
Pound Wlk CB10.........22 C2
Powell CI CO5 ..........179 E5
**POWERS HALL END** ....176 E3
**Powers Hall Inf Sch**
CM8 ..................176 D3
**Powers Hall Jun Sch**
CM8 ..................176 D3
Powling Rd IP3 .........18 A2
Pownall Cres CO2 .......135 F4
Pownall Rd IP3............17 E4
Poynter PI CO13 ........170 E7
Prail Ct CO6 ...........130 F2
Pratts Farm La CM3 ....191 D4
Pratt's La IP9 ..........38 A2
Prentice Hall La CM9 ...213 B7
Prentice Mews IP3 ......38 C8
Prentice Rd CO5 .........97 A4
President Rd CO3 ........134 E5
Preston Rd CO15 ........189 D5
Prestwick Dr CM23 .....119 B1
Pretoria Rd CO9 ........76 F2
**Prettygate Inf Sch**
CO3 ..................135 B4
**Prettygate Jun Sch**
CO3 ..................135 B4
Prettygate Rd CO3 ......135 A4
**Prettyman Rd**
Felixstowe IP11.........221 C1
Ipswich IP3 .............18 B3
Prime's CI CB10 .........22 D1
Primrose CI CM23 .......145 C6
**Primrose Hill**
Chelmsford CM1 .......204 F3
Haverhill CB9 ..........8 F7
Holbrook IP9 ...........62 D4
Ipswich IP2 ............16 F4
**Primrose La**
Ramsey CO12 ..........89 A1
Tiptree CO5 ...........179 C5
Primrose PI CM8 ........176 E4
Primrose Rd CO15 ......189 E6
**Primrose Wlk**
Colchester CO4 ........136 E7
Maldon CM9.............210 B1
Primula CI CO16.........188 C4
Primula Way CM1........206 A6
Prince Albert Rd CO5 ...201 D6
**Prince Charles CI**
Clacton-on-S CO15.....188 C6
Sudbury CO10 ..........33 F8
**Prince Charles Rd**
CO2 ..................136 A2
Princel La CO7 .........84 F7
Princel Mews CO7 ......84 F7
**Prince Of Wales Dr**
IP2 ...................17 B2
**Prince of Wales Ind Est**
CO6 ..................133 B4
Prince Of Wales Rd CM3...196 A3
**Prince of Wales Rdbt**
CO6 ..................133 B4
**Prince Philip Ave**
CO15 .................188 C1
Prince Philip Rd CO2 ...136 A1
Princes CI CM23 ........145 C7
Prince's Espl CO14 .....144 D1
Princes Gate CO14 .....144 D1
Princes Gdns IP11......221 C7
**Princes Rd**
Chelmsford CM2 ......216 B7
Clacton-on-S CO15.....189 D5
Felixstowe IP11.........221 E4
Harwich CO12 ..........91 B3
Maldon CM9.............210 A2
**Princess Anne CI**
CO15 .................188 C1
Princess Dr CO4 ........110 C5
Princess St CO12 .......90 F5
Princes St IP1 ..........17 B5
Princess Way CO9 ......8 E8
Prince St CO10 .........33 E8
Princes Well CO10 ......45 F7
Princethorpe Rd IP3.....18 C4
Princeton Mews CO4 ...110 B4
Prior's CI CM2 ..........102 D8
Priors **8** CM23 ..........141 F2
**Priors Hall Barn** *
CB11 ..................67 D4
Priors Way CO6 .........131 A3
**Prior's Wood Rd**
CM22 .................148 C7
Prior Way CO4 ..........109 E2
Priory Ave CO6 .........8 F7
**Priory CI**
Chelmsford CM1 .......204 E2
Hatfield Peverel CM3 ...194 B1
Ickleton CB10 ..........3 A3
Seawick CO16 .........203 A6
Priory Cotts CO2 ........160 E6
**Priory Ct**
Bishop's Stortford
CM23 .................145 F7
Colchester CO1 .........135 E7
Hatfield Peverel CM3 ...194 A4
Ipswich IP10 ...........38 C6

Priory Dr CM24 .........119 E5
Priory Farm Rd CM3 ..194 B2
Priory Gdns CO10.......33 E6
PRIORY HEATH .........18 D1
Priory La
  Bicknacre CM3.........218 E5
  Great Notley CM77 .....154 C8
Priory Mews CM3.......194 C2
Priory Pk
  Ipswich IP3 ...........38 B6
  St Osyth CO16 ........187 A4
Priory Prim Sch CM3 ..218 F2
Priory Rd
  Bicknacre CM3.........218 E1
  Chappel CO6 ..........106 B3
  Clacton-on-S CO15....188 E3
  Sudbury CO10 .........15 D1
Priory St
  Colchester CO1 .......136 A7
  Earls Colne CO6.......105 B7
Priory The CM1 .......215 B8
Priory Wlk
  **22** Colchester CO1 .....135 F7
  Sudbury CO10 .........33 E7
Priory Wood CO7 ......51 E4
Priory Wood Rdbt
  CM22 ..................147 A8
Prittlewell Cl IP2.......16 F1
Proctor Cl CO5.........163 B2
Proctors Way CM23....146 A4
Proctor Way CO6 .......132 E3
Progress Ct CM7 ......127 E3
Progress Way CO16....168 C1
Promenade
  Clacton-on-S CO15.....203 D6
  Harwich CO12..........91 E4
  Harwich, Dovercourt
  CO12.................91 C2
Promenade Way CO7...185 E5
Propelair Way CO4 ....109 D2
Prospect Cl CM3.......194 A3
Prospect Hill CO10.....34 D3
Prospect Pk CO13 .....170 A5
Prospect Pl CB11 ......22 F2
Prospect Rd IP1........17 A7
Prospero Ct CO4.......136 F8
Provan Ct IP3 .........18 B4
Provence Cl CO3 ......134 C7
Providence La IP1......17 A7
Providence Pl CO1....136 B6
Providence St **6** IP1 ..17 C6
Prunus Ct CO2 ........163 A7
Prykes Dr CM1 ........205 A2
Pryor Cl CM8..........177 A1
Pryors Cl CM23.........146 A6
Pryors Rd CM7 ........216 C2
Pudding La CO2........161 B3
Puffinsdale CO15 ......188 F5
Pulford Pl CM.........
Pulpitfield Cl CO14 ...171 A8
Pumphill SG9 .........64 A2
Pump Hill
  Great Baddow CM2 ....216 F6
  St Osyth CO16 ........187 D4
Pump Hill Cvn Pk
  CO16 .................187 C4
Pump Ho The **13**
  CM23 .................146 A7
Pump La
  Chelmsford CM1 ......205 E6
  Danbury CM3..........218 D5
  Purleigh CM3..........220 D1
Pumpyard Cotts CO9..31 E1
Punchard Way IP11.....221 A8
Punders Field CM7 ....128 D1
Purbeck Ct
  **4** Colchester CO1 .....136 D7
  Great Baddow CM2....216 E6
Purcell Cl CO4.........136 E6
Purcell Cole ..........204 A1
Purcell Rd CM8.........194 E7
Purdis Ave IP3 ........18 F2
Purdis Farm La IP3.....18 F2
PURLEIGH ............220 C1
Purleigh Com Prim Sch
  CM3 ..................220 D1
Purley Way CO16 .....188 B6
Purplett Ho IP2........17 D4
Purplett St IP2........17 D4
Purvis Way CO4 .......110 B5
Putticks La CO2 .......59 E3
PUTTOCK END .........31 C6
PUTTOCK'S END .......148 E4
Pyecat's Cnr CO7......137 C7
Pye Cnr CO... ........51 E4
Pyefleet Cl
  Brightlingsea CO7.....185 E7
  Fingringhoe CO5......164 C6
Pyefleet Ho CO5.......201 D7
Pyefleet View CO15....163 B3
Pye Gdns CM23........145 E8
Pyesand CO13 .........170 C8
PYE'S GREEN .........153 C5
Pygot Pl CM7.........127 E4
Pyms Rd CM2 .........216 B3
Pynchbek CM23 .......145 E3
Pynchon Mews CM1 ..205 D3
Pyne Gate CM1........216 B1

**Q**

QM Ind Pk IP3.........18 C1
Quadling St IP1........17 C5
Quadrangle Ctr The
  IP3..................18 C1
Quaker's La CB9.......9 A7
Quale Rd CM2.........206 B4
Quantock La IP5.......18 F7
Quay Ctyd **2** CO11....86 D4
Quay La
  Beaumont CO16.......142 B5
  Kirby-le-S CO13 ......143 D1
  Sudbury CO10 ........33 E6
Quayside Dr CO2 .....136 D5
Quayside Ind Est CM9..210 A4
Quay St
  **1** Manningtree CO11...86 D4
  Wivenhoe CO7........164 B8
Quay The
  Harwich CO12.........91 D6
  Wivenhoe CO7........164 B7
Quay Theatre* CO10...33 E6
Queech La IP9.........87 C8
Queech The IP9........35 B2
Queen Anne Dr CO5 ..201 D6
Queen Anne Gdns
  CO5 .................201 D6
Queen Anne Rd CO5...201 D7
Queenborough Gr
  CM77 ................154 C8
Queenborough La
  Great Notley CM77 ...154 D8
  Rayne CM77..........154 B8
Queenbury Cl CO5.....201 E6
Queen Edith Dr CB9 ..27 B6
Queen Elizabeth Ave
  CO15 ................188 C1
Queen Elizabeth Way
  CO2 .................136 A2
Queen Mary Ave CO2..135 F4
Queen's Ave CM9......210 A1
Queensberry Rd IP3...18 A1
Queensbury Ave CO6 ..133 D5
Queens Cl
  Stansted Mountfitchet
  CM24 ...............119 E8
  Sudbury CO10 .......33 E8
Queenscliffe Rd IP2...17 A3
Queen's Cnr CO5......201 D7
Queen's Cotts CO6....105 B7
Queens Cres CM23....145 E5
Queens Ct
  **5** Sudbury CO10 .....33 F8
  West Mersea CO5.....201 D7
Queen's Ct
  Clacton-on-S CO15....189 D4
  **6** Haverhill CB9 .....8 E8
Queensgate Dr IP4....17 F8
Queen's Gdns CM7....127 B7
Queen's Head Rd CO4..82 E3
Queen's Ho CO4.......170 F4
Queensland Cres
  CM1 .................204 E5
Queens Mews CO5....201 B6
Queens Rd
  Braintree CM7 .......127 F5
  Sudbury CO10 .......33 E8
  Chelmsford CM2 .....205 D2
  Clacton-on-S CO15....188 D7
  Colchester CO3 ......135 C6
  Earls Colne CO6......105 B7
  Felixstowe IP11......221 E4
  Frinton-on-S CO13....170 F4
  Harwich CO12........91 A2
  West Bergholt CO6...108 D3
  Wivenhoe CO7........164 C8
Queens Sq **5** CB9 ....9 A8
Queen's Sq IP3........18 B2
Queen St
  Brightlingsea CO7....185 F6
  Castle Hedingham CO9..51 E3
  Chelmsford CM2 .....205 A1
  Coggeshall CO6 .....131 A2
  Colchester CO1 ......135 F7
  Felixstowe IP11......221 C6
  Great Oakley CO12 ...116 C4
  Haverhill CB9 ........8 D7
  Ipswich IP1..........17 C5
  Maldon CM9..........210 A2
  Sible Hedingham CO9..75 F6
Queens Terr CO10.....34 A7
Queensway
  Clacton-on-S CO15....189 D5
  Great Cornard CO10...34 B5
  Haverhill CB9 ........8 D8
  Lawford CO11........86 C4
  Tiptree CO5..........179 C6
Queen's Way IP3......18 B2
Queen Victoria Dr IP9..91 B8
QUENDON ............66 F2
Quendon Pl **17** IP9...9 B8
Quendon Way CO13....171 A6
Quentin Cl IP1........16 E8
Quickset Rd CB11.....20 C5
Quicksie Hill CB11.....20 C5
Quilberry Dr CM77....154 D8
Quilp Dr CM1..........204 F7
Quilter Dr IP8.........16 C1
Quilter Rd IP11.......221 F4
Quilters Cl CO15......158 B2
Quilter's Gn CO5......107 D6
Quince Cl CO1........60 D1
Quince Ct CO5........179 D4
Quinion Cl CM1........204 D7

Quintons Cnr CO7 .....59 D4
Quinton's La IP11......221 F7
Quintons Rd CO7.......59 D4

**R**

R A Butler Jun & Inf Schs
  CB11 ................22 E1
RACECOURSE .........18 B2
Rachael Cl **1** CM2....205 B1
Rachael Gdns CM8....156 E4
Rachel Ct **2** IP4......17 D6
Radcliffe Dr IP2.......16 D2
Radiator Rd CO10......34 A5
RADLEY'S END .........97 A2
Radveld Chase CO3...134 E4
RADWINTER ...........45 F8
Radwinter CE Prim Sch
  CB10 ................45 F7
RADWINTER END ......25 B4
Radwinter Rd
  Ashdon CB10 ........24 B7
  Saffron Walden CB10..23 B1
  Sewards End CB10....23 F1
Raeburn Cl CO13......170 F7
Raeburn Ct CM1.......205 E6
Raeburn Rd IP3.......18 A1
Raeburn Rd S IP3.....17 F1
Ragley Cl CM7........154 B6
Raglan Rd CO15.......188 C3
Raglan Rd CO13.......171 A5
Ragley Cl CM7........154 B6
Raile Wlk CO10.......15 D8
Railey Rd CB11.......43 E8
Railway App IP11......221 E5
Railway Cotts
  Thorpe-le-S CO16....168 F7
  Wendens Ambo CB11..42 F5
Railway Sq CM1.......205 A3
Railway St
  Braintree CM7.......128 A3
  Chelmsford CM1 .....205 A3
  Manningtree CO11....86 D4
Railway Terr
  Clacton-on-S CO15....188 F3
  **1** Manningtree CO11..86 D4
Rainbow Cl CO12......91 D4
Rainbow Mead CM3 ..194 A5
Rainbow Mews CM9 ..209 F5
Rainbow Rd CO5 .....201 D6
Rainbow Way CO6 ....77 F1
Raine Ave CB9........8 D8
Rainham Way CO13...171 B6
Rainsborowe Rd CO2..135 C4
Rainsford Ave CM1....204 F3
Rainsford La CM1......204 F2
Rainsford Rd
  Chelmsford CM1 .....204 F3
  Stansted Mountfitchet
  CM24 ...............119 E8
Rambler Cl CO3.......134 D7
Rampart Cotts CO6 ...109 B7
Ramparts Cl CO6 .....109 B7
Ramplings Ave CO15..188 E5
Ramsden Cl CO15.....189 A5
RAMSEY ..............90 A2
Ramsey Cl
  Heybridge CM9 ......210 D4
  Ipswich IP2..........17 A1
Ramsey Mews CO2 ...136 A4
Ramsey Rd
  Halstead CO9.........103 D8
  Harwich CO12........90 C2
Ramsey Sch (Priory Hall)
  The CO9..............77 A2
Ramsey Sch The CO9..77 A2
Ramsgate Dr IP3 .....18 B3
Ramshaw Dr CM2.....205 F3
Rana Ct CM7..........127 F4
Rana Dr CM7..........127 F4
Randall Cl
  Great Dunmow CM6 ..123 D1
  Witham CM8..........194 F7
Randolph Ave CM7 ...73 C6
Randolph Cl
  Ipswich IP3..........18 B5
  Maldon CM9..........220 F8
Rands Way IP3........18 B2
Randulph Terr CM1...205 D3
Randwell Cl IP4.......18 C8
Ranelagh Ct IP11......221 E4
Ranelagh Prim Sch
  IP2..................16 F5
Ranelagh Rd
  Felixstowe IP11......221 E4
  Ipswich IP2..........17 A5
Ranger Hts **4** CM7...127 F3
Ranger Wlk CO2......136 B3
Range Way CO2.......135 B1
RANK'S GREEN .......174 D8
Ransome Cl IP8.......16 A6
Ransome Cres IP8....16 B2
Ransome Rd IP3 ......18 B3
Ransomes Europark
  IP3..................38 E8
Ransomes Way
  Chelmsford CM1 .....205 B4
  Ipswich IP3..........38 D8
Ransom Rd CO5.......179 C5
Ranulf Rd CM4........161 E6
Ranulph Way CM3 ....194 B3
Raphael Dr CM1 ......204 F7
Rapier St IP2..........17 C3
Ratcliff Ct CO5........158 B2
Ratcliffe Ct
  Colchester CO1 ......136 A6
  Frinton-on-S CO13....170 F5
Ratcliffe Rd CO3......134 E6

Rat Hill IP9 ...........63 F2
Ravel Ave CM8........194 F7
Ravens Ave CO9......76 F1
Ravensbourne Dr
  CM1 .................204 E2
Ravens Cres CM6.....152 E6
Ravenscroft Prim Sch
  CO16 ...............188 B4
Ravensdale CO15......188 F6
Ravenswood **11** CO1 ..16 B4
Ravenswood Ave IP3..38 C8
Ravenswood Com Prim
  Sch IP3..............38 C8
Rawden Cl CO12......91 B4
Rawden Way CM9.....109 E4
Rawlings Cres CO4....110 B5
Rawstorn Rd CO3.....135 E2
Ray Ave CO12.........91 A3
Raycliff Ave CO15.....188 E7
RAYDON ..............58 E8
Raydon Way CO10....34 C6
Rayfield Cl CM6.......151 A4
Rayhaven CO12.......90 D2
Ray Ho CO5...........201 D7
Ray La
  Harwich CO12........90 E5
  Ramsey CO12........90 A3
Rayleigh Cl
  Braintree CM7.......128 C4
  Colchester CO4 .....110 B1
Rayleigh Mans CO2...135 C5
Rayleighs The CO2....135 C5
Ray Mead CM3 .......190 F7
Rayments Bglws CB10..45 E3
Raymouth Ho CO2....135 E2
RAYNE ...............154 B6
Rayne Prim Sch
  CM7 .................126 F2
Rayne Rd CM7 .......127 D3
Rayner Rd CO2.......135 B4
Rayners Ct CO4.......83 F4
Rayner Way CO9.....76 E1
Raynham Cl CM23....146 C7
Raynham Rd CM23...146 B8
Raynhams CB10.......22 D1
Ray The CM1..........205 E5
Reade Rd IP9.........62 D5
Reader's Cnr CM2....216 E5
Readers Ct CM2......216 E6
Reading Rd IP4.......18 B7
Reaper Rd CO3.......135 A5
Rebecca Gdns CM8...156 E4
Rebecca Rd CO5......189 A3
Rebecca Meade CM6..122 F8
Rebow Rd
  Harwich CO12........91 A2
  Wivenhoe CO7........164 B8
Rebow St CO1.........136 B6
Reckitts Cl CO15......189 B4
Recreation Cl IP11 ...221 D6
Recreation Ground
  Sible Hedingham CO9..75 D8
  Stansted Mountfitchet
  CM24 ...............119 E6
Recreation Ho CO2...136 B5
Recreation La IP11....221 D6
Recreation Rd
  Clacton-on-S CO15....188 F3
  Colchester CO1 ......136 C5
  Haverhill CB9 ........8 A5
  Sible Hedingham CO9..75 D8
Recreation Way
  Brightlingsea CO7....185 F7
  Ipswich IP3..........18 E2
Recreation Wlk CO10..34 B5
Rectory Cl
  Bishop's Stortford
  CM23 ...............145 D3
  **5** Colchester CO4...109 E2
  Glemsford CO10 .....2 B5
  Littlebury CB11 ......21 F4
  Little Waltham CM3...191 C6
Rectory Cotts CO15 ..138 F1
Rectory Dr CM23 .....118 D6
Rectory Field IP9.....63 E7
Rectory Hill
  East Bergholt CO7....59 C1
  Stoke-by-N CO6......56 D7
Rectory Ct CO7.......137 C1
Rectory La
  Abberton CO5 .......163 A3
  Ashdon CB10 ........6 A1
  Brantham CO11......60 E1
  Chelmsford CM1 .....205 B4
  Farnham CM23 ......118 D6
  Great Leighs CM3....173 D7
  Ramsey CO12........90 A1
  Rivenhall CM8 .......177 A6
  Wickham St P CO9...53 C6
  Woodham Mortimer
  CM9 ................219 F6
Rectory Mdw CM7....129 C2
Rectory Mdws CO9...51 D1
Rectory Rd
  Aldham CO6.........132 F7
  Copford CO6.........133 C1
  Frating Green CO7...138 B1
  Great Henny CO10....33 E4
  Great Holland CO13..170 A3
  Harkstead IP9........63 C2
  Ipswich IP2..........17 C4
  Langham CO4........83 F7
  Little Bentley CO7....139 E8
  Little Oakley CO12...117 A7
  Rowhedge CO5......163 B8

Rectory Rd continued
  Sible Hedingham CO9..51 D1
  Stisted CM77.........129 B7
  Tiptree CO5..........179 C5
  Tolleshunt Knights
  CM9 .................180 C1
  Weeley Heath CO16..167 F3
  Wivenhoe CO7........137 C2
  Woodham Walter CM9..208 D3
  Wrabness CO11......89 A3
  Writtle CM1..........215 B8
Redan St IP1..........17 B7
Red Barn La CO12....116 B2
Red Barn Rd CO7.....185 F8
Redbridge Rd CO15...188 F8
Redcliffe Rd **3** CM2..205 C4
Reddells Cl **3** CO10...33 F8
Reddings Cl CB11.....43 E7
Rede Way CO10.......34 C6
Redgate La IP9........37 D5
Redgates La CB10 ....23 E3
Redgates Pl CM2.....205 D4
Redhill Cl IP11.........16 F8
Redhouse La CO4.....82 D2
Red House La
  Great Cornard CO10...34 A4
  Sudbury CO10 .......33 E7
Red La IP9............60 A8
Red Lion Ct **4** CM23..146 A4
Red Lion Yd **17** CO1..135 F7
Redmayne Dr CM2....215 F8
Redmill CO3..........135 A3
Redrose Wlk CO16....188 C8
Redruth Cl CM1.......205 E5
Redshank Cl CM9 ....9 C7
Redshank Dr CM9 ....210 C5
Red Sleeve **5** IP9 ....35 A1
Redvers Cl CM23 .....119 A2
Redwing Cl IP2........16 D3
Redwood Cl
  Colchester CO4 .....110 E1
  Witham CM8 .........177 A5
Redwood Ct **2** CO4...136 E8
Redwoods The CM23..145 D8
Reed Cl CO16 ........188 C5
Reedland Way IP11...221 B5
Reeds La CB9.........9 A8
Refinery Rd CO12.....90 E5
Regal Cl CM2.........216 D8
Regency Cl
  Bishop's Stortford
  CM23 ...............145 E7
  Chelmsford CM2 .....205 D3
Regency Ct
  Heybridge CM9 ......210 A5
  Ipswich IP3..........17 F5
Regency Gn CO15.....188 E5
Regent Cl CO15.......188 E5
Regent Ct CO5........164 A8
Regent Rd CO7.......185 F7
Regents Cl CO4.......110 C5
Regent St
  Ipswich IP4..........17 E6
  **9** Manningtree CO11..86 D4
  Rowhedge CO5......164 A8
Regimental Way CO12..90 C1
Regina Cl IP4.........18 B5
Regina Rd CM1.......205 C3
Reigate Ave CO16.....188 D6
Reigate Cl IP3.........18 B3
Rembrandt Gr CM1...205 E6
Rembrandt Way CO3..135 B5
Rembrow Rd IP9......35 A1
Remembrance Ave
  CM3 .................194 A3
Remercie Rd CO11....87 A4
Remus Cl CO4.........109 F5
Rendlesham Ct **8** IP1..17 A7
Rendlesham Rd
  Felixstowe IP11......221 B5
  Ipswich IP1..........17 A6
Renfrew Rd IP4.......18 B8
Rennie Pl CM2........206 B3
Rennie Wlk CM9......210 C4
Renoir Pl CM1.........205 F7
Retreat The
  West Bergholt CO6...108 D3
  Witham CM8 .........177 A1
Reuben Wlk CO1.....105 B6
Reverdy Ho CO2......135 E2
Rex Mott Ct CM8.....176 F2
Reydon Ct CB9.......9 A8
Reydon Ho IP3........18 A2
Reymead Cl CO5......201 C6
Reynard Copse CM23..118 F1
Reynard Hts CM4.....136 C8
Reynards Cl CO13.....170 D6
Reynards Copse CO4..110 A3
Reynard Way CM7....216 F6
Reynolds Ave
  Colchester CO3 .....135 B5
  Ipswich IP3..........38 A8
Reynolds Ct IP11......221 B5
Reynolds Rd IP3......18 A1
Rhodes Ave CM23....145 F5
Riby Rd IP11..........221 D3
Rice Bridge Ind Est
  CO16 ...............169 A7
Richard Ave
  Brightlingsea CO7....185 F6
  Wivenhoe CO7........137 C2
Richard Burn Way
  CO10 ...............15 E2
Richard de Clare Com
  Prim Sch CO9........76 F1
Richards Cl CM8.......176 F1
Richardson Pl CM1 ...204 F4

Richardson Rd C07 . . . . . . .59 D3
Richardsons La IP9 . . . . . . .63 D8
Richardson Wlk
  Colchester CO3 . . . . . . . .134 F5
  Witham CM8 . . . . . . . . . .177 B2
Richards Wlk CO15 . . . . . .188 E6
Richard Whittington Prim
  Sch CM23 . . . . . . . . . . .145 E4
Rich Cl CM3 . . . . . . . . . . .173 F7
Riche Cl CM6 . . . . . . . . . .152 B5
Richmond Cl CM23 . . . . . .145 C2
Richmond Cres CO12 . . . . .91 B2
Richmond Dr CO15 . . . . . .188 A1
Richmond Ho ⑪ IP4 . . . . . .17 D5
Richmond Rd
  Chelmsford CM2 . . . . . . .206 A4
  Ipswich IP1 . . . . . . . . . . . .16 F8
  West Mersea CO5 . . . . . . .201 D6
RICHMOND'S GREEN . . . . . .97 D7
RICKLING . . . . . . . . . . . . . .66 B3
Rickling CE Prim Sch
  CM8 . . . . . . . . . . . . . . . .93 E8
RICKLING GREEN . . . . . . . . .93 D8
Rickling Green Rd
  Quendon CB11 . . . . . . . . .66 E1
  Rickling Green CB11 . . . . . .93 E8
Rickling Rd CB11 . . . . . . . . .66 B6
Rickstones Rd CM8 . . . . . .177 A6
Rickstones Sch The
  CM8 . . . . . . . . . . . . . . .176 F6
Riddiford Dr CM1 . . . . . . .204 F4
Riddles Dr CO7 . . . . . . . . .109 F2
Ridge The
  Braintree CM7 . . . . . . . . .128 B6
  Little Baddow CM3 . . . . . .207 E2
  Walton-on-t-N CO14 . . . . .171 B8
Ridgeway CO4 . . . . . . . . . .110 A4
Ridgeway The
  Braintree CM7 . . . . . . . . .128 A1
  Harwich CO12 . . . . . . . . . .91 B3
RIDGEWELL . . . . . . . . . . . . .29 B7
Ridgewell Ave CM1 . . . . . .204 F4
Ridgewell CE Prim Sch
  CO9 . . . . . . . . . . . . . . . . .29 B6
Ridgewell Rd
  Ashen CO10 . . . . . . . . . . .11 C1
  Birdbrook CO9 . . . . . . . . .10 E2
  Great Yeldham CO9 . . . . . .29 E3
Ridgewell Way CO2 . . . . . .135 F1
Ridings Ave CM77 . . . . . . .154 B7
Ridings The
  Bishop's Stortford
  CM23 . . . . . . . . . . . . . .145 D4
  Great Baddow CM2 . . . . . .216 D7
Ridlands Cl CM77 . . . . . . .155 E6
Ridley Gdns CM22 . . . . . . .94 C2
Ridley Rd CM1 . . . . . . . . . .205 B8
Riffhams Chase CM3 . . . . .207 D2
Riffhams Dr CM2 . . . . . . . .217 A7
Riffhams La
  Danbury CM3 . . . . . . . . . .218 C8
  Little Baddow CM3 . . . . . .207 C1
Rifle Hill CM7 . . . . . . . . . . .127 F1
Rifle Hill Works CM7 . . . . .127 F1
Rigby Ave CO11 . . . . . . . . .86 E4
Rignal's La CM2 . . . . . . . . .216 D3
Riley Ave CO15 . . . . . . . . .203 E6
Rimini Cl CO2 . . . . . . . . . .135 C3
Ringham Rd IP4 . . . . . . . . .18 A6
RINGTAIL GREEN . . . . . . . .172 B5
Ripley Cl CM23 . . . . . . . . . .188 B6
Rippers Ct CO9 . . . . . . . . . .51 E2
Ripple Way CO4 . . . . . . . . .110 B1
Risby Cl
  Clacton-on-S CO16 . . . . . .188 A4
  Ipswich IP4 . . . . . . . . . . . .18 B6
Rise The CO6 . . . . . . . . . . .134 A8
Ritabrook Rd IP2 . . . . . . . . .16 E1
RIVENHALL . . . . . . . . . . . . .177 B8
Rivenhall CE Prim Sch
  CM8 . . . . . . . . . . . . . . . .177 B8
Rivenhall End CO10 . . . . . . .12 C7
River Cl CO9 . . . . . . . . . . . .76 F1
River Cotts CM3 . . . . . . . . .206 F8
Riverdale Ct IP11 . . . . . . . .221 D3
River Hill
  Ipswich IP8 . . . . . . . . . . . .16 C8
  Terling CM3 . . . . . . . . . . .175 B3
River Hill Cotts CM3 . . . . . .175 B3
River Mead CM7 . . . . . . . . .128 A4
Rivermead Gate CM1 . . . . .205 B4
Rivermead Ind Est
  CM1 . . . . . . . . . . . . . . . .205 B4
Rivers Ho CO14 . . . . . . . . .144 D2
Riverside
  Bishop's Stortford
  CM23 . . . . . . . . . . . . . .145 F7
  Bradwell CM77 . . . . . . . .129 D3
  Chelmsford CM1 . . . . . . .205 C3
  Great Dunmow CM6 . . . . .123 E1
Riverside Ave E CO11 . . . . .86 C5
Riverside Ave W CO11 . . . . .86 C5
Riverside Bsns Pk
  Earls Colne CO6 . . . . . . . .104 F8
  Stansted Mountfitchet
  CM24 . . . . . . . . . . . . . .119 E6
Riverside Cotts CO11 . . . . . .86 C7
Riverside Ct CO9 . . . . . . . . .76 E2
Riverside Ind Est CM9 . . . .209 F4
Riverside Ind Pk IP2 . . . . . .17 D3
Riverside Maltings
  CO6 . . . . . . . . . . . . . . . .130 F1
Riverside Pk CM1 . . . . . . . .205 C3
Riverside Rd IP1 . . . . . . . . .16 F7
Riverside Way
  Kelvedon CO5 . . . . . . . . .158 C2
  Sible Hedingham CO9 . . . . .51 E1

Riverside Wlk
  ⑯ Bishop's Stortford
  CM23 . . . . . . . . . . . . . .145 F7
  Colchester CO1 . . . . . . . .135 E8
Rivers St IP4 . . . . . . . . . . . .17 F7
Riverton Dr CM0 . . . . . . . .213 B1
River View
  Braintree CM7 . . . . . . . . .127 F1
  Holbrook IP9 . . . . . . . . . . .62 D5
  Manningtree CO11 . . . . . . .86 C4
  Witham CM8 . . . . . . . . . .195 A8
River View Rd IP9 . . . . . . . .63 B2
Rivish La CO10 . . . . . . . . . .15 C7
Roach Vale CO4 . . . . . . . . .110 E1
Roach Vale Prim Sch
  CO4 . . . . . . . . . . . . . . . .110 E1
Roast Gn CB11 . . . . . . . . . .64 F6
Robeck Rd IP3 . . . . . . . . . .17 F1
Robert Cl CM2 . . . . . . . . . .205 F4
Roberts Ct CM2 . . . . . . . . .216 E7
Robert's Hill CO8 . . . . . . . . .79 F3
Roberts Rd CO1, CO2 . . . . .136 A5
Robert Suckling Ct
  CB9 . . . . . . . . . . . . . . . . .27 B6
Robert Wallace Cl
  CM23 . . . . . . . . . . . . . .118 F1
Robert Way CO7 . . . . . . . . .137 C3
Robin Cl
  Great Bentley CO7 . . . . . .166 D8
  Haverhill CB9 . . . . . . . . . . .9 C7
Robin Cres CO3 . . . . . . . . .134 B4
Robin Dr IP2 . . . . . . . . . . . .16 D3
ROBINHOOD END . . . . . . . .49 B6
Robin Hood Rd CM22 . . . . . .94 C1
Robinia Ct ⑪ CO4 . . . . . . . .136 F7
Robin Jeffrey Ct ⑱
  CM23 . . . . . . . . . . . . . .145 F6
Robinsbridge Rd CO6 . . . . .130 F2
Robinsdale CO15 . . . . . . . .188 F6
Robinson Cl CM23 . . . . . . .145 F5
Robinson Rd CO7 . . . . . . . .186 A7
Robin Way
  Chelmsford CM2 . . . . . . .216 B5
  Sudbury CO10 . . . . . . . . . .33 C5
Robjohns Ho ⑪ CM2 . . . . .205 C2
Robjohns Rd CM1 . . . . . . .215 E8
Robletts Way CO6 . . . . . . . .80 E4
Rochdale Way CO4 . . . . . . .136 E6
Rochelle Cl CM6 . . . . . . . . .70 A3
Rochester Cl CM7 . . . . . . .128 D4
Rochester Ct CO16 . . . . . . .22 F2
Rochester Way CO10 . . . . . .15 D2
Rochford Cl CM24 . . . . . . .119 E5
Rochford Ho CO14 . . . . . . .144 E2
Rochford Rd
  Bishop's Stortford
  CM23 . . . . . . . . . . . . . .119 C1
  Chelmsford CM2 . . . . . . .205 C1
  St Osyth CO16 . . . . . . . . .187 B4
Rochford Way
  Frinton-on-S CO13 . . . . . .170 F7
  Walton-on-t-N CO14 . . . . .171 A7
Rockall Cl CB9 . . . . . . . . . . .9 D7
Rockells Farm* CB11 . . . . .41 B5
Rockhampton Wlk ⑩
  CO2 . . . . . . . . . . . . . . . .136 A1
Rockingham Cl CO4 . . . . . .110 D3
RODBRIDGE CORNER . . . . . .15 C4
Rodbridge Hill CO10 . . . . . .15 B5
Rodbridge Nature
  Reserve* CO10 . . . . . . . . .15 B4
Roddam Cl CO3 . . . . . . . . .135 C6
Roding Ct CM7 . . . . . . . . . .128 D1
Rodney Gdns CM7 . . . . . . .128 C4
Rodney Way CM1 . . . . . . . .215 E7
Rogation Cl CO3 . . . . . . . .134 D6
Roger Browning Ho ⑧
  CO1 . . . . . . . . . . . . . . . .135 F7
Rogers Cl IP11 . . . . . . . . . .221 D6
ROGERS END . . . . . . . . . . . .6 B1
Rokell Way CO13 . . . . . . . .170 F6
Rolands Cl CM1 . . . . . . . . .205 B7
Rollerworld* CO1 . . . . . . . .136 B7
Rolley La CO5 . . . . . . . . . . .158 C2
Rolph CE Prim Sch
  CO16 . . . . . . . . . . . . . . .141 F1
Rolph Cl CO16 . . . . . . . . . .142 A2
Rolphs Cotts CM8 . . . . . . .156 D5
ROLPHY GREEN . . . . . . . . .172 A4
Roman Ct CM7 . . . . . . . . . .209 F4
Roman Ct
  Braintree CM7 . . . . . . . . .128 C1
  Saffron Walden CB11 . . . . .43 E7
Roman Hill CO2 . . . . . . . . .163 B7
Roman Ho ⑧ CM2 . . . . . . .205 B1
Romanhurst CM9 . . . . . . . .210 A4
Roman La CM24 . . . . . . . . .120 B2
Roman Rd
  Chelmsford CM2 . . . . . . .205 B1
  Colchester CO1 . . . . . . . .136 A7
  Little Waltham CM3 . . . . . .191 B5
Romans Pl CM1 . . . . . . . . .204 B1
Roman Way
  Braintree CM7 . . . . . . . . .127 C6
  Brightlingsea CO7 . . . . . . .165 E1
  Clacton-on-S CO16 . . . . . .188 D5
  Kirby Cross CO13 . . . . . . .170 E7
Romford Cl CO4 . . . . . . . . .136 B8
Romney Cl
  Braintree CM7 . . . . . . . . .127 C6
  Brightlingsea CO7 . . . . . . .165 E1
  Clacton-on-S CO16 . . . . . .188 D5
Romney Rd IP3 . . . . . . . . . .38 A8
Romulus Cl CM77 . . . . . . .109 F5
Ronald Rd CO9 . . . . . . . . . .103 E8

ROOK END . . . . . . . . . . . . .68 A5
Rook End La CB11 . . . . . . . .68 B5
Rookeries The CO6 . . . . . . .133 B4
Rookery Chase CO7 . . . . . . .84 E2
Rookery Cl
  Great Chesterford CB10 . . . .3 D3
  Hatfield Peverel CM3 . . . . .194 A5
Rookery La
  Great Totham CM9 . . . . . .196 E2
  Tiptree CO5 . . . . . . . . . . .179 C7
  Wendens Ambo CB11 . . . . .42 E4
Rookery The
  Lawford CO11 . . . . . . . . . .86 C4
  Stansted Mountfitchet
  CM24 . . . . . . . . . . . . . .119 E8
Rookes CB10 . . . . . . . . . . . .22 D3
Rookes Cres CM1 . . . . . . . .215 F8
Rookwood Cl CO15 . . . . . . .188 D7
Rookwood Way CM9 . . . . . . .9 A6
Roosevelt Way CO2 . . . . . .136 B4
Roos Hill Debden Rd
  CB11 . . . . . . . . . . . . . . . .43 E5
Roothings The CM9 . . . . . .210 B5
Roots La CM8 . . . . . . . . . . .195 E5
Roper Cl CO4 . . . . . . . . . . .110 B6
Roper Ct IP4 . . . . . . . . . . . .18 C5
Roper's Chase CM1 . . . . . .215 A4
Ropers La CO10 . . . . . . . . .15 B5
Rope Wlk
  Ipswich IP4 . . . . . . . . . . . .17 C5
  Maldon CM9 . . . . . . . . . .210 A1
Rosabelle Ave CO7 . . . . . . .137 B1
Rosalind Cl CO4 . . . . . . . . .136 F7
Rose Acre CO7 . . . . . . . . . .58 F6
Roseacres CM2 . . . . . . . . .148 C7
Rose Allen Ave CO2 . . . . . .162 F8
Rose Ave CO3 . . . . . . . . . .134 C4
Rosebank
  Harwich CO12 . . . . . . . . . .91 A3
  West Mersea CO5 . . . . . . .201 B6
Rosebank Ct CO15 . . . . . . .189 A2
Rosebank Rd CO5 . . . . . . . .201 B6
Rosebay Cl CM8 . . . . . . . . .176 D3
Rosebery CM23 . . . . . . . . .146 C6
Rosebery Ave CM1 . . . . . . .136 A7
Rosebery Ct IP11 . . . . . . . .221 D2
Rosebery Rd
  Chelmsford CM1 . . . . . . .216 B8
  Felixstowe IP11 . . . . . . . .221 F4
  Ipswich IP4 . . . . . . . . . . . .17 F5
Rose Cotts
  Brent Pelham SG9 . . . . . . .64 A5
  Great Sampford CM7 . . . . . .47 E5
Rose Cres CO4 . . . . . . . . . .109 D2
Rosecroft Cl CO15 . . . . . . .188 E6
Rose & Crown Wlk
  CB10 . . . . . . . . . . . . . . . .22 D2
Rose Ct CO2 . . . . . . . . . . .163 B8
Rosedale Cotts CO3 . . . . . .133 F5
Rosefinch Cl CB9 . . . . . . . . .9 C7
Rose Gdns
  Braintree CM7 . . . . . . . . .128 A2
  Seawick CO16 . . . . . . . . .187 A1
Rose Glen CM2 . . . . . . . . . .216 C7
ROSE GREEN . . . . . . . . . . .106 E5
Rose Green Cotts
  CO6 . . . . . . . . . . . . . . . .106 E5
ROSE HILL . . . . . . . . . . . . . .18 A4
Rose Hill CM7 . . . . . . . . . .128 A2
Rosehill Cres IP3 . . . . . . . . .17 F4
Rose Hill Prim Sch
  IP3 . . . . . . . . . . . . . . . . .17 F4
Rosehill Rd IP3 . . . . . . . . . .17 F4
Rose Ho ⑫ CO1 . . . . . . . . .136 A6
Rose La
  Great Chesterford CB10 . . . .3 D3
  Ipswich IP4 . . . . . . . . . . . .17 C5
  Salcott-c-V CM9 . . . . . . . .199 B8
  Wivenhoe CO7 . . . . . . . . .164 B7
Roseland Cotts CO15 . . . . .188 E3
Roselawn Fields CM1 . . . . .205 B8
Rosemary Ave
  Braintree CM7 . . . . . . . . .127 F4
  Felixstowe IP11 . . . . . . . .221 F6
Rosemary Cl
  Castle Hedingham CO9 . . . .52 A5
  Great Dunmow CM6 . . . . .123 C1
Rosemary Cotts CM3 . . . . .192 E1
Rosemary Cres
  Clacton-on-S CO15 . . . . . .188 F2
  Great Dunmow CM6 . . . . .123 C1
  Tiptree CO5 . . . . . . . . . . .179 C5
Rosemary Ct
  ② Colchester CO4 . . . . . .136 D8
  Tiptree CO5 . . . . . . . . . . .179 C5
Rosemary Gdns CO15 . . . . .15 F2
Rosemary La
  Halstead CO9 . . . . . . . . . . .76 E2
  Ipswich IP4 . . . . . . . . . . . .17 D5
Rosemary Rd CO15 . . . . . .188 F2
Rosemary Rd W CO15 . . . . .188 E2
Rosemary Way CO15 . . . . .203 G7
Rosemount IP11 . . . . . . . . .221 F4
Rosery Ho IP11 . . . . . . . . .221 F4
Rosery Mews CO13 . . . . . .170 A4
Rosetta Cl CO7 . . . . . . . . . .137 B2
Rose Wlk CO4 . . . . . . . . . .110 A4
Rosewood Cl CO4 . . . . . . . .109 C2
Roslings Cl CM1 . . . . . . . . .204 D1
Ross Cl
  Haverhill CB9 . . . . . . . . . . .9 D7
  Saffron Walden CB11 . . . . .43 E6
Rossendale CM1 . . . . . . . . .204 E1
Rossendale Cl CM1 . . . . . .110 D3
Rosseter Cl CM2 . . . . . . . .216 D7

Rosslyn Terr CO5 . . . . . . . .158 C3
Rotary Way CO3 . . . . . . . . .135 E8
Rothbury Rd CM1 . . . . . . . .204 D1
Rothesay Ave CM2 . . . . . . .216 A8
Rothmans Ave CM2 . . . . . .216 E6
ROTTEN END . . . . . . . . . . .101 A7
Roughtons CM2 . . . . . . . . .216 C3
Roundacre CO9 . . . . . . . . .103 E8
Roundbush Cnr
  Birch Green CO5 . . . . . . . .160 D3
  Great Totham CM9 . . . . . .196 D6
Roundbush Rd CO5 . . . . . .160 D2
Round Cl CO3 . . . . . . . . . . .135 B7
Round Coppice Rd
  Great Hallingbury
  CM24 . . . . . . . . . . . . . .147 A8
  Stansted Mountfitchet
  CM24 . . . . . . . . . . . . . .120 B1
Roundridge Rd IP9 . . . . . . .35 B2
Roundwood Rd IP4 . . . . . . .18 A7
Rous Chase CM2 . . . . . . . .216 B1
Rouse Way CO1 . . . . . . . . .136 B7
Routh Ave IP3 . . . . . . . . . . .18 F1
Rover Ave CO15 . . . . . . . . .203 E6
Rowallan Cl CO3 . . . . . . . .135 A3
Rowan Chase CO5 . . . . . . .179 C6
Rowan Cl
  Clacton-on-S CO15 . . . . . .188 C3
  Colchester CO3 . . . . . . . .134 D4
  Great Bentley CO7 . . . . . .166 F8
  Harwich CO12 . . . . . . . . . .91 B3
  Ipswich IP3 . . . . . . . . . . . .18 D2
Rowan Dr CM9 . . . . . . . . . .210 C5
Rowanhayes Cl IP2 . . . . . . .17 B3
Rowan Pl CO1 . . . . . . . . . .109 E1
Rowan Way
  Great Dunmow CM6 . . . . .123 C1
  Hatfield Peverel CM3 . . . . .194 A3
  Witham CM8 . . . . . . . . . .177 A5
ROW GREEN . . . . . . . . . . .154 D6
ROW HEATH . . . . . . . . . . . .167 F4
ROWHEDGE . . . . . . . . . . . .163 F8
Rowhedge Ct CO7 . . . . . . .136 F4
Rowhedge Ferry Rd
  CO7 . . . . . . . . . . . . . . . .164 A8
Rowhedge Rd CO2,
  CO5 . . . . . . . . . . . . . . . .136 E1
Rowherns La CO7 . . . . . . . .139 F4
Rowland Ho IP11 . . . . . . . .221 B5
Rowland's Yd CO12 . . . . . . .90 E2
Rowland's Yd CO12 . . . . . . .90 E2
Rowley Cotts The CO6 . . . . .56 D5
Rowley Ct CB9 . . . . . . . . . . .9 E5
Rowley Hill CB9 . . . . . . . . . .9 E5
Rowney Ave CB10 . . . . . . . .44 E2
Rowntree Way CB11 . . . . . .43 D7
Row The
  Hadstock CB1 . . . . . . . . . . .5 B7
  Stratford St M CO7 . . . . . .58 C2
Roxborough Cl CO16 . . . . .132 E3
Roxburghe Rd CO16 . . . . . .167 F6
Roxwell Ave CM1 . . . . . . . .204 D3
Roxwell Rd
  Chelmsford CM1 . . . . . . .204 C4
  Writtle CM1 . . . . . . . . . . .204 A4
Royal Ct
  Colchester CO1 . . . . . . . .110 C1
  Maldon CM9 . . . . . . . . . .210 A1
Royal Hospital Sch
  IP9 . . . . . . . . . . . . . . . . .62 D3
Royal Oak Gdns ⑥
  CM23 . . . . . . . . . . . . . .145 F6
Royal Sq CO7 . . . . . . . . . . .84 F7
Roy Ave IP3 . . . . . . . . . . . .18 B5
Roydon Way CO13 . . . . . . .170 F6
Royston Dr IP2 . . . . . . . . . .16 D2
Royston La CB11 . . . . . . . . .20 C6
Royston Rd CB11 . . . . . . . . .42 C5
Ruaton Dr CO16 . . . . . . . . .188 B3
Rubens Gate CM1 . . . . . . .205 F7
Rubens Rd IP3 . . . . . . . . . . .18 A1
Rudd Cl CO4 . . . . . . . . . . .110 F1
Rudkin Rd CO4 . . . . . . . . . .109 F5
Rudlands IP8 . . . . . . . . . . . .16 C1
RUDLEY GREEN . . . . . . . . .220 C2
Rudsdale Way CO3 . . . . . . .134 F5
Rue De Jeunes ⑧
  CM7 . . . . . . . . . . . . . . . .127 F2
Ruffels Field CM6 . . . . . . . .124 E4
Ruffles Rd CB9 . . . . . . . . . . .9 C7
Rugby Rd CO10 . . . . . . . . . .34 B4
Rugosa Cl CO3 . . . . . . . . . .134 C7
Rumballs Ct CM23 . . . . . . .145 C4
Rumsey Fields CM3 . . . . . .218 F7
Rumsey Row CM1 . . . . . . .204 B1
Runnacles St CM8 . . . . . . .156 C5
Runnacles Way IP11 . . . . . .221 B5
Running Mare La
  CM2 . . . . . . . . . . . . . . . .216 A3
Runsell Cl CM3 . . . . . . . . . .218 F7
Runsell La CM3 . . . . . . . . .218 F8
RUNSELL GREEN . . . . . . . .219 B7
Runsell View CM3 . . . . . . .219 A7
Rurik Ct CM7 . . . . . . . . . . .220 F8
Rush Cl CM3 . . . . . . . . . . .192 C8
Rush Cl IP4 . . . . . . . . . . . . .94 C1
Rushes Ct CM23 . . . . . . . .146 A5
Rush Green Rd CO16 . . . . .188 B2
Rush La CM22 . . . . . . . . . . .94 C1
Rushleigh Gn CM23 . . . . . .145 D4
Rushleigh Rd CM1 . . . . . . .205 E5
RUSHLEY GREEN . . . . . . . . .51 F6
Rushleys Cl CO5 . . . . . . . . .201 D6
Rushmere Pl ⑪ CM1 . . . . . .9 B8
Rushmere Rd IP3 . . . . . . . . .18 B7
RUSHMERE ST ANDREW
  . . . . . . . . . . . . . . . . . . . .18 E7

Rushmere St
  Ipswich IP4, IP5 . . . . . . . .18 D8
  Rushmere St A IP5 . . . . . . .18 E8
Rushmoor Dr CM7 . . . . . . .128 B1
Ruskin Cl CO13 . . . . . . . . .170 E7
Ruskin Rd
  Chelmsford CM2 . . . . . . .205 E2
  Ipswich IP4 . . . . . . . . . . . .17 F5
Ruskins The CM77 . . . . . . .126 F1
Russell Cl CM8 . . . . . . . . . .194 F7
Russell Ct
  Colchester CO2 . . . . . . . .136 B4
  Felixstowe IP11 . . . . . . . .221 C1
Russell Gdns CM2 . . . . . . .216 A4
RUSSELL GREEN . . . . . . . .192 D6
Russell Rd
  Clacton-on-S CO15 . . . . . .189 A3
  Felixstowe IP11 . . . . . . . .221 D2
  Ipswich IP1 . . . . . . . . . . . .17 B5
Russell's Rd
  Gosfield CO9 . . . . . . . . . . .76 A1
  Halstead CO9 . . . . . . . . . . .76 A1
Russet Way CM1 . . . . . . . .215 E7
Russet Ct CM7 . . . . . . . . . .128 A1
Russets CM2 . . . . . . . . . . .216 D3
Russett Cl CB9 . . . . . . . . . . .8 C8
Rustic Cl CM7 . . . . . . . . . .128 C3
Rutherfords CM1 . . . . . . . .191 B1
Rutland Ave CO4 . . . . . . . .135 B3
Rutland Ct ⑪ CM2 . . . . . . .8 E7
Rutland Gdns CM7 . . . . . . .128 A4
Rutland Pl CM1 . . . . . . . . . .72 B2
Rutland Rd CM1 . . . . . . . . .205 A7
Rydal Way CM77 . . . . . . . .154 C6
Rydal Wlk IP3 . . . . . . . . . . .18 E2
Ryde Ave CO15 . . . . . . . . .189 A8
Rye Cl
  Brightlingsea CO7 . . . . . . .165 E1
  Colchester CO3 . . . . . . . .134 E5
  Hatfield Peverel CM3 . . . . .194 A3
  Ipswich IP3 . . . . . . . . . . . .18 D4
Rye Ct ⑧ CB9 . . . . . . . . . . .8 F7
Rye Field The CM3 . . . . . . .207 D3
Ryegate Rd CO1 . . . . . . . . .135 F7
Rye Grass Way CM7 . . . . . .128 B1
Rye Hills CO9 . . . . . . . . . . .103 F8
Rye La CO2 . . . . . . . . . . . .162 A4
Rye Mill La CO5 . . . . . . . . .158 D4
Ryes La CO10 . . . . . . . . . . .33 A2
Rye St CM23 . . . . . . . . . . .118 F1
Rylands IP9 . . . . . . . . . . . . .35 A2
Ryle The CM1 . . . . . . . . . . .215 A8
Rylstone Way CB11 . . . . . . .43 F8
Rysley CM3 . . . . . . . . . . . .207 D4

# S

Sacketts Grove Cvn Pk
  CO15 . . . . . . . . . . . . . . .187 F2
Sackett's Grove Cvn Pk
  CO16 . . . . . . . . . . . . . . .188 A2
Sackville Cl CM1 . . . . . . . . .204 E3
Sackville Way CO16 . . . . . .108 D4
Saddle Mews CO4 . . . . . . .134 C6
Saddle Rise CM1 . . . . . . . .205 E8
Saddlers Cl
  Bishop's Stortford
  CM23 . . . . . . . . . . . . . .145 C4
  Great Notley CM77 . . . . . .154 B7
Sadds Yd CO15 . . . . . . . . .188 F3
Sadler Cl CM2 . . . . . . . . . .136 B4
Sadlers Cl CO13 . . . . . . . . .170 C6
Saffron Bsns Ctr CB10 . . . .22 E2
Saffron Cl CM7 . . . . . . . . . .73 C3
Saffron Croft CM7 . . . . . . .209 E2
Saffron Ct CB11 . . . . . . . . .22 D1
Saffron Gdns CM7 . . . . . . . .73 C3
SAFFRON WALDEN . . . . . . .22 E3
Saffron Walden Cty High
  Sch CB11 . . . . . . . . . . . .43 C8
Saffron Walden Mus*
  CB10 . . . . . . . . . . . . . . . .22 D2
Saffron Walden Hospl
  CB11 . . . . . . . . . . . . . . . .23 A2
Saffron Way CO5 . . . . . . . .179 C4
Saffron Wlk CM7 . . . . . . . . .73 B3
Sagehayes Cl IP2 . . . . . . . .17 B3
Sage Rd CO2 . . . . . . . . . . .136 A2
Sages CM22 . . . . . . . . . . . .94 F5
Sages End Rd CB9 . . . . . . . .26 B8
Sage Wlk CO5 . . . . . . . . . .179 C4
St Agnes Way IP5 . . . . . . . .18 F6
St Alban's RC High Sch
  IP4 . . . . . . . . . . . . . . . . .18 C7
St Alban's Rd
  Clacton-on-S CO15 . . . . . .189 A3
  Colchester CO1 . . . . . . . .135 C7
St Andrew's Ave
  Colchester CO4 . . . . . . . .136 D6
  Wivenhoe CO7 . . . . . . . . .137 A5
St Andrew's CE Prim Sch
  Bulmer CO10 . . . . . . . . . .32 F3
  Great Yeldham CO9 . . . . . .29 F2
  Halstead CO9 . . . . . . . . . .77 A3
  Marks Tey CO6 . . . . . . . . .132 C3
  Weeley CO16 . . . . . . . . . .167 F8
  Wormingford CO6 . . . . . . .80 E5
St Andrews Cl
  Alresford CO7 . . . . . . . . . .165 B7
  Ipswich IP4 . . . . . . . . . . . .18 D5
St Andrew's Cotts
  CM3 . . . . . . . . . . . . . . . .194 B3

St Andrews Ct 3
  CO4 . . . . . 136 C8
St Andrew's Dr IP9 . . . . .63 E7
St Andrews Gdns
  CO4 . . . . . 136 C8
St Andrew's Jun & Inf
  Schs CO4 . . . . . 136 D7
St Andrews Pl CO7 . . . .165 E1
St Andrews Rd
  Boreham CM3 . . . . .192 F1
  Great Cornard CO10 . . .34 A6
  Halstead CO9. . . . . . .76 F1
St Andrew's Rd
  Clacton-on-S CO15. . . .188 C3
  Felixstowe IP11. . . . . .221 E5
  Hatfield Peverel CM3 . .194 A4
  Weeley CO16. . . . . . .140 F1
St Andrew's Rise CO10. . .32 E5
St Andrew Wlk IP4 . . . . .18 F4
St Annes Ct CO6. . . . .131 B2
St Annes Ct CM1 . . . .205 C3
St Anne's Rd CO4. . . . .136 C8
St Anns Ct CM2 . . . . .205 A1
St Anns Rd CO15. . . . .188 E4
St Anthonys Cres CM1 . . .4 E8
St Anthony's Dr CM2. . .216 C2
St Aubins Ct CO15. . . .189 B4
St Aubyns Rd IP4. . . . . .18 A5
St Augustine Ct CM6. . .151 F6
St Augustine Mews
  CO1 . . . . . 136 A7
St Augustine Rd IP3 . . .18 D4
St Augustine's Gdns
  IP3 . . . . . 18 C3
St Augustine's Way
  CM1 . . . . . 205 F6
St Austell Rd CO4 . . . .110 D2
St Austin's La CO12. . . .91 E6
St Bartholomew Cl
  CO4 . . . . . 110 C3
St Bartholomews La
  CO10 . . . . . 15 D2
St Benedict's RC Coll
  CO3 . . . . . 135 B6
St Bernard Rd CO4 . . . .110 D2
St Botolph's Church Wlk
  7 CO2. . . . . .135 F6
St Botolph's Cir 8
  CO2 . . . . . 135 F6
St Botolph's Pl 1 CB9. . .8 F7
St Botolph's St 6
  CO2 . . . . . 135 F6
St Botolph's Terr 11
  CO13 . . . . . 171 C8
St Botolph's Way CB9. . . .8 F8
St Brelades Ct CO15 . . .189 B5
St Bride Ct CO4 . . . . .110 D2
St Catherines Cl CO2 . .135 D1
St Catherines Ct
  CM23 . . . . . 145 E7
St Catherine's Ct IP2 . . .16 E1
St Catherine's Rd
  Chelmsford CM1 . . . . .204 E2
  Long Melford CO10 . . . .15 C7
St Cedd's Sch CM1 . . . .205 A4
St Christopher Ct
  CO4 . . . . . 110 D2
St Christopher Rd
  CO4 . . . . . 110 D2
St Christophers Way
  CO15 . . . . . 203 G7
St Clair Cl CO15 . . . . .188 F8
St Clair's Dr CO16 . . . .187 B5
St Clair's Rd CO16 . . . .187 B5
St Clare Dr CO3 . . . . .135 C7
St Clare Rd CO3 . . . . .135 A6
St Clare's RC Prim Sch
  CO16 . . . . . 188 B4
St Clement Rd CO4 . . . .110 D2
St Clements CM6 . . . . . .70 A2
St Clement's Church La 18
  IP4. . . . . .17 D5
St Clement's Ct CO16. . .188 B5
St Clement's Hospl IP3 . . .18 B4
St Cleres Hall La
  CO16 . . . . . 187 B3
St Cleres Way CM3 . . . .218 D7
St Columb Ct CO4 . . . .110 C2
St Cyrus Rd CO4 . . . . .110 D3
St Davids Cl CO4 . . . . .136 C7
St David's Rd IP3 . . . . . .18 B3
St Denis Cl CO12. . . . . .91 A1
St Dominic Rd CO4 . . . .110 D2
St Edmundsbury Ho
  IP4. . . . . .17 F6
St Edmunds Cl CO12. . . .91 A1
St Edmunds Croft
  CM6 . . . . . 123 E1
St Edmund's Ct CO4 . . .136 C8
St Edmunds Fields
  CM6 . . . . . 123 E2
St Edmund's Hill CO8,
  CO10 . . . . . 55 D6
St Edmunds Ho CO4 . . .136 E8
St Edmunds La
  Bures CO8. . . . . . . .55 F1
  Great Dunmow CM6 . . . .123 E1
St Edmund's Pl IP1. . . . .17 C8
St Edmund's Rd
  Felixstowe IP11. . . . . .221 D2
  Ipswich IP1. . . . . . . .17 B8
St Fabian's Dr CM1. . . .204 E4
St Faith Rd CO4 . . . . .110 D2
St Felix RC Prim Sch
  CB9 . . . . . .8 D7

St Fillan Rd CO4. . . . . .110 D2
St Francis RC Prim Sch
  Braintree CM7. . . . . . .127 E4
  Maldon CM9. . . . . . . .209 F3
St George's Ave CO12. . . .91 C2
St George's CE Prim Sch
  CO7 . . . . . 112 E1
St Georges Cl CM9 . . . .210 E3
St George's Cl CO7 . . . .112 E1
St George's Ct CM8 . . . .176 F1
St George's St 17 IP1. . . .17 C6
St George's Inf Sch
  CO2 . . . . . 136 A4
St George's New Town
  Jun Sch CO2. . . . . . .136 A5
St George's St IP1. . . . . .17 C5
St Giles CE Prim Sch
  CO2 . . . . . 52 D2
St Giles Cl
  Great Maplestead CO9 . . .52 D2
  Maldon CM9. . . . . . . .209 E2
St Giles Cres CM9 . . . .209 E2
St Gregory CE Prim Sch
  CO10 . . . . . 33 D7
St Gregory's Ct CO10 . . . .33 D8
St Helena Mews CO3 . . .135 D5
St Helena Rd CO3 . . . . .135 D5
St Helena Sch CO3 . . . .135 C6
St Helens Ave CO3 . . . .189 A8
St Helen's Gn CO12. . . . .91 E5
St Helen's La 7 CO1. . . .135 F7
St Helen's Prim Sch
  IP4. . . . . .17 E6
St Helen's St IP4. . . . . .17 D6
St Helier Ct CO15. . . . .189 B4
St Ives Cl CO12. . . . . .188 B3
St Ives Rd CO5 . . . . . .182 E6
St James' CE Prim Sch
  CO1 . . . . . 136 A7
St James Ct
  Brightlingsea CO7 . . . . .185 E6
  Clacton-on-S CO15. . . . .188 E1
  Haverhill CB9. . . . . . . .8 E8
  8 Saffron Walden CB10. . . .22 F2
St James' Ct 8 CO1 . . . .136 A7
St James Pk CM1. . . . . .204 D4
St James Rd CM7. . . . . .127 F5
St James' Rise CO1 . . . .136 A7
St James's St CM7 . . . . .51 F4
St James Way CM23 . . . .145 C3
St Jean Wlk CO5 . . . . .179 D6
St John Gdns CO15 . . . .188 E6
St John Payne RC Comp
  Sch CM1. . . . . . . .205 A6
St Johns Ave CO7 . . . . .127 F2
St John's Ave
  Chelmsford CM2 . . . . . .216 B8
  2 Colchester CO2 . . . . .135 F6
St John's CE Prim Sch
  Colchester CO4 . . . . . .110 D4
  Ipswich IP4. . . . . . . .18 A7
St Johns Cl
  Great Chesterford CB10 . . .3 D2
  Saffron Walden CB11. . . .43 D7
St John's Cl CO4 . . . . .110 D4
St John's Cres CO24. . . .119 E7
St Johns Ct IP11 . . . . .221 D4
St John's Ct
  Ipswich IP4. . . . . . . .18 A6
  Tollesbury CM9 . . . . . .199 C1
St John's Danbury CE
  Prim Sch CM3. . . . . .218 E7
St John's Gn
  Colchester CO2 . . . . . .135 F6
  Writtle CM1. . . . . . . .204 B1
St John's Green Prim Sch
  CO2 . . . . . 135 F6
St John's Hospl CM2. . . .215 F6
St John's La CM24. . . . .119 E7
St John's Pl CO2 . . . . .135 F6
St John's Rd
  Chelmsford CM2 . . . . . .216 B8
  Clacton-on-S CO16. . . . .188 C5
  Colchester CO2 . . . . . .110 D3
  Ipswich IP4. . . . . . . .18 A6
  Stansted Mountfitchet
  CM24 . . . . . 119 E7
  Wivenhoe CO7. . . . . . .164 C7
  Writtle CM1. . . . . . . .204 B1
St John's St
  Colchester CO2 . . . . . .135 F6
  Tollesbury CM9 . . . . . .199 C1
St John's Terr CM7 . . . . .72 B2
St John The Baptist CE
  Prim Sch CO9. . . . . . .78 B8
St Joseph Rd CO4 . . . . .110 C3
St Joseph's Coll IP2 . . . .17 A3
St Joseph's Prim Sch
  CO10 . . . . . 33 E8
St Joseph's RC Prim Sch
  Bishop's Stortford
  CM23 . . . . . 145 E6
  Harwich CO12 . . . . . . .91 B2
St Jude Gdns CO4 . . . . .110 E2
St Judes Cl CO4 . . . . .110 D2
St Julian Gr CO1 . . . . .136 A6
ST LAWRENCE . . . . . .213 B1
St Lawrence CE Prim Sch
  CO2 . . . . . 163 E8
St Lawrence Ct 3
  CM7 . . . . . 127 F3
St Lawrence Dr CM0. . . .213 B1
St Lawrence Rd CO4 . . .110 D2
St Lawrence St 11 IP1. . . .17 C6
St Leonards Cl IP11. . . . .43 A2
St Leonard's Hospl
  CO10 . . . . . 33 F7
St Leonards Rd IP3. . . . .18 B3

St Leonard's Rd CO1. . . .136 C6
St Leonards School Ho 8
  CO1 . . . . . 136 C6
St Leonards Terr 7
  CO1 . . . . . 136 C6
St Luke's Chase CO5. . . .179 D5
St Luke's Cl CO5. . . . . .179 D5
St Luke's Cl CO4 . . . . .110 D2
St Margaret's CE Prim Sch
  Ipswich IP4. . . . . . . .17 D6
  Toppesfield CO9 . . . . . .50 C7
St Margaret's Cross
  CO4 . . . . . 83 F4
St Margaret's Ct
  CO16 . . . . . 188 C4
St Margaret's Gn 2
  IP4. . . . . .17 D6
St Margaret's Plain 1
  IP4. . . . . .17 D6
St Margaret's Rd CM2 . .205 E3
St Margaret's Sch
  CO9 . . . . . 102 D8
St Margaret's St 1 IP4. . . .17 D6
St Mark Dr CO4 . . . . .110 D2
St Marks RC Prim Sch
  IP2. . . . . .16 F3
St Marks Rd CO15 . . . .188 E4
St Martins Cl CO15 . . . .188 E4
St Mary Magdalen Ho
  CO1 . . . . . 136 B6
St Mary's Art Ctr*
  CO1 . . . . . 135 E7
St Mary's Cath* CM1 . . .205 B2
St Mary's CE Foundation
  Prim Sch CM24. . . . . .119 E7
  Ardleigh CO7. . . . . . .111 E7
  Saffron Walden CB10. . . . .22 D2
St Mary's Cl
  Great Baddow CM2 . . . . .216 F6
  Panfield CM7. . . . . . . .127 B7
St Mary's Cotts CO10 . . . .2 C5
St Mary's Cres IP11 . . . .221 D6
St Mary's Ct CO15 . . . .188 E3
St Mary's Dr CM24 . . . .119 F5
St Mary's Fields CO3 . . .135 E7
St Mary's La CM9 . . . . .210 B2
St Marys Mead CM1 . . .191 A1
St Marys Mews
  Frinton-on-S CO13. . . . .171 A5
  Tollesbury CM9 . . . . . .199 D2
St Mary's Pl CM6 . . . . .151 D7
St Mary's RC Sch
  IP4. . . . . .17 D7
St Mary's RC Sch
  CM23 . . . . . 145 E7
St Mary's Rd
  Braintree CM7. . . . . . .128 B3
  Clacton-on-S CO15. . . . .188 E4
  Frinton-on-S CO13. . . . .171 A5
  Great Bentley CO7. . . . .166 F6
  Ipswich IP4. . . . . . . .17 D7
  Kelvedon CO5 . . . . . . .158 C2
  Rivenhall CM8. . . . . . .177 B7
St Mary's Sch
  Colchester CO3 . . . . . .135 C7
  Copford CO3 . . . . . . .133 F5
St Mary's Sq CO5 . . . . .158 B3
St Marys Terr CO3 . . . . .135 C6
St Mary's View CB10. . . . .22 E4
St Mary's Villas CM7 . . . .72 B1
St Mary's Wlk CB9 . . . . .27 B6
St Matthew's Ho 4 IP1. . . .17 B6
St Matthew's CE Prim Sch
  IP1. . . . . .17 B6
St Matthew's St IP1 . . . . .17 B6
St Michael's CE Jun Sch
  CM2 . . . . . 216 C2
St Michael's CE Prim Sch
  Bishop's Stortford
  CM23 . . . . . 145 F7
  Braintree CM7. . . . . . .127 D2
St Michael's Chase
  CO6 . . . . . 133 D2
St Michaels Ct 6
  CO11 . . . . . 86 D1
St Michael's Ct 11
  CM7 . . . . . 127 F2
St Michael's Hospl
  CM7 . . . . . 127 F2
St Michael's La 2
  CM7 . . . . . 127 F2
ST MICHAEL'S MEAD
  CM23 . . . . . 145 C5
St Michaels Mews 5
  CM7 . . . . . 127 F2
St Michael's Prim Sch
  CO2 . . . . . 135 C1
St Michaels Rd CO15 . . .135 D1
St Michael's Rd
  Braintree CM7. . . . . . .127 F2
  Chelmsford CM2 . . . . . .216 B8
  Harwich CO12 . . . . . . .91 B2
  Thorpe-le-S CO16. . . . .141 F2
St Michaels Wlk CM2 . . .216 C2
St Mildreds Rd CM2 . . . .216 B8
St Monance Way CO4. . . .110 D2
St Nazaire Rd CM2. . . . .205 F3
St Neots Cl CO4 . . . . .110 D2
St Nicholas Cl CM8 . . . .176 F4
St Nicholas Ct
  Harwich CO12 . . . . . . .91 D6
  Ipswich IP1. . . . . . . .17 C5
St Nicholas Field CM23 . .92 B8
St Nicholas' Gdns
  CM7 . . . . . 127 F8

St Nicholas Pas 18
  CO1 . . . . . 135 F7
St Nicholas Rd CM8. . . .176 F4
St Nicholas Rdbt CO12. . .91 A4
St Nicholas St
  22 Colchester CO1 . . . .135 F7
  Ipswich IP1. . . . . . . .17 C5
St Nicholas Way CO6 . . .131 A4
ST OSYTH . . . . . . . .187 B4
St Osyth CE Prim Sch
  Clacton-on-S CO15. . . . .188 D3
St Osyth Gn CO16. . . . .187 B4
St Osyth Pl 7 IP2. . . . . .36 F8
ST OSYTH HEATH . . . .167 D1
St Osyth Priory*
  CO16 . . . . . 187 A4
St Osyth Rd
  Alresford CO7. . . . . . .165 D7
  Clacton-on-S CO15. . . . .188 D3
  Little Clacton CO16. . . . .168 B1
St Osyth Rd E CO16 . . . .168 C2
St Osyth Rd W CO16 . . .168 C1
St Pauls Mews CM2 . . . .210 C4
St Paul's Rd
  Clacton-on-S CO15. . . . .189 A3
  Colchester CO1 . . . . . .135 E8
St Peter's Ave CM9 . . . .209 F2
St Peter's CE Prim Sch
  Coggeshall CO6 . . . . . .131 B2
  Sible Hedingham CO9 . . . .75 D8
St Peters Cl CO7 . . . . .127 F4
St Peter's Cl CM7. . . . .127 F4
St Peters Coll CM1 . . . .204 E5
St Peters Ct
  Clacton-on-S CO15. . . . .189 B5
  Clare CO10 . . . . . . . .12 B7
  Colchester CO1 . . . . . .135 E8
  18 Sudbury CO10 . . . . .33 E7
St Peter's Hospl CM9 . . .209 F2
St Peter's-In-the-Fields
  CM7 . . . . . 127 F4
St Peter's Rd
  Braintree CM7. . . . . . .127 F4
  Chelmsford CM1 . . . . . .204 E2
  Coggeshall CO6 . . . . . .131 B2
  West Mersea CO5 . . . . .201 B6
St Peter's St
  Colchester CO1 . . . . . .135 F8
  Ipswich IP1. . . . . . . .17 C5
St Peters View CO9 . . . . .51 D1
St Peters Wlk CM9. . . . .196 B3
St Peter's Wlk CM7 . . . .127 F3
St Philip's Priory Sch
  CM2 . . . . . 216 A8
St Philomena's Sch
  CO13 . . . . . 170 F5
St Pius X RC Prim Sch
  CM1 . . . . . 204 F6
St Runwalds St 9
  CO1 . . . . . 135 F7
St Saviour Cl CO4 . . . .110 D2
St Stephens La 8 IP1 . . . .17 C6
St Swithins Cotts
  CM2 . . . . . 217 C3
St Teresa's RC Prim Sch
  CO15 . . . . . 134 E5
St Thomas Ct CO4 . . . .110 E2
St Thomas More RC Prim
  Sch IP1. . . . . . . .43 E8
St Thomas More's RC Prim
  Sch CO1 . . . . . . .136 A7
St Valery CM22 . . . . . .148 C7
St Vincent Chase
  CM7 . . . . . 128 B5
St Vincent Rd CO15 . . . .188 E1
St Vincents Rd CM2 . . . .216 B8
Sainty Cl CO7 . . . . . .164 C8
Salamanca Way CO10 . . .135 C2
Salary Cl CO4 . . . . . .110 F1
Salcombe Ho CO4 . . . . .136 C8
Salcott Creek Ct CM2 . . .128 D1
SALCOTT-CUM-VIRLEY
  . . . . . . . . 199 B7
Salehurst Rd IP3 . . . . . .18 E3
Salerno Cres CO2. . . . .135 C2
Salerno Way CM1. . . . .204 E6
Saling Hall Gdns*
  CM7 . . . . . 126 A8
Salisbury Ave CO3 . . . .135 E6
Salisbury Cl CM23 . . . .145 F5
Salisbury Ct
  Clacton-on-S CO15. . . . .189 D5
  Ipswich IP3. . . . . . . .18 A4
Salisbury Rd
  Clacton-on-S CO15. . . . .189 D5
  Ipswich IP3. . . . . . . .18 A4
Salisbury Terr 1 CO10. . . .33 E8
Sallows Cl IP7 . . . . . . .16 F7
Salmet Cl IP2 . . . . . . .16 E1
Salmon Cl CO3 . . . . . .134 E4
Salmon Par CM1. . . . . .205 B3
Salmons Cl CM6 . . . . .151 A5
Salmon's Cnr CO6 . . . . .132 A3
Salmon's La CO6. . . . . .132 A4
Salter Cl CO3 . . . . . . .135 C7
Salter Pl CM2 . . . . . . .205 F2
Salters CM23 . . . . . . .145 C4
Salters Hall Mews
  CO10 . . . . . 33 D7
Salter's Mdw CM9 . . . .198 D4
Salthouse St 16 IP4. . . . .17 C5
Saltings Cres CO1 . . . . .201 E7
Salvia Cl CO16. . . . . .188 C4
Samford Cl CM9. . . . . . .62 D7
Samford Ct IP8. . . . . . .61 D7

Samford Pl IP8. . . . . . .16 B6
Samian Cl CM9 . . . . . .209 F5
Samphire Cl CM8. . . . . .176 D3
Sampson Dr CO10 . . . . .15 D8
Sampsons La CO5. . . . .182 F3
Samson's La CO5 . . . . .182 F3
Samsons Cl CO7 . . . . .165 D1
Samson's Rd CO7. . . . .165 E1
Samuel Ct IP4 . . . . . . .17 C6
Samuel Manor CM2. . . .205 F3
Sanderling Gdns CM9. . .210 C5
Sanders Cl CM24 . . . . .119 D7
Sanders Dr CO3 . . . . .135 B7
Sanderson Mews CO5. . .163 F8
Sandford Cl CO7 . . . . .164 C8
Sandford Mill Rd
  Chelmsford CM2 . . . . . .205 F2
  Chelmsford CM2 . . . . . .206 B2
  Great Baddow CM2 . . . . .217 C8
Sandford Rd CM2. . . . .205 E3
Sandhills Cotts CM7 . . . .73 D1
Sandhurst Ave IP3 . . . . .17 F4
Sandle Rd CM23 . . . . .145 E4
Sandling Cres CM9 . . . . .18 E5
Sandlings The IP3 . . . . .18 D1
Sandmartin Cres CO3 . .134 C4
SANDON . . . . . . . .217 D6
Sandon Brook Manor
  CM2 . . . . . 217 E8
Sandon Brook Pl
  CM2 . . . . . 217 E8
Sandon Cl CO3 . . . . . .109 C2
SANDON GREEN . . . .217 C6
Sandon Hall Bridleway
  CM2 . . . . . 217 D4
Sandon Hill CM3. . . . . .172 A6
Sandon Sch The CM2. . . .217 B6
Sandown Cl CO15. . . . .189 A8
Sandpiper Cl
  Colchester CO4 . . . . . .137 A8
  Haverhill CB9. . . . . . . .9 C8
  Heybridge CM9 . . . . . .210 C5
Sandpiper Ct 18
  CM23 . . . . . 145 F6
Sandpiper Rd IP2 . . . . .16 E2
Sandpiper Wlk CM2. . . .216 C6
Sandpit Cl CO4 . . . . . .18 F5
Sandra Ct 5 CO2. . . . . .127 F3
Sandringham Cl IP2 . . . . .16 F2
Sandringham Ct CO10 . . .34 A7
Sandringham Dr CO2 . . .136 A4
Sandringham Gdns 6
  CM23 . . . . . 145 E5
Sandringham Pl CM2 . . .205 C2
Sandwich Ct CM7 . . . . .127 E6
Sandwich Rd
  Brightlingsea CO7 . . . . .185 F8
  Clacton-on-S CO15. . . . .203 J8
Sandy Hill CO6 . . . . . . .80 D5
Sandyhill La IP3. . . . . . .17 E1
Sandy La
  Bulmer CO10 . . . . . . .32 F5
  Sudbury CO10 . . . . . . .33 B5
Santiago Cotts CO7. . . .185 E6
Sapling Pl IP4. . . . . . .17 F5
Sapphire Cl IP1 . . . . . .16 D8
Sarah's Wlk CM22 . . . . .148 B7
Saran Ct CO7 . . . . . . .137 A2
Sarcel CM77. . . . . . . .129 C6
Sargeant Cl CO2 . . . . .136 B3
Sarre Way CM3 . . . . . .185 E8
Sassoon Way 3 CM9. . . .210 A1
Saturn Rd IP1. . . . . . . .16 D8
Saul's Ave CM8 . . . . . .195 B8
Sauls Bridge Cl CM8 . . .195 A8
Saunders Ave CM7. . . . .127 E3
Saunders Cl CM22 . . . . .94 C1
Savernake Rd CM1. . . . .204 E1
Saville Cl CB11. . . . . . .65 C4
Savill Rd CO2 . . . . . . .136 C2
Sawkins Ave CM2 . . . . .216 D6
Sawkins Cl
  Abberton CO5 . . . . . . .163 B2
  Chelmsford CM2 . . . . . .216 D6
Sawkins Gdns CM2 . . . .216 D6
Sawney Brook CM1 . . . .204 A1
Sawpit La CM23 . . . . . .92 D7
Sawston Cl IP2. . . . . . .17 A2
Sawyers Cl 3 IP9 . . . . . .35 A1
Sawyer's Rd CM9 . . . . .197 C5
Saxmundham Way
  CO16 . . . . . 188 A3
Saxon Bank CM7 . . . . .128 B2
Saxon Cl
  Colchester CO3 . . . . . .134 F4
  Halstead CO9. . . . . . . .76 F2
Saxon Ct CM9 . . . . . .210 A3
Saxon Dr CM8 . . . . . . .176 E3
Saxon La IP8. . . . . . . .35 D7
Saxon Way
  Chelmsford CM1 . . . . . .205 B7
  Holland-on-S CO15 . . . . .189 F6
  Maldon CM9. . . . . . . .210 B1
  Point Clear B CO16 . . . . .185 F3
  Saffron Walden CB11. . . .22 C1
Saxstead Dr CO16 . . . . .188 A4
Sayers Ho CO7 . . . . . .127 F3
Saywell Brook CM2 . . . .206 A2
Scarfe's Cnr CO6. . . . . .82 B4
Scarfe Way CO4 . . . . .136 E6
Scarletts Chase CO6. . . .108 E6
Scarletts Cl CM8. . . . . .195 A7
Scarletts Rd CO1 . . . . .136 C4
Sceptre Cl CM9 . . . . . .199 D2
Scholars Mews CM9. . . .196 B3

**School Barn Cotts**
CO10 . . . . . . . . . . . . . .13 E7
School Chase CO9 . . . . . .103 E8
School Cl IP9 . . . . . . . . . .35 A1
School Ct CO12 . . . . . . . .91 D4
Schoolfield
Birdbrook CO9 . . . . . . . .28 A6
Glemsford CO10 . . . . . . .2 B5
SCHOOL GREEN . . . . . . .74 A3
School Hill
Birch CO2 . . . . . . . . . . .161 A4
Washbrook IP8 . . . . . . . .35 F8
School Ho
**I** Colchester CO1 . . . .136 A6
Shalford CM7 . . . . . . . . .100 E5
School La
Birch CO2 . . . . . . . . . . .161 A3
Brantham CO11 . . . . . . . .60 D1
Broomfield CM1 . . . . . . .191 B1
Chelmsford CM1 . . . . . .204 F8
Dedham CO7 . . . . . . . . . .84 F7
Duddenhoe End CB11 . . . .41 A7
Great Bentley CO7 . . . . .166 A8
Great Horkesley CO6 . . . .82 A2
Great Leighs CM3 . . . . . .173 F8
Great Wigborough CO5 . .181 F3
Haverhill CB9 . . . . . . . . . .8 E7
Henham CM22 . . . . . . . . .94 F5
Lawford CO11 . . . . . . . . .86 A2
Little Horkesley CO6 . . . . .81 D5
Mistley CO11 . . . . . . . . . .86 F4
Newport CB11 . . . . . . . . .42 F1
Stratford St M CO7 . . . . . .58 D2
Takeley CM22 . . . . . . . .121 D6
West Bergholt CO6 . . . . .108 E4
School Mews CO6 . . . . . .130 F2
School Rd
Blackmore End CM7 . . . . .74 C2
Colchester CO2 . . . . . . . .136 A2
Copford CO6 . . . . . . . . .133 D3
Elmstead Market CO7 . . .138 A4
Frinton-on-S CO13 . . . . .170 E5
Great Oakley CO12 . . . . .116 C3
Great Totham CM9 . . . . .196 B3
Langham CO4 . . . . . . . . .83 E4
Little Horkesley CO6 . . . . .81 D4
Little Maplestead CO9 . . .77 B8
Little Totham CM9 . . . . .197 B3
Little Waltham CM3 . . . . .30 D3
Messing CO5 . . . . . . . . .159 D2
Pentlow CO10 . . . . . . . . .13 F6
Rayne CM7 . . . . . . . . . .153 E8
Shotley Gate IP9 . . . . . . .91 B8
Sible Hedingham CO9 . . . .75 D8
Silver End CM8 . . . . . . . .156 E3
Tattingstone IP9 . . . . . . .36 D1
Tendring CO16 . . . . . . . .140 E6
Wickham Bishops CM8 . .195 F5
Wickham St P CO9 . . . . . .53 C5
School St
Foxearth CO10 . . . . . . . .14 D6
Great Chesterford CB10 . . .3 D2
Stoke-by-N CO6 . . . . . . .56 D5
Sudbury CO10 . . . . . . . . .33 E7
School Terr CM7 . . . . . . .127 E2
School View Rd CM1 . . .204 F3
School Villas
Great Easton CM6 . . . . . .123 A8
Henham CM6 . . . . . . . . . .95 F2
Lindsell CM6 . . . . . . . . . .97 F4
Takeley CM22 . . . . . . . .121 C6
School Wlk CM7 . . . . . . .127 F3
Schreiber Rd IP4 . . . . . . .18 B7
Scofield Ct CO10 . . . . . . .34 A6
Scotland St CO6 . . . . . . .56 E6
SCOTLAND STREET . . . .56 D6
SCOT'S GREEN . . . . . . .204 F8
Scott Ave CM7 . . . . . . . . .73 D6
Scott Cl CM7 . . . . . . . . .155 A8
Scott Dr CO3 . . . . . . . . .134 F6
Scott Rd
Bishop's Stortford
CM23 . . . . . . . . . . . .145 E6
Ipswich IP1 . . . . . . . . . .18 B1
Scotts Wlk CM1 . . . . . . .204 D5
Scraley Rd CM9 . . . . . . .210 E6
Scrips CO6 . . . . . . . . . . .157 F6
Scrip's Rd CO6 . . . . . . . .158 A7
Scrivener Dr IP2 . . . . . . . .16 C2
Scurvy Hall La
Howe Street CM3 . . . . .173 C1
Little Waltham CM3 . . . .191 B8
Scylla Cl CM9 . . . . . . . .210 C6
Scythe Way CO3 . . . . . .134 F4
Seabrook Gdns CM3 . . . .192 F1
Seabrook Rd CM2 . . . . .217 A6
Seabrooks The CO10 . . . . .2 B3
Sea Cornflower Way
CO15 . . . . . . . . . . . . .203 G7
Sea Cres CO15 . . . . . . . .203 F6
Seafield Ave CO11 . . . . . .87 B4
Seafield Rd CO12 . . . . . . .91 B2
Seafields Gdns CO15 . . .189 C5
Seafields Rd CO15 . . . . .189 C5
Sea Flowers Way
CO15 . . . . . . . . . . . . .203 G7
Seagers CM9 . . . . . . . . .196 B4
Sea Glebe Way CO15 . . .203 G7
Sea Holly Way CO15 . . . .203 G6
Sea King Cres CO4 . . . . .110 B4
Sea Lavender Way
CO15 . . . . . . . . . . . . .203 G6
Sea Pink Way CO15 . . . .203 G6
Sea Rd IP1 . . . . . . . . . . .221 D2
Searle Cl CM2 . . . . . . . .216 D7
Searles Cotts CO6 . . . . .133 D2
Searle Way CO6 . . . . . . .108 B1

**Sea Rosemary Way**
CO15 . . . . . . . . . . . . .203 G7
Sea Shell Way CO15 . . . .203 G6
Sea Thistle Way
CO15 . . . . . . . . . . . . .203 G7
Seaton Cl CO11 . . . . . . . .86 B3
Seaton Rd IP11 . . . . . . .221 D5
Seaview Ave
Little Oakley CO12 . . . . .117 C7
West Mersea CO5 . . . . .201 E6
Seaview Ct CO15 . . . . . .189 A2
Seaview Cvn Pk CO5 . . . .201 F6
Seaview Gdns CO7 . . . . .185 F7
Seaview Hts CO14 . . . . . .171 C7
Sea View Par CM0 . . . . .213 C1
Sea View Prom CM0 . . . .213 B1
Seaview Rd
Brightlingsea CO7 . . . . .185 F7
Seawick CO16 . . . . . . . .203 B7
Seaview Terr CO16 . . . . .186 A3
Sea Way CO15 . . . . . . . .203 F6
SEAWICK . . . . . . . . . . .203 C7
Seawick Rd CO16 . . . . . .203 B6
Sebastian Cl CO4 . . . . . .136 F7
Seckford Cl IP4 . . . . . . . .18 F5
Second Ave
Chelmsford CM1 . . . . .205 B5
Clacton-on-S CO15 . . . .189 B4
Frinton-on-S CO13 . . . .170 E3
Glemsford CO10 . . . . . . .2 C5
Halstead CO9 . . . . . . . . .77 B1
Harwich CO12 . . . . . . . .91 C3
Seawick CO16 . . . . . . . .203 C6
Stansted Mountfitchet
CM24 . . . . . . . . . . . .120 B2
Sudbury CO10 . . . . . . . . .15 F1
Trimley St M IP11 . . . . .221 A7
Walton-on-t-N CO14 . . .144 E3
Weeley CO16 . . . . . . . .167 F8
Secundus Dr CO2 . . . . . .135 F3
Seden Ct CO15 . . . . . . . .169 B1
Sedgefield Way CM7 . . .128 B1
Sedop Cl CB11 . . . . . . . . .43 D7
Seedbed Ctr CO4 . . . . . .110 C6
Seedfield The CO5 . . . . .201 B6
Selby Cl CM7 . . . . . . . . .135 D1
Seldon Rd CO5 . . . . . . . .179 D5
Selhurst Ct CO14 . . . . . .170 F7
Selkirk Rd IP4 . . . . . . . . .18 B8
Selsey Ave CO15 . . . . . .203 I8
Selvale Way IP11 . . . . . .221 C4
Selwyn Cl IP2 . . . . . . . . .17 C4
Septimus Dr CO4 . . . . . .110 A5
Serenus Ct **I** IP1 . . . . . .17 C5
Serpentine Rd IP3 . . . . . .18 C2
Serpentine Wlk CO1 . . . .109 E1
Seven Ash Gn CM1 . . . . .205 C5
Seven Devils La CB11 . . . .43 B6
SEVEN STAR GREEN . . .133 F8
Seventh Ave
Chelmsford CM1 . . . . .205 B6
Stansted Mountfitchet
CM24 . . . . . . . . . . . .120 B2
Severalls La CO4 . . . . . .110 B6
Severn Rd
Clacton-on-S CO15 . . . .188 F5
Ipswich IP3 . . . . . . . . . .17 F3
Sewards End CO10 . . . . . .23 E1
Sewell's La CO10 . . . . . . .13 B1
Sexton Cl CO2 . . . . . . . .163 B8
Sextons La CM8 . . . . . . .178 B1
Seymore Dr CB9 . . . . . . . .8 D7
Seymour Rd
Ipswich IP2 . . . . . . . . . .17 C4
Jaywick CO15 . . . . . . . .187 F1
Seymour St CM2 . . . . . .205 A1
Shackleton Cl CO12 . . . . .90 F1
Shackleton Gdns
CM23 . . . . . . . . . . . .145 E6
Shackleton Rd IP3 . . . . . .18 B3
Shackleton Sq IP3 . . . . . .18 B3
SHAFTENHOE END . . . . .39 B8
Shaftenhoe End Rd
SG8 . . . . . . . . . . . . . .39 A8
Shaftesbury Ave CO12 . . .91 B4
Shaftesbury Ct **I** CB9 . . . .8 E7
Shaftesbury Sq **I** IP4 . . .17 D5
Shafto Rd IP11 . . . . . . . .16 E8
Shair La
Great Bentley CO7 . . . . .167 B8
Weeley CO16 . . . . . . . .140 B2
Shakespeare Cl CM7 . . .155 A7
Shakespeare Dr CM9 . . .210 A1
Shakespeare Rd CO3 . . .134 F6
Shakeston Cl CM1 . . . . .215 B8
Shalfleet Ct CO15 . . . . . .188 F8
SHALFORD . . . . . . . . . .100 E7
SHALFORD GREEN . . . .100 C3
Shalford Lo CM1 . . . . . .205 B8
Shalford Prim Sch
CM7 . . . . . . . . . . . . .100 E5
Shalford Rd CM7 . . . . . .126 E3
Shalom Hall* CO7 . . . . .181 B8
Shamrock Ave IP2 . . . . . .16 E4
Shamrock Cl CM9 . . . . . .199 D2
Shamrock Ho CO15 . . . .203 J8
Shangani Rd CM23 . . . . .145 F5
Shanklin Cl CO15 . . . . . .189 A8
Shannon Cl CB9 . . . . . . . .9 D7
Shannon Rd IP3 . . . . . . . .38 A8
Shardelowe Ave CM1 . . .206 A8
Shardlois Bsns Pk
CM7 . . . . . . . . . . . . .156 A6
Shardlowe's Farm CM7 . . .75 E1
Sharlands Row CM9 . . . .199 A8
Sharpington Cl CM2 . . . .216 C3
Shatters Rd CO2 . . . . . . .161 A1

**Shaw Cl** CO13 . . . . . . . .170 F7
Shaw Dr CM7 . . . . . . . . .73 D7
Shawlands Ave CO10 . . . .34 B7
Shaw Rd
Long Melford CO10 . . . . .15 D8
Witham CM8 . . . . . . . . .176 F5
Shearers Ct CM23 . . . . .145 C4
Shearers Way CM3 . . . . .192 F1
Shearman Ct **I** CB9 . . . . . .9 A7
Shears Cres CO5 . . . . . .201 D5
Shears Ct CO5 . . . . . . . .201 D5
Sheds La CB10 . . . . . . . .22 E2
Sheene Ct CM7 . . . . . . . .128 D5
Sheepcoates La CM9 . . .196 F2
Sheepcote La CM23 . . . . .92 E3
Sheepcotes CM2 . . . . . . .206 B5
Sheepcotes La
Little Waltham CM3 . . . .191 C7
Silver End CM8 . . . . . . .156 E5
Sheepcot Rd CO9 . . . . . . .51 F3
Sheepen Rd CO3 . . . . . .135 E8
Sheepen Rd CO3 . . . . . .135 D8
Sheepshead Hill CO10 . . .34 C6
Sheepshead Wlk CO2 . . .135 F2
Sheerwater Mews
CO4 . . . . . . . . . . . . .137 A8
Sheldrake Dr IP2 . . . . . . .16 C2
Sheldrick Link CM2 . . . .206 B4
Shellcroft . . . . . . . . . . . .77 F1
Shellduck Cres CM7 . . . .154 C5
Shelley Ave
Great Cornard CO10 . . . .34 B6
Tiptree CO5 . . . . . . . . .179 E5
Shelley La CO4 . . . . . . . .168 F2
Shelley Rd
Chelmsford CM2 . . . . .205 D2
Clacton-on-S CO16 . . . .188 A5
Colchester CO3 . . . . . .134 F6
Shelley St **I** IP2 . . . . . . .17 C4
Shelley Wlk CM7 . . . . . .155 A8
Sheltons The CO13 . . . . .170 B6
Shelley Rd IP3 . . . . . . . . .18 B1
Shepherd Dr
Colchester CO4 . . . . . .109 E3
Ipswich IP8 . . . . . . . . . .16 C2
Shepherds Cl CM23 . . . .145 C4
Shepherds Croft CO3 . . .134 D5
Shepherds Ct **I** CB9 . . . . .8 E7
Shepherds La CO10 . . . . . .2 A6
Shepherds Way CM10 . . .22 F2
Sheppard Cl CO16 . . . . .188 D6
Sheppard Dr CM2 . . . . . .206 A4
Sherborne Rd CM1 . . . . .205 D5
Sherbourne Cl CO13 . . . .170 F7
Sherbourne Rd CO4 . . . .136 F7
Sheridan Wlk CO3 . . . . .134 F6
Sheriffs Way CO15 . . . . .188 E7
Sheringham Dr CM7 . . . .154 C5
Sherrington Rd IP1 . . . . .17 A8
Sherwood Cl CO4 . . . . . .136 D7
Sherwood Ct CM23 . . . .145 F7
Sherwood Dr
Chelmsford CM1 . . . . .204 D1
Clacton-on-S CO15 . . . .188 E6
Sherwood Way CO5 . . . .158 D4
Shetland Cl IP4 . . . . . . . .18 A8
Shetland Rd CB9 . . . . . . . .9 D8
Sherwood Wlk CO1 . . . .135 E7
Shillito Cl CO3 . . . . . . . .134 F3
Shimbrooks CM3 . . . . . .173 F7
Ship La CO11 . . . . . . . . . .87 E3
Ship Launch Rd IP3 . . . . .17 E3
Shipwrights The CO7 . . .164 B8
Shipyard Est CO7 . . . . . .185 F5
Shire Cl CM1 . . . . . . . . .205 F7
Shire Ct **I** CB9 . . . . . . . . .9 A7
Shire Hall Yd **I** IP4 . . . . .17 D5
Shire Hill CB11 . . . . . . . .22 F1
Shire Hill Ind Est CB11 . . .22 F1
Shire Hill La CB10 . . . . . .44 A8
Shire La CO6 . . . . . . . . .108 F4
Shires Cl CM7 . . . . . . . .154 B7
Shirley Cl CO15 . . . . . . .188 A1
Shoebridge's Hill CO7 . . .84 E6
Shoemenders La CM0 . . .214 E4
Shop La CO5 . . . . . . . . .184 F3
Shop Rd CO11 . . . . . . . .113 B6
Shops The CM8 . . . . . . .156 D4
Shorefields Sch CO15 . . .189 B4
Shoreham Rd CO15 . . . .203 I8
Shore La
Bradfield CO11 . . . . . . . .87 E3
Harkstead IP9 . . . . . . . .63 A2
Shortcroft CM23 . . . . . .146 D7
Short Cut Rd CO1 . . . . . .135 E7
Short La CO13 . . . . . . . .170 C3
Shortlands IP8 . . . . . . . . .16 D1
Shotlands Pl CM23 . . . . .145 F8
Shortridge Ct CM8 . . . . .194 F8
Short Wyre St **I** CO1 . . .135 F7
Shotley Cl
Clacton-on-S CO16 . . . .188 A3
Felixstowe IP11 . . . . . .221 B4
Ipswich IP2 . . . . . . . . . .16 C2
SHOTLEY GATE . . . . . . .91 A8
Shotley Mews CM8 . . . . . .8 C8
Shropshire Cl CM2 . . . . .216 F5
Shrubbery Cl IP11 . . . . . .221 D4
SHRUB END . . . . . . . . .135 A3
Shrub End Rd CO3 . . . . .135 B4
Shrubland Cl CO15 . . . . .189 B5
Shrubland Dr IP4 . . . . . . .18 F5
Shrubland Rd
**I** Colchester CO2 . . .136 A6
New Mistley CO11 . . . . .87 A3
Shrublands CB10 . . . . . . .22 E3
Shrublands Cl CM2 . . . . .205 C2
SHUDY CAMPS . . . . . . . . .7 B6

**Shums Hill** CO13 . . . . . .170 C8
Shut La CO6 . . . . . . . . . .105 B6
Siam Pl CO10 . . . . . . . . .33 E7
SIBLE HEDINGHAM . . . . .51 E1
SIBLEY'S GREEN . . . . . .97 B5
Sidegate Ave IP4 . . . . . . .18 A8
Sidegate La IP4 . . . . . . . .18 A8
Sidegate Prim Sch IP4 . . .18 A8
Sidings Pl **I** CM7 . . . . . .128 A2
Sidings The CO10 . . . . . . .2 C2
Sidmouth Rd CM1 . . . . .205 E6
Sidney Pl CM1 . . . . . . . .206 A7
Sidney Terr CM23 . . . . . .145 F6
Siena Mews CO2 . . . . . .136 B4
Siggin's La CB1 . . . . . . . . .5 D7
Silcock Cl CO4 . . . . . . . .110 C2
Silcott St CO7 . . . . . . . .185 E6
Silent St IP1 . . . . . . . . . .17 C5
Silk Factory Row CO10 . . .2 B6
Silk St IP4 . . . . . . . . . . . .17 D6
Silks Way CM7 . . . . . . . .127 F2
Sillett Cl CO16 . . . . . . . .188 D6
Siloam Pl IP3 . . . . . . . . . .17 E4
Silvanus Cl CO10 . . . . . .135 D6
Silverdale Ct CO15 . . . . .189 B5
Silver Dawn Touring Pk
CO16 . . . . . . . . . . . . .188 D3
SILVER END . . . . . . . . . .156 E4
Silver End Prim Sch
CM8 . . . . . . . . . . . . .156 E3
Silver Leys IP9 . . . . . . . . .60 E6
Silver Row CB11 . . . . . . .42 F5
Silver St
Maldon CM9 . . . . . . . .209 F3
Silver End CM8 . . . . . . .156 D4
Stansted Mountfitchet
CM24 . . . . . . . . . . . .119 D6
Silverthorn Cl CO15 . . . .179 F5
Silverthorne Cl CO2 . . . .136 A3
Silvester Way CM2 . . . . .206 B4
Simmonds Way CM8 . . . .218 F8
Simon Ho IP4 . . . . . . . . .17 F6
Simons Flats CO15 . . . . .179 C7
Simons La CO1 . . . . . . . .136 B6
Simpson Cl IP3 . . . . . . . .17 F1
Simpsons La CO5 . . . . . .179 A3
Sims Cl CO6 . . . . . . . . .105 B7
Sinclair Cl CO4 . . . . . . . .110 C2
Sinclair Dr IP2 . . . . . . . . .17 C3
Singer Ave CO15 . . . . . .203 F7
Singleton Ct CO10 . . . . . .34 A5
Sinnington End CO4 . . . .110 C4
Sioux Cl CO4 . . . . . . . . .110 C4
Sir Alf Ramsey Way
IP1 . . . . . . . . . . . . . . .17 B5
Sir Charles Lucas Arts Coll
CO4 . . . . . . . . . . . . . .136 E8
Sir Isaac's Wlk CM7 . . . .135 F7
Siskin Cl CO4 . . . . . . . . .136 F8
Sittang Cl CO12 . . . . . . .135 C1
Sitwell Cl CO11 . . . . . . . .86 B4
Siward Rd CM8 . . . . . . . .194 D8
Six Bells Ct CM7 . . . . . . .127 F5
Sixth Ave
Chelmsford CM1 . . . . .205 B6
Stansted Mountfitchet
CM24 . . . . . . . . . . . .120 C3
Sixth Form Coll The
CO1 . . . . . . . . . . . . . .135 E7
Skate's Hill CO10 . . . . . . .2 B2
Skeins Way CM11 . . . . . .65 C4
Skelmersdale Rd
CO15 . . . . . . . . . . . . .188 F3
Skelton Cl CO11 . . . . . . . .86 C4
Skerry Rise CM1 . . . . . . .205 B7
Skiddaw Cl CM7 . . . . . . .154 D7
Skighaugh CO12 . . . . . . .141 C8
Skinner's La CM7 . . . . . .216 B3
Skinners St CM23 . . . . . .145 C4
Skipper Ct CM7 . . . . . . .154 F8
Skipper Rd IP8 . . . . . . . . .36 E8
Skitts Hill CM7 . . . . . . . .128 B3
Skitts Hill Ind Est
CM7 . . . . . . . . . . . . .128 B1
Skreens Ct CM1 . . . . . . .204 D4
SKYE GREEN . . . . . . . . .131 E1
Sky Hall Hill CO4 . . . . . . .83 D7
Skylark La IP8 . . . . . . . . .16 C2
Skylark Wlk CM2 . . . . . .216 F6
Skymans Fee CO13 . . . . .170 E6
Sladburys La CO15 . . . . .189 C6
Sladbury's La CO15 . . . .189 C6
Slade Rd CO15 . . . . . . . .189 D8
Slades Cl CO10 . . . . . . . . .2 C5
Slade's La CM2 . . . . . . . .216 A3
Slade St **I** IP4 . . . . . . . .17 D5
Slade The CB10 . . . . . . . .22 F7
Slate CO9 . . . . . . . . . . . .76 F1
Slaters Cl CO13 . . . . . . .170 E6
Sleaford Cl IP2 . . . . . . . .17 A3
Slipes Cnr CO1 . . . . . . . .87 C1
Sloeberry Rd IP3 . . . . . . .38 C7
Sloe Hill CO9 . . . . . . . . . .76 C2
Slough Farm Rd CO9 . . . .76 D2
Slough House Cl
CM7 . . . . . . . . . . . . .128 D1
Slough La
Ardleigh CO7 . . . . . . . .111 D4
Cock Clarks CM3 . . . . .219 D3
Elmstead Market CO7 . .137 D4
Slough Rd
Brantham CO7, CO11 . . .60 D2
Danbury CM3 . . . . . . . .219 C3
Slushy La IP9 . . . . . . . . . .63 B3
Smaley La CO10 . . . . . . .15 C8
Smallbridge Entry CO8 . . .80 D8

**Smallwood Rd** CO2 . . . .135 B3
Smart St **II** CM7 . . . . . . . .17 D5
Smeaton Cl CO4 . . . . . . .110 C6
Smeetham Hall La
CO10 . . . . . . . . . . . . .32 E6
Smithers Cl IP9 . . . . . . . .35 A1
Smithers Dr CM2 . . . . . .217 A6
Smiths Cotts CM22 . . . . .93 E4
SMITH'S END . . . . . . . . .39 A8
Smith's End La SG8 . . . . .39 A8
Smiths Field
Colchester CO1 . . . . . .136 C5
Rayne CM7 . . . . . . . . .126 F2
Smiths Gn CB11 . . . . . . . .68 C6
SMITH'S GREEN . . . . . . . . . . . . . . .
Steeple Bumpstead . . . . .26 F4
Takeley . . . . . . . . . . . . .148 D7
Smith's Green Cotts
CB9 . . . . . . . . . . . . . . .27 A5
Smithy La CO15 . . . . . . .188 C6
SMYTHE'S GREEN . . . . .160 C2
Smythies Ave CO1 . . . . .136 B4
Snakes La
Stansted Mountfitchet
CM24 . . . . . . . . . . . .93 F2
Ugley CM22 . . . . . . . . .94 A3
Snape Cl CO16 . . . . . . . .188 A4
Snape Way CO13 . . . . . .170 F7
Sneating Hall La
CO13 . . . . . . . . . . . . .169 E8
Sneezor Way CM8 . . . . .194 E7
Snelling Gr CM2 . . . . . . .216 F6
Sniveller's La CO5 . . . . . .157 D3
Snowberry Ct CM7 . . . . .128 D4
Snowberry Gr CO2 . . . . .136 A3
Snowcroft IP9 . . . . . . . . .35 A1
Snowdon Cl **I** CB9 . . . . . .8 E6
Snowdon Rd IP2 . . . . . . .17 B2
Snowdrop Cl
Bishop's Stortford
CM23 . . . . . . . . . . . .145 C6
Chelmsford CM1 . . . . .205 E7
Witham CM8 . . . . . . . .176 E4
Snow Hill La CO6 . . . . . . .57 D5
Snowley Par CM23 . . . . .119 B1
Snows Way CO11 . . . . . . .86 D8
Soane St IP4 . . . . . . . . . .17 D6
Sodbury Ho CO15 . . . . . .188 F5
Soft Rd CO10 . . . . . . . . . .31 F5
Soils The CO12 . . . . . . . .116 E5
Solway Ct **I** CO4 . . . . . .136 E8
Somerset Cl CO2 . . . . . .135 B3
Somerset Ct **I** CB9 . . . . . .8 E7
Somerset Pl CM1 . . . . . .205 A7
Somerset Rd IP4 . . . . . . .17 F8
Somerset Way CO15 . . . .187 F1
Somers Rd CO3 . . . . . . .135 A4
Somerton Ct IP11 . . . . . .221 F4
Sonell Ct CO7 . . . . . . . . .137 B2
Songers Cotts CO4 . . . . .83 B6
Sorrel Cl
Colchester CO4 . . . . . .109 C2
Ipswich IP2 . . . . . . . . . .16 F3
Sorrel Gr CM77 . . . . . . . .154 B7
Sorrel Horse Mews **II**
IP4 . . . . . . . . . . . . . . .17 D5
Sorrell Cl
Goldhanger CM9 . . . . . .211 E7
Little Waltham CM3 . . . .191 B6
Sorrel Wlk CB9 . . . . . . . . .8 D8
South Area IP1 . . . . . . . . .16 C7
Southborough Rd
CM2 . . . . . . . . . . . . .216 A8
South Cl
Halstead CO9 . . . . . . . .103 E8
Ipswich IP4 . . . . . . . . . .17 E8
St Osyth CO16 . . . . . . .187 B4
Southcliff Ct
Clacton-on-S CO15 . . . .189 B4
Walton-on-t-N CO14 . . .171 C7
Southcliff Hall CO15 . . . .188 F2
Southcliff Pk CO15 . . . . .189 A4
Southcliff Prom CO14 . . .171 C7
Southcote Rd CM8 . . . . .176 F4
Southcroft Cl CO13 . . . . .170 C6
Southend Rd
Great Baddow CM2 . . . .217 B4
Howe Green CM2 . . . . .217 D2
Woodham Mortimer
CM9 . . . . . . . . . . . . .219 C5
Southey Cl CM9 . . . . . . .210 C4
SOUTHEY GREEN . . . . . .75 D5
Southfield CB10 . . . . . . . . .3 A3
Southfields CO7 . . . . . . . .84 F6
Southgate Cres CO15 . . .179 E5
Southgate Gdns CO10 . . .15 C6
Southgate Rd IP8 . . . . . . .16 B1
Southgate St and Pk
CB10 . . . . . . . . . . . . .43 F7
Southgate St CO10 . . . . .15 C6
South Gn CB11 . . . . . . . .64 D8
SOUTH GREEN . . . . . . .164 A3
Southgreen Gdns
CO16 . . . . . . . . . . . . .188 C5
South Green Rd CO15 . . .163 F3
SOUTH HEATH . . . . . . .167 A3
South Heath Rd CO7 . . .166 F3
South Hill IP11 . . . . . . . .221 D3
South Hill Cl CM3 . . . . . .218 D6
South Ho CO13 . . . . . . . .170 F4
Southland Cl CO4 . . . . . .110 C1
Southlands Chase
CM2 . . . . . . . . . . . . .217 E4
Southmill Ct CM23 . . . . .146 A6

**Southmill Rd** CM23 . . . . 146 A5
**Southmill Trad Ctr**
CM23 . . . . . . . . . . . . . . . . 146 A6
**South Primrose Hill**
CM1 . . . . . . . . . . . . . . . . . 204 F3
**South Rd**
Bishop's Stortford
CM23 . . . . . . . . . . . . . . . 146 A5
Saffron Walden CB11 . . . . . . 22 E1
Takeley CM22 . . . . . . . . . . 148 C8
**South St Commercial Ctr**
**1** CM23 . . . . . . . . . . . . . 145 F6
**South St**
Bishop's Stortford
CM23 . . . . . . . . . . . . . . . 145 F6
Braintree CM7 . . . . . . . . . . 127 F2
Colchester CO2 . . . . . . . . . 135 E6
Great Chesterford CB10 . . . . 3 D2
Great Waltham CM3 . . . . . . 190 E7
Ipswich IP1 . . . . . . . . . . . . . 17 B7
Manningtree CO11 . . . . . . . . 86 D4
Tolleshunt D'arcy CM9 . . . . 198 D4
**South Strand** CO11 . . . . . . 86 C5
**South Suffolk Bsns Ctr**
CO10 . . . . . . . . . . . . . . . . . 34 A7
**Southview 10** CM7 . . . . . . 128 A2
**South View** CM6 . . . . . . . . 150 C8
**Southview Dr**
Holland-on-S CO15 . . . . . . 189 F6
Walton-on-t-N CO14 . . . . . 171 C7
**South View Gn** IP9 . . . . . . . 60 E6
**South View La** CM8 . . . . . . 218 D6
**Southview Terr** CM3 . . . . . 218 D6
**Southway**
Brightlingsea CO7 . . . . . . . 185 F7
Colchester CO1 . . . . . . . . . 135 E6
**Southwold Way** CO16 . . . . 188 A5
**Southwood Chase**
CM23 . . . . . . . . . . . . . . . 219 A4
**Sovereign Cl** CM7 . . . . . . . 128 D4
**Sovereign Cres** CO3 . . . . . 135 C6
**Sovereign Dr** IP1 . . . . . . . . 16 C7
**Sowerberry Cl** CM1 . . . . . . 204 F7
**Spa Dr** CM0 . . . . . . . . . . . 213 B1
**SPAIN'S END** . . . . . . . . . . . 47 E6
**Spains Hall Rd** CM7 . . . . . . 72 C8
**Spalding Ave** CM1 . . . . . . . 204 E5
**Spalding Cl** CM7 . . . . . . . . 127 E4
**Spalding Ct** CM1 . . . . . . . . 205 A3
**Spalding Way** CM2 . . . . . . 216 F8
**Spanbies Rd** CO7 . . . . . . . . 58 D2
**Spansey Ct 1** CO9 . . . . . . . 76 D1
**Spa Rd**
Feering CO5 . . . . . . . . . . . 158 E4
Witham CM8 . . . . . . . . . . 176 C2
**Sparepenny La N** CB10 . . . 47 A4
**Sparepenny La S** CB10 . . . . 47 B4
**Sparkey Cl** CM6 . . . . . . . . . 195 A7
**Sparks La** CO9 . . . . . . . . . . 29 A6
**Spar La** CM3 . . . . . . . . . . . 220 C3
**Sparlings The** CO13 . . . . . 170 C8
**Sparrow Cl** CO9 . . . . . . . . . 75 D8
**Sparrow Rd** CO10 . . . . . . . . 34 B6
**Sparrows Cnr** CO12 . . . . . . 116 E5
**Sparrowsend Cotts**
CB11 . . . . . . . . . . . . . . . . . 43 A4
**Sparrowsend Hill** CB11 . . . . 43 A5
**Sparrows Herne**
CO15 . . . . . . . . . . . . . . . . 188 F6
**Sparrows Ho** CO7 . . . . . . . 185 E6
**Spartan Cl** CB9 . . . . . . . . . . . 8 C8
**Speckled Wood Cl** IP8 . . . . 36 D8
**Speckled Wood Ct**
CM7 . . . . . . . . . . . . . . . . . 154 E8
**Speedwell Cl** CM8 . . . . . . 176 D4
**Speedwell Rd**
Colchester CO2 . . . . . . . . . 136 D2
Ipswich IP2 . . . . . . . . . . . . 16 F4
**Spencer Cl**
Elsenham CM22 . . . . . . . . . 94 C3
Stansted Mountfitchet
CM24 . . . . . . . . . . . . . . . 119 E6
**Spencer Ho** CM24 . . . . . . . 119 D7
**Spencer Rd**
Great Chesterford CB10 . . . . 3 D3
Thorpe-le-S CO16 . . . . . . . 142 A2
**Spencers Piece** CM24 . . . . . 83 E4
**Spencer Sq** CM7 . . . . . . . . 127 F8
**Spendells Cl** CO14 . . . . . . 144 D2
**Spendells Ho** CO14 . . . . . . 144 E2
**Spenlow Dr** CM1 . . . . . . . . 204 D7
**Spennells The** CM24 . . . . . 142 A4
**Spenser Way** CO15 . . . . . . 187 F1
**Spicers La** CO10 . . . . . . . . . 15 C8
**Spike The 7** CB10 . . . . . . . . 22 F2
**Spindle Rd** CB9 . . . . . . . . . . 8 D8
**Spindle Wood** CO4 . . . . . . 110 B4
**Spindrift Way** CO7 . . . . . . 164 B8
**Spinks La** CM8 . . . . . . . . . 176 F1
**Spinnaker Cl** CO15 . . . . . . 203 J8
**Spinnaker Dr** CM9 . . . . . . 210 E3
**Spinnel's Hill** CO11 . . . . . . 88 B1
**Spinnel's La**
Wix CO11 . . . . . . . . . . . . . 115 D7
Wrabness CO11 . . . . . . . . . 88 C1
**Spinner Cl** IP1 . . . . . . . . . . 16 D8
**Spinneyfields** CO5 . . . . . . 179 D6
**Spinney The**
Braintree CM7 . . . . . . . . . 128 C1
Earls Colne CO6 . . . . . . . . 105 A6
Hatfield Peverel CM3 . . . . . 194 B3
Jaywick CO16 . . . . . . . . . . 188 A2
Long Melford CO10 . . . . . . . 15 C7

**Spinney The** continued
Newport CB11 . . . . . . . . . . 67 A7
Rushmere St A IP4 . . . . . . 18 F4
Stansted Mountfitchet
CM24 . . . . . . . . . . . . . . . 119 E6
**Spires The**
Bishop's Stortford
CM23 . . . . . . . . . . . . . . . 145 D7
Great Baddow CM2 . . . . . . 216 F6
**Spiritus Ho** CO2 . . . . . . . . 136 D5
**Spital Rd**
Maldon CM9 . . . . . . . . . . 209 F2
Maldon CM9 . . . . . . . . . . 220 D7
**Spitfire Cl** IP3 . . . . . . . . . . . 18 B1
**Sporehams La**
Danbury CM3 . . . . . . . . . . 218 C4
Howe Green CM2, CM3 . . . 217 F4
**Sportsmans La** CM3 . . . . . 194 A2
**Sportsway** CO1 . . . . . . . . 135 F8
**Spots Wlk** CM2 . . . . . . . . . 216 D3
**Spout La** CO10 . . . . . . . . . . 55 D7
**Spratts La** CO11 . . . . . . . . 113 B4
**Springbank Ave** CO11 . . . . . 86 B3
**Springbok Ho** CM2 . . . . . . 216 F5
**Spring Chase**
Brightlingsea CO7 . . . . . . . 185 E7
Wivenhoe CO7 . . . . . . . . . 137 B2
**Spring Cl**
Clacton-on-S CO16 . . . . . . 188 C5
Colchester CO4 . . . . . . . . . 110 C3
Little Baddow CM3 . . . . . . 207 D5
**Spring Cotts** CB9 . . . . . . . . . 9 C6
**Spring Elms La** CM3 . . . . . 207 F3
**Springett Pl** CM77 . . . . . . 155 E6
**Springett's Hill** CO8 . . . . . . 55 D2
**SPRINGFIELD** . . . . . . . . . . 205 E6
**Springfield Ave** IP11 . . . . . 221 E5
**Springfield Basin 10**
CM2 . . . . . . . . . . . . . . . . 205 C2
**Springfield Cotts**
CM3 . . . . . . . . . . . . . . . . 210 B5
**Springfield Ct**
Bishop's Stortford
CM23 . . . . . . . . . . . . . . . 145 E8
Clacton-on-S CO15 . . . . . . 188 C3
**Springfield Gn** CM1 . . . . . 205 E4
**Springfield Hospl** (private)
CM1 . . . . . . . . . . . . . . . . 205 D7
**Springfield Inf Sch** IP1 . . . . 16 F8
**Springfield Jun Sch**
IP1 . . . . . . . . . . . . . . . . . . 16 F8
**Springfield La** CM1 . . . . . . 205 E7
**Springfield Lyons App**
CM2 . . . . . . . . . . . . . . . . 206 A5
**Springfield Mdws**
CO16 . . . . . . . . . . . . . . . 168 C4
**Springfield Park Ave**
CM1 . . . . . . . . . . . . . . . . 205 D2
**Springfield Park Hill**
CM2 . . . . . . . . . . . . . . . . 205 D2
**Springfield Park La**
CM2 . . . . . . . . . . . . . . . . 205 D2
**Springfield Park Par**
CM2 . . . . . . . . . . . . . . . . 205 D2
**Springfield Park Rd**
CM2 . . . . . . . . . . . . . . . . 205 D2
**Springfield Pl** CM1 . . . . . . 205 E5
**Springfield Prim Sch**
CM1 . . . . . . . . . . . . . . . . 205 E7
**Springfield Rd**
Chelmsford CM1 . . . . . . . 205 E4
Sudbury CO10 . . . . . . . . . . 15 E1
**Springfields**
Braintree CM77 . . . . . . . . 127 C2
Brightlingsea CO7 . . . . . . . 185 F7
Great Dunmow CM6 . . . . . 150 D8
**Springfields Dr** CO2 . . . . . 135 A3
**Springfield Terr 2**
CO10 . . . . . . . . . . . . . . . . 33 F8
**Spring Gardens Rd**
CO6 . . . . . . . . . . . . . . . . 106 E6
**Spring Gdns** CO10 . . . . . . . 15 C8
**Springham Dr** CO4 . . . . . . 110 A6
**Springhill Cl** CB11 . . . . . . . 22 A1
**Springhill Ct** CO7 . . . . . . . 138 E8
**Springhill Rd** CB11 . . . . . . . 43 D8
**Springhurst Cl** IP4 . . . . . . . 17 F6
**Spring La**
Colchester CO3 . . . . . . . . . 135 A7
Colchester, Lexden
CO3 . . . . . . . . . . . . . . . . 135 A8
Eight Ash G CO3 . . . . . . . 108 B1
Great Totham CM9 . . . . . . 196 D7
Hatfield Peverel CM3,
CM3 . . . . . . . . . . . . . . . . 194 F2
Maldon CM9 . . . . . . . . . . 210 B4
West Bergholt CO6 . . . . . . 108 E3
Wivenhoe CO7 . . . . . . . . . 137 B2
**Springland Cl** IP4 . . . . . . . . 18 A6
**Springlands Way** CO10 . . . 15 F2
**Spring Lane Rdbt**
CO3 . . . . . . . . . . . . . . . . 135 A7
**Spring Mdw** CO10 . . . . . . . . 2 B6
**Springmead** CM77 . . . . . . 154 D7
**Spring Meadow Prim Sch**
CO12 . . . . . . . . . . . . . . . . 91 A3
**Spring Pond Cl** CM2 . . . . . 216 E8
**Spring Rd**
Brightlingsea CO7 . . . . . . . 185 F7
Ipswich IP4 . . . . . . . . . . . . 18 A6
St Osyth CO16 . . . . . . . . . 187 A3
Tiptree CO5 . . . . . . . . . . . 179 C4
**Spring Rise**
Galleywood CM2 . . . . . . . 216 C2
Haverhill CB9 . . . . . . . . . . . 9 C6
**Spring Sedge Cl** CO3 . . . . 134 C7
**Springtail Rd** IP8 . . . . . . . . 36 E8
**Springvalley La** CO7 . . . . . 111 C4

**Spring Way** CO9 . . . . . . . . 51 E1
**SPRINGWELL** . . . . . . . . . . . 22 A7
**Springwell Rd** CB10,
CB11 . . . . . . . . . . . . . . . . 22 A5
**Springwood Ct** CM7 . . . . . 127 D3
**Springwood Dr** CM7 . . . . . 127 C4
**Springwood Ind Est**
CM7 . . . . . . . . . . . . . . . . 127 D3
**Sprites End** IP11 . . . . . . . . 221 E1
**Spriteshall La** IP11 . . . . . . 221 B7
**Sprites La** IP8, IP2 . . . . . . . 16 C2
**Sprites Prim Sch** IP2 . . . . . 16 C2
**SPROUGHTON** . . . . . . . . . . 16 A6
**Sproughton Bsns Pk**
IP1 . . . . . . . . . . . . . . . . . . 16 C8
**Sproughton CE Prim Sch**
IP8 . . . . . . . . . . . . . . . . . 16 B6
**Sproughton Rd** IP1 . . . . . . 16 D7
**Spruce Ave**
Colchester CO4 . . . . . . . . 136 E8
Great Dunmow CM6 . . . . . 123 B1
**Spruce Cl**
West Mersea CO5 . . . . . . . 201 B7
Witham CM8 . . . . . . . . . . 177 A4
**Spurgeon Cl** CM7 . . . . . . . . 51 E1
**Spurgeon Pl** CO5 . . . . . . . 158 C2
**Spurgeon St** CO1 . . . . . . . 136 C6
**Square The**
Colchester CO2 . . . . . . . . 135 B3
Heybridge CM9 . . . . . . . . 210 A5
Stansted Mountfitchet
CM22 . . . . . . . . . . . . . . . . 93 F3
**Squires Cl** CM23 . . . . . . . 145 D6
**Squires Ct** CO6 . . . . . . . . . 105 B6
**Squire's Ct 1** CB9 . . . . . . . . 8 E7
**Squirrells Cl** CM1 . . . . . . . 204 F5
**Squirrels Cl 2** CM23 . . . . . 145 D6
**Squirrels Field** CO4 . . . . . 109 F5
**Squirrels The** IP9 . . . . . . . . 35 A2
**Stable Cl**
Colchester CO3 . . . . . . . . 134 E6
West Mersea CO5 . . . . . . . 201 E7
**Stablecroft** CM1 . . . . . . . . 205 F7
**Stable Rd** CO14 . . . . . . . . 171 A7
**Stable Mews** CO5 . . . . . . . 201 E7
**Stable Yard Cotts**
CM6 . . . . . . . . . . . . . . . . 122 C4
**Stacey Ct 3** CM23 . . . . . . 145 F6
**Stackyard The** CB10 . . . . . . 3 A3
**Stacy Ct** CM6 . . . . . . . . . 123 C1
**Stafford Cl** CO13 . . . . . . . 170 E6
**Stafford Cres** CM7 . . . . . . 128 D4
**Stafford Rd** CM23 . . . . . . . 145 F5
**STAFFORD'S CORNER** . . . . 181 E5
**Stainer Cl** CM7 . . . . . . . . 154 F7
**Stainers** CM23 . . . . . . . . . 145 C5
**Stalin Rd** CO2 . . . . . . . . . 136 B4
**Stallards Cres** CO13 . . . . . 170 E6
**STAMBOURNE** . . . . . . . . . . 28 D3
**STAMBOURNE GREEN**
. . . . . . . . . . . . . . . . . . . . 28 A1
**Stambourne Rd**
Great Yeldham CO9 . . . . . . 29 D3
Ridgewell CO9 . . . . . . . . . 28 F5
Toppesfield CO9 . . . . . . . . 50 B8
**Stambridge Rd** CO15 . . . . 188 C4
**Stamford Cl** IP2 . . . . . . . . . 36 F8
**Stammers Rd** CO4 . . . . . . 109 F4
**STANBROOK** . . . . . . . . . . . . 96 E7
**Standard Ave** CO15 . . . . . 203 D6
**Standard Rd 8** CO1 . . . . . 136 C6
**Standley Rd** CM4 . . . . . . . 144 D1
**Standrums** CM6 . . . . . . . . 150 D8
**Stane Cl** CM23 . . . . . . . . . 118 F1
**Stane Field** CO6 . . . . . . . . 132 E3
**Stanes Rd** CM7 . . . . . . . . 127 F6
**Stanfield Cl** CO3 . . . . . . . 134 E3
**Stanfield Mdw** CM8 . . . . . 155 F1
**Stanley Ave**
Brightlingsea CO7 . . . . . . . 186 A7
Ipswich IP3 . . . . . . . . . . . . 18 A4
**Stanley Drapkin Prim Sch**
CB9 . . . . . . . . . . . . . . . . . 27 B6
**Stanley Rd**
Clacton-on-S CO15 . . . . . . 188 C2
Felixstowe IP11 . . . . . . . . 221 E3
Great Chesterford CB10 . . . . 3 E3
Halstead CO9 . . . . . . . . . . 76 D2
Sudbury CO10 . . . . . . . . . . 33 E8
Wivenhoe CO7 . . . . . . . . . 137 C1
**Stanley Rise** CM2 . . . . . . . 205 F3
**Stanleys Farm Rd**
CB11 . . . . . . . . . . . . . . . . . 43 F8
**Stanley Wood Ave**
CO10 . . . . . . . . . . . . . . . . 15 F1
**Stanley Wooster Way**
CO4 . . . . . . . . . . . . . . . . 136 E7
**Stanmore Cl** CO16 . . . . . . 188 D5
**Stanmore Way** CO16 . . . . 187 B6
**Stannard Way** CO10 . . . . . 34 A6
**STANSTEAD** . . . . . . . . . . . . 2 F7
**Stansted Pl** CO7 . . . . . . . . 103 F8
**Stansted Rd** CO7 . . . . . . . 103 F8
**Stansted Airport Sta**
CM24 . . . . . . . . . . . . . . . 121 B4
**Stansted Cl** CM1 . . . . . . . 204 E1
**Stansted Ctyd** CM24 . . . . . 121 B1
**STANSTED**
**MOUNTFITCHET** . . . . . . . 119 C8
**Stansted Mountfitchet Sta**
CM24 . . . . . . . . . . . . . . . 119 E6
**Stansted Rd**
Birchanger CM23 . . . . . . . 119 C4

**Stansted Rd** continued
Bishop's Stortford
CM23 . . . . . . . . . . . . . . . 119 B2
Colchester CO2 . . . . . . . . 136 A1
Elsenham CM22 . . . . . . . . 94 C1
**Stansted Way** CO13 . . . . . 171 A6
**Stanstreete Field**
CM7 . . . . . . . . . . . . . . . . 154 B5
**Stanton Pl 3** CB9 . . . . . . . . 9 B8
**STANWAY** . . . . . . . . . . . . . 134 C5
**Stanway Cl** CO10 . . . . . . . . 2 C5
**Stanway Ctr The** CO3 . . . . 134 E4
**Stanway Fiveways Prim**
Sch CO3 . . . . . . . . . . . . . 134 C5
**STANWAY GREEN** . . . . . . . 134 D3
**Stanway Prim Sch**
CO3 . . . . . . . . . . . . . . . . 134 C6
**Stanway Sch The**
CO3 . . . . . . . . . . . . . . . . 134 C6
**Stanwell St 9** CO2 . . . . . . 135 F6
**Stanwyn Ave** CO15 . . . . . 188 E3
**Stapleford Cl** CM2 . . . . . . 205 A1
**Staplers Cl** CM9 . . . . . . . . 196 B4
**Staplers Heath** CM9 . . . . . 196 B4
**Staplers Wlk** CM9 . . . . . . 196 B4
**Starfield Cl** IP4 . . . . . . . . . 18 B6
**Star La**
Great Dunmow CM6 . . . . . 123 D1
Ipswich IP4 . . . . . . . . . . . . 17 D5
**Starling Cl 17** CM23 . . . . . 145 F6
**STARLING'S GREEN** . . . . . . 64 F3
**Starling's Hill** CO9 . . . . . . . 75 E4
**Star Mead** CM6 . . . . . . . . . 70 A2
**Star Rd** CM2 . . . . . . . . . . . 94 F5
**START HILL** . . . . . . . . . . . . 147 A7
**Station App**
Braintree CM7 . . . . . . . . . 128 A2
Frinton-on-S CO13 . . . . . . 170 F5
**Station Hill** CO8 . . . . . . . . 79 E8
**Station La** CO12 . . . . . . . . . 91 C4
**Station Rd**
Alresford CO7 . . . . . . . . . 165 A8
Ardleigh CO7 . . . . . . . . . . 111 E7
Bentley IP9 . . . . . . . . . . . . 60 E6
Birdbrook CO9 . . . . . . . . . 10 D1
Bishop's Stortford
CM23 . . . . . . . . . . . . . . . 146 A3
Bradfield CO11 . . . . . . . . . 87 E3
Braintree CM7 . . . . . . . . . 127 F2
Brightlingsea CO7 . . . . . . . 185 E6
Clacton-on-S CO15 . . . . . . 188 F3
Clare CO10 . . . . . . . . . . . . 12 C7
Colne Engaine CO6 . . . . . . 77 F1
Cressing CM8 . . . . . . . . . 156 A3
Earls Colne CO6 . . . . . . . . 105 A7
Elsenham CM22 . . . . . . . . . 94 C2
Felsted CM6 . . . . . . . . . . 151 F6
Great Bentley CO7 . . . . . . 166 E8
Great Dunmow CM6 . . . . . 150 E8
Harwich, Bath Side CO12 . . 91 E5
Harwich CO12 . . . . . . . . . . 90 F5
Harwich, Dovercourt
CO12 . . . . . . . . . . . . . . . . 91 D4
Hatfield Peverel CM3 . . . . 193 F5
Haverhill CB9 . . . . . . . . . . . 9 A8
Kelvedon CO5 . . . . . . . . . 158 C3
Kirby Cross CO13 . . . . . . . 170 B6
Long Melford CO10 . . . . . . 15 C5
Maldon CM9 . . . . . . . . . . 210 A3
Manningtree CO11 . . . . . . 86 C5
Marks Tey CO6 . . . . . . . . 133 B4
Newport CB11 . . . . . . . . . 67 A8
Rayne CM77 . . . . . . . . . . 126 D1
Saffron Walden CB11 . . . . 22 D1
Sible Hedingham CO9 . . . . 51 E2
Stansted Mountfitchet
CM24 . . . . . . . . . . . . . . . 119 E6
Sudbury CO10 . . . . . . . . . . 33 E7
Takeley CM22 . . . . . . . . . 148 C2
Thorpe-le-S CO16 . . . . . . . 168 F8
Thorrington CO7 . . . . . . . 166 A6
Tiptree CO5 . . . . . . . . . . . 179 C4
Tollesbury CM9 . . . . . . . . 199 D2
Tolleshunt D'arcy CM9 . . . 198 E5
Trimley St M IP11 . . . . . . 221 A3
Wendens Ambo CB11 . . . . . 42 F5
White Notley CM8 . . . . . . 155 F2
Wickham Bishops CM8 . . . 195 C4
Witham CM8 . . . . . . . . . . 177 A3
Wivenhoe CO7 . . . . . . . . . 164 B8
Wrabness CO11 . . . . . . . . . 88 F3
**Station Road Ind Est**
Great Dunmow CM6 . . . . . 150 E7
Tolleshunt D'arcy CM9 . . . 198 E5
**Station St**
Ipswich IP2 . . . . . . . . . . . . 17 C3
Saffron Walden CB11 . . . . 22 D1
Walton-on-t-N CO14 . . . . 171 C6
**Station Terr** CM3 . . . . . . . 193 F5
**Station Yd** IP2 . . . . . . . . . . 17 B4
**Steamer Terr 2** CM1 . . . . 205 A4
**Steam Mill Rd** CO11 . . . . . 114 B8
**Stebbens Way** CM7 . . . . . 210 B4
**STEBBING** . . . . . . . . . . . . 124 E5
**Stebbing Prim Sch**
CM6 . . . . . . . . . . . . . . . . 124 E5
**Stebbing Rd** CM6 . . . . . . . 152 B7
**Stedman Ct** CO15 . . . . . . 203 D6
**Steed Cres** CO2 . . . . . . . . 136 C4
**Steeds Mdw** CO10 . . . . . . . 15 C8
**Steele Cl** CO6 . . . . . . . . . 133 B5
**STEEPLE BUMPSTEAD**
. . . . . . . . . . . . . . . . . . . . 27 B8
**Steeple Bumpstead Rd**
CB9 . . . . . . . . . . . . . . . . . 26 E7
**Steeple Cl** CM9 . . . . . . . . 210 D5

**Steeple View** CM23 . . . . . 145 F6
**Steerforth Cl** CM1 . . . . . . 204 D7
**Stella Maris** IP2 . . . . . . . . . 16 D5
**Stepfield** CM8 . . . . . . . . . 177 B2
**Stephen Cl**
Haverhill CB9 . . . . . . . . . . . 8 F8
Long Melford CO10 . . . . . . 15 B5
**Stephen Cranfield Cl**
CO5 . . . . . . . . . . . . . . . . 164 A7
**Stephen Marshall Ave**
CM7 . . . . . . . . . . . . . . . . 72 C6
**Stephen Neville Ct**
CB11 . . . . . . . . . . . . . . . . . 43 D8
**Stephen's Ct** IP4 . . . . . . . . 18 B6
**Stephenson Rd**
Braintree CM7 . . . . . . . . . 128 A1
Clacton-on-S CO15 . . . . . . 189 B8
Colchester CO4 . . . . . . . . 110 D6
**Stephenson Rd W**
CO15 . . . . . . . . . . . . . . . 169 A1
**Sterling Cl** CO3 . . . . . . . . 134 E5
**Sterling Complex** IP1 . . . . . 16 D7
**Stevens Cl** CO4 . . . . . . . . 109 E3
**Stevens La** CM6 . . . . . . . . 152 F6
**Stevenson Rd** IP1 . . . . . . . 17 B6
**Stevens Rd** CM8 . . . . . . . 176 E1
**Stevens Wlk** CO4 . . . . . . . 136 F7
**STEVENTON END** . . . . . . . . 6 C2
**Stewards Cl** CO13 . . . . . . . 170 F7
**Stewart Rd** CM2 . . . . . . . 216 A6
**Stewarts The** CM23 . . . . . 145 C6
**Stewarts Way** CM23 . . . . . 92 F2
**STICKLING GREEN** . . . . . . . 65 C5
**Stilemans Wood** CM7 . . . . 128 D1
**Stiles The** CM9 . . . . . . . . 210 E3
**Stirling Dr** CB9 . . . . . . . . . . 8 E8
**Stirrup Cl** CM1 . . . . . . . . . 205 E7
**Stirrup Mews** CO3 . . . . . . 134 E6
**STISTED** . . . . . . . . . . . . . . 129 C6
**Stisted CE Prim Sch**
CM7 . . . . . . . . . . . . . . . . 129 B6
**Stivvy's Rd** CM9 . . . . . . . 208 C3
**Stock Chase** CM9 . . . . . . . 210 B5
**Stockhouse Cl** CM9 . . . . . 180 B2
**Stockhouse Rd** CO5 . . . . . 180 B7
**STOCKING GREEN** . . . . . . . 24 C1
**Stocking La** SG8 . . . . . . . . 39 C1
**Stockley Cl** CB9 . . . . . . . . . 9 C7
**Stockman Terr** CM77 . . . . 154 C8
**Stockmen Field** CM23 . . . . 145 C5
**Stockmers End 1** IP9 . . . . . 35 A1
**Stock Rd** CM2 . . . . . . . . . 216 B2
**STOCKS GREEN** . . . . . . . . 158 F6
**STOCKSTREET** . . . . . . . . . 130 B2
**Stock Terr** CM9 . . . . . . . . 210 B5
**Stockwell 5** CO1 . . . . . . . 135 F7
**STOKE** . . . . . . . . . . . . . . . . 17 D3
**Stokeash Cl** CO16 . . . . . . 188 A3
**STOKE BY CLARE** . . . . . . . . 11 C4
**STOKE-BY-NAYLAND** . . . . . 56 E5
**Stoke-by-Nayland Mid**
Sch CO6 . . . . . . . . . . . . . 56 C6
**Stoke-by-Nayland Prim**
Sch CO6 . . . . . . . . . . . . . 56 C6
**Stoke Coll** CO10 . . . . . . . . 11 C3
**Stoke Hall Rd** CO10 . . . . . 15 C5
**Stoke High Sch** IP2 . . . . . . 17 C2
**STOKE HILL** . . . . . . . . . . . . 17 B4
**STOKE PARK** . . . . . . . . . . . 17 A1
**Stoke Park Dr** IP2 . . . . . . . 17 A1
**Stoke Park Gdns** IP2 . . . . . 17 A1
**Stoke Quay** IP2 . . . . . . . . . 17 D4
**Stoke Rd**
Clare CO10 . . . . . . . . . . . . 12 A6
Nayland CO6 . . . . . . . . . . 56 B2
**Stoke St** IP2 . . . . . . . . . . . 17 C4
**Stokes The** CO14 . . . . . . . 171 B8
**Stonebridge Hill** CO6 . . . . 104 E7
**Stonechat Rd** CM11 . . . . . 16 D2
**Stone Cl** CM7 . . . . . . . . . 127 F2
**Stone Cotts**
Great Maplestead CO9 . . . . 52 D2
Greenstead Green CO9 . . . 104 A5
**Stonecrop** CO4 . . . . . . . . 109 C2
**Stonegrove Rd** IP11 . . . . . 221 B1
**Stone Hall** CO10 . . . . . . . . 12 B7
**Stonehall Dr** CO16 . . . . . . 168 D1
**Stonehall La** CO12 . . . . . . 115 B1
**Stoneham St** CO6 . . . . . . . 130 F2
**Stonehill Way** CO5 . . . . . . 201 A6
**Stone La**
Tiptree CO5 . . . . . . . . . . . 179 A2
Wrabness CO11 . . . . . . . . . 88 F5
**Stonelands Ho** IP11 . . . . . 221 B6
**Stoneleigh Pk** CO3 . . . . . . 134 F4
**Stone Lodge La** IP2 . . . . . . 17 C2
**Stone Lodge La W** IP2 . . . . 16 F3
**Stone Path Dr** CM3 . . . . . 193 F3
**Stone Rd** CO7 . . . . . . . . . 113 B1
**STONES GREEN** . . . . . . . . 115 D2
**Stone's Green Rd**
CO12 . . . . . . . . . . . . . . . 114 E2
**Stoney Comm** CM24 . . . . . 119 C5
**Stoney Common Rd**
CM24 . . . . . . . . . . . . . . . 119 D5
**Stoneyfield Dr** CM24 . . . . 119 C5
**Stoney La** CO7 . . . . . . . . . 186 A8
**Stoney Pl** CM24 . . . . . . . . 119 C5
**Stonham Ave** CO16 . . . . . 188 A4
**Stony La** CM9 . . . . . . . . . . 70 A2
**Stopes Ho 3** CO1 . . . . . . . 136 A7
**Stopford Ct 2** IP1 . . . . . . . 17 A6
**Stores Rd** CO5 . . . . . . . . . 179 C6

Storms Way CM2 .....206 B2
Stortford Hall Ind Pk
CM23 .....146 B7
Stortford Hall Pk
CM23 .....146 B8
Stortford Hall Rd 3 .....146 B8
STORTFORD PARK .....145 C8
Stortford Rd
Clavering CB11 .....65 C4
Great Dunmow CM6 .....123 C1
Takeley CM6 .....149 D7
Stort Lo CM23 .....145 D8
Stort Rd CM23 .....145 F6
Stort Valley Ind Pk
CM23 .....119 B2
Stour Ave IP11 .....221 C3
Stour Cl
Glemsford CO10 .....2 C2
Harwich CO12 .....90 D2
Stour Ct CM7 .....128 D1
Stourdale Cl CO11 .....86 A3
Stour Estuary Nature
Reserve* CO12 .....89 C3
Stour Gdns CO10 .....34 B4
Stour Gn CO10 .....12 B6
Stour Rd CO12 .....91 D5
Stourside IP9 .....91 A8
Stour St
Cavendish CO10 .....13 C8
Manningtree CO11 .....86 D4
Sudbury CO10 .....33 E7
Stourton Rd CM8 .....176 E3
Stour Vale
Clare CO10 .....12 A6
Stoke by C CO10 .....10 D2
Stour Valley Rd CB9 .....9 B7
Stourview Ave CO11 .....87 A4
Stourview Cl CO11 .....87 B4
Stour View Cl CO12 .....91 D5
Stour Wlk CO4 .....110 E2
Stour Ct CO4 .....109 F5
Stradbroke Rd IP4 .....18 A7
Straight Rd
Boxted CO4 .....82 F2
Bradfield CO11 .....87 C1
Colchester CO3 .....134 F5
Great Bentley CO7 .....167 A4
Straight Way CO2 .....161 A2
Strand The IP2 .....37 C8
Stranger's Gn CO7 .....185 D8
Strasbourg Sq 6 CB9 .....9 B8
Stratford Pl 4 CO14 .....171 C8
Stratford Rd
Clacton-on-S CO15 .....189 D6
Dedham CO4 .....84 D7
STRATFORD ST MARY
.....58 C2
Stratford St Mary Prim
Sch CO7 .....58 C1
Strawberry CM7 .....128 A1
Strawberry Fields CB9 .....8 D7
Strawberry La CO5 .....179 F3
Strawbrook Hill CM3 .....173 E4
Straw La CO10 .....33 D7
Street Farm Bglws
CO11 .....61 A2
Street The
Ardleigh CO7 .....111 E8
Ashen CO10 .....11 D1
Belchamp Otten CO10 .....31 C8
Belstead IP8 .....36 C6
Berden CM23 .....92 B8
Birdbrook CO9 .....28 B7
Bradfield CO11 .....87 E1
Bradwell CM77 .....129 D3
Brantham CO11 .....61 A1
Bulmer CO10 .....32 E5
Capel St M IP9 .....35 A1
Chappel CO6 .....106 D5
Cressing CM77 .....156 A6
East Bergholt CO7 .....59 B2
Feering CO5 .....158 E5
Foxearth CO10 .....14 C6
Galleywood CM2 .....216 B2
Gosfield CO9 .....102 E7
Great Hallingbury
CM22 .....147 B4
Great Henny CO10 .....13 E3
Great Tey CO6 .....132 C8
Harkstead IP9 .....63 B2
Hatfield Peverel CM3 .....193 F4
Holbrook IP9 .....62 D6
Kirby-le-S CO13 .....143 B1
Little Clacton CO16 .....168 C3
Little Dunmow CM6 .....151 D7
Little Totham CM9 .....197 B5
Little Waltham CM3 .....191 B6
Maldon CM9 .....210 B4
Manuden CM23 .....93 D7
Messing CO5 .....159 D2
Pebmarsh CO9 .....78 A8
Pentlow CO10 .....14 A8
Purleigh CM3, CM9 .....220 F1
Ramsey CO12 .....90 A1
Rayne CM77 .....126 F2
Salcott-c-V CM9 .....199 B8
Shalford CM7 .....100 E7
Stisted CM7 .....129 C6
Stoke by C CO10 .....11 B3
Stratford St M CO7 .....84 D8
Tendring CO16 .....140 E5
Terling CM3 .....175 C2
Tiptree CO5 .....179 A8
Toppesfield CO9 .....50 B7
Washbrook IP8 .....35 F8
Weeley IP8 .....140 F1
Wherstead IP9 .....37 B6

Street The continued
White Notley CM8 .....155 E1
Wickham Bishops CM8 .....195 C4
Woodham Walter CM9 .....208 D2
Stretford Ct CM8 .....156 D3
STRETHALL .....20 F4
Strethall Rd CB11 .....21 C4
Strickmere CO7 .....58 D2
Strood Cl CO5 .....201 B7
Strood The CO5 .....183 C3
Strudwick Cl 15 CM7 .....127 F2
Strutt Cl CM3 .....194 A4
Stuart Cl
Great Baddow CM2 .....217 B6
Ipswich IP3 .....17 F7
Stuart Ct 2 CM7 .....128 B2
Stuart Ho CO10 .....135 F8
Stuart Pawsey Ct
CO7 .....137 C1
Stuarts Dr CO10 .....34 A7
Stuarts Way CM7 .....128 B2
Stubbs Cl
Ipswich IP3 .....18 A1
Kirby Cross CO13 .....170 E7
Stubbs La CO4 .....86 B4
Stubbs La CM7 .....128 C1
Studd's La CO4 .....109 D4
Stump Cross CO10 .....3 C5
Stump La CM1 .....205 D4
Stump's Cross CO9 .....29 A2
Sturdee Ave IP3 .....18 B3
STURMER .....9 F4
Sturmer Ct 3 CO2 .....136 A1
Sturmer End Ind Est
CB9 .....9 C6
Sturmer Rd
Haverhill, Calford Green
CB9 .....9 F7
Haverhill CB9 .....9 E6
Sturrick La CO7 .....139 D1
STUTTON .....61 F2
Stutton CE Prim Sch
IP9 .....62 A2
Stutton Cl IP9 .....62 A2
Stutton Gn IP9 .....62 C1
Stutton La IP9 .....61 C5
Stutton Rd CO11 .....61 A2
Styles CO11 .....71 D2
Sub-Station Rd IP11 .....221 B2
Sucklings Yd CB9 .....27 C7
SUCKSTED GREEN .....96 A6
Sudbourne Ave CO16 .....188 A4
Sudbourne Rd IP11 .....221 B5
SUDBURY .....33 D8
Sudbury Rd
Bulmer CO10 .....32 F6
Bures CO8 .....55 F1
Castle Hedingham CO9 .....52 B4
Felixstowe IP11 .....221 A4
Gestingthorpe CO9 .....31 F2
Great Cornard CO10 .....34 F7
Great Maplestead CO9 .....53 C2
Halstead CO9 .....76 F3
Long Melford CO10 .....15 C3
Stoke-by-N CO6 .....56 C6
Sudbury Sta CO10 .....33 F7
Sue Ryder Foundation
Mus* CO10 .....1 D1
Suffolk Ave CO5 .....201 D7
Suffolk Cl
Clacton-on-S CO15 .....189 E7
Colchester CO4 .....110 B1
Suffolk Coll
Ipswich IP4 .....17 E6
Ipswich IP4 .....17 E5
Suffolk Coll (Argyll St
Annexe) IP4 .....17 C6
Suffolk Dr CM2 .....206 A4
Suffolk Knowle CO8 .....55 F1
Suffolk Rd
Ipswich IP4 .....17 D7
Maldon CM9 .....209 E1
Sudbury CO10 .....33 E8
Suffolk Ret Pk IP1 .....17 A6
Suffolk Ski Ctr* IP2 .....37 B8
Suffolk Sq CO10 .....33 E8
Suffolk St CO14 .....171 C8
Sugar La CO9 .....74 E7
Sulleys Hill IP7 .....58 B8
Sullivan Cl CO4 .....136 E6
Summercroft Prim Sch
IP4 .....18 D8
Summerfield Cl IP4 .....18 D8
Summerfield Ct IP4 .....18 D8
Summerfields CO9 .....51 E1
Summerhill Rd CB11 .....43 D8
Summerleaze Ct
CM77 .....154 D7
Sunbank CM6 .....150 E7
Sunbeam Ave CO15 .....203 E6
Sunbeam Cl CO5 .....164 A8
Sunbury Way CM9 .....220 F8
Sundale Cl CO15 .....189 F6
Sunfield Cl IP4 .....18 B6
Sunflower Cl 5 CM8 .....205 F6
Sun Lido Square Gdns
CM77 .....127 C2
Sunningdale CM23 .....145 E6
Sunningdale Ave
Felixstowe IP11 .....221 F6
Ipswich IP4 .....18 D5
Sunningdale Dr IP11 .....221 F6
Sunningdale Fall
CM3 .....194 B4
Sunningdale Rd CM1 .....204 E4

Sunningdale Way
CO13 .....170 E7
Sunnyfields Rd CM7 .....102 D2
Sunny Point CO14 .....144 E3
Sunnyside
Braintree CM7 .....127 E3
Stansted Mountfitchet
CM24 .....119 E6
Sunnyside Rd CO6 .....107 D5
Sunnyside Way CO16 .....168 C1
Sunnyway Cotts CM3 .....218 E3
Sunray Ave IP11 .....221 F6
Sunrise Ave CM1 .....205 A5
Surbiton Rd IP1 .....16 F8
SURREX .....131 E2
Surrex Cotts CO6 .....131 D2
Surrex Farm Units
.....131 D2
Surrey Cl CO15 .....189 A2
Surrey La CO5 .....179 C4
Surrey Rd
Felixstowe IP11 .....221 D4
Ipswich IP1 .....17 A6
Sussex Cl CM1 .....204 F8
Sussex Gdns CO15 .....189 E6
Sussex Rd CO3 .....135 C7
Sutherland Ho CM1 .....205 A4
Sutor Cl CM8 .....176 E1
Sutton Mead CM2 .....206 A4
Sutton Park Ave CO3 .....135 A3
Swains Croft CO10 .....32 E5
Swallow Cl
Harwich CO12 .....90 E1
Layer de la H CO2 .....162 A5
Colchester CM23 .....146 A6
Swallowdale
Clacton-on-S CO15 .....188 F6
Colchester CO2 .....136 C3
Swallow Field CO6 .....105 B6
Swallow Path CM2 .....216 B5
Swallow Rd IP2 .....16 C3
Swallow's Row CO7 .....167 B8
Swallow's Row CO7 .....140 B1
Swallowtail Cl IP9 .....36 E8
Swallow Wlk CO9 .....76 F1
Swanbridge Ind Pk
CM8 .....177 B3
Swan Chase CO9 .....75 E8
Swan Cl
Colchester CO4 .....136 E5
Hatfield Peverel CM3 .....193 F4
Colchester CM3 .....193 F4
Swan Ct
2 Bishop's Stortford
CM23 .....145 F6
Maldon CM9 .....210 B4
New Mistley CO11 .....87 A3
Sible Hedingham CO9 .....75 E8
Swan Farm Mews IP8 .....16 A1
Swanfield CO10 .....15 C7
Swan Gr CO6 .....106 C5
Swan Hill IP8 .....16 A2
Swan La
Haverhill CB9 .....9 A8
Long Melford CO10 .....15 C7
Swan Mdw CO7 .....58 C1
Swan Pas 13 CO1 .....135 E7
Swan Rd CO16 .....141 D5
Swanscomb Rd CO6 .....105 F4
Swansea Ave IP2 .....17 B1
Swan Side CM7 .....127 F3
Swans Pasture CM1 .....205 D6
Swan St
Chappel CO6 .....106 C3
Kelvedon CO5 .....158 D3
Sible Hedingham CO9 .....51 E1
SWAN STREET .....106 C3
Swan Vale Ind Est
CM8 .....177 B3
Swan Yd CO6 .....131 A2
Swatchway Cl IP3 .....38 B8
Swaynes CM7 .....58 C2
Sweden Cl CO12 .....90 F4
Swedish Est CO11 .....61 B8
Sweet Briar Cl IP8 .....145 B6
Sweet Briar Rd CO3 .....134 C7
Sweet Mead CB10 .....22 E3
Swift Ave
Clacton-on-S CO15 .....203 F6
Colchester CO3 .....134 C4
Swift Cl CM7 .....155 A7
Swinbourne Dr CM7 .....127 D3
Swinton Cl IP7 .....146 A6
Swiss Ave CM1 .....205 A4
Sworders Yd 3 CM23 .....145 F7
Sycamore Cl
Clacton-on-S CO15 .....203 F6
Great Cornard CO10 .....34 B7
Heybridge CM9 .....210 C6
Sycamores The CM23 .....146 B6
Sycamore Way
Brantham CO11 .....60 D1
Clacton-on-S CO15 .....188 C3
Kirby Cross CO13 .....170 D6
Sydner Cl CM2 .....217 A5
Sydney St
Brightlingsea CO7 .....185 F6
Colchester CO2 .....136 B1
Syers Field CM7 .....74 B2

Sylvan Cl CM2 .....216 B6
Symmons Cl CM77 .....126 F1
Symonds Ct 6 CO9 .....76 F2
Syringa Cl 6 CO4 .....136 E7

T

Taber Pl CM8 .....177 B3
Tabor Ave CM7 .....127 E3
Tabor Cl CO7 .....185 F8
Tabor Rd CO1 .....136 C7
Tabors Ave CM2 .....216 F8
Tabor Science Coll
CM7 .....127 D4
Tabor's Hill CM2 .....216 F7
Tacket St IP4 .....17 D5
Tacon Cl IP11 .....221 C1
Tacon Rd IP11 .....221 C1
Tailors CM23 .....145 B5
Tailors Cl CM7 .....154 C8
Tait Mews CM9 .....210 A2
TAKELEY .....148 C7
Takeley Bsns Ctr
CM22 .....148 C7
Takeley Pk CM22 .....148 C6
Takeley Prim Sch
CM22 .....148 C8
TAKELEY STREET .....147 E7
Talavera Cres CO2 .....135 C2
Talbot Ave CO2 .....203 F6
Talbot Rd
Little Clacton CO16 .....168 C4
Sudbury CO10 .....15 F2
Talbots IP11 .....221 D3
Talbot St CO12 .....91 D5
Talcott Rd CO2 .....136 A2
Talisman Cl CO5 .....179 D6
Talisman Wlk CO5 .....179 D6
Tall Trees CO4 .....109 E3
Tall Trees Cvn Pk
CM24 .....120 A4
Tally Ho CO4 .....110 B4
Tally Ho Cnr CO7 .....58 D1
Talmash Gdns IP2 .....17 A4
Tamar Ave CM8 .....176 E2
Tamarisk Way
Clacton-on-S CO15 .....203 F6
Colchester CO4 .....136 E8
Tamar Rise CM1 .....205 C6
Tambour Cl CO4 .....132 C8
Tamdown Way CM7 .....127 C4
Tamworth Chase CO2 .....136 A6
Tangerine Cl CM2 .....136 D6
Tan La CO16 .....168 F4
Tanner Cl CO16 .....188 B3
Tanners Mdw CM7 .....128 C2
Tanners View IP2 .....16 F7
Tanners Way CB10 .....22 E1
Tanton Rd CM6 .....151 E6
Tanyard The CM6 .....70 A2
Tapestry Ct CO6 .....105 B6
Tapestry Wlk CM7 .....128 D2
Tapley Rd CM1 .....204 F7
Tapsworth Cl CO16 .....188 D5
Tapwoods CO3 .....135 A7
Tara Cl CO4 .....110 D1
Tarragona Mews CO2 .....136 B4
Taragon Cl CO5 .....179 C4
Tarrett Dr 11 CO1 .....136 C6
Tasman Ct CM1 .....204 E5
Tasmania Rd IP4 .....18 D6
Tasman Rd IP3 .....9 C7
Tattersall Way CM1 .....215 C4
TATTINGSTONE .....61 C7
Tattingstone CE Prim Sch
IP9 .....61 D7
Taunton Rd
Chelmsford CM1 .....205 E5
Felixstowe IP11 .....221 D6
Taverners Wlk CM8 .....176 F4
Tavern St IP1 .....17 C6
Tavistock Rd CM1 .....205 E5
Tawell Mews CO5 .....179 D5
Tawney Cl IP9 .....35 A1
Tawneys Ride CO8 .....80 A8
Tayberry PI IP3 .....38 C7
Taylor Ave CM1 .....204 E5
Taylor Ct CO1 .....135 F7
Taylor Dr CO11 .....86 C4
Taylors End Rd CM24 .....120 E1
Taylor's Rd CO5 .....163 F8
Tayspill Ct CO2 .....135 B3
Teak Wlk CM8 .....177 A4
Teal Cl
Colchester CO4 .....137 A8
Great Notley CM77 .....154 B5
Ipswich IP2 .....16 D2
Teal Way CO5 .....158 D2
Teapot Cnr IP7 .....57 E8
Tedder Cl CO2 .....136 A4
Tees Cl CM8 .....176 E2
Tees Rd CM1 .....205 C6
Teign Dr CM8 .....176 D2
Telford PI CM1 .....205 D4
Telford Rd
Braintree CM7 .....128 A1
Clacton-on-S CO15 .....189 C8
Telford Way CO4 .....110 D6
Temperance Yd CO6 .....105 B6
Templar Rd CM7 .....154 C8
Templars CI CM8 .....176 F4
Templar's Ct CO9 .....8 E7
Templars Inf Sch
CM8 .....176 F5
Templars Jun Sch
CM8 .....176 F5
Temple Cl CO13 .....171 A6

Temple Ct CO4 .....110 D2
TEMPLE END .....14 B4
Temple La CM8, CM7 .....156 C3
Templemead CM8 .....176 F3
Temple Pattle CO11 .....86 C7
Temple Rd
Colchester CO2 .....135 A2
Ipswich IP3 .....18 C4
Templeton Ct CM7 .....128 A3
Temple Way CM7 .....209 F5
Ten Acre App CM9 .....209 F5
Tenby Rd IP2 .....17 A2
TENDRING .....140 F5
TENDRING GREEN .....140 E8
TENDRING HEATH .....114 D1
Tendring Prim Sch
CO16 .....140 F6
Tendring Rd
Little Bentley CO7 .....140 A8
Thorpe-le-S CO16 .....141 D4
Tendring Tech Coll
Thorpe-le-S CO16 .....142 A1
Walton-on-t-N CO13 .....171 A7
Tennyson Cl CM7 .....154 F8
Tennyson Rd
Chelmsford CM1 .....204 F5
Ipswich IP4 .....17 F5
Tenpenny Hill CO7 .....165 E5
Tenterfield Cl CM7 .....127 F5
Tenterfield CM6 .....150 E8
Tenter Field CO7 .....58 D1
Tenterfield Rd CM9 .....210 A2
Tenterfields .....42 F1
Tenth Ave CM24 .....120 C2
TERLING .....175 C3
Terling CE Prim Sch
CM3 .....175 C3
Terling Cl CO2 .....136 A1
Terling Hall Cotts
CM3 .....193 B7
Terling Hall Rd CM3 .....193 C7
Terling Rd
Hatfield Peverel CM3 .....193 F6
Witham CM8 .....176 B3
Terminal Rd N CM22,
CM24 .....121 B4
Terminal Rd S CM22,
CM24 .....121 B4
Termitts Chase CM3 .....194 A7
Tern Cl
Haverhill CB9 .....9 C7
Kelvedon CO5 .....158 D3
Terndale CO15 .....188 F6
Tern Mews CO7 .....164 B8
Tern Rd IP2 .....16 E2
Terrace Hall Chase
CO6 .....109 D6
Terrace The
Cavendish CO10 .....1 D1
Felsted CM6 .....152 B5
Hatfield Peverel CM3 .....194 B5
Terra Cotta PI CO10 .....2 E8
Tew Cl CO5 .....179 D5
Tewkesbury Rd CO15 .....188 F4
Tey Rd
Aldham CO6 .....106 E1
Coggeshall CO6 .....131 C4
Earls Colne CO6 .....105 D4
Tey Road Cl CO6 .....105 D6
Thackeray Cl CM7 .....155 A8
Thames Ave CM1 .....204 D4
Thames Cl CM7 .....128 A1
Thanet Rd IP4 .....18 B6
Thanet Wlk CO5 .....164 A8
Thatchers Dr CO7 .....137 F6
Thatchers The CM23 .....145 C5
Thatchers Way CM77 .....154 C8
THAXTED .....70 A3
Thaxted Prim Sch CM6 .....70 A2
Thaxted Rd
Debden CB11 .....68 C6
Great Sampford CB10 .....44 C4
Saffron Walden CB10 .....43 F8
Thaxted CB10 .....69 E8
Thaxted Wlk CO2 .....163 A8
Thebe Cl IP1 .....16 D8
Theberton Rd IP3 .....18 B1
The Bglws CM7 .....100 F5
THE HEATH .....61 B6
Thelsford Wlk CO4 .....166 A5
Theobalds Rd CO10 .....15 B5
Thetford Ct CM1 .....204 D1
Thetford Rd 11 IP1 .....17 A7
Thieves' Cnr CM1 .....204 A4
Third Ave
Chelmsford CM1 .....205 B5
Clacton-on-S CO15 .....189 C4
Frinton-on-S CO13 .....170 E4
Glemsford CO10 .....2 C5
Halstead CO9 .....77 B1
Harwich CO12 .....91 C3
Seawick CO16 .....203 B6
Stansted Mountfitchet
CM24 .....120 B2
Walton-on-t-N CO14 .....144 E6
Thirlmere Cl CM77 .....154 D7
Thirslet Dr CM9 .....210 C4
Thirtle Cl CO15 .....188 D6
Thistle Cl IP2 .....16 F4
Thistledown
Colchester CO4 .....110 B3
Panfield CM7 .....127 A7
Thistley Cl CM9 .....211 E6

Thistley Cres CB11 . . . . . . . 66 E1
THISTLEY GREEN
 Braintree . . . . . . . . . 128 B7
 Felsted . . . . . . . . . . 153 A3
Thistley Green Rd
 CM7 . . . . . . . . . . . 128 B7
Thomas Ave IP11 . . . . . 221 A8
Thomas Bell Rd CO6 . . . 105 A6
Thomas Benold Wlk
 CO2 . . . . . . . . . . . 162 F8
Thomas Cl CM2 . . . . . . 205 F3
Thomas Heskin Ct [10]
 CM23 . . . . . . . . . . 146 A7
Thomas Lord Audley Sch
 & Language Coll The
 CO2 . . . . . . . . . . . 135 F2
Thomas Rd CO15 . . . . . 188 D4
Thomas St CO7 . . . . . . 109 F5
Thomas Wakley Cl
 CO4 . . . . . . . . . . . 109 F5
Thomas Wlk CB11 . . . . . 20 F1
Thompson Ave CO3 . . . 134 F6
Thompson Rd IP1 . . . . . 16 C8
Thorington Cl CM77 . . . 154 C6
THORINGTON STREET
 . . . . . . . . . . . . . . . 57 B4
THORLEY . . . . . . . . . . 145 D2
Thorley Hall Stables
 CM23 . . . . . . . . . . 145 D2
Thorley High CM23 . . . . 145 F1
Thorley Hill CM23 . . . . . 145 F5
Thorley Hill Prim Sch
 CM23 . . . . . . . . . . 145 F4
THORLEY HOUSES . . . . 145 A5
Thorley La
 Bishop's Stortford, Thorley
  Houses CM23 . . . . . 145 B5
 Bishop's Stortford, Thorley
  Park CM23 . . . . . . . 145 D3
 Bishop's Stortford, Thorley
  Street CM23 . . . . . . 145 F3
Thorley Neighbourhood
 Ctr CM23 . . . . . . . . 145 D4
THORLEY PARK . . . . . . 145 D4
Thorley Park Rd
 CM23 . . . . . . . . . . 145 F5
THORLEY STREET . . . . 145 F3
Thornbera Cl CM23 . . . . 145 F4
Thornbera Gdns
 CM23 . . . . . . . . . . 145 F4
Thornbera Rd CM23 . . . 145 F4
Thornberry Ave CO16 . . 140 F1
Thornbury Rd CO15 . . . 158 F4
Thornbush La IP8 . . . . . 16 A8
Thorncroft CB10 . . . . . . 22 F2
Thorndon Cl CO16 . . . . 188 A4
Thorne Rd CO5 . . . . . . 158 B2
Thorney Rd IP9 . . . . . . 35 A1
Thornfield Ct CO2 . . . . . 136 D2
Thornfield Rd CM23 . . . 145 E8
Thorn Gr CM23 . . . . . . 145 F3
Thorn Grove Prim Sch
 CM23 . . . . . . . . . . 146 B6
Thornhayes Cl IP2 . . . . . 17 A3
Thornhill CM3 . . . . . . . 220 D1
Thornhill Cl CO13 . . . . . 170 F7
Thornley Dr IP4 . . . . . . 18 C8
Thorns Way CM1 . . . . . 171 A8
Thornton Dr CO4 . . . . . 109 F2
Thornton Rd CM6 . . . . . 148 F7
Thorn Way IP11 . . . . . . 221 C4
Thornwood CO4 . . . . . . 109 F4
Thornwood Cl CO5 . . . . 201 D6
Thoroughfare [9] IP1 . . . 17 C6
Thoroughgood Rd
 CO15 . . . . . . . . . . 188 F3
Thorpe Cross CO16 . . . 141 E8
THORPE GREEN . . . . . 141 E2
THORPE-le-SOKEN . . . . 142 B1
Thorpe-le-Soken Sta
 CO16 . . . . . . . . . . 168 F7
Thorpe Mews CM7 . . . . 128 C3
Thorpe Park La CO16 . . 169 F8
Thorpe Rd
 Beaumont CO16 . . . . 142 B5
 Clacton-on-S CO15 . . 188 F7
 Kirby Cross CO13 . . . 169 E7
 Tendring CO16 . . . . . 169 C7
 Weeley CO16 . . . . . . 141 A2
Thorpe Wlk CO4 . . . . . 136 F7
THORRINGTON . . . . . . 166 A5
Thorrington Cross
 CO7 . . . . . . . . . . . 165 F5
Thorrington Rd
 Great Bentley CO7 . . . 166 F8
 Little Clacton CO16 . . 168 C4
Thorrington Tide Mill*
 CO7 . . . . . . . . . . . 165 E3
Thracian Cl CO2 . . . . . 135 A3
Threadneedle St
 [2] Chelmsford CM1 . . 205 B2
 Dedham CO7 . . . . . . 84 F7
Three Acres CO16 . . . . 187 A4
Three Crowns Rd CO4 . . 89 E7
Three Gates Cl CO9 . . . 103 D8
Three Mile Hill CM4 . . . 215 C2
Thremhall Ave
 Bishop's Stortford
 CM23 . . . . . . . . . . 146 F8
 Great Hallingbury CM22,
 CM24 . . . . . . . . . . 147 C8
Takeley CM24 . . . . . . 121 A2
Threshelfords Bsns Pk
 CO5 . . . . . . . . . . . 158 E3
Thresher Cl CM23 . . . . 145 C5

Thresher Rise CM77 . . . 154 C8
Threshers End CO3 . . . 134 D5
Thrift Wood CM3 . . . . . 218 F1
Thriftwood Sch CM2 . . . 216 B3
Thrimley La CM23 . . . . 118 C6
Thrushdale CO15 . . . . . 188 F6
Thurlow Pl [10] CB9 . . . . 9 B8
Thurlston Cl CO4 . . . . . 110 D1
Thurstable Cl CM9 . . . . 199 E2
Thurstable Rd CM9 . . . 199 D2
Thurstable Sch CO5 . . . 179 D6
Thurstable Way CM9 . . . 199 E2
Thurston Ct IP11 . . . . . 221 A3
Thyme Mews CM8 . . . . 176 E3
Thyme Rd CO5 . . . . . . 179 C5
Tiberius Cl
 Colchester CO4 . . . . . 110 B6
 Haverhill CB9 . . . . . . . 9 D7
Tiberius Gdns CM8 . . . . 194 E8
Tideswell Cl CM7 . . . . . 128 D4
Tidings Hill CO9 . . . . . . 103 E8
Tiffin Dr CO15 . . . . . . . 179 E5
TILBURY GREEN . . . . . 179 E5
TILBURY JUXTA CLARE
 . . . . . . . . . . . . . . . 30 A5
Tilbury Rd
 Great Yeldham CO9 . . . 30 A3
 Ridgewell CO9 . . . . . . 29 C7
Tildesley Cl CO13 . . . . . 170 A6
Tile Barn La CO11 . . . . . 85 C2
Tile House La CO6 . . . . 109 B8
TILKEY . . . . . . . . . . . 130 F3
Tilkey Rd CO6 . . . . . . . 130 F3
Tillwicks Cl CO6 . . . . . . 105 A7
TILTY . . . . . . . . . . . . . 96 D2
Timber Hill CO1 . . . . . . 136 C6
Timbers Cl CM77 . . . . . 154 B7
Timber Yd CM7 . . . . . . 128 A2
Timsons La CM2 . . . . . 205 E4
Tinabrook Cl IP2 . . . . . . 16 C1
Tindal Sq [3] CM1 . . . . . 205 B2
Tindal St CM1 . . . . . . . 205 B2
TINDON END . . . . . . . . 46 A1
Tindon End Rd CB10 . . . 46 A2
Tinker Ave CM7 . . . . . . 73 C6
TINKERS GREEN . . . . . . 47 F5
Tinnocks La CM9 . . . . . 116 D8
Tintagel Way CM9 . . . . 220 E8
Tintern Cl IP2 . . . . . . . . 17 A2
Tippett Cl CO4 . . . . . . . 136 E6
TIPTREE . . . . . . . . . . . 179 D5
Tiptree Hall La CO5 . . . 179 B2
TIPTREE HEATH . . . . . . 179 A2
Tiptree Heath Prim Sch
 CO5 . . . . . . . . . . . 179 B3
Tiptree Mews* CO5 . . . 179 D5
Tiptree Rd
 Great Braxted CM8,
 CM9 . . . . . . . . . . . 196 B8
 Wickham Bishops CM8 . 195 F6
Titan Ct IP1 . . . . . . . . . 16 D7
Titania Cl CO4 . . . . . . . 136 F7
Titchwell Dr IP3 . . . . . . 38 D7
Tithe Cl CM6 . . . . . . . . 176 E3
Titus Way CO4 . . . . . . . 110 B6
Tobruk Rd CM1 . . . . . . 204 F6
Tofts Chase CM3 . . . . . 207 E5
Tofts Wlk [15] CM7 . . . . 127 F3
Toga Ct CM22 . . . . . . . 135 A2
Toga La
 Great Horkesley CO6 . . 82 A3
 Little Horkesley CO6 . . 81 F3
Tokely Rd CO7 . . . . . . . 196 B5
Tokio Rd IP4 . . . . . . . . 18 A6
Toller Rd IP3 . . . . . . . . 17 E3
TOLLESBURY . . . . . . . 199 D2
Tollesbury Rd CM9 . . . . 198 F3
Tollesbury Sch CM9 . . . 199 D1
TOLLESHUNT D'ARCY
 . . . . . . . . . . . . . . . 198 D4
Tolleshunt D'arcy Rd
 CM9 . . . . . . . . . . . 197 F3
Tolleshunt D'arcy St
 Nicholas Prim Sch
 CM9 . . . . . . . . . . . 198 D4
TOLLESHUNT KNIGHTS
 . . . . . . . . . . . . . . . 180 A2
TOLLESHUNT MAJOR
 . . . . . . . . . . . . . . . 180 A2
Tollgate Ct CO3 . . . . . . 134 C6
Tollgate Dr CO3 . . . . . . 134 B6
Tollgate E CO3 . . . . . . . 134 C6
Tollgate S CO3 . . . . . . . 134 C6
Tollgate W CO3 . . . . . . 134 B5
Tolliday Cl CO7 . . . . . . . 137 A2
Tolworth Rd IP4 . . . . . . 18 A6
Tom Davies Ho [8]
 CM7 . . . . . . . . . . . 127 F2
Tomline Rd
 Felixstowe IP11 . . . . . 221 E4
 Ipswich IP3 . . . . . . . 18 A4
Tomlinson Rd CM6 . . . . 151 E6
Tom La CM7 . . . . . . . . 72 A6
Tom Tit La CM9 . . . . . . 219 E7
Tony Webb Cl CO4 . . . . 110 C4
Tooley's Ct (Almshouses)
 [9] IP4 . . . . . . . . . . . 17 C5
TOPPESFIELD . . . . . . . 50 C7
Toppesfield Rd CO9 . . . 50 F8
Top Rd
 Tolleshunt Knights
 CM9 . . . . . . . . . . . 180 A2
 Wimbish DB10 . . . . . . 45 A3
 Woodham Walter CM9 . 208 D2
Torquay Rd CM1 . . . . . 205 D5

Torrington Cl CM1 . . . . 205 E5
Tortoiseshell Cl IP8 . . . . 36 E8
Tortoiseshell Way
 CM7 . . . . . . . . . . . 127 E1
Tortosa Cl CO1 . . . . . . 136 B4
Torver Cl CM7 . . . . . . . 154 C6
TOTHAM HILL . . . . . . . 196 E5
Totham Hill Gn CM9 . . . 196 E6
Tot La CM23, CM24 . . . 119 D4
Totlands Dr CO15 . . . . . 189 A7
Totnes Wlk CM1 . . . . . 205 E6
Totteridge Cl CO16 . . . 188 D5
Toucan Way CO15 . . . . 188 C4
Toulmin Rd CM3 . . . . . 194 A4
Tovell's Rd IP4 . . . . . . . 17 F6
Tower Ave CM1 . . . . . . 204 F4
Tower Ct [4] CB9 . . . . . . 8 E7
Tower Cut CO7 . . . . . . 185 F6
Tower Cvn Pk CO15 . . . 203 D6
Tower Est CO3 . . . . . . . 185 E4
Tower Hill Redoubt Fort*
 CO2 . . . . . . . . . . . 91 E5
Tower Mill Rd IP1 . . . . . 91 C5
Tower Ramparts IP1 . . . 17 C6
Tower Ramparts Ctr [8]
 IP1 . . . . . . . . . . . . 17 C6
Tower Rd
 Clacton-on-S CO15 . . 188 E1
 Felixstowe IP11 . . . . . 221 D3
Towers Rd CM9 . . . . . . 210 C5
Tower St
 Brightlingsea CO7 . . . 185 F6
 Ipswich IP1 . . . . . . . 17 C6
Towers The CO15 . . . . 189 A2
Town Croft CM1 . . . . . 205 A5
Town End Field CM8 . . . 194 F8
Townfield St CM1 . . . . . 205 B3
Townsend CM2 . . . . . . 206 A5
Townsend Rd CO15 . . . 179 C7
Town St CM6 . . . . . . . . 70 A2
Towse Cl CO16 . . . . . . 188 C5
Traddles Ct CO16 . . . . 204 F6
Trafalgar Ct IP4 . . . . . . 17 F6
Trafalgar Cotts CO12 . . 90 F3
Trafalgar Ct
 Braintree CM7 . . . . . . 128 B4
 Brightlingsea CO7 . . . 185 F8
Trafalgar Ho [4] CM7 . . 127 F2
Trafalgar Rd
 Clacton-on-S CO15 . . 188 E1
 Colchester CO3 . . . . . 134 E6
Trafalgar Way CM7 . . . 128 B4
Trajan Cl CO4 . . . . . . . 110 B6
Tranter Dr CO4 . . . . . . 109 E4
Tredgetts CB10 . . . . . . . 6 B1
Tree Cl CO15 . . . . . . . 188 F7
Treetops
 Colchester CO4 . . . . . 110 B3
 Felixstowe IP11 . . . . . 221 C6
Treetops Ct CO15 . . . . 109 F5
Trefoil Cl IP2 . . . . . . . . 18 E4
Trefoil Ct [4] CB9 . . . . . . 8 F7
Trelawn CM3 . . . . . . . . 206 E8
Trelawny Ho IP11 . . . . . 221 B1
Trenchard Cres CM1 . . 205 D8
Trenchard Lo CM1 . . . . 205 D7
Trent Rd
 Chelmsford CM1 . . . . 204 D5
 Ipswich IP3 . . . . . . . 17 F2
Trevose IP11 . . . . . . . . 221 F4
Trews Gdns CO15 . . . . 158 C3
Triangle Garage CM9 . . 210 E5
Triangle Sh Ctr CO14 . . 170 F7
Trickett Ct CO7 . . . . . . 137 B1
Tricketts La CM7 . . . . . . 73 E4
Trimley Cl CO16 . . . . . 188 B4
TRIMLEY ST MARY . . . 221 B8
Trimley St Mary Prim Sch
 IP11 . . . . . . . . . . . 221 A7
Trimley St James IP11 . . 221 A7
Trimly Ave IP11 . . . . . . 221 A4
Trinity Cl
 Bishop's Stortford
 CM23 . . . . . . . . . . 145 F6
 Chelmsford CM2 . . . . 205 D3
 Manningtree CO11 . . . 86 D3
 Rushmere St A IP5 . . . 18 F7
 West Mersea CO5 . . . 201 C7
 Wivenhoe CO7 . . . . . 137 C1
Trinity Ct CO9 . . . . . . . 76 E2
Trinity Farm Ct [12]
 CO11 . . . . . . . . . . . 86 D4
Trinity Mews CO5 . . . . 201 C7
Trinity Rd
 Chelmsford CM2 . . . . 205 D2
 Halstead CO9 . . . . . . 76 D1
 Manningtree CO11 . . . 86 D3
Trinity Road Prim Sch
 CM2 . . . . . . . . . . . 205 D2
Trinity Sq [13] CO1 . . . . 135 F7
Trinity St
 Bishop's Stortford
 CM23 . . . . . . . . . . 145 F6
 Colchester CO1 . . . . . 135 F7
 Halstead CO9 . . . . . . 76 D2
 Ipswich IP3 . . . . . . . 17 E4
Trinity Ter [3] CO9 . . . . 76 D1
Trinity Way CM23 . . . . 145 F6
Trinovantian Way
 CM7 . . . . . . . . . . . 128 A2
Trinity Ho CO4 . . . . . . 136 E7
Trippier Ho CO4 . . . . . 136 E7
Triumph Ave CO15 . . . 203 E7
Triumph Cl CO4 . . . . . 136 E5
Troon Gdns IP4 . . . . . . 18 B8
Trotters Field CM7 . . . 128 B3
Trotwood Cl CM1 . . . . 204 E7

Troys Chase CM3 . . . . 175 C6
Trunette Rd CO15 . . . . 188 C3
Trusses Rd CM0 . . . . . 214 F3
Truswell Terr CO11 . . . 86 D7
Tryon Cl [3] CO9 . . . . . 76 D1
Tucker Dr CM6 . . . . . . 176 F1
Tucker's Row [4]
 CM23 . . . . . . . . . . 145 F6
Tuddenham Ave IP4 . . . 17 E7
Tuddenham Rd IP4 . . . 17 E8
Tudor CE Prim Sch
 CO10 . . . . . . . . . . 15 F1
Tudor Cl
 Brightlingsea CO7 . . . 185 E8
 Jaywick CO15 . . . . . 188 A1
 Sudbury CO10 . . . . . 15 E1
 Walton-on-t-N CO14 . . 144 D2
 Witham CM8 . . . . . . 176 F1
Tudor Ct
 [3] Braintree CM7 . . . 128 B2
 West Mersea CO5 . . . 201 C7
Tudor Gn
 Jaywick CO15 . . . . . 187 F1
 Sudbury CO10 . . . . . 15 E2
Tudor Par CO15 . . . . . 203 G8
Tudor Pl [3] IP4 . . . . . . 17 D6
Tudor Rd CO10 . . . . . . 15 E1
Tudor Rose Cl CO3 . . . 134 C7
Tudwick Rd CM9 . . . . . 197 E6
Tufnell Way CO4 . . . . . 199 D2
Tufted Cl CM7 . . . . . . . 154 C5
Tugby Pl CM1 . . . . . . . 204 E6
Tukes Way CB11 . . . . . 43 F7
Tulip Cl CM1 . . . . . . . . 205 E7
Tulip Way CO16 . . . . . . 188 C4
Tulip Wlk CO4 . . . . . . . 188 C4
TUMBLER'S GREEN . . . 129 E8
Tumulus Way CO2 . . . . 135 A3
Tunstall Cl CO16 . . . . . 187 B5
Tupman Cl CM4 . . . . . 204 D6
Turin St IP2 . . . . . . . . . 17 E4
Turkentine Cl CO10 . . . 34 D5
Turkey Cock La CO3,
 CO6 . . . . . . . . . . . 133 E7
Turkey Oaks CM1 . . . . 205 D3
Turner Ave CO11 . . . . . 86 B5
Turner Ct
 Black Notley CM7 . . . . 155 B4
 Wivenhoe CO7 . . . . . 137 C1
Turner Rd
 Colchester CO4 . . . . . 109 F3
 Ipswich IP3 . . . . . . . 38 A8
Turners Cres CM23 . . . 145 C4
Turnpike Cl CO7 . . . . . 110 E8
Turnpike Rd CM2 . . . . 128 A3
Turnstone End [3]
 CO4 . . . . . . . . . . . 136 F8
Turpins Cl CO15 . . . . . 189 C5
Turpins Ct CO15 . . . . . 189 C5
Turpins La
 Kirby Cross CO13 . . . 170 E7
 Kirby-le-S CO13 . . . . 170 E7
Turret Green Ct [7] IP1 . 17 C5
Turret Ho CO15 . . . . . 189 A2
Turret La IP4 . . . . . . . . 17 C5
Turstan Rd CM8 . . . . . 194 E8
Tusser Cl CM4 . . . . . . 177 B7
Tusser Rd CM2 . . . . . . 216 D8
Tusset Mews CO3 . . . . 134 C7
Tweed Ct CO9 . . . . . . 103 D8
Twelve Acres CM7 . . . . 128 D3
Twenty First St CM24 . . 120 F3
Twining Rd CO3 . . . . . 134 E4
Twin Oaks CM2 . . . . . . 106 B8
TWINSTEAD . . . . . . . . 54 C6
TWINSTEAD GREEN . . . 54 A5
Twitten La CM2 . . . . . . 216 B2
Twitty Fee CM3 . . . . . . 219 A8
Two Acres IP9 . . . . . . . 35 B2
Two Village CE Prim Sch
 CO12 . . . . . . . . . . 90 B1
Twyford Bsns Ctr The
 CM23 . . . . . . . . . . 146 A4
Twyford Bury La CM22,
 CM23 . . . . . . . . . . 146 A5
Twyford Cl CM23 . . . . 146 A5
Twyford Gdns CM23 . . 145 F4
Twyford Ind Est
 CM23 . . . . . . . . . . 146 A5
Twyford Mews CM22 . . 146 A3
Twyford Mill CM22 . . . 146 A3
Twyford Rd CM23 . . . . 146 A4
Tyburn Hill CO6 . . . . . . 106 A6
Tydeman Cl CO3 . . . . . 134 C4
Tye Cnr CO10 . . . . . . . 32 F2
Tyed Croft CO3 . . . . . . 134 D4
Tye Gn CO10 . . . . . . . . 2 B5
TYE GREEN
 Elmstead Market CO7 . 137 C4
 Ipswich IP3 . . . . . . . 17 E4
Tye Rd The CO7 . . . . . 167 B7
Tyler Ave
 Clacton-on-S CO16 . . 188 B3
 Little Dunmow CM6 . . 151 E5
Tylers CO13 . . . . . . . . 23 E1
Tylers Cl CM2 . . . . . . . 216 B6

Tylers Gn IP11 . . . . . . . 221 A7
Tyler St
 Harwich CO12 . . . . . . 90 F5
 Ipswich IP2 . . . . . . . 17 D4
Tylneys Rd CO9 . . . . . 77 A3
Tymperley Ct [8] CO1 . . 136 A6
Tymperleys Clock Mus*
 CO1 . . . . . . . . . . . 135 F7
Tyndale Dr CO15 . . . . . 188 A1
Tyndales La CM3 . . . . . 219 B5
Tynedale Ct CO4 . . . . . 110 B4
Tynedale Sq CO4 . . . . 110 B4
Tyne Way CM1 . . . . . . 204 D5
Tyrells Cl CM2 . . . . . . 205 E4
Tyrells Way CM2 . . . . . 216 F7
Tyrrells Sch The CM1 . . 205 E5
Tyssen Mead CM3 . . . . 206 E8
Tythe Cl CM1 . . . . . . . 205 E8
Tythings The
 Halstead CO9 . . . . . . 103 D8
 Howe Green CM2 . . . 217 D2

## U

Ufford Pl [8] CB9 . . . . . . 9 B8
UGLEY . . . . . . . . . . . . 93 E6
UGLEY GREEN . . . . . . 94 A3
Ullswater CM77 . . . . . . 154 C6
ULTING . . . . . . . . . . . 208 C6
Ulting Hall Rd CM9 . . . 208 E7
Ulting La CM9 . . . . . . . 208 E6
Ulting Rd
 Hatfield Peverel CM3 . . 194 C2
 Ulting CM9 . . . . . . . 208 C8
Una Rd CO12 . . . . . . . 90 F5
Undercliff Rd W IP11 . . 221 D3
Union Rd CO15 . . . . . . 203 G8
Unity Cl CO3 . . . . . . . . 15 D6
Unity Ct CO2 . . . . . . . 156 B4
Unity St IP3 . . . . . . . . 17 E4
Univ of Essex CO4 . . . . 136 F4
Upland Cres CO5 . . . . . 201 C7
Upland Dr CO4 . . . . . . 110 C2
Upland Rd
 Ipswich IP4 . . . . . . . 18 A6
 West Mersea CO5 . . . 201 C7
Uplands Com Mid Sch
 CO10 . . . . . . . . . . 15 F1
Uplands Cres CO15 . . . 15 E1
Uplands Ct CO15 . . . . 188 D1
Uplands Dr CM1 . . . . . 205 D7
Uplands Rd
 Clacton-on-S CO15 . . 188 D1
 Sudbury CO10 . . . . . 15 E1
Uppingham Ho CM1 . . 204 E3
UPPEND . . . . . . . . . . . 92 B1
Upper Acres CM4 . . . . 176 F5
Upper Barclay St [12]
 IP4 . . . . . . . . . . . . 17 D6
Upper Branston Rd
 CO15 . . . . . . . . . . 188 D4
Upper Bridge Rd
 CM2 . . . . . . . . . . . 205 A1
Upper Brook St IP4 . . . 17 C5
Upper Cavendish St
 IP3 . . . . . . . . . . . . 18 A5
Upper Chapel St CO9 . . 76 E2
Upper Chase [2] CM2 . . 216 A8
Upper Cotts CO2 . . . . . 162 A5
UPPER DOVERCOURT . . 90 E3
Upper East St CO10 . . . 33 F8
Upper Fenn Rd CO10 . . 29 D8
Upper Fenn Rd CO9 . . . 77 A2
Upperfield Dr IP11 . . . . 221 F6
Upper Fourth Ave
 CO13 . . . . . . . . . . 170 F5
Upper Gn
 Alphamstone CO8 . . . 54 F3
 Stoke by C CO10 . . . . 11 C4
UPPER GREEN
 Langley . . . . . . . . . . 40 D3
 Radwinter . . . . . . . . 45 C4
Upper High St [1] IP1 . . 17 C6
Upper Holt St CO6 . . . 105 C6
Upper Houses CO10 . . . 32 D3
Upper Mill Field CM6 . . 150 E7
Upper Moors CM3 . . . . 190 F1
Upper Orwell St IP4 . . . 17 D5
Upper Park Rd
 Brightlingsea CO7 . . . 185 E7
 Clacton-on-S CO15 . . 188 D3
UPPER POND STREET
 . . . . . . . . . . . . . . .
Upper Rd CO10 . . . . . 55 E8
Upper Roman Rd
 CM2 . . . . . . . . . . . 205 B1
Upper Second Ave
 CO13 . . . . . . . . . . 170 E5
Upper Sq CB10 . . . . . . 22 D2
Upper St
 Stanstead CO10 . . . . . 2 E8
 Stratford St M CO7 . . . 58 D1
UPPER STREET . . . . . . 61 D2
Upper Third Ave
 CO13 . . . . . . . . . . 170 E5
Upper Trinity Rd CO9 . . 76 E1
Upshires CO11 . . . . . . 43 F8
Upton Cl
 Ipswich IP1 . . . . . . . 17 E6
 West Bergholt CO6 . . . 108 D4
Urban Hive CM77 . . . . 154 B8
Urban Rd CM23 . . . . . 146 B7
Usterdale Rd CB10 . . . . 22 E3
Uxbridge Cres IP3 . . . . 18 C1

## V


Valance Rd CB11 ........65 A7
Vale Cl CO4 ............110 E2
Vale End CM2 ..........216 C3
Vale La IP9..............61 B4
Valens Cl CO4 ..........110 A6
Valenta Cl CO1 .........136 C6
Valentine Ct CM7........127 E4
Valentines Dr CO4.......110 C1
Valentine Way CM8......156 D3
Valentinus Cres CO2.....135 F3
Valfreda Way CO7 .......137 B2
Valkyrie Cl CM9 ........199 D2
Valletta Cl CM1.........205 A3
Valley Bridge CM1 .......205 B6
Valleybridge Rd CO15...189 A5
Valley Cl
Brantham CO11...........60 D1
Colchester CO3 .........134 E3
Valley Cres CO6 .........108 E3
Valley Ct CM23 ..........145 E5
Valley Farm Holiday Pk
CO15 ...................189 B5
Valley La
Tattingstone IP9 ..........36 F4
Wherstead IP9 ...........37 A3
Valley Rd
Braintree CM7..........128 A4
Clacton-on-S CO15.......189 A5
Colchester CO4..........136 F4
Harwich CO12............90 D2
Ipswich IP1..............17 B8
Sudbury CO10............34 F8
Wivenhoe CO7..........164 C8
Valley View
Finchingfield CM7 .........72 D6
Stanstead CO10............2 F7
West Bergholt CO6 .......108 E3
Valley View Cl CO4......110 A4
Valleyview Dr IP4 ........18 F4
Valley Wlk
Felixstowe IP11.........221 D5
Walton-on-t-N CO14 .....171 A7
Vallis Way CO5 .........179 E5
Valonia Dr CO7..........164 B8
Vandenburg Circ CM7.....73 D6
Van Diemans Ct CM2 ...216 C8
Van Dieman's La CM2...216 C8
Van Dieman's Rd
CM2 ...................216 C8
Vandyck Rd IP3 ..........38 A8
Van Dyck Rd CO3........135 B5
Vane Ct CM8 ...........177 A5
Vane La CO6 ............131 A2
Vanessa Dr CO7 .........137 B1
Vange Pl 7 CB9............9 B8
Vanguard Way CM7.......128 B4
Vanners Rd CB9 ...........9 A7
Vansittart St CO12 ........91 D5
Varden Cl CM1 ..........204 F6
Vaughan Cl CM77.........126 F2
Vaughan St 8 IP2.........17 C4
Vaux Ave CO12 ...........90 F1
Vauxhall Ave CO15.......203 E6
Vauxhall Dr CM7.........127 D2
Vega Cl CO1............136 C6
Vellacotts CM1 ..........205 B7
Venmore Dr CM6 ........150 E8
Ventnor Dr CO15 ........189 A8
Ventris Cl IP2 ...........16 D5
Ventura Dr CO1.........136 C6
Vermeer Ride CM1.......205 F7
Vermont Cl CO15 ........189 A4
Vermont Cres IP4 .........17 D7
Vermont Rd IP4 ..........17 D7
Vernon Ct CM23 .........145 E4
Vernon's Cl CM22.........94 F4
Vernons Rd CO6 .........106 E5
Vernon St IP2............17 C4
Vernon Way CM7 ........128 C5
Veronica Wlk CO4 .......136 E7
Vesta Cl CO6 ...........130 F2
Veyses End CO7 ..........58 D2
Viaduct Rd CM1 ........205 A2
Viborg Gdns CM9........220 E8
Vica Cotts CM3 .........207 D5
Vicarage Ave CM8 .......155 F1
Vicarage Cl
18 Bishop's Stortford
CM23 ..................145 F7
Panfield CM7............126 A8
Tolleshunt D'arcy CM9 ...198 D4
Vicarage Cres CM3 ......194 B4
Vicarage Ct
Colchester CO3 .........135 A3
Halstead CO9.............76 D2
Vicarage Field CO10......34 B5
Vicarage Gdns CO15.....188 E2
Vicarage La
Berden CM23.............92 B8
Great Baddow CM2.......216 F5
Thaxted CM6 .............70 A3
Thorpe-le-S CO16 ........141 F2
Ugley CM22..............93 E5
2 Walton-on-t-N
CO14..................171 C8
Wherstead IP9 ...........37 B5
Vicarage Mdw CO9 .......76 E1
Vicarage Mead 1 CM6....70 A3
Vicarage Mead Bglws 3
CM6 ....................70 A3
Vicarage Mews CM2 .....216 F6
Vicarage Rd
Belchamp St P CO10 ......13 A1
Chelmsford CM2 .........216 B8
Felixstowe IP11.........221 C4
Vicarage Rd *continued*
Finchingfield CM7 .........72 D6
Vicars Orch CO10.........32 E5
Vicerons Pl CM23.......145 D4
Viceroy Cl CO2 ..........136 B3
Victoria Ave
Kirby-le-S CO13 .........170 D8
Saffron Walden CB11.......22 E1
Victoria Chase CO1......135 E8
Victoria Cl CO7..........137 B2
Victoria Cotts CM9......210 A5
Victoria Cres
Chelmsford CM1 ........205 A3
Lawford CO11 ............86 C4
Victoria Ct
4 Braintree CM7 ........128 A2
Chelmsford CM1 .........205 B3
Clacton-on-S CO15.......188 F3
Colchester CO3 ..........134 F7
Harwich CO12 ............91 C3
Victoria Espl CO5........201 E5
Victoria Gdns
Colchester CO4 ..........110 B3
Saffron Walden CB11.......22 E1
Victoria Ho
Felixstowe IP11..........221 E4
Ipswich IP2...............17 B4
Victoria Mews CO5 .....201 D6
Victoria Pl
Brightlingsea CO7 ........185 F6
Colchester CO1 ..........136 B6
Victoria Rd
Chelmsford CM1 ..........205 B3
Clacton-on-S CO15.......189 A3
Colchester CO3 .........135 C6
Felixstowe IP11.........221 D3
Haverhill CB9..............8 D7
Maldon CM9............210 A2
Walton-on-t-N CO14 .....171 C8
Weeley Heath CO16 ......168 B5
Victoria Rd S CM1 .......205 B2
Victoria St
Braintree CM7...........128 A2
Felixstowe IP11..........221 E4
Harwich CO12 ............91 D4
Ipswich IP1..............17 A6
Victor Rd CO1 ..........136 B6
Victory Cl CO7...........166 B4
Victory Ct
Clacton-on-S CO15........188 E1
Colchester CO3 ..........134 E6
Victory Gdns CM7 .......128 B4
Victory Rd
Clacton-on-S CO15.......188 D3
Ipswich IP4..............18 A7
West Mersea CO5 ........201 A6
Vienna Cl CO12...........91 A1
Viking Rd CM9...........209 E1
Viking Way CO15 ........189 F6
Villa Ct 4 CO1 .........136 C6
Village Cl
Kirby Cross CO13 .......170 D7
Little Clacton CO16 ......168 D1
Village Gate CM2 ........206 A2
Village Sq CM2 ..........206 A3
Village Way CO13........170 D6
Villa Ho CO3 ...........134 C6
Villa Rd CO3............134 C5
Villiers Pl CM3 ..........206 E8
Villiers-Sur-Marne Ave
CM23 ..................145 D4
Vince Cl CO5 ...........201 C6
Vincent Cl IP1............16 E8
Vine Dr CO7 ............137 C3
Vine Farm Rd CO7 .......137 C3
Vine Par CO7............137 C3
Viner Cotts CM3 .........175 B3
Vine Rd CO5.............179 C6
Vinesse Rd CO6 ..........81 D3
Vine St CM7..............72 B2
Vineway The CO12........91 B4
Vine Wlk IP9..............35 A1
Vineyard Gate 4 CO2....135 F6
Vineyard St CO2 .........135 F6
Vineyards The* CM7....153 D6
Vineyards The CM2 ......216 F7
Vinnicombe Ct 3 IP2.....16 E1
Vint Cres CO3 ..........135 C6
Viola Wlk CO4...........136 E7
Violet Cl
Chelmsford CM1 .........205 E7
Ipswich IP2...............16 F4
Virgil Rd CM8 ...........176 F5
Virginia Cl CO15.........188 A1
Virley Cl CM9............210 D4
Viscount Dr CO4.........110 C5
Visitor Ctr & Country
Wlk* CB9 ................9 C6
Vista Ave CO13 .........143 D1
Vista Ct IP2..............17 B4
Vista Rd CO15 ..........189 A3
Vitllus Cl CO4 ..........110 B6
Vitoria Mews CO2 .......135 C2
Vivian Ct CO14 .........171 C8
Volwycke Ave CM9.......220 F8
Vyntoner Ho CO16 .......187 A4


## W


Waddesdon Rd CO12......91 D4
Wade Rd CO15 ..........189 B8
Wade Reach CO14........171 B8
Wadgate Rd IP11.......221 C4
Wadhurst Rd IP3 .........18 D3
Wadley Cl CO5 ..........179 E5
Wagtail Dr CM9 .........210 C5
Wagtail Pl CO5 .........158 C2
Wainsfield Villas CM6.....70 B2
Wainwright Ave
CM77 ..................154 D8
Wainwright St CM23....145 C5
Wakefield Cl
Colchester CO1 .........136 A8
Great Chesterford CB10 .....3 D3
Wakelin Way CM8 .......177 B2
WAKES COLNE ........106 C6
WAKES COLNE GREEN
.........................79 C1
Wakes Hall Bsns Ctr
CO6 ...................106 B6
Wakeshall La C10.........30 C8
Wakes St CO6 ..........106 C6
Waldeck Ct CB11 .........43 D7
Waldegrave Cl CO11 ......86 B3
Waldegrave Rd CO11 .....86 C3
Waldegraves Farm Cvn
Site CO5...............201 G6
Waldegraves La CO5....201 G7
Waldegraves The CO8.....79 F8
Waldegrave Way CO11....86 B3
Walden Ave CB10..........44 E2
Walden Castle* CB10.....22 D2
Walden Cl CM9..........196 A4
Walden Ho CO13.........170 F4
Walden House Rd CM8,
CM9 ...................196 A4
Walden Pl CB10 ..........22 D2
Walden Rd
Ashdon CB10.............23 E6
Great Chesterford CB10 .....3 E3
Hadstock CB1 .............5 B6
Littlebury CB10 ...........21 F4
Radwinter CB10...........45 D7
Sewards End CB10 ........23 D1
Thaxted CM6 .............69 F5
Wendens Ambo CB11 ......42 F6
Wendons Ambo CB11 ......43 A6
Walden Way CO13 ......171 A6
Waldgrooms CM6........123 C1
Waldingfield Rd CO10.....33 F8
WALES END ..............1 A7
Walford Cl CO6 .........131 A2
Walford Pl CM2..........205 F2
Walford Way CO6........131 A2
Walker Cl IP3 ............18 C5
Walkers Cl CM1 ........205 D7
Walkfares CM3 ..........206 F8
Walk The
Eight Ash G CO6 ........134 A8
Felixstowe IP11.........221 C5
10 Ipswich IP1 ...........17 C6
Wallace Binder Cl
CM9 ...................209 F1
Wallace Cres CM2 ......216 D8
Wallace La CM3 .........172 B7
Wallace Rd
1 Colchester CO4........109 E2
Ipswich IP1..............16 E8
Wallace's La CM3........192 F4
Wallasea Gdns CM1......205 F5
Wall Ct 6 CM7 ..........127 F1
Waller's Gr IP2...........16 F4
Wallflower Ct 11 CM1....205 F6
Wallis Ct CO3 ...........134 E3
Wall La CO11 .............88 D4
Wall St CO16 ...........202 D6
Walls The CO11...........86 E4
Walmer Cl CO7 ..........185 F7
Walnut Dr
Bishop's Stortford
CM23 ..................145 D3
Colchester CO4 .........109 D5
Witham CM8 ...........177 A4
Walnut Gr CM7 ..........127 E2
Walnut Tree Cotts
CM3 ...................190 E5
Walnut Tree Ho CO3 .....135 B4
Walnuttree Hospl
CO10 ...................33 D7
Walnut Tree La
Harkstead IP9............63 B2
Sudbury CO10 ............33 D7
Walnut Tree Way
Colchester CO2 ..........135 B3
Tiptree CO5............179 C7
Walnut Way
Brightlingsea CO7 ........185 E7
Clacton-on-S CO15.......188 C2
Walnut Wlk CM6.........123 B1
Walsingham Cl CO10......34 C5
Walsingham Ct IP2.......37 A8
Walsingham Rd CO2 .....135 F6
Walter Porter Ct CO4 ...110 D1
Walter Radcliffe Way
CO7 ...................164 C7
Walters Cl CM2.........216 C3
Walters Yd 6 CO1 .......135 F7
Walter Way CM8.........156 D4
Waltham Cl IP2 ..........17 A2
Waltham Glen CM2 .....216 C7
Waltham Rd
Boreham CM3 ..........193 A3
Terling CM3.............175 A2
Waltham Way CO13.....171 A5
WALTON ..............221 D6
Walton Ave IP11........221 A2
Walton Ct
Colchester CO4 ..........136 F4
Felixstowe IP11.........221 D6
Walton Hall La CM3......220 B1
Walton Ho
4 Ipswich IP1 ...........17 A6
Walton-on-t-N CO14 ......171 B8
Walton Maritme Mus*
CO14 ..................144 D1
Walton-On-Naze Sta
CO14 ..................171 C7
WALTON-ON-THE-NAZE
.......................171 D8
Walton-on-the-Naze Prim
Sch CO14 .............144 D1
Walton Rd
Clacton-on-S CO15.......189 A3
Frinton-on-S CO13........170 F6
Kirby-le-S CO13..........170 E8
Thorpe-le-S CO13,
CO16.................142 D2
Walton-on-t-N CO13,
CO14..................171 B7
Wantz Chase CM9 ......210 A2
Wantz Haven CM9 ......210 A2
Wantz Rd CM9..........210 A2
Wapping La CO7.........165 B2
Warburton Ave CO9.......75 D8
Ward Cres CM23.........145 E6
Warde Chase CO14 ......171 B8
Warder Cl CM6 ..........123 E1
Wardle Way CM1 ........204 E7
Wardley Cl IP2 ...........16 D1
Ward Path CM2..........206 B4
Ward Rd IP8 .............16 B2
Wards Croft CB11.........43 D7
Wareham Ave IP3 ........18 D3
Warehouse Rd CM6......124 F4
Warehouse Villas
CM6 ...................125 A4
Ware View Terr 4
CM9 ...................209 F2
Wargrave Rd CO15......188 D4
Warham Rd CO12.........90 F1
Warish Hall Farm
CM24 ..................121 D1
Warley Cl CM7..........128 C4
Warley Way CO13........171 B6
Warner Cl CM77 .........126 F1
Warner Dr CM7.........127 D4
Warners CM6............150 D8
Warners Mill 13 CM7.....127 F2
Warner Textile Archive
(Mus)* CM7 ...........127 F2
Warner Way CO10 ........34 A8
Warnham Cl CO16 .......188 B6
Warren Cl
Broomfield CM1.........191 B3
Takeley CM22 ..........148 D7
Warren Ct 12 CB9..........8 E7
WARREN HEATH ..........18 F1
Warren Heath Ave IP3....18 D2
Warren Heath Rd IP3.....18 D2
Warren La CO3 .........134 C2
Warren Lingley Way
CO5 ...................179 E6
Warren Rd
Braintree CM7..........128 C2
Halstead CO9.............76 D1
Warrenside CM7........155 A8
Warrens The
Kirby Cross CO13 ........170 E6
Wickham Bishops CM8 .....195 F5
Warrington Rd IP1 .......17 B7
Warwick Bailey Cl
CO4 ...................109 D2
Warwick Cl
Braintree CM7...........128 B4
Little Easton CM6 ........122 F5
Maldon CM9............210 A1
Warwick Cres
Clacton-on-S CO15........188 E3
Maldon CM9.............210 A1
Warwick Ct 2 CB9 ........8 E8
Warwick Dr CM9 .......210 A1
Warwick Rd
Bishop's Stortford
CM23 ..................146 B6
Clacton-on-S CO15........188 E3
Ipswich IP4..............17 E6
Takeley CM6 ............148 E7
Warwick Sq CM1 .......204 F4
Washall Dr CM77 .......154 D8
WASHBROOK ............35 E8
Wash Cnr
Aldham CO6............107 C3
Ramsey CO12 ............89 E1
Washford Gdns CO15 ...188 D2
Washington Cl CM9......209 E1
Washington Ct CO3......134 E5
Washington Rd
Harwich CO12 ............91 A2
Maldon CM9.............209 F1
Wash La
Clacton-on-S CO15.......188 D1
Goldhanger CM9 .........211 B7
Wasses Cnr CO16.......141 D5
WATCH HOUSE GREEN
.......................152 E7
Watch House Rd CM6....124 F5
Watch House Villas
CM6 ...................152 D7
Watchouse Rd CM2.....216 C3
WATER END .............24 B6
Waterfront Terr
CO14 ..................144 D1
Waterglade Ret Pk
CO15 ..................188 E2
Water Hall La CM7.......100 F6
Waterhouse Bsns Pk
CM1 ...................204 F1
Waterhouse La
Ardleigh CO7............112 B5
Chelmsford CM1 .........204 F1
Waterhouse St CM1......204 F1
Water La
Bishop's Stortford
CM23 ..................145 F8
Bures CO8 ...............55 E1
Cavendish CO10 ...........1 D2
Colchester CO3 .........135 D8
Debden CB11.............44 B1
Great Easton CM6 .......122 C7
Helions Bumpstead CB9 ....26 D7
Little Horkesley CO6 .......81 E6
Newport CB11............43 A1
Pebmarsh CO9............78 A7
Radwinter CB10...........45 E8
Shalford CM7...........100 F3
Stansted Mountfitchet
CM24 ..................119 E6
Steeple Bumpstead CB9 ....27 B6
Stisted CM77............129 C5
Stoke-by-N CO6 ...........56 E8
Sturmer CB9 ..............9 F5
Waterloo La CM1 .......205 C2
Waterloo Rd IP1 .........17 A7
Watermill La CM23,
CM24 ..................119 B5
Watermill Rd CO5 .......158 E4
Waterside
Brightlingsea CO7 ........185 F5
Stansted Mountfitchet
CM24 ..................119 E6
Waterside Bsns Pk
CM8 ...................177 B4
Waterside La CO2 ......136 D4
Waterside Rd CM0.......214 F3
Waterson Vale CM2 .....216 C8
Waterville Mews CO2....136 B3
Waterwick Hill CB11......40 B1
Waterworks Cl CO2......161 E3
Waterworks Cotts
CO5 ...................179 A6
Waterworks Dr CO16.....188 B5
Waterworks Rd CM9 ....199 D2
Waterworks St 6 IP4 ....17 D5
Watery La
Coggeshall CO6.........130 A1
Great Dunmow CM6 .....150 A2
Manuden CM23 ...........92 C1
Watling La CM6 ..........69 F3
Watling St CM6...........70 A3
Watsham Pl CO7........137 C2
Watson Rd CO15.........188 E3
Watson's Cl CB10.........47 B4
Watsons Yd 9 CM23.....145 F8
Watts Cl CM6............151 B4
Watts Ct IP4 .............17 D5
Watts Rd CO2 ...........135 B2
Watts Yd CM23 ...........93 A2
Wat Tyler Wlk 1 CO1....135 F7
Wave Bridge Ct CM9.....210 B5
Wavell Ave CO2.........135 C4
Wavell Cl CM1..........205 D8
Waveney Dr CM1 .......205 C6
Waveney Rd
Felixstowe IP11.........221 C3
Ipswich IP1..............16 E8
Waveney Terr CB9 .........9 A7
Wavring Ave CO13 .......170 E7
Wayback The CB10........22 E2
Way Bank La CO10........10 E7
Waylands Dr CO16.......140 E1
Wayletts Dr CM23........146 B7
Wayside CM3............218 E8
Waytemore Castle*
CM23 ..................146 A7
Waytemore Rd CM23.....145 E6
Wear Dr CM1...........205 D6
Weathervane Cotts
CM7 ....................72 B1
Weaver Cl IP1............16 D8
Weaverhead Cl CM6 ......70 A3
Weaverhead La CM6......70 A3
Weavers Cl
Braintree CM7...........127 F3
Colchester CO3 ..........134 F5
Weavers Ct
Halstead CO9.............76 E1
Harwich CO12 ............91 D4
6 Sudbury CO10 .........33 E7
Weavers Dr CO10 ..........2 B4
Weaversfield CM8 ......156 C5
Weavers Gn CO6........107 D6
Weavers La CO10 .........33 E7
Weavers Row CO9 ........76 F1
Weaver St CM23.........145 C4
Weavers Terr 7 CO10.....33 E7
Webb Cl CM2............206 B3
Webb Rd CM6 ...........151 E6
Webb St IP2 .............17 C3
Webster Cl CO9 ..........75 D8
Weddell Rd CB9 ...........9 C6
Wedgewood Dr 4
CO4....................109 E2
Wedgewood End CM7.....72 B2
Wedow Rd CM6...........70 A3
WEELEY ................140 E1
Weeley By-Pass Rd
CO16 ..................140 E1
WEELEY HEATH .......168 A5
Weeley Rd
Great Bentley, Aingers
Green CO7 ............166 F5
Great Bentley CO7........166 F8
Little Clacton CO16 ......168 C4
Weeley Sta CO16 ........167 F8
Weetmans Dr CO4 ......110 A5
Weggs Willow CO4 .....136 C7

Weighbridge Ct CB11 .....43 D8
Weight Rd CM2 .....205 C2
Weir La CO2, CO5 .....163 C7
Welbeck Ct IP11 .....221 A7
Welhams Way CO11 .....86 D8
Welland Ave CM1 .....204 C5
Wellands CM8 .....195 E5
Wellands Cl CM8 .....195 D5
Weller Gr CM1 .....204 E7
Wellesley Ho 7 CO3 .....135 E6
Wellesley Rd
  Clacton-on-S CO15 .....188 E4
  Colchester CO3 .....135 E6
  Ipswich IP4 .....17 F5
Wellfield CM1 .....204 A1
Well Field CO9 .....103 F8
Wellfield Way CO13 .....170 D7
Well-Green Cl CM8 .....43 E7
Wellhouse Ave CO5 .....201 E7
Wellington Cl
  Braintree CM7 .....128 C4
  Chelmsford CM1 .....204 D5
Wellington Ct 5 IP1 .....17 A7
Wellington Rd
  Harwich CO12 .....91 E6
  Maldon CM9 .....209 F2
Wellington St
  Brightlingsea CO7 .....185 F6
  4 Colchester CO2 .....135 E6
  Ipswich IP1 .....17 A7
Wellington Terr 7 CB9 .....8 E7
Well La
  Clare CO10 .....12 B7
  Danbury CM3 .....218 C7
  Easthorpe CO5 .....160 A6
  Galleywood CM2 .....216 B2
Wellmeads CM2 .....216 B8
Wells Cl 4 IP4 .....17 E6
Wells Ct 7 CM1 .....205 A3
Wells Ct
  Chelmsford CM1 .....205 D5
  Great Dunmow CM6 .....123 C1
Wells Hall Com Prim Sch
  CO10 .....34 B4
Wells Mead CO10 .....34 C4
Well Side CO6 .....132 E3
Wells Rd CO10 .....136 B8
Well's St CM1 .....205 A3
Well St CO7 .....185 E7
Well Terr CM9 .....210 B5
Wellum Cl 8 CB9 .....8 E7
WELSHWOOD PARK .....110 F2
Welshwood Park Rd
  CO4 .....110 C2
Welwyn Ct CO15 .....188 D1
Wenden Rd CB11 .....43 E7
WENDENS AMBO .....42 E5
Wendy Cl IP7 .....63 F7
Wenham La CO7 .....59 D6
Wenham Rd IP8 .....35 C7
Wenlock Rd CO16 .....167 F6
Wenlock Way CM9 .....210 A3
Wentford St CB9 .....8 C8
Wents Cl CO7 .....139 E1
Wentworth Cl CM3 .....194 B4
Wentworth Cres CM7 .....127 F5
Wentworth Dr
  Bishop's Stortford
  CM23 .....145 D6
  Ipswich IP8 .....16 C2
Wentworth Mdws
  CM9 .....209 F2
Wentworth Prim Sch
  CM9 .....209 F1
Wentworth Terr 8 CB9 .....8 E8
Wesel Ave IP11 .....221 B3
Wesley Ave CM4 .....136 C8
WESLEY END .....28 E4
Wesley End Rd CO9 .....28 D4
Wesley Way IP1 .....16 F8
West Acre CO3 .....135 B7
West Area IP1 .....16 C7
West Ave
  Chelmsford CM1 .....204 F5
  Clacton-on-S CO15 .....188 E2
West Bank Ferry Terminal
  IP2 .....17 C2
West Belvedere CM3 .....218 F7
WEST BERGHOLT .....108 D4
WESTBOURNE .....16 F7
Westbourne Ct 1 CB9 .....9 A8
Westbourne Gr CM2 .....216 D7
Westbourne Rd IP1 .....16 F8
West Bowers Rd CM9 .....208 C4
Westbury Cl CO6 .....133 D5
Westbury Ct CO13 .....170 F4
Weyland
  Great Holland CO13 .....170 A5
  Ipswich IP4 .....18 B8
West Chase CM9 .....209 F3
Westcliff Ct CO15 .....188 E4
Westcott Cl CO16 .....188 D6
West Dock Rd CO12 .....90 E5
West Dr CO7 .....73 C3
West End La CO12 .....91 B1
West End Mews CO3 .....135 B7
West End Rd
  Ipswich IP1 .....17 A5
  Tiptree CO5 .....179 A3
Westerdale CM1 .....205 D7
Westerfield Ct IP4 .....17 D7
Westerfield Rd IP4 .....17 D8
Westergreen Mdw
  CM7 .....127 E1

Westerings
  Bicknacre CM3 .....218 F2
  Purleigh CM3 .....220 D1
Westerings The CM2 .....216 F5
Westerlings The
  CM77 .....155 E6
Western Cl
  Rushmere St A IP4 .....18 F4
  Silver End CM8 .....156 E3
Western Ho CO5 .....158 C2
Western La CM8 .....156 E3
Western Prom
  Brightlingsea CO7 .....185 D5
  Point Clear End CO16 .....185 E4
Western Rd
  Brightlingsea CO7 .....185 E6
  Silver End CM8 .....156 F3
Western's End CO11 .....86 D8
Westfield CO10 .....12 A6
Westfield Ave CM1 .....205 A4
Westfield Cl CM8 .....145 E8
Westfield Com Prim Sch
  CB9 .....9 B7
Westfield Dr CO6 .....131 A3
Westfield Rd CM23 .....145 E8
West Fields IP1 .....43 E8
Westgate St IP1 .....17 C6
West Green Cotts
  CO11 .....86 A7
West Hanningfield Rd
  CM2 .....217 A3
Westholme Rd IP1 .....17 A8
Westlake Cres CO7 .....137 A2
Westlands Com Prim Sch
  CM1 .....204 E2
West Lawn
  Galleywood CM2 .....216 C2
  Ipswich IP4 .....18 C8
Westleton Way IP11 .....221 B5
Westley La CB10 .....22 D5
West Lo CO3 .....135 C6
West Lodge Rd CO3 .....135 D6
WEST MERSEA .....201 C5
West Mill Gn IP9 .....60 E6
Westminster Ct IP4 .....18 B5
Westminster Ct
  Clacton-on-S CO15 .....189 B3
  Colchester CO3 .....136 C4
Westminster Gdns
  CM7 .....128 B4
Westmorland Cl CO11 .....87 B3
Weston Rd CO7 .....73 C3
West Quay CO7 .....164 B7
West Rd
  Bishop's Stortford
  CM23 .....145 E6
  Clacton-on-S CO15 .....203 H8
  Halstead CO9 .....76 E1
  Ipswich IP3 .....38 E8
  Saffron Walden CB11 .....43 D8
  Stansted Mountfitchet
  CM24 .....119 E6
Westridge Way CO15 .....189 A6
Westropps CO10 .....15 C5
Westside Ctr CO3 .....134 A5
West Sq CM9 .....209 F3
West St
  Coggeshall CO6 .....130 E1
  Colchester CO2 .....135 E6
  Harwich CO12 .....91 D6
  Rowhedge CO5 .....163 F8
  Tollesbury CM9 .....199 C1
  Walton-on-t-N CO14 .....171 C8
  Wivenhoe CO7 .....164 B8
West Station Ind Est
  CM9 .....209 E2
West Station Rd CM9 .....209 E1
West Station Yd CM9 .....220 E8
West Stockwell St
  CO1 .....135 F7
West View CM22 .....148 C8
West View CO14 .....110 B3
Westway
  Chelmsford CM1 .....215 E8
  Colchester CO3, CO3 .....135 E8
Westwood Ave IP1 .....17 A8
Westwood Ct IP1 .....17 A7
Westwood Dr CO5 .....201 E6
West Wood Hill CO4 .....109 B3
West Yd CO9 .....103 E8
Wetherfield CM24 .....119 D7
WETHERSFIELD .....73 C3
Wethersfield CE Prim Sch
  CM7 .....73 C3
Wethersfield Rd
  Blackheath CO2 .....163 A8
  Shalford CM7 .....100 E8
  Sible Hedingham CO9 .....51 C1
Wet La CO4 .....82 E5
Wetzlar Ct CO2 .....136 B4

Wheatfield Rd CO3 .....134 D5
Wheatfield Way CM1 .....204 F3
Wheatlands
  Ardleigh CO7 .....111 E7
  Elmstead Market CO7 .....137 F6
Wheatley Ave CM7 .....128 C3
Wheaton Rd CM8 .....177 B2
Wheatsheaf Cl CO11 .....88 D3
Wheatsheaf Ct 14
  CO1 .....136 A6
Wheatsheaf La CO11 .....88 D3
Wheeler Cl CO4 .....136 E6
Wheeler's Hill CM3 .....191 D6
Wheelwrights Cl
  CM23 .....145 C4
Wheelwrights The
  IP11 .....221 A8
Wherry La 15 IP4 .....17 D5
Wherry Quay IP7 .....17 D5
WHERSTEAD .....37 B6
Wherstead Rd IP2 .....17 C2
Whinchat Cl IP2 .....16 D3
Whinfield Ave CO2 .....136 D6
Whitbreads Farm La
  CM3 .....173 D4
Whitby Rd IP4 .....17 F8
White Arch Pl CO4 .....83 B6
WHITEASH GREEN .....76 B2
White Barns CM3 .....172 B6
Whitebeam Cl
  Chelmsford CM2 .....215 F7
  Colchester CO6 .....109 D5
White Bear CM24 .....119 E8
White Caville CB9 .....8 C8
WHITE COLNE .....105 E6
White Cotts CM3 .....174 E5
White Court Prim Sch
  CM77 .....154 C6
White Cross CO1 .....89 A2
Whiteditch La CB11 .....42 F2
White Elm Rd CM3 .....219 A2
White Elm St IP3 .....17 E4
Whitefriars Way CO3 .....135 A5
Whitegate Rd CO7 .....186 A6
Whitegates CM6 .....97 F4
Whitehall Cl CO7 .....154 C6
Whitehall Cl CM8 .....177 A2
Whitehall Ind Est
  CO2 .....136 D4
Whitehall La
  Bishop's Stortford
  CM23 .....118 F1
  Thorpe-le-S CO16 .....141 C3
Whitehall Rd
  Bishop's Stortford
  CM23 .....118 E1
  Colchester CO2 .....136 D4
White Hart Cotts
  CM2 .....206 A6
Whitehart Cl CO12 .....91 D6
White Hart La
  Chelmsford CM1 .....205 F8
  West Bergholt CO6 .....108 E5
Whitehead Cl CM1 .....215 B8
White Horse Ave CO9 .....103 D8
White Horse Cotts IP9 .....36 D1
White Horse Hill IP9 .....36 D1
White Horse La
  Maldon CM9 .....209 F2
  Newport CB11 .....43 A1
  Witham CM8 .....176 F3
White Horse Rd
  Capel St M IP9 .....35 B1
  East Bergholt CO7 .....59 E1
Whitehouse Cres
  CM2 .....216 D8
Whitehouse Hill CM9 .....199 A7
Whitehouse La
  Belchamp St P CO10 .....13 B2
  West Bergholt CO6 .....108 D3
Whitehouse Rd CM6 .....124 F5
White Lodge Cres
  CO4 .....142 C1
White Mead CM1 .....191 B2
WHITE NOTLEY .....155 E1
White Notley CE Prim Sch
  CM8 .....155 F1
Whitepost St CM23 .....146 A5
White Post Field CM8 .....150 E8
Whitesbridge La CM3 .....215 D1
Whites Field CO7 .....59 B3
Whiteshot Way CB10 .....22 F2
Whites La CM3 .....173 E6
White St CM6 .....150 D8
Whitethorn Cl CO4 .....136 D6
Whitethorn Gdns
  CM2 .....216 C7
Whitethorn Rd IP3 .....18 F1
Whiteways CB10 .....3 C5
Whiteways CM8 .....176 E3
Whitewell Rd 10 CO2 .....135 F6
Whitfield Link CM2 .....216 D7
Whitland Cl IP2 .....37 A8
Whitlands CO10 .....2 B6
Whitley's Chase CM7 .....48 D5
Whitlock Dr CO9 .....29 F1
Whittaker Way CO5 .....206 B4
Whittaker Way CO5 .....201 B7
Whittington Way
  CM23 .....145 F3
Whittle Rd CM2 .....216 F6
Whitworth Cl IP2 .....16 D2
Whybrews 4 CO4 .....136 C8
Whytes Cotts CO6 .....133 B8
Whyverne Cl CM1 .....205 E6

WICKEN BONHUNT .....66 C7
Wicken Rd
  Arkesden CB11 .....41 F1
  Newport CB11 .....66 F8
Wickfield Ash CM1 .....204 D6
Wickham Bishop Rd
  CM3 .....194 D4
WICKHAM BISHOPS .....195 D5
Wickhambrook Ct
  IP11 .....221 A4
Wickham Cres
  Braintree CM7 .....128 A2
  Chelmsford CM1 .....204 F6
Wickham Hall La
  CM8 .....195 D3
Wickham Rd
  Colchester CO3 .....135 D6
  Witham CM8 .....194 F8
WICKHAM ST PAUL .....53 C6
Wickham's Chase
  CM3 .....219 C2
Wickhay Cotts CM3 .....207 D5
Wick La
  Ardleigh CO7 .....111 B8
  Fingringhoe CO5 .....164 C3
  Harwich CO12 .....91 B2
  St Osyth Heath CO7,
  CO16 .....167 C3
Wicklow Ave CM1 .....204 D6
Wick Rd
  Colchester CO2 .....136 D2
  Great Bentley CO7 .....167 B5
  Langham CO4 .....83 F3
  Thorington Street CO4,
  CO6 .....57 C2
Wicks Cl CM7 .....127 C4
Wicks Pl CM1 .....205 A3
Wick Terr CO4 .....83 F3
WIDDINGTON .....67 E4
WIDFORD .....215 E6
Widford Chase CM2 .....215 F7
Widford Cl CM2 .....215 F7
Widford Gr CM2 .....215 F7
Widford Ind Est CM2 .....215 E8
Widford Lodge Prep Sch
  CM2 .....215 F7
Widford Lodge Sch
  CM2 .....215 F7
Widford Park Pl CM2 .....215 F7
Widford Rd CM2 .....215 F7
Widgeon Cl IP2 .....16 D3
Widgeon Pl CO5 .....158 C2
Widleybrook La
  Blackmore End CM7 .....74 A2
  Wethersfield CM7 .....73 F3
Wigborough Rd
  Layer de la H CO2 .....161 E2
  Peldon CO5 .....182 C5
Wigborough Wick La
  CO5 .....186 F2
Wigeon Cl CM7 .....154 C5
WIGGENS GREEN .....8 E1
Wiggins View CM2 .....206 B4
Wigmore Cl IP2 .....16 F1
Wignall St CO11 .....85 F3
Wilberforce St IP1 .....17 A4
Wilbye Cl CM7 .....135 B4
Wilbye Ho CO3 .....135 A7
Wild Boar Field CM7 .....128 D3
Wilding Rd IP8 .....16 B1
Wilkes Way CM6 .....151 E6
Wilkin Cl CO3 .....135 A4
Wilkin Dr CO5 .....179 E5
Wilkinson Gr CM77 .....155 B5
Wilkinson Pl CM1 .....194 A3
Wilkinsons Mead
  CM2 .....206 A4
Willets Pond CO7 .....59 E1
Willett Rd CO2 .....135 E3
Willetts Field CB10 .....47 A3
William Booth Way
  IP11 .....221 B5
William Boys Cl 1
  CO4 .....136 D8
William Cl CO7 .....137 C4
William Dr CO15 .....188 D2
William Groom Ave
  CO12 .....91 A2
William Harris Way
  Beerchurch CO2 .....162 F8
  Colchester CO2 .....135 F1
William Hunter Way 7
  CM1 .....17 D6
William Julien Courtauld
  Hospl CM7 .....127 C2
William Paul Housing
  Trust 3 CM7 .....17 C4
Williams Dr CM7 .....127 F4
Williamson Ho 2
  CO1 .....136 A6
William Sparrow Ct
  CO7 .....137 C2
Williams Rd CM1 .....191 B1
William St 3 IP1 .....17 C6
William's Wlk 6 CO1 .....135 F7
William Wood Ho 16
  CO10 .....33 E7
Willingale Rd CM7 .....128 D4
Willingham Way CO4 .....136 E7
Willis Almshouses
  CM9 .....196 B3
Willoughby Ave CO5 .....201 D6
Willoughby Dr CM2 .....205 F2
Willoughby Rd IP2 .....17 B4
Willoughby's La CM7 .....128 C8
Willow Ave
  Kirby Cross CO13 .....170 D6
  Seawick CO16 .....203 B6
Willowbank CM2 .....216 B3

Willow Brook Prim Sch
  CO4 .....110 C1
Willow Cl
  Ardleigh CO7 .....110 D3
  Bishop's Stortford
  CM23 .....145 E8
  Brightlingsea CO7 .....185 D6
  Broomfield CM1 .....191 B1
  Sudbury CO10 .....33 E6
Willow Cres CM3 .....194 A3
Willow Dene CO9 .....51 D2
Willow Hall La CO11 .....115 D8
Willow Mdws CO9 .....75 E8
Willowmere Cvn Pk
  CO4 .....34 B2
Willow Pk
  Copford CO6 .....133 E5
  Weeley Heath CO16 .....168 A6
Willow Rd CM6 .....123 C1
Willow Rise CM8 .....177 A5
WILLOWS GREEN .....153 E4
Willows Prim Sch The
  IP2 .....16 F2
Willows The
  Boreham CM3 .....206 F8
  Chelmsford CM1 .....205 A2
  Colchester CO2 .....136 A3
  Frinton-on-S CO13 .....170 F5
  Great Chesterford CB10 .....3 D8
Willow Tree Ct 1
  CO4 .....136 E8
Willow Tree Way CO6 .....105 B6
Willow Way
  Clacton-on-S CO15 .....203 G7
  Halstead CO9 .....76 D1
  Harwich CO12 .....90 F2
Willow Wlk
  Heybridge CM9 .....210 C6
  Tiptree CO5 .....179 C7
  Weeley CO16 .....167 F8
Will's Ayley La CB10 .....2 B1
Wills Gn CO5 .....158 F6
Willum Ho CB10 .....22 D1
Wilmington Rd CO4 .....110 C2
Wimslow Dr IP2 .....16 C2
Wilshire Ave CM2 .....205 F3
Wilson Cl
  Bishop's Stortford
  CM23 .....145 F5
  Wivenhoe CO7 .....137 A2
Wilson Ct CO15 .....189 B8
Wilson Marriage Rd
  CO4 .....110 C1
Wilson Rd IP8 .....16 B1
Wilson's Ct CM9 .....210 B2
Wilson's La CO6 .....132 E3
Wilton Ho CO16 .....188 C5
WIMBISH .....45 C6
WIMBISH GREEN .....45 E3
Wimbish Prim Sch
  CB10 .....45 C4
Wimbish Wlk CB10 .....44 E2
Wimborne Ave IP3 .....18 E4
Wimborne Gdns
  CO13 .....170 F7
Wimbourne Ho CO12 .....91 D3
Wimpole Cl IP5 .....18 F6
Wimpole Rd CO1 .....136 B5
Wimsey Ct CM8 .....177 A5
Wincelow Hall Rd
  CB10 .....25 E2
Winchelsea Dr CM2 .....216 E7
Winchelsea Pl CO7 .....185 F8
Winchester Cl CM23 .....145 D4
Winchester Ct
  Chelmsford CM1 .....205 A5
  Frinton-on-S CO13 .....171 A5
Winchester Rd
  Colchester CO2 .....136 B5
  Frinton-on-S CO13 .....171 A5
Winchester Way IP2 .....36 F8
Winckford Cl CM3 .....191 B6
Windermere Cl IP3 .....38 B8
Windermere Ct CO15 .....188 F2
Windermere Dr CM77 .....154 C6
Windermere Rd
  Clacton-on-S CO15 .....189 C6
  Great Notley CM77 .....154 C7
  Sudbury CO10 .....34 A8
Windham Rd CO10 .....34 B8
Windmill Dr CM23 .....145 E7
Windmill Old Rd CM23 .....145 E7
Windmill Prim Sch
  CM23 .....145 E6
Winding Piece IP9 .....35 A1
Windley Tye CM23 .....204 E3
Windmill Cl
  Clacton-on-S CO15 .....188 F5
  Colchester CO4 .....109 E4
  Copford CO6 .....133 D4
Windmill Fields CO10 .....130 F3
Windmill Gdns CM7 .....128 A8
Windmill Hill CB10,
  CB11 .....22 B3
Windmill Pk CO15 .....188 F5
Windmill Pl CO10 .....2 E7
Windmill Rd
  Bradfield CO11 .....87 C1
  Halstead CO9 .....76 D1
Windmill Row CO10 .....2 C5
Windmills CO6 .....106 C1

...mills The CM1 ......191 B3
...mill The CM24 ....119 D6
...mill Way CO5 ....179 C6
...rush Dr CM1.....205 C6
...sor Ave CO15 ......188 D3
...sor Cl
...chester CO2 .......136 A2
...ham CM8 .........194 F8
...sor Ct
...Braintree CM7 ......128 B2
...ghtlingsea CO7 .....185 F6
...Colchester CO1 ....136 C6
...sor Gdns
...shop's Stortford
CM23 ...............145 C7
...intree CM7.......128 B4
...sor Ho CO5.......201 D7
...sor Pl CO10 .......34 A7
...sor Rd
...cton-on-S CO15.....188 D3
...xstowe IP11.......221 C3
...wich IP1..........16 F7
...t Mersea CO5 ......201 D7
...sor Terr CB9........8 E8
...sor View CO9 ......53 C6
...sor Way CM1 ....204 E1
...ield Terr CO14.....144 D2
...rith Rd IP3 ........18 D4
...gate Cl CM7 .....127 E5
...gate Ho IP1 ....17 A7
...sley Rd CO1 .....136 B6
...sley Sq CO1 ......136 B4
...stanley Rd CB11 ...43 E7
...ston Ave
...chester CO3 ......135 B4
...wich IP4 ..........18 C8
...ree CO5...........179 E5
...ston Ct
...intree CM7........127 E6
...xstowe IP11.......221 B5
...ston Ct CO13 .....170 F4
...ston Way CO9 .....77 A3
...tree Cl CO2.......161 F5
...tree Cl CO3 ......134 C4
...tree Rd CO3 ......134 D5
...erbournes CO14...171 A7
...er's Hill CO2.......160 F1
...er's Rd CO5.......160 E1
...oms Gn CO6 ......131 B3
...SINGTON ...........81 D7
...aria Pl CO16 ......188 C5
...eria Ct CO4.....136 E7
...eria Lo CM1 ...205 F6
...eria CM7.......81 D8
...n Elm CO12 ........90 F2
...eria Lo CM6 ......131 B8
...ntree La CB10......25 F3
...MAM ...............176 E4
...am Lo CM8 ........194 D7
...am Rd
...k Notley CM77,
...ssing CM77 ........156 B3
...gford CM9 ........209 D7
...ng CM3 ...........175 E2
...eshunt Major CM9 ..197 D5
...kham Bishops CM8 ..195 E6
...am Sta CM8.......177 A3
...ERMARSH GREEN
.................57 C7
...ersfield Rd CB9......8 F8
...poll St IP4.........17 D6
...ick Wlk CO16.......187 A5
...ng Cl CO16 .......188 D5
...n Wood Rd
.................170 E5
...NHOE ............137 C2
...nhoe Bsns Ctr
.................164 C8

Wivenhoe Cross CO7.... 137 C2
WIVENHOE PARK .... 137 A4
Wivenhoe Rd
  Alresford CO7 ...........165 B7
  Colchester CO7 .........111 C1
Wivenhoe Sta CO7.......164 B8
WIX ................115 C5
Wix By-Pass CO11 ......115 C6
WIX GREEN .........115 D5
Wix Rd
  Beaumont CO16.........141 E8
  Bradfield CO11 ..........87 E1
  Great Oakley CO12 ......116 B3
  Ramsey CO12 ...........89 F1
  Tendring CO11...........114 F8
  Wix CO11...............115 C3
Wix & Wrabness Prim Sch
  CO11..................115 B5
Woburn Ave
  Bishop's Stortford
  CM23 .................145 C7
  Kirby Cross CO13 .......170 D7
Woburn Ct CM2 ........205 A1
Woden Ave CO3 ........134 D4
Wolfe Ave CO1, CO2 ....136 A5
Wolmers Hey CM3.......190 F7
Wolseley Ave CO15 .....203 E6
Wolseley Rd CM2 .......205 A1
Wolsey Art Gall* IP4 ......17
DéWolsey Ct IP11.......221 E3
Wolsey Gdns IP11 ......221 E3
Wolsey St IP1 ........17 C5
Wolton Rd CO2 .........135 B2
Wolves Hall La CO16....114 F1
Wood Barn La CO16.....16 C1
Woodberry Way
  CO14 .................171 C7
Woodbridge Gr CO16 ...188 A4
Woodbridge Rd
  Ipswich, California IP5 ....18 B7
  Ipswich IP4.............17 E6
  Rushmere St A IP5 ......18 E7
Woodbridge Rd E IP4....18 D7
Wood Cnr
  Fordham Heath CO6 .....107 F1
  Wivenhoe CO7...........137 B1
Woodcock Cl
  Colchester CO4 .........136 E6
  Haverhill CB9............9 C7
Woodcock Rd IP2 .......16 E2
Wood Dale CM2 ........216 E6
Wood End CB11 ........67 D3
WOODEND GREEN ......95 A6
Woodfield Cl
  Stansted Mountfitchet
  ...................119 E6
  Walton-on-t-N CO14 ....171 A7
Woodfield Cotts CM9 ...210 C6
Woodfield Dr CO5 ......201 B7
Wood Field End CO2....162 A5
Woodfield La IP9 .......61 E3
Woodfield Rd CM47.....128 A3
Woodfields CM24 .......119 E6
Woodfield Terr CM4....119 E6
Woodfield Way CM3 ....194 A4
Woodford Cl CO15 ......188 F8
Woodgates IP11........221 B6
WOODGATES END .....121 D7
Woodgates Farm
  CM6 ..................121 E7
Woodgates Rd CO7 .....59 D5
Wood Green Est CO7 ...166 F5
WOOD HALL ..........65 D8
Woodhall Bsns Pk
  CO10 .................15 F2
Woodhall Cl CO10 ......15 E1
Woodhall Com Prim Sch
  CO10 .................15 F2
Woodhall Gr CM23.....145 D6
Woodhall Hill CM1.....190 C2
Woodhall Par CM1......205 A7
Woodhall Rd
  Chelmsford CM1 ........205 A7
  Sudbury CO10 ..........15 E1
WOODHAM MORTIMER
  ...................219 F6
Woodham Mortimer Rd
  CM9 ..................219 E8

WOODHAM WALTER ....208 E2
Woodham Walter CE Prim
  Sch CM9...............208 D3
WOODHILL ...........218 B5
Woodhill Common Rd
  CM3 ..................218 B5
Woodhill Rd
  Chelmsford CM2 ........217 E6
  Danbury CM3............218 B6
Woodhouse La
  Broomfield CM3.........191 A4
  Great Horkesley CO6....109 A6
Woodhouse Sq IP4 ...17 D5
Wood La
  Birchanger CM23.......119 E2
  Brent Pelham SG9 ......64 A6
  Clacton-on-S CO15......169 C2
  Fordham Heath CO3 ....107 F1
  Heybridge CM9 .........210 A5
Woodland Chase CO3...107 F1
Woodland Ave CO4 ....205 A5
Woodland Dr CO3 ......134 F5
WOODLAND GREEN .....9 E6
Woodland Rd CM1 .....205 A4
Woodlands
  Bishop's Stortford
  CM23 .................146 C8
  Braintree CM7..........128 C3
  Broomfield CM1.........191 A4
  Colchester CO4 .........63 E7
  Great Oakley CO12 .....116 B2
  Great Waltham CM1 ....190 F4
  Ipswich IP8.............16 C1
  Jaywick CO16 ..........188 A1
Woodlands Cl CO15.....189 A8
Woodlands Park Dr
  CM6 ..................171 B5
Woodlands Rd IP9......62 D7
Woodlands Rise CO16...140 F1
Woodlands The CO7 ....185 E8
Woodlands Way CM3 ...190 F4
Woodlands Wlk CM6....123 B1
Woodland Way
  Gosfield CO9 ...........102 A8
  Wivenhoe CO7...........137 B1
Woodlark Cl IP2 ........16 E1
Woodlyn Ct CO15.......189 E6
Woodpecker Cl
  Bishop's Stortford
  CM23 .................145 C6
  Colchester CO4 ......136 F8
Woodpecker Rd IP2 ....16 D3
Wood Rd CM9 ..........210 B6
Woodroffe Cl CM2 .....206 A3
Woodrolfe Farm La
  CM9 ..................199 E1
Woodrolfe Pk CM99.....199
F2Woodrolfe Rd CM9....199 E2
Woodrose Lo CM1 ...205 F6
Woodrows La CO16 .....188 B5
Woodrow Way CO4 .....136 E7
Woodrush End CO3 .....134 B6
Woodrush Rd IP3........18 E2
Woods Cl CB9...........9 E5
Woods Ct CO4 .........109 D2
Woodside
  Bishop's Stortford
  CM23 .....154...146 D8
  Great Totham CM9......196 B3
  Little Baddow CM3 .....207 F1
  Walton-on-t-N CO14 ....171 B7
Woodside Cl CO4 .......110 E1
WOODSIDE GREEN .....146 F1
Woodside Way CM6....123 A1
Woodspring Cl IP2...17 A2
Woods Rd CM3 .........172 B6
Wood St CM2 ..........216 A7
Woodstock CO5 ........201 C7
Woodstock Pl CM2 .....216 F5
Woodview Cl CO4 ......110 D4
Woodview Cotts CO5 ...180 C8
Woodview Dr CM3 .....174 A7
Woodview Rd CM6......150 D8
Woodville Rd IP4.......17 F3
Woodward Cl IP2.......16 D5
Wood Way CM77.......154 B6
Woodyards CM0 ........214 F3
Woollards Cl IP1 .......17 A6

Woollards Gdns CO10......15 C8
Woolner Rd CO16.......188 D6
Woolnough Cl CM9......27 B6
Woolpack La CM7......127 F5
Woolpit Downs CO8 .....79 E8
Woolpit's Rd CM7 ......99 E1
Woolridge Pl CM8 ......195 E5
WOOLVERSTONE .......38 A1
Woolverstone Cl IP2....16 C1
Woolwich Rd CO16 .....188 C5
Wootton Dr IP1 ........17 C8
Worcester Cl CM7 ......128 A1
Worcester Cres CO7 ...165 B8
Worcester Ct
  Clacton-on-S CO15......188 E1
  Great Baddow CM2 .....217 A5
Worcester Ho CB9......9 B6
Worcester Rd
  Colchester CO1 .........136 A8
  Ipswich IP3.............38 B8
Worcester Rd CM1 .....205 A5
Wordsworth Rd
  Braintree CM7..........127 F7
  Colchester CO3 .........134 F6
Wordsworths Way
  CO16 .................188 A5
Workhouse Cnr CO12 ...116 C3
WORKHOUSE GREEN ....55 E7
WORKHOUSE HILL ......82 C4
Workhouse Hill CO4 ....82 E4
Workhouse Rd CO6 .....81 C2
Worlds End La CO5 .....158 D3
WORMINGFORD .........80 E4
Worrin Rd CM6 .........151 E6
Worsdell Way CO4 .....109 F2
Worsley Cl IP2 .........16 D2
Worsnop Ho CO2 .......136 B5
Wortham Pl CM9.........9 A8
Worthing Mews CO15...203 18
Worthington Way
  CO3 ..................134 F4
WRABNESS .............88 E4
Wrabness Local Nature
  Reserve* CO11 ........88 C4
Wrabness Rd
  Ramsey CO12 ..........90 A2
  Wrabness CO12.........89 D3
Wrabness Sta CO11.....89 A4
Wraglins The CM3 ......146 B5
Wratting Rd CB9 .......9 A4
Wren Ave IP2 ..........16 D3
Wrenbrook Rd CM23....145 F6
Wren Cl
  Colchester CO3 .........134 C4
  Great Bentley CO7......139 D1
Wrendale CO15.........188 F6
Wren Ho CO3...........134 F5
Wright Ct CM2 ......127 F3
Wright Mead CM2 .....206 B4
Wright Rd IP3...........18 C2
Wright's Ave CM77.....155 E6
Wright's Piece CM22....95 A6
WRITTLE ..............204 A2
Writtle Coll CM1 .......188 B4
Writtle Coll CM1 .......204 B3
Writtle Jun & Inf Schs
  CM1 ..................215 A8
Writtle Rd CM1 ........215 E8
Wroxham Cl CO3 .......135 B6
Wroxham Rd IP3........17 F3
Wryneck Cl CO4 .......109 F3
Wulvesford CM8 ........194 D8
Wyatts La CO10 ........55 D8
Wych Elm CO2 .........136 A3
Wycke Hill CM9 ........220 D8
Wycke Hill Bsns Pk
  CM9 ..................220 E8
Wycke La CM9..........213 E8
Wycliffe Gr CO1........109 E1
Wycliffe Ho CM1.......205 E5
Wydale Dr CO3 .........134 A3
Wye Rd IP3 ...........18 A3
Wykeham Rd CM1 .....204 B1
Wykes Bishop St IP3....17 E4
Wyncolls Rd CO4 .......110 D6
Wyndam Cl CO2........163 B8
Wyndham Cres CO15...189 A5

Wynterton Cl IP3........18 B1
Wynyard Rd CB10......22 E2
Wyseman Pl CO11 ......86 C7
Wyvern Ct CO7 ........137 B1
Wyverne CM6 .........151 A5
Wyvern Rd IP3 ........18 C1

**Y**
Yale Bsns Pk IP3........38 E8
Yale Mews CO4........110 B4
Yardley Hall La CM6 ....69 D6
Yard The CM7..........128 A2
Yare Ave CM8..........176 D2
Yarmouth Cl CO16......188 E6
Yarmouth Pl CB9 .......9 A8
Yarmouth Rd IP1 .......17 A6
Yarwood Rd CM2.......205 E2
Yeldham Lock CM2 .....206 A2
Yeldham Pl CB9 .......9 A8
Yeldham Rd CO9........51 D3
Yeoman Cl IP2 .........16 F6
Yeoman Lo CM2 .......205 F3
Yeoman Rd IP11........221 B3
Yeomans Cl CM23......145 D6
Yerril Gdn CB9 .........8 E7
Yeton Ward Ho IP11 ...221 C5
Yew Cl CM8 ...........177 B5
Yew Ct IP2..............17 B3
Yew Tree Cl
  Colchester CO4 .........136 E8
  Hatfield Peverel CM3 ...194 A5
Yewtree Gdns CM2 .....216 C6
Yewtree Gr IP5.........18 F2
Yew Tree Pl CM23......145 F8
Yewtree Rise IP8........16 C1
Yew Way CO15.........203 F6
Yonge Cl CM3 .........192 E1
Yorick Ave CO5.........201 C6
Yorick Rd CO5..........201 C6
York Cl CO10 ..........33 E8
York Ct CM7 ........128 B2
York Gdns CM7........128 B4
York Mans CO15 .......189 E5
York Pl CO1 ...........136 A8
York Rd
  Brightlingsea CO7 ......185 E6
  Chelmsford CM2 .......216 A8
  Clacton-on-S CO15......189 E5
  Earls Colne CO6.........105 B6
  Felixstowe IP11.........221 E4
  Haverhill CB9...........8 E7
  Ipswich IP3.............18 A4
  Sudbury CO10 .........33 E8
York St CO11 ........86 C4
Young Cl CO16 .........188 C5
YOUNGS END ..........154 B3
Ypres Cotts CO2 .......162 A4
Ypres Rd CO2 .........135 F4

**Z**
Zambesi Rd CM23 ......145 F5
Zinnia Mews CO16......188 C4

# PHILIP'S MAPS

## the Gold Standard for drivers

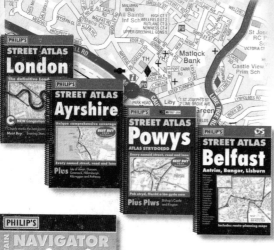